Military Living's™ U.S. Forces Travel Guide to

U.S. Military Installations

L. Ann Crawford, Publisher,
Military Living Publications, and
Vice-President, Military Marketing Services, Inc.

William Roy Crawford, Sr., Ph.D., President,
Military Living Publications, and
Military Marketing Services, Inc.

Editor: Nicole Clark

Assistant Editors: Elizabeth Ksiazek, Donna Russell,
Kathie Russell and Margaret Volpe

Cover Design: Susan Druzak

Vice President-Marketing: R.J. Crawford

Office Staff:
Timothy Brown, TSgt, USAF (Ret), AnnaBelle Causey,
Nigel Fellers, Maureen Fleegal, Irene Kearney,
Lourdes Medina, Sandy Moore, Tin Ngo,
Karme Raggio, Joel Thomas, MSG, USA (Ret),
Ricardo Thomas, Larry Williamson.

Military Living Publications
P. O. Box 2347
Falls Church, Virginia 22042-0347
TEL: (703) 237-0203
FAX: (703) 237-2233
E-mail:milliving@aol.com

NOTICE

The information in this book has been compiled and edited either from the activity/installation listed, its superior headquarters, or from other sources that may or may not be noted by the authors. Information about the facilities listed, including contact phone numbers and rate structures, could change. This book should be used as a guide to the listed facilities with this understanding. Please forward any corrections or additions to: **Military Living Publications, P. O. Box 2347, Falls Church, Virginia 22042-0347. TEL: 703-237-0203, FAX: 703-237-2233.**

This directory is published by Military Marketing Services, Inc., T/A Military Living Publications, a private business in no way connected with the U.S. Federal or any other government. This book is copyrighted by L. Ann and William Roy Crawford, Sr. Opinions expressed by the publisher and authors of this book are their own and are not to be considered an official expression by any government agency or official.

The information and statements contained in this directory have been compiled from sources believed to be reliable and to represent the best current opinion (at press time) on the subject. No warranty, guarantee, or representation is made by Military Marketing Services, Inc., as to the absolute correctness or sufficiency of any representation contained in this or other publications and we can assume no responsibility.

MILITARY MARKETING SERVICES, INC.,
(T/A MILITARY LIVING PUBLICATIONS)
First Printing - August 1997

Library of Congress Cataloging-in-Publication Data

Crawford, Ann Caddell.
U.S. forces travel guide to U.S. military installations / L. Ann Crawford, William Roy Crawford; editor Nicole Clark, assistant editors, Elizabeth Ksiazek, Donna Russell, and Margaret Volpe.
p. cm.
Includes index.
ISBN: 0-914862-63-4
1. United States--Armed Forces--Barracks and quarters--Directories. 2. Military bases, American--Directories.
I. Crawford, William Roy, 1932- . II. Clark, Nicole. III> Title.
UC403.C7223 1997
355.7'025'73--dc21 97-28319
CIP

ISBN 0-914862-63-4

HOW TO USE THIS DIRECTORY

Each listing has similar information, listed in the following order:

Name of Installation (AL01R2)

Street/PO Box (if required)
City/APO/FPO, State, ZIP Code

LOCATION IDENTIFIER: Example (AL01R2). The first two characters (letters) are Country/State abbreviations used in Military Living's books (Appendix A). The next two characters are random numbers (00-99) assigned to a specific location. The fifth character is an R indicating region and the sixth character is the region number.

TELEPHONE NUMBER INFORMATION: C- This is the commercial telephone service for the installation's main or information/operator assistance number, the designation has also been used for other commercial numbers in this directory. Within the North American Area Code System, the first three digits are the area code. The next three digits are the area telephone exchange/switch number. The last four digits are usually the information or operator assistance number, or the line number of a specific telephone.

D- This is the Department of Defense, worldwide, Defense Switched Network (DSN). We have, at the request of our readers, included the DSN prefix with most numbers in each listing. In most cases, the number given is for information/operator assistance. ***Note: The 312 area code on defense number is for calls from outside North America. When calling within North America the 312 is not needed.***

FAX: Telefax numbers are listed as available.

E-MAIL: Electronic mail on worldwide web numbers are listed as available.

LOCATION: Specific driving instructions to the installation from local major cities, interstate highways and routes are given. More than one routing may be provided. **USMRA:** is **MILITARY LIVING'S "United States Military Road Atlas"** reference to the location. **NMC:** is the nearest major city. The distance and direction from the installation to the NMC are given.

GENERAL: Major activities, organizations, military units and special information concerning the installation, if any, are provided in this section.

TEMPORARY MILITARY LODGING: The billeting/lodging office or registration/check-in point, location and complete telephone/fax contact/reservation numbers are provided. Hours of operation are noted. Category of persons accommodated is specified and special contact numbers for DV/VIP (Distinguished Visitor/Very Important Person, both officer and enlisted grades) are provided. **Detailed information at over 425 installations worldwide is contained in Military Living's all-time best-selling title, *Temporary Military Lodging Around the World*. See coupons in this book for ordering information.**

LOGISTICAL SUPPORT: The scope of support facilities available at the installation is specified and the telephone for the facility is provided. Space limitations preclude listing all support numbers; however, the telephone numbers for facilities not listed are available through the information operator number in each listing.

HEALTH & WELFARE: The installation or nearest medical emergency information and/or appointment service numbers are listed. The installation or servicing medical inpatient numbers are provided as well. Chaplain support and chapel service contact numbers are specified.

RECREATION: The contact telephone number for most rest, recreation, athletic facilities, and opportunities are given for each installation. Information about camping and recreation areas on the installation, controlled by the installation, or near the installation is provided. **Complete camping and recreation area details are contained in *Military Living's Military RV, Camping and Rec Areas Around the World*. See coupons in this book for ordering information.**

SPACE-A: The location, hours of operation, contact telephone numbers and flight-location opportunities are specified for departure locations on each installation. The numbers provided are the Space-A information numbers at specified departure locations. If no Space-A is available at the given installation, the name of the nearest installation with Space-A opportunities is provided. **Full Space-A information such as arrival locations, aircraft used, schedules, terminal facilities, eligibility, rules, travel documents needed and more, are all contained in Military Living's best-selling book, *Military Space-A Air Opportunities Around the World*. See coupons in this book for ordering information.**

ATTRACTIONS: This section provides information to the traveler about attractions on the installation or in the surrounding area.

Please review the appendices for abbreviations used in this book and for other helpful information. **Address your questions regarding this title or other Military Living books to: Military Living Publications, P.O. Box 2347, Falls Church, Virginia 22042-0347. ATTN: Ann or Roy Crawford. You may telephone us at 703-237-0203, FAX 703-237-2233 or E-mail milliving@aol.com. No collect calls accepted.**

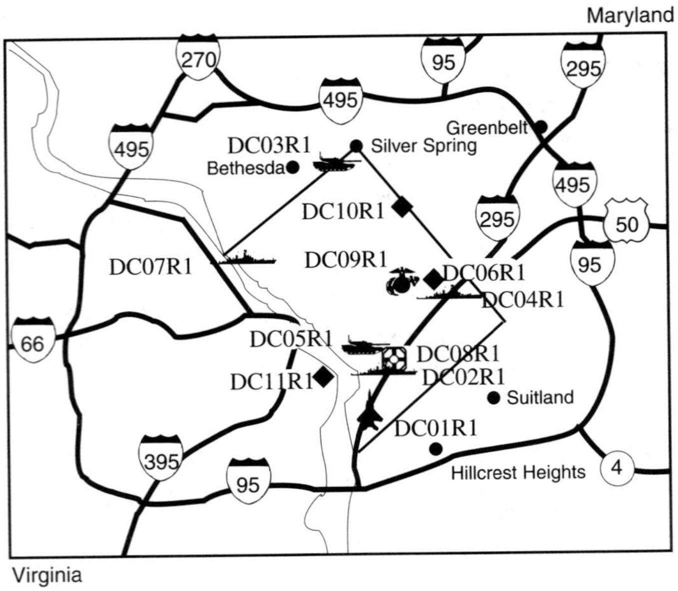

MAP LEGEND

- Army
- Navy
- Marine Corps
- Coast Guard
- Air Force, Air Force Reserves, Air National Guard
- International Airport
- Recreation Area
- Space Center
- Defense Installation

BASE CLOSURES

The 1995 Defense Base Closure and Realignment Commission's Report was accepted by Congress and became Public Law on 28 September 1995.

The 1995 law, along with previous directed closures and realignments in the basic law in 1988, 1990, 1991 and 1993, complete the base closure and realignments which have been approved by Congress. These directed closures have been noted at the beginning of each listing affected with the DoD estimated date of final closure. Some bases have already closed and consequently have been deleted from this edition.

It should also be noted that final closure dates will be established for each installation. These dates could change as the DoD completes the final closure plans and as funding becomes available to effect the closures. Support facilities on the affected bases will normally decrease gradually; therefore, it is best to check with each military installation scheduled for closure or realignment before you go.

Lastly, it should be noted that the 1995 Defense Base Closure and Realignment Law, along with previous base closure laws, only apply to domestic United States Bases and United States Bases located in United States possessions.

Some Words About Our Changing World

The military is undergoing sweeping changes which have made this book both challenging and interesting to publish. Some installations are closing and others are realigning. We have included the dates of expected closure as provided to us at the beginning of each listing. Installations which will close prior to 30 September 1997 have been excluded from this book. Also, we have not included installations which do not have support facilities and consequently are of limited value to our readers. The information in this book is as accurate as we can make it. The information in this book has been provided by military installations in the Continental United States (CONUS), Alaska, Hawaii and US possessions overseas. However, as with all directories, there are changes that happen daily that cause inaccuracies. **Military Living Publications** has always relied on its readers to write or call when information has become outdated. It is the secret of our success. Please do not hesitate to let us know when information is incorrect, or if we have missed an installation for your fellow travelers. Enjoy.

HOW TO SAVE MONEY ON YOUR TRAVEL

Travel on less per day....the military way!™

STAY WITH "FAMILY" - Right! Military families can stay with "family" as they travel around the United States and its territories. No matter where you go, there is probably a military installation en route! Our family always got that "back-home feeling" the minute they entered the front gate of a military installation, does yours?

MAKE EVERY MOVE A MINI-VACATION! Military installations not only offer temporary military lodging to those military ID card holders on the road again, all kinds of facilities are available to help cut your cost on the way.

EATING - You have the added advantage of being able to pick up provisions at the commissary to make many of your meals while on the road. The savings are great - just like back home at your military post, base or station. Stop at a military fast-food outlet, a military club or at the golf course for a bite to eat and take a break. It's not good to keep moving without stopping - and the kids need a rest, too.

GASOLINE & AUTO REPAIRS - Stop at military exchange gas stations and save. Should you run into auto trouble, check and see if there is a military auto repair shop close by - these facilities are part of the military support facilities. You will know who you are dealing with and have someone to talk to if you are not satisfied!

PICK UP NEEDED TRAVEL ITEMS at your military exchange. Buy a telephone card to use instead of costly third-party dialing and collect calls. Cash checks. Use restrooms! Whatever was available to you at your home installation is almost always available to you when traveling.

HAVE SOME FUN! - Take a swim in a military pool, play a round of golf, or at some places on the water - a sail! You are not limited to using morale, welfare and recreation (MWR) facilities or Services at your home base. Show the kids how the other Services live! The whole military network is yours!

SPLURGE - By saving on much of your travel, you may be able to make a special memory by stopping at amusement parks and other attractions. Their tickets are available at real savings at military ticket and tour offices. In addition, you may want to stay at civilian lodging sometimes - but don't forget to show your ID and ask for their military rates!

STOP EARLY! USE MILITARY LODGING - Play it safer and stop sooner in the afternoon to stay at a military lodging facility. All the military armed services offer lodging at reasonable rates. Here are two toll-free phone numbers to keep in mind for your next trip - 1-800-GO-ARMY-1 (1-800-46-2769-1) and 1-800-NAVY INN (1-800-628-9466).

The Army Central Reservations Line offers reservations at many Army lodging facilities, and the Navy operates a fine Navy Lodge system, as well. This book will give you the phone numbers for the direct dial to these military lodging facilities as well as to those not listed at the toll-free numbers.

The Air Force, at our press time, had not made a toll-free reservations number available as yet, but there is good news for travelers! In a change in regulation, you can now make reservations at an Air Force lodging facility within 24 hours of your arrival and for up to three days. Air Force lodging numbers are in this book. You will be surprised at how reasonable Air Force lodging can be.

The big news in savings is for our **Guard** and **Reserve** families. They can now use temporary military lodging and military RV, camping and recreation areas on the same basis as active duty personnel and their families.

CAMP OUT - Most military outdoor recreation offices offer camping gear from tents to small mobile units for rent. You will be surprised at how many military installations have on base or nearby military RV, camping and rec areas.

YES! You can stay with family on your next move - your military family! Plan your trip to include staying at military installations and for shopping en route. You will find savings, familiar surroundings and more safety - no matter where you go. Let ***U.S. Forces Travel Guide to U.S. Military Installations*** be your guide to finding savings, fun and security on your next trip!

CONTENTS

UNITED STATES

LOCATION IDENTIFIER	INSTALLATION	PAGE

NOTE: Bases scheduled for closure are designated by a date in parenthesis.

ALABAMA

ALASKA

ARIZONA

ARKANSAS

CALIFORNIA

Other Installations in California

COLORADO

Other Installations in Colorado

CONNECTICUT

DELAWARE

Other Installations in Delaware

DISTRICT OF COLUMBIA

Other Installations in District of Columbia

FLORIDA

Other Installations in Florida

GEORGIA

Other Installations in Georgia

HAWAII

Other Installations in Hawaii

IDAHO

ILLINOIS

Other Installations in Illinois

INDIANA

Other Installations in Indiana

IOWA

Other Installations in Iowa

KANSAS

KENTUCKY

Other Installations in Kentucky

LOUISIANA

MAINE

Other Installations in Maine

MARYLAND

Other Installations in Maryland

MASSACHUSETTS

Other Installations in Massachusetts

MICHIGAN

Other Installations in Michigan

MINNESOTA

Other Installations in Minnesota

MISSISSIPPI

Other Installations in Mississippi

MISSOURI

Other Installations in Missouri

MONTANA

Other Installations in Montana

NEBRASKA

Other Installations in Nebraska

NEVADA

NEW HAMPSHIRE

NEW JERSEY

NORTH DAKOTA

OHIO

OKLAHOMA

OREGON

PENNSYLVANIA

TERMS & CONDITIONS FOR 10% DISCOUNT OFF DINNER

- Effective through Dec. 31, 1998 at participating Holiday Inn® hotel restaurants.
- Valid for use only by government/military travelers and federal cost reimbursable contractors (CRC's) in conjunction with an official stay (at the government/military rate) at any participating Holiday Inn hotel.
- Traveler must present coupon at time of seating to receive the dinner discount.
- Discount may not be applied on any other meal charges.
- Not valid on room service.
- Taxes, gratuities and alcoholic beverages not included.
- Limit one coupon for each night's stay.
- Void where prohibited, restricted, taxed or license required.
- Coupon is not redeemable for cash. Non-negotiable. Coupon value 1/100th of 1 cent. No copies or facsimiles accepted.

TERMS & CONDITIONS FOR FREE LOCAL CALL

- Effective through Dec. 31, 1998 at participating Holiday Inn® hotel restaurants.
- Valid for use only by government/military travelers and federal cost reimbursable contractors (CRC's) in conjunction with an official stay (at the government/military rate) at any participating Holiday Inn hotel.
- Traveler must present coupon at time of seating to receive free continental breakfast.
- Not valid on room service.
- Taxes, gratuities and alcoholic beverages not included.
- Limit one coupon for each night's stay.
- Void where prohibited, restricted, taxed or license required.
- Coupon is not redeemable for cash. Non-negotiable. Coupon value 1/100th of 1 cent. No copies or facsimiles accepted.

TERMS & CONDITIONS FOR FREE CONTINENTAL BREAK

- Effective through Dec. 31, 1998 at participating Holiday Inn® hotel restaurants.
- Valid for use only by government/military travelers and federal cost reimbursable contractors (CRC's) in conjunction with an official stay (at the government/milita at any participating Holiday Inn hotel.
- Traveler must present coupon at time of seating to receive free continental breakfa
- Not valid on room service.
- Taxes, gratuities and alcoholic beverages not included.
- Limit one coupon for each night's stay.
- Void where prohibited, restricted, taxed or license required.
- Coupon is not redeemable for cash. Non-negotiable. Coupon value 1/100th of 1 cent. No copies or facsimiles accepted.

TEXAS

Other Installations in Texas

UTAH

Other Installations in Utah

VERMONT

Installations in Vermont

VIRGINIA

WISCONSIN

WYOMING

UNITED STATES POSSESSIONS

AMERICAN SAMOA

GUAM

PUERTO RICO

VIRGIN ISLANDS

APPENDICES

PHOTO CREDITS

The Fun Begins With . . . MILITARY Living™ PUBLICATIONS

These photos on our cover are just a few of the military locations offering traveling military ID card holders opportunities to "travel on less per day . . the military way!™ Check them out in this money-saving guide.

Photo credits beginning with upper left:

The Medal of Honor golf course at Quantico, VA. Photo by Richard Standen.

The new Mologne House Hotel at Walter Reed Army Medical Center, Washington D.C. Photo by RJ Crawford.

Camp and save - you can often rent pop-ups and other campers at an en route installation. Photo taken at Key West, FL by Ann Crawford.

The new Exchange in Key West. Photo by Ann Crawford.

Make every move or trip a mini-vacation! This big fish was caught near the Seward Resort, AK. Photo courtesy of Seward Resort.

New combined BX-Mart at Fort Worth Naval Air Station/Joint Reserve Base,TX. Photo by Ann Crawford.

Another great place to stay in Hawaii - the Inn at Schofield Barracks. Photo courtesy of the hotel.

UNITED STATES

ALABAMA

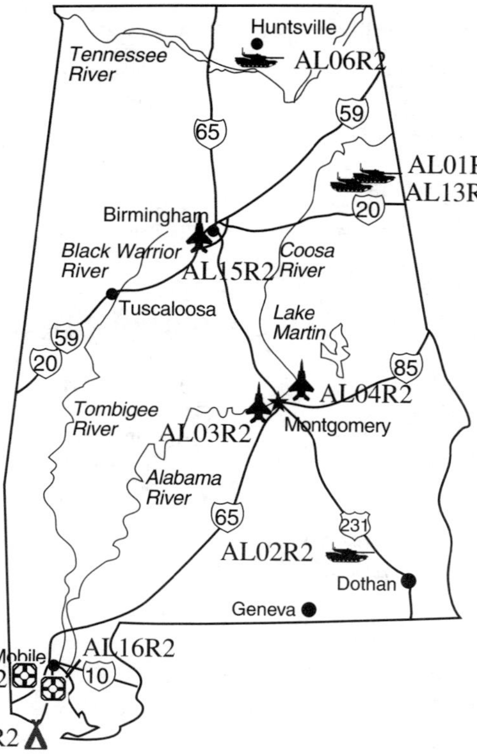

ALABAMA AIR NATIONAL GUARD BASE (AL15R2)

5401 Eastlake Boulevard
Birmingham, AL 35217-3595

TELEPHONE NUMBER INFORMATION: Main Installation Numbers: C-205-714-2000, D-312-778-2000.

LOCATION: Exit I-59/20 at Tallapoosa Street, north for one-half mile to a right on Eastlake Blvd to installation. USMRA: Page 36 (D,E-4). NMC: Birmingham, in city limits.

GENERAL INFORMATION: 117th Air Refueling Wing (KC-135R). The base is open Tue-Fri from 0700L-1730L hours and some weekends.

TEMPORARY MILITARY LODGING: None. See Fort McClellan listing, C-205-848-4338, D-312-865-4338.

RV, CAMPING/FAMCAMP: None. See Fort McClellan listing, C-205-848-5663, D-312-865-5649.

SPACE-A: Pax Terminal C-205-714-2208, D-312-778-2208. Some unscheduled flights available on MEDEVAC and KC-135s.

LOGISTICAL SUPPORT:

Exchange-714-2348	Gas Station-714-2294

ADMINISTRATIVE SUPPORT:	Police-714-2240
HEALTH & WELFARE:	Medical-714-2213

REST & RECREATION: None. See Fort McClellan listing, C-205-848-3526.

ATTRACTIONS: Vulcan (Iron Man Statue) on Red Mountain. The largest shopping mall in the Southeast is located in Birmingham.

ANNISTON ARMY DEPOT (AL13R2)

ATTN: SIOAN-CO
7 Frankford Avenue
Anniston, AL 36201-4199

TELEPHONE NUMBER INFORMATION: Main installation numbers: C-205-235-7501, D-312-571-7501.

LOCATION: From I-20 take Oxford exit onto Highway US-78 and follow signs to the depot. USMRA: Page 36 (F-3). NMC: Anniston, ten miles east.

GENERAL INFORMATION: Units at the Depot include the Defense Reutilization and Marketing Office, the TMDE Support Center, the CECOM Liaison Office, the Defense Logistics Agency and the Anniston Chemical Activity.

TEMPORARY MILITARY LODGING: None. See Fort McClellan listing, C-205-848-4338, D-312-865-4338.

RV, CAMPING/FAMCAMP: None. See Fort McClellan listing, C-205-848-5663, D-312-865-5649.

SPACE-A: None. See Alabama ANGB listing, C-205-714-2208, D-312-778-2441, Fax: C-205-841-9219.

LOGISTICAL SUPPORT:

Carlson Wagonlit Travel-820-3983	Exchange-237-9159

ADMINISTRATIVE SUPPORT:

Fire Department-235-6171	Legal-235-6334
Locator-235-7501	Public Affairs-235-6281

HEALTH & WELFARE:	Medical-235-7521

REST & RECREATION:

Camping Equipment-235-7170	Fitness Center-235-6385
MWR-235-7170	Recreation-235-6385

ATTRACTIONS: Anniston Museum of Natural History and the Berman Museum, also located in Anniston.

DAUPHIN ISLAND COAST GUARD RECREATION FACILITY (AL07R2)

P.O. Box 436
Dauphin Island, AL 36528-0436

TELEPHONE NUMBER INFORMATION: Main installation number: C-334-861-7113.

LOCATION: On Gulf of Mexico approximately 40 miles south of Mobile. I-10 to Highway 193 south (exit 17); south approximately 35 miles to Dauphin Island. Left at dead end to east end of island. Follow signs to complex. USMRA: Page 36 (B-10). NMC: Mobile, 40 miles north. NMI: Mobile Coast Guard Group (Brookley), 40 miles north.

GENERAL INFORMATION: Dauphin Island offers a variety of outdoor sightseeing activities. Operated by Mobile Coast Guard Group, off base year round. Military personnel active, retired and DoD. Check in 1600-2000, check out 1200 Fri-Sun. Reservations: Required by phone, C-205-861-7113, then followed by reservation request form sent with payment. Payment due before check in. Active Duty Coast Guard up to 60 days in advance. Other active branches and reserve up to 45 days in advance. Retired and DoD Civilians up to 30 days in advance. No pets or firearms allowed. Seven day limit for cottages; fourteen day limit for camper sites.

ALABAMA
Dauphin Island Coast Guard Recreation Facility, continued

TEMPORARY MILITARY LODGING: Three bedroom cottages, furnished kitchen, CATV, microwave, full cooking/eating utensils, all linens (except wash and dishcloths) (13). Handicap accessible units available (3). Rates: $100-120 Fri-Sun; $140-160 Sun-Fri (5 day week); $240-280 Fri-Fri or Sun-Sun (7 day week). Monthly Rate available Oct-Nov.

RV, CAMPING/FAMCAMP: Camper spaces with full hookups (5); camper/tent spaces with no hookups (100). Rates: $10 with hookups; $5 without hookups.

ADMINISTRATIVE SUPPORT:
Police-861-5523

REST & RECREATION: Bicycling, Boating, Fishing, Rec Equipment, Swimming.

OTHER SUPPORT & FACILITIES AVAILABLE: Bath House, Beach/private, Convenience Store, Fishing Poles/Bait, Food Vending, Grills, Laundry, Picnic Area, Playground, PX/small, Restrooms*, Sewage Dump, Showers*, Sun Deck. Also see Mobile Coast Guard Group, C-334-441-6217.

** Handicap accessible.*

ATTRACTIONS: Explore old Fort Gaines, ancient Indian Shell mounds or Audubon Bird Sanctuary.

FORT McCLELLAN (AL01R2)

Building 51, Buckner Circle
ATTN: ATZN-GN
Fort McClellan, AL 36205-5000
Scheduled to close September 1999

TELEPHONE NUMBER INFORMATION: Main installation numbers: C-205-848-4611, D-312-865-1110.

LOCATION: From I-20 take AL-21 north nine miles to fort. From I-59 take US-431 25 miles southeast to fort. USMRA: Page 36 (F-3). NMC: Anniston, three miles southeast.

GENERAL INFORMATION: US Army Chemical and Military Police Centers and Fort McClellan, Training Brigade, DoD Polygraph Institute, US Marine Corps Detachment, US Navy Detachment, and US Air Force Civil Engineer Readiness School.

TEMPORARY MILITARY LODGING: Lodging office, Building 3295, 14th Street and Summerall Road, 24 hours daily, C-205-848-4338, D-312-865-4338. All ranks. DV/VIP C-205-848-3808/5616.

RV, CAMPING/FAMCAMP: McClellan Recreation Area & Campground located on post, year round, C-205-848-5663, D-312-865-5649, eight camping spaces with W/E hookups, four camping spaces without hookups.

SPACE-A: None. See Maxwell AFB listing, C-205-953-6454, D-312-493-6454, Fax: C-334-953-6114.

LOGISTICAL SUPPORT:
Bank-820-2500
Carlson Wagonlit Travel-820-3483
Child Development Center-848-5331
Conv Store-820-9280
Credit Union-820-1500
Exchange-820-9400
Package Store-820-9280
Shoppette-820-9530
Travel Office-820-6372
Cafeteria-820-2000
Child Care-848-3693/3632
Class Six-820-9280
Commissary-848-3130
Dining Facilities-848-5674
Gas Station-820-9250
Postal Service-848-3194
Snack Bar-820-2000
Visitor Center-848-3546/4338

ADMINISTRATIVE SUPPORT:
Fire Dept-848-5936
Legal-848-5435
ID Office-848-3641
Public Affairs-848-3743
Housing Office-848-3215
Locator-848-3281/3795
Police-848-5555/4531
SDO-848-3821

HEALTH & WELFARE:
ACS-848-4525
CHAMPUS-848-2126
Dental-848-5510
  Appointments-848-5458
  Clinic-848-3911
  Emergency-848-4635
TRICARE-820-7129
Veterinary Services-848-7095
Army Emergency Relief-848-5444
Chapel 848-5351
Medical 848-2543
  Appointments-848-2543
  Clinic-848-2313/2388/2107
  Health Advisor-848-2126
  Hospital-848-2357
  Information-848-2200

REST & RECREATION:
Auto Hobby Shop-ext 5146
Bowling-848-5149
Golf Course-848-3623
ITT Office-820-6372
McClellan Club-848-5301
Skeet/Trap-ext 3700
Rec Services-ext 4323
Youth Services-848-3607
Bingo-820-6699
Fitness Center-848-5249
Gym-848-4802
Library-848-3715
MWR-848-3526
Swimming-ext 4656
Theater-848-3861

OTHER SUPPORT AVAILABLE: American Red Cross, Barber Shop, Beauty Shop, Dry Cleaner, Education Office.

ATTRACTIONS: Military Police, Chemical Corps and WAC Museums on post. Natural History Museum located nearby. Fort adjacent to Talladega National Forest. Berman Museum (military artifacts) in nearby Anniston. Birmingham; 40 minute drive.

Note: The US Military Police and the US Army Chemical Schools will move from Fort McClellan to Fort Leonard Wood, MO in late 1999.

FORT RUCKER (AL02R2)

Building 122
ATTN: ATZQ-GSC
Fort Rucker, AL 36362-5000

TELEPHONE NUMBER INFORMATION: Main installation numbers: C-334-255-1110, D-312-558-1110.

LOCATION: Eighty miles southeast of Montgomery, midway between the capital city and the Florida Gulf Coast, and seven miles south of Ozark, off US-231 on AL-249. Clearly marked. USMRA: Page 36 (F,G-8). NMC: Dothan, 26 miles southeast.

GENERAL INFORMATION: US Army Aviation Center NCO Academy, First Aviation Brigade, Aviation Training Brigade, Army Air Traffic Control Activity, Army Aero-medical Center, Army Aero-medical Research Laboratory, Army Aviation Technical Text Center, US Army Safety Center and US Army School of Aviation Medicine.

TEMPORARY MILITARY LODGING: Lodging office, Building 308, 6th Avenue, 24 hours daily, C-334-255-3780, D-312-558-3780. All ranks. DV/VIP, Building 114, C-344-255-3100/3400.

RV, CAMPING/FAMCAMP: On-post recreation area at Lake Tholocco, year round (camping area closed Nov-Feb), Outdoor Rec C-334-255-4305, D-312-558-4305, 18 camper spaces with W/E hookups.

SPACE-A: Cairns Army Airfield, Building 30501, C-334-255-8563, D-312-558-8563, flights via executive aircraft to CONUS locations.

LOGISTICAL SUPPORT:
Bank-598-2401
Beauty Shop-598-4315
Barber Shop-598-4315
Carlson Wagonlit Travel-255-9034

ALABAMA
Fort Rucker, continued

Child Dev Center-255-3564
Commissary-255-3610
Education Office-255-3359
Gas Station-503-9044
Recycling-255-9505
Shoppette-503-9044
Class Six-503-9044
Credit Union-598-4411
Exchange-503-9044
Postal Service-598-6446
SATO-255-9034
Travel Office-598-1574

ADMINISTRATIVE SUPPORT:
Fire Dept-255-2511
Legal-255-3482
Public Affairs-255-2252
Housing Office-255-2318
Police-255-2222
SDO/NCO-255-3400

HEALTH & WELFARE:
American Red Cross-255-1055
Army Emergency Relief-255-3643
Chapel-255-2989
Family Services-255-2341
Retiree Services-255-9124
TRICARE-598-6500
Veterinary Services-255-2159
ACS-255-9251
CHAMPUS-255-7233
Dental-255-2367
Medical
  Central Appts-255-7000
  Emergency-255-7900
  Health Benefits-255-7229
  Hospital-255-7000
  Information-255-7000

REST & RECREATION:
Arts & Crafts-255-9131
Bowling-255-9503
Equestrian Center- 598-3384
Fitness Center-255-2393
Golf Course-255-9539
ITR Office-255-9517
MWR-255-2292/598-5311
Theater-255-2408
Auto Hobby Shop-255-9725
Clubs
  NCO-598-2492
  O-598-2462
Gym-255-9567
Library 255-3885
Swimming-ext 3998
Youth Services-255-9108

ATTRACTIONS: National Peanut Festival, first week of Nov in Dothan. Monument to the Boll Weevil, Enterprise, AL, seven miles west. US Army Aviation Museum on post, 0900-1600 daily; group tours and library usage, C-334-255-3036.

GUNTER ANNEX TO MAXWELL AIR FORCE BASE (AL04R2)

60 West Maxwell Boulevard
Maxwell Air Force Base, AL 36112-6307

TELEPHONE NUMBER INFORMATION: Main installation numbers: C-334-953-1110, D-312-493-5496.

LOCATION: Take I-65 to Northern Bypass, six miles to exit on AL-231, continue west one mile to AFB. Coming from the opposite direction, from I-85, follow signs and take Eastern Bypass north one mile to AL-231. Go west one mile to AFB. USMRA: Page 36 (E,F-6). NMC: Montgomery, two miles southwest.

GENERAL INFORMATION: Standard Systems Group, Extension Course Institute, USAF Senior NCO Academy and educational activities.

TEMPORARY MILITARY LODGING: Lodging office, Building 826, 24 hours daily, C-334-416-3360, D-312-596-3360. Extensive facilities. DV/VIP call Maxwell AFB, C-334-253-2095, D-312-875-2095.

RV, CAMPING/FAMCAMP: Run by Maxwell AFB, Lake Martin Maxwell/Gunter Recreation Area and Lake Pippin Maxwell/Gunter Recreation Area C-334-953-3509, D-312-493-3509.

SPACE-A: None. See Maxwell AFB listing, C-334-953-6454, D-312-493-6454, Fax: C-334-953-6114.

LOGISTICAL SUPPORT:
Commissary-953-2343
Gas Station-265-7773
Visitor Center-953-2014
Exchange-834-5946
SATO-263-5500

ADMINISTRATIVE SUPPORT:
Fire Dept-953-7360
Locator-953-5027
Legal-953-2786
Police-953-7222

HEALTH & WELFARE:
CHAMPUS-953-7854
Chaplain-953-2862
Medical-953-6985
Chapel-279-4131
Child Care-953-6667

REST & RECREATION:
Arts & Crafts-ext 3118
Bowling-ext 3186
Family Services-953-3850
Golf Course-263-7588
Gym-ext 3175
ITT Office-953-7370
Picnic Area-ext 4888
Recreation-953-5675
Wood Hobby Shop at Maxwell
Auto Hobby Shop-ext 3119
Clubs
  EM-953-6399
  NCO-262-8364
  O-264-6423
Library-ext 3179
Rec Center-ext 4802
Theater-953-7411
Youth Activities-ext 4802

ATTRACTIONS: Alabama state capital, Alabama Shakespeare Festival, Coliseum, Montgomery Museum of Fine Arts, monument to powered flight at Maxwell AFB, First White House of the Confederacy, Civil Rights Memorial, and the new Alabama State Farmers Market..."largest in the southeastern US."

MAXWELL AIR FORCE BASE (AL03R2)

50 LeMay Plaza South
Maxwell Air Force Base, AL 36112-6334

TELEPHONE NUMBER INFORMATION: Main installation numbers: C-334-953-1110, D-312-493-1110.

LOCATION: Take I-85 south to I-65 north. Take Herron Street exit to Bell Street and follow signs to Bell Street Gate Visitor Center. USMRA: Page 36 (E-6). NMC: Montgomery, one-and-a-half miles southeast.

GENERAL INFORMATION: Headquarters Air University (AETC), professional military education center for USAF.

TEMPORARY MILITARY LODGING: Lodging office, Building 157, 351 West Dr., 24 hours daily, C-334-953-2401/7390, D-312-493-2401/7390. Extensive facilities. DV/VIP C-334-953-2095.

RV, CAMPING/FAMCAMP: Lake Martin Maxwell/Gunter Recreation Area, off base near Dadeville C-334-953-3509, D-312-493-3509, year round, 61 camper spaces with W/E hookups, 12 Mobile Homes, 15 tent spaces; Lake Pippin Maxwell/Gunter Recreation Area near Niceville, FL, year round, C-334-953-3509, D-312-493-3509, 23 camper spaces with W/E hookups, 10 tent spaces, and 8 Mobile Homes. FAMCAMP on base, C-334-953-5161, year round, 31 camper spaces with full hookups.

SPACE-A: Pax Term/Lounge, Building 844, 0700-1700 Mon-Fri, C-334-953-6454, D-312-493-6454, Fax: C-334-953-6114. DV/VIP lounge C-334-953-6961. Flights scheduled 24 hours in advance, most via executive aircraft.

LOGISTICAL SUPPORT:
Cafeteria-263-6044
Commissary-953-6209
Exchange-834-5946
Package Store-265-7472
Visitor Center-953-4283
Child Care-953-6667
Conv Store-265-7773
Gas Station-265-7773
SATO-264-0076

ADMINISTRATIVE SUPPORT:
Legal-953-2786
Police-953-7222
SDO/NCO-953-2862
Locator-953-5027
Public Affairs-953-2014

ALABAMA
Maxwell Air Force Base, continued

HEALTH & WELFARE:
CHAMPUS-953-7854
Family Services-953-5002
Retiree Services-953-6725
Chapel-953-2111
Medical-953-2333

REST & RECREATION:
Clubs
  Aero- ext 7342
  EM-262-8364
  NCO-262-8364
  O-264-6423
Golf Course-263-9587
ITT Office-953-6351
Library-ext 5947
Theater-953-7411

ATTRACTIONS: State capital, Shakespeare Theater, historic houses and buildings in Montgomery, including First White House of the Confederacy, Montgomery Museum of Fine Arts, Civil Rights Memorial Monument.

MOBILE COAST GUARD AVIATION TRAINING CENTER (AL08R2)

USCG Aviation Training Center
85011 Tanner Williams Road
Mobile, AL 36608-9682

TELEPHONE NUMBER INFORMATION: Main installation numbers: C-334-639-6117, after hours C-334-639-6110, D-312-649-3635.

LOCATION: Take Airport Blvd exit west from I-65, eight miles from base, turn right on Schillinger Road, turn left on Tanner Williams Road, one mile. Clearly marked. USMRA: Page 36 (B-9). NMC: Mobile, one mile northwest.

GENERAL INFORMATION: The Aviation Training Center for the US Coast Guard and home for the Gulf Strike Team.

TEMPORARY MILITARY LODGING: Extremely limited. Usually filled by TDY students. C-334-639-6361. See Keesler AFB, MS, C-601-377-2631/3660.

RV, CAMPING/FAMCAMP: None. See Mobile CGB, Dauphin Island Recreational Complex, C-334-861-7113.

SPACE-A: Extremely limited. Main hangar, 0800-1600 Mon-Fri, C-334-639-6161, D-312-436-3635, Fax: C-334-639-6435, flights to east and midwest.

LOGISTICAL SUPPORT:
Barber Shop-639-6494
Conv Store-639-6496
Credit Union-639-6326
Education Office-639-6131
Gas Station-639-6496
Package Store-639-6390
Beauty Shop-639-6495
Commissary-639-6390
Dining Facilities-639-6148
Exchange-639-6390
Grocery Annex-639-6379
Shoppette-639-6496

ADMINISTRATIVE SUPPORT:
Housing Office-441-6326
OOD-639-6110
Police-639-6100
Quarter Deck-639-6110
Locator-639-6117
Pass/ID Office-639-6117
Public Affairs-639-6428

HEALTH & WELFARE:
American Red Cross-438-2571
Chapel-639-6038
Medical
  Central Appts-639-6401 (AD)
  639-6725 (Dependents)
  Health Benefits-639-6037
  Information-639-6400
CHAMPUS-639-6038
Dental
  Central Appts-639-6404
  Clinic-639-6404
  Emergency-639-6410
TRICARE-639-6037

REST & RECREATION:
Auto Hobby Shop-639-6135
Fitness Center-639-6384
MWR-639-6130
Clubs
  EM-639-6359
  O-639-6358
Outdoor Rec-639-6136
  Rental Equipment
  Outdoor Racquet Courts
  Weight Room Complex
  Jogging Trail
  Walter's Park Picnic Area (fee)
  Swimming Pool (fee)

ATTRACTIONS: Mobile is one of the largest commercial seaports in the country. Historic houses and beautiful flowers in the Mobile Bay area. Bellingrath Gardens (year round), USS *Alabama*, and Battleship Park.

***NOTE:** ATC will be installing a new phone system in early 1997. Phone numbers will start with the prefix 441-XXXX. Fifty percent of the last four digits will remain the same, but the other 50% will change. Contact the PAO office or the main installation number to verify the number you are trying to reach.*

MOBILE COAST GUARD BASE (AL16R2)

South Broad Street
Brookley Complex Building 101
Mobile, AL 36615-1390

TELEPHONE NUMBER INFORMATION: Main installation numbers: C-334-441-6217.

LOCATION: From I-10, exit on Broad Street, go south approximately three-quarters of a mile to base. USMRA: Page 36 (B-9,10). NMI: Pensacola NAS, Pensacola, FL, 55 miles east. NMC: Mobile, one mile north

GENERAL INFORMATION: US Coast Guard Group activities.

TEMPORARY MILITARY LODGING: None. See Keesler AFB, MS listing, C-601-377-2631/3660.

RV, CAMPING/FAMCAMP: Operates Dauphin Island Recreation Area, 40 miles south of post. See Dauphin Island Recreation Area for more information.

SPACE-A: None. See Keesler AFB, MS listing, C-601-377-4538, D-312-597-4538.

LOGISTICAL SUPPORT:
Conv Store-441-5097
Gas Station-441-5097
Exchange-441-5090
Package Store-441-5091

ADMINISTRATIVE SUPPORT:
Locator-441-6217
Public Affairs-441-6007

HEALTH & WELFARE: None. See Keesler AFB, MS listing, C-601-377-6550. Also see Pensacola Naval Hospital, FL listing, C-850-505-6601.

REST & RECREATION:
All Hands Club-441-5098/5099
MWR-441-6198

ATTRACTIONS: Mobile Bay, Battleship Park, *USS Alabama* and other military displays, Bellingrath Gardens.

REDSTONE ARSENAL (AL06R2)

Commander US Army Missile Command
Building 5300, ATTN: AMSMI-RA
Redstone Arsenal, AL 35898-5020

TELEPHONE NUMBER INFORMATION: Main installation numbers: C-205-876-2151, D-312-746-0011.

LOCATION: Off US-231 go south on Martin Road to main gate. For uniformed personnel, Gate 8 is on Drake Avenue, take US-72 onto Jordan Lane, then west on Drake. Drake becomes Goss Road on the Arsenal. Coming from I-595, take the Ride Out Road exit to Redstone Arsenal, entering through Gate 9. USMRA: Page 36 (E-1). NMC: Huntsville, adjacent.

ALABAMA
Redstone Arsenal, continued

GENERAL INFORMATION: Headquarters US Army Missile Command, US Army ORDNANCE Missile & Munitions Center & School and NASA.

TEMPORARY MILITARY LODGING: Lodging office, Building 244, Goss Road, 24 hours daily, C-205-837-4130, D-312-746-5713/8026, Fax: C-205-837-1911; other SDO, Building 5300, C-205-876-3331. All ranks. DV/VIP call Billeting Office C-205-876-5713, D-205-746-5713.

RV, CAMPING/FAMCAMP: C-205-876-6854, D-205-746-6854, Fax: C-205-842-9134, D-205-788-9134. Building 5132, 0930-1700 daily. Arsenal campground on post, year round, 23 camper spaces with W/E hookups; only electricity hookups during winter months. Outdoor Rec, Building 5132, C-205-876-6854.

SPACE-A: Redstone Arsenal Army Airfield, Building 4809, 0730-1630 Mon-Fri, C-205-876-1916, D-312-746-1916, Fax: C-205-842-0562, D-312-788-0562. Space available transit military air available periodically.

LOGISTICAL SUPPORT:
Bank-535-0246
Beauty Shop-883-1450
Carlson Wagonlit Travel-880-8196
Child Dev Center-876-3704
Commissary-955-6627
Dining Facilities-876-6743
Education Office-876-9761
Gas Station-883-0367
Postal Service-881-8883
Snack Bar-881-7986
Barber Shop-881-7409
Cafeteria-876-8894
Child Care-876-7880
Class Six-883-0367
Credit Union-722-3740
Dry Cleaner-882-3529
Exchange-883-6100
Laundry-882-3529
Shoppette-883-0367
Travel Office-880-3601

ADMINISTRATIVE SUPPORT:
Fire Dept-876-5974
Legal-876-9005
OOD-876-3331
Public Affairs-876-4161
Housing-876-5016
Locator-876-3331
Police-876-2222
SDO/SNCO-876-3331

HEALTH & WELFARE:
American Red Cross-876-4427
Army Emergency Relief-876-5468
Chapel-876-5751
Family Services-876-2859
Retiree Services-876-2022
TRICARE-882-7404
Veterinary Services-876-2441
ACS-876-5397
CHAMPUS-876-2960
Dental-876-2616/1643
Medical
  Central Appts-955-8888
  Emergency-876-8287
  Health Benefits-876-2690

REST & RECREATION:
Arts & Crafts-876-7951
Bowling-876-6634
Fitness Center-313-6091
Golf Course-876-6888
Gym-876-6701
ITR-876-4531
Outdoor Rec-876-6854
Wood Hobby Shop-876-7974
Youth Services-876-2255
Auto Hobby Shop-955-7727
Clubs
  NCO-837-0750
  O-830-2582
Indoor Rec-876-4531
Library-876-4741
Wellness Center-955-6844
Youth Center-876-2255

ATTRACTIONS: Alabama Space and Rocket Center, Alabama Constitution Village, Burritt Museum and Park, Huntsville Depot Museum and Trolley, Huntsville/Madison County Botanical Garden, Old Town Historic District, Twickenham Historic District and the Tennessee River.

ALASKA

CLEAR AIR STATION (AK18R5)

13 SWS, P.O. Box 40013
Clear Air Station, AK 99704-0013

TELEPHONE NUMBER INFORMATION: Main Installation numbers: C-907-585-6409, D-317-585-6416/6110.

LOCATION: Located on Fairbanks/ Anchorage Highway. USMRA: Page 128 (F-4). NMC: Fairbanks, 80 miles northeast.

GENERAL INFORMATION: 13th Space Warning Squadron.

TEMPORARY MILITARY LODGING: Lodging office, Building 200, C-907-585-6224. All ranks.

RV, CAMPING/FAMCAMP: None. See Eielson AFB listing, Birch Lake Recreation Area, C-907-488-6161, D-317-377-4214.

SPACE-A: None. See Eielson Air Force Base listing, C-907-377-1854, D-317-377-1854, Fax: C-907-377-2287.

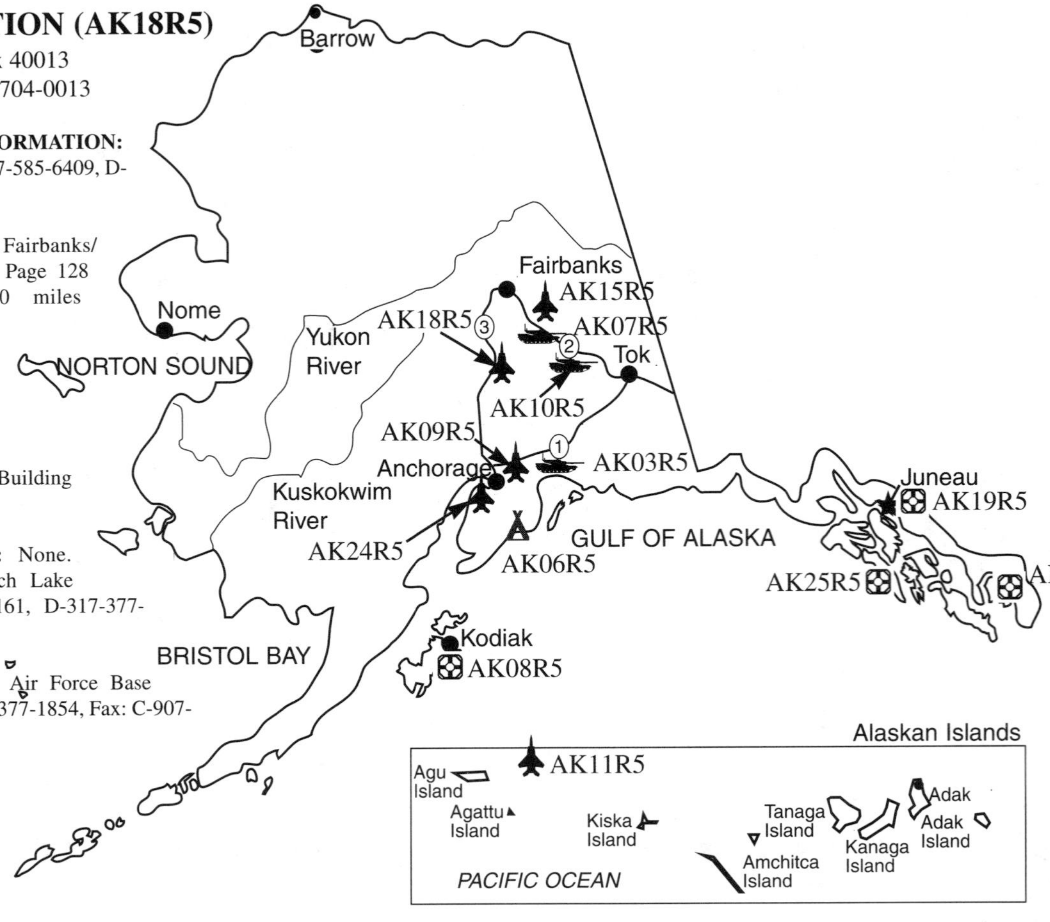

LOGISTICAL SUPPORT:

Exchange-585-6457	Mail Room-585-6224
Post Office-585-6268	SATO-585-6364

ADMINISTRATIVE SUPPORT:

Duty Manager-585-6224	Fire Dept-585-6321/911
Locator-585-1110	NCO-585-6409
Pass/ID Office-585-6293	Police-585-6433/911

HEALTH & WELFARE:	Medical-585-6414

REST & RECREATION:

Bowling-585-6546	Clubs
MWR-585-6276	Com-585-6409
Public Affairs-585-6416	NCO/O-585-6536
Recreation Services-585-6576	Polar Bar-585-6536
Services-585-6519	

ATTRACTIONS: Near Mount McKinley National Park. Hunting, Fishing, and other outdoor activities.

EIELSON AIR FORCE BASE (AK15R5)

3112 Broadway Avenue, Unit 15A
Eielson Air Force Base, AK 99702-1895

TELEPHONE NUMBER INFORMATION: Main installation numbers: C-907-377-1110, D-317-377-1110.

LOCATION: M16 Post 341 on Richardson Highway (AK-2). AFB is clearly marked. USMRA: Page 128 (F,G-4). NMC: Fairbanks, 26 miles northwest.

GENERAL INFORMATION: 354th Fighter Wing, and 168th Air Refueling Wing (ANG), Det 1, 210th Rescue Squadron (ANG), support activities. Major activity: COPE THUNDER-summer air combat training exercises.

TEMPORARY MILITARY LODGING: Lodging Office, 354 SVS/SVRO, 3112 Broadway U-6B, Building 2270, Eielson AFB, AK 99702-1885, 24 hours daily, C-907-377-1844, D-317-377-1844. All ranks. DV/VIP C-907-377-7686.

RV, CAMPING/FAMCAMP: FAMCAMP on base 354 SVS/SVRO, 3112 Broadway U-6B, Eielson AFB, AK 99702-1885, 15 May-7 Sep, C-907-377-1232, D-317-377-1232. Fax: C-907-377-2770, D-317-377-2770, 24 camper spaces with full hookups; Ravenwood Ski Lodge, on base, Nov-Mar, C-907-377-1328, day use only, snow skiing, rec room and support facilities; Birch Lake Recreation Area, 38 miles south of the AFB, May-Sep, C-907-488-6161, D-317-377-4214, 40 camper spaces with E hookups, two deluxe cabins, 16 family cabins, four smaller cabins, and many tent spaces.

SPACE-A: Pax Term/Lounge, Building 1190, Flightline Avenue, Suite 1, Eielson AFB, AK 99702, 0730-1630 daily, or as required, C-907-377-1854, D-317-377-1854 Fax: C-907-377-2287, flights to CONUS and Alaska locations.

LOGISTICAL SUPPORT:

Barber Shop-372-2237	Beauty Shop-372-3265
Burger King- 372-4343	Cafeteria-377-1341
Child Care-377-3636	Child Dev Center-377-3237
Class Six-377-2210	Commissary-377-5134
Conv Store-377-2210	Credit Union-372-6111

ALASKA
Eielson Air Force Base, continued

Dining Facilities-377-2563
Education Office-377-3177
Laundry-372-3541
Postal Service-377-2289
Shoppette-377-2210
Visitor Center-377-3807
Dry Cleaner-372-3541
Exchange-377-4154
Gas Station-377-1218
SATO-377-2288
Snack Bar-377-5154

ADMINISTRATIVE SUPPORT:
Command Post-377-1500
Housing Office-377-1840
Locator-377-1841
 Non Duty-377-7885
Public Affairs-377-2116
Fire Dept-377-4156
Legal-377-4114
Pass/ID Office-377-1033
Police-377-5130

HEALTH & WELFARE:
Air Force Aid Society-377-3351
CHAMPUS-377-5155-ext 299
Dental
 Central Appts-377-1846-ext 203
 Clinic-377-1846-ext 261
 Emergency-377-2296
Retiree Services-377-3192
Veterinary Services-377-1146
American Red Cross-377-1855
Chapel-377-2130
Family Services-377-2242
Medical
 Central Appts-377-1847
 Clinic-377-2259
 Emergency-377-2296
 Health Benefits-377-5155-ext 299
 Information-377-1847

REST & RECREATION:
Arts & Crafts-377-4880
Boat Shop-ext 1232
Clubs
 Com-377-5219
 Flying-ext 1121
 O-377-2051
MWR-377-1839
Rec Equipment-ext 1232
Swimming-ext 1231
Wood Hobby Shop-377-1168
Auto Hobby Shop-377-3190
Bowling-377-1129
Fitness Center-377-1231
Gym-ext 1231
ITT-377-2722
Library-377-3174
Recreation-377-1232
Services-377-2857
Theater-377-1172
Youth Center-377-5437

ATTRACTIONS: Fairbanks and North Pole, Denali National Park, outdoor sports, and recreation.

ELMENDORF AIR FORCE BASE (AK09R5)

3rd Wing/PA
6920 12th Street
Elmendorf Air Force Base, AK 99506-2530

TELEPHONE NUMBER INFORMATION: Main installation numbers: C-907-552-1110, D-317-552-1110.

LOCATION: Off Glenn Highway adjacent to north Anchorage. Take Boniface Parkway Exit. Take either Elmendorf Access Road or Post Road. The base is adjacent to Fort Richardson. USMRA: Page 128 (F-5), page 131 (B,C,D,E-1). NMC: Anchorage, two miles southwest.

GENERAL INFORMATION: Pacific Air Forces Base. Headquarters Alaskan Command, 3rd Wing, Headquarters Alaska NORAD Region, Headquarters 11th Air Force.

TEMPORARY MILITARY LODGING: Lodging office, North Star Inn, Building 31-250, Acacia Street, 24 hours daily, C-907-552-2454, D-317-552-2454, Fax: C-907-552-8276. All ranks. DV/VIP C-907-552-3210.

RV, CAMPING/FAMCAMP: FAMCAMP, on base, May-Sep, C-907-552-4599, 39 camper spaces with W/E hookups, 10 tent spaces.

SPACE-A: Pax Term/Lounge, Building 32-233 24 hours daily, C-907-552-3781/4616, D-317-552-3781/4616, Fax: C-907-552-3996. Flights to CONUS, Alaska, and foreign locations.

LOGISTICAL SUPPORT:
Child Care-753-5113
Exchange-753-4208
Package Store-753-5151
Snack Bar-753-6146
Commissary-552-4877
Gas Station-753-2134
SATO-753-0509

ADMINISTRATIVE SUPPORT:
Legal-552-3046
Police-552-3421
SDO/NCO-552-3013
Locator-552-4860
Public Affairs-552-8151

HEALTH & WELFARE:
CHAMPUS-552-3430
Family Services-552-2694
Retiree Services-552-2337
Chapel-552-4422
Medical
 Central Appts-552-2748
 Emergency-552-5555

REST & RECREATION:
Arts & Crafts-ext 2470
Clubs
 Aero-753-4167
 EM-753-5190
 Jogging -ext 5353/3504
 NCO-753-5190
 O-753-3131
 Riding -ext 4987
Riding Stables-ext 4987
Ski Area-ext 4838
Theater-753-2344
Youth Center-ext 2266
Bowling-ext 4108
Community Center-ext 8529
Field House-ext 5353/3504
Golf Course-ext 3821
ITT-552-5191
Library-ext 3787
Racquetball-ext 5353
Rec Equip-ext 2023
Services Squadron-ext 2468
Swimming-ext 3504
Tennis-ext 8529/5353

ATTRACTIONS: Anchorage, outdoor sports and recreation, Portage Glacier, Earthquake Park.

FORT GREELY (AK10R5)

ATTN: APVR-GPC
502 2nd Street
APO AP 96508-6050

TELEPHONE NUMBER INFORMATION: Main installation numbers: C-907-873-4113, D-317-873-4113.

LOCATION: Off AK-4, six miles south of junction of AK-2 and AK-4. Five miles south of Delta Junction. USMRA: Page 128 (F,G-4). NMC: Fairbanks, 105 miles northwest.

GENERAL INFORMATION: Army Northern Warfare Training Center, Army Cold Region Test Center and support units.

TEMPORARY MILITARY LODGING: Limited availability with TDY and new arrivals having priority. Lodging office, Building 663, First Street, 0730-1530 Mon, Tue, Thurs & Fri, 0730-1130 Wed, C-907-873-3285, D-317-873-3285. Other hours, SDO, Building 501, C-907-873-4720. All ranks.

RV, CAMPING/FAMCAMP: None. See Eielson AFB, Birch Lake Recreation Area, C-907-488-6161, D-317-377-4214.

SPACE-A: None. See Elmendorf AFB listing, C-907-552-3337, D-317-552-4616, Fax: C-907-552-3996.

LOGISTICAL SUPPORT:
Child Care-873-4593
Exchange-869-3135
SATO-873-3107
Commissary-873-4404
Gas Station-869-3210
Snack Bar-869-3110

ADMINISTRATIVE SUPPORT:
Legal-873-3250
SDO/NCO-873-4720
Locator-873-3255

ALASKA
Fort Greely, continued

HEALTH & WELFARE:
Army Emergency Relief-873-3288
Emergency-911
Medical-873-4498
Chapel-873-4610
Family Services-873-3284/7
Police-873-1111

REST & RECREATION:
Arts & Crafts-873-3181
Bowling-873-2695
Library-873-3217
Outdoor Sports Center-873-3183/1115
Theater-873-3283
Auto Crafts-873-3293
Com Club-895-3105
MWR-873-4207
Rec Center-873-1115

ATTRACTIONS: Outdoor sports and recreation.

FORT RICHARDSON (AK03R5)

600 Richardson Drive, #5900
Fort Richardson, AK 99505-5900

TELEPHONE NUMBER INFORMATION: Main installation numbers: C-907-384-1110, D-317-384-1110.

LOCATION: Main gate is on Glenn Highway, eight miles south of Eagle River. USMRA: Page 128 (F-5), page 131 (E-1). NMC: Anchorage, eight miles southwest.

GENERAL INFORMATION: Headquarters for US Army, Alaska: Arctic Support Brigade; 1st Battalion (Airborne), 501st Infantry, and other support units.

TEMPORARY MILITARY LODGING: Lodging office, Building 600, Richardson Drive, 0600-2230 Mon-Fri, 1000-1730 Sat-Sun, C-907-384-0436, D-317-384-0436. All ranks.

RV, CAMPING/FAMCAMP: Black Spruce Travel Camp on post, 1 May-1 Sep, C-907-384-1745, 22 camper spaces with W/E hookups, and 20 camper/tent spaces at Upper Otter Lake Campground; operates Seward Resort at Resurrection Bay near Seward, 133 miles south of post. See Seward Resort listing for more information.

SPACE-A: None. See Elmendorf AFB listing, C-907-552-4616, D-317-552-4616, Fax: C-907-552-3996.

LOGISTICAL SUPPORT:
Cafeteria-428-1314
Commissary-384-1565
Exchange-428-1233
Package Store-384-3190
Snack Bar-428-1314
Child Care-384-7483
Conv Store-428-3190
Gas Station-428-1248
SATO-384-1663

ADMINISTRATIVE SUPPORT:
Fire Dept-384-0774
Locator-384-0306
Public Affairs-384-2113
Legal-384-0371
Police-384-0823
SDO/NCO-384-6665

HEALTH & WELFARE:
ACS-384-1518
Chapel-384-1468
Family Services-384-1518
Retiree Services-1-800-478-7384
CHAMPUS-552-3430
Emergency-911
Medical-384-0600

REST & RECREATION:
Arts & Crafts-ext 3717
Bowling-ext 1840
Golf Course-428-0056
Library-ext 1648
Otter Lake Lodge-ext 6246
Recreation-384-1649/1480
Skeet Range-ext 1480
Swimming-ext 1301
Youth Center-ext 1508/1516
Auto Hobby Shop-ext 3718
Fitness Center-ext 1308
ITR Office-384-1649
MWR-384-1300
Outdoor Rec Center-428-0001
Rec Equipment-ext 1745
Ski Slope/Lodge-ext 2975/6
Theater-428-1200

ATTRACTIONS: Great outdoors and Anchorage.

FORT WAINWRIGHT (AK07R5)

ATTN: AFVR-WPC
1060 Gaffney Road, #6050
Fort Wainwright, AK 99703-5900

TELEPHONE NUMBER INFORMATION: Main installation numbers: C-907-353-1110, D-317-353-1110. HP: http://143.213.254/ home.htm.

LOCATION: From Fairbanks, take Airport Way east which leads to the Main Gate of the post. USMRA: Page 128 (F-4). NMC: Fairbanks, adjacent.

GENERAL INFORMATION: Infantry Brigade, Aviation Brigade and other support units.

TEMPORARY MILITARY LODGING: Lodging office, Building 1045 (Murphy Hall), Gaffney Road, 0730-1630 Mon-Fri, C-907-353-6294/7291, D-317-353-6294/7291, Fax: C-907-353-7409, D-317-353-7409. All ranks. DV/VIP C-907-353-6671.

RV, CAMPING/FAMCAMP: Glass Park, on post, year round, C-907-353-2706, D-317-353-2706, camper spaces in open area, no hookups.

SPACE-A: None. See Eielson AFB listing, C-907-377-1854, D-317-377-1854, Fax: C-907-377-2287.

LOGISTICAL SUPPORT:
Barber Shop-356-1070
Burger King-356-3130
Class Six-356-1044
Conv Store-356-7259
Dry Cleaner-356-1359
Exchange-356-1345
Postal Service-356-1980
Shoppette-356-7529
Beauty Shop-356-2727
Child Care-353-7331
Commissary-353-7805
Credit Union-356-1262
Education Office-353-7486
Gas Station-353-1263
SATO-353-1166
Snack Bar-353-1976

ADMINISTRATIVE SUPPORT:
Fire Dept-353-6485
Legal-353-6534
Pass/ID Office-353-2243
Public Affairs-353-6701
Housing-353-1190
Locator-353-6815
Police-353-7535
SDO/NCO-353-7500

HEALTH & WELFARE:
American Red Cross-353-7234
Army Emergency Relief-353-4237
Chapel-353-6271
Family Services-353-7331
Retiree Services-353-2102
Veterinary Services-353-7179
ACS-353-4227
CHAMPUS-353-5340
Dental-353-5135
Medical-1-800-478-5172 or -353-5172
Central Appts-353-4000
Emergency-353-5143
Health Benefits-353-5340

REST & RECREATION:
Arts & Crafts-ext 7520
Boat Shop/Outdoor Equip-ext 6349
Clubs
Arctic Oasis-353-1085
Flying-ext 6671
Last Frontier Club-353-1609
Library-ext 7131
Recreation-353-1998
Swimming-ext 1993
Wood Hobby Shop-353-7520
Auto Hobby Shop-ext 7436
Bowling-353-2654
Fitness Center-353-7272
Golf Course-353-6223
Gym-353-1994
ITR-353-2652
Rec Center-ext 7882
Ski Lodge-ext 6780
Theater-353-6792
Youth Center/Services-353-9661

ATTRACTIONS: Fairbanks, North Pole, Golden Days (mid-July), World Eskimo Indian Olympics, Tanana Valley State Fair, Jesse Owens Games, area tours, gold panning, riverboat tours, hiking, rafting, boating, hunting, fishing, camping, Alaskaland, Denali National Park, Mount McKinley (highest point in North America), Northern Lights, Luge Run (Bobsled), skiing, hunting, ice fishing, Chena Hot Springs, Dog Sled Races, Eskimo Winter Olympics, Special Olympics, Nenana Ice Classic, Ice Festival. Continuous daylight in summer; 2-three hours light in winter.

JUNEAU COAST GUARD AIR STATION (AK19R5)

345 Eagan Drive
Juneau, AK 99801-1701

TELEPHONE NUMBER INFORMATION: Main installation number: C-907-463-2365.

LOCATION: Accessible by air or boat. From the ferry go right (southeast) 13 miles to Eagan Drive, follow signs. USMRA: Page 128 (I-6). NMC: Juneau, in city limits.

GENERAL INFORMATION: Juneau is home to the Seventeenth Coast District Offices, which has operational control over all Coast Guard units in Alaska.

TEMPORARY MILITARY LODGING: None. Nearest facility is more than 100 miles away.

RV, CAMPING/FAMCAMP: None. Nearest facility is more than 100 miles away.

SPACE-A: None. See Sitka Coast Guard Air Station listing, C-907-966-5420, Fax: C-907-966-5428.

LOGISTICAL SUPPORT: Exchange-463-2385

ADMINISTRATIVE SUPPORT: Buoy Deck-463-2370

HEALTH & WELFARE: Medical-463-2146
Clinic-463-2140

REST & RECREATION: Consol Club-463-2382

ATTRACTIONS: Beautiful Alaskan countryside. Hunting, fishing, and camping.

KETCHIKAN COAST GUARD INTEGRATED SUPPORT COMMAND (AK21R5)

1300 Stedman Street
Ketchikan, AK 99901-6698

TELEPHONE NUMBER INFORMATION: Main installation numbers: C-907-228-0222.

LOCATION: Accessible only via AK-7, also known as North and South Tongass. Located three miles south of the ferry terminals on AK-7. USMRA: Page 128 (J-7). NMC: Ketchikan, in the city.

GENERAL INFORMATION: Industrial Support Facility, responsible for area search-and-rescue and other Coast Guard operations. Also host The Cutter *Plane Tree*, the Cutter *Naushon* and STATION Ketchikan.

TEMPORARY MILITARY LODGING: None. Nearest facility is more than 100 miles away.

RV, CAMPING/FAMCAMP: None. Nearest facility is more than 100 miles away.

SPACE-A: None. See Sitka Coast Guard Air Station listing, C-907-966-5420, Fax: C-907-966-5428.

LOGISTICAL SUPPORT:
Cafeteria-228-0258
Exchange-225-4528
Commissary-225-4528
Package Store-225-4528

ADMINISTRATIVE SUPPORT:
OOD-228-0222
Pass/ID Office-228-0311

HEALTH & WELFARE:
CHAMPUS-228-0320
Medical-228-0320
Family Services-228-0211

REST & RECREATION:
Auto Hobby Shop-228-0330
Clubs
  All Hands-228-0254
  CPO/EM-228-0230
Public Affairs-228-0344
Camping/Rec Equip-ext 0389
Fitness Center-228-0211
Morale Boats-228-0389
MWR-228-0250
Recreation-228-0250

ATTRACTIONS: Sport fishing and hunting abundant.

KODIAK COAST GUARD INTEGRATED SUPPORT COMMAND (AK08R5)

P.O. Box 195014
Kodiak, AK 99619-5014

TELEPHONE NUMBER INFORMATION: Main installation numbers: C-907-487-5760.

LOCATION: From Kodiak City, take Chiniak Highway southwest for seven miles. Base is on left side. USMRA: Page 128 (E-7). NMC: Kodiak, seven miles northeast.

GENERAL INFORMATION: ISC, Air Station, Communication Station, LORAN station, Electronic Support Unit, North Pacific Regional Fisheries Training Center, Marine Safety Detachment and Public Affairs Detachment. Also home to three USCG Cutters: Storis, Ironwood and Firebush.

TEMPORARY MILITARY LODGING: Guest house, Building N-30, 0800-1700 daily, C-907-487-5446, D-317-487-5446. All ranks. PCS or official duty, all others Space-A. DV/VIP C-907-487-5265.

RV, CAMPING/FAMCAMP: None. Nearest facility is more than 100 miles away.

SPACE-A: Pax Term, Hangar #1, 0800-1600 Mon-Fri, C-907-487-5149, D-317-487-5149, Fax: C-907-487-5273, flights to Alaska locations and Sacramento.

LOGISTICAL SUPPORT:
Barber Shop-487-5847
Cafeteria-487-5440
Child Dev Center-487-5481
Conv Store-487-5519
Dry Cleaner-487-5450
Exchange-487-5373/5113
Laundry-487-5450
Postal Service-487-5263
Snack Bar-487-5715
Beauty Shop-487-5432
Child Care-487-5922
Commissary-487-5015
Dining Facilities-487-5235
Education Office-487-5119
Gas Station-487-5107
Package Store-487-5519
SATO-487-2500

ADMINISTRATIVE SUPPORT:
Fire Dept-487-5808
Legal-487-5474
OOD-487-5267
Police-487-5266, ext 010
Housing-487-5310, ext 141
Locator-487-5267
Pass/ID Office-487-5170, ext 157
Public Affairs-487-5170, ext 186

ALASKA
Kodiak Coast Guard Integrated Support Command, continued

HEALTH & WELFARE:
American Red Cross-487-5200
Chapel-487-5745
Family Services-487-5542
Medical-487-5757
Central Appts-487-5757, ext 125
Emergency-487-5222
Health Benefits-487-5757, ext 131
Information-487-5757, ext 125
CHAMPUS-487-5757, ext 131
Dental-487-5757
Central Appts-487-5757, ext 115
Retiree Services-487-5761

REST & RECREATION:
Arts & Crafts-487-5493
Boat House-ext 5047
Clubs
Com-487-5798
CPO/O-487-5798
EM-487-5110
MWR-487-5108
Racquetball-ext 5272
Theater-487-5884
Wood Hobby Shop-487-5550
Auto Hobby Shop-487-5844
Bowling-487-5401
Community Center-487-5250
Golf Course-486-7561
Gym-487-5272
Library-487-5661
Outdoor Sports-ext 5272
Teen Center-ext 5271
Weight Room-ext 5272
Youth Services-487-5457

ATTRACTIONS: Hunting and fishing paradise, National Wildlife Refuge-home of Kodiak brown bear, sightseeing and local museums display Alutiiq and Russian History.

KULIS AIR NATIONAL GUARD BASE (AK24R5)

5005 Raspberry Road
Anchorage, AK 99502-1998

TELEPHONE NUMBER INFORMATION: Main installation numbers: C-907-249-1176, D-317-626-1176.

LOCATION: Take International Airport Road to Jewel Lake Road, turn right onto Raspberry Road. Main gate is approximately one mile on right. USMRA: Page 128 (F-5), page 131 (A-4). NMC: Anchorage, in city limits.

GENERAL INFORMATION: 176th Wing.

TEMPORARY MILITARY LODGING: None. See Elmendorf AFB listing, C-907-552-2454, D-317-552-2454, Fax: C-907-552-8276.

RV, CAMPING/FAMCAMP: None. See Steward Resort listing, C-907-224-5559, 1-800-770-1858, D-317-384-FISH (3474)/LINE (5463).

SPACE-A: Base Ops, C-907-249-1225, D-317-626-1225, Fax: C-907-249-1648.

LOGISTICAL SUPPORT:
Cafeteria-249-1454
SATO-249-1206

ADMINISTRATIVE SUPPORT:
Fire Department 249-1394
Locator-249-1176
Public Affairs 249-1342
Legal-249-1100
Police-249-1271
SDO/NCO-249-1131

HEALTH & WELFARE:
Chapel-249-1141
Medical-249-1415

REST & RECREATION:
NCO Club-249-1234

ATTRACTIONS: Great opportunity for skiing, hunting, fishing, camping, sightseeing, and bird watching.

SEWARD RESORT (AK06R5)

P.O. Box 329
Seward, AK 99664-5000

TELEPHONE NUMBER INFORMATION: Main installation numbers: C-907-384-1110, D-317-384-1110.

LOCATION: 124 miles south of Anchorage off AK-1 to AK-9. Follow signs. USMRA: Page 128 (F-6). NMC: Anchorage, 124 miles north. NMI: Fort Richardson, 133 miles north.

GENERAL INFORMATION: Superb fishing for salmon, halibut, snapper, ling cod, black bass and flounder. Nearby streams offer outstanding trout fishing. Operated by Fort Richardson, off base 1 May-15 September 0600-2300, 16 September-30 April 1100-1900. Military personnel active, retired, reserve, DoD, NAF and contract civilians. Reservations: call for specific information 0600-2300 local time, seven days a week, C-907-224-5559, 1-800-770-1858, D-317-384-FISH (3474)/LINE (5463). No reservations may be made by mail. Visa, MasterCard, American Express and Diners accepted. Pets are not permitted in Cabins, Motel units or Common buildings. Pets must be kept on a short leash (six feet and under); are not to be left unattended; are not allowed on boats; owner must clean up after pets. Seven day limit; manager approval for up to 14. No open fires; grills and fire rings may be used. No fish cleaning in motels or cabins. No smoking in cabins, motel units or common buildings.

TEMPORARY MILITARY LODGING: Motel, two double beds, full bath, linens, microwave, small refrigerator (56). Handicap accessible rooms available (3). Rates: E1-E5 $59; E6-E9, W1-CW3, O1-O3 $79; CW4-CW5, O4-O10, DoD/NAF and others $89. Premier Cabins w/ boat sleeps six, one bedroom, sleeper sofa, loft, furnished, linens, complete kitchen, fireplace, six person boat w/ driver (2). Deluxe Cabins sleep six, one bedroom, sleeper sofa, loft, furnished, linens, complete kitchen, fireplace (2). Standard Cabins sleep six, one bedroom, sleeper sofa, loft, furnished, linens, complete kitchen, one handicapped unit (10). Rates: Premier Cabins E1-E5 $300; E6-E9, W1-CW3, O1-O3 $350; CW4-CW5, O4-O10, DoD/NAF and others $400; Deluxe Cabins E1-E5 $124; E6-E9, W1-CW3, O1-O3 $144; CW4-CW5, O4-O10, DoD/NAF and others $164; Standard Cabins E1-E5 $99; E6-E9, W1-CW3, O1-O3 $119; CW4-CW5, O4-O10, DoD/NAF and others $139.

RV, CAMPING/FAMCAMP: 40 gravel RV/Trailer Spaces with W/E hookups. 10 tent spaces no hookups. Rates: RV Spaces E1-E5 $17; E6-E9, W1-CW3, O1-O3 $19; CW4-CW5, O4-O10, DoD/NAF and others $21; Tent Spaces E1-E5 $7; E6-E9, W1-CW3, O1-O3 $10; CW4-CW5, O4-O10, DoD/NAF and others $12.

REST & RECREATION: Basketball, Fishing/license, Hiking, Hunting/license, Volleyball, Wildlife Tour/fee.

OTHER SUPPORT & FACILITIES AVAILABLE: Boat Rental*, Fish Cleaning Facility, Fish Freezer, Fishing Rods, Grills, Laundry Facility, Playground, Picnic Area, Rec Center, Restrooms, Sewage Dump Station, Showers, Snack Bar/BX Annex, Vending Machines. Also, see Fort Richardson listing, C-907-384-1110, D-317-384-1110.

** Deep-sea fishing, by drawing/free. Deep-sea fishing charters/fee.*

ATTRACTIONS: Area is a photographer's dream. Late July to mid August see active salmon spawning areas on drive to Seward.

SITKA COAST GUARD AIR STATION (AK25R5)

611 Airport Road
Sitka, AK 99835-6500

TELEPHONE NUMBER INFORMATION: Main installation numbers: C-907-966-5434.

LOCATION: Located at end of Airport Road on Jponski Island, five miles north of airport terminal. USMRA: Page 128 (I-7). NMC: Juneau, 90 miles by air or ferry.

ALASKA
Sitka Coast Guard Air Station, continued

GENERAL INFORMATION: Air Station Sitka primarily involved in search and rescue throughout southeast Alaska. Additionally, performs law enforcement, fisheries patrols and aids to navigation support.

TEMPORARY MILITARY LODGING: None. Nearest facility is more than 100 miles away.

RV, CAMPING/FAMCAMP: None. Nearest facility is more than 100 miles away.

SPACE-A: Very limited. C-907-966-5420, Fax: C-907-966-5428.

LOGISTICAL SUPPORT:
Cafeteria-966-5546
Conv Store-966-5436
Exchange-966-5436
Class Six-966-5436
Dining Facilities-966-5546

ADMINISTRATIVE SUPPORT:
Locator-966-5431
SDO/NCO-966-5420

HEALTH & WELFARE:
CHAMPUS-966-5438
Medical-966-5438
Emergency-911

REST & RECREATION:
Camping Equip-ext 5581
Gym-ext 5511
Rec Equipment-ext 5581
Support Services-ext 5581
Clubs
Com-966-5516
O-966-5596

ATTRACTIONS: Sport fishing and hunting abundant. Sitka National Historical Park, totem poles and Sitka shoreline. Russian Bishop's House; St Michael's Russian Orthodox Church, with many precious icons on display; Castle Hill, site of 1867 transfer of Alaska territory from Russia to the US.

Other Installations in Alaska

Eareckson Air Station (AK11R5), 616th ALSS/TRO, Shemya AK, APO AP 96512-5000. Contracted flights from Reeves Air, call C-907-392-3401. Limited billeting, call C-907-392-3240.

ARIZONA

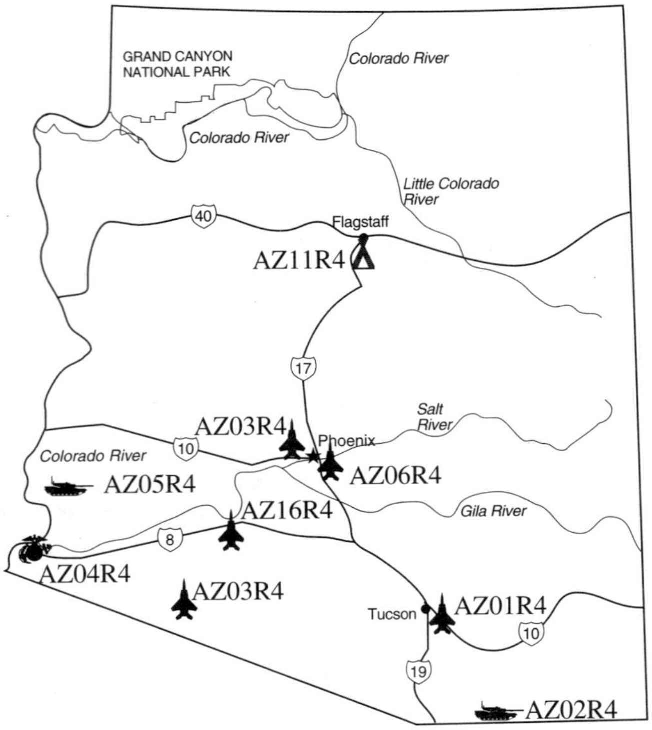

DAVIS-MONTHAN AIR FORCE BASE (AZ01R4)

355th Wing, Hq 12th Air Force
5275 East Granite Street
Davis-Monthan Air Force Base, AZ 85707-3010

TELEPHONE NUMBER INFORMATION: Main installation numbers: C-520-228-3900, D-312-228-1110. HP: www.dm.af.mil.

LOCATION: From the east on I-10, exit Kolb Road; north to Golf Links Road, left to Craycroft Road, left to main gate. From the west on I-10, exit Alvernon Way; turn left, following road around to the base. (Alvernon Way turns into Golf Links Road at Ajo intersection.) USMRA: Page 108 (F-9). NMC: Tucson, in city limits.

GENERAL INFORMATION: Air Combat Command Base, 355th Wing (host unit), HQ 12th Air Force, AAC Air Ops, and Aerospace Maintenance and Regeneration Center (AMARC) and 305th Rescue Squadron (AFRES).

TEMPORARY MILITARY LODGING: Lodging office, Building 2350, 10th Street, 24 hours daily, C-520-748-1500, D-312-748-3230. All ranks. DV/VIP 520-228-3600.

RV, CAMPING/FAMCAMP: Davis-Monthan FAMCAMP on base, C-520-747-9144, year round, 73 camper spaces with full hookups, 35 overflow camper spaces without hookups.

SPACE-A: Pax Term/Ops in Building 4819, 0700-1600 Mon-Fri, C-520-228-2322, D-312-228-2322, Fax: C-520-228-7229.

LOGISTICAL SUPPORT:
Bank-792-7027
Barber Shop-571-1604
Beauty Shop-748-8334
Cafeteria-790-6150
Child Care-228-3336
Child Dev Center-228-3336
Class Six-747-1365
Clothing & Sales-228-4408
Commissary-228-3116
Conv Store-748-8076
Credit Union-298-7882
Dining Facilities-228-3072
Dry Cleaner-790-1701
Education Office-228-4813
Exchange-748-7887
Gas Station-748-8212
Package Store-747-1365
Postal Service-748-1651
SATO-228-4841
Shoppette-745-3866
Snack Bar-790-6150
Visitor Center-228-4886

ADMINISTRATIVE SUPPORT:
Fire Dept-228-4758
Housing Office-228-3687
Legal-228-5242
Locator-228-3347
Pass/ID Office-228-5246
Police-228-3200
Public Affairs-228-3204
SDO/NCO-750-3121

HEALTH & WELFARE:
Air Force Aid Society-228-3891
CHAMPUS-228-2606
Dental-Hospital
Central Appts-228-2652
Clinic-228-2651
Retiree Services-228-5100
TRICARE-228-3835
Veterinary Services-228-3529
American Red Cross-228-3205
Chapel-228-5411
Family Services-228-3369
Medical-Hospital
Central Appts-228-2778
Emergency-228-2828
Health Benefits-228-2606
Information-228-2564

REST & RECREATION:
Arts & Crafts-228-4385
Bowling-228-3461
Clubs
Aero-ext 3603
EM-228-3100
NCO-228-3100
O-228-3301
Saddle-885-9049
Picnic Area-ext 3846
Swimming-ext 3579
Wood Hobby Shop-228-4385
Auto Hobby Shop-228-3614
Ceramics-ext 4385/4028
Community Center-228-3717
Fitness Center-228-3714
Golf Course-228-3734
Gym-ext 3714
Library-228-4381
Outdoor Rec-228-3736
Rec Center/Tickets-ext 3717
Theater-228-3623
Youth Center-228-4565

ATTRACTIONS: Old Tucson, movie sets, Reid Park, zoo, Arizona-Sonora Desert, Pima Air and Space Museum, Titan Missile Museum, University of Arizona, Kitt Peak Observatory, Biosphere II, and Mount Lemon hiking and skiing. Also, twice weekly tours at AMARC.

FORT HUACHUCA (AZ02R4)

USAIC & Fort Huachuca
ATTN: ATZS-CDR
Fort Huachuca, AZ 85613-6000

TELEPHONE NUMBER INFORMATION: Main installation numbers: C-520-538-7111, D-312-821-7111.

LOCATION: From I-10 take State Route AZ-90 south approximately 30 miles to Sierra Vista and main gate to fort. USMRA: Page 108 (F,G-9,10). NMI: Davis Monthan AFB, 75 miles northwest. NMC: Tucson, 75 miles northwest.

GENERAL INFORMATION: US Army Intelligence Center and Fort Huachuca, US Army Signal Command, US Army Electronic Proving Ground, Joint Interoperability Command and 11th Signal Brigade.

TEMPORARY MILITARY LODGING: Lodging office, Building 43083, Service Road, 24 hours daily, C-520-533-2222, D-312-821-2222. Extensive facilities. All ranks. DV/VIP C-520-533-1231, D-312-821-1231.

RV, CAMPING/FAMCAMP: Apache Flats Campground on post, Building 15423, 1100-1900 hours Wed through Fri, 1000-1800 hours Sat and Sun, C-520-533-7085/6, D-312-821-7085/6. 24 camper spaces with W/E hookups and a limited number of tent spaces.

SPACE-A: Limited flights from Libby Army Airfield on post via executive aircraft, C-520-538-2860.

ARIZONA
Fort Huachuca, continued

LOGISTICAL SUPPORT:

Barber Shop-459-1172	Beauty Shop-458-7140
Carlson Wagonlit Travel-515-0914	Child Care-533-5209
Child Dev Center-533-5209	Class Six-458-8389
Commissary-533-5540	Credit Union-459-1860
Dry Cleaner-458-2111	Exchange-458-7831
Gas Station-458-4022	Laundry-533-2661
Postal Service-458-4411	Shoppette-458-8389
Snack Bar-533-5759	

ADMINISTRATIVE SUPPORT:

Fire Dept-533-2116 or 911	Housing Office-533-3083
Legal-533-2095	Locator-533-7111
Pass/ID Office-533-1608	Police-533-2181 or 911
Public Affairs-533-2752	SDO/NCO-533-2291

HEALTH & WELFARE:

American Red Cross-533-3883/3895	ACS-533-3234
Army Emergency Relief-533-5972	Chapel-533-5559
Dental-533-3147	Family Services-533-2330
Central Appts-533-5151	Medical
Retiree Services-533-5733	Emergency-533-5132
TRICARE-515-5840	Veterinary Services-533-2767

REST & RECREATION:

Arts & Crafts-533-2015	Auto Hobby Shop-538-1690
Barnes Field House (Gym)-538-2022	Bowling 533-2849
Clubs	Eilfer Fitness Center-533-1723
EM (Ozone)-533-0861	Golf Course-533-7092
NCO (LaHacienta)-533-7322	ITT/ITR-533-2404
O/Civ (Lakeside)-533-2193	Library-533-4101
MWR-533-3107/1315	Outdoor Rec-533-6706
Picnic Reservations-538-7085	Riding-533-5220
Swimming-533-3858/3853	Theater-533-2950
Youth Center-533-3205	

OTHER SUPPORT AVAILABLE: Bank, Cafeteria, Community Center, Education Office, civilian and military personnel offices and Defense Finance and Accounting Service.

ATTRACTIONS: Two post historical museum and original cantonment, now a national historical landmark. Tombstone, AZ, home of the famous OK Corral and the gun fight between the Earps and Doc Holiday and the Clantons; a 25 minute drive east on Charleston Road.

FORT TUTHILL RECREATION AREA (AZ11R4)

Luke Recreation Area
HC 30, Box 5
Flagstaff, AZ 86001-8701

TELEPHONE NUMBER INFORMATION: Main installation numbers: C-602-856-0111, D-312-896-0111.

LOCATION: Located at an elevation of 7,000 feet at the base of the San Francisco Peaks. Four miles south of Flagstaff. Take I-17 to exit 337 (Airport/Sedona). Enter park area at Fort Tuthill (adjoins Coconino County fairgrounds). Take first road to left.. USMRA: Page 108 (E-4). NMC: Flagstaff, four miles north. NMI: Luke Air Force Base (Glendale), 138 miles southwest.

GENERAL INFORMATION: Fort Tuthill Recreation Area was created in 1928 as a National Guard summer camp, it is operated by Luke Air Force Base, off base hotels, chalets, cabins and yurts: year round; camping area: May-Oct. Military personnel active, retired, reserve and DoD civilians. Check in after 1500, check out 1100; office open 24 hours. Reservations: Required, confirm with credit card or mail deposit. C-800-552-6268 or C-602-856-7990, Fax C-602-856-7990, D-312-896-3401. Reservations accepted at Fort Tuthill. Active Duty military may make reservations for any 12 month period beginning with the month in which the reservation made. All other authorized personnel may make reservations for any six (6) month period beginning with the month in which the reservation is made. Reservations should be confirmed with a credit card. Check guarantees are due within 10 days after the date the reservation is made. Cancellations must be received at least 48 hours in advance of arrival to avoid penalty fees. Visa, Mastercard and American Express accepted. No pets in any rental unit. Pets allowed on leash in RV AREA ONLY. Firearms are permitted but must remain unloaded and secured in vehicle at all times.

TEMPORARY MILITARY LODGING: Furnished, three bedroom multi family chalet (1); furnished, two bedroom chalet with full hookups (11); furnished cabin with full hookups (1). Rates: multi family chalet $150 daily; chalet $75 daily. Hotel with full hookups: double, occupancy four (8), queen, occupancy two (8), queen, handicapped, occupancy two (2), queen, kitchenette, occupancy two (2). Rates: double $35 daily, queen; queen with kitchenette $40 daily.

RV, CAMPING/FAMCAMP: Yurts* with E hookup;camper space with W&E hookups (21); camper/tent spaces with no hookups (13). Rates: yurts $25 daily; camper spaces with hookups $14 daily, camper spaces with no hookups $9 daily.

*A "yurt" is a cabin/tent structure, 24 feet in diameter with woden floor, deck and door, two windows and stretched-canvas covering with skylight. It is furnished, but has no bathroom or kitchen.

ADMINISTRATIVE SUPPORT: Police-911

OTHER SUPPORT & FACILITIES AVAILABLE: Arcade, Country Store, Golf, Grills, Handball, Jacuzzi, Laundry, Lodge, Picnic Area, Playground, Rec Equipment, Restrooms, RV Storage, Sewage Dump, Showers, Sports Fields, Theaters and Tennis Courts. Also, see Luke Air Force Base listing, C-602-856-7411, D-312-896-1110.

REST & RECREATION: Boating, Day Trips, Fishing, Hiking, Horseback Riding, Hunting, Mountain Biking, Nature Trails, Outdoor Adventure Trips, Sledding/Tubing, Snowskiing. Many opportunities for both sports person and tourist within a 30-mile radius.

ATTRACTIONS: Tall pines, mild summer temperatures, and skiing in the winter make this an ideal vacation spot.

GILA BEND AIR FORCE AUXILIARY FIELD (AZ16R4)

3096 First Street
Gila Bend Air Force Auxiliary Field, AZ 85337-5000

TELEPHONE NUMBER INFORMATION: Main installation numbers: C-520-683-6200, D-312-853-5200 (Answered by Gila Bend Security Police).

LOCATION: From I-10 west of Phoenix take exit 112 (Yuma/Gila Bend); south on AZ-85 through Gila Bend; right at Gila Bend AFAF/Ajo sign approximately three-and-a-half miles to the AFAF. USMRA: Page 108 (C-7,8). NMC: Phoenix, 69 miles northeast.

GENERAL INFORMATION: Primarily responsible for Barry M. Goldwater Air Force Gunnery Range, which covers 2.7 million acres.

TEMPORARY MILITARY LODGING: Lodging office, Building 4300, C-520-683-6238, D-312-853-5238.

RV, CAMPING/FAMCAMP: FAMCAMP on base, year round, C-520-683-6238, D-312-853-5238, 35 camper spaces with full hookups with cable TV, picnic tables, various tent sites without hookups. Outdoor basketball and tennis courts. Picnic Area with horseshoe pits, volleyball court and softball field.

SPACE-A: None. See Luke AFB listing, C-602-856-7131, D-312-896-7131.

LOGISTICAL SUPPORT: Police-683-6220

ADMINISTRATIVE SUPPORT: None. See Luke AFB listing, C-520-856-6405.

HEALTH & WELFARE: None. See Luke AFB listing, C-602-856-7506.

REST & RECREATION: None. See Luke AFB listing, C-602-856-6000.

ATTRACTIONS: Pleasant weather year round. Mountain areas and Mexico within easy driving distance. Luke AFB, 65 miles away, has full support facilities.

LUKE AIR FORCE BASE (AZ03R4)

7131 North Litchfield Road
Luke Air Force Base, AZ 85309-1534

TELEPHONE NUMBER INFORMATION: Main installation numbers: C-602-856-7411, D-312-896-1110.

LOCATION: From Phoenix, west on I-10 to Litchfield Rd Exit 128, north on Litchfield Rd approximately five miles. Also, from Phoenix, on I-17 to Glendale Avenue, west on Glendale Avenue to intersection of Glendale Avenue and Litchfield Rd, approximately 10 miles. USMRA: Page 108 (D-6,7). NMC: Phoenix, 20 miles east.

GENERAL INFORMATION: Air Education Training Command Base. Largest fighter wing in free world.

TEMPORARY MILITARY LODGING: Lodging office, Building 660, Bong Lane, 24 hours daily, C-602-856-3941. All ranks. DV/VIP EX-C-602-856-5840.

RV, CAMPING/FAMCAMP: Operates Fort Tuthill Rec Area, 150 miles north on I-17, four miles south of Flagstaff. See Fort Tuthill Recreation Area listing for more information. Gila Bend FAMCAMP at Auxiliary Field, on base year round, Lodging Office, HC01 Box 22, Gila Bend AFAF, AZ 85337-5000, C-520-683-6238, D-312-896-5238, 35 camper spaces with full hookups.

SPACE-A: Pax Term/Lounge, Building 439, 0630-2230 Mon-Fri, 0730-1800 Sat, Sun, Holidays, C-602-856-7131, D-312-896-7131, flights to Midwest and West Coast.

LOGISTICAL SUPPORT:

Child Care-856-6339	Commissary-935-3821
Conv Store-935-2414	Exchange-935-2671
Gas Station-935-4953	SATO-856-6891
Snack Bar-856-7102	

ADMINISTRATIVE SUPPORT:

Legal-856-6901	Locator-856-6405
Police-856-5970	Public Affairs-856-6011
SDO/NCO-856-5800	

HEALTH & WELFARE:

CHAMPUS-856-7600	Chapel-856-6211
Medical-856-7506	Retiree Services-856-6827

REST & RECREATION:

Arts & Crafts-856-6502	Auto Hobby Shop-856-6107
Bowling-856-6946	Clubs
Fitness Center-856-6241	EM-856-7136
ITT Office-856-6000	O-856-6446
Library-856-7191	Rec Center-856-7152
Theater-856-6461	Wood Hobby Shop-856-6566
Youth Center-856-6225	

ATTRACTIONS: Colorful Scottsdale nearby. Arizona state capital, fairgrounds and coliseum in Phoenix. ASU in Tempe. Lots of sunshine, hot summers, cool winters.

PHOENIX AIR NATIONAL GUARD BASE (AZ06R4)

161st Air Refueling Wing (ANG)
3200 East Old Tower Road
Phoenix, AZ 85034-6098

Note: In 1997, this unit will undergo a massive construction effort in which the entire base will be demolished to make room for a third runway at Sky Harbor IAP. An entirely new base will be re-built by the city of Phoenix south of the base's present location.

TELEPHONE NUMBER INFORMATION: Main installation numbers: C-602-302-9000.

LOCATION: From I-10 in Phoenix, take the 24th street exit; go north one-quarter mile, turn east on Old Tower Road; follow Old Tower Road to the front gate of post. USMRA: Page 108 (D-7). NMI: Luke AFB, 30 miles west. NMC: Phoenix, five miles west.

GENERAL INFORMATION: Home to 161st ARW (ANG), direct connection to Sky Harbor IAP.

TEMPORARY MILITARY LODGING: None. See Luke AFB listing, C-602-856-3941.

RV, CAMPING/FAMCAMP: None. See Luke AFB listing, C-602-856-7990, Fax: C-602-856-7990, D-312-896-3401.

SPACE-A: Sky Harbor IAP, Pax Term, 0630-1600 Tue-Fri, C-602-302-9162, D-312-853-9162, Fax: C-602-302-9288, D-312-853-9288, flights via KC-135 Aerial Refuelers; CONUS and OCONUS year round.

LOGISTICAL SUPPORT: None. See Luke AFB listing, C-602-856-7411, D-312-896-1110.

ADMINISTRATIVE SUPPORT: Public Affairs-302-9235

HEALTH & WELFARE: None. See Luke AFB listing, C-602-856-7411, D-312-896-1110.

REST & RECREATION: Fitness Center, Gym, Phoenix ANG Club, Swimming Pool.

OTHER SUPPORT AVAILABLE: Fire Dept, Police.

ATTRACTIONS: Located in downtown Phoenix, warm weather year round offers every opportunity for sightseeing, Phoenix Suns basketball, NFL Arizona Cardinals and Arizona State University.

OTHER INFORMATION: For military members and travelers Phoenix ANGB has limited facilities, however Luke AFB is only 30 miles west and offers every amenity and support available while the city of Phoenix offers plenty of amenities including hotels, motels, restaurants of all kinds and many recreational opportunities.

YUMA ARMY PROVING GROUND (AZ05R4)

ATTN: STEYP-CO
Building 2100
Yuma Army Proving Ground, AZ 85365-9124

TELEPHONE NUMBER INFORMATION: Main installation numbers: C-520-328-2020, D-312-899-2151.

LOCATION: Northeast of I-8 turn right on US-95. Southwest of I-10 turn left on US-95. US-95 bisects Army Proving Ground. USMRA: Page 108 (A-6,7,8; B-7,8). NMC: Yuma, 27 miles southwest.

GENERAL INFORMATION: Army Materiel Test Facility with instrumented ranges.

ARIZONA
Yuma Army Proving Ground, continued

TEMPORARY MILITARY LODGING: Lodging office, Building 1003, 5th Street & Barranca Road, 0700-1800 daily, C-520-328-2127/2129, D-312-899-2127/2129. All ranks. DV/VIP C-520-328-2020.

RV, CAMPING/FAMCAMP: Yuma Proving Ground Travel Camp on post, C-520-329-8710, 40 camper spaces with full hookups

SPACE-A: None. See Yuma MCAS listing, C-520-341-2729, D-312-951-2729.

LOGISTICAL SUPPORT:
Child Care-328-2588
Commissary-328-2240
Conv Store-328-2252
Exchange-328-2252
Gas Station-343-1365
Leisure Travel Office-ext 2/3/4586

ADMINISTRATIVE SUPPORT:
Fire Dept-328-2949
Legal-328-2608
Locator-328-2151/2430
Police-328-2720
Public Affairs-328-6189/6533

HEALTH & WELFARE:
ACS-328-2513
CHAMPUS-328-2502
Chapel-328-3465
Family Services-328-2711
Medical-328-2502
  Central Appts-328-2502
  Emergency-328-2911

REST & RECREATION:
Bowling-ext 2790
Com Club-328-2097
Fitness Center-ext 2400
ITT-329-6374
MWR-328-2223
Swimming-ext 2209
Tennis Courts-ext 2400
Outdoor Rec-ext 4586

ATTRACTIONS: Isolated post, next to Kofa National Wildlife Refuge and the Colorado River; boating on the Colorado River.

YUMA MARINE CORPS AIR STATION (AZ04R4)

Box 99100
Yuma Marine Corps Air Station, AZ 85369-9100

TELEPHONE NUMBER INFORMATION: Main installation numbers: C-520-341-2011, D-312-951-2011.

LOCATION: From I-8 take Avenue 3E south for one mile to base on right, adjacent to Yuma IAP. USMRA: Page 108 (A-8). NMC: Yuma, three miles northwest.

GENERAL INFORMATION: The premier Marine Corps Combat Air Training Base. Near perfect flying conditions and range facilities are available.

TEMPORARY MILITARY LODGING: Lodging office, Sta S-4, Billeting fund, Building 1058, Martini Avenue, 24 hours daily, C-520-341-3578/3094, D-312-951-3578/3094. All ranks. Hostess House C-520-341-2262.

RV, CAMPING/FAMCAMP: Operates Martinez Lake Rec Area, C-520-341-2278, D-312-951-2007, year round, on the Colorado River, 38 miles north of Yuma MCAS off US-95, 17 camper spaces with W/E hookups, three camper/tent spaces, five cabins and four mobile homes.

SPACE-A: Pax Term/Lounge and Ops, Building 151, 0700-1530 daily, C-520-341-2729, D-312-951-2729.

LOGISTICAL SUPPORT:
Child Care-341-2350
Commissary-341-2248
Conv Store-341-3567
Exchange-341-2256
Gas Station-341-2110
Package Store-341-3567
SATO-341-2755

ADMINISTRATIVE SUPPORT:
Legal-341-2481
Locator-341-2011
Police-341-2205/2361
Public Affairs-341-2275
SDO/NCO-341-2253

HEALTH & WELFARE:
CHAMPUS-341-2916
Chapel-341-2371
Family Services-341-3421
Medical-341-2772
  Emergency-341-2111

REST & RECREATION:
Athletic/Picnic Facilities-ext 2778
Auto Hobby Shop-ext 2395
Bowling-726-8320
Camping Equipment-ext 2848
Clubs
  EM-341-2457
  O-341-2711
  SNCO-341-2711
Gym-ext 2727
Library-ext 2785
Services-ext 2278
Swimming
  EM-ext 2926
  O-ext 3474
Theater-341-2358

ATTRACTIONS: Desert type climate, Colorado River.

ARKANSAS

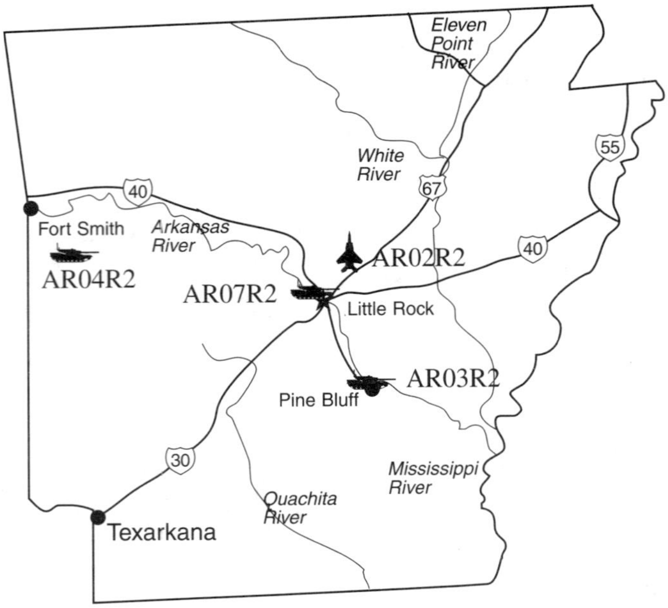

CAMP JOSEPH T. ROBINSON (AR07R2)

ATTN: TAG-AR-PR
Building 6000
North Little Rock, AR 72199-9600

TELEPHONE NUMBER INFORMATION: Main installation numbers: C-501-212-5100, D-312-962-5100.

LOCATION: Take Burns Park exit off I-40, follow signs to camp (two miles). USMRA: Page 76 (D-5). NMC: North Little Rock, one mile south.

GENERAL INFORMATION: Headquarters Arkansas National Guard, 90th Regional Support Command.

TEMPORARY MILITARY LODGING: Lodging office, Building 6300, 6th Street and Missouri Avenue, 0700-1530 Mon-Thu, 0700-2200 Fri, 0700-1630 Sat, 0600-1530 Sun, C-501-212-5274.

RV, CAMPING/FAMCAMP: None. See Little Rock AFB listing, Little Rock FAMCAMP, C-501-988-3365, D-312-731-3365, Fax: C-501-988-6164, D-312-731-6164.

SPACE-A: None. See Little Rock AFB, listing, C-501-988-3684, D-312-731-3684, Fax: C-501-988-6726.

LOGISTICAL SUPPORT:
Exchange-753-9017 | Dining Facilities-758-8468
Snack Bar-753-9017

ADMINISTRATIVE SUPPORT:
Fire Dept-212-5280 | Legal-212-5030
Locator-212-5100 | Police-212-5280
Public Affairs-212-5020

HEALTH & WELFARE:
Chapel-212-5926 | Medical-212-5262

REST & RECREATION:
All Ranks Club-758-5076 | Golf Course-753-5608
Gym-212-5639 | Fitness Center-212-5639
Lounge-212-5693 | Rec Equipment-212-5639
Swimming Pool-212-5639 | Support Services-753-9017
MWR-753-9017

ATTRACTIONS: State Capitol, Burns Park, Wild River Country, Quapaw District, Little Rock Zoo, Arkansas Arts Center, Governor's Mansion, Old Mill, Pinnacle Mountain, War Memorial Park, Arkansas Travelers baseball.

FORT CHAFFEE (AR04R2)

Building 1370, ATTN: ATZR-ZC
Fort Chaffee, AR 72905-5000
Scheduled to close September 30, 1997.
Transferring to Arkansas National Guard.

TELEPHONE NUMBER INFORMATION: Main installation numbers: C-501-481-2141, D-312-962-2111.

LOCATION: From I-40, take the I-540 exit west in Fort Smith. From I-540, exit onto AR-22 East (Rogers Avenue) and continue through the town of Barling to Fort Chaffee, one mile east of Barling. USMRA: Page 76 (A,B-4,5). NMC: Fort Smith, six miles northwest.

GENERAL INFORMATION: Active Army and Reserve Component training support, USAR NCO Academy, Regional Training Brigade.

TEMPORARY MILITARY LODGING: Lodging office, Building 1370, Fort Smith Blvd, 0730-1630 Mon-Fri, 0700-1600 Sat & Sun, C-501-484-2252/2917, D-312-962-2252. After duty hours contact SDO C-501-484-2666.

RV, CAMPING/FAMCAMP: Chaffee Trailer Park on post, C-501-484-2770, D-312-962-2252, 39 camper spaces with full hookups.

SPACE-A: None. See Little Rock AFB, listing, C-501-988-3684, D-312-731-3684, Fax: C-501-988-6726.

LOGISTICAL SUPPORT: | Exchange-484-2229

ADMINISTRATIVE SUPPORT:
CDO/OOD-484-2666 | Fire Dept-484-2127
Locator-484-2460 | Police-484-2666
Public Affairs-484-2905 | SDO/NCO-484-2666

HEALTH & WELFARE:
Medical-484-2488 | Retiree Services-484-3130
Emergency-484-6241
Information-484-6100

REST & RECREATION:
Golf Course-484-2326 | Gym-ext 2550
Library-ext 2550 | MWR-484-2550
Rec Equipment-ext 2550 | Rec Center-ext 2550

ATTRACTIONS: Ouachita and Ozark National Forests, city of Fort Smith, Arkansas River. Fayetteville, home of the University of Arkansas Razorbacks, offers great opportunity for sporting events.

LITTLE ROCK AIR FORCE BASE (AR02R2)

314 AW/PA
1250 Thomas Avenue, Suite 154
Little Rock Air Force Base, AR 72099-5028

TELEPHONE NUMBER INFORMATION: Main installation numbers: C-501-988-3131, D-312-731-1110. E-mail: 314awpa@314-1.littlerock.af.mil.

LOCATION: From US-67/167 to Jacksonville, follow signs to main gate. USMRA: Page 76 (D,E-5). NMC: Little Rock, 18 miles southwest.

GENERAL INFORMATION: Air Education and Training Command Base Group with two AMC tenant units, C-130 Training, USAF Combat Aerial Delivery School, Headquarters Arkansas Air National Guard, and other missions.

ARKANSAS
Little Rock Air Force Base, continued

TEMPORARY MILITARY LODGING: P.O. Box 1192, Building 1024, Cannon Circle, 24 hours daily, C-501-988-6652/6753, D-312-731-6652/6753, Fax: C-501-988-7769, D-312-731-6652. DV/VIP 501-988-6828.

RV, CAMPING/FAMCAMP: On base. Little Rock FAMCAMP, year round, C-501-988-3365, D-312-731-3365, Fax:C-501-988-6164, D-312-731-6164, 23 camper spaces with W/E hookups, six tent spaces.

SPACE-A: Pax Term/Lounge, Building 430, 0730-1630 Mon-Fri, C-501-988-3342/3684, D-312-731-3342/3684, Fax: C-501-988-6726, D-312-731-6726, flights to CONUS, OCONUS and foreign locations.

LOGISTICAL SUPPORT:
Bank-985-4025
Beauty Shop-988-1900
Child Dev Center-988-6139
Commissary-988-6990
Dry Cleaner-988-2139
Exchange-988-1150
Postal Service-988-3478
Snack Bar-988-3908
Barber Shop-988-1160
Child Care-988-6139
Class Six-988-1374
Conv Store-988-4841
Education Office-988-3417
Gas Station-988-2301
SATO-988-4117

ADMINISTRATIVE SUPPORT:
CDO/OOD 988-3200
Housing Office-988-6373
Locator-988-6025
Police-988-3221
Fire Dept-988-3737
Legal-988-7886
Pass/ID Office-988-6338
Public Affairs-988-3601

HEALTH & WELFARE:
Air Force Aid Society-988-6801
CHAMPUS-988-7458
Dental-988-8811
Medical-988-8811
TRICARE-988-7270
American Red Cross-988-3428
Chapel-988-6014
Family Services-988-6451
Retiree Services-988-6095
Veterinary Services-988-7249

REST & RECREATION:
Auto Hobby Shop-988-6761
Clubs
  EM-988-3760
  O-988-1111
ITT-988-3216
MWR-988-3365
Theater-988-6461
Youth Center-988-7718
Bowling-ext 3793
Community Center-988-7588
Fitness Center-988-3742
Golf Course-988-6199
Library-988-6979
Outdoor Rec-988-3365
Wood Hobby Shop-988-6761

ATTRACTIONS: Little Rock, Governor's Mansion, State Capitol, Old State House, River Market, Quapaw Quarter, Museum of Science and History, Little Rock Zoo, Children's Museum, Pinnacle and Petit Jean Mountains, Burns Park, War Memorial Stadium, Arkansas River, and Lake Conway.

PINE BLUFF ARSENAL (AR03R2)

ATTN: SMCPB-CO
10020 Kabrich Circle
Pine Bluff Arsenal, AR 71602-9500

TELEPHONE NUMBER INFORMATION: Main installation numbers: C-501-540-3000, D-312-966-3000.

LOCATION: Southeast of Little Rock, take US-65 south to exit 32, then east to AR-256 to main gate. Off US-65 northwest of Pine Bluff. Take AR-256, cross AR-365 into main gate of arsenal. USMRA: Page 76 (E-6). NMC: Pine Bluff, eight miles southeast. NMI: Little Rock Air Force Base, 32 miles northwest.

GENERAL INFORMATION: A design, development, manufacturer and disposal of chemical defenses, 52nd Explosive Detachment, Technical Escort Unit, Test management and Diagnostic Equipment Support Center, USA Health Clinic and Pine Bluff Chemical Activity.

TEMPORARY MILITARY LODGING: Lodging office, Building 15-390, Sibert Road, 0730-1400 daily, C-501-540-3008, D-312-966-3008. DV/VIP facilities available.

RV, CAMPING/FAMCAMP: None. See Little Rock AFB listing, C-501-988-3365, D-312-731-3365, Fax: C-501-988-6164, D-312-731-6164.

SPACE-A: None. See Little Rock AFB listing, C-501-988-3684, D-312-731-3684.

LOGISTICAL SUPPORT:
Child Care-540-3612
Credit Union-535-2441
Education Office-540-3092
Travel Office-540-3611
Child Dev Center-540-3421
Dining Facilities-536-6708
Exchange-540-3474

ADMINISTRATIVE SUPPORT:
Fire Dept-540-3507
Legal-540-3131
Pass/ID Office-540-3495
Public Affairs-540-3421
Housing Office-540-3008
Locator-540-3000
Police-540-3505/3506
SDO/NCO-540-3176

HEALTH & WELFARE:
Army Emergency Relief-540-3031
Medical-540-3409
  Health Benefits-540-3814
CHAMPUS-540-3410

REST & RECREATION:
Bowling-540-3779
Golf Course-540-3028
MWR-540-2775
Fitness Center-540-3779
Gym-540-3779
Youth Center-540-3612

ATTRACTIONS: Hot Springs National Park, Ozarks Mountains, University of Arkansas at Pine Bluff and the Arkansas River. Arkansas..."The Natural State".

CALIFORNIA

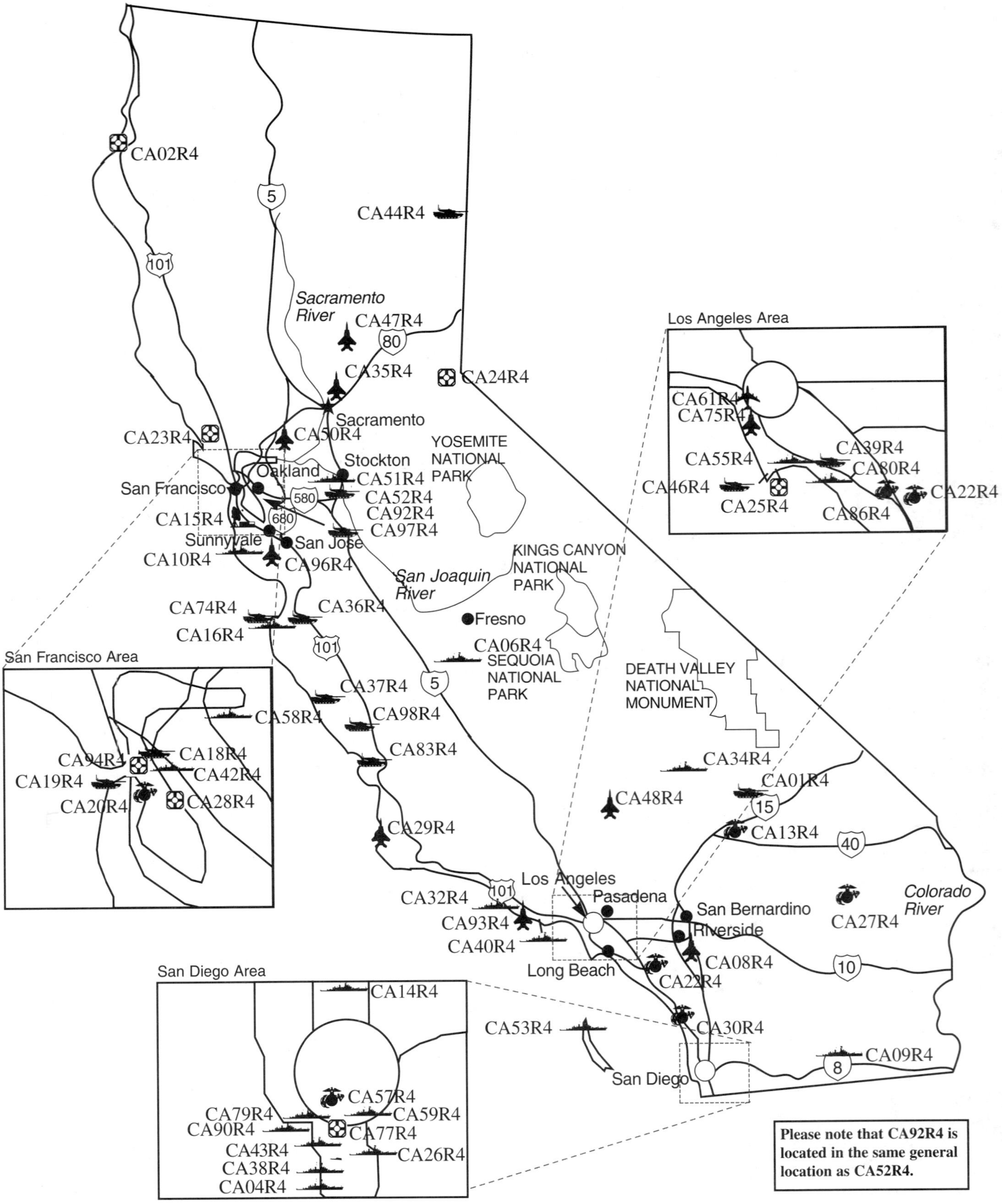

Please note that CA92R4 is located in the same general location as CA52R4.

ALAMEDA COAST GUARD INTEGRATED SUPPORT COMMAND (CA28R4)

Coast Guard Island, Building 21
Alameda, CA 94501-5100

TELEPHONE NUMBER INFORMATION: Main installation numbers: C-510-437-2905.

LOCATION: From the north: take US-880 south to 16th Street/Embarcadero exit; left on Embarcadero follow signs to causeway and island. Signs posted. From the south: take US-880 north to 29th Street, exit; Left U-turn at first left, cross overpass, then first right through the light, follow signs around to causeway and island. USMRA: Page 119 (D-5). NMC: Oakland, one mile northwest.

GENERAL INFORMATION: Major Coast Guard Support Base in San Francisco area.

TEMPORARY MILITARY LODGING: Housing office, Building 21, McCullough Drive, 0730-1530 daily, C-510-437-3180; other hours OOD, Building 3, C-510-437-3304. Limited facilities. DV/VIP C-510-437-3303. Duty personnel only.

RV, CAMPING/FAMCAMP: None. See Oakland Army Base listing, Lake Tahoe Oakland Condominiums, C-510-444-8107, D-312-859-3113.

SPACE-A: None. See Travis AFB, C-707-424-1854 or 1-800-787-2534.

LOGISTICAL SUPPORT:

Carlson Wagonlit Travel-437-3686	Child Care-437-2740
Class Six-437-3165	Conv Store-437-3165
Dining Facilities-437-3303	Exchange-437-3165
Gas Station-437-3165	Postal Service-437-3161
Special Services-437-3577	

ADMINISTRATIVE SUPPORT:

CDO-437-3151	Housing Office-437-5936
Legal-437-3330	Locator-437-2904
Police-437-3156	Public Affairs-437-3325

HEALTH & WELFARE:

Chapel-437-3067	Dental-437-3582/3
Medical	
Central Appts-437-3582	
Clinic-437-3581	

REST & RECREATION:

Auto Hobby Shop-437-3883	Gym-437-3580
Marina-437-3285	MWR-437-3545

OTHER FACILITIES AVAILABLE: Balboa Travel, Outdoor Rec, Racquetball, Swimming, Tennis, Ticket Office.

ATTRACTIONS: San Francisco and the exciting San Francisco Bay Area nearby.

BARSTOW MARINE CORPS LOGISTICS BASE (CA13R4)

Command Headquarters, Box 110100
Barstow Marine Corps Logistics Base, CA 92311-5001

TELEPHONE NUMBER INFORMATION: Main installation numbers: C-760-577-6211, D-312-282-6444.

LOCATION: On I-40, one-and-a-half miles east of Barstow. Take I-15 northeast from San Bernardino, or west from Las Vegas, NV. Signs mark direction to MCLB. USMRA: Page 111 (G-12,13). NMC: San Bernardino, 75 miles southwest.

GENERAL INFORMATION: The Marine Corps Logistics Base serving the western part of the US.

TEMPORARY MILITARY LODGING: Lodging office, Building 171, 0700-1530 daily, C-760-577-6418, D-312-282-6418, Fax: C-760-577-6542. Other hours OD, Building 30, Room 8, ext 6611. All ranks. DV/VIP C-760-577-6555, D-312-282-6555. Oasis ext 6550 Active Duty, Retired Military and guests of the same.

RV, CAMPING/FAMCAMP: None. See El Toro MCAS listing, Big Bear Recreation Facilities, C-714-726-2626.

SPACE-A: None. See Edwards AFB listing, C-805-277-4412/4185, D-312-527-2222.

LOGISTICAL SUPPORT:

Cafeteria-577-6428	Child Care-577-6287
Commissary-577-6403	Conv Store-256-8974
Exchange-256-8974	Gas Station-256-9411
SATO-577-6135	Snack Bar-577-6264

ADMINISTRATIVE SUPPORT:

CDO/OOD-577-6611	Fire Dept-577-6731
Legal-577-6874	Locator (Civ)-577-6485
Police-577-6669	(Mil)-577-6675
Public Affairs-577-6430	SDO/NCO-577-6009

HEALTH & WELFARE:

CHAMPUS-577-6593	Chapel-577-5402/6846
Family Services-577-6533	Medical
	Central Appts-577-6591
	Emergency-577-6577

REST & RECREATION:

Auto Hobby Shop-577-6441	Bowling-577-6264
Ceramics-577-6228	Clubs
Golf Course-577-6431	EM/NCO-577-6532
Gym-577-6899	ITT-577-6541
Library-577-6395	Rec Equipment-577-6898
Wood/Rock Hobby-577-6441	Services-577-6541

ATTRACTIONS: Calico Ghost Town, Solar One, Lake Dolores.

BEALE AIR FORCE BASE (CA47R4)

5900 C Street
Beale Air Force Base, CA 95903-1221

TELEPHONE NUMBER INFORMATION: Main installation numbers: C-916-634-3000, D-312-368-3000. HP: http://www.beale.af.mil.

LOCATION: From CA-70 North, take Feather River Blvd exit (south of Marysville), follow to North Beale Road, take left (follow signs to Beale), continue for 10 miles until road dead ends at main gate of AFB. USMRA: Page 110 (C,D-5,6). NMC: Sacramento, 35 miles southwest.

GENERAL INFORMATION: Air Combat Command Base, home of the 9th Reconnaissance Wing and high-altitude reconnaissance aircraft training, 7th Space Warning Squadron and AF Combat and Munitions Center (AFCOMAC) training school.

TEMPORARY MILITARY LODGING: Lodging office, 5786 A Street, 24 hours daily, C-916-634-2953, D-312-368-2953. Fax: C-916-634-2755, D-312-368-2755. All ranks. DV/VIP C-916-788-0216.

RV, CAMPING/FAMCAMP: Beale FAMCAMP on base, year round, 9 SVS/SVRO, 17630 Doolittle Drive, 0900-2200 daily, C-916-634-3382, D-312-368-3382, Fax: C-916-634-2269, D-312-368-2269. Forty-three camper spaces with full hookups.

SPACE-A: None. See McClellan AFB listing, C-916-643-4105, D-312-633-4105, Fax: C-916-643-5616, D-312-633-5616.

CALIFORNIA
Beale Air Force, continued

LOGISTICAL SUPPORT:

Barber Shop-634-3437	Beauty Shop-788-0053
Cafeteria-788-2270	Child Care-634-4717
Child Dev Center-634-4717	Class Six-788-0224
Commissary-634-2421	Conv Store-788-1915
Credit Union-788-0265	Dry Cleaner-788-0300
Education Office-634-2525	Exchange-634-2987
Gas Station-788-0214	Omega (official)-634-2940
Postal Service-788-2401	(leisure)-634-2264
Shoppette-788-1271	Snack Bar-788-1550

ADMINISTRATIVE SUPPORT:

Fire Dept-634-8675	Housing Office-634-2792
Legal-634-2928	Locator-634-2113
Pass/ID Office-634-3154	Police-634-2131
Public Affairs-634-8890	

HEALTH & WELFARE:

Air Force Aid Society-ext 4-2843	American Red Cross-ext 4-2078
Chapel-634-2306	Dental
Family Services-634-2860	Central Appts-ext 4-4781
Medical	Clinic-ext 4-4782
Central Appts-ext 4-2941	Emergency-ext 4-4444
Emergency-ext 4-4444	Retiree Services-634-2157
Health Benefits-788-1160	TRICARE-1-800-242-6788
Information-ext 4-4849	Veterinary Services-ext 4-2104

REST & RECREATION:

Arts & Crafts-ext 4-2294	Auto Hobby Shop-ext 4-2296
Bowling-ext 4-2299	Clubs
Community Center-ext 4-2275	Aero-ext 4-9011
Fitness Center Annex-634-2260	Consol-634-4948
Golf Course-634-2124	Rod/Gun-788-2473
Gym-ext 4-2259	ITT-ext 4-3942
Library-ext 4-2314	MWR-ext 4-2819
Rec Center-ext 4-2264	Rec Equip-ext 4-3340
Services-ext 4-2273	Swimming-contact clubs
Theater-634-2520	Youth Center-ext 4-4953
Youth Services-ext 4-3543	

ATTRACTIONS: 9-hole golf course on base, WW II German POW site-National Historical Landmark. Within a two-hour drive: Lake Tahoe and Reno, Nevada, Sacramento, Sutter's Fort, Zoo, Grass Valley and Nevada City nearby. Napa Valley Wineries and San Francisco is less than three hours south.

CAMP PARKS/PARKS RESERVE FORCES TRAINING AREA (CA97R4)

Building 790
Dublin, CA 94568-5000

TELEPHONE NUMBER INFORMATION: Main installation numbers: C-510-803-5648.

LOCATION: East Bay Area; westbound 580 to Dublin. USMRA: Page 119 (G-6). NMC: San Francisco, 30 miles west.

TEMPORARY MILITARY LODGING: None. See Oakland Army Base listing, C-510-466-3113, D-312-859-3113.

RV, CAMPING/FAMCAMP: None. See Oakland Army Base listing, Lake Tahoe Oakland Condominiums, C-510-444-8107, D-312-859-3113.

SPACE-A: None. See Travis AFB listing, C-707-424-1854, D-312-837-1854, Fax: C-707-424-2048

LOGISTICAL SUPPORT: Exchange-829-7780

ADMINISTRATIVE SUPPORT:

Fire Dept-803-5613	Police-803-5604
Public Affairs-803-5636	

HEALTH & WELFARE: Medical-803-5606

REST & RECREATION:

Com Club-803-5615	Recreation-803-5618

ATTRACTIONS: San Francisco and Bay Area. Many exciting things to see and do in and around Oakland. Jack London Square shopping area at the foot of Broadway in Oakland is a waterfront promenade lined with stores, restaurants and entertainment.

CAMP PENDLETON MARINE CORPS BASE (CA30R4)

Box 555019
Camp Pendleton, CA 92055-5019

TELEPHONE NUMBER INFORMATION: Main installation numbers: C-619-725-4111, D-312-365-4111.

LOCATION: From San Diego: on I-5 which is adjacent to Camp Pendleton main gate. Take "Camp Pendleton Only" off ramp I-5 at Oceanside. USMRA: Page 111 (F-14,15). NMC: Oceanside, adjacent to Base southeast.

GENERAL INFORMATION: The only Marine Corps Amphibious Training Base on the West Coast.

TEMPORARY MILITARY LODGING: Lodging office, Building 1310 (Mainside), 24 hours daily, C-619-725-5304, D-312-365-5304. All ranks. DV/VIP C-619-725-5194.

RV, CAMPING/FAMCAMP: Operates three camping facilities on base, year round: Lake O'Neill Recreation Park, C-619-725-4241, D-312-365-4241, five camper spaces with full hookups, 40 camper spaces with W/E hookups, 20 camper spaces with W only, 52 camper/tent spaces without hookups; Del Mar Beach Cottages, C-619-725-2134, 84 camper spaces with W/E hookups; 8 mobile homes; San Onofre Recreation Beach on base, year round, C-619-725-7935 (campsites), C-619-725-7629 (cottages), D-312-365-7935, 36 mobile homes/cottages, 80 camper spaces with W/E hookups, 26 camper spaces without hookups, 42 camper/tent spaces with W only.

SPACE-A: None. See El Toro Marine Corps Air Station listing, C-714-726-3920, D-312-997-3920.

LOGISTICAL SUPPORT:

Barber Shop-725-5128	Beauty Shop-725-5938
Child Care-725-6112	Child Dev Center-725-6112
Commissary-725-4012	Conv Store-725-3585
Credit Union-725-4491	Dry Cleaner-725-5581
Education Office-725-6593	Exchange-725-6233
Gas Station-725-5828	Laundry-725-5581
Package Store-725-3585	Postal Service-725-5832
SATO-725-4396	

ADMINISTRATIVE SUPPORT:

CDO/OOD-725-5617	Fire Department-725-3377
Housing Office-725-6246	Legal-725-6172
Locator-725-5171	Pass/ID Office-725-2768
Police-725-3888	Public Affairs-725-5011
SDO/NCO-725-5617	

HEALTH & WELFARE:

American Red Cross-725-6877	CHAMPUS-725-1616
Chapel-725-4700	Dental-725-5992
Family Services-725-5361	Central Appts-725-5782
Medical	N-MC Relief Society-725-5337
Central Appts-725-1288	Retiree Services-725-9052
Clinic-725-1507	Veterinary Services-725-3439

CALIFORNIA
Camp Pendleton Marine Corps Base, continued

Emergency-725-3258
Health Benefits-725-1616
Hospital-725-1437
Information-725-1288

REST & RECREATION:

Archery-ext 6288	Arts & Crafts-725-4880
Auto Hobby Shop-725-5963	Bowling-725-6784
Beach Info-ext 2463/7935	Clubs
Community Center-725-9717	EM-725-6122
Equipment Rental-ext 5296	Flying-ext 4910
Fitness Center-723-5331	O-725-6571
Golf Course-725-5331	Gym-725-5205
Indoor Rec-725-5945	ITT-725-5864
ITR-725-7447	Library-725-5669
Marinas-725-2802	MWR-725-5355
Outdoor Rec-725-6722	Riding Stables-ext 5094
Services-ext 6288	Skeet/Trap-ext 4832
Swimming Pool-ext 4344/5084	Theater-725-7735
Youth Center-725-5374	Youth Services-725-6614

ATTRACTIONS: Sandy beaches, Old California Missions, Disneyland, Knott's Berry Farm, Magic Mountain, Sea World, Wild Animal Park, Lion Country Safari, San Diego Zoo, Balboa Park, Maritime Museum, Carlsbad Raceway, Palomar Observatory; race tracks at Hollywood Park, Del Mar, Santa Anita or Los Alamitos.

CAMP ROBERTS (CA98R4)

California Army National Guard
Western Mobilization and Training Complex Installation
Headquarters, Building 109
Camp Roberts, CA 93451-5000

TELEPHONE NUMBER INFORMATION: Main installation numbers: C-805-238-3100, D-312-949-8210.

LOCATION: On Highway 101, halfway between Los Angeles and San Francisco. USMRA: Page 111 (C-10). NMC: Paso Robles, 12 miles north.

TEMPORARY MILITARY LODGING: Camp Roberts, Billeting Office, Building 6038, 0800-1630 Mon to Fri, C-805-238-8304, D-312-949-8304, Fax C-805-238-8384.

RV, CAMPING/FAMCAMP: Camp Roberts, on base year round, Billeting, Building 6038, Camp Roberts, CA 93451-5000, C-805-238-8312, D-312-949-8312, Fax C-805-238-8384. 12 camper spaces with full hookups.

SPACE-A: None. See Lemoore NAS listing, C-209-998-1683, D-312-949-1683, Fax: C-209-998-3046.

LOGISTICAL SUPPORT:

Consol Mess-238-8237	Exchange-238-8195
Postal Service-238-8209	Snack Bar-238-8120

ADMINISTRATIVE SUPPORT:

Fire Dept-238-8220	Housing Office-238-8312
Locator-238-8390	Public Affairs-238-8203

HEALTH & WELFARE: Chapel-238-8185

REST & RECREATION: MWR-238-8203

OTHER FACILITIES AVAILABLE: Athletic field/track, fitness center, gym, recreation center, pizza pub, laundry.

ATTRACTIONS: A short drive to the Hearst Castle and the Pacific Ocean, hunting, fishing, military museum, California Missions nearby.

CAMP SAN LUIS OBISPO (CA83R4)

California Army National Guard
Western Mobilization and Training Complex Installation
P.O. Box 4360, Highway 1, Headquarters Building 738
San Luis Obispo, CA 93403-4360

TELEPHONE NUMBER INFORMATION: Main installation numbers: C-805-594-6500/1, D-312-630-6500/1.

LOCATION: On Highway 1 between San Luis Obispo and Morro Bay, USMRA: Page 111 (C-11). NMC: San Luis Obispo, five miles east.

GENERAL INFORMATION: Permanent tenant facilities include USPFO for California, National Interagency Counter Drug Institute, California Special Training Institute, California Conservation Corps, Federal Youth Program and 223rd Infantry Regiment.

TEMPORARY MILITARY LODGING: Lodging office, Building 738, 0800-1630 Mon-Fri, C-805-594-6500, D-312-630-9800.

RV, CAMPING/FAMCAMP: Camp San Luis Obispo RV Park, on post year round, Billeting Office, Camp San Luis Obispo, P.O. Box 4360, San Luis Obispo, CA 93403-4360, C-805-594-6500. Four camper spaces with full hookups, eight camper spaces with W/E hookups, primitive tent spaces with no hookups.

SPACE-A: None. Edwards AFB listing, C-805-277-4412/4185, D-312-527-2222, Fax: C-805-277-5544.

LOGISTICAL SUPPORT: Exchange-549-3912

ADMINISTRATIVE SUPPORT:

Locator-549-6500	Public Affairs-594-6501

HEALTH & WELFARE: None. See Edwards AFB listing, C-805-277-1110, D-312-527-1110.

REST & RECREATION:

MWR-594-6501	O'Club-541-6168

ATTRACTIONS: Twelve miles from Pacific Ocean and scenic central coast of California, thirty-five miles from Hearst Castle, midway between Los Angeles and San Francisco.

CHINA LAKE NAVAL AIR WARFARE CENTER WEAPONS DIVISION/ NAVAL AIR WEAPONS STATION (CA34R4)

1 Administration Circle, Building 00001
China Lake, CA 93555-6001

TELEPHONE NUMBER INFORMATION: Main installation numbers: C-619-939-2303, D-312-437-2303. E-mail: steveboster@imdgw.chinalake.navy.mil. HP: http://www.chinalake.navy.mil//

LOCATION: From US-395 or CA-14, take CA-178 to Ridgecrest and the main gate. USMRA: Page 111 (G-10,11,12; H-11). NMC: Los Angeles, 150 miles south.

GENERAL INFORMATION: A major Navy Research, Development, and Test Center for Naval Weapons Systems principally for air warfare. Located in the upper Mojave Desert.

TEMPORARY MILITARY LODGING: Lodging office, CD 823620D CBO, 24 hours daily, C-619-939-3146, D-312-437-3146, Fax: C-619-939-2789. All ranks. DV/VIP C-619-939-3039/2338, Fax: C-619-939-3152.

RV, CAMPING/FAMCAMP: None. See El Toro MCAS listing, Big Bear Recreation Facilities, C-714-726-2626.

CALIFORNIA
China Lake Naval Air Warfare Center Weapons Division/ Naval Air Weapons Station, continued

SPACE-A: Armitage Air Field at Center for test flights. Very limited. C-619-939-2303, D-312-437-5308, Fax: C-616-446-7204.

LOGISTICAL SUPPORT:

Barber Shop-446-8862	Beauty Shop-446-8822
Child Care-939-6683	Child Dev Center-939-3171
Class Six-446-2078	Commissary-939-3138
Credit Union-371-7130	Education Office-927-3649
Exchange-446-2586	Gas Station-446-5044
Postal Service-446-5251	Shoppette-446-2078
SATO-446-9047	Snack Bar-446-2415
Visitor Center-939-3105	

ADMINISTRATIVE SUPPORT:

Fire Dept-939-2085	Housing Office-939-4449
Legal-939-2203	Locator-939-9011
Police-939-3323	Public Affairs-939-3511
Quarter Deck-939-2303	SDO/NCO-939-2303

HEALTH & WELFARE:

American Red Cross-678-5441	CHAMPUS-939-8019
Chapel-939-3506	Dental-939-8040
Family Services-927-1545	Medical
N-MC Relief Society-939-2921	Central Appts-939-8000
Retiree Services-678-5441	Clinic-939-8000 (duty)
	939-2911 (after hours)
	Emergency-see Clinic #s
	Health Benefits-939-8019

REST & RECREATION:

Arts & Crafts-939-3252	Auto Hobby Shop-939-2346
Bowling-939-3471	Ceramics-ext 3252
Clubs	Fitness Center-939-2334
Com-939-8660	Golf Course-939-2990
NCO-939-8661	Gym-939-2334
O-939-3116	ITT-939-8660
Library-939-2595	MWR-932-2010
Swimming-ext 2334	Wood Hobby Shop-939-3252
Youth Center-927-TEEN	Youth Services-939-2909

ATTRACTIONS: Weapons Exhibit Facility for air-launched Navy & Marine Corps weaponry. Desert type attractions and recreation, isolated area.

CONCORD NAVAL WEAPONS STATION (CA58R4)

10 Delta Street
Concord Naval Weapons Station, CA 94520-5100

TELEPHONE NUMBER INFORMATION: Main installation numbers: C-510-246-2000, D-312-350-2000.

LOCATION: From I-680 take exit in Concord to CA-242/CA-4, exit Chicago Highway, Weapons Station is clearly marked. USMRA: Page 119 (F-2,3). NMC: San Francisco, 35 miles southwest.

GENERAL INFORMATION: Department of Defense Ammunition Transshipment and Naval Weapons Support for Pacific Fleet.

TEMPORARY MILITARY LODGING: None. See Oakland Army Base listing, C-510-466-3113, D-312-858-3113, Fax: C-510-466-2997, D-312-859-2997.

RV, CAMPING/FAMCAMP: None. Oakland Army Base listing, C-510-444-8107, D-312-859-3113, Fax: C-510-466-2997.

SPACE-A: None. See Travis AFB, C-707-424-1854, D-312-837-1854, Fax: C-707-424-2048.

LOGISTICAL SUPPORT:

Bank-671-9191	Barber Shop-246-2922
Conv Store-246-2924	Education Office-246-5773
Exchange-246-2924	SATO(ITT)-246-5061
Snack Bar	
Station Grill-246-5795	

ADMINISTRATIVE SUPPORT:

CDO-246-5553	Fire Dept-246-2078
Housing Office-246-5810	Emergency-3911
Legal-246-2085	Locator-246-2000
Pass/ID Office-246-5531	Police-246-5553
Public Affairs-246-5592	

HEALTH & WELFARE:

CHAMPUS-246-5869	Chapel-246-5594
Dental-246-5885	Medical-246-2933
Retiree Services-246-5040	Emergency-246-3911
TRICARE-246-5869	

REST & RECREATION:

Auto Hobby Shop-246-2156	Fitness Center-246-2021
Gym-246-2021	ITT-246-5795
MWR-246-5341	Outdoor Rec-246-2154
Sports/All Hands Club-246-2153	Swimming-ext 2144
Youth Center-246-3137	

ATTRACTIONS: The Weapons Station is a wildlife preserve: deer, elk, eagles, quail, fox, to name a few. Beautiful San Francisco, 35 miles southwest.

CORONADO NAVAL AMPHIBIOUS BASE (CA38R4)

3420 Guadalcanal Road, Building 16
San Diego, CA 92155-5001

TELEPHONE NUMBER INFORMATION: Main installation numbers: C-619-437-2011, D-312-577-2011.

LOCATION: From San Diego, take I-5 south to Coronado-San Diego Bay Bridge ($1 toll for non-carpool, free to motorcycles and carpools). Left on Orange Avenue for three miles; pass Hotel del Coronado and watch for signs to base (left turn at fourth light after hotel). USMRA: Page 118 (C,D-7,8). NMI: North Island Naval Air Station, three miles northwest. NMC: San Diego, five miles north.

GENERAL INFORMATION: West Coast Naval Amphibious Training Base, Naval Surface, Expeditionary Warfare Training Group Pacific, Special Warfare Group, and 27 Tenant Commands.

TEMPORARY MILITARY LODGING: Lodging office, Building 500, Tulagi Street, 24 hours daily, C-619-437-3494, D-312-577-3494, BOQ C-619-437-3860, D-312-577-3860, BEQ C-437-3496, EM C-619-437-3494, Officers C-619-437-3859, Fax: C-619-577-3475.

RV, CAMPING/FAMCAMP: Fiddlers Cove, one-and-a-half miles south of base, year round, C-619-435-8788, Fax: C-619-437-1389, 50 camper spaces with W/E hookups.

SPACE-A: None. See North Island NAS listing, C-619-545-9567, D-312-735-9567.

LOGISTICAL SUPPORT:

Barber Shop-522-7404/18	Child Care-437-2119
Child Dev Center-437-2119	Conv Store-522-7403
Credit Union-1-800-220-1872	Dining Facilities-437-2046
-ext 431	Dry Cleaner-522-7416
Education Office-437-2651	Exchange-522-7403
Gas Station-522-7415	Laundry-522-7416
Postal Service-437-2470	SATO-435-4414
Shoppette-522-7414	Snack Bar-437-2188

CALIFORNIA
Coronado Naval Amphibious Base, continued

ADMINISTRATIVE SUPPORT:

CDO-437-3432
Housing Office-556-8027
Locator-437-2011
Police-437-3432
SDO/NCO/OOD-437-3432
Fire Dept-437-2931
Legal-437-2080
Pass/ID Office-437-3021
Public Affairs-437-3024

HEALTH & WELFARE:

Chapel-437-2070
Medical-437-3047
Central Appts-437-2981
Clinic-437-3048
Health Benefits-437-3048
Dental-437-2954
Retiree Services-437-2780/2107
TRICARE-437-2526

REST & RECREATION

Athletics-ext 2185/86
Bowling-437-3016
Clubs
All Hands-437-3171
EM-437-3171
Restaurant-437-3040
Library-437-3026
MWR-437-3339
Rec Center-437-5135
Theater-437-3027
Auto Hobby Shop-437-3834
Catering-437-2181
Fitness Center-437-3066
Gym-437-3066
Indoor Rec (Q-Zone)-437-5135
ITT-437-3018
Marina-435-8788
Outdoor Rec-437-3028
Camping Gear
Youth Center-435-5056

ATTRACTIONS: Downtown Gaslamp District, Horton Plaza Shopping Center, San Diego Bay Area, Seaport Village, San Diego Zoo, Balboa Park, Sea World, and Wild Animal Park.

DEFENSE DISTRIBUTION REGION WEST-SHARPE SITE (CA52R4)

700 East Roth Road, Building S-10
Stockton, CA 95296-0002

TELEPHONE NUMBER INFORMATION: Main installation numbers: C-209-982-2000.

LOCATION: Off I-5 at Roth Road; or from CA-99 north, left on CA-120, north on Airport Way, left on Roth Road to Depot. USMRA: Page 110 (C-7,8). NMC: Stockton, seven miles north.

GENERAL INFORMATION: Joint Service Command under the Defense Logistics Agency flag to continue the unified mission of supply and support to the military services.

TEMPORARY MILITARY LODGING: None. See Travis AFB listing, C-707-437-2987, D-312-837-2987.

RV, CAMPING/FAMCAMP: Sharpe Travel Camp on post, year round, C-209-982-2232, D-312-462-2232. 12 camper spaces with full hookups.

SPACE-A: None. See Travis AFB, C-707-424-1854, D-312-837-1854, Fax: C-707-424-2048.

LOGISTICAL SUPPORT:

Exchange-982-3886
SATO-982-2233

ADMINISTRATIVE SUPPORT:

Locator-982-2000
Post Rest-982-2262
Police-982-2560

HEALTH & WELFARE:

CHAMPUS-982-3836
Retiree Services-982-2213
Medical-982-3831

REST & RECREATION:

Consol-982-2265
Services-ext 2237

OTHER FACILITIES AVAILABLE: Arts & Crafts, Library, Racquetball and Tennis Courts, Swimming, Youth Center.

ATTRACTIONS: San Joaquin and Sacramento Valleys. San Francisco and Bay Area, 90 miles west. Reno/Tahoe to north; Yosemite National Park to south.

EDWARDS AIR FORCE BASE (CA48R4)

1 South Rosamond Boulevard
Edwards Air Force Base, CA 93524-1031

TELEPHONE NUMBER INFORMATION: Main installation numbers: C-805-277-1110, D-312-527-1110. HP: http://www.cpo.edwards.af.mil/afftchtm.

LOCATION: Eighteen miles east of Rosamond, and 30 miles northeast of Lancaster, off CA-14. Also, 10 miles southwest of Boron, off CA-58. USMRA: Page 111 (F,G-12). NMC: Los Angeles, 90 miles southwest. NMI: China Lake Naval Weapons Center, two miles north.

GENERAL INFORMATION: Major Units: 412 Test Wing, Benefield Anacheic Chamber, Base Conducts a full range of flight and system testing. NASA Dryder Flight Research Facility located on base. Alternate landing field for the space shuttle. Home of the world's premiere flight test facility. Air Force Materiel Command Base. Air Force Flight Test Center, and USAF Test Pilot School.

TEMPORARY MILITARY LODGING: Lodging office, Building 5602, 24 hours daily, C-805-277-3394, D-312-527-3394. All ranks. DV/VIP C-805-277-3326.

RV, CAMPING/FAMCAMP: FAMCAMP on base, year round, C-805-277-3394, D-312-527-3394, 26 camper spaces with full hookups, 10 without hookups.

SPACE-A: Pax Term/Lounge, Building 1200, 0600-2200 daily, C-805-277-4412/4185, D-312-527-2222, Fax: C-805-277-5544, limited flights to CONUS and foreign locations.

LOGISTICAL SUPPORT:

Barber Shop-277-2946
Cafeteria-277-3489
Child Care-258-2883
Class Six-258-5817
Conv Store-258-4797
Dining Facilities-277-3489
Education Office-277-2713
Gas Station-258-5037
Postal Service-277-4315
Snack Bar-277-6507
Beauty Shop-258-5371
Car Rental-258-1586
Child Dev Center-258-2883
Commissary-277-4589
Credit Union-258-4407
Dry Cleaner-258-4606
Exchange-258-6573
Laundry-258-4606
SATO-277-3160
Travel Office-277-7488

ADMINISTRATIVE SUPPORT:

Fire Dept-277-4540
Legal-277-4310
OOD-277-7964
Public Affairs-277-4127
Housing Office-277-4060
Locator-277-2777
Police-277-3348
SDO/NCO-277-3040

HEALTH & WELFARE:

CHAMPUS-277-2662
Dental-277-2872
Medical
Central Appts-277-3730
Clinic-277-4386
Emergency-277-2331
Health Benefits-277-8480
Hospital-277-2744
Information-277-2744
Chapel-277-2110
Family Services-277-2246
Retiree Services-277-4931
TRICARE-277-2662
Veterinary Services-277-3205

CALIFORNIA
Edwards Air Force Base, continued

REST & RECREATION:

Arts & Crafts-277-2783	Auto Hobby Shop-277-4275
Bowling-277-2590	Ceramics-ext 4171
Clubs	Community Center-277-7488
Aero-277-5251	Fitness Center-277-5220
Com-277-2830	Golf Course-277-3469
EM-277-0810	Gym-277-3077
Rod/Gun-277-3182	Horse Stables-277-2898
Indoor Rec-ext 3546	ITT-275-7488
Library-277-2375	MWR-277-3004
Outdoor Rec-277-2895	Services-277-4240
Theater-277-4178	Wood Hobby Shop-ext 3139
Youth Center-ext 2217	Youth Services-277-3004

ATTRACTIONS: Mojave Desert area. Adjacent to mountain and winter sports areas; 90 minutes from beaches; historic mining and ghost towns nearby, 150 miles from Disneyland, 70 miles from Magic Mountain.

EL CENTRO NAVAL AIR FACILITY (CA09R4)

Naval Air Facility Command
ATTN: Public Affairs
El Centro, CA 92243-5001

TELEPHONE NUMBER INFORMATION: Main installation numbers: C-619-339-2524, D-312-958-2524.

LOCATION: Take I-8, two miles west of El Centro, to Forrester Road exit, one-and-a-half miles to Evan Hewes Highway left (west) for four miles, right on Bennet Road to main gate. USMRA: Page 111 (H-15,16). NMC: El Centro, seven miles east.

GENERAL INFORMATION: Operates bombing and gunnery ranges in support of fleet operations. Ideal flying conditions.

TEMPORARY MILITARY LODGING: Lodging office, Building 270, B & 2nd Streets, 24 hours daily, C-619-339-2408, D-312-958-8408. DV/VIP Officers, C-619-339-8535, Fax: C-619-353-1492.

RV, CAMPING/FAMCAMP: Campground on base, year round, C-619-339-2489, D-312-958-8489, 59 camper spaces with full hookups.

SPACE-A: Pax Term, Building 519, 0700-2300 Mon-Sat, C-619-339-2426, D-312-958-8426, limited Space-A flights to CONUS and OCONUS locations.

LOGISTICAL SUPPORT:

Child Care-399-2560	Commissary-339-2483
Conv Store-339-2670	Exchange-339-2478
Gas Station-339-7535	Package Store-339-2670

ADMINISTRATIVE SUPPORT:

Legal-339-2594	Police-339-2525
SDO/NCO-339-2699	

HEALTH & WELFARE:

CHAMPUS-339-2674	Chapel-339-2457
Medical-339-2675/2674	

REST & RECREATION:

Consol-339-2491	Rec Services-ext 2481

ATTRACTIONS: Winter (Jan-Mar) home of the Navy Blue Angels. Imperial Valley, near Mexico.

EL TORO MARINE CORPS AIR STATION (CA22R4)

P.O. Box 95002
Santa Ana, CA 92709-5000
Scheduled to close December 1999

TELEPHONE NUMBER INFORMATION: Main installation numbers: C-714-726-2100, D-312-997-2100.

LOCATION: Take I-5 to Sand Canyon Road exit; East to Trabuco Road then right to main gate. USMRA: Page 111 (F-14); Page 117 (G,H-7,8). NMC: Anaheim, 15 miles northwest.

GENERAL INFORMATION: Marine Corps Air Bases, Western Area, Headquarters 3rd Marine Aircraft Wing, and supporting units.

TEMPORARY MILITARY LODGING: Building 58, 0700-2000 daily, C-714-726-2381, D-312-997-22381. After hours, SDO, C-714-726-3901. All ranks.

RV, CAMPING/FAMCAMP: Operates Big Bear Recreation Facilities in San Bernardino National Forest, year round, C-714-726-2626, El Toro Campgrounds on base, year round, C-714-726-2626, D-312-997-2626, four camper spaces with full hookups, 11 with W/E hookups.

SPACE-A: Pax Term/Lounge, Building 624, 0700-2200 Mon-Fri, 0900-1800 Sat-Sun, C-714-726-3920, D-312-997-3920, CONUS, OCONUS and overseas flights.

LOGISTICAL SUPPORT:

Cafeteria-726-3340	Child Care-726-2153
Commissary-726-3828	Conv Store-726-3340
Exchange-726-3340	Gas Station-726-3340
Package Store-726-3340	SATO-559-1511
Snack Bar-726-3340	Special Services-726-2571

ADMINISTRATIVE SUPPORT:

Legal-726-2507	Locator-726-3736
Police-726-2901	SDO/NCO-726-3901

HEALTH & WELFARE:

CHAMPUS-726-2888	Chapel-726-3825
Family Services-726-2771	Medical
Retiree Services-726-2989	Central Appts-726-3175
	Emergency-726-9911

REST & RECREATION:

Auto Hobby Shop-ext 2481	Bowling-ext 2576
Camping Equipment-ext 2509	Clubs
Golf Course-ext 2577	Aero-ext 2480
Gym-ext 2993	EM-726-2476
ITT-726-2626	NCO-726-2476
Library-ext 2569	O-726-2465
Stables-ext 2911	SNCO-726-2566
Swimming-ext 2469	

ATTRACTIONS: Orange County and greater Los Angeles area, Disneyland in Anaheim, Anaheim Stadium (home of the Anaheim Angels baseball team), Knott's Berry Farm in Buena Park, Marineland located at the tip of the Palo Verdes peninsula, Movieland Wax Museum in Buena Park, Crystal Cathedral in Garden Grove, beaches, boating.

FORT HUNTER LIGGETT (CA37R4)

US Army Garrison, Building 205
ATTN: AFRC-FMH-CDR, P.O. Box 7000
Fort Hunter Liggett, CA 93928-7000

TELEPHONE NUMBER INFORMATION: Main installation numbers: C-408-386-3000, D-312-686-2291.

LOCATION: From US-101 S exit at King City to CA-14, S to main gate. USMRA: Page 111 (C-10). NMC: King City, 25 miles.

GENERAL INFORMATION: Sub-Installation of Fort McCoy. Primary training area for 40th Infantry Division (MECH) CALGD, and testing area for USA TEXCOM.

TEMPORARY MILITARY LODGING: Lodging office, Building 105, 0800-1630 daily, C-408-386-2511, D-312-686-2511. All ranks. DV/VIP C-408-386-2025. Other hours, SDO, Building 205, EX-2503.

RV, CAMPING/FAMCAMP: Fort Hunter Liggett Primitive Campground, on post year round, Outdoor Recreation, Fort Hunter Liggett, P.O. Box 7130, Jolon, CA 93928-7130, C-408-386-3310, 20 graded camper/tent spaces with central W.

SPACE-A: None. See Lemoore NAS listing, C-209-998-1683, D-312-949-1683, Fax: C-209-998-2036.

LOGISTICAL SUPPORT:
Child Care-386-2313
Exchange-385-4585
SATO-386-2406
Theater-386-2645
Commissary-386-2190
Gas Station-386-6032
Snack Bar-386-2645

ADMINISTRATIVE SUPPORT:
Fire Dept-386-2527
Locator-386-2030
Public Affairs-386-2505
Legal-386-2202
Police-386-2613
SDO/NCO-386-2503

HEALTH & WELFARE:
ACS-386-2762
Chapel-386-4363
Medical-386-2516
CHAMPUS-386-2771
Family Services-386-2762

REST & RECREATION:
Com Club-386-2588
MWR-386-2762
Rec Center-ext 2406
ITT-386-2406
Recreation-386-2612

OTHER FACILITIES AVAILABLE: Bowling, Craft Shops, Gym, Hunting and Fishing, Library.

ATTRACTIONS: Old California, hacienda formerly owned by the Hearst family, San Antonio Mission, Prime hunting and fishing area.

FORT IRWIN NATIONAL TRAINING CENTER (CA01R4)

ATTN: AFZJ-GC
Interloop Road, Building 237
Fort Irwin National Training Center, CA 92310-5000

TELEPHONE NUMBER INFORMATION: Main installation numbers: C-619-380-4111, D-312-470-4111.

LOCATION: Take I-15 east from Los Angeles for 125 miles or I-15 west from Las Vegas, NV for 150 miles. Fort is north of I-15 near Barstow. Watch for signs. USMRA: Page 111 (G,H-11,12). NMC: San Bernardino, 60 miles southwest.

GENERAL INFORMATION: The US Army National Training Center, Home of the 11th Armored Cavalry Regiment, NTC Support Battalion & Operations Group.

TEMPORARY MILITARY LODGING: Lodging office, Building 109, 1st Avenue 0800-1630 daily, C-619-380-4599, D-312-470-4599. All ranks. DV/VIP C-619-380-3000. Very limited.

RV, CAMPING/FAMCAMP: None. See Edwards AFB listing, C-805-277-3394, D-312-527-3394.

SPACE-A: None. See China Lake NAWSCWD listing, C-619-939-2302, D-312-437-5308, Fax: C-619-446-7204.

LOGISTICAL SUPPORT:
Child Care-380-1029
Conv Store-380-2417
Gas Station-386-2417
Travel Office-380-3652 (official)
Commissary-380-3422
Exchange-386-2060
Package Store-386-2417

ADMINISTRATIVE SUPPORT:
Legal-380-6359
IG-380-3038
SDO/NCO-380-3750
Locator-380-3369
Police-380-4444/3474

HEALTH & WELFARE:
Chapel-380-3562
Family Services-380-3513
Veterinary Clinic-380-3025
Dental-380-3166
Medical
Central Appts-380-3124
Emergency-380-3777

REST & RECREATION:
Arts & Crafts-ext 3431
Batting Cages-ext 4653
Clubs
EM-380-8646
NCO-380-3293
O-380-3293
Mini-Golf Course-ext 4653
Rec Center-ext 3585
Riding Stables-ext 4796
Teen Center-ext 5685
Youth Activities-ext 4163
Auto Hobby Shop-ext 3531
Bowling-ext 4249
Golf Course-ext 4653
Gym-ext 3810
Library-ext 3462
ITT-380-4767
Morale Support Hq-ext 3582
Rec Equip-ext 3434
Swimming-ext 4951/ 3046
Theater-380-3490

ATTRACTIONS: Goldstone Deep Space Station. Painted Rock, Opposing Force Display Yard, Rainbow Basin, Calico Ghost Town, and NTC/11th ACR Museum.

FORT MacARTHUR (CA46R4)

2400 South Pacific Avenue, Building 37
San Pedro, CA 90731-2960

TELEPHONE NUMBER INFORMATION: Main installation numbers: C-310-363-8292, D-312-833-8292. HP: http://www.laafb.af.mil.

LOCATION: From I-110 (Harbor Freeway) go south to San Pedro, left to Gaffney Street, left on 19th Street right to Pacific Avenue, on the left approximately one-quarter mile. USMRA: Page 117 (C-7). NMI: Los Angeles AFB, 18 miles north. NMC: Los Angeles, in city limits.

GENERAL INFORMATION: Military family housing annex, located 18 miles from Los Angeles AFB.

TEMPORARY MILITARY LODGING: Billeting Manager, Building 37, Patton Quadrangle, 24 hours daily, C-310-363-8296. DV/VIP C-310-363-3751.

RV, CAMPING/FAMCAMP: None. See Los Angeles AFB listing, C-310-363-2081, D-312-833-2081.

SPACE-A: None. See Los Angeles AFB listing, C-310-363-0714, D-312-833-0714, Fax: C-310-216-2670.

LOGISTICAL SUPPORT: Exchange-832-9611

ADMINISTRATIVE SUPPORT: Police-363-8385

HEALTH & WELFARE: Medical-363-8301

REST & RECREATION: None. See Los Angeles AFB listing, C-310-363-2190.

CALIFORNIA
Fort MacArthur, continued

ATTRACTIONS: Hollywood and beaches within easy driving distance, major league sports attractions; Los Angeles Dodgers, Los Angeles Lakers, Los Angeles Clippers, and the Los Angeles Kings.

HUMBOLDT BAY COAST GUARD GROUP (CA02R4)

1296 Chestnut Street
Eureka, CA 95501-5000

TELEPHONE NUMBER INFORMATION: Main installation numbers: C-707-839-6123.

LOCATION: Take Highway 101 past Eureka, Airport Road exit, keep right. First left onto Coast Guard Road, left at "T," follow road to gate. USMRA: Page110 (A-2,3). NMC: Eureka, 20 miles south.

GENERAL INFORMATION: Small Group/Air Station, three helicopters, 150 people. Small Boat Station in Eureka with TML-1 unit, call for reservations and priority.

TEMPORARY MILITARY LODGING: Limited. SAR ready crew, 0700-2200, C-707-443-2212/3, Fax: C-707-269-2541.

RV, CAMPING/FAMCAMP: None. Nearest facility is more than 100 miles away.

SPACE-A: None. Nearest facility is more than 100 miles away.

LOGISTICAL SUPPORT: Exchange-443-7796

ADMINISTRATIVE SUPPORT: Public Affairs-839-6114/6113

HEALTH & WELFARE: Medical Clinic-839-6176

REST & RECREATION: None. Nearest facility is more than 100 miles away.

OTHER SUPPORT & FACILITIES AVAILABLE: Convenient store and shoppette.

ATTRACTIONS: Fishing communities, dairy farms, logging. Rio Dell/Scotia Lumber Mill-free tours. Museums-local artists, Orick-Redwood Burl and chainsaw art.

IMPERIAL BEACH OUTLYING LANDING FIELD (CA04R4)

ATTN: PAO
Imperial Beach, CA 91932-5000

TELEPHONE NUMBER INFORMATION: Main installation numbers: C-619-437-9428.

LOCATION: From I-5 south, right on Palm Avenue left on 13th Street, fork right to base. USMRA: Page. 118 (D,E-10). NMC: San Diego, five miles south.

TEMPORARY MILITARY LODGING: None. See Coronado NAB listing, Billeting Office C-619-437-3860/3494, D-312-577-3860/3494.

RV, CAMPING/FAMCAMP: None. See Coronado NAB listing, Fiddlers Cove RV Park, C-619-435-8788/4700, Fax: C-619-437-1389.

SPACE-A: None. See North Island listing, C-619-545-9567, D-312-735-9567.

LOGISTICAL SUPPORT:
Commissary-437-9481/2
Exchange-424-2900
Service Station-424-2938/8

ADMINISTRATIVE SUPPORT: Public Affairs-437-8167

HEALTH & WELFARE: None. See Coronado NAB listing, C-619-437-3047.

REST & RECREATION: None. See Coronado NAB listing, C-619-437-3339.

ATTRACTIONS: San Diego Bay area, San Diego Zoo, Mexico approximately two miles south.

LEMOORE NAVAL AIR STATION (CA06R4)

700 Avenger Avenue
Lemoore Naval Air Station, CA 93246-5001

TELEPHONE NUMBER INFORMATION: Main installation numbers: C-209-998-0100, D-312-949-0100. HP: http://www.lemoore.navy.mil.

LOCATION: On CA-198, 24 miles east of I-5, 30 miles west of CA-99 in the south central part of the state. USMRA: Page 111 (D-10). NMC: Fresno, 40 miles north.

GENERAL INFORMATION: Navy's newest and largest master jet air station.

TEMPORARY MILITARY LODGING: Lodging office, Building 852, Hancock Circle, 24 hours daily, C-209-998-4784, D-312-949-4784. All ranks. BOQ, C-209-998-4609, D-312-949-4609, DV/VIP - E7-E9, C-209-998-3344, Fax: C-209-998-4587. Navy Lodge C-209-998-5791.

RV, CAMPING/FAMCAMP: None. See Camp Roberts listing, C-805-238-8312, D-312-949-8312, Fax: C-805-238-8384.

SPACE-A: Pax Term/Lounge, Building 180, 24 hours daily, C-209-998-1683, D-312-949-1683, Fax: C-805-238-8384, flights to CONUS Naval Air Stations and other locations.

LOGISTICAL SUPPORT:
Barber Shop-998-4644
Beauty Shop-998-4644
Child Care-998-4919
Child Dev Center-998-4919
Commissary-998-4667
Conv Store-998-4939
Credit Union-998-4578
Dining Facilities-998-4812
Dry Cleaner-998-4703
Education Office-998-3857
Exchange-998-4661
Gas Station-998-4729
Postal Service-998-1850
PSO Travel-998-3993
Snack Bar-998-1850

ADMINISTRATIVE SUPPORT:
CDO-998-3301
Fire Dept-998-4507
Housing Office-998-2000
Legal-998-3873
OOD/Locator-998-3300
Pass/ID Office-998-3386
Police-998-4749
Public Affairs-998-3394
Quarter Deck-998-3300

HEALTH & WELFARE:
American Red Cross-998-3383
Chapel-998-4618
Family Services-998-4042
Medical-998-4481
- Central Appts-998-4448
- Emergency-998-4435
- Health Benefits-998-4490
- Hospital-998-4481
- Information-998-4481

CHAMPUS-998-4490
Dental
- Central Appts-998-4219
- Clinic-998-4300
- Emergency-998-4220

N-MC Relief Society-998-4045
Veterinary Services-998-5195

REST & RECREATION:
Arts & Crafts-997-8904
Bowling-998-4647
Electronics Hobby-ext 4904
Fitness Center-998-4141
Gym-998-4141
ITT-998-8905
Library-998-4633
MWR-998-4886

Auto Hobby Shop-998-4908
Clubs
- Combined-998-4877
- CPO-998-4858
- EM(Tailgates)-998-4877
- Flying-ext 3526
- O-998-4857

Outdoor Rec-998-4897

Rec Center-ext 4804
Theater-998-4643
Services-998-4898
Youth Center-998-4936

ATTRACTIONS: Sequoia National Park. Ski areas within a 200 mile radius.

LONG BEACH NAVAL SHIPYARD (CA55R4)

ATTN: PAO
300 Skipjack Road
Long Beach, CA 90822-5099
Scheduled to close September 1997, call ahead to verify support availability.

TELEPHONE NUMBER INFORMATION: Main installation numbers: C-310-980-2798.

LOCATION: Take Long Beach Freeway, CA-710, to Terminal Island exit to Naval Shipyard. Clearly marked. USMRA: Page 117 (C,D-7). NMI: San Diego Naval Station, 110 miles south. NMC: Long Beach, two miles east.

GENERAL INFORMATION: Shipyard is in process of closing.

TEMPORARY MILITARY LODGING: None. See Fort MacArthur listing, C-310-363-8296.

RV, CAMPING/FAMCAMP: None. See Los Angeles AFB listing, C-310-363-2081, D-312-833-2081.

SPACE-A: None. See Los Angeles AFB listing, C-310-363-0714, D-312-833-0714, Fax: C-310-216-2670.

LOGISTICAL SUPPORT: None. See Los Angeles AFB listing, C-310-363-1110, D-312-833-1110.

ADMINISTRATIVE SUPPORT:
CDO-980-6964
Housing Office-980-6633/6003/6335
Pass/ID Office-980-2641/2444
Public Affairs-980-2798
Fire Dept-980-6333
Legal-980-5124/5130
Police-980-2731/32

HEALTH & WELFARE:
CHAMPUS-519-8182
Retiree Services-980-5436
Medical-980-2736

REST & RECREATION: None. See Los Angeles AFB listing, C-310-363-1110, D-312-833-1110.

ATTRACTIONS: Greater Los Angeles area, Long Beach and Hollywood. Amphitheater and parks on base.

LOS ALAMITOS/ARMY NATIONAL GUARD ARMED FORCES RESERVE CENTER (CA39R4)

Building 15, Post Headquarters
Los Alamitos, CA 90720-5001

TELEPHONE NUMBER INFORMATION: Main installation numbers: C-562-795-2000, D-312-972-2011.

LOCATION: Off I-605. Clearly marked. USMRA: Page 117 (E-6,7). NMC: Los Angeles, five miles north.

GENERAL INFORMATION: Armed Forces Reserve Center (AFRC), supporting all active military and reservists from all branches of the Armed Forces, including, retired military, DoD Personnel, certain State active duty and Civil Service personnel, and quasi-military personnel.

TEMPORARY MILITARY LODGING: Transient Quarters, Building 19, Hq AFRC, 0800-1630 hours, C-562-795-2124, Fax: C-562-795-2125.

RV, CAMPING/FAMCAMP: None. See Los Angeles AFB listing, C-310-363-2081.

SPACE-A: C-562-795-2571, D-312-972-2571, Fax: C-310-792-2571.

LOGISTICAL SUPPORT:
Beauty Shop-430-3698
Clothing Sales-795-2059
Exchange-430-1076
Carlson Wagonlit Travel-430-4936
Dry Cleaners-594-5503
Package Store-795-1076

ADMINISTRATIVE SUPPORT:
Fire Dept-795-2144
SDO/NCO-795-2090
Police-795-2100

HEALTH & WELFARE: None. See Los Angeles AFB listing, C-310-363-0964.

REST & RECREATION:
Golf Course-430-9913

ATTRACTIONS: Los Angeles, Hollywood and Orange County.

LOS ANGELES AIR FORCE BASE (CA75R4)

2430 East El Segundo Boulevard, Suite 4049
Los Angeles Air Force Base, CA 90045-4687

TELEPHONE NUMBER INFORMATION: Main installation numbers: C-310-363-1110, D-312-833-2582.

LOCATION: From I-405 (San Diego Freeway) take El Segundo Blvd exit, one-quarter mile on right. USMRA: Page 117 (B-5). NMC: Los Angeles, 10 miles northeast.

GENERAL INFORMATION: Space and Missile Systems Center, manages research, development and acquisition of DoD space systems; 61st Air Base Group.

TEMPORARY MILITARY LODGING: Limited. Fort MacArthur Inn, C-310-363-8296, D-312-833-8296.

RV, CAMPING/FAMCAMP: FAMCAMP on base, year round, C-310-363-2081, D-312-833-2081, 15 camper spaces with W/E hookups.

SPACE-A: Available at Los Angeles IAP, 0730-2030 daily, C-310-363-0714, D-312-833-0714, Fax: C-310-216-2670. Limited number of flights to CONUS and foreign locations via Air Force contract commercial aircraft.

LOGISTICAL SUPPORT:
Child Care-363-1792
Exchange-640-0129
Package Store-322-7533
Commissary-833-1426
Gas Station-615-0295
SATO-363-1130

ADMINISTRATIVE SUPPORT:
Legal-363-2483
Police-363-2123
Locator-363-1876
Public Affairs-363-0030

HEALTH & WELFARE:
Chapel-363-5355
Medical-363-5029
  Clinic-363-0964
Family Services-363-1121
Retiree Services-363-5120

REST & RECREATION:
Auto Skills Center-363-1705
Equipment Rental-363-2081
Swimming Pool-363-8260
Consol Club-363-2230
Fitness Center-363-2269
Tickets & Tours-363-2190

ATTRACTIONS: Several Southern California area attractions, Hollywood, beaches.

MARCH AIR RESERVE BASE (CA08R4)

452 AMW/PA
2145 Graeber Street, Suite 211
March Air Reserve Base, CA 92518-1671

TELEPHONE NUMBER INFORMATION: C-909-655-1110, D-312-947-1110. E-mail: pa452@tecnet2.jcte.jcs.mil. HP: http:////www.afres.com.

LOCATION: From Highway 60 in Riverside, approximately 10 miles the road will fork, bear right on Interstate I-215 south, exit at March ARB. Second light is main gate. USMRA: Page 111 (G-14). NMC: Riverside, nine miles northwest.

GENERAL INFORMATION: Air Force Reserve Base, 452nd Air Mobility Wing (AFRES host); Home of the 163rd Air Refueling Wing (CA, ANG); 119th Fighter Group (ND, ANG); Armed Forces Radio and Television Services; Defense Visual Info Center; Air Force Audit Agency; US Customs Service; Domestic Air Interdiction Coordination Center; Base activated 1918, named after 2nd Lt Peyton C. March, Jr. who died in Texas in a crash, 19 February 1918. Base converted to ARB, 1 April 1996.

TEMPORARY MILITARY LODGING: The March Inn, C-909-655-3347, Fax: C-909-655-4574.

RV, CAMPING/FAMCAMP: NEW!! Outdoor Rec, 452 SVS/SVRO, Bldg 803, March ARB, CA 92518. C-909-655-2816, Fax: C-909-655-5221. Twelve sites with W/E/S for $10 daily and 5 sites without hookups for $5 daily. Picnic tables and BBQ pits available.

SPACE-A: C-909-655-2001. Pax Terminal: C-909-655-2397.

LOGISTICAL SUPPORT:
Commissary-655-3967 Exchange-655-3111

ADMINISTRATIVE SUPPORT: Public Affairs-655-4137

HEALTH & WELFARE: None. See El Toro MCAS, C-714-726-3175.

REST & RECREATION:
Hap Arnold Club-655-2121 MWR-655-4303

ATTRACTIONS: Sunny California.

MARINES' MEMORIAL CLUB (CA20R4)

609 Sutter Street
San Francisco, CA 94102-1022

TELEPHONE NUMBER INFORMATION: Main installation numbers: C-415-673- 6672. Reservations, 1-800-5-MARINE or 415-673-6604 (direct). E-mail: marineclub@msn.com. HP: http://www.marineclub.com/marine club.

LOCATION: From CA-580, cross the Bay Bridge, take 5th Street exit to O'Farrell, right to Powell Street, left to Sutter Street USMRA: Page 119 (C-5). NMC: San Francisco, in city limits.

GENERAL INFORMATION: The Marines' Memorial Club is a club/hotel exclusively for uniformed services personnel, active duty and retirees and their guests. **The club is not a part of the government but is a private, non-profit organization and is completely self supporting.** This club/hotel is a living memorial to Marines who lost their lives in the Pacific during WW II. It opened on the Marine Corps' Birthday, November 10, 1946, and chose as its motto "A tribute to those Marines who have gone before; and a service to those who carry on."

TEMPORARY MILITARY LODGING: Hotel, all ranks, leave or official duty. Guest rooms (137); deluxe suites (11); family suites (3). Reservations required. C-1-800-5-MARINE or 415-673-6672 (direct). Average room $75-100, average suite $175.

RV, CAMPING/FAMCAMP: None. See Travis AFB listing, C-707-424-3583, D-312-837-3583.

SPACE-A: None. See Travis AFB listing, C-707-424-1854, D-312-837-1854.

LOGISTICAL SUPPORT: Club facilities include coin-operated launderette, valet, exchange store, package store, rooms for private parties, and a dining room and lounge in the Skyroom on the 12th floor, overlooking San Francisco. Conv Store/news stand and coffee shop outside hotel adjacent to entrance. Hotel discount parking on Sutter Street, ask at desk. *Military Living books, maps and atlases are sold in the Club exchange, first floor.*

ADMINISTRATIVE SUPPORT: None. See Travis AFB listing, C-707-424-2798.

HEALTH AND WELFARE: None. See Travis AFB listing, C-707-423-3000.

REST & RECREATION: Theater, library/museum, swimming, gym.

ATTRACTIONS: In the heart of San Francisco, within walking distance of Cable Cars; Union Square is just one-and-a-half blocks away. Many major attractions.

McCLELLAN AIR FORCE BASE (CA35R4)

3237 Peacekeeper Way, Suite 5
McClellan Air Force Base, CA 95652-1048
Scheduled to close July 2001

TELEPHONE NUMBER INFORMATION: Main installation numbers: C-916-643-2111, D-312-633-2111.

LOCATION: Off I-80 north. From I-80 take Madison Avenue or Watt Avenue exit. Clearly marked. USMRA: Page 110 (C-6). NMC: Sacramento, nine miles southwest.

GENERAL INFORMATION: Air Force Materiel Command Base. Headquarters Sacramento Air Logistics Center. US Coast Guard Station McClellan. Also AMC, ACC AFCC, and AFRES units.

TEMPORARY MILITARY LODGING: Lodging office, Building 89, 54 O'Malley Avenue, 24 hours daily, C-916-643-3267, D-312-633-6223. DV/VIP C-916-643-4311. All ranks.

RV, CAMPING/FAMCAMP: None. See Beale AFB listing, C-916-634-3382, D-312-368-3382.

SPACE-A: Pax Term, Building 251, 0730-1615 daily, C-916-643-4105, D-312-633-4105, Fax: C-916-643-5616, flights to CONUS and foreign locations. Also, try the Coast Guard Air Station Ops at the AFB.

LOGISTICAL SUPPORT:
Cafeteria-643-3598
Commissary-925-8754*
Exchange-920-0537*
Package Store-643-3080
Snack Bar-920-6660
Child Care-643-3611
Conv Store-332-3872
Gas Station-922-8868
SATO-643-4410

** Facility will remain open after base closure.*

ADMINISTRATIVE SUPPORT:
CDO/OOD-643-2751
Locator-643-4113
Public Affairs-643-6127
Legal-643-3150
Police-643-6160

HEALTH & WELFARE:
CHAMPUS-646-9320
Family Services-643-3815
Retiree Services-643-2207
Chapel-643-6021
Medical
Central Appts-646-8400
Clinic-646-8537
Inpatient-643-7107

REST & RECREATION:
Arts & Crafts-ext 3004
Clubs
Aero-ext 3264
EM-922-9657
NCO-643-5977
O-643-3526
MWR-643-6660
Picnic Area-ext 2596
Rec Equipment-ext 6034
Swimming-ext 2259
Youth Center-ext 3946
Bowling-ext 5752
Gym-ext 2596
Golf Course-643-3313
Hobby Shop-ext 2323
ITT-643-2259
Library-ext 4640
Outdoor Rec-ext 2738
Rec Center-ext 2259
Rec News-ext 5311
Theater-643-8706

ATTRACTIONS: Lake Tahoe and Reno, NV, San Francisco Bay Area. Air Museum on base, C-916-643-3192, 0900-1500 Mon-Sat, closed Sun and federal holidays.

MIRAMAR NAVAL AIR STATION (CA14R4)

45249 Miramar Way
Miramar Naval Air Station, CA 92145-5005
Disestablishing October 1, 1997 & retitled
Miramar MCAS under 1995 BRAC Mandates.

TELEPHONE NUMBER INFORMATION: Main installation numbers: C-619-537-1011, D-312-577-1011.

LOCATION: From I-15 north of San Diego, take Miramar Way exit. USMRA: Page 118 (C,D-2,3,4; E,F-2,3). NMC: San Diego, 15 miles southwest.

GENERAL INFORMATION: Commander Airborne Early Warning Wing Pacific, Commander 3rd Marine Air Wing, Commander Marine Air Group 11, Commander Air Group 46.

TEMPORARY MILITARY LODGING: Lodging office, Building M-312 (BOQ), 24 hours daily, C-619-537-4233, D-312-577-4235; Building 638 (BEQ), C-619-537-4233, D-312-577-4235. DV/VIP EM C-619-537-6221, Officers C-619-537-1221, Fax: C-619-537-4243. Navy Lodge, Building 516, C-619-271-7111 or 1-800-NAVY-INN.

RV, CAMPING/FAMCAMP: RV Park on base, year round, C-619-537-4149, D-312-577-4149, 36 camper spaces with full hookups, 12 camper spaces with with E.

SPACE-A: Limited. C-619-537-4284, D-312-577-4284, Fax: C-619-537-4261/1721.

LOGISTICAL SUPPORT:
Cafeteria-695-7278
Commissary-537-4513
Gas Station-695-7251
SATO-537-4126
Child Care-537-4144
Exchange-695-7200
Package Store-695-7344

ADMINISTRATIVE SUPPORT:
Legal-537-1241
OOD-537-1227

HEALTH & WELFARE:
American Red Cross-537-4107
Chapel-537-1333
Medical-537-4653
Central Appts-537-4656
Emergency-537-4655
CHAMPUS-537-4653
Family Services-537-4099
Navy Relief-537-1807
Retiree Services-537-4806

CALIFORNIA
Miramar Naval Air Station, continued

REST & RECREATION:
Arts & Crafts-ext 4134
Bowling-ext 1215
Golf Course-ext 4155
Gym-ext 4128
Library-ext 1261
Rec Supply-ext 4149
Swimming-ext 4140
Tickets-ext 4126
Youth Center-ext 4136
Auto Hobby Shop-ext 1215
Clubs
EM-ext 4140
O-537-4809
Picnic Area-ext 3526
Services-ext 4117
Theater-537-4143
Wood Hobby Shop-ext 4134

ATTRACTIONS: Old Town San Diego, Sea World, San Diego Zoo, Wild Animal Park, beautiful beaches and boardwalk, Mission Blvd.

MOFFETT FEDERAL AIRFIELD NASA/AMES RESEARCH CENTER (CA15R4)

ATTN: PAO
P.O. Box 0128
Moffett Federal Airfield, CA 94035-5000

TELEPHONE NUMBER INFORMATION: Main installation numbers: C-415-604-5000, D-312-359-5000.

LOCATION: On Bayshore Freeway, US-101, 35 miles south of San Francisco. USMRA: Page 119 (F-9). NMC: San Jose, seven miles south, San Francisco, 35 miles north.

GENERAL INFORMATION: NASA-AMES Research Center. Santa Clara Naval Air Reserve, and Onizuka AS Annex are tenants.

TEMPORARY MILITARY LODGING: Lodging office, Building 20, 24 hours daily, C-415-603-9503, D-312-359-9503, Fax: C-415-603-9805. Navy Lodge C-415-962-1542 or 800-NAVY-INN. All ranks.

RV, CAMPING/FAMCAMP: None. See Defense Distribution Region West-Sharpe Site listing, Sharpe Travel Camp, C-209-982-2232, D-312-462-2232.

SPACE-A: Pax Term, Building 158, 24 hours daily, C-415-604-5231, D-312-494-5231, flights to CONUS, OCONUS and foreign locations.

NASA/AMES

LOGISTICAL SUPPORT:
Cafeteria-604-5969
Visitor Center-604-6274

ADMINISTRATIVE SUPPORT:
Locator-604-5000
Public Affairs-604-9000
Police-604-5461

REST & RECREATION: Moffett Club-604-1680

ONIZUKA AS ANNEX (TENANT)

LOGISTICAL SUPPORT:
Child Care-940-1869
Commissary-603-9976
Education Office-603-8045
Child Dev Center-940-1884
Credit Union-969-6222

ADMINISTRATIVE SUPPORT: Housing Office-603-8100

HEALTH & WELFARE:
Air Force Aid Society-603-8002
Chapel-603-8073
Family Services-603-8004
Medical-603-8220
Central Appts-603-8251
Clinic-603-8220
Health Benefits-603-8228
CHAMPUS-603-0815
Dental-603-8265
Central Appts-603-8251
Clinic-603-8220
Retiree Services-603-8047
TRICARE-960-0816

REST & RECREATION:
Auto Hobby Shop-603-9717
Youth Center-691-1216
Golf Course-603-8026

SANTA CLARA NAVY AIR RESERVE STATION (NARS) (TENANT)

LOGISTICAL SUPPORT:
Child Care-940-1884
Conv Store-603-9927
SATO-604-1686
Commissary-603-9976
Exchange-603-9907

ADMINISTRATIVE SUPPORT:
CDO/OOD-603-9527
Legal-603-9515

HEALTH & WELFARE:
CHAMPUS-603-8227
Family Services-603-8016
Chapel-404-4100
Clinic-608-8251
Emergency-608-8251

REST & RECREATION:
Auto Hobby Shop-ext 8046
Golf-ext 4702
NASA Field House-ext 1686
Rec Services-691-1216
Swimming-ext 4712
Ticket Office-ext 4757
Bowling-ext 4709
Gym-ext 4697
Racquetball-ext 1686
Softball-ext 1686
Tennis-ext 1686
Youth Activities-965-2716

ATTRACTIONS: Paramount Great America Park is five miles south. Located in the heart of the "Silicon Valley." San Jose and Santa Cruz are nearby.

Note: As of 1 August 1997, a new area code, 650, has replaced some 415 and 916 area codes. There is a six month grace period for those numbers effected.

MONTEREY NAVAL POSTGRADUATE SCHOOL (CA16R4)

1 University Circle
Monterey, CA 93943-5000

TELEPHONE NUMBER INFORMATION: Main installation numbers: C-408-656-2441, D-312-878-2441.

LOCATION: Take CA-1 to central Monterey exit, right at light onto Camino Aguajito. Then first right (right fork) onto 10th Street, turn left at stop sign onto Sloat Avenue, and right at 10th Street gate. Or N on CA-1, Aguajito Road exit to Mark Thomas Drive, to left on Sloat Avenue, right at 10th Street gate. USMRA: Page 111 (B-9). NMC: Monterey, in city limits.

GENERAL INFORMATION: Naval Postgraduate School, Defense Resource Management Institute, Fleet Numerical Oceanography Center, and Naval Support Activity-Monterey Bay.

TEMPORARY MILITARY LODGING: Lodging office, Building 220, Herrmann Hall, 1 University Circle, 24 hours daily, C-408-656-2060, D-312-878-2060, Fax: C-408-646-3024.

RV, CAMPING/FAMCAMP: None. See Fort Hunter Liggett listing, C-408-386-3310.

SPACE-A: None. See Lemoore NAS listing, C-209-998-1683, D-312-949-1683.

LOGISTICAL SUPPORT:
Child Care-656-2734
Conv Store-375-0959
Gas Station-373-7271
SATO-656-3357
Commissary-242-3418
Exchange-375-3737
Package Store-373-7511
Snack Bar-373-0557

ADMINISTRATIVE SUPPORT:
CDO/OOD-656-2441
Legal-656-2506
Police-656-2555
Fire Dept-656-2334
Locator-656-2441
Public Affairs-656-2023

CALIFORNIA
Monterey Naval Postgraduate School, continued

HEALTH & WELFARE:
Chapel-656-2241
Medical
Central Appts-242-5741
Emergency-242-5234
Family Services-656-3141
Retiree Services-242-5595

REST & RECREATION:
Clubs
O-656-2170
MWR-656-3223
Rec Equipment-ext 3118
Swimming-ext 2275
Golf Course-656-2167
Gym-ext 2167
Recreation-656-2275
Rec Office-ext 2467

ATTRACTIONS: Beaches, seafood, Carmel Valley, Carmel-By-The-Sea, Pebble Beach, Big Sur coastline, Salinas Valley. Beautiful area, Monterey Bay Aquarium and Cannery Row.

NORTH ISLAND NAVAL AIR STATION (CA43R4)

Building 605, McCain Boulevard
P.O. Box 357033
North Island Naval Air Station, CA 92135-7033

TELEPHONE NUMBER INFORMATION: Main installation numbers: C-619-545-8123, D-312-735-8123. E-mail: bwelk@emh.nasni.navy.mil. HP: http://www.nasni.navy.mil.

LOCATION: From I-5 exit at Coronado Bridge (toll). Also, from CA-75 north to CA-282 to base. In Coronado. USMRA: Page 118 (B,C-6,7). NMC: San Diego, four miles northeast.

GENERAL INFORMATION: Largest Naval Industrial Complex on the West Coast.

TEMPORARY MILITARY LODGING: Lodging office, Building I (BOQ), 24 hours daily, BEQ, C-619-545-9551, D-312-735-7489 Fax: C-619-545-9042, BOQ, C-619-545-7489, D-312-735-7489. Navy Lodge, Building 1402, 24 hours daily, C-619-545-6940, D-312-735-6940. DV/VIP EM C-619-545-9551, Officers C-619-545-7545, Fax: C-619-545-9072. All ranks.

RV, CAMPING/FAMCAMP: None. See Coronado NAB listing, Fiddlers Cove RV Park, C-619-435-8788, Fax: C-619-437-1389.

SPACE-A: Pax Term/Lounge, Building 700, 24 hours daily, C-619-545-9567, D-312-735-9567, flights to CONUS. Some to foreign locations.

LOGISTICAL SUPPORT:
Barber Shop-522-7230
Cafeteria-522-7265
Commissary-545-6566
Credit Union-656-1600
Education Office-545-7923
Gas Station-522-7281
Package Store-545-7279
SATO-545-7937
Beauty Shop-522-7229
Child Care-545-7226
Conv Store-522-7277
Dry Cleaner-522-7231
Exchange-522-7266
Laundry-522-7231
Postal Service-545-4380
Snack Bar-522-7266/69

ADMINISTRATIVE SUPPORT:
CDO/OOD-545-8123
Legal-545-8141
Pass/ID Office-525-7916
Public Affairs-545-8167
Fire Dept-524-6250
Locator-524-0444
Police-545-9446
Quarter Deck-545-8123

HEALTH & WELFARE:
American Red Cross-435-4285
CHAMPUS-545-4319
ACS-232-1133
Chapel-545-8213
Dental
Central Appts-545-6938
Clinic-545-6397
Emergency-545-6397
N-MC Relief Society-545-7202
Family Services-545-6071
Medical
Central Appts-545-4263
Clinic-545-4268
Emergency-9-911
Hospital-532-6400
Information-545-4265

REST & RECREATION:
Auto Hobby Shop-545-7237
Clubs
CPO-545-7223
EM-545-7205
O-545-6945
Library-ext 5-8230
Outdoor Rec-545-7237
Recreation-545-9206
Skeet/Trap Range-ext 7225
Theater-545-9479
Wood Hobby Shop-545-7236
Bowling-545-7240
Fitness Center-ext 2876
Golf Course-545-9659
Gym-522-2877
ITT-545-9576
MWR-545-8032
Pool
Crew-ext 2880
Officers-ext 7228
Women's Spa-522-2871

ATTRACTIONS: Beaches, sport fishing, Old San Diego, Sea World, Bay Area, San Diego Zoo, and Mexico nearby.

OAKLAND ARMY BASE (CA18R4)

ATTN: MTWGA-C
56 Alaska Street
Oakland Army Base, CA 94626-5780
Scheduled to close July 31, 2001

TELEPHONE NUMBER INFORMATION: Main installation numbers: C-510-466-9111, D-312-859-9111.

LOCATION: Near junction of I-80 and I-880, south of San Francisco-Oakland Bay Bridge, look for signs. USMRA: Page. 119 (D-5). NMC: Oakland, two miles southeast.

GENERAL INFORMATION: Western Headquarters for Military Traffic Management Command and other Western Area Army support units. Vehicle Processing Center (VPC) for overseas shipment and pick-up (1-800-446-0443).

TEMPORARY MILITARY LODGING: Lodging office, Building 650, 24 hours daily, C-510-466-3113, D-312-859-3113, Fax: C-510-466-2997, D-312-859-2997. All ranks. **Fort Mason Officers' Club,** overlooking Fisherman's Wharf in San Francisco, has a limited number of suites and rooms available for officers (all grades); contact the Club Manager for reservations up to 30 days in advance, C-415-441-7700, D-312-859-0111.

RV, CAMPING/FAMCAMP: Lake Tahoe Oakland Condominiums off base, year round, C-510-444-8107, D-312-859-3113, two three-bedroom condominiums on Lake Tahoe.

SPACE-A: None. See Travis AFB listing, C-707-424-1854, D-312-837-1854, Fax: C-707-424-2048.

LOGISTICAL SUPPORT:
Carlson Wagonlit Travel-466-2100
Commissary-466-2004
Dining Facilities
Gateway Club-466-3598
Strike Zone Snack Bar-466-3573
Snack Bar-465-3175
Child Care-466-2687
Conv Store-465-3176
Exchange-836-4277
Gas Station-465-3176
Postal Service-839-7110
Travel Office-466-2100

ADMINISTRATIVE SUPPORT:
CDO/OOD-466-3131
Legal-466-2921
Pass/ID Office-466-2195
Public Affairs-466-3021
Fire Dept-466-2762
Locator-466-9111
Police-466-3333
SDO/NCO-466-3131

CALIFORNIA
Oakland Army Base, continued

HEALTH & WELFARE:
ACS-466-3459
Chapel-466-2616
Medical
Central Appts-466-2918
Emergency-466-2161/2245
Army Emergency Relief-466-3477
Family Services-466-3472
Retiree Services-466-2765

REST & RECREATION:
Arts & Crafts-466-3541
Bowling-466-3020
Fitness Center-466-2246
ITT-466-2141
MWR-466-3516
Youth Center-ext 3040
Auto Hobby Shop-466-3068
Clubs
Gateway-466-3598
O-415-441-7700
Recreation-466-3470

ATTRACTIONS: San Francisco and Bay area. Many exciting things to see and do in and around Oakland. Jack London Square shopping area at the foot of Broadway in Oakland is a waterfront promenade lined with stores, restaurants and entertainment.

OAKLAND FLEET & INDUSTRIAL SUPPLY CENTER (CA42R4)

250 Executive Way
Oakland, CA 94625-5000
Scheduled to close September 1998

TELEPHONE NUMBER INFORMATION: Main installation numbers: C-510-302-2000, D-312-672-2000.

LOCATION: Can be reached from I-880 and CA-24 from the east. Clearly marked. USMRA: Page 119 (D-5). NMC: Oakland, four miles east.

GENERAL INFORMATION: Support Activity for Navy Resale System.

TEMPORARY MILITARY LODGING: None. See Oakland Army Base listing, C-510-466-3113, D-312-859-3113.

RV, CAMPING/FAMCAMP: None. See Oakland Army Base listing, Lake Tahoe Oakland Condominiums, C-510-444-8107, D-312-859-3113.

SPACE-A: None. See Travis AFB, C-707-424-1854, D-312-837-1854, Fax: C-707-424-2048.

LOGISTICAL SUPPORT:
Exchange-302-5405

ADMINISTRATIVE SUPPORT:
CDO/OOD-302-5713
Locator-302-2000
Public Affairs-302-4794/4967
Fire Dept-302-6421
Police-302-6421

HEALTH & WELFARE: None. See Travis AFB listing, C-707-423-3000. Chapels available at Oakland Army Base.

REST & RECREATION:
MWR-302-6759
Recreation-302-6759

OTHER SUPPORT AVAILABLE: Credit Union, Postal Service, Shoppette.

ATTRACTIONS: San Francisco, Oakland and Bay area.

ONIZUKA AIR STATION (CA96R4)

1080 Lockheed Way, Box 053
Sunnyvale, CA 94089-1236

TELEPHONE NUMBER INFORMATION: Main installation numbers: C-408-752-3000, D-312-561-3000.

LOCATION: Clearly marked from Highway 101 or Highway 237, follow signs to base. USMRA: Page 119 (F-9). NMC: San Jose, 10 miles northwest.

GENERAL INFORMATION: 750th Space Group, Det 2 & Det 6, SMC, tenant of Moffett Federal Airfield/NASA Ames.

TEMPORARY MILITARY LODGING: None. See Moffett Federal Airfield listing BEQ C-415-603-9503, D-312-359-9503, Fax: C-415-603-9805.

RV, CAMPING/FAMCAMP: None. See Defense Distribution Region West-Sharpe Site listing, Sharpe Travel Camp, C-209-982-2232, D-312-462-2232.

SPACE-A: None. See Moffett Federal Airfield/NASA Ames listing, C-415-404-5231, D-312-494-5231.

LOGISTICAL SUPPORT:
Barber Shop-752-4600
Exchange-752-4601
Conv Store-752-4601

ADMINISTRATIVE SUPPORT:
Legal-752-4622
Pass/ID Office-752-6605
Public Affairs-752-4026
Locator-752-4539
Police-752-3200

HEALTH & WELFARE: None. See Moffett Federal Airfield/NASA Ames listing for available support.

REST & RECREATION:
Camping/Rec Equipment-752-4556
MWR-752-4556
ITT-752-4556

ATTRACTIONS: San Francisco, a one hour drive. Monterey (south) and Napa Valley (north), under two hour drives. Day trips to Lake Tahoe, Yosemite National Park.

Note: Most of Onizuka AS support is located at Moffett Federal Airfield/NASA Ames, 3 miles away.

PETALUMA COAST GUARD TRAINING CENTER (CA23R4)

599 Tomales Road
Petaluma, CA 94952-5000

TELEPHONE NUMBER INFORMATION: Main installation numbers: C-707-765-7212/7215.

LOCATION: Exit US-101 North to E Washington Avenue, nine miles west to Coast Guard Training Center. USMRA: Page 110 (B-6,7). NMC: San Francisco, 58 miles south.

GENERAL INFORMATION: The major West Coast Coast Guard Training Center.

TEMPORARY MILITARY LODGING: Guest Housing, Building T-134, Nevada Avenue, 0730-1600, C-707-765-7248. All ranks.

RV, CAMPING/FAMCAMP: Petaluma Lake Area Campsites, on base, year round, C-707-765-7348. Six camper spaces without hookups, 25 tent spaces.

SPACE-A: None. See Travis AFB listing, C-707-424-1854, D-312-837-1854, Fax: C-707-424-2048.

LOGISTICAL SUPPORT:
Cafeteria-765-7168
Conv Store-765-7252
Gas Station-765-7254
SATO-765-7362
Child Care-765-7334
Exchange-765-7241
Package Store-765-7252

CALIFORNIA
Petaluma Coast Guard Training Center, continued

ADMINISTRATIVE SUPPORT:
CDO/OOD-765-7212
Locator-765-7212
Public Affairs-765-7145
Fire Dept-765-7355
Police-765-7215

HEALTH & WELFARE:
CHAMPUS-765-7563
Family Services-765-7326
Chapel-765-7330
Medical-765-7200
Emergency-765-7200

REST & RECREATION:
Consol Club-765-7248
MWR-765-7340
Driving Range-765-7348
Theater-765-7346

OTHER FACILITIES AVAILABLE: Bowling, Fitness Course, Gym, Library, Swimming Pool.

ATTRACTIONS: The base is a federal game preserve.

POINT MUGU NAVAL AIR WARFARE CENTER, WEAPONS DIVISION (CA40R4)

521 9th Street, Building 1, Room 117
Point Mugu, CA 93042-5001

TELEPHONE NUMBER INFORMATION: Main installation numbers: C-805-989-1110, D-312-351-1110.

LOCATION: Eight miles south of Oxnard and 40 miles north of Santa Monica, on Pacific Coast Highway (PCH), CA-1. USMRA: Page 111 (E-13). NMC: Oxnard, seven miles north.

GENERAL INFORMATION: Naval Air Warfare Center Weapons Division, Naval Air Weapons Station, Navy Weapons Test Squadron, Air Test & Evaluation Squadron 9 Detachment, Antarctic Development Squadron 6, Explosive Ordnance Disposal MU 3 Detachment, Helicopter Combat Support Squadron 5, Marine Aviation Detachment, Naval Satellite Operations Center, Naval Air Reserve Forces, Patrol Squadron 5, Naval Air Reserve. No general visits permitted.

TEMPORARY MILITARY LODGING: Protocol Code 08AE00E, NAWCWPNS, 521 9th Street, Point Mugu, CA 93042-5001, Protocol office, Building 36, Mon-Thurs 0730-1630 hours, C-805-989-7532/8672, D-312-351-8672, Fax: C-805-939-4358, D-312-351-4358. All ranks. VIP EM/Officers C-805-989-8672, Fax: C-805-989-7470.

RV, CAMPING/FAMCAMP: Point Mugu Recreation Facilities on base, year round, MWR Beach Motel, Code 860000E, NAWS, 521 9th Street, Point Mugu, CA 93042-5001, C-805-989-8407, D-312-351-8407, 51 camper spaces with full hookups, six camper spaces without hookups, 24 motel units, beach motel located in Building 774 on 18th street.

SPACE-A: Pax Terminal, Building 339, Mon-Thurs 0600-1800, every other Fri 0600-1800, C-805-989-7731, D-312-351-7731, Fax: C-805-989-4085, D-312-351-4085, flights to CONUS and foreign locations.

LOGISTICAL SUPPORT:
Bank-989-8787
Beauty Shop-989-8701
Child Care-989-8375
Commissary-989-7891
Dining Facilities
Mugu's Pizza-989-7747
The Point-989-8570
Gas Station-488-0161
Package Store-989-8896
SATO-989-8378 (official)
Barber Shop-989-7271
Cafeteria-989-8898
Child Dev Center-989-7481
Credit Union-989-8787
Dry Cleaner-989-5111
Education Office-989-8457
Exchange-989-8896
Laundry-989-5111
Postal Service-989-8707
Travel Office-488-1084 (leisure)

ADMINISTRATIVE SUPPORT:
CDO/OOD-989-7209
Housing Office-989-7250
Locator-703-614-9221*
Police-989-7058
Quarter Deck-989-7209
Fire Dept-989-7034/7035
Legal-989-7309
Pass/ID Office-989-7670/7648
Public Affairs-989-8094/95

**off base*

HEALTH & WELFARE:
American Red Cross-989-7393 or 982-3074
Dental
Central Appts-989-7126/7603
Clinic-989-7126/7603
Emergency-989-7126/7603
N-MC Relief Society-989-8918
TRICARE-981-2819
CHAMPUS-982-6322
Chapel-989-7967
Family Services-989-8146
Medical
Central Appts-989-8932
Clinic-989-8815/16
Emergency-911

REST & RECREATION:
Auto Hobby Shop-989-7353
Clubs
CPO-989-8570
EM-989-7747
O-989-8849
ITT-989-7628
Library-989-7771
Swimming-ext 7788
Youth Center-989-7580
Bowling-989-7667
Community Center-989-7580
Fitness Center-989-7728
Golf Course-989-7109
Gym-989-7728
ITT Recording-989-8349
MWR-989-7509
Theater-989-8249

ATTRACTIONS: Beautiful beaches and Los Angeles area nearby. Annual Point Mugu Air Show in the Fall. Disneyland, Marineland, Movieland, Universal Studios, Queen Mary, and Spruce Goose, Lion Country Safari and more. Ronald Reagan Presidential Library in Simi Valley (C-805-522-8444).

PORT HUENEME NAVAL CONSTRUCTION BATTALION CENTER (CA32R4)

Commanding Officer
1000 23rd Avenue
Port Hueneme, CA 93043-4301

TELEPHONE NUMBER INFORMATION: Main installation numbers: C-805-982-4711, D-312-551-4711.

LOCATION: From US-101, exit south on Ventura Road, right to Pleasant Valley Road. USMRA: Page 111 (D,E-13). NMC: Los Angeles, 50 miles southeast.

GENERAL INFORMATION: Major units include Naval Mobile Construction Battalions THREE, FOUR, FIVE and FORTY and Underwater Construction Team TWO, 31st Naval Construction Regiment; Naval Support Force Antarctica; Naval Construction Training Center, Engineering Duty Officers School; Port Hueneme Naval Reserve Center; Naval School, Civil Engineer Corps Officers; Naval Facilities Engineering Services Center; Air Force Detachment 1, 345 TRS, Vehicle Maintenance Training School.

TEMPORARY MILITARY LODGING: Central reservation number (officer and enlisted) C-805-982-4115. Navy Lodge, Building 1172, C-805-985-2624.

RV, CAMPING/FAMCAMP: None. See Point Mugu NAWS listing, C-805-989-8407, D-312-351-8407.

SPACE-A: None. See Point Mugu NAWS listing, C-805-989-7731, D-312-351-7731, Fax: C-805-989-4085.

LOGISTICAL SUPPORT:
Barber/Beauty Shop-982-9420
Commissary-982-9451
Education Office-982-2913
Gas Station-982-4768
Mini Mart-982-9400
Travel Office (leisure)-982-4276
Child Dev Center-982-4849
Credit Union-982-3405
Exchange-982-9400
Laundry-982-9421
Postal Service-982-4761
Travel Office (official)-982-3536

CALIFORNIA
Port Hueneme Naval Construction Battalion Center, continued

ADMINISTRATIVE SUPPORT:
CDO/OOD-982-2007
Housing Office-982-4321
Locator-982-5333 (Mil)
982-4711 (Civ)
Public Affairs-982-4493
Fire Dept-982-4595
Legal-982-3124
Pass & ID Office-982-2018
Police-982-4591
Quarter Deck-982-4576

HEALTH & WELFARE:
American Red Cross-982-3074
Chapel-982-4358
Family Services-982-5037
Medical-982-6301
Central Appts-984-8433
1-800-446-5271
Emergency-911
CHAMPUS-982-6322
Dental-982-5584
N-MC Relief Society-982-4409
Retiree Services-982-5037
TRICARE-982-6322

REST & RECREATION:
Auto Hobby Shop-982-4392
Clubs
EM-982-5293
O-982-2754
ITT-982-4284
Museum-982-5163
Rec Equip-982-4695
Theater-982-5491
Bowling-982-2619
Community Center-982-4282
Golf Course-982-2620
Gym-982-5173
Library-982-4743
MWR-982-4556
Swimming-982-4752
Youth Center-982-4218

ATTRACTIONS: CEC/Seabee Museum, the Navy's second oldest museum. Annual open house - Seabee Days, local attractions with beautiful beaches, two marinas, Channel Islands, historic sites. Santa Barbara and Los Angeles nearby. Attractions include zoo, Disneyland, Universal Studios, Knott's Berry Farm, waterparks and museums.

PRESIDIO OF MONTEREY (CA74R4)

Building 614, Room 142
Presidio of Monterey, CA 93944-5006

TELEPHONE NUMBER INFORMATION: Main installation numbers: C-408-242-5000, D-312-878-5000.

LOCATION: From CA-1 in Monterey, exit to Del Monte Blvd, west to Lighthouse Avenue Enter from Lighthouse Avenue USMRA: Page 111 (B-9). NMC: Monterey, in city limits.

GENERAL INFORMATION: Defense Language Institute, Foreign Language Center.

TEMPORARY MILITARY LODGING: C-408-242-5091, Fax: C-408-242-5298.

RV, CAMPING/FAMCAMP: South Lake Tahoe Recreation Housing off post, year round, C-408-242-5506, D-312-878-5506, one A-Frame chalet, one cabin, two condominiums and motel lodgings.

SPACE-A: None. See Lemoore NAS, CA listing, C-209-998-1683, D-312-949-1683.

LOGISTICAL SUPPORT:
Commissary-242-7671
Exchange-242-9602
Package Store-899-2336
Snack Bar-647-9606
Child Care-242-1058
Gas Station-372-0702
SATO-648-8045

ADMINISTRATIVE SUPPORT:
Fire Dept-242-7701
Legal-242-5083/84
Police-242-5634
SDO/SNCO-242-5119
Housing Office-656-2321
Locator-242-5119
Public Affairs-242-5104

HEALTH & WELFARE:
ACS-242-7650/60
Chapel-242-5281
Medical-242-5234
CHAMPUS-242-0304
Chaplain-242-7620

REST & RECREATION:
Consol Club-649-1823
Golf Course-899-2351
MWR-242-6995
Sports Arena-ext 5295
Youth Center-ext 5277
Fitness Center-ext 5641
ITT-242-5377
Rec Center-242-5447
Theater-373-2234

ATTRACTIONS: Beaches, seafood, Carmel Valley, Carmel-by-the-Sea, Salinas Valley. Beautiful location on a hill above the bay.

PRESIDIO OF MONTEREY ANNEX (CA36R4)

Building 614, Room 142
Presidio of Monterey, CA 93944-5006

TELEPHONE NUMBER INFORMATION: Main installation numbers: C-408-242-2211, D-312-929-1110.

LOCATION: From US-101 Fort Ord exit to main gate of post. USMRA: Page 111 (B,C-9). NMC: Monterey, seven miles south.

TEMPORARY MILITARY LODGING: None. See Presidio of Monterey listing, C-408-242-5091, Fax: C-408-242-5298.

RV, CAMPING/FAMCAMP: None. See Presidio of Monterey listing, C-408-242-5506, D-312-878-5506.

SPACE-A: None. See Lemoore NAS, CA listing, C-209-998-1683, D-312-949-1683.

LOGISTICAL SUPPORT:
Commissary-242-7671
Gas Station-394-2443
Exchange-899-2336

ADMINISTRATIVE SUPPORT:
Locator-242-2271
Public Affairs-242-5555/5104
Police-242-7851

HEALTH & WELFARE: None. See Presidio of Monterey listing, C-408-647-6995.

REST & RECREATION: None. See Presidio of Monterey listing, C-408-647-5234.

ATTRACTIONS: Beaches, seafood, Carmel Valley, Carmel-by-the-Sea, Salinas Valley. Beautiful location on a hill above the bay.

PRESIDIO OF SAN FRANCISCO (CA19R4)

Mason Street
Presidio of San Francisco, CA 94129-7000

TELEPHONE NUMBER INFORMATION: Only Exchange and Commissary at this facility. See numbers below.

LOCATION: Off Highway 101 near Golden Gate Bridge. USMRA: Page 119 (C-5). NMC: San Francisco, in the city.

TEMPORARY MILITARY LODGING: None. See Travis AFB listing, C-707-437-2987, D-312-837-2987.

RV, CAMPING/FAMCAMP: None. See Travis AFB listing, C-707-424-3583, D-312-837-3583.

SPACE-A: None. See Travis AFB listing, C-707-424-1854, D-312-837-1854.

CALIFORNIA
Presidio of San Francisco, continued

LOGISTICAL SUPPORT:
Commissary-561-2382 Exchange-922-4591

ATTRACTIONS: Golden Gate Park and Bridge nearby. Bus service to downtown and Fisherman's Warf.

SAN CLEMENTE ISLAND NAVAL AUXILIARY LANDING FIELD (CA53R4)

P.O. Box 357054
San Diego, CA 92135-7054

TELEPHONE NUMBER INFORMATION: Main installation numbers: C-619-524-9214, D-312-524-9214.

LOCATION: Visitors must be sponsored by military stationed on the island. USMRA: Page 111 (E-15). NMC: Los Angeles, 50 miles northeast.

GENERAL INFORMATION: This is a closed island, accessible by air or boat only.

TEMPORARY MILITARY LODGING: Billeting Office C-619-524-9202.

RV, CAMPING/FAMCAMP: None. See Camp Pendleton MCB listing, C-619-725-4241, D-312-365-4241.

SPACE-A: None. See Los Angeles AFB listing, C-310-363-0714, D-312-833-0714, Fax: C-310-216-2670.

LOGISTICAL SUPPORT: Exchange-524-9147

ADMINISTRATIVE SUPPORT:
CDO/OOD-524-9214 Fire Dept-524-9212
Police-524-9214

HEALTH & WELFARE: None. See Camp Pendleton listing, C-619-725-1288.

REST & RECREATION: Consol Club-524-9227

ATTRACTIONS: Beaches, and wildlife.

SAN DIEGO COAST GUARD AIR STATION (CA77R4)

2710 North Harbor Drive
San Diego, CA 92101-1079

TELEPHONE NUMBER INFORMATION: Main installation numbers: C-619-683-6333.

LOCATION: Take I-5 south to Sassafras Street/Airport exit. Follow Sassafras Street to Grape Street, Right Grape Street, then right on North Harbor Drive. Front gate one mile on the left. USMRA: Page 118 (C-6). NMC: San Diego, city limits.

GENERAL INFORMATION: Responsible for search and rescue missions, law enforcement, marine environment protection and providing aids to navigation. Marine Safety Office, ATON unit, and Coast Guard Station.

TEMPORARY MILITARY LODGING: None. See San Diego NSB listing, C-619-524-4788, D-312-524-4788.

RV, CAMPING/FAMCAMP: None. See Camp Pendleton MCB listing, C-619-553-7533/9381, D-312-553-7533/9381.

SPACE-A: CG Hangar, C-619-557-6510. Fixed wing Space-A opportunities extremely limited, also see North Island Naval Air Station listing.

LOGISTICAL SUPPORT: Exchange-557-6388

ADMINISTRATIVE SUPPORT:
CDO/OOD-683-6470 Locator-683-6333
Public Affairs-683-6320 SDO/NCO-683-6470

HEALTH & WELFARE:
CHAMPUS-532-8329 Family Services-683-6336
Medical-683-6380
Emergency-532-8275
Information-532-6400

REST & RECREATION: None. See San Diego MCRD listing, C-619-524-4435.

ATTRACTIONS: City of San Diego, Del Mar Racetrack, San Diego Zoo, Balboa Park, Sea World, Mission San Luis Rey.

SAN DIEGO FLEET COMBAT TRAINING CENTER, PACIFIC (CA90R4)

53690 Tomahawk Drive, Suite 144
San Diego, CA 92147-5000

TELEPHONE NUMBER INFORMATION: Main installation numbers: C-619-553-8123, D-312-533-8123.

LOCATION: West to Rosecrans, north to Canon, then west to Catalina. USMRA: Page 118 (A,B-6). NMC: San Diego, 10 miles.

GENERAL INFORMATION: Naval Command Control & Ocean Surveillance Center (NCCCSC, Navy Center for Tactical Systems Inter-operability (NCTSI) & Det 1 Tactical Training Group, Pacific (TATRAGRUPAC).

TEMPORARY MILITARY LODGING: None. See San Diego NSB listing, C-619-553-7533/9381, D-312-553-7533/9381.

RV, CAMPING/FAMCAMP: None. See Camp Pendleton MCB listing, C-619-725-4241, D-312-365-4241.

SPACE-A: None. See North Island NAS listing, C-619-545-9567, D-312-735-9567.

LOGISTICAL SUPPORT:
Barber Shop-221-2056 Cafeteria-221-2054
Conv Store-221-2053 Dry Cleaner-221-2653
Education Office-553-8176 Exchange-221-2053
Postal Service-553-8121

ADMINISTRATIVE SUPPORT:
CDO/OOD-553-8225 Legal-553-8110
Pass/ID Office-553-8328 Police-553-8329
Public Affairs-553-8110

HEALTH & WELFARE: None. See San Diego NMC listing, C-619-532-6400.

REST & RECREATION: None. See San Diego NS listing, C-619-556-7029.

OTHER FACILITIES AVAILABLE: Fitness Center.

ATTRACTIONS: Sea World, San Diego Zoo, Balboa Park, city of San Diego.

SAN DIEGO MARINE CORPS RECRUIT DEPOT (CA57R4)

1600 Henderson Avenue, Suite 120
San Diego, CA 92140-5093

TELEPHONE NUMBER INFORMATION: Main installation numbers: C-619-524-8762.

CALIFORNIA
San Diego Marine Corps Recruit Depot, continued

LOCATION: From I-5 use Old Town Avenue exit and follow signs. USMRA: Page 118 (C-6). NMC: San Diego, two miles southeast; adjacent to the west side of Lindbergh Field.

GENERAL INFORMATION: Recruit Training Regiment, Headquarters and Service Battalion, Drill Instructor School, Recruiters School, Headquarters 12th Marine Corps Recruiting District, USCG Pacific Area Tactical Law Enforcement Team.

TEMPORARY MILITARY LODGING: Lodging office, Building 625, 0700-2230 daily, C-619-524-4401. All ranks.

RV, CAMPING/FAMCAMP: None. See Camp Pendleton MCB listing, C-619-725-4241, D-312-365-4241.

SPACE-A: None. See North Island NAS listing, C-619-545-9567, D-312-735-9567.

LOGISTICAL SUPPORT:

Barber Shop-524-4432	Child Care-524-4430
Child Dev Center-524-4430	Conv Store-524-4435
Credit Union-524-9400	Dining Facilities-524-6878
Dry Cleaner-524-1958	Education Office-524-6865
Exchange-297-2500	Gas Station-296-3987
Package Store-524-4435 ext 651	Postal Service-524-4398
SATO-295-7286	Travel Office-295-7286
Visitor Center-524-6038	

ADMINISTRATIVE SUPPORT:

Fire Dept-524-4222	Housing Office-524-4401
Legal-524-4110/1	Locator-524-1719
OOD-524-8700*	Pass/ID Office-524-4200
Police-524-4202	Public Affairs-524-8727

** After 1600 on weekdays and weekends*

HEALTH & WELFARE:

American Red Cross- 524-5727	CHAMPUS-557-7500
Chapel-524-8820	Dental-524-4008
Family Services-524-5728	Central Appts-524-4005
Medical	Clinic-524-4005
Central Appts-524-4036	N-MC Relief Society-524-5734
Clinic-524-4036	
Emergency-9-911	

REST & RECREATION:

Auto Hobby Shop-524-5240	Bowling-524-4446
Camping Equipment-524-6180	Clubs
Fitness Center-524-4428	Combined-524-6878
Gym-524-4428	NCO-524-4448
ITT-524-6772	Library-524-1850
Marina-524-5269	Museum-524-6038
Boat Rental	MWR-524-4435
Outdoor Rec-524-6769	Services-524-5055
Visitor Center-524-6038	

ATTRACTIONS: Sea World, San Diego Zoo, Balboa Park, city of San Diego, Wild Animal Park, Command Museum, Mexico nearby.

SAN DIEGO NAVAL MEDICAL CENTER (CA59R4)

34800 Bob Wilson Drive
San Diego, CA 92134-5000

TELEPHONE NUMBER INFORMATION: Main installation numbers: C-619-532-6400, D-312-522-6400.

LOCATION: Exit from I-5 to Pershing Drive and west on Florida Canyon Drive. to entrance. USMRA: Page 118 (D-6). NMC: San Diego, three miles northeast.

GENERAL INFORMATION: Large Naval medical treatment facility serving the San Diego area.

TEMPORARY MILITARY LODGING: None. See San Diego NS listing, C-619-556-8672.

RV, CAMPING/FAMCAMP: None. See Camp Pendleton MCB listing, C-619-725-4241, D-312-365-4241.

SPACE-A: None. See North Island NAS listing, C-619-545-9567, D-312-735-9567.

LOGISTICAL SUPPORT:

Child Care-532-6665	Exchange-525-1502
SATO-532-6607	

ADMINISTRATIVE SUPPORT:

CDO/OOD-532-6400	Fire Dept-911
Public Affairs-532-9380	

HEALTH & WELFARE:

CHAMPUS-532-8328	Medical
TRICARE-1-800-242-6788	Emergency-532-8275

REST & RECREATION:

Fitness Center-532-7260	Library-532-7950
MWR-532-7245	Rec Services Office-532-7245
Swimming Pool-532-8516	Tickets-532-7255

ATTRACTIONS: Zoo, Sea World, Balboa Park, city of San Diego, Wild Animal Park, Mexico nearby.

SAN DIEGO NAVAL STATION (CA26R4)

3445 Surface Navy Boulevard
San Diego, CA 92136-5000

TELEPHONE NUMBER INFORMATION: Main installation numbers: C-619-556-1011, D-312-526-1011.

LOCATION: Off I-5, seven miles south of San Diego. Take 28th St exit. Station is at 28th & Main Streets. USMRA: Page 118 (D-7,8). NMC: San Diego, in the city.

GENERAL INFORMATION: Pacific Fleet Training Center, Public Works Center, and home port for major ships of the Pacific Fleet.

TEMPORARY MILITARY LODGING: Lodging office, 0730-1630 daily, Building 3362 (BEQ) C-619-556-8672; and Building 3104 (BOQ) C-619-556-8156. DV/VIP C-619-556-8672/8163, Fax: C-619-556-9325. Navy Lodge near Harbor Dr, 24 hours daily, C-619-234-6142, D-312-958-6142. Reservations: 1-800-628-9466. All ranks.

RV, CAMPING/FAMCAMP: Admiral Baker Field Campground off base, year round, C-619-556-5525, 27 camper spaces with W/E hookups, 12 camper spaces without hookups.

SPACE-A: None. See North Island NAS listing, C-619-545-9567, D-312-735-9567.

LOGISTICAL SUPPORT:

Cafeteria-544-2228	Child Care-556-7475
Commissary-556-7202	Exchange-544-2111
Gas Station-544-2289	Package Store-544-2252
SATO-231-7361	

CALIFORNIA
San Diego Naval Station, continued

ADMINISTRATIVE SUPPORT:

CDO/OOD-556-1246/47	Fire Dept-524-6250
Legal-556-1663	Locator-556-1011
Police-556-1841	Public Affairs-556-7356

HEALTH & WELFARE:

CHAMPUS-557-7505	Chapel-556-1921/6025
Family Services-556-7436	Medical-556-8114
Retiree Services-556-7404	Emergency-556-8114

REST & RECREATION:

Admiral Robinson Center-ext 7486	Arts & Crafts-ext 7030
Auto Hobby Shop-ext 5008/9	Bowling-ext 7486
Clubs	Golf Course-556-5162
CPO-556-7050	ITT-556-7498
EM-556-1915	MWR-556-7029
O-556-7948	Rec Services-ext 7029/7455
Sports Director-ext 7444	Theater-556-6062

ATTRACTIONS: Zoo, Sea World, Balboa Park, City of San Diego, Wild Animal Park, Mexico nearby.

SAN DIEGO NAVAL SUBMARINE BASE (CA79R4)

140 Sylvester Road
San Diego, CA 92106-3521

TELEPHONE NUMBER INFORMATION: Main installation numbers: C-619-553-7533, D-312-553-7533.

LOCATION: Take I-5 or I-8 to Rosecrans exit. Follow Rosecrans south to main gate. USMRA: Page 118 (B-6). NMC: San Diego, five miles southeast.

GENERAL INFORMATION: Submarine Training Facility, Submarine Development Group One.

TEMPORARY MILITARY LODGING: Lodging office, Building 601, 24 hours daily, BEQ C-619-553-7533, D-312-553-7533, BOQ C-619-553-9381, D-312-553-9381. DV/VIP C-619-553-9381, D-312-553-9381, Fax: C-619-553-0613.

RV, CAMPING/FAMCAMP: None. See Camp Pendleton MCB listing, C-619-725-4241, D-312-365-4241.

SPACE-A: None. See North Island Naval Air Station listing, C-619-545-9567, D-312-735-9567.

LOGISTICAL SUPPORT:

Conv Store-221-2011	Exchange-221-2011
Gas Station-221-1095	SATO-222-3632

ADMINISTRATIVE SUPPORT:

Legal-553-8594	Police-553-7070
Public Affairs-553-8644	SDO/NCO-553-7533

HEALTH & WELFARE:

CHAMPUS-532-8300	Chapel-553-7201
Family Services-553-7505	

REST & RECREATION:

Archery-ext 7549	Arts & Crafts-ext 7162
Auto Hobby Shop-ext7162	Bowling-ext 7521
Camping Equipment-ext 7549	Ceramics-ext 7545
Clubs	Gym-ext 7552
CPO-553-7597	Hobby Shop-ext 7549
EM-553-7519	Library-ext 9851
O-553-9384	ITT-553-7162
Rec Center-ext 7552	Services-ext 7162
Swimming-ext 7552	

ATTRACTIONS: City of San Diego, San Diego Zoo, Balboa Park, Sea World, Mission San Luis Rey. Pacific Ocean, mountains, and deserts within a short driving distance.

SAN PEDRO COAST GUARD INTEGRATED SUPPORT COMMAND (CA25R4)

Commanding Officer
P.O. Box 8, Terminal Island Station
San Pedro, CA 90731-0208

TELEPHONE NUMBER INFORMATION: Main installation numbers: C-310-732-7400.

LOCATION: On Coast Guard Base, Terminal Island. USMRA: Page 117 (C-7). NMC: Long Beach, two miles east.

GENERAL INFORMATION: Integrated Support Command for the Los Angeles area.

TEMPORARY MILITARY LODGING: Local Housing Authority, PCS, Base PO Box 8, Terminal Island Station, San Pedro, 0700-1530 daily, C-310-732-7560. BEQ only at CG ISC San Pedro. All ranks. DV/VIP 310-732-7400.

RV, CAMPING/FAMCAMP: None. See El Toro MCAS listing, Big Bear Recreation Facilities, C-714-726-2626.

SPACE-A: Available at Los Angeles IAP; see Los Angeles AFB listing, C-310-363-0714, D-312-833-0714, Fax: C-310-216-2670.

LOGISTICAL SUPPORT: Exchange-732-7555

ADMINISTRATIVE SUPPORT:

Housing Office-ext 7560	OOD-ext 7400
Pass/ID Office-ext 7420	Public Affairs-ext 7354

HEALTH & WELFARE:

CHAMPUS-ext 7500	Dental-ext 7511
Family Services-ext 7583	

REST & RECREATION: None. See Los Angeles AFB listing, C-310-363-2190.

OTHER SUPPORT AVAILABLE: Barber Shop, Conv Store, Dining Facilities, Laundry, Education Office, Postal Service.

ATTRACTIONS: Greater Los Angeles area.

SANTA CLARA NAVAL AIR RESERVE STATION (CA10R4)

500 Shenandoah Plaza
Moffett Federal Air Field, CA 94035-5000

TELEPHONE NUMBER INFORMATION: Main installation numbers: C-415-604-5000, D-312-359-5000.

LOCATION: On Bayshore Freeway, US-101, 35 miles south of San Francisco. USMRA: Page 119 (F-9). NMC: San Jose, seven miles south.

GENERAL INFORMATION: 129th Air Rescue Group, CALIFORNIA NG, and Naval Air Reserve Units. Santa Clara Naval Air Reserve is the Navy local area coordinator for the South Bay area. NAVAIRES Santa Clara is a tenant on Moffett Federal Airfield (operated by NASA).

TEMPORARY MILITARY LODGING: Lodging office, Building 593, 0800-1600 daily, BEQ C-415-404-8299, D-312-494-8299, BOQ C-415-404-6170, D-312-462-6170, DV/VIP C-415-404-8299, D-312-462-8299, Fax: C-415-404-6156. Navy Lodge C-415-962-1542 or 1-800-NAVY-INN. All ranks.

CALIFORNIA
Santa Clara Naval Air Reserve Station, continued

RV, CAMPING/FAMCAMP: None. See Defense Distribution Region West-Sharpe Site listing, Sharpe Travel Camp, C-209-982-2232, D-312-462-2232.

SPACE-A: Pax Term, Building 158, 24 hours daily, C-415-604-5231, D-312-494-5231, flights to CONUS, OCONUS and foreign locations.

LOGISTICAL SUPPORT:
Child Care-940-1884
Conv Store-603-9927
Gas Station-603-9939
SATO-604-1686
Commissary-603-9976
Exchange-603-9907
Package Store-603-9927
Snack Bar-603-9930

ADMINISTRATIVE SUPPORT:
CDO/OOD-603-9527
Legal-603-9515
Police-604-1623
Fire Dept-604-5416
Locator-603-5000
Public Affairs-603-9539

HEALTH & WELFARE:
CHAMPUS-603-8227
Family Services-603-8016
Retiree Services-603-4069
Chapel-603-8073/4100
Medical-603-8251
Emergency-603-8251

REST & RECREATION:
Auto Hobby Shop-ext 8046
Clubs
...CPO/O-603-4716
EM-603-8959
NCO-603-8959
MWR-603-9717
Swimming-ext 4712
Youth Activities 965-2716
Bowling-ext 4709
Golf Course-ext 4702 or 603-8026
Gym-ext 4697
ITT-604-1686
Rec Services 691-1216
Ticket Office-ext 4757

ATTRACTIONS: Paramount's Great America Park, five miles south. Located in the heart of the "Silicon Valley." San Jose and Santa Cruz are nearby.

SEAL BEACH NAVAL WEAPONS STATION (CA80R4)

800 Seal Beach Boulevard
Seal Beach, CA 90740-5050

TELEPHONE NUMBER INFORMATION: Main installation numbers: C-562-626-7301, D-312-873-7301.

LOCATION: Take I-405 to Seal Beach Blvd exit. Turn right (South). Continue to main gate on left. USMRA: Page 117 (E-7). NMC: Long Beach, adjacent.

GENERAL INFORMATION: Home of the Fish & Wildlife Services, National Wildlife Refuge.

TEMPORARY MILITARY LODGING: BEQ: C-562-626-7227.

RV, CAMPING/FAMCAMP: None. See El Toro MCAS listing, C-714-726-2626, D-312-997-2626.

SPACE-A: None. See El Toro MCAS listing, C-714-726-3920, D-312-997-3920.

LOGISTICAL SUPPORT:
Exchange-626-7292
Snack Bar-626-7555

ADMINISTRATIVE SUPPORT:
CDO/OOD-626-7229
Legal-626-7603
Pass/ID Office-626-7230
Public Affairs-626-7215
Fire Dept-626-7280
Locator-626-7692
Police-626-7210

HEALTH & WELFARE:
Chapel-626-7229
Medical-626-7444
Emergency-594-7285
After hours-594-7333

REST & RECREATION:
All Hands Club-626-7105
Boy Scout Campsite-ext 7215
Golf Course-430-9913
MWR-626-7227
Special Services-ext 7215
Bowling-ext 7278
Camping Equip-ext 7555/7576
Gym-ext 7278
Rec Center/Equip-ext 7278
Youth Activities-ext 7278

ATTRACTIONS: Greater Los Angeles area, Hollywood.

SIERRA ARMY DEPOT (CA44R4)

ATTN: SIOSI-CO
First Street, Building P-1
Herlong, CA 96113-5000
On November 1, 1997, the area code for Sierra Army Depot will change from 916 to 530.

TELEPHONE NUMBER INFORMATION: Main installation numbers: C-916-827-2111, D-312-855-4910. E-mail: SIOSI-PA@Sierra-emh.army.mil. HP: http://www.sierra.army.mil.

LOCATION: Fifty-five miles northwest of Reno, NV, off US-395. Right on CA-A26 from Reno. When traveling south on US-395, left on CA-A25. USMRA: Page 110 (E-4). NMC: Reno, NV, 55 miles southeast.

GENERAL INFORMATION: Major Army Materiel Command Depot, maintenance and storage activities.

TEMPORARY MILITARY LODGING: Lodging office, Building P-144, Mon-Thurs 0630-1700; other hours, Building P-100, C-916-827-4544/4345. All ranks.

RV, CAMPING/FAMCAMP: None. See Oakland Army Base listing, Lake Tahoe Oakland Condominiums, C-510-444-8107, D-312-859-3113.

SPACE-A: None. See Travis AFB listing, C-704-424-1854, D-312-837-1854, Fax: C-707-424-2048.

LOGISTICAL SUPPORT:
Conv Store-827-3292
Commissary-827-4480
Gas Station-827-3292
Snack Bar-827-4442
Commercial Travel-827-4175
Credit Union-827-2191
Postal Service-827-3074
Travel Office-827-4602

ADMINISTRATIVE SUPPORT:
Fire Dept-827-4323
Legal-827-4548
Pass/ID Office-827-4408
Public Affairs-827-4343
Housing Office-827-5350
Locator-827-4407
Police-827-4345
SDO/NCO-827-4345/4555

HEALTH & WELFARE:
ACS-827-4425
CHAMPUS-827-4141
Medical-827-4575
Emergency-827-4911
Army Emergency Relief-827-4570
Family Services-827-4425
Retiree Services-827-4555

REST & RECREATION:
Bowling-ext 4442
Fitness Center-827-4132
ITT-827-4602
Outdoor Rec-827-4354
Swimming-ext 4602 *summer ONLY*
Community Club-827-4360
Gym-827-4655
Library-827-4157
Services-ext 4602
Youth Services-827-4696

ATTRACTIONS: Reno for entertainment, casinos, Lake Tahoe is a one-and-a-half hour drive south.

STOCKTON NAVAL COMMUNICATIONS STATION (CA51R4)

305 Fyffee Avenue
Stockton, CA 95203-4920
Scheduled to close October 31, 1997.

TELEPHONE NUMBER INFORMATION: Main installation numbers: C-209-944-0395/0225, D-312-466-7395/7225.

LOCATION: From I-5 north exit at Rough & Ready Island, right at Fresno Street to Washington Street to station. USMRA: Page 110 (C-7). NMC: Stockton, in the city.

GENERAL INFORMATION: Major Naval Communications Station on the West Coast.

TEMPORARY MILITARY LODGING: None. See Travis AFB listing, C-707-437-2987, D-312-837-2987.

RV, CAMPING/FAMCAMP: None. See DDRW - Sharpe Site listing, Sharpe Travel Camp on post, year round, C-209-982-2232, D-312-462-2232.

SPACE-A: None. See Travis AFB listing, C-707-424-1854, D-312-837-1854, Fax: C-707-424-2048.

LOGISTICAL SUPPORT:
Commissary-944-0224
Gas Station-944-0479
Exchange-944-0200/0393

ADMINISTRATIVE SUPPORT:
Fire Dept-944-0333
Public Affairs-944-0513
Police-944-0336

HEALTH & WELFARE: None. See DDRW - Sharpe Site listing, C-209-982-3831.

REST & RECREATION:
Golf Course-944-0442
Racquetball-ext 0330
MWR-944-0582
Services-944-0582

ATTRACTIONS: Equal distance to Sacramento and San Francisco.

TRAVIS AIR FORCE BASE (CA50R4)

540 Airlift Drive, Building 381
Travis Air Force Base, CA 94535-2127

TELEPHONE NUMBER INFORMATION: Main installation numbers: C-707-424-1110, D-312-837-1110.

LOCATION: Off I-80 North, take Airbase Parkway exit. Clearly marked. USMRA: Page 110 (B,C-7). NMC: San Francisco, 45 miles southwest.

GENERAL INFORMATION: Air Mobility Command Base, 60th Air Mobility Wing, Headquarters 15th Air Force, 349th Air Mobility Wing (AFRES).

TEMPORARY MILITARY LODGING: Lodging office, Building 404, Sevedge Drive, 24 hours daily, C-707-437-2987. D-312-837-2987. All ranks. DV/VIP 707-424-3185.

RV, CAMPING/FAMCAMP: Travis FAMCAMP on base, year round, C-707-424-3583, D-312-837-3583, 70 camper spaces with full hookups, eight camper/tent spaces without hookups.

SPACE-A: Pax Term/Lounge, Building P-3, 24 hours daily, C-707-424-1854 or 1-800-787-2534, D-312-837-1854, Fax: C-707-424-2048, flights to CONUS, OCONUS, and foreign locations.

LOGISTICAL SUPPORT:
Cafeteria-437-2092
Commissary-437-9211
Gas Station-437-2232
SATO-437-7380
Child Care-424-0341
Exchange-437-3305
Package Store-437-3692
Shoppette-437-6606

ADMINISTRATIVE SUPPORT:
Legal-424-3251
Police-424-3293
Locator-424-2798

HEALTH & WELFARE:
CHAMPUS-437-7100
Family Services-424-2486
Retiree Services-424-3904
Chapel-424-3217
Medical
  Central Appts-423-3000
  Emergency-423-3826

REST & RECREATION:
Bowling-ext 5048
Fitness Center-ext 5680
Golf Course-ext 5797
Hobby Shops-ext 1338
Library-ext 3279
Museum-ext 5605
Youth Center-ext 5392
Clubs
  Aero-437-3470
  EM-424-5071
  O-424-2745
  Saddle-437-9060
Rec Center-ext 5659
Theater-437-3855

ATTRACTIONS: Travis Air Museum, San Francisco 55 miles southwest, Sacramento 45 miles northeast, discount outlet stores in Vacaville, Solano Mall in Fairfield, Busch Brewery, Western Railway Museum, Jelly-Belly Factory.

TUSTIN MARINE CORPS AIR STATION (CA86R4)

ATTN: Public Affairs
Tustin, CA 92710-5001
Scheduled to close December 1997

TELEPHONE NUMBER INFORMATION: Main installation numbers: C-714-726-2100, D-312-997-2100.

LOCATION: From I-5 (Santa Ana Freeway) left at Sand Canyon exit; to light at Trabuco, right to main gate. USMRA: Page 117 (G-7). NMC: Irvine 10 miles northwest.

TEMPORARY MILITARY LODGING: Billeting Office C-714-726-3001/7984, D-312-997-3001/7984, DV/VIP C-714-726-7301, D-312-997-7301.

RV, CAMPING/FAMCAMP: None. See Big Bear Rec Facilities, C-714-726-2626.

SPACE-A: None. See El Toro MCAS listing, C-714-726-3920, D-312-997-3920.

LOGISTICAL SUPPORT: Exchange-726-3340

ADMINISTRATIVE SUPPORT:
Locator-726-3736
Police-726-9911/7666

HEALTH & WELFARE: Medical-726-7256
  Clinic-726-7231

REST & RECREATION: Clubs
  EM -726-7219
  NCO-726-7219
  O' Club-726-7330

ATTRACTIONS: Orange County and greater Los Angeles area, Disneyland in Anaheim, Anaheim Stadium (home of the California Angels baseball team), Knott's Berry Farm in Buena Park, Marineland located at the tip of the Palo Verdes peninsula, Movieland Wax Museum in Buena Park, Crystal Cathedral in Garden Grove, beaches, boating.

CALIFORNIA

TWENTYNINE PALMS MARINE CORPS AIR/GROUND COMBAT CENTER (CA27R4)

Box 788101
Twentynine Palms, CA 92278-8101

TELEPHONE NUMBER INFORMATION: Main installation numbers: C-619-830-6000, D-312-957-6000.

LOCATION: I-10 to Highway 62. Take Highway 62 to town of Twentynine Palms. Once in town take Adobe Road north to base, approximately five miles. USMRA: Page 111 (H,I-13,14). NMC: Palm Springs, 60 miles southwest.

GENERAL INFORMATION: Headquarters Battalion, Marine Corps Communication-Electronics School, 7th Marine Regiment, Combat Service Support Group-1, Aviation Ground Support Element, Marine Unmanned Aerial Vehicle Squadron-1, "D" Company, 3rd Assault Amphibian Battalion, 1st Tank Battalion, 3rd Battalion, 11th Marines, 3rd Light Armored Reconnaissance Battalion.

TEMPORARY MILITARY LODGING: Building 1565, 5th Street, 24 hours daily, C-619-830-6573, D-312-957-6573. All ranks. DV/VIP C-619-830-6109.

RV, CAMPING/FAMCAMP: See El Toro MCAS listing Big Bear Rec Facilities, C-714-726-2626.

SPACE-A: None. See Los Angeles AFB listing, C-310-363-0714, D-312-833-0714, Fax: C-310-216-2670.

LOGISTICAL SUPPORT:

Barber Shop-830-6163
Cafeteria-830-6989
Child Care-830-6269
Conv Store-830-6138
Dry Cleaner-830-6163
Exchange-830-6163
Laundry-830-6163
SATO-830-6622
Visitor Center-830-5153
Beauty Shop-830-6163
Car Rental-830-6337
Child Dev Center-830-5589
Commissary-830-7573
Education Office-830-4702
Gas Station-830-6693
Package Store-830-6860
Snack Bar-830-6163

ADMINISTRATIVE SUPPORT:

CDO/OOD-830-7200
Housing Office-830-6075
Locator-830-6000
Police-830-5457
Quarter Deck-830-2037
Fire Dept-830-5239
Legal-830-5270
Pass/ID Office-830-7440
Public Affairs-830-6213

HEALTH & WELFARE:

American Red Cross-830-6685
Chapel-830-6464
Family Services-830-6344
Medical-830-2037
  Central Appts-830-2286
  Emergency-830-2398
  Health Benefits-830-2572
  Information-830-2872
Veterinary Services-830-7521
CHAMPUS-830-2572
Dental-830-7663
  Central Appts-830-7053
  Clinic-830-7664
  Emergency-830-7043
N-MC Relief Society-830-7451
Retiree Services-830-7550
TRICARE-830-2572

REST & RECREATION:

Auto Hobby Shop-830-4179
Clubs
  Combined-830-4138
  EM-830-6696
  O-830-6706
Library-830-6875
Outdoor Rec-830-7235
Theater-830-5236 ext 264
Wood Hobby Shop-830-7214
Youth Center-830-6269
Youth Services-830-6269
Bowling-830-5422
Fitness Center-830-6451
Golf Course-830-6132
Gym-830-6440
ITT Office-830-6163 ext 264
MWR-830-6807
Services-830-6163
  Hunting
  Riding Stables
  Skeet Range
  Swimming

ATTRACTIONS: Joshua Tree National Monument. Locale is in the center of Southern California's attraction areas: Two-and-a-half hours to Los Angeles, three-and-a-half hours to San Diego, one-and-a-half hours to Palm Springs, three hours to Las Vegas, NV and one-and-a-half hours to Laughlin, NV.

VANDENBERG AIR FORCE BASE (CA29R4)

30 SW/PA
747 Nebraska Avenue, Suite 7, Building 10577, Room A-103
Vandenberg Air Force Base, CA 93437-6267

TELEPHONE NUMBER INFORMATION: Main installation numbers: C-805-734-8232, D-312-276-3595. For extension numbers below: call main installation number and wait for recording, then dial extension or "0" for operator assistance. E-mail: pubaffairs@plans.vafb.af.mil. HP: http://www.30sw.vafb.af.mil.

LOCATION: Base is located 55 miles north of Santa Barbara, 25 miles south of Santa Maria and six miles north of Lompoc, on California Highway 1. USMRA: Page 111 (C-12). NMC: Santa Barbara, 55 miles south.

GENERAL INFORMATION: Air Force Space Command, 30th Space Wing.

TEMPORARY MILITARY LODGING: Lodging office, Building 13005, 24 hours daily, C-805-734-1111. All ranks. Two suites for handicapped. DV/VIP C-805-734-3711.

RV, CAMPING/FAMCAMP: FAMCAMP on base, year round, Building 10122, C-805-734-8232 ext 6-8579, D-312-276-8579, 20 camper spaces with full hookups, 30 camper spaces with W/E, 19 camper spaces without hookups, 15 tent spaces.

SPACE-A: Pax Term: Building 1749, 0800-1700 daily, C-805-734-8232 ext 6-7742, D-312-276-7742, Fax: C-805-734-8232, ext 6-8038

LOGISTICAL SUPPORT:

Barber Shop-734-1259
Cafeteria-ext 6-7540
Child Dev Center-ext 6-1555
Commissary-ext 5-8813
Credit Union-734-8550
Dry Cleaner-734-3039
Exchange-734-5521
Laundry-734-3039
Postal Service-ext 6-3766
Shoppette-ext 5-8269
Beauty Shop-734-1264
Child Care-ext 6-4639
Class Six-ext 5-8269
Conv Store-ext 5-8269
Dining Facilities-ext 6-7540
Education Office-ext 6-5933
Gas Station-734-2185
Package Store-ext 5-8269
SATO-734-4381
Visitor Center-ext 6-7662

ADMINISTRATIVE SUPPORT:

Fire Dept-ext 6-4680
Legal-ext 5-6218
Pass/ID Office-ext 6-1853
Public Affairs-ext 6-3595
Housing Office-ext 6-3434
Locator-ext 6-1841
Police-ext 6-3911

HEALTH & WELFARE:

Air Force Aid Society-ext 5-8551
CHAMPUS-734-1878
Dental-ext 6-1846
Medical-ext 6-4077
TRICARE-734-1878
American Red Cross-ext 6-1855
Chapel-ext 6-5773
Family Services-ext 6-5484
Retiree Services-ext 6-5474
Veterinary Services-ext 6-3019

REST & RECREATION:

Arts & Crafts-ext 6-6438
Bowling-734-1310
Clubs
  Aero-734-2733
  Co-located-734-4376
  Rod & Gun-ext 6-4560
ITT-ext 6-3824
MWR-ext 6-5908
Rec Center-ext 6-7976
Swimming-ext -6-3581
Wood Hobby Shop-ext 6-4567
Auto Hobby Shop-ext 6-6014
Ceramics-ext 6-5209
Community Center-ext 6-7976
Fitness Center Annex-ext 6-4826
Golf Course-ext 6-6262
Gym-ext 6-3832
Library-ext 6-6050
Outdoor Rec-ext 6-0960
Services-ext 6-5031
Theater-734-1315
Youth Center-ext 6-0035

CALIFORNIA
Vandenberg Air Force Base, continued

ATTRACTIONS: Great beaches, historic missions, Hearst Castle, north of AFB.

Other Installations in California

Channel Islands ANGS (CA93R4), Point Mugu, CA 93041-4001. USMRA: Page 111 (D,E-13). C-805-986-8000, D-312-893-7000, Space-A-986-7997.

Lake Tahoe Coast Guard Station (CA24R4), P.O. Box 882, Tahoe City, CA 96145-0882. USMRA: Page 110 (E-6). C-916-583-7438, RVC-583-7438.

Los Angeles International Airport (CA61R4), 200 World Way, Box 2, Los Angeles, CA 90045-5810. USMRA: Page 117 (B-5). C-310-363-0715, D-312-833-0715, Space-A-363-0715.

San Francisco Coast Guard Station (CA94R4), Yerba Buena Island, San Francisco, CA 94130-5013, USMRA: Page 119 (C-5). C-415-399-3400, Exchange-399-3478.

Tracy Defense Depot Activity (CA92R4), Stockton, CA 95376-5000. USMRA: Page110 (C-7). C-209-832-9049.

COLORADO

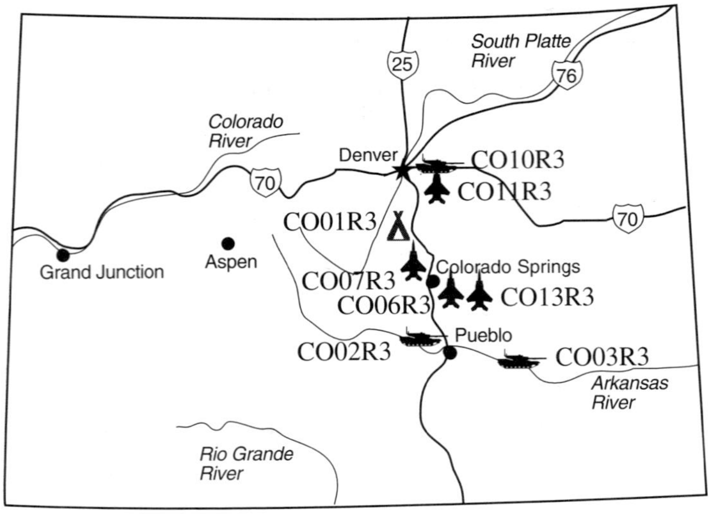

BUCKLEY AIR NATIONAL GUARD BASE (CO11R3)

18500 East Sixth Street
Buckley ANGB, CO 80011-9599

Buckley is undergoing changes due to construction, mission changes, etc, therefore some of the active duty activities are located at Fitzsimons US Army Garrison until facilities are available on base.

TELEPHONE NUMBER INFORMATION: Main installation numbers: C-303-677-9011, D-312-877-9011.

LOCATION: On East 6th Avenue, off of I-225, clearly marked. USMRA: Page 109 (G-3), page 116 (C,D-3,4). NMC: Denver, 21 miles west.

GENERAL INFORMATION: 140th Wing, 200th Airlift Squadron, 2nd Space Warning Squadron, 821st Space Group, Navy/Marine Reserve Training Center, and Army Aviation Support Facility.

TEMPORARY MILITARY LODGING: None. See Fitzsimons US Army Garrison listing, C-303-361-8903, D-312-943-8903.

RV, CAMPING/FAMCAMP: None. See USAF Academy listing, Farish Rec Area, C-719-687-9098.

SPACE-A: None. See Peterson AFB listing, C-719-556-4707, D-312-834-4707.

LOGISTICAL SUPPORT:
Child Dev Center-677-6174
Credit Union-677-9829
Education Office-677-9703/9589

ADMINISTRATIVE SUPPORT:
Fire Dept-677-9924 (non emergency)
Pass/Registration Office-677-9935
Police-677-9930
Public Affairs-677-9431

HEALTH & WELFARE:
Medical-677-6464

REST & RECREATION:
All Ranks Club-677-9840
ITT-677-6853

ATTRACTIONS: Denver nearby. Snow sports, Pro sports teams, National Western Stock Show and Rodeo in January. Fitzsimons Army Garrison five miles northwest.

FARISH RECREATION AREA (CO01R3)

P.O. Box 146
Woodland Park, CO 80866-0146

TELEPHONE NUMBER INFORMATION: Main installation numbers: C-719-333-1818, D-312-259-3110.

LOCATION: Located on 655 acres of magnificent woodland at an altitude of 9,150 feet in the Rocky Mountains. Surrounded by Pike National Forest 15 miles north of Pikes Peak. From I-25 at Colorado Springs, take exit 141 west for 18 miles to Woodland Park; turn right (near McDonald's) on Rampart Range Road approximately seven miles. Follow the Farish signs. USMRA: page 109 (F-4). NMC: Colorado Springs, 30 miles southeast. NMI: US Air Force Academy, 35 miles east; Peterson AFB and Fort Carson, 40 miles southeast.

GENERAL INFORMATION: Operated by US Air Force Academy, off base year round for lodge and cottage and day use; limited campsites available during the winter. Call for conditions during winter months. Military personnel active, retired, reserve, DoD civilians and retired/NAF civilians. Check in 1400, check out 1200 for lodge and cottage; check in and out 1200 for camping area. Questions may be addressed to Farish Management, C-719-687-9098. Reservations: Advance reservations required. Accepted up to 90 days in advance; Academy active duty and their family members and guests have first priority. C-719-687-9098/9306, Fax C-719-686-1437. Visa, MasterCard, American Express and Diners are accepted. No pets allowed in lodge or cottage; allowed on leash in camping area; owner must clean up after pet. No sewage dump station. Fishing is restricted to Government military and civilian employees, retirees, guests, and family members; special USAF Academy permits are available for overnight guests. Patrons with campers more than 26 feet long should contact the Farish staff for directions to an alternate entrance. All visitors are advised to call for road and weather conditions before making the trip especially in winter, fall and spring. Gate fee. No firearms allowed.

TEMPORARY MILITARY LODGING: Two bedroom cottage (sleeps eight) basic linens, towels and cooking utensils provided (1); Sleeping Lodge, private bath in Room 1, shared bath with others, kitchen facilities available, no maid service (4 rooms); Entire Lodge, sleeps 17; camper cabins, guest provides own bedding (4). Rates: Cottage $65 daily; sleeping lodge $36-$65 daily; entire lodge $157 daily; camper cabins $20.

RV, CAMPING/FAMCAMP: Yurt* (1); In place Scamp Travel Trailers with E hookup (3); gravel camper spaces with E hookup (15); gravel camper space pavilion with E hookup (1); gravel camper/tent spaces with no hookups (15); primitive tent spaces (unlimited). Rates: Yurt $20 daily; scamp travel trailer $20 daily, camper spaces with hookup $9 daily; camper pavilion $15 daily; camper/tent spaces $7.50 daily; primitive tent spaces $7.50.

*A "yurt" is a cabin/tent structure, 24 feet in diameter with wooden floor, deck and door, two windows, and stretched-canvas covering with skylight. It is furnished, but has no bathroom or kitchen.

REST & RECREATION: Fishing, Hiking, Horseshoes, Ice Fishing, Ice Skating, Mountain Biking, Paddle Boats, Sledding, Skiing, Tubing, Volleyball, Outdoor Adventure Program.

OTHER SUPPORT & FACILITIES AVAILABLE: Chapel/outdoor, Grills, Grocery/small, Mountain Bike Rental, Pavilions/fee, Picnic Area, Playground, Port-a-Potties, Recreation Equipment, Trails. Also see US Air Force Academy listing, C-719-333-1818, D-312-259-3110.

ATTRACTIONS: Abundant wildlife and three fishing lakes. Enjoy a mountain getaway with a real backwoods feel within driving distance of area attractions.

FITZSIMONS US ARMY GARRISON (CO10R3)

ATTN: MCHG-ZX
12101 East Colfax Avenue
Aurora, CO 80045-5002

Scheduled to close September 1999

COLORADO
Fitzsimons US Army Garrison, continued

TELEPHONE NUMBER INFORMATION: Main installation numbers: C-303-361-8241, D-312-943-1101.

LOCATION: From I-70 take Peoria Avenue (281), exit south, one mile on left is West Gate (Note: West Gate is for walk in only). Continue onto ColFax: C-Avenue Center on left. From I-25 take I-225 north to ColFax: C-Avenue, west on ColFax: C-Avenue to Center on right. USMRA: Page 116 (C-3). NMC: Denver, eight miles east.

GENERAL INFORMATION: One of the US Army's largest Medical Research, Teaching, and Treatment Facilities.

TEMPORARY MILITARY LODGING: Lodging office and Guest House, ("Fitzsimons Lodge"), Building 400, W Bruns Avenue, 0730-2130 Mon-Fri, C-303-361-8903, D-312-943-8903. All ranks. DV/VIP C-303-361-8824.

RV, CAMPING/FAMCAMP: Dillon Recreation Area off post, C-303-361-8956, D-312-943-8956, 30 camper/tent spaces with E hookups, three camper/tent spaces without hookups.

SPACE-A: None. See Peterson AFB listing, C-719-556-4707, D-312-834-4707.

LOGISTICAL SUPPORT:

Barber Shop-340-1759	Beauty Shop-340-1870
Carlson Wagonlit Travel-361-8066	Child Care-361-8574
Child Dev Center-361-8574	Class Six-340-1066
Commissary-361-8270	Conv Store-340-1066
Credit Union-340-3343	Dining Facilities-361-8459
Dry Cleaner-340-1634	Education Office-361-8193
Exchange-340-1100	Gas Station-340-1543
Postal Service-364-7176	SATO-361-8066
Snack Bar-361-8475	

ADMINISTRATIVE SUPPORT:

Fire Dept-361-8641	Housing Office-361-8692
Legal-361-8262	Locator-361-8800
Pass/ID Office-361-3157	Police-361-8728
Public Affairs-361-3952	SDO/NCO-361-8181

HEALTH & WELFARE:

American Red Cross-361-4606	ACS-361-8659
Army Emergency Relief-361-4560	CHAMPUS-361-8780
Chapel-361-3988	Dental-361-8923
Family Services-361-8659	Medical
Retiree Services-361-8517	Central Appts-361-8350
Veterinary Services-361-8817	Health Benefits-361-8780
	Information-361-8181

REST & RECREATION:

Golf Course-340-8622	Gym-361-8686
ITR-361-8622	Tickets-ext 2135
Indoor/Outdoor Rec	
MWR	

ATTRACTIONS: Many snow ski areas nearby, Denver, Central City Gambling.

FORT CARSON (CO02R3)

4TH ID & Fort Carson
ATTN: AFZC-GC
Building 1544
Fort Carson, CO 80913-5000

TELEPHONE NUMBER INFORMATION: Main installation numbers: C-719-526-5811, D-312-691-5811.

LOCATION: From Colorado Springs, take I-25 to exit 135 or CO-115 S to main gate, clearly marked. USMRA: Page 109 (F,G-5,6), page 115 (C,D-6,7). NMC: Colorado Springs, six miles north.

GENERAL INFORMATION: 3rd Armored Cavalry Regiment; 3rd Brigade, 4th Infantry Division; 43rd Support Group and 10th Special Forces Group.

TEMPORARY MILITARY LODGING: Lodging office, Building 731, Woodfill Road, Colorado Inn, 24 hours daily, C-719-526-4832, D-312-691-4832. All ranks. DV/VIP C-719-526-5811.

RV, CAMPING/FAMCAMP: Turkey Creek Ranch, 12 miles south on CO-115, Rec Area and Ranch House, C-719-526-3905.

SPACE-A: See Peterson AFB listing, C-719-556-4521, D-312-834-4521, Fax: C-719-556-4979.

LOGISTICAL SUPPORT:

Child Care-526-4188	Commissary-526-5644
Conv Store-576-7298	Exchange-576-6313
Gas Station-576-4096	Package Store-576-6126

ADMINISTRATIVE SUPPORT:

Fire Dept-526-5615	Legal-526-5572
Locator-526-0227	Police-526-2333
Public Affairs-526-3420	SDO/SNCO-526-3400

HEALTH & WELFARE:

ACS-526-4590	Chapel-526-0480
Family Services-526-4590	Medical-526-7298
TRICARE-526-7256	Central Appts-264-5000
	Emergency-526-7111

REST & RECREATION:

Arts & Crafts-526-0900	Auto Hobby Shop-526-2147
Bowling-526-5542	All Ranks Club-576-7540
Events Center-576-6646	Fitness Center-526-2597
Golf Course-526-4122	ITT-526-5366
Library-526-2350	MWR-526-1992
Outdoor Rec-526-2083	Rec Equipment-526-1992/3
Swimming	Wood Hobby Shop-526-3487
Indoor-526-5739	Youth Activities-526-2680
Outdoor-526-4456	

ATTRACTIONS: USAF Academy, guided tours, Colorado Springs, Pikes Peak, museums, Seven Falls.

PETERSON AIR FORCE BASE (CO06R3)

21st Space Wing
775 Loring Avenue, Suite 241
Peterson Air Force Base, CO 80914-1294

TELEPHONE NUMBER INFORMATION: Main installation numbers: C-719-556-7321, D-312-834-7011. HP: http://www.spacecom.af.mil.

LOCATION: Off US-24 (Platte Avenue) east of Colorado Springs. Clearly marked. USMRA: Page 109 (G-5), page 115 (D,E-5,6). NMC: Colorado Springs, six miles west.

GENERAL INFORMATION: US Space Command, Air Force Space Command, Army Space Command, North American Aerospace Defense Command, 302nd Tactical Airlift Wing (Reserve), 21st Space Wing.

TEMPORARY MILITARY LODGING: Lodging office, Building 1042, Stewart Avenue, 24 hours daily, C-719-556-8048, D-312-834-8048, Fax: C-719-556-7852, D- 312-834-7852. All ranks. DV/VIP C-719-556-5007.

RV, CAMPING/FAMCAMP: None. See USAF Academy listing, Farish Rec Area, C-719-687-9098.

COLORADO
Peterson Air Force Base, continued

SPACE-A: Pax Term/Lounge, Building 123, 0730-1630 Mon-Fri, C-719-556-4707, D-312-834-4707, flights to CONUS locations.

LOGISTICAL SUPPORT:

Bank-574-2777	Barber Shop-597-8307
Beauty Shop-596-0579	Child Care-556-7460
Child Dev Center-556-7460	Class Six-597-5041
Commissary-556-4247	Conv Store-597-5041
Credit Union-574-1100	Dining Facilities-556-4180
Dry Cleaner-597-3050	Education Office-556-4064
Exchange-596-7270	Gas Station-597-0360
Laundry-597-3050	Package Store-596-5685
Postal Service-556-4596	Professional Travel-556-4199
Shoppette-597-5041	Visitor Center-556-6406

ADMINISTRATIVE SUPPORT:

Fire Dept-556-4790	Housing Office-556-4364
Legal-556-4871	Locator-556-4020
Pass/ID Office-556-6406	Police-556-4805
Public Affairs-556-4696	

HEALTH & WELFARE:

Air Force Aid Society-556-6141	American Red Cross-556-7570
CHAMPUS-556-1057	Chapel-556-4442
Dental-556-1000	Family Services-556-7614
Medical-556-1000	Retiree Services-556-7153
Health Benefits-556-1657	TRICARE-556-1053

REST & RECREATION:

Auto Hobby Shop-556-4481	Bowling-556-4607
Clubs	Community Center-556-7671
Aero-ext 4310	Fitness Center-556-8069
NCO-556-4194	Golf Course-556-7414
O-576-4181	ITT-556-7671
Rod/Gun-ext 7688	Hobby Shops
Library-556-7462	Museum-556-4915
Outdoor Rec-556-4867	Rec Center-ext 7941
Camping Equipment	Rec Equipment-ext 7751
Skeet/Trap-ext 7688	Ski Shop-ext 4487
Swimming-ext 4608	Youth Center-ext 7413
Youth Services-556-7220	

ATTRACTIONS: Fine Arts Center, Seven Falls, Museums, Pikes Peak Cog Railway in Manitou Springs, ski resorts, US Olympic Training Center.

UNITED STATES AIR FORCE ACADEMY (CO07R3)

2304 Cadet Drive, Suite 316
United States Air Force Academy, CO 80840-5001

TELEPHONE NUMBER INFORMATION: Main installation numbers: C-719-333-1818, D-312-259-3110.

LOCATION: West of I-25 north from Colorado Springs. Two gates, about five miles apart, provide access from I-25, clearly marked. USMRA: Page 109 (F-4,5), page 115 (A,B-1,2 C-1,2,3). NMC: Colorado Springs, eight miles south.

GENERAL INFORMATION: US Air Force Academy, education of future Air Force officers, and other tenant units.

TEMPORARY MILITARY LODGING: Lodging office, Building 3130, Academy Drive, C-719-333-3061. All ranks. DV/VIP C-719-472-3540.

RV, CAMPING/FAMCAMP: Operates Farish Recreation Area off base, 35 miles west of post. See Farish Recreation Area listing for more information. Peregrine Pines FAMCAMP on base, year-round, C-719-333-4356, 53 camping sites, including 40 sites with with E/S, picnic tables, barbecue grills, and 13other sites for tent camping, 45 camper spaces with full hookups, 33 camper spaces without hookups.

SPACE-A: None. See Peterson AFB listing, C-719-556-4707, D-312-692-4707.

LOGISTICAL SUPPORT:

Barber Shop-472-1369	Beauty Shop-472-1495
Child Care-333-4733	Child Dev Center-333-4166
Class Six-472-0554	Commissary-333-3610
Conv Store-472-0395	Credit Union-472-1090
Dining Facilities	Dry Cleaning-472-6216
Airmen's Dining Hall-333-4730	Education Office-333-2269
Exchange-472-0861	Gas Station-472-0395
Laundry-472-6216	Package Store-472-0554
Postal Service-333-3505	Professional Travel-472-6644
Snack Bar-472-1321	Visitor Center-333-2555

ADMINISTRATIVE SUPPORT:

Housing Office-333-2100	Legal-333-3642
Locator-333-4262	Police-333-2000
Public Affairs-333-4050	

HEALTH & WELFARE:

CHAMPUS-333-4983	Chapel-333-3300
Family Services-333-3444	Medical
	Central Appts-264-5000
	Emergency-333-5000

REST & RECREATION:

Arts & Crafts-333-4579	Auto Hobby Shop-333-4752
Bowling-333-4709	Clubs
Golf Course-333-4735	EM-472-0061/333-4377
Gym-333-4522	O-333-4253
ITT-333-3241	Library-333-4665
Pool-333-4430	Sports Info-800-666-8723
Sports Tickets-472-1895	Stables-333-4607

ATTRACTIONS: Pikes Peak, snow skiing, ghost towns, Colorado Springs.

Other Installations in Colorado

Falcon Air Force Base (CO13R3), 300 O'Malley Avenue, Falcon Air Force Base, CO 80912-3024. Main installation numbers: C-719-567-4113, D-560-4113. This is a closed security base. 50th Space Wing, Ballistic Missile Defense Organization, Space Warfare Center. Visitor Center-567-5643/5620, Fire Dept-567-3370, Legal-567-5050, Police-567-5643, Public Affairs-567-5040, Chapel-567-3705, Dental-567-5065, Medical-567-6666, Fitness Center-567-2666, ITT-567-6050.

Pueblo Depot Activity (CO03R3), ***Scheduled to close under the 1995 BRAC. No scheduled date has been established.*** 45825 Highway 96E, Pueblo, CO 81006-9330. Main installation numbers: C-719-549-4111, D-312-749-4111. Take US-50 E from Pueblo, 13 miles, base is clearly marked. USMRA: Page 109 (G-5,6). NMC: Pueblo, 13 miles west. Police-549-4236, Public Affairs-549-4135, Medical-549-4176, MWR-549-4716.

CONNECTICUT

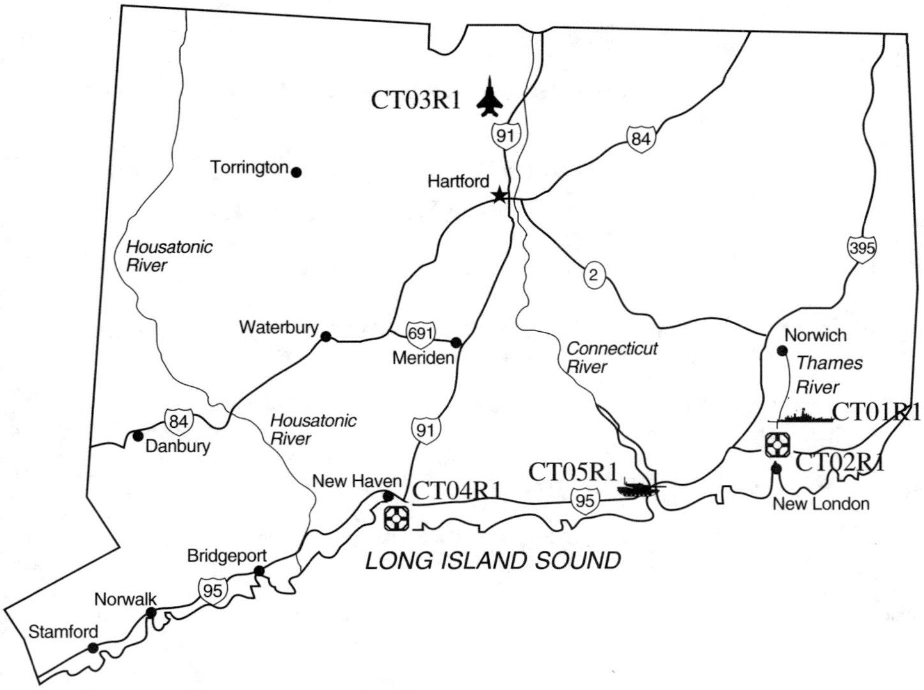

BRADLEY AIR NATIONAL GUARD BASE (CT03R1)

100 Nicholson Road
East Granby, CT 06026-9390

TELEPHONE NUMBER INFORMATION: Main installation numbers: C-860-623-8291, D-312-636-8310.

LOCATION: Take I-91 to exit 40. Follow signs to route 20 (East Granby) and base. USMRA: Page 16 (E-5,6). NMC: Hartford, 10 miles south.

GENERAL INFORMATION: 103rd Fighter Wing, "The Flying Yankees," 118th Tactical Fighter Squadron and other support units and facilities.

TEMPORARY MILITARY LODGING: None. See Westover ARB, MA listing, C-413-557-2700, D-312-589-2700.

RV, CAMPING/FAMCAMP: None. See United States Coast Guard Academy listing, C-860-444-8474, or C-860-437-6809.

SPACE-A: Bradley IAP, Pax Term, 24 hours daily, C-860-292-2356, D-312-636-8356.

LOGISTICAL SUPPORT: Exchange-653-6994

ADMINISTRATIVE SUPPORT:
Legal-292-2478 Locator-623-8291
Police-292-2312 Public Affairs-292-2506

HEALTH & WELFARE: Chapel-292-2445

REST & RECREATION: None. See New London NSB listing, C-203-449-4636, D-312-241-4636.

ATTRACTIONS: Historic Newgate Prison and the homes of Mark Twain and Harriet Beecher Stowe located within one hour's drive. New England Air Museum adjacent to Bradley IAP.

CAMP ROWLAND ARMY NATIONAL GUARD TRAINING SITE (CT05R1)

38 Smith Street
Niantic, CT 06357-2597

TELEPHONE NUMBER INFORMATION: Main installation numbers: C-203-691-6000, D-312-636-6000.

LOCATION: From I-95, exit 74, follow Route 161 towards Niantic Center. turn right onto Smith Street. USMRA: Page 16 (F,G-9). NMC: New London, 11 miles north.

GENERAL INFORMATION: Tenant activities: Northeast Leadership Training Regiment; Co C 280th Signal Battalion; 208th Personnel Detachment.

TEMPORARY MILITARY LODGING: 38 Smith Street, 0800-1600 Mon-Fri, C-860-691-6001, D-312-636-6000.

RV, CAMPING/FAMCAMP: None. See Newport NETC, RI listing, C-401-841-3116, Fax: C-401-841-4500.

SPACE-A: None. See Bradley ANG listing, C-860-292-2356.

LOGISTICAL SUPPORT:
Exchange-739-9672 Visitor Center-691-6001

ADMINISTRATIVE SUPPORT: Police-691-6008

HEALTH & WELFARE: None. See United States Coast Guard Academy listing, C-860-444-8474 or 860-437-6809.

REST & RECREATION: None. See United States Coast Guard Academy listing, C-860-444-8474, or C-860-437-6809.

OTHER SUPPORT & FACILITIES AVAILABLE: Fitness Center, Laundry, Locator, Outdoor Rec (basketball, baseball, soccer) available.

ATTRACTIONS: State parks.

LONG ISLAND SOUND COAST GUARD GROUP (CT04R1)

120 Woodward Avenue
New Haven, CT 06512-3698

TELEPHONE NUMBER INFORMATION: Main installation numbers: C-203-468-4451.

LOCATION: Take I-95 north to exit 50, right at light, Unit is one mile on right. Take I-95 south to the New Haven Airport exit 51 (Frontage Road). Pass shopping center, left at second light, Unit is one mile on the right. USMRA: Page 16 (E-9). NMC: New Haven, in city limits.

GENERAL INFORMATION: MSO, Long Island Sound, Aid to Navigation Team, Long Island Sound, USCGC BOLLARD and CGSTA New Haven.

TEMPORARY MILITARY LODGING: None. See New London NSB listing, Navy Lodge C-860-466-1160, D-312-241-1160, or BEQ/BOQ C-860-449-2408/2105.

RV, CAMPING/FAMCAMP: None. See Newport NETC, RI listing, C-401-841-3116, Fax: C-401-841-4500.

CONNECTICUT
Long Island Sound Coast Guard Group, continued

SPACE-A: None. See Stewart ANGB, NY listing, C-914-563-2285/6, D-312-247-2285/6.

LOGISTICAL SUPPORT: Exchange-468-2712

ADMINISTRATIVE SUPPORT:
CDO-468-4401
Pass/ID Office-468-4450
OOD-468-4455
Public Affairs-468-4464

HEALTH & WELFARE: CHAMPUS-468-4415

REST & RECREATION: None. See New London NSB listing, C-860-449-3238.

ATTRACTIONS: New Haven: Yale University, museums, boating, shopping.

NEW LONDON NAVAL SUBMARINE BASE (CT01R1)

Route 12 and Crystal Lake Road
Groton, CT 06349-5044

TELEPHONE NUMBER INFORMATION: Main installation numbers: C-860-449-4636, D-312-241-4636.

LOCATION: From I-95 N take exit 86 to CT-12 & Crystal Lake Road. Base clearly marked. USMRA: Page 16 (G,H-8), pg 25 (C,D-1). NMC: Hartford, 50 miles northwest.

GENERAL INFORMATION: Naval Submarine School, Naval Underwater Medical Institute, Naval Hospital, Commander Submarine Group Two, Submarine Squadrons Two and Twelve.

TEMPORARY MILITARY LODGING: Navy Lodge, Building CT-380, 77 Dewey Avenue, 0700-2300 daily, Check in 1500-1800, Check out 1200, C-860-446-1160, D-312-241-1160. All ranks, BEQ C-860-449-2408, BOQ C-860-449-2105. DV/VIP C-860-449-2105.

RV, CAMPING/FAMCAMP: None. See Newport NETC, RI listing, C-401-841-3116, Fax: C-401-841-4500.

SPACE-A: None. See Stewart ANGB, NY listing, C-914-563-2285/6, D-312-247-2285/6.

LOGISTICAL SUPPORT:
Child Care-449-3519
Conv Store-446-8593
Exchange-449-3811
Gas Station-449-3626
SATO-449-3404
Commissary-449-3911
Dining Facilities
  Enlisted Galley-449-3679
Package Store-449-3535

ADMINISTRATIVE SUPPORT:
CDO/COD-449-3777
Legal-449-3741
Pass/ID Office-449-3224
Public Affairs-449-3889
Fire Dept-449-3333
Locator-449-3087
Police-449-3222

HEALTH & WELFARE:
CHAMPUS-449-4968
Family Services-449-3383
Retiree Services-449-3284
Chapel-449-3232
Medical-449-3428
  Central Appts-449-4877
  Emergency-449-3333

REST & RECREATION:
Auto Hobby Shop-ext 3582
Clubs
  CPO-449-3721
  EM-449-3050
Bowling-ext-3477
Golf Course-449-3763
Gym-ext 4205
Hobby Shops-ext 3217
ITT-449-3238
Marina-ext 3164
Recreation-449-3238
Swimming-ext 3562
Library-ext 3723
MWR-449-3238
Services-ext 3687
Theater-449-3358

ATTRACTIONS: USCG Academy, *Nautilus* Memorial/Submarine Library and Museum.

UNITED STATES COAST GUARD ACADEMY (CT02R1)

15 Mohegan Avenue
New London, CT 06320-4195

TELEPHONE NUMBER INFORMATION: Main installation numbers: C-860-444-8474, or 860-437-6809.

LOCATION: From southbound I-95 take exit 83 in New London. From northbound I-95 take exit 82A. Follow signs, clearly marked. USMRA: Page 16 (G-8,9), Page 25 (C-2). NMI: New London NSB, across the Thames. NMC: New Haven, 40 miles west.

GENERAL INFORMATION: The Officer Education and Training Academy for the US Coast Guard.

TEMPORARY MILITARY LODGING: Billeting Office, Building 3130, Academy Dr., 24 hours daily, C-860-446-1160.

RV, CAMPING/FAMCAMP: None. See Newport NETC, RI listing, C-401-841-3116, Fax: C-401-841-4500.

SPACE-A: None. See Stewart ANGB, NY listing, C-914-563-2285/6, D-312-247-2285/6.

LOGISTICAL SUPPORT:
Barber Shop-444-8454
Cafeteria-444-8148
Conv Store-444-6761
Dining Facilities-444-8148
Exchange-444-8488/87
Main Gate-444-8614
Personnel Support Center-444-8689
Snack Bar-444-8473
Visitor Center-444-8611
Bookstore-444-8308
Child Dev Center-ext 8329
Credit Union-439-0780
Dry Cleaner-437-1212
Gas Station-444-8494
Package Store-444-8491
Postal Service-444-6752
Travel Office-440-0696

ADMINISTRATIVE SUPPORT:
Housing Office-444-8211
OOD-444-8452
Police-444-8597
SDO/NCO-444-8450/1
Legal-444-8253
Pass/ID Office-444-8208
Public Affairs-444-8270

HEALTH & WELFARE:
American Red Cross-444-8400
Chapel-444-8480
Medical
  Central Appts-444-8401
  Health Benefits-444-8408
CHAMPUS-444-8432
Dental-444-8424

REST & RECREATION:
Bowling-444-8470
Equipment Rental-ext 8476
Events Recording-442-1092
Fitness Center/Gym-ext 8600
Library-444-8510
MWR Office 444-8474
Clubs
  EM-444-8456
  O-444-8458
Hobby Shop-ext 8489
Musical Activities-ext 8471
Ticket Office-ext 8154

ATTRACTIONS: Self-guided tours of the Academy; Visitor's Pavilion (May-Oct); Museum (year round); when in port, the barque *EAGLE* is open to the public; formal reviews by the Corps of Cadets are held on the Washington parade ground on Fridays (fall & spring); Mystic Seaport; Casinos.

DELAWARE

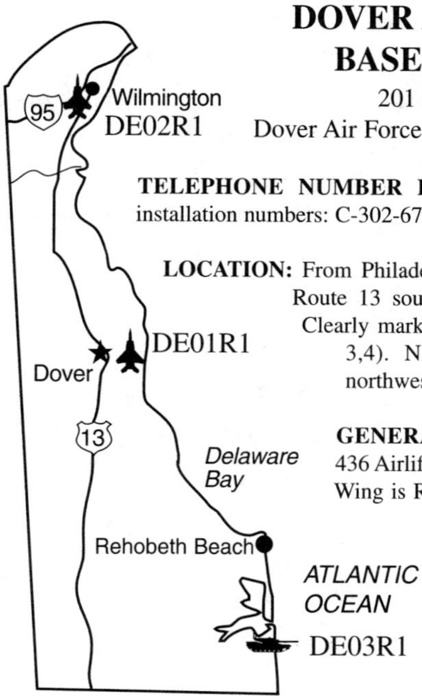

DOVER AIR FORCE BASE (DE01R1)

201 Eagle Way
Dover Air Force Base, DE 19902-7219

TELEPHONE NUMBER INFORMATION: Main installation numbers: C-302-677-3000, D-312-445-3000.

LOCATION: From Philadelphia, take I-95 south to Route 13 south, follow signs to base. Clearly marked. USMRA: Page 42 (I-3,4). NMC: Dover, five miles northwest.

GENERAL INFORMATION: 436 Airlift is host unit; 512th Airlift Wing is Reserve Wing (Associate); East Coast Port Mortuary, Air Mobility Command Base. Largest air cargo port on the East Coast. AFRES units.

TEMPORARY MILITARY LODGING: Lodging office, Building 846, 14th Street, 24 hours daily, C-302-677-2841, D-312-445-2841. All ranks. DV/VIP C-302-677-6649.

RV, CAMPING/FAMCAMP: None. See Newport NETC, RI listing, C-401-841-3116, Fax: C-401-841-4500.

SPACE-A: Pax Term, Building 500, 24 hours, C-302-677-4090, D-312-445-2854, Fax: C-302-677-2953. Flights to CONUS and overseas. Also try New Castle County Airport, Building 2812, 0800-1630 Mon-Fri, C-302-323-3525, D-312-445-3525, flights to CONUS and OCONUS locations. ANG units.

LOGISTICAL SUPPORT:
Barber Shop-677-6344
Child Care-677-3716
Class Six-677-6301
Conv Store-674-3551
Dining Facilities-677-3924
Education Office-677-4619
Gas Station-674-4228
Rogers Travel-736-1668
Shoppette-674-3551
Visitor Center-677-3921
Beauty Shop-734-8262
Child Dev Center-677-3716
Commissary-674-4189
Credit Union-678-8000
Dry Cleaner-678-3069
Exchange-674-4862
Postal Service-677-6198
Services Squadron-677-6901
Snack Bar-674-3380

ADMINISTRATIVE SUPPORT:
Fire Dept-677-4401
Legal-677-3300
Pass/ID Office-677-2853
Public Affairs-667-3372
Housing Office-677-6969
Locator-677-3000
Police-677-6666

HEALTH & WELFARE:
Air Force Aid Society-677-6930
CHAMPUS-677-2530
Dental
  Central Appts-677-2846
  Clinic-677-2846
American Red Cross-677-2855
Chapel-677-3932
Family Services-677-6941
Medical-677-2600
  Emergency-677-2600
  Emergency-677-2600
Retiree Services-677-4612
Veterinary Services-677-5252
  Information-677-2567
TRICARE-677-2486

REST & RECREATION:
Arts & Crafts-677-3245
Bowling-ext 3946
Community Center-677-6899
Equipment Rental-ext 3959
Fitness Center-677-3962
Golf Course-677-6039
Library-677-3992
Skeet-ext 6380
Tennis-ext 3963
Youth Activities-ext 6376
Auto Skills Center-677-3249
Clubs
  EM-677-6351
  O-677-6022
  "The Club"-677-6024
ITT-677-3955
Outdoor Rec-677-5553
Swimming-ext 3963
Theater-678-8711
Youth Center-677-6379

ATTRACTIONS: State capital, Dover Air Force Base Museum, great beaches and the Delaware Bay, Dover Downs racing and gambling.

NEW CASTLE COUNTY AIRPORT/ DELAWARE AIR NATIONAL GUARD (DE02R1)

2600 Spruance Drive, Corporate Commons
New Castle, DE 19720-2495

TELEPHONE NUMBER INFORMATION: Main installation numbers: C-302-323-3525, D-312-445-7525.

LOCATION: From I-95 take exit 5 to DE-141 south for one mile to intersection of DE-37 (Corporate Commons Blvd). Turn right Corporate Commons Blvd then left onto Spruance Drive and follow to gate entrance. USMRA: Page 42 (I-2). NMC: Wilmington, seven miles northeast.

GENERAL INFORMATION: Delaware Air National Guard Base.

TEMPORARY MILITARY LODGING: None. See Aberdeen Proving Ground, MD listing, C-410-278-5148, D-312-298-5148.

RV, CAMPING/FAMCAMP: None. See Aberdeen Proving Ground, MD listing, C-410-278-4124, D-312-298-4124.

SPACE-A: Pax Term, Building 2812, C-302-323-3525, D-312-445-3525, Fax: c-302-323-3330. Flights to CONUS and overseas. 0800-1630, ANG units.

LOGISTICAL SUPPORT: Exchange-322-5988

ADMINISTRATIVE SUPPORT:
Fire Dept-323-3450
Police-323-3440

HEALTH & WELFARE: Medical-323-3385
  Clinic-445-7418/9

REST & RECREATION: None. See Aberdeen Proving Ground, MD listing, C-301-278-7134.

ATTRACTIONS: State parks and the Chesapeake and Delaware Canal.

Other Installations in Delaware

Delaware Army National Guard (DE03R1), Bethany Beach Training Site, Route 1, Bethany Beach, DE 19930-5000. C-302-854-7900, D-312-440-7900. USMRA: Page 42 (J-6). TML/RVC-302-854-7902, D-312-40-7902, Fax: C-302-854-7999, D-312-440-7999. Twenty three mobile homes, four apartments and 10 campsites.

DISTRICT OF COLUMBIA

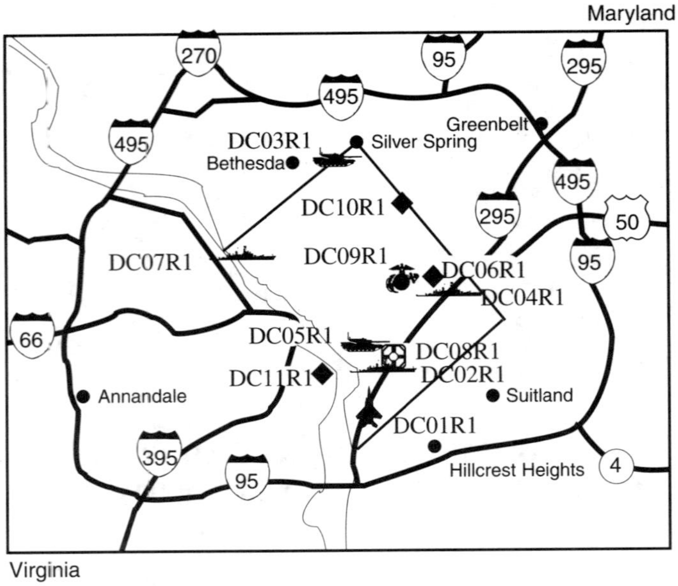

BOLLING AIR FORCE BASE (DC01R1)

20 MacDill Boulevard, Suite 230
Bolling Air Force Base, DC 20332-5100

TELEPHONE NUMBER INFORMATION: Main installation numbers: C-202-545-6700, D-312-297-4080. HP: http://www.bolling.af.mil.

LOCATION: Take I-95 (east portion of Capital Beltway, I-495), exit to I-295 north, exit to Portland Street, and main entrance to AFB. Also, I-395 north, exit South Capitol Street, main entrance to AFB on right. Visitors entrance is at south gate one mile south of main gate. Clearly marked. USMRA: Page 54 (F-6). NMC: Washington, DC, in southeast section of the city.

GENERAL INFORMATION: 11th Wing. Support for Air Force activities of the National Capital Region.

TEMPORARY MILITARY LODGING: Bolling Inn, Building 602, Thiesen Street, 24 hours, C-202-767-5316, D-312-297-5316/5741. All ranks. DV/VIP C-202-767-5584, Officer retirees Space-A.

RV, CAMPING/FAMCAMP: None. See Andrews AFB, MD listing, C-301-981-4109.

SPACE-A: None. See Andrews AFB, MD listing, C-301-981-1854, D-312-858-1854, Fax: C-301-981-4241.

LOGISTICAL SUPPORT:

Cafeteria-562-4419	Child Care-767-2890
Child Dev Center-ext 3047	Command Post-767-1111
Commissary-767-4695	Conv Store-563-6490
Exchange-562-3000	SATO
Gas Station-563-6490	Official-574-5182
Visitor Center-767-5505	Leisure-574-0120

ADMINISTRATIVE SUPPORT:

Fire Dept-767-5777	Legal-767-4772
Locator-767-4522	Police-767-5000
Public Affairs-767-4781	

HEALTH & WELFARE:

CHAMPUS-767-5540	Chapel-767-5900
Family Services-767-4464	Medical
Retiree Services-767-5244	Central Appts-767-5520
	Clinic-767-5532
	Emergency-767-5532

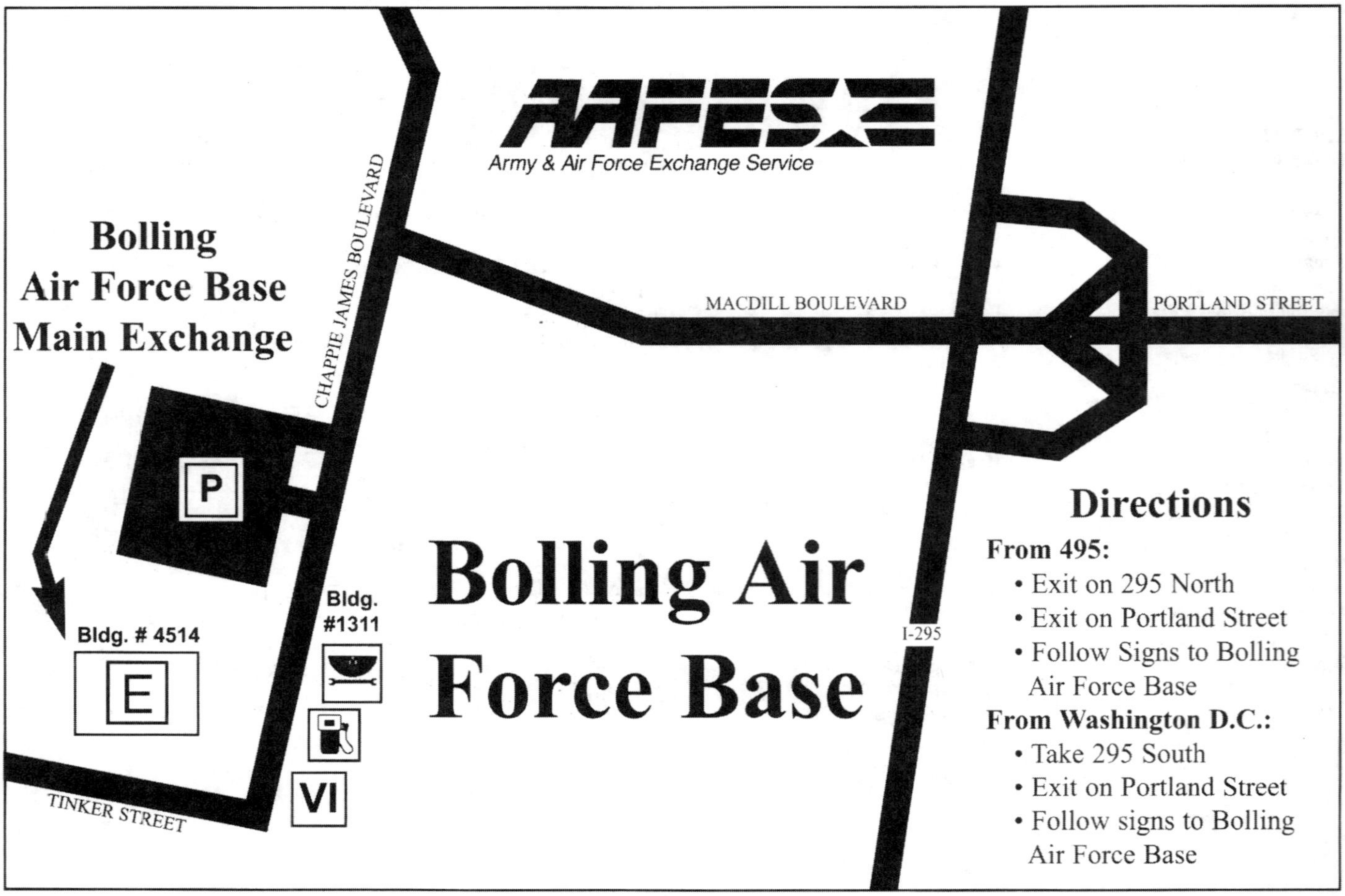

REST & RECREATION:

Arts & Crafts-ext 4422	Auto Hobby Shop-ext 5471
Bowling-563-4054	Camping Equipment-767-9135
Clubs	Fitness Center-ext 5895
NCO-767-5222	Library-ext 5578
O-563-8400	Marina-ext 4651
Outdoor Rec-767-9136	Rec Center-ext 3847
Rec Equipment-ext 9136	Swimming Pool-767-4942
Youth Center-767-4575	

ATTRACTIONS: Washington, DC, with its many museums, galleries, monuments and other attractions. Kennedy Center for the Performing Arts.

FORT LESLEY J. McNAIR (DC05R1)

103 3rd Avenue
Washington, DC 20319-5058

TELEPHONE NUMBER INFORMATION: Main installation numbers: C-202-685-2892, D-312-325-2888. E-mail: ANPA@mcnair-emh2.army.mil. HP: http://www.mdw.army.mil.

LOCATION: At confluence of Anacostia River and Washington Channel, southwest. Enter on P Street, SW. Take Maine Avenue, SW, to right on 4th Street, SW, to dead end at P Street Left, then immediate right into main gate. USMRA: Page 54 (F-5), page 55 (E-4). NMC: Washington, DC, in southwest section of city.

GENERAL INFORMATION: Headquarters US Army Military District of Washington, Co A, 3rd US Infantry (The Old Guard) "Commander in Chief's Guard," home to the National Defense University, consisting of the National War College (NWC) and the Industrial College of the Armed Forces (ICAF); home to the Inter-American Defense College (IADC).

TEMPORARY MILITARY LODGING: Lodging office, Fort Myer, Building 50, Johnson Lane, 24 hours daily, C-703-696-3576/3577. Limited VOQ facilities (Building 54, 24 hours daily) at Fort McNair. DV/VIP C-703-697-7051, D-312-297-7051.

RV, CAMPING/FAMCAMP: None. See Andrews AFB, MD listing, C-301-981-4109.

SPACE-A: None. See Andrews AFB, MD listing, C-301-981-1854/3526/3604, D-312-858-1854, Fax: C-301-981-4241.

LOGISTICAL SUPPORT:

Barber Shop-863-1130	Beauty Shop-484-0921
Child Care-696-3095	Conv Store-484-5823
Credit Union-(703) 706-5126	Dry Cleaner-863-1251
Gas Station-484-5823	Laundry-863-1251
Package Store-484-5833	Shoppette-484-5823
Snack Bar-685-3038	

ADMINISTRATIVE SUPPORT:

Fire Dept-911	Housing Office-696-3576
Legal-696-0762	Locator-475-2005
Police-685-3139	Public Affairs-685-2892
SDO/NCO-475-0918	

HEALTH & WELFARE:

ACS-696-3510	Army Emergency Relief-696-8435
CHAMPUS-696-3030	Chapel-475-0706
Dental-685-3388	Medical
Clinic-685-3100	Central Appts-685-3100
Emergency-911	Clinic-685-3100
	Emergency-911
	Health Benefits-685-3100
	Information-685-3100

REST & RECREATION:

Ball Field-ext 1964	Bowling-685-3038
Fitness Center-685-3117	Gym-ext 1964
Golf Course-685-3138/3415/3570	Library-287-9490
Multi Craft Shop-ext 2000	O'Club-484-5800
Swimming-ext 0504	Tennis-ext 1964

ATTRACTIONS: Included in the original plans for the District of Columbia, and is nearly 200 years old. Second only to West Point in length of service. Site of the trial and execution of President Lincoln's conspirators and where Walter Reed did his research work. Washington waterfront with restaurants, seafood markets, monuments and scenic Potomac River nearby.

MARINE BARRACKS (DC09R1)

8th and I Streets, SE
Washington, DC 20390-5000

TELEPHONE NUMBER INFORMATION: Main installation numbers: C-202-433-4073, D-312-288-4073.

LOCATION: At 8th & I Streets SE. From I-395 north, take 6th Street exit, drive east two blocks to 8th Street, turn left. From I-295/I-395 north interchange area, continue to follow I-295 north, 6th Street exit, follow as above. From I-295 south take exit 13, US Naval Station/Suitland Parkway exit, follow exit ramp around to reenter I-295 north. From I-495 (Capital Beltway), take Pennsylvania Avenue west exit, follow Pennsylvania Avenue to 8th Street, turn left and follow to I Street USMRA: Page 54 (F,G-5). NMC: Washington DC, in SE section of the city.

GENERAL INFORMATION: USMC light infantry battalion. **Note:** the Marine Barracks is a closed post for all practical purposes. **Facilities are not available unless user, if not permanently stationed at barracks, is escorted by a Marine stationed there.**

TEMPORARY MILITARY LODGING: None. See Bolling AFB listing, C-202-767-5316, D-312-297-5316/5741.

RV, CAMPING/FAMCAMP: None. See Andrews AFB, MD listing, C-301-981-4109.

SPACE-A: None. See Andrews AFB, MD listing, C-301-981-1854, D-312-858-1854, Fax: C-301-981-4241.

LOGISTICAL SUPPORT: Exchange-433-4961

ADMINISTRATIVE SUPPORT:

Legal-433-3180	Public Affairs-433-4173

HEALTH & WELFARE: Chaplain-433-6201

REST & RECREATION:

ITT-433-2338	MWR-433-2338
NCO-433-2528	

ATTRACTIONS: Evening Parades are held every Friday, Sunset Parades are held every Tuesday (May through August) for information and reservations call C-202-433-4073. Smithsonian Institution, Lincoln and Jefferson Memorials, Washington Monument, National Archives, Library of Congress, the US Mint, National Gallery of Art, Navy Memorial Museum and the Marine Corps Museum at the Washington Navy Yard and many other attractions.

USO WORLD HEADQUARTERS (DC06R1)

901 M Street, SE
Washington, DC 20374-5096

TELEPHONE NUMBER INFORMATION: Main installation numbers: C-202-610-5700. E-mail: Info@USO.org. HP: http://www.USO.org. *For a list of USOs worldwide, see Appendix C.*

DISTRICT OF COLUMBIA
USO World Headquarters, continued

LOCATION: In the Washington Navy Yard, Building 198. The offices of the USO World Headquarters are on the first and second floors. See receptionist on second floor. USMRA: Page 54 (F,G-5).

GENERAL INFORMATION: The administrative branch of the USO network worldwide; there are more than 160 USO centers worldwide.

RECREATION: Free tickets for shows and sporting events. Ticket and information hot line: 703-696-2551. USO Metro Washington's Service. There are nine Outreach Locations of the USO in the greater Washington DC area serving uniformed personnel and their families. See Appendix C in this book for addresses and telephone numbers.

UNITED STATES SOLDIERS' AND AIRMEN'S HOME (DC10R1)

3700 N Capitol Street, NW
Washington, DC 20317-5000

TELEPHONE NUMBER INFORMATION: Main installation number: C-800-422-9988. HP: http://www.afrh.com.

LOCATION: Two and one-half miles north of the Capitol off North Capitol Street Across the street from VA Hospital and Shrine of the Emaculate Conception. USMRA: Page 54 (F-3). NMI: Walter Reed Army Medical Center,. NMC: Washington DC, in city limits.

LOGISTICAL SUPPORT: Exchange-291-6252

ADMINISTRATIVE SUPPORT:
Locator-722-3111
Police-722-3111
Public Affairs-722-3556

OTHER SUPPORT AND FACILITIES AVAILABLE: Arts & Crafts, Auto Hobby Shop, Bank, Barber Shop, Beauty Shop, Bowling, Cafeteria,Chapel, Conv Store, Credit Union, Dental, Dining Facilities, Dry Cleaner, Fitness Center, Golf Course, Gym, Indoor Rec, Library, Medical, Outdoor Rec, Postal Retiree Services, Services, Shoppette, Snack Bar, Theater, Wood Hobby Shop.

ATTRACTIONS: Smithsonian, monuments, Capitol, etc.

WALTER REED ARMY MEDICAL CENTER (DC03R1)

ATTN: MCHL-GC
6825 16th Street NW
Washington, DC 20307-5001

TELEPHONE NUMBER INFORMATION: Main installation numbers: C-202-782-3501, D-312-662-3501.

LOCATION: From I-495 (Capital Beltway) take Georgia Avenue/Silver Spring exit south to Medical Center. To reach the Forest Glen support facilities from Georgia Avenue south, right turn onto Linden Lane, cross over B&O railroad bridge, support facilities on left (three-quarter miles from Georgia Avenue). USMRA: Page 54 (F-2). NMC: Washington, DC, in city limits.

GENERAL INFORMATION: The major Army Medical Research, Teaching, and Treatment Facility; Armed Forces Institute of Pathology (AFIP) located on main post. Forest Glen Annex, located in Silver Spring, MD, has large Commissary and Exchange. Walter Reed Institute of Research to be completed by year 2000.

TEMPORARY MILITARY LODGING: Fisher House I, Forest Glen Annex, (for families of critically ill patients), C-301-295-7374. Fisher House II, C-202-356-7564. Guest House, Building 17, priority to PCS, members of immediate family of seriously ill patients and MEDEVAC/AIRVAC, C-202-782-0068/3044. Mologne House Hotel, P.O. Box 59728, Washington, DC 20012, 24 hours daily, C-202-782-4600, D-312-662-4600. Walter Reed Inn, Building 6825, Georgia Avenue at Butternut Street, 24 hours daily, C-202-782-7076/2096, D-312-291-2076/2096. All ranks.

RV, CAMPING/FAMCAMP: None. See Andrews AFB, MD listing, C-301-981-4109.

SPACE-A: None. See Andrews AFB, MD listing, C-301-981-1854, D-312-858-1854, Fax: C-301-981-4241.

LOGISTICAL SUPPORT:
Carlson Wagonlit Travel
  Official-882-0303
  Leisure-882-1919
Gas Station-588-1602*
Child Dev Center-782-5024
Commissary-295-8041*
Exchange-565-0900*
Snack Bar-423-5401/2

ADMINISTRATIVE SUPPORT:
Fire Dept-782-3318
Locator
  Civilian 782-0546
  Military-782-1150
Legal-782-1550/5810
Police-782-3325
Public Affairs-782-7177

HEALTH & WELFARE:
ACS-782-3412
Chapel-782-6308
Medical
  Central Appts-782-3501
CHAMPUS-782-6136/1336
Family Services-782-3412
Retiree Services-782-3412

REST & RECREATION:
Arts & Crafts-295-7386/8011*
Bowling-295-7368/9*
DPCA-782-4946
Fitness Center-782-7324/7022
ITR-782-0600
MWR-782-7034/7377
Sports-295-7709/10*
Tennis-ext 2324
Auto Crafts-782-4972/7433
Clubs
  Abrams Lounge-782-3383
  Patients Lounge-782-6359
Library-782-6314/5
Outdoor Rec-295-8010/8008*
Swimming-ext 2324

** denotes 301 area code; facility located at Forest Glen Annex.*

ATTRACTIONS: Washington, DC, White House, Capitol, National Zoo, Washington National Cathedral, Arlington Cemetery, Smithsonian.

WASHINGTON NAVAL SECURITY STATION (DC07R1)

3801 Nebraska Avenue, NW
Washington, DC 20393-5440.

TELEPHONE NUMBER INFORMATION: Main installation numbers: C-202-764-0211, D-312-764-0211.

LOCATION: From Virginia cross the Key Bridge, turn left onto Foxhall Road. Go approximately two and a half miles to Nebraska Avenue and turn right. Station is half a mile on your right. USMRA: Page 54 (D,E-3,4). NMC: Washington, DC, in the city.

GENERAL INFORMATION: Naval Security Station, and assigned units.

TEMPORARY MILITARY LODGING: BEQ C-202-764-0254, D-202-764-0211.

RV, CAMPING/FAMCAMP: None. See Andrews AFB, MD listing, C-301-981-4109.

SPACE-A: None. See Andrews AFB, MD listing, C-301-981-1854, D-312-858-1854, Fax: C-301-981-4241, D-312-858-4241.

LOGISTICAL SUPPORT:
Barber Shop-764-0249
Visitor Center-764-0211
Credit Union-255-8440

DISTRICT OF COLUMBIA
Washington Naval Security Station, continued

ADMINISTRATIVE SUPPORT:

CDO-764-0220	Locator-764-2296
OOD-764-0211	Police-764-0294
Quarter Deck-764-0211	

HEALTH & WELFARE:

Chapel-764-0313	Dental-764-0204
Medical-764-0224	

REST & RECREATION: Gym-764-0295

ATTRACTIONS: Washington, DC, with its many museums, galleries, monuments and other attractions. Kennedy Center for the Performing Arts.

WASHINGTON NAVAL STATION-ANACOSTIA ANNEX (DC02R1)

2701 South Capitol Street, SW
Washington, DC 20373-5800

TELEPHONE NUMBER INFORMATION: Main installation numbers: C-703-545-6700, D-312-227-0101. (Note: The area code for the following numbers is 202.)

LOCATION: From I-395, exit South Capitol Street, cross South Capitol Street Bridge, main entrance is on right. USMRA: Page 54, (F,G-5). NMC: Washington, DC, in southeast section.

GENERAL INFORMATION: Naval Media Center, White House Communications Agency, US Navy Ceremonial Guard.

TEMPORARY MILITARY LODGING: Limited transient billeting, C-202-433-8796/0806, D-312-288-8796/0806. Navy Lodge in Bellevue Navy Housing area, Building 4412, C-202-563-6950 or 1-800-NAVY-INN.

RV, CAMPING/FAMCAMP: None. See Andrews AFB, MD listing, C-301-981-4109.

SPACE-A: None. See Andrews AFB, MD listing, C-301-981-1854, D-312-858-1854, Fax: C-301-981-4241, D-312-858-4241.

LOGISTICAL SUPPORT: Child Care-433-0771

ADMINISTRATIVE SUPPORT:

CDO/OOD-433-2231/32	Locator-545-6700
Fire Dept-433-3334	Police-433-2411
PSD Anacostia-685-0667	Public Affairs-433-2218
SDO/SNCO-433-2231/32	

HEALTH & WELFARE:

Chapel-433-2058	Family Services-433-6150
Retiree Services-433-6150	

REST & RECREATION:

All Hands Club-433-4070	Fitness Center-685-0898
ITT-433-6666	MWR-433-3005
Recreation-433-2269	

ATTRACTIONS: On the Potomac, and in sight of the Capitol and many famous monuments. Museums, and professional sports.

WASHINGTON NAVY YARD/ NAVAL STATION (DC04R1)

901 M Street SE
Washington, DC 20374-5000

TELEPHONE NUMBER INFORMATION: Main installation numbers: C-703-545-6700, D-312-277-0101. (Note: The area code for the following numbers is 202.) HP: http://www.ndw.navy.mil.

LOCATION: Exit I-395 N at 6th Street SE/Navy Yard, proceed to 8th Street, turn right to M Street, turn left to Main Gate at 9th and M Streets, SE. USMRA: Page 54 (F,G-5), page 55 (F-4). NMC: Washington, DC, in southeast section.

GENERAL INFORMATION: Headquarters Naval District Washington, Military Sealift Command, Naval Criminal Investigative Service, and the Navy Band.

TEMPORARY MILITARY LODGING: Lodging office, in the Anacostia complex adjacent to Bolling AFB. From I-95 (Beltway east) take I-295 north, exit at South Capitol Street NDW Anacostia is clearly marked. C-202-433-8796/0806, D-312-288-8796/0806, 0730-1600 daily, other hours-ext 2193. Navy Lodge in Bellevue Navy Housing area, exit I-395 N at South Capitol St, proceed to I-295S, exit at Naval Research Laboratory. Clearly marked, 24 hours daily, C-202-563-6950.

RV, CAMPING/FAMCAMP: None. See Andrews AFB, MD listing, C-301-981-4109.

SPACE-A: None. See Andrews AFB, MD listing, C-301-981-1854, D-312-858-1854, Fax: C-301-981-4241, D-312-858-4241.

LOGISTICAL SUPPORT:

Child Care-433-0771	Credit Union-(703) 255-8055
Exchange-889-7534	

ADMINISTRATIVE SUPPORT:

CDO/OOD-433-0960	Family Housing-685-1187
Fire Dept-433-3334	Legal-433-4331
Pass/ID Office-433-3017	Police-433-2411
PSD Anacostia-685-0667	Public Affairs-433-2218

HEALTH & WELFARE:

Chapel-433-2058	Dental-433-3115
Family Services-433-6150	Medical-433-6529/3976/3407
N-MC Relief Society-433-3365	Emergency-433-3269
Retiree Services-433-6150	

REST & RECREATION:

Fitness Center 433-2063	ITT-433-6666
Library 433-4132	MWR-433-3005
O'Club-433-3041	Recreation-433-2269 Equipment
Tennis 433-2829	

ATTRACTIONS: Navy Memorial Museum, Navy Art Gallery, Display Ship *Barry*, Marine Corps Museum. *Concerts on the Avenue* at the US Navy Memorial located at 701 Pennsylvania Avenue, NW, on Tuesday evenings beginning at 8 pm. The summer concerts, performed weekly between June and August by the US Navy Band specialty groups, are free and open to the public and no reservations are required. Call 433-2525 for more information.

Note: In 1997, headquarters for Naval Facilities Engineering Command and the office of the Judge Advocate General of the Navy will move to the Washington Navy Yard (some 400 people) from leased space in Alexandria, VA.

Other Installations in the District of Columbia

Armed Forces Hostess Association (DC11R1), Room 1A736 The Pentagon, 6604 Army Pentagon, Washington, DC 20310-6604. USMRA: Page 54 (E-5). C-703-697-3180/6857, D-312-227-6857, Fax: C-703-693-9510.
US Coast Guard Headquarters (DC08R1), 2100 2nd Street, SW, Washington, DC 20593. USMRA: Page 54 (F-5,6), page 55 (F-4). C-202-267-2100, Exchange-267-2372, Medical-366-0892.

FLORIDA

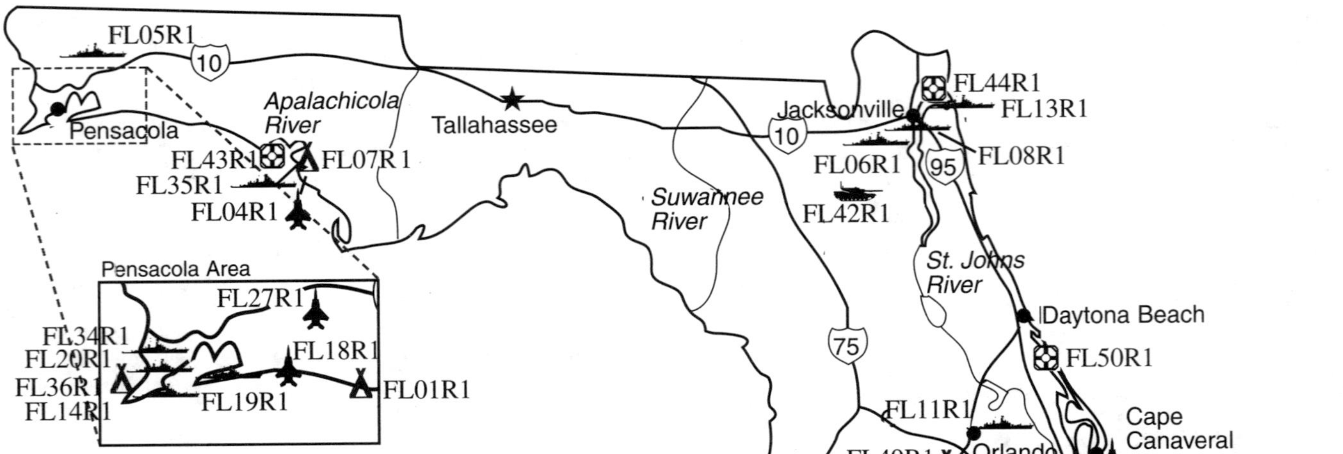
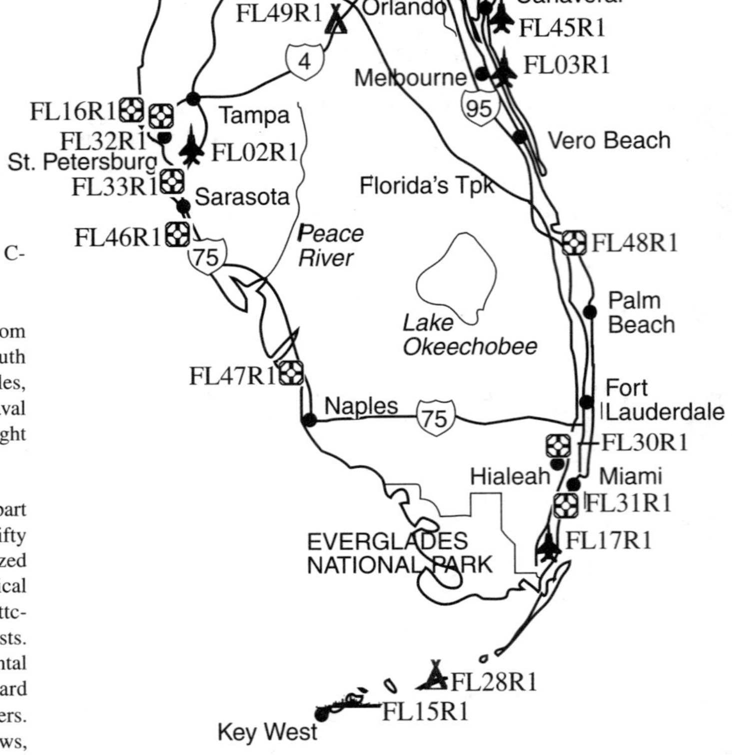

BLUE ANGEL NAVAL RECREATION AREA (FL36R1)

2100 Bronson Field Road
Pensacola, FL 32506-5000

TELEPHONE NUMBER INFORMATION: Main installation numbers: C-850-452-2000, D-312-922-0111.

LOCATION: Situated on Perdido Bay amid oak trees and Spanish moss. From I-10 west of Pensacola, take Exit 2 (FL-297/Pine Forest Road) south approximately one-and-a-half miles to Blue Angel Parkway; south eight miles, then west on US-98 for three miles. Watch for sign to Bronson Field Naval Recreation Area on left. USMRA: page 39 (A-13). NMC: Pensacola, eight miles east. NMI: Corry Station, eight miles northeast.

GENERAL INFORMATION: As there are no currents or drop-offs in this part of the bay, its sandy bottom creates an ideal swimming area for children. Fifty acres of the complex have been reserved for youth activities. Organized activities and annual events. Operated by Corry Station Naval Technical Training Center, off base year round. E-mail: nttc-pen.mwr-0720@nttc-pen.navy.mil. Military personnel active, retired, DoD civilians and guests. Check in 1400, check out 0800-1100. Reservations: Recommended for rental campers, C-850-453-9435, Fax C-850-453-1147. Visa and MasterCard accepted. Pets allowed on leash in park, no pets allowed in rental campers. Nominal admission charge for park. Absolutely NO firearms, bows and arrows, BB guns, or other items which could be considered to be weapons, and NO fireworks.

RV, CAMPING/FAMCAMP: Rental campers with W&E hookups (17); camper/RV spaces with W&E hookups (138); primitive tent spaces with no hookups (unlimited). Rates: rental campers $15 daily, camper/RV spaces $7 daily, tent spaces $3 daily.

ADMINISTRATIVE SUPPORT: Police-453-2030/4530

OTHER SUPPORT & FACILITIES AVAILABLE: BBQ Pits, Boat Launch, Boat Rental, Camp Equipment, Country Store, Dry Storage, Fishing Pier*, Ice, Jogging Trail, Laundry, LP Gas, Paddle Boats, Pavilions*, Pay Telephones, Picnic Area, Restrooms*, Sewage Dump, Showers*, Vending Machine, Walking Trails. Also, see Corry Station listing, C-850-452-2000, D-312-922-0111.

** Handicap accessible.*

REST & RECREATION: Boating, Fishing/license, Rec Equipment, Swimming, Volleyball, Water Skiing.

ATTRACTIONS: The park offers spectacular camping, boating, swimming and picnic areas.

CAMP BLANDING/FLORIDA NATIONAL GUARD POST (FL42R1)

Route 1, Box 465
Starke, FL 32091-9703

TELEPHONE NUMBER INFORMATION: Main installation number: C-850-533-2268, D-312-960-3100.

LOCATION: Thirty-one miles west of I-95; exit onto Route 16. USMRA: Page 38 (F,G-4). NMC: Jacksonville, 30 miles north.

GENERAL INFORMATION: Installation Support Unit, 653rd Engineering Det, 221st Ordnance Detachment, Florida Regional Training Institute, Headquarters 3rd Battalion, 20th Special Forces, 202nd Civil Engineering Squadron, 159th Weather Flight, 159 Weather School, and other support units.

TEMPORARY MILITARY LODGING: Lodging office, Building 2392 Jacksonville Road, 0800-1630 daily, C-850-533-3381, D-312-960-3381 (Closed Sundays).

RV, CAMPING/FAMCAMP: RV Park & Campsites on post year round, Billeting Office Campsites, Camp Blanding Training Site, Route 1, Box 465, Starke, FL 32091-9703, C-850-533-3381, D-312-533-3104, Fax C-850-533-3540, 15 camper spaces with full hookups, 50 primitive camper/tent spaces with W hookups.

SPACE-A: None. See Cecil Field NAS listing C-904-778-5536/5481, D-312-860-5536/5481, Fax: C-904-778-5833.

LOGISTICAL SUPPORT:

Barber Shop-533-3195
Credit Union-533-2184
Exchange-533-3513
Beauty Shop-533-3195
Dry Cleaner-533-3369
Laundry-533-3369

ADMINISTRATIVE SUPPORT:

Housing Office-533-3381/2
Police-533-3526
SDO/SNCO-533-3462
Pass/ID Office-533-3566
Public Affairs-533-3407

HEALTH & WELFARE:

Chapel-533-3231
Medical-533-3105
  Information-533-3514

REST & RECREATION:

O'Club-533-3320

ATTRACTIONS: Under one hour drives to Gainesville, Jacksonville and St Augustine, three hours to Disney and the Orlando area. Kingsley Lakes on post; one of the best bass fishing lakes in area.

CAPE CANAVERAL AIR STATION (FL45R1)

1201 Minuteman Street, Suite C
Patrick Air Force Base, FL 32925-5000

TELEPHONE NUMBER INFORMATION: Main installation numbers: C-407-494-1110, D-312-467-1110.

LOCATION: From I-95 take 528 E, exit 401 to AFS. USMRA: Page 38, (I-7). NMC: Cocoa Beach, 2 miles north.

GENERAL INFORMATION: Home of space shuttle launches.

TML: None. See Patrick AFB, C-407-494-6570, D-312-854-7597.

RV, CAMPING/FAMCAMP: None. See Patrick AFB, C-407-494-4787, D-312-854-4787.

SPACE-A: None. See Patrick AFB, C-407-494-5631, D-312-854-5631.

LOGISTICAL SUPPORT:

Commissary-853-3196
Visitor Center-494-2659
Exchange-853-3196

ADMINISTRATIVE SUPPORT: None. See Patrick AFB, C-407-494-1110, D-312-854-1110.

HEALTH & WELFARE: None. See Patrick AFB, C-407-494-1110, D-312-854-1110.

REST & RECREATION: None. See Patrick AFB, C-407-494-1110, D-312-854-1110.

ATTRACTIONS: Shuttle launches. At Patrick AFB, Air Force Space Museum, John F. Kennedy Space Center, Disney World, Daytona Beach, Epcot Center, Spaceport USA, Sea World.

CECIL FIELD NAVAL AIR STATION (FL06R1)

P.O. Box 111
Cecil Field Naval Air Station, FL 32215-0111
Scheduled to close (operational) December 1998; total closure August 1999.

TELEPHONE NUMBER INFORMATION: Main installation numbers: C-904-778-5627, D-312-860-5627. HP: http://www.cecilfield.com.

LOCATION: Take Normandy Blvd (FL-228) exit W off I-295 to main gate. From I-10 take Whitehouse/Chaffee Road. Proceed four miles south, taking a right onto Normandy Blvd. Follow four miles to main gate. USMRA: Page 38 (G-3). NMC: Jacksonville, 13 miles east.

GENERAL INFORMATION: Naval Combat Aircraft Support and Training Base; tenants: Twelve Strike-Fighter (FA-18 Hornet) Squadrons, Five Sea Control (S-3B) Squadrons, and one Fleet Air Reconnaissance (ES-31) Squadron.

TEMPORARY MILITARY LODGING: BOQ/DV/VIP, Building 331, 24 hours daily, C-904-778-5255, D-312-860-5255. BEQ, Building 92, 24 hours daily, C-904-778-6191, D-312-860-6191.

RV, CAMPING/FAMCAMP: Lake Fretwell Recreation Area on base, year round, C-904-778-6112, D-312-860-6112, four camper spaces with W/E hookups.

SPACE-A: Pax Term/Lounge, Building 47, 0700-1600 Mon-Fri, C-904-778-5536/5481, D-312-860-5536/5481, Fax: C-904-778-5833, flights to CONUS locations. Also see Jacksonville NAS listing.

LOGISTICAL SUPPORT:

Barber Shop-778-3198
Child Care-778-6910
Conv Store-772-0656
Dining Facilities
  McDonald's-771-7887
  Flightline Galley-778-5312
Postal Service-778-6292
Snack Bars
  Bowling Center-778-5290
  Golf Course-778-7887
Beauty Shop-771-0351
Commissary-778-5703
Credit Union-777-6000
Exchange-778-3571
Gas Station-778-0778
Package Store-778-3571
SATO-778-5676

ADMINISTRATIVE SUPPORT:

CDO/OOD-778-5627
Housing Office-778-5550
Locator-778-5240
Police-778-5381
Public Affairs-778-6055
Fire Dept-778-5333
Legal-778-6088
Pass/Tag Office-778-5288
  ID Cards-778-5358
Quarterdeck-778-5627

HEALTH & WELFARE:

American Red Cross-778-5337
Chapel-778-5340
Family Services-778-5194
Medical
  Central Appts-778-5717
  Clinic-778-5406
  Dependent Clinic-778-5508
  Emergency-778-5212
CHAMPUS-778-6711
Dental
  Clinic-778-6260
  Emergency-778-5212
N-MC Relief Society-778-6171

REST & RECREATION:

Auto Hobby Shop-778-5651
Clubs
  CPO-778-5390
  EM-778-6107
  O-778-5110
ITT-778-6112
MWR-778-6004/5478
Thrift Store-778-6461
Bowling-778-5591
Equipment Rental-772-0947
Golf Course-778-5425
Gym-778-5498
Hobby Shops-778-5651
Library-778-6211
Skeet Range-778-5181
Youth Center-777-8247

FLORIDA
Cecil Field Naval Air Station, continued

ATTRACTIONS: Beaches, golf, museums, Busch Gardens tours, minor league baseball and proximity to central Florida tourist attractions.

CLEARWATER COAST GUARD AIR STATION (FL32R1)

15100 Rescue Way
Clearwater, FL 34622-2990

TELEPHONE NUMBER INFORMATION: Main installation numbers: C-813-535-1437 (ask for extensions).

LOCATION: From I-275, take 60 west to 611 south. Follow signs to air station. USMRA: Page 38 (E-8), page 56 (C-3). NMI: MacDill AFB, 30 miles east. NMC: Tampa, 20 miles east.

GENERAL INFORMATION: The Coast Guard Air Station is responsible for search-and-rescue, law enforcement, and other Coast Guard operations throughout Florida, the Gulf of Mexico and the Caribbean.

TEMPORARY MILITARY LODGING: None. See MacDill AFB listing, C-813-828-2661, D-312-968-4259.

RV, CAMPING/FAMCAMP: None. See MacDill AFB listing, Coon's Creek Rec Area, C-813-840-6919, 800-821-4982, Fax: C-813-828-7507.

SPACE-A: Limited flights. C-813-535-1437, ext 1223.

LOGISTICAL SUPPORT:
Barber Shop-ext 1712
Exchange-ext 1710

ADMINISTRATIVE SUPPORT:
CDO/OOD-ext 1210
Public Affairs-ext 1145
Housing Office-ext 1160

HEALTH & WELFARE: Medical-ext 1606

REST & RECREATION: MWR-ext 1180

ATTRACTIONS: Busch Gardens—The Dark Continent, Salvador Dali Museum, The Pier in St Petersburg, Adventure Island Water Park, Tampa's Latin Quarter, beaches, water sports.

CORRY STATION NAVAL TECHNICAL TRAINING CENTER (FL19R1)

640 Roberts Avenue
Pensacola, FL 32511-5138

TELEPHONE NUMBER INFORMATION: Main installation numbers: C-850-452-2000, D-312-922-0111.

LOCATION: Off US-98, three miles north of Pensacola NAS. USMRA: Page 38 (A,B-13), page 53 (B-4). NMC: Pensacola, five miles northeast.

GENERAL INFORMATION: Home of the Naval Technical Training Center.

TEMPORARY MILITARY LODGING: BQ: C-850-452-6609, D-312-922-6609.

RV, CAMPING/FAMCAMP: See Blue Angel Naval Recreation Area listing, C-850-453-9435, for more information.

SPACE-A: None. See Pensacola NAS listing, C-850-452-3311, D-312-922-3311, Fax: C-850-452-2512.

LOGISTICAL SUPPORT:
Child Care-452-6138
Exchange-453-5311
Conv Store-453-5311
SATO-452-6291

ADMINISTRATIVE SUPPORT:
Legal-452-6334
Police-452-6130
SDO/NCO-452-6512
Locator-452-6512
Public Affairs-452-6318

HEALTH & WELFARE:
CHAMPUS-452-6709
Medical-452-5242
Chapel-452-6376
Retiree Services-452-6529

REST & RECREATION:
Clubs
CPO-452-6330
EM-452-6347
Rec Center 452-6520
ITT-452-6143
MWR-452-6568
Recreation-453-2129
RV/Camping-453-2129

OTHER FACILITIES AVAILABLE: Archery, Bowling, Hobby Shop, Swimming, Tennis.

ATTRACTIONS: Visit the historic section of Pensacola, beaches. Naval Aviation Museum at NAS Pensacola.

DESTIN ARMY INFANTRY CENTER RECREATION AREA (FL01R1)

557 Calhoun Avenue
Destin, FL 32541-5000

TELEPHONE NUMBER INFORMATION: Main installation numbers: C-706-545-2011, D-312-835-2011.

LOCATION: Located on 15-acre site on Choctawhatchee Bay in Destin FL. US-231 south to I-10, west to US-331, south to US-98, west to Benning Drive; right to area. ***OR*** I-10 to FL-85; south to Fort Walton Beach; US-98 east to Destin; left at Benning Drive to area. USMRA: page 39 (C-13). NMC: Pensacola, 45 miles west. NMI: Eglin AFB, 17 miles north.

GENERAL INFORMATION: Operated by Fort Benning, GA, off post year round. Military personnel active, retired, National Guard, reserves and DoD civilians. Check in at office 1600-2000, check out 1100. Reservations: Required for cabins, motel and charter boat, C-850-837-2725; not accepted for camper spaces; up to six months in advance for active duty at Fort Benning, four months in advance for others. **Reservations, C-800-642-0466.** Reservations may also be made at Fort Benning, C-706-545-5600. *Information only,* C-850-837-6423, Fax: C-850-837-5706. Visa, MasterCard and American Express accepted. No pets or firearms allowed.

TEMPORARY MILITARY LODGING: Three bedroom duplex, private bath, kitchen, microwave, cable TV, phone (free local calls), linens, pots and pans (5); two bedroom duplex, private bath, kitchen, microwave, cable TV, phone (free local calls), linens, pots and pans (17); Motel, two double beds; refrigerator, microwave, coffeepot, cable TV, phone (free local calls), linens (54). Five duplex rooms handicap accessible. Rates: three bedroom duplex $50-$65 daily (includes immediate family only; additional fee for guests. Off-season rates available 15 Oct-16 Mar); two bedroom duplex $44-$58 daily; Motel $38-$49 daily.

RV, CAMPING/FAMCAMP: Camper spaces with full hookups (43); primitive camper/tent spaces with E and central W (23). Rates: camper spaces $11-$14 daily; primitive camper/tent spaces $6 daily.

ADMINISTRATIVE SUPPORT: Police-651-7400/911.

REST & RECREATION: Boating, Deep-Sea Fishing, Jet Skis, Pontoon Boats, Rec Equipment, Swimming.

OTHER SUPPORT & FACILITIES AVAILABLE: Beach, Boat Launch, Boat Rental, Boat Slip Rental, Deep-Sea Charter, Fishing Pier, Game Room,

Grills, Laundry, Marina, Party Boat, Picnic Area, Playground, Restrooms, Sewage Dump, Showers, TV Room, Swimming Pool, Vending Machine, Water Sports , Equipment Rental. Also, see Eglin Air Force Base listing, C-850-882-1110, D-312-872-1110.

ATTRACTIONS: Enjoy sparkling sugar-white quartz sands of Emerald Coast. Gulf of Mexico fishing and swimming areas approximately two miles from recreation area. Area also offers golf at six public courses, two greyhound race tracks within 45 miles, Destin Fishing Museum, Gulfariam, Zoo, and Indian Temple Mound Museum.

EGLIN AIR FORCE BASE (FL27R1)

101 West D Avenue, Suite 129
Eglin Air Force Base, FL 32542-5498

TELEPHONE NUMBER INFORMATION: Main installation numbers: C-850-882-1110, D-312-872-1110.

LOCATION: Exit I-10 at Crestview. Follow signs to Niceville and Valparaiso (Eglin AFB). USMRA: Page 39 (B,C,D,-13), page 53 (E-2,3; F-1,2,3; G,H-1,2,3,4). NMC: Fort Walton Beach, seven miles south.

GENERAL INFORMATION: Air Force Materiel Command Base. Largest AFB in the Free World, Air Force Development Test Center, 33rd Fighter Wing, AFRES units.

TEMPORARY MILITARY LODGING: Lodging office, Building 11001, Boatner Road, 24 hours daily, C-850-882-8761, D-312-872-8761. All ranks. DV/VIP C-850-882-3011. Navy CBQ (Officers & EM) C-850-882-5683, D-312-872-5683 DV/VIP.

RV, CAMPING/FAMCAMP: FAMCAMP on base, year round, C-850-882-5058 22 camper spaces with W/E hookups, 20 tent spaces.

SPACE-A: Pax Term/Lounge, Building 60, 0600-1800 Mon-Fri, 0800-1600 Sat-Sun, C-850-882-4757, D-312-872-4757, Fax: C-850-882-2655, flights to CONUS locations.

LOGISTICAL SUPPORT:

Child Care-882-5519	Commissary-882-3172
Exchange-651-2512	Gas Station-678-7222
SATO-882-8016	

ADMINISTRATIVE SUPPORT:

Legal-882-4611	Locator-882-4478
Police-882-2502	

HEALTH & WELFARE:

CHAMPUS-882-7249	Chapel-882-4426/2111
Family Services-882-2893	Medical-883-8221
Retiree Services-882-5916	Appts-882-4131
	Emergency-882-7227

REST & RECREATION:

Clubs	Golf-882-2695
NCO-678-5127	Hobby Shops-882-3570
O-651-1010	ITT-882-5930
Library-882-2460	Theater-882-3813
Youth Activities-882-5074	

OTHER FACILITIES AVAILABLE: Bowling, Gym, Fishing, large and small Game Hunting on the AFB, Skeet and Swimming.

ATTRACTIONS: Fort Walton Beach and beach areas, sport fishing, deep sea fishing, dog races, Pensacola, 35 miles west.

HOMESTEAD AIR RESERVE BASE (FL17R1)

360 Coral Sea Boulevard
Homestead ARB, FL 33039-1299

TELEPHONE NUMBER INFORMATION: Main installation numbers: C-305-224-7000, D-312-791-7000.

LOCATION: Exit 6 off Florida Turnpike, left at bottom of the ramp, approximately one-half mile to traffic light (SW 288th Street), then left to main gate. USMRA: Page 39 (I-14), page 51 (A,B-10). NMC: Miami, 30 miles northeast.

GENERAL INFORMATION: Home of the 482nd Fighter Wing.

TEMPORARY MILITARY LODGING: Lodging Office, Homestead Inn, 0700-2100 hours daily; holiday hours are 0900-1800 hours, C-305-224-7168, D-312-791-7168, Fax: C-305-224-7290, D-312-224-7290.

RV, CAMPING/FAMCAMP: None. See Marathon Rec Cottages listing, C-305-536-5850, Fax: C-305-536-4216.

SPACE-A: Pax Terminal/lounge Building 701, C-305-224-7518, D-312-791-7518, flights to CONUS locations.

LOGISTICAL SUPPORT:

Conv Store-224-7464	Exchange-224-7464
Package Store-224-7464	SATO-224-7051

ADMINISTRATIVE SUPPORT:

CDO/OOD-224-7023	Fire Dept-224-7117
Legal-224-7063	Locator-224-7000
Police-224-7115	Public Affairs-224-7303

HEALTH & WELFARE:

CHAMPUS-265-3104	Chapel-224-7093
Family Services-224-7329	Retiree Services-224-7580

REST & RECREATION:	Consol-224-7517

ATTRACTIONS: Biscayne Bay, deep sea fishing, Everglades National Park, horse and dog racing, boating, and water sports.

HURLBURT FIELD (FL18R1)

131 Bartley Street, Suite 326
Hurlburt Field, FL 32544-5271

TELEPHONE NUMBER INFORMATION: Main installation numbers: C-850-884-1110 (Eglin Base info), D-312-579-1110, ask for Hurlburt.

LOCATION: Off US-98, five miles west of Fort Walton Beach. Clearly marked. USMRA: Page 39 (C-13), page 53 (H-4). NMC: Pensacola, 35 miles west.

GENERAL INFORMATION: Air Force Special Operations Command Base, on the Eglin AFB reservation, US Special Operations Command AF Component, 16th Special Operations Wing, Air Force Air Ground Operations School, USAF Special Operations School.

TEMPORARY MILITARY LODGING: Billeting Office, Building 90509, 24 hours daily, C-850-884-6245/7115, D-312-579-6245/7115, Fax: C-850-884-5043, D-312-579-5043. All ranks. DV/VIP C-850-884-2308.

RV, CAMPING/FAMCAMP: Hurlburt FAMCAMP off base year round, 16 SVS/SVRL, Hurlburt Field, FL 32544-5000, C-850-884-6939. Twenty-five camp spaces with full hook ups, 10 tent spaces with no hook ups.

SPACE-A: Base Ops, C-850-884-7806. Also see Eglin AFB listing C-850-882-4757, D-312-872-4757.

FLORIDA
Hurlburt Field, continued

LOGISTICAL SUPPORT:
Bank-581-2222
Beauty Shop-581-3524
Child Dev Center-884-6937
Commissary-881-2139
Dining Facilities-884-6935/1276
Education Office-884-6724
Laundry-581-3614
Postal Service-884-7646
Shoppette-581-0488
Bay Area Travel-884-4771
Child Care-884-6937
Class Six-581-0488
Credit Union-862-0111
Dry Cleaner-581-3614
Exchange-581-0030
Gas Station-581-2224
SATO-884-6344

ADMINISTRATIVE SUPPORT:
Fire Dept-884-1357/911
Legal-884-7821
Pass/ID Office-884-5125
Public Affairs-884-7464
Housing Office-884-7505
Locator-882-3300
Police-884-6423
Command Post-884-7774

HEALTH & WELFARE:
Air Force Aid Society-884-5441
CHAMPUS-881-3912
Dental-884-7881
Medical
Central Appts-884-7882
Clinic-881-5177
Emergency-911
or Eglin ER-883-8227
Health Benefits-881-3912
Information-883-8242
American Red Cross-884-6107/6246
Chapel-884-7795
Family Services-884-6201
TRICARE-881-3912

REST & RECREATION:
Arts & Crafts-884-6942/7405
Bowling-884-6941
Community Center-884-6105
Fitness Center-884-6949
Golf Course-884-6940/581-0007
Gym-884-6884/6905
Library-884-6947/7143
MWR-884-4099
Recreation-884-7397
Services-884-4684
Theater-884-7648
Wood Hobby Shop-884-7244
Auto Hobby Shop-884-6674
Clubs
Consol-884-6469
O-884-7507
Soundside-581-3110/3111
Indoor Rec-884-6105
Marina-884-0939
Outdoor Rec-884-6939
Equipment Rental
Swimming-884-6866
Tickets & Tours-884-6105
Youth Center-884-6355

ATTRACTIONS: Zoo, Gulf Islands National Seashore, Pensacola Historical Museum, Naval Air Museum, Air Force Armament Museum, Navaree Beach Campgrounds, Gulfarium, Ft. Walton Beach Art Museum, Numerous golf courses, sport fishing, boating, water sports, beaches, shopping, Indian Temple Mound Museum, Pensacola (west) and Panama City (east), both short drives.

JACKSONVILLE NAVAL AIR STATION (FL08R1)

P.O. Box 102
Jacksonville Naval Air Station, FL 32212-5000

TELEPHONE NUMBER INFORMATION: Main installation numbers: C-904-542-2345/2346, D-312-942-2345/2346.

LOCATION: Access from US-17 south. USMRA: Page 38 (G-3), page 50 (B,C-6,7). NMC: Jacksonville, nine miles northeast.

GENERAL INFORMATION: Fixed and rotary wing anti-submarine warfare aircraft support and training, Naval Hospital, Naval Aviation Depot, Naval Supply Center.

TEMPORARY MILITARY LODGING: Lodging office, Building 11, 24 hours daily, C-904-542-3138 (EM), 904-542-3537 (Officer). DV/VIP C-904-542-3147/3148. Navy Lodge: C-904-542-6000, D-312-942-6000 or 1-800-NAVY-INN.

RV, CAMPING/FAMCAMP: RV Park on base, year round, C-904-542-3227, D-312-942-3227, eight camper spaces with full hookups, four camper spaces with W/E, 14 camper/tent spaces without hookups.

SPACE-A: Pax Term/Lounge, Building 118, 24 hours daily, C-904-542-3956, D-312-942-3956, Fax: C-904-942-2514, flights to CONUS and Caribbean area.

LOGISTICAL SUPPORT:
Child Care-542-5529
Conv Store-777-7285
Gas Station-778-7142
SATO-1-800-949-7286
Commissary-573-5010
Exchange-777-7200
Navy Campus-542-2477
Snack Bar-542-2936

ADMINISTRATIVE SUPPORT:
CDO/OOD-542-2338
Legal-542-3481
Police-542-2661
Fire Dept-542-2451
Locator-542-2340
Public Affairs-542-4032

HEALTH & WELFARE:
CHAMPUS-573-3300
Family Services-542-2766
Retiree Services-542-5783
Veterinary Services-542-3786
Chapel-542-3051/3440
Medical-777-7300
Central Appts-777-7467
Emergency-777-7340

REST & RECREATION:
Archery-542-3111
Auto Hobby Shop-ext 3227
Clubs
EM-542-3521
O-542-3041
Library-ext 3415
MWR-542-3112
Storage-ext 3227
Wood Hobby Shop-ext 3681
Athletic Director-ext 3239
Bowling-ext 3403
Fitness Center -ext 3518
Golf Course-542-3249
ITT-542-3318
Marina-ext 3260
Recreation-542-3112
Swimming-ext 2930

ATTRACTIONS: Golfing, beaches, deep sea fishing, St Augustine, Orlando. Museum of Science and History in Jacksonville, art museums, planetarium.

KEY WEST NAVAL AIR STATION (FL15R1)

Code 01J, P.O. Box 9001
Key West Naval Air Station, FL 33040-9001

TELEPHONE NUMBER INFORMATION: Main installation numbers: C-305-293-2268, D-312-483-2268. E-mail: naskwpao@norfolk.navy.com.

LOCATION: Take Florida Turnpike, US-1 south to exit signs for Key West NAS on Boca Chica Key, seven miles north of Key West. USMRA: Page 39 (G-16). NMC: Miami, 150 miles north.

GENERAL INFORMATION: Search and Rescue helicopters, Tactical Aircrew Combat Training (TACTS), Joint Interagency Task Force East (JIATF East), USCGG Key West, Caribbean Regional Operations Center (CARIBROC), US Army Special Forces Underwater Operations School, Tactical aircraft and rescue aircraft operations; pilot training, Coast Guard, reserve and other services support detachments.

TEMPORARY MILITARY LODGING: Consolidated Bachelor Quarters, P.O. Box 9058, 24 hours daily, C-305-293-4143, D-312-483-4143, Fax: C-305-293-4302, D-312-483-4302. (BOQ) C-305-293-5571, BEQ: C-305-293-2488. Navy Lodge: C-305-292-7556 or 1-800-NAVY-INN.

RV, CAMPING/FAMCAMP: Sigsbee RV Park on base, year round, C-305-293-4434, 70 camper spaces with full hookups, 200 camper spaces with W, unlimited tent spaces.

SPACE-A: Check at Control Tower, Boca Chica Annex, 0730-1630 daily, C-305-293-2774, D-312-483-2774, Fax: C-305-293-2755, D-312-483-2416, flights to CONUS locations.

FLORIDA
Key West Naval Air Station, continued

LOGISTICAL SUPPORT:

Banks-294-6622	Barber Shop-292-7223
Beauty Shop-292-7223	Child Care-293-4376
Child Dev Center-293-4376	Commissary-293-4402
Conv Store-292-7226	Credit Union-294-6622
Dining Facilities-293-2435	Dry Cleaner-292-7229
Education Office-293-2705	Exchange-292-7210
Laundry-292-7229	Gas Station-292-7219
Mini Mart-293-7216	Package Store-292-7226
Postal Service-293-2406	SATO-294-8470
Shoppette-293-7216	Travel Office-293-4434

ADMINISTRATIVE SUPPORT:

CDO/OOD-293-2268	Fire Dept-293-3145
Housing Office-293-4417	Legal-293-4310
Locator-293-2256	Pass/ID Office-293-2803
Police-293-2531	Public Affairs-293-2627
Quarter Deck-293-2268	

HEALTH & WELFARE:

Chapel-293-2318	Dental-293-2309
Family Service-293-4408	Medical
N-MC Relief Society-293-2169	Central Appts-293-4500
TRICARE-293-4543	Clinic-293-2444
Veterinary Services-293-2364	Emergency-293-2337
	Health Benefits-293-4543
	Hospital-293-4500
	Information-293-4500

REST & RECREATION:

Auto Hobby Shop-293-2615	Bowling-293-2976
Clubs	Community Center-293-4432
CPO-293-2407	Fitness Center-293-2480
Consol-293-2495	Gym-293-2480
EM-293-2495	ITT-293-4433
Flying-ext 5081	Library-293-2116
NCO-293-2495	Marina-293-4434
O-293-2480	MWR-293-2112
Outdoor Rec-293-2682	Rec Center-ext 2112
Water Rec-ext 2468	Youth Center-293-4437

ATTRACTIONS: Audubon House, Aquarium, Looe Key Reef, Ernest Hemingway Home and Museum, Harry Truman Little White House, Mel Fischer's Maritime Museum, Shipwreck Historium, boating, diving, snorkeling, sport fishing, water sports.

MacDILL AIR FORCE BASE (FL02R1)

8208 Hangar Loop Drive, Suite 51
MacDill Air Force Base, FL 33621-5502

TELEPHONE NUMBER INFORMATION: Main installation numbers: C-813-828-1110, D-312-968-1110.

LOCATION: Take I-75 south to I-275 south, exit at Dale Mabry Highway (US-92), south five miles to MacDill AFB main gate. USMRA: Page 38 (E,F-8), page 56 (E,F-3,4). NMC: Tampa, five miles north.

GENERAL INFORMATION: Air Mobility Command Base. Headquarters US Special Operations Command, US Central Command and 6th Air Refueling Wing.

TEMPORARY MILITARY LODGING: Lodging office, Building 411, corner Garden Drive & Tampa Blvd, 24 hours daily, C-813-828-2661, D-312-968-4259. All ranks. DV/VIP C-813-828-2056.

RV, CAMPING/FAMCAMP: Coon's Creek Recreation Area on base, year round, C-813-840-6919 or 1-800-821-4982, D-312-968-4982, Fax: C-813-828-7507 199 camper spaces with full hookups, 57 camper spaces with W/E hookups, 33 spaces without hookups, and 34 tent spaces without hookups.

SPACE-A: Pax Term/Lounges, Hangar 4, 0730-1630 Mon-Fri, C-813-828-2310, D-312-968-2310, Fax: C-813-828-3202, flights to CONUS locations and MEDEVAC.

LOGISTICAL SUPPORT:

Cafeteria-840-0511	Child Care-828-3332
Commissary-828-3196	Conv Store-840-2077
Exchange-840-0511	Gas Station-839-7089
Package Store-840-2323	SATO-828-4327
Snack Bar-840-2211	

ADMINISTRATIVE SUPPORT:

Fire Dept-828-3438	Legal-828-4421
Locator-828-2444	Police-828-3322
Public Affairs-828-2215	

HEALTH & WELFARE:

ACS-828-4413	CHAMPUS-828-5220
Chapel-828-3621	Family Services-828-2221
Medical	Retiree Services-828-4555
Central Appts-839-5711	
Emergency-828-3334	

REST & RECREATION:

Arts & Crafts-ext 4413	Auto Hobby Shop-ext 4553
Bowling-ext 3008	Clubs
Golf Course-828-4494	EM-828-3357
Gym-ext 4496	NCO-828-3357
ITT-828-2478	O-837-1031
Library-ext 3607	Marina-ext 4983
MWR-ext 4983	Rec Center-ext 4518
Theater-828-3973	Youth Activities-ext 4244

ATTRACTIONS: Busch Gardens, Disney World, professional sports (football, hockey, baseball (spring training), sport fishing, water sports.

MARATHON RECREATION COTTAGES (FL28R1)

Commanding Officer (PM)
USCG, Integrated Support Command
100 MacArthur Causeway
Miami Beach, FL 33139-5101

TELEPHONE NUMBER INFORMATION: Main installation number: C-305-535-4300.

LOCATION: Situated on Marathon Key in the heart of the Florida Keys. In the Florida Keys on US-1 (Overseas Highway) at mile marker 48 at Marathon. Enter recreation area from US-1. USMRA: page 39 (H-15). NMC: Miami, 111 miles northeast. NMI: Key West Naval Air Station on Boca Chica Key, 40 miles south.

GENERAL INFORMATION: Topography is similar to that of islands in the eastern Caribbean. Beaches on Atlantic and Gulf sides. Operated by Miami CG Integrated Support Command, on base year round. Military personnel active, retired and reserve. Check in after 1600 with OOD, Coast Guard Station Marathon, 1800 Overseas Highway C-305-743-3549, check out 1200. Reservations: No advance reservations for RV spaces; required for cottages with full payment in advance, by application only, at least eight weeks in advance. Application may be obtained by phone C-305-536-5850, Fax C-305-536-4216; reservations cannot be made by phone. (For information on RV spaces, C-305-743-3549). No pets allowed. Twelve day limit, to include only one weekend for cottages; 14 day limit for RV spaces. No cribs provided. Swimming not allowed on CG Station; diving and fishing areas accessible by boat. No firearms allowed. No waste dumping allowed.

FLORIDA
Marathon Recreation Cottages, continued

TEMPORARY MILITARY LODGING: cottages, one bedroom; one double bed, two single sofa beds, one rollaway bed; sleeps five adults; fully furnished, including kitchen; AC, TV. Bring extra towels; recently renovated (4). Rates: $20-35 daily, depending on rank.

RV, CAMPING/FAMCAMP: Paved RV spaces with W&E hookups. Rates: $12 daily.

REST & RECREATION: Basketball, Bicycling, Boating, Fishing/license, Hiking, Swimming, Volleyball.

OTHER SUPPORT & FACILITIES AVAILABLE: Boat Rental, Boat Dock, Grills, Picnic Tables. Also, see Key West Naval Air Station listing, C-305-293-2268, D-312-483-2268.

ATTRACTIONS: The Florida Keys, beautiful beaches and the Florida sun.

MAYPORT NAVAL STATION (FL13R1)

Box 32
Mayport Naval Station, FL 32228-0112

TELEPHONE NUMBER INFORMATION: Main installation numbers: C-904-270-5011, D-312-960-5011.

LOCATION: From Jacksonville take Atlantic Blvd (FL-10) east to Mayport Road (FL-A1A), left to Naval Station. USMRA: Page 38 (H-3), page 50 (G-3,4). NMC: Jacksonville, 10 miles west.

GENERAL INFORMATION: Homeport for 23 ships. Major commands include Commander, Western Hemisphere Group, Commander Carrier Group Six, Commander Cruiser Destroyer Group Twelve.

TEMPORARY MILITARY LODGING: Lodging office, Building 1586, Bailey Avenue, 24 hours daily, C-904-247-1376, D-312-960-5707, BEQ: C-904-270-5575, D-312-960-5575, BOQ: C-904-270-5423, D-312-960-5423. All ranks. DV/VIP (EM) C-904-270-5707, D-312-960-5707, (Officers) C-904-270-5423, D-312-960-5423. Navy Lodge, 1-800-NAVY-INN.

RV, CAMPING/FAMCAMP: None. See Jacksonville NAS listing, C-904-542-3227, D-312-942-3227.

SPACE-A: None. See Jacksonville NAS listing, C-904-542-3956, D-312-942-3956, Fax: C-904-942-2514.

LOGISTICAL SUPPORT:
Bank-270-5600
Beauty Shop-247-5752
Child Care-270-5339
Commissary-249-7362
Credit Union-270-5358
Education Office-270-6341
Gas Station-270-5712
SATO-270-5605
Barber Shop-247-5752
Car Rental-249-0955
Child Dev Center-270-5339
Conv Store-270-5449
Dry Cleaner-270-5449
Exchange-247-5752
Postal Service-270-5560
Snack Bar-270-5143

ADMINISTRATIVE SUPPORT:
CDO/OOD-270-5401
Housing Office-270-5730
Locator-270-5401
Police-270-5583
Quarter Deck-270-5401
Fire Dept-270-5334
Legal-270-5647
Pass/ID Office-270-5585
Public Affairs-270-5226
SDO/NCO-270-5401

HEALTH & WELFARE:
American Red Cross-270-5241
Chapel-270-5212
Family Services-270-5392
N-MC Relief Society-270-5418
Retiree Services-270-5783
TRICARE-270-5763
CHAMPUS-270-5763
Dental-270-5351
Medical
  Clinic-270-5675
  Hospital-777-7300
Veterinary Services-270-5763

REST & RECREATION:
Arts & Crafts-ext 5540
Bowling-270-5377
Golf Course-270-5380
Gym-270-5451
Intramural Sports-ext 5451
ITT-270-5145
Rec Center-ext 5680
Tennis-ext 5717
Auto Hobby Shop-270-5392
Clubs
  CPO-270-5432
  EM-270-7197
  O-270-5313
Library-270-5393
Swimming-ext 5425
Youth Services-270-5680

ATTRACTIONS: Zoo, beaches, deep sea fishing. Three-hour drive to Orlando.

MIAMI COAST GUARD AIR STATION (FL30R1)

Opa Locka Airport
ATTN: PAO
Opa Locka, FL 33054-2397

TELEPHONE NUMBER INFORMATION: Main installation number: C-305-953-2100.

LOCATION: Take exit 14 from I-95 onto NW 135th Street (Opa Locka Blvd, also FL-916) west to Lejeune Road, then north to the airport. Turn left on Wright, Air Station is at the end of the road. USMRA: Page 39 (J-13), page 51 (B-4,5). NMC: Miami, 10 miles southeast.

GENERAL INFORMATION: A Coast Guard Air Station with regional search-and-rescue and drug-interdiction responsibilities.

TEMPORARY MILITARY LODGING: None. See Key West NAS listing, C-305-293-4143. (BOQ) C-305-293-5571, BEQ: C-305-293-2488.

RV, CAMPING/FAMCAMP: None. See Marathon Rec Cottages listing, C-305-536-5850, Fax: C-305-536-4216.

SPACE-A: No regularly scheduled flights from the Air Station. See Key West NAS listing, C-305-293-2774, D-312-483-2774, Fax: C-305-293-2755, D-312-483-2416.

LOGISTICAL SUPPORT:
Commissary-953-2290
Package Store-953-2290
Exchange-685-1661-ext 42

ADMINISTRATIVE SUPPORT:
CDO/OOD-953-2280
SDO/NCO-953-2130/2140
Public Affairs-953-2151

HEALTH & WELFARE:
CHAMPUS-953-2265/2266
Family Services-953-2110
Dental-953-2265
Medical-953-2266

REST & RECREATION:
All Hands Club-953-2291
MWR-953-2115
Auto Hobby Shop-953-2115

OTHER SUPPORT AVAILABLE: Barber Shop, Beauty Shop, Dining Facilities, Police, Public Affairs.

ATTRACTIONS: Hollywood/Rembroke Pines Area, city of Miami, Gratigny Park, Spanish Monastery, Vizcaya Art Museum, Hialeah Park, Miami Seaquarium, Miami Serpentarium, Dade City Art Museum, beaches.

MIAMI COAST GUARD INTEGRATED SUPPORT COMMAND (FL31R1)

100 MacArthur Causeway
Miami Beach, FL 33139-5119

TELEPHONE NUMBER INFORMATION: Main installation number: C-305-535-4300.

FLORIDA
Miami Coast Guard Integrated Support Command, continued

LOCATION: Take I-95 to MacArthur Causeway (also I-359) east. USMRA: Page 39 (J-13), page 51 (D-6). NMC: Miami Beach, in city limits.

GENERAL INFORMATION: The Coast Guard Base in Miami is responsible for regional search-and-rescue, drug-interdiction missions and aids to navigation.

TEMPORARY MILITARY LODGING: None. See Homestead ARB listing, C-305-224-7168, D-312-791-7168.

RV, CAMPING/FAMCAMP: Operates Marathon Rec Cottages off base. See Marathon Rec Cottages listing for more information.

SPACE-A: None. See Key West NAS listing, C-305-293-2751/2769, D-312-483-2751/2769.

LOGISTICAL SUPPORT: Exchange-535-4354/4410

ADMINISTRATIVE SUPPORT: SDO/NCO-535-4361

HEALTH & WELFARE:
CHAMPUS-535-4350
Medical-535-4350

REST & RECREATION: None. See Miami CGAS listing, C-305-953-2100.

ATTRACTIONS: City of Miami (tours available), Gratigny Park, Spanish Monastery, Vizcaya Art Museum, beaches, water sports.

ORLANDO NAVAL TRAINING CENTER (FL11R1)

4551 Kitty Hawk Street
Orlando, FL 32813-8360
Scheduled to close April 1999

TELEPHONE NUMBER INFORMATION: Main installation numbers: C-407-646-4501, D-312-791-4501.

LOCATION: From I-4 in Orlando take FL-50 (Colonial Drive) east about three miles; then north on Maguire for one-half mile to NTC. USMRA: Page 38 (H-7), page 53 (D-1). NMI: Patrick AFB, one hour, near Cocoa Beach. NMC: Orlando, three miles from downtown.

GENERAL INFORMATION: Training Center, schools, and Naval Nuclear Power Training Command. Annex is adjacent to Orlando IAP on site of the old McCoy AFB, 10 miles south.

TEMPORARY MILITARY LODGING: Lodging office, Building 375, 1200 Leahy Street, 0730-1600 Mon-Fri, front desk manned 24 hours daily, C-407-646-5614, D-312-791-5614.

RV, CAMPING/FAMCAMP: Lake Baldwin Picnic Grounds ext 5161. Travel Trailer Park, on base, at Annex year round, C-407-857-2120, 48 camper spaces with full hookups, 13 spaces with W/E, 10 spaces without hookups.

SPACE-A: None. See Patrick AFB listing, C-407-494-5631, D-312-854-5631, Fax: C-407-494-7991.

LOGISTICAL SUPPORT:
Barber Shop-646-5511
Cafeteria-646-5826
Child Dev Center-646-5131
Conv Store-646-4456
Dry Cleaner-646-5800
Exchange-646-5950
Package Store-646-4890
Snack Bar-646-4291
Beauty Shop-646-5511
Child Care-646-5131
Commissary-857-1520
Credit Union-277-5045
Education Office-646-4397
Gas Station-646-5979
SATO-895-4664

ADMINISTRATIVE SUPPORT:
CDO/OOD-646-4501
Locator-646-4501
Public Affairs-646-4430
Legal-646-5180
Police-646-5108
Quarter Deck-646-4501

HEALTH & WELFARE:
American Red Cross-646-4611
Dental-646-4267
Medical-646-4267
Retiree Services-646-5778
Veterinary Services-646-4613
Chapel-646-5751
Family Services-646-5283
N-MC Relief Society-646-5132
TRICARE-673-5800

REST & RECREATION:
Bowling-646-5048
Clubs
  Consol-646-4867
  EM-646-4127
  Flying-898-3311
  O-646-4529
MWR-646-5135
Swimming-646-5196
Wood Hobby Shop-646-5024
Ceramics-646-5808
Fitness Center-646-5088
Golf Course-646-5736
Gym-646-5161
ITT-646-5164
Library-646-5137
Sailing-ext 4492
Water Sports-646-5850

OTHER SUPPORT AVAILABLE: Fire Dept, Housing Office, Pass/ID Office.

ATTRACTIONS: The playground of Florida, Disney World, Busch Gardens, Cypress Gardens, Sea World, Epcot Center, Universal Studios, Church Street Station.

PANAMA CITY COASTAL SYSTEMS STATION, NAVAL SURFACE WARFARE CENTER (FL35R1)

6703 West Highway 98
Panama City, FL 32407-7001

TELEPHONE NUMBER INFORMATION: Main installation numbers: C-850-234-4100, D-312-436-4100.

LOCATION: Located on US-98 at the foot of the Hathaway Bridge in Panama City Beach. USMRA: Page 39 (D,E-14). NMC: Panama City, adjacent.

GENERAL INFORMATION: The Station is a Navy Research and Development Laboratory responsible for coastal and harbor defense activities.

TEMPORARY MILITARY LODGING: BEQ, Building 304, C-850-234-4756, BOQ, Building 349, C-850-234-4556, 24 hours daily. DV/VIP (Officers) C-850-234-5464, D-312-436-5464.

RV, CAMPING/FAMCAMP: Operates Panama City CSS Outdoor Rec/Marina on base; see listing for more information.

SPACE-A: None. See Pensacola NAS listing, C-850-452-3311/2431, D-312-922-3311, Fax: C-850-452-2512.

LOGISTICAL SUPPORT: Exchange-235-2778

ADMINISTRATIVE SUPPORT: Police-234-4332

HEALTH & WELFARE: Medical-234-4177

REST & RECREATION: Fitness Center-234-4370

ATTRACTIONS: Beaches, water sports.

FLORIDA

PANAMA CITY CSS OUTDOOR RECREATION/MARINA (FL07R1)

MWR, 6703 W Highway 98
Panama City Coastal Systems Station, FL 32408-5000

TELEPHONE NUMBER INFORMATION: Main installation numbers: C-850-234-4100, D-312-436-4100.

LOCATION: On base. Located on US-98 at the foot of the Hathaway Bridge in Panama City Beach. USMRA: page 39 (D,E-14). NMC: Panama City, adjacent.

GENERAL INFORMATION: Panama City Beach is considered one of the world's most beautiful beaches because of the brilliant white sand and emerald waters of the Gulf of Mexico. Operated by Panama City Coastal Systems Station, Naval Surface Warfare Center, on base 1 Apr-31 Oct, Mon-Thu, 0900-1800; Fri-Sun, Holidays, 0700-1900; 1 Nov-31 Mar, Mon-Fri, 0900-1700. Military personnel active, retired, reserve, DoD civilians at Coastal Systems Station. Check in at marina, check out 1200. Reservations: Accepted 6 months in advance. For campers/boats, call the Marina, C-850-234-4402 or write to address above. List dates/times of arrival. A deposit of 50% is required. Fax: C-850-234-4334. Visa, MasterCard and American Express accepted. Pets allowed on leash, except in mobile homes. No firearms allowed. Campfires are not permitted on sites.

TEMPORARY MILITARY LODGING: Park model mobile home, one bedroom includes linens (3). Rates: Military $35 daily, $45 DoD civilian.

RV, CAMPING/FAMCAMP: Hardstand camper spaces with full hookups (29); wet boat slips (13); dry boat slips (35). Rates: camper spaces-Military $10 daily/$250 monthly, DoD civilian $15 daily/$300 monthly; wet boat slip-Military $70 monthly, DoD civilian $85 monthly; dry boat slip-Military $35 monthly, DoD civilian $45 monthly.

ADMINISTRATIVE SUPPORT: Police-234-4373

OTHER SUPPORT & FACILITIES AVAILABLE: Beach, Boat Ramp, Boat Rental, Camping Equipment, Consolidated Mess, Exchange, Gas, Grills, Grocery/nearby, Gym, Ice, Laundry/nearby, Marina, Pavilions, Picnic Area, Playground, Racquetball, Restrooms, Showers, Sports Equipment, Sports FielD, Swimming Pool, Tennis Courts, Trails.

REST & RECREATION: Bicycling, Boating, Fishing, Horseshoes, Picnicking, Rec Equipment, Sailing, Scuba Diving, Snorkeling, Swimming, Tours, Water Skiing.

ATTRACTIONS: Water sports (jet skiing, sailing, boating, swimming, etc).

PATRICK AIR FORCE BASE (FL03R1)

1201 Minuteman Street, Suite C-133
Patrick Air Force Base, FL 32925-3237

TELEPHONE NUMBER INFORMATION: Main installation numbers: C-407-494-1110, D-312-854-1110.

LOCATION: Take I-95 south to exit 73 (Wickham Road), three miles to FL-404 (Pineda Causeway), left on South Patrick Drive to Patrick AFB. USMRA: Page 38 (I-8) NMC: Orlando, 45 miles northwest.

GENERAL INFORMATION: Air Force Space Command Base, 45th Space Wing, support to DoD and NASA.

TEMPORARY MILITARY LODGING: Billeting Office, Building 720, 820 Falcon Avenue, 24 hours daily, C-407-494-6570, D-312-854-7597. All ranks. DV/VIP-407-494-4506.

RV, CAMPING/FAMCAMP: Manatee Cove Campground on base, year round, C-407-494-4787, D-312-854-4787, 56 camper spaces with W/E, five spaces without hookups.

SPACE-A: Pax Term/Lounge, Building 800, 0730-1630 Mon-Fri, C-407-494-5631, D-312-854-5631, Fax: C-407-494-7991, flights to CONUS and Caribbean locations.

LOGISTICAL SUPPORT:

Child Care-494-7028	Commissary-494-4060
Conv Store-494-4555	Dinette-494-4248
Exchange-799-1300	Gas Station-494-2655
Package Store-494-6686	SATO-494-4155
Snack Bar-494-5614	Visitor Center-494-2659

ADMINISTRATIVE SUPPORT:

Fire Department-494-7642	Legal-494-7357
Locator-494-4542	Police-494-2008
Public Affairs-494-5933	SDO/NCO-494-7001

HEALTH & WELFARE:

CHAMPUS-494-8112	Chapel-494-4073
Family Services-494-4907	Medical-494-8229
Retiree Services-494-5464	Central Appts-494-8134
	Emergency-494-8134

REST & RECREATION:

Auto Hobby Shop-ext 2537	Bowling-ext 2958
Clubs	Golf Course-494-7856
Aero-ext 4356	Gym-ext 6697
EM-494-7491	Hobby Shops-ext 2482
NCO-494-7491	ITT-494-5158
O-494-4011	Library-ext 6881
MWR-494-8382	Recreation-853-1287
Rec Center-ext 5523	Skeet-ext 4787
Swimming-ext 6796	Theater-494-2057
Youth Center-ext 4747	

ATTRACTIONS: Air Force Space Museum, John F. Kennedy Space Center, Disney World, Daytona Beach, Epcot Center, Spaceport USA, Sea World.

PENSACOLA NAVAL AIR STATION (FL14R1)

190 Radford Boulevard
Pensacola Naval Air Station, FL 32508-5217

TELEPHONE NUMBER INFORMATION: Main installation numbers: C-850-452-0111, D-312-922-0111.

LOCATION: Four miles south of US-98, and 12 miles south of I-10. Take Navy Blvd from US-98 or US-29 directly to NAS. USMRA: Page 39 (A,B-13,14), page 53 (A,B-4,5). NMC: Pensacola, eight miles north.

GENERAL INFORMATION: Chief of Naval Education & Training, Naval Aviation Schools Command, home of Navy Blue Angels, Navy Public Works Center, Naval Air Technical Training Center.

TEMPORARY MILITARY LODGING: Lodging office, 24 hours daily, Building 600, C-850-452-2756, D-312-922-2756, Fax: C-850-452-3188. Navy Lodge C-800-628-9466.

RV, CAMPING/FAMCAMP: Oak Grove Park on base, year round, C-850-452-2535, D-312-922-2535, 0800-1630 (winter), 0830-1700 (summer), 12 cabins, 42 camper spaces with W/E hookups, 15 tent sites.

SPACE-A: Pax Term/Lounge, Building 1852, 0600-2100 daily, C-850-452-3311, D-312-922-3311, Fax: C-850-452-2512, flights to CONUS locations.

LOGISTICAL SUPPORT:

Bank-453-3411	Barber Shop-458-3339
Beauty Shop-458-3328	Cafeteria-458-3271
Child Care-452-4569	Child Dev Center-452-2211
Commissary-452-6889	Conv Store-453-3356
Credit Union-453-4341	Dry Cleaner-458-3275
Education Office-452-4119	Exchange-458-3317
Gas Station-458-3220	Laundry-458-3275
Omega-453-8922	Package Store-455-3356
Postal Service-452-2627	SATO-452-2589
Shoppette-458-3356	Snack Bar-452-3899
Travel Office-453-8922	Visitor Center-452-4412

ADMINISTRATIVE SUPPORT:

CDO/OOD-452-2353	Fire Dept-452-2896
Housing Office-452-4412	Legal-452-4321
Locator-452-0111	Pass/ID Office-452-4153
Police-452-2453	Public Affairs-452-2311
Quarter Deck-452-2353	

HEALTH & WELFARE:

American Red Cross-452-2492	CHAMPUS-452-6711
Chapel-452-2341	Dental-452-5616
Family Services-452-5990	Central Appts-452-5600
Medical-452-5662	N-MC Relief Society-452-2492
Central Appts-452-5242	Retiree Services-452-5991
Clinic-452-5242	TRICARE-457-7878
Emergency-452-4138	Veterinary Services-452-3530
Health Benefits-452-6711	
Hospital-452-5242	
Information-452-5242	

REST & RECREATION:

Auto Hobby Shop-452-2039	Beach-ext 4391
Bowling-ext 4630	Clubs
Fitness Center-452-2317	EM-452-4357
Golf Course-452-2454	NCO-452-2443
Gym-452-2317	O-455-2276/8860
Indoor Rec-452-2317	ITT-452-4229
Library-452-4362	Marinas-452-3369
MWR-452-3806	Outdoor Rec-452-4931
Sailing-ext 3369	Services-458-3356
Wood Hobby Shop-452-2039	Swimming 452-8293
Youth Center-452-2417	Youth Services-452-2417

ATTRACTIONS: Sport fishing, water sports, golf, National Museum of Naval Aviation, Fiesta of Five Flags, Fort Pickens, Fort Barrancas, annual Blue Angels Marathon, annual Blue Angels Homecoming Air Show (Nov).

PENSACOLA NAVAL HOSPITAL (FL20R1)

6000 West Highway 98
Pensacola, FL 32512-0003

TELEPHONE NUMBER INFORMATION: Main installation numbers: C-850-505-6601, D-312-534-6601. HP: http://www.pcnh-srv.medweb.navy.mil.

LOCATION: On US-98 between Navy Blvd and Fairfield Drive in Pensacola. USMRA: Page 39 (A,B-13), page 53 (B-4). NMC: Pensacola, in city limits.

GENERAL INFORMATION: The Naval Hospital, built in 1976, supports four naval training bases and has four branch medical clinics in the area. Also has four other branch medical clinics it supports at Panama City, Florida, Pascagoula, Gulfport and Meridian, Mississippi.

TEMPORARY MILITARY LODGING: None. See Pensacola NAS listing, BOQ C-850-452-2756, D-312-922-2756, Fax: 904-452-3188 and Whiting Field NAS, C-850-623-7605/6, D-312-868-7605/6.

RV, CAMPING/FAMCAMP: None. See Pensacola NAS listing, Oak Grove Trailer Park, C-850-452-2535, D-312-922-2535.

SPACE-A: None. See Pensacola NAS listing, C-850-452-3311, D-312-922-3311.

LOGISTICAL SUPPORT:

Conv Store-455-9649	Snack Bar-455-6267

ADMINISTRATIVE SUPPORT:

CDO-505-6601	Legal-505-6844
OOD-505-6604	Public Affairs-505-6796
Quarter Deck-505-6601	

HEALTH & WELFARE:

CHAMPUS-505-6709	Chapel-505-6481
Medical	TRICARE-457-7878
Emergency-505-6730/1/88	
Health Benefits-505-6709	
Information-505-6601	

REST & RECREATION: None. See Pensacola NAS (C-850-452-3806) and Corry NTTC (C-850-452-6568) listings.

OTHER SUPPORT AVAILABLE: Dining Facilities, Postal Service.

ATTRACTIONS: The Blue Angels, beaches, fishing.

ST PETERSBURG COAST GUARD GROUP/STATION (FL33R1)

600 8th Avenue SE
St. Petersburg, FL 33701-5030

TELEPHONE NUMBER INFORMATION: Main installation numbers: C-813-824-7638, 1-800-732-6864.

LOCATION: Take I-275 to I-175 east, exit 9, right to Group/Station. Located adjacent to Albert Whitted Airport. USMRA: Page 38 (E-8), page 54 (D-5). NMC: St Petersburg, in city limits.

TEMPORARY MILITARY LODGING: None. See MacDill AFB listing, C-813-828-2661, D-312-968-4259.

RV, CAMPING/FAMCAMP: None. See MacDill AFB listing, Coon's Creek Rec Area, C-813-840-6919, 800-821-4982, Fax: C-813-828-7507.

SPACE-A: None. See MacDill AFB listing, C-813-828-2310, D-312-968-2310, Fax: C-813-828-3202.

FLORIDA
St Petersburg Coast Guard Group/Station, continued

LOGISTICAL SUPPORT:
Barber Shop-896-2816
Galley-824-7651
Package Store-896-2816
Exchange-896-2816
Minimart-824-7667
SDO/NCO-824-7501

ADMINISTRATIVE SUPPORT:
CDO/OOD-824-7519
Police-825-7599
Locator-824-7506
Public Affairs-824-7564

HEALTH & WELFARE:
CHAMPUS-824-7579
Family Services-824-7684
Retiree Services-824-7504
Chapel-823-3454
Medical-824-7579
  Emergency-824-7579

REST & RECREATION:
Clubs
  All Hands-824-7658
  Consol-824-7658
  CPO/O' Club-824-7582
MWR-824-7598

OTHER FACILITIES AVAILABLE: Swimming pool with picnic area.

ATTRACTIONS: Close to beaches, boating, fishing, skin diving, scuba diving, snorkeling, water skiing, St Petersburg sights, professional sports (NHL Tampa Bay Lightning, NFL Tampa Bay Buccaneers, MLB -in 1998- Tampa Bay Devil Rays), MLB spring training, minor league baseball, Salvador Dali Museum.

SAUFLEY FIELD (FL34R1)

NETPDTC
6490 Saufley Field Road
Pensacola, FL 32509-5237

TELEPHONE NUMBER INFORMATION: Main installation numbers: C-850-452-1628, D-312-922-1628.

LOCATION: From I-10 take exit 2 to FL-297 (Pine Forest Road) south to a right onto Blue Angel Parkway south then take a right onto Saufley Field Road to main gate of base. USMRA: Page 39 (A,B-13), page 53 (A,B-3). NMC: Pensacola, in the city.

GENERAL INFORMATION: Host unit at Saufley Field is the Naval Education and Training Professional Development and Technology Center (NETPDTC). Tenant units include the Defense Activity for Non-Traditional Education Support (DANTES), Federal Prison Camp, Finance and Accounting Service Center, Naval Reserve Center, and other minor units.

TEMPORARY MILITARY LODGING: None. See Pensacola NAS listing, C-850-452-2756, D-312-922-2756, Fax: C-850-452-3188.

RV, CAMPING/FAMCAMP: None. See Pensacola NAS listing, Oak Grove Trailer Park, C-850-452-2535, D-312-922-2535.

SPACE-A: None. See Pensacola NAS listing, C-850-452-3311, D-312-922-3311, Fax: C-850-452-2512.

LOGISTICAL SUPPORT: None. See Pensacola NAS listing, C-850-452-0111.

ADMINISTRATIVE SUPPORT:
CDO-452-1628
MSO-452-1519

HEALTH & WELFARE:
Chapel-452-1655
Medical
  Emergency-452-3333
Dental-452-5600

REST & RECREATION:
CMO Club-452-1556
Gym-ext 1071
  Handball
  Racquetball
  Tennis
Golf Course-ext 1097
Services-452-1071 (Corry Annex)

ATTRACTIONS: Gulf Islands National Seashore (Fort Pickens, Fort Barrancas, Fort Barrancas Advanced Redoubt), Naval Museum of Aviation.

SHADES OF GREEN™ ON WALT DISNEY WORLD® RESORT (FL49R1)

P.O. Box 22789
Lake Buena Vista, FL 32830-2789

TELEPHONE NUMBER INFORMATION: Main installation number: C-407-824-3400.

LOCATION: From Orlando take I-4 west, exit 26B, Walt Disney World®, follow Magic Kingdom Resort signs, go through Magic Kingdom toll booth, stay in far right lane following signs to resort and hotels, at first light turn left, Seven Seas Drive past Polynesian Resort, come to three way stop, turn right on Floridian Way, driveway is first road to the left, Magnolia Palm Drive. USMRA: Page 38 (G-7), page 53 (A-2). NMC: Orlando, 15 miles northeast.

GENERAL INFORMATION: The Army announced on November 3, 1993 that it had leased the Disney Inn at Walt Disney World® in Lake Buena Vista, Florida, to serve as an Armed Forces Rec Center (AFRC). The Disney Inn was renamed "Shades of Green™ on Walt Disney World® Resort." It is very popular with families because of its large rooms and easy access to transportation to various parts of Disney World. Season of Operation: Year round. Military personnel, active, retired, Guard & Reserve, family members and DoD employees. Reservations: Required; make reservations by calling (407) 824-3600 or Fax C-(407) 824-3665. You may also write for reservation and information packet. Visa, MasterCard, American Express, Diners and Discover accepted. No pets allowed. Kennel facilities available through Disney.

TEMPORARY MILITARY LODGING: Deluxe rooms with two queen-size beds, sofa bed, private bath (287); Suite with two queen-size beds, sofa bed, private bath (1). Rates: E1-5 $57; E6-9, O1-3, WO1-CW3, GS1-10, NF1-3 $81; O4-6, CW4-5, GS11-15, NF4-5 $89; O7-10, foreign military, Retired DoD civilians, NF6 $95. Rates are for double occupancy. Single occupancy subtract $2. There will be an added charge of $10 per additional adult above two per room.

LOGISTICAL SUPPORT:
Car Rental-824-3600
Gift Shop-824-3400
Travel Office-824-3600
Dining Facility-824-3574
  Garden Gallery Restaurant/
  Evergreens Sport Bar & Grill

REST & RECREATION: AAFES Gift Shop, Children's Play Area, Fitness Center, Golf Course, Laundry Facilities, Swimming Pool (2), Tennis Courts (2), Toddler Pool.

ATTRACTIONS: A child's dream come true, a visit to Walt Disney World®, Epcot Center and Disney MGM Studios Theme Park. Located on the Magic Kingdom Resort area with transportation available to all Walt Disney World® attractions. Shades of Green™ lies directly adjacent to two PGA Championship Golf Courses, home of the Walt Disney World®/Oldsmobile Golf Classic. If that is not enough to keep you busy, there is golf, swimming, and tennis all without leaving the resort.

TYNDALL AIR FORCE BASE (FL04R1)

445 Suwannee Road, Building 662, Suite 101
Tyndall Air Force Base, FL 32403-5541

TELEPHONE NUMBER INFORMATION: Main installation number: C-850-283-1110. HP: http://www.tyndall.af.mil.

FLORIDA
Tyndall Air Force Base, continued

LOCATION: Take I-10, exit to US-231 south to US-98 east. Clearly marked. USMRA: Page 39 (E-14). NMC: Panama City, 10 miles northwest.

GENERAL INFORMATION: Air Education and Training Command Base, 325th Fighter Wing, 1st Air Force Headquarters Southeast Air Defense Sector, Headquarters USAF Civil Engineering Support Agency, 475th Weapons Evaluation Group.

TEMPORARY MILITARY LODGING: Billeting Office, Building 1329, C-850-283-4210/4211. All ranks. DV/VIP C-850-283-2232.

RV, CAMPING/FAMCAMP: FAMCAMP on base, year round, C-850-283-2798, D-312-523-2798, three cottages, 76 camper spaces with full hookups, 14 camper spaces with W/E, eight tent spaces.

SPACE-A: Base Ops, Building 149, C-850-283-4244, D-523-4244. Also see Pensacola NAS listing.

LOGISTICAL SUPPORT:

Barber Shop-286-4300	Child Care-283-2266
Child Dev Center-283-4747	Commissary-283-4825
Conv Store-286-5804	Credit Union-769-9999
Dining Facilities-283-2239	Education Office-283-4285
Exchange-283-4110	Gas Station-286-5826
Package Store-286-5886	Postal Service-283-2366
SATO-283-2581	Shoppette-286-5852
Snack Bar-283-2814	Travel Office-283-3177
Visitor Center-283-3860	

ADMINISTRATIVE SUPPORT:

Command Post-283-2115	Fire Dept-283-4777
Housing Office-283-2706	Legal-283-4681
Locator-283-2138/4210	Pass/ID Office-283-4191
Police-283-2254	Public Affairs-283-2983
SDO/NCO-283-4145	

HEALTH & WELFARE:

Air Force Aid Society-283-4205	American Red Cross-283-2770
CHAMPUS-283-3883	Chapel-283-2925
Dental	Family Services-283-2963
Central Appts-283-7572	Medical
Clinic-283-7579	Central Appts-283-2778
Retiree Services-283-2737	Emergency-911
TRICARE-283-7168	Hospital-283-7515
Veterinary Services-283-2434	Information-283-7583

REST & RECREATION:

Arts & Crafts-283-4511	Auto Hobby Shop-283-4542
Bowling-283-2380	Clubs
Community Center-283-2495	Flying-283-2495
Golf Course-286-2565	NCO/EM-283-4146
Gym-283-2631	O-286-5171
ITT-283-2230	Library-283-4287
Marinas-286-9911	MWR-283-2501
Outdoor Rec-283-4473	Swimming-283-2495
Tennis-283-2495	Theater-283-2594
Wood Hobby Shop-283-2594	Youth Center-283-4366
Youth Services-283-2517	

ATTRACTIONS: Panama City and beautiful white sand beaches.

WHITING FIELD NAVAL AIR STATION (FL05R1)

7550 USS Essex Street
Milton, FL 32570-6155

TELEPHONE NUMBER INFORMATION: Main installation numbers: C-850-623-7011, D-312-868-7011.

LOCATION: From US-90 east exit, FL-87 north for eight miles to NAS. USMRA: Page 39 (B-13). NMC: Pensacola, 30 miles southwest.

GENERAL INFORMATION: Naval Aviation Training, fixed- and rotary-wing aircraft.

TEMPORARY MILITARY LODGING: Lodging office, Building 2942, 24 hours daily, C-850-623-7605/6, D-312-868-7605/6. All ranks. DV/VIP C-850-623-7201/7605.

RV, CAMPING/FAMCAMP: None. See Pensacola NAS listing, Oak Grove Trailer Park, C-850-452-2535, D-312-922-2535.

SPACE-A: None. See Pensacola NAS listing, C-850-452-3311, D-312-922-3311, Fax: C-850-452-2521.

LOGISTICAL SUPPORT:

Child Care-623-7472	Commissary-623-7131
Exchange-623-8066	Gas Station-623-8088
Package Store-623-7198	

ADMINISTRATIVE SUPPORT:

CDO/OOD-623-7437	Fire Dept-623-7331
Legal-623-7231	Locator-623-7437
Police-623-7431/2	Public Affairs-623-7651

HEALTH & WELFARE:

CHAMPUS-623-7657	Chapel-623-7211
Chapel-623-7395	Family Services-623-7234
Medical-623-7151	Retiree Services-623-7177

REST & RECREATION:

Boat Dock-623-2383	Bowling-623-7545
Consol Club-623-7311	Fitness Center-623-7412
Golf Course/Pro Shop-623-7348	Gym-623-7798
Hobby Shop-623-7445	Library-623-7274
MWR-623-7221	Racquetball-623-7412
Recreation-623-7502	

ATTRACTIONS: Deep sea fishing, hunting, water sports, golf, dog races, stock car racing, Pensacola Symphony Orchestra.

Other Installations in Florida

Cortez Coast Guard Station (FL46R1), 4530 124th Street, Court West, Cortez, FL 34215-9999. USMRA: Page 39 (E,F-9). C-941-794-1262, Exchange-795-2805.
Fort Myers Beach Coast Guard Station (FL47R1), 719 San Carlos Drive, Fort Myers, FL 33931-2221. USMRA: Page 39 (F,G-11). C-941-463-5754. Exchange-463-3009.
Jupiter Coast Guard Station (FL48R1), US-1, Lighthouse Park, Jupiter, FL 33469-5000. USMRA: Page 39 (J-10). C-561-746-5402. Exchange-746-5402.
Mayport Coast Guard Base (FL44R1), 4200 Ocean Street, Mayport, FL 32267-0385. USMRA: Page 38 (H-3), page 50 (F-3). C-904-247-7301. Exchange-247-8737/8.
New Smyrna Beach Coast Guard Station (FL50R1), 2999 North Peninsula Avenue, New Smyrna Beach, FL 32169-0370. USMRA: Page 38 (I-6). C-904-428-9085. Exchange-427-2786.
Panama City Coast Guard Station (FL43R1), 1700 Thomas Drive, Panama City, FL 32407-5898. USMRA: Page 39 (D-14). C-850-234-2475. See Panama City Coastal Systems Station for full range of support.
Sand Key Coast Guard Station (FL16R1), 1375 Gulf Boulevard, Clearwater, FL 34630-5000. USMRA: Page38 (E-8). C-813-596-8540. Exchange-596-8744.

GEORGIA

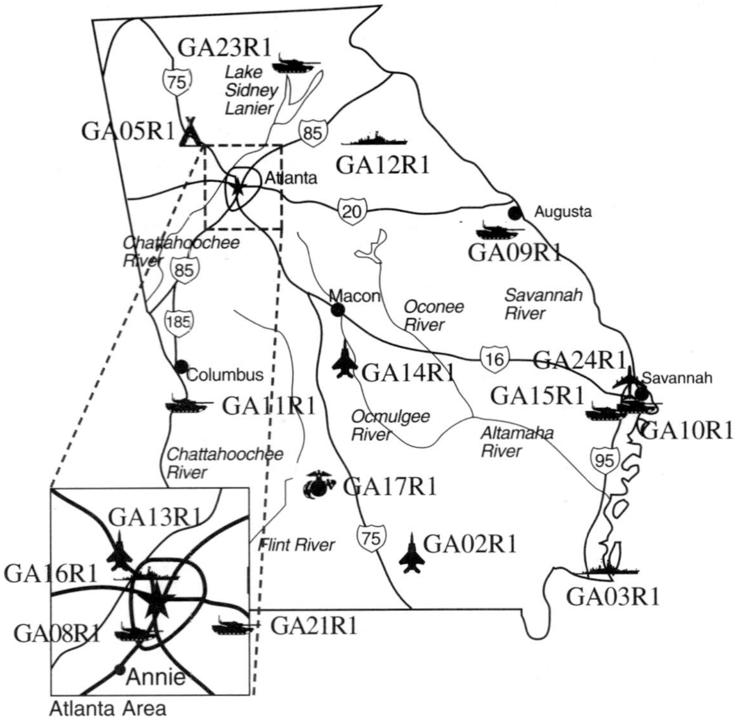

ALBANY MARINE CORPS LOGISTICS BASE (GA17R1)

814 Radford Boulevard
Albany, GA 31704-1128

TELEPHONE NUMBER INFORMATION: Main installation numbers: C-912-439-5000, D-312-567-5000.

LOCATION: Off US-82, take Mock Road south from 5-Points to Fleming Road. Go east to main gate. USMRA: Page 37 (C-8). NMC: Albany, three miles west.

GENERAL INFORMATION: The East Coast main Marine Corps Logistics Base.

TEMPORARY MILITARY LODGING: Housing office, Building 3600, 0800-1630 daily. C-912-439-5614, D-312-567-5614.

RV, CAMPING/FAMCAMP: None. See Moody AFB listing, Grassy Pond Rec Area, C-912-559-5840, D-312-460-5840.

SPACE-A: None. See Moody AFB listing, C-912-257-2465, D-312-460-2465.

LOGISTICAL SUPPORT:
Child Care-439-5247
Conv Store-435-8352
Gas Station-436-8352
Omega Travel-435-1946
Commissary-435-1721
Exchange-888-6801
Package Store-888-6801
Snack Bar-432-2759

ADMINISTRATIVE SUPPORT:
Legal-439-5212
Police-439-5181
Locator-439-5000/5206
SDO/NCO-439-5206

HEALTH & WELFARE:
CHAMPUS-435-5544
Family Services-439-5276
Chapel-439-5282
Medical
  Central Appts-435-5984
  Emergency-435-0806

REST & RECREATION:
Bowling-ext 5233
Covella Pond Picnic Area-ext 5234
Golf Course-ext 5211
Gym-ext 5246
Hobby Shops-ext 5226
Library-ext 5242
Swimming-ext 5234
Clubs
  NCO-439-5223
  O-439-5239
  Rod/Gun Club-ext 5000
  SNCO-439-5197
Skeet Range-ext 5234
Theater-439-5166

ATTRACTIONS: MCLB Band, Wildlife Refuge, Tallahassee, FL, easy drive south.

ATHENS NAVAL SUPPLY CORPS SCHOOL (GA12R1)

1425 Prince Avenue
Athens, GA 30606-2205

TELEPHONE NUMBER INFORMATION: Main installation numbers: C-706-354-1500, D-312-588-1500.

LOCATION: From Atlanta, take I-85 north to highway 316, east to Athens perimeter loop. Follow loop west to Prince Avenue exit, left onto Prince Avenue. Base is on the right. USMRA: Page 37 (D-3), page 49 (A-1). NMC: Atlanta, 70 miles west.

GENERAL INFORMATION: Navy Supply Corps School, Personnel Support Detach.

TEMPORARY MILITARY LODGING: Lodging office, Brown Hall, 0800-1600 daily, BEQ/BOQ/DV/VIP C-706-354-7360, D-312-588-7360, Fax: C-706-354-7360.

RV, CAMPING/FAMCAMP: None. See Fort Gordon listing, C-706-541-1057, Fax: C-706-541-1963.

SPACE-A: None. See Atlanta NAS listing, C-770-919-6359, D-312-925-6359.

LOGISTICAL SUPPORT:
Child Care-543-6113
Conv Store-354-8761
Gas Station-354-8761
SATO-354-7369
Commissary-354-7371
Exchange-354-3850
Package Store-354-8761

ADMINISTRATIVE SUPPORT:
CDO/OOD-354-1500
Public Affairs-354-7316
Police-354-7355

HEALTH & WELFARE:
CHAMPUS-354-7321
Medical-354-7321
Chapel-354-7208
Retiree Services-354-7335

REST & RECREATION:
Clubs
  CPO-354-7381
  O-354-7381
Recreation-354-7374
Tennis-ext 7205
Gym-ext 7377
Library-ext 7217
MWR-354-7363
Swimming-ext 7300

ATTRACTIONS: Athens, University of Georgia, Naval Supply Corps Museum.

ATLANTA NAVAL AIR STATION (GA16R1)

1000 Halsey Avenue
Marietta, GA 30060-5099

TELEPHONE NUMBER INFORMATION: Main installation numbers: C-770-919-6392, D-312-925-6392.

GEORGIA
Atlanta Naval Air Station, continued

LOCATION: From I-75, take exit 111 Windy Hill. Proceed west on Windy Hill to Atlanta Road. Take right, north on Atlanta Road to Richardson Road. Take right, east. Main Gate on left. USMRA: Page 37 (B-3), page 49 (A-1). NMC: Atlanta, 15 miles southeast.

GENERAL INFORMATION: Navy and Marine Corps tactical aircraft and crew training, training and administration of Naval Reservists.

RV, CAMPING/FAMCAMP: World Famous Navy Lake Site, off base, C-770-974-6309, nine cabins, one camper with W/E, 10 camper spaces with W/E hookups, two camper spaces without hookups, three tent spaces.

TEMPORARY MILITARY LODGING: Lodging office, Building 54, 24 hours daily. Very limited. BEQ/BOQ/DV/VIP C-770-919-6393, D-312-925-6393.

SPACE-A: C-770-919-6359, D-312-925-6359.

LOGISTICAL SUPPORT:

Child Care-919-6590	Exchange-428-1274
Gas Station-427-4400	Package Store-419-0776
SATO-424-3909	Visitor Center-919-6735

ADMINISTRATIVE SUPPORT:

CDO/OOD-919-6392	Legal-919-6396
Police-919-6394	Public Affairs-919-6406/6241

HEALTH & WELFARE:

CHAMPUS-919-5314	Chapel-919-6472
Family Services-919-6735	Medical-919-5300
Retiree Services-919-6735	Central Appts-919-5302
	Emergency-919-5304

REST & RECREATION:

Clubs	ITT-919-6499
CPO-919-6508	Quality of Life-919-6510
NCO-919-6508	Auto Hobby Shop
O-919-6508	Bowling
	Fitness Center
	Flying Club

ATTRACTIONS: Atlanta, Stone Mountain State Park, Six Flags Over Georgia, and other attractions are within 30 miles of NAS.

CAMP FRANK D. MERRILL (GA23R1)

Wahsega Road
Dahlonega, GA 30533-9499

TELEPHONE NUMBER INFORMATION: Main installation numbers: C-706-864-3327, D-312-797-5770.

LOCATION: From GA 400 take Highway 60 north to Dahlonega, follow 60 and US 19 approximately three miles take left on Wahsega Rd. Camp is approximately nine miles. USMRA: Page 37 (C-2). NMC: Gainesville 25 miles south.

GENERAL INFORMATION: Mountain training phase of Ranger School.

TEMPORARY MILITARY LODGING: Small lodging facility (two units), C-706-864-3327 ext-187. All ranks. (Can be bumped by incoming assigned duty status personnel)

RV, CAMPING/FAMCAMP: None. See Dobbins ARB listing, C-770-919-4870, D-312-925-4870.

SPACE-A: See Dobbins ARB listing, C-770-919-4903, D-312-925-4903, Fax: C-770-919-5105.

LOGISTICAL SUPPORT:

Commissary-ext-109	Exchange-ext-188

ADMINISTRATIVE SUPPORT:

Fire Dept-ext-130	Public Affairs-ext-102
SDO-864-3327	

HEALTH & WELFARE:

CHAMPUS-ext-189	Medical-ext-189
	Clinic-864-3327
	Emergency-864-6136

REST & RECREATION:

All Ranks Club-ext-158	Sauna-ext 126

OTHER FACILITIES AVAILABLE: Gym, Horseshoe Ring, Outdoor Grills, Picnic Areas, Racquetball, Swimming Pool.

ATTRACTIONS: Old gold mining town of Dahlonega-site of first gold rush, Blue Ridge Mountains, State parks, Appalachian Trail, North Georgia College-formerly a military college-built in 1873, abundant opportunity for hunting and fishing. One hour drive to Atlanta.

DOBBINS AIR RESERVE BASE (GA13R1)

1492 First Street
Dobbins Air Reserve Base, GA 30069-5010

TELEPHONE NUMBER INFORMATION: Main installation numbers: C-770-919-5000, D-312-925-5000.

LOCATION: From Atlanta take 75 north to the Lockheed/Dobbins Exit (#111) turn right onto Highway 41. Follow signs to Dobbins main gate. USMRA: Page 37 (B-3), Page 49 (A-1). NMC: Atlanta, 16 miles northeast.

GENERAL INFORMATION: Air Reserve Training Base, Headquarters 22nd Air Force (AFRES), 94th Airlift Wing (AFRES).

TEMPORARY MILITARY LODGING: Lodging Office, Dobbins Inn, Building 800, 1295 Barracks Court, 24 hours daily, C-770-919-5185, D-312-925-4783. All ranks. DV/VIP 770-919-4520.

RV, CAMPING/FAMCAMP: Lakeside FAMCAMP on base, year round, C-770-919-4870, D-312-925-4870, 16 camping spaces with W/E hookups.

SPACE-A: Pax Term/Lounge, Building 737, 0700-2300 daily, C-770-919-4903, D-312-925-4903, Fax: C-770-919-5105. Flights to CONUS locations. Reserve units.

LOGISTICAL SUPPORT:

Bank-422-4469	Barber Shop-425-3092
Class Six-428-1122	Credit Union-422-4469
Education Office-919-5043	Exchange-428-3054
SATO-919-4848	Shoppette-428-1122
Travel Office-919-4850/5788	

ADMINISTRATIVE SUPPORT:

Fire Dept-919-4839	Legal-919-5199
Locator-919-5000	Pass/ID Office-919-5738
Police-919-4908	Public Affairs-919-5055
SDO/NCO-919-5000	

HEALTH & WELFARE:

CHAMPUS-919-5305/5314	Chapel-919-4955
Family Services-919-5004	Medical-919-5300
	Emergency-919-5302

REST & RECREATION:

Clubs	Fitness Center-919-4872
Consol-919-4594	ITT-919-6502 (NAS Atlanta)
Flying-919-4870	Gym-919-4872
MWR-919-4870	

GEORGIA
Dobbins Air Reserve Base, continued

ATTRACTIONS: Jimmy Carter Presidential Library, Stone Mountain, Six Flags, Metro Atlanta, Underground Atlanta, Atlanta Braves baseball, Piedmont Park, The Fox Theater, Hight Museum of Art, Atlanta Art Gallery.

FORT BENNING (GA11R1)

U.S. Army Infantry Center
ATTN: ATZB-GC
Fort Benning, GA 31905-5065

TELEPHONE NUMBER INFORMATION: Main installation numbers: C-706-545-2011, D-312-835-2011.

LOCATION: Off I-185 and US-27/280. USMRA: Page 37 (B-6). NMC: Columbus, five miles northwest.

GENERAL INFORMATION: Army Infantry Center and School, Army Infantry Training Brigade, School of the Americas, 75th Ranger Regiment, 29th Infantry Regiment, 36th Engineer Group, 11th Infantry Regiment, 3rd Brigade, 3rd Infantry Division, Ranger Training Brigade, US Army Marksmanship Unit, US Physical Fitness School.

TEMPORARY MILITARY LODGING: Lodging office, Building 399, 24 hours daily. C-706-689-0067, D-312-835-3145. All ranks. DV/VIP 706-545-5724.

RV, CAMPING/FAMCAMP: Uchee Creek Rec Area on post, year round, C-706-545-4053, D-312-835-4053, 22 cabins, 38 camper spaces with full hookups, 27 camper spaces with W/E hookups. Also, operates Destin Army Infantry Center Recreation Area, FL, on Choctawatchee Bay. See Destin Army Infantry Center Recreation Area listing for more information.

SPACE-A: Lawson Army Airfield on post, limited flights via executive Army aircraft, C-706-545-3524, D-312-835-3524.

LOGISTICAL SUPPORT:

Child Care-689-8698	Commissary-544-3663
Conv Store-682-0473	Exchange-682-0826
Gas Station-687-6520	Package Store-687-9674
SATO-682-0622	Snack Bar-687-0349

ADMINISTRATIVE SUPPORT:

Legal-545-3281	Locator-545-5217
Police-545-5222	

HEALTH & WELFARE:

CHAMPUS-544-3401	Chapel-545-2288
Family Services-545-1169	Medical
Retiree Services-545-2715	Central Appts-544-2041
SDO/NCO-545-2218	Emergency-544-1502

REST & RECREATION:

Arts & Crafts-545-4436/3677	Bowling-545-4436/3677
Clubs	Golf Course-687-1940
EM-689-0887	Gym-545-4436/3677
NCO-687-1232	Hobby Shops-545-4436/3677
O-682-1861	Intramural Sports-545-4436/3677
Rod/Gun-545-4436/3677	Library-545-4436/3677
Pool-545-4436/3677	Rec Center-545-4436/3677
Tennis-545-4436/3577	Theater-682-0562
Youth Center-545-4436/3677	

ATTRACTIONS: National Infantry Museum on post, Springer Opera House, Columbus, Callaway Gardens, Pine Mountain, Roosevelt Little White House.

FORT GILLEM (GA21R1)

4705 North Wheeler Drive
Forest Park, GA 30297-5000

TELEPHONE NUMBER INFORMATION: Main installation numbers: C-404-362-7311, D-312-797-7311.

LOCATION: From I-75, east on I-285 to I-675, south to Fort Gillem exit, right to Anvil Block Road, go one-half mile to light at main gate. Fort is five miles from Hartsfield (Atlanta) IAP. USMRA: Page 37 (C-4), page 49 (C-4). NMC: Atlanta, 10 miles northwest.

GENERAL INFORMATION: Subpost of Fort McPherson. Headquarters 1st US Army, 2nd US Army Recruiting Brigade (SW), 3rd CID Region, Army CID Lab, Army and Air Force Exchange Distribution Region, and other tenant agencies.

TEMPORARY MILITARY LODGING: Lodging office, Building 816, Hood Avenue, 0730-1600 Mon-Fri, C-404-363-5410, D-312-797-5410. All ranks. DV/VIP 404-363-5431.

RV, CAMPING/FAMCAMP: None. See Dobbins ARB listing, Lakeside FAMCAMP, C-770-919-4870, D-312-925-4870.

SPACE-A: None. See Dobbins ARB listing, C-770-919-4903, D-312-925-4903, Fax: C-770-919-5105.

LOGISTICAL SUPPORT:

Commissary-363-5126	Exchange-363-5430
Package Store-363-9047	

ADMINISTRATIVE SUPPORT:

Fire Dept-363-5532	Police-363-5981
Public Affairs-464-3392	

HEALTH & WELFARE:

Chapel-362-7395	Family Services-362-7764

REST & RECREATION:

Com Club-363-3830	Gym-ext 5843
Tennis-ext 5853	

ATTRACTIONS: Atlanta Braves, Six Flags, Stone Mountain.

FORT GORDON (GA09R1)

US Army Signal Center
ATTN: ATZH-GC
Building 29808, Chamberlain Avenue
Fort Gordon, GA 30905-5000

TELEPHONE NUMBER INFORMATION: Main installation numbers: C-706-791-0110, D-312-780-0110. HP: http://www.gordon.army.mil.

LOCATION: Between US-78/278 and US-1. Gates are on both US-78 & US-1. USMRA: Page 37 (F-4). NMC: Augusta, 12 miles northeast.

GENERAL INFORMATION: 15th Regimental Signal Brigade, Regimental Noncommissioned Officer Academy, Dwight David Eisenhower Army Medical Center, 63rd Signal Battalion, 67th Signal Battalion, 73rd Ordnance Battalion, 513th Military Intelligence Brigade, Regional Signal Intelligence Operations Center.

TEMPORARY MILITARY LODGING: Lodging office, Griffith Hall, Building 250, Chamberlain Avenue, 0730-2400 daily, C-706-791-2277/3103, D-312-780-2277. Stinson Guest House C-706-793-7160.

RV, CAMPING/FAMCAMP: Recreation Area off base, year round, C-706-541-1057, Fax: C-706-541-1963. Nine cabins, eight mobile homes, one bunk house, 60 camper spaces with full hookups, 30 camper spaces with E, 50 tent spaces.

GEORGIA
Fort Gordon, continued

SPACE-A: May be obtained through the Fort Gordon Operational Support Airlift. C-706-791-6251/2019.

LOGISTICAL SUPPORT:

Bank-771-5960
Beauty Shop
793-0185
793-5070
793-0230
791-8015
Child Care-791-6494
Class Six-793-5366
Conv Store-793-1160
Dining Facilities-791-4507
Anthony's-798-1947
Burger King-793-8542
Burger King-798-1947
Food Court-772-9742
Education Office-791-2000
Gas Station-793-8363
Package Store-793-5366
Postal Service-790-3651
Shoppette-793-7177
Snack Bar-798-2190
Visitor Center-791-3579
Barber Shop
787-7282
791-6516
Book Store-791-7019
Cafeteria-771-6921
Carlson Wagonlit Travel-798-0990
Child Dev Center-791-6494
Commissary-791-2354
Credit Union
798-9869 (on post)
793-0012 (off post)
Dry Cleaner
798-1888
793-0818
Exchange-793-7171
Laundry
798-1888
798-7100
798-9999
Travel Office-798-7966

ADMINISTRATIVE SUPPORT:

CDO-791-4517
Housing Office-791-5116
Legal-791-7812
Public Affairs-791-7003
Fire Dept-791-1201
ID Office-791-1927
Police-791-4380
SDO/NCO-791-4517

HEALTH & WELFARE:

American Red Cross-791-3169
Army Emergency Relief-791-4525
Chapel-791-4683
Family Services-791-6967
Retiree Services-791-2654
TRICARE-1-800-444-5445
ACS-791-3579
CHAMPUS-791-6261
Dental-787-5304
Medical-787-5811
Family Practice Appts-791-7300
Health Benefits-787-6346
Hospital-787-5811
Information-787-5811
Patient Rep-787-4656

REST & RECREATION:

Auto Hobby Shop-791-2390
Clubs
Cafe-771-6921
EM-791-6780
NCO-791-6780
O-791-2205
Golf Courses
Center-791-8319
Gordon Lakes-791-2433
Indoor Pool-791-3034
ITR-798-0990
ITT-798-7956
Libraries
Conrad Tech-791-4605
Eisenhower-787-6763
Woodworth-791-2449
Services-791-2013/2887
Youth Services-791-5104
Bowling
Gordon Lanes-791-3446
Ten Pin Alley-791-5106
Community Activities-791-6491
Fish & Wildlife-ext 5025
Fitness Center-791-6872
Gyms
#1 791-2849
#3 791-2864
#4 791-3692
#5 791-7370
#6 791-6872
MWR-791-4140
Outdoor Rec-791-2390
Rec Center-341-1057
Riding Stables-ext 4864
Theaters
Musical-791-4603
Signal-791-3982

ATTRACTIONS: Augusta Masters Golf Tournament, many golf courses, and historical sites in old Augusta.

FORT McPHERSON (GA08R1)

1386 Troop Row, SW
Fort McPherson, GA 30330-1069

TELEPHONE NUMBER INFORMATION: Main installation numbers: C-404-464-3113, D-312-367-3113. E-mail: ID then @ftmcphsn.army.mil. HP: http://www.mcpherson.army.mil.

LOCATION: Off I-75, take Lakewood Freeway (GA-166), exit west past MARTA Station to main gate. USMRA: Page 49 (B-3). NMC: Atlanta, in city limits.

GENERAL INFORMATION: Headquarters Forces Command, Headquarters Third Army, US Army Reserve Command.

TEMPORARY MILITARY LODGING: Billeting Office, Lodging T-22, 0630-2330 daily. C-770-464-3833/2253, D-312-367-2253/3833. DVQ: C-707-669-6196. All ranks. DV/VIP 404-464-4145.

RV, CAMPING/FAMCAMP: Operates Lake Allatoona Army Recreation Area off post. See Lake Allatoona Army Recreation Area listing for more information.

SPACE-A: None. See Dobbins ARB listing, C-404-919-4903, D-312-925-4903, Fax: C-404-919-5105.

LOGISTICAL SUPPORT:

Child Care-464-3945
Exchange-753-6258
Package Store-753-4537
Commissary-464-2231
Gas Station-753-2114

ADMINISTRATIVE SUPPORT:

Legal-464-2626/3394
SDO/NCO-464-2980/3602
Police-464-3050/HELP
Public Affairs-464-2204

HEALTH & WELFARE:

ACS-464-2475
Chapel-464-3954
Medical-464-2778
Army Clinic-464-3139
Appts-464-2184
Appts-464-2183 (Ret)
CHAMPUS-464-2044
Chapel-464-2004
Retiree Services-464-3219

REST & RECREATION:

Arts & Crafts-ext 2221
Bowling-ext 2479
Golf Course-ext 2178/2078
Library-ext 2665
Tickets-ext 3677/4392
Auto Hobby Shop-ext 2070
Community Club-464-3828
Gym-ext-3034
Rec Center-ext 3677
Youth Center-ext 2763

ATTRACTIONS: Six Flags, Cyclorama, pro sports, Stone Mountain.

FORT STEWART (GA15R1)

3rd Infantry Division (Mech) & Fort Stewart
ATTN: AFZP-GC
Fort Stewart, GA 31314-5000

TELEPHONE NUMBER INFORMATION: Main installation numbers: C-912-767-1110, D-312-870-1110.

LOCATION: On US-84. Accessible from US-17 or I-95. Also GA-119 or GA-144 crosses the post but may be closed occasionally. USMRA: Page 37 (G-7). NMC: Savannah, 35 miles northeast.

GENERAL INFORMATION: Hq 3rd Infantry Division (mechanized).

TEMPORARY MILITARY LODGING: Billeting Office, Building 4951, 0730-2400 daily, C-912-767-8384, D-312-870-8384. Other hours, SDO, Building1, C-912-767-8666. All ranks. DV/VIP 912-767-8610.

GEORGIA
Fort Stewart, continued

RV, CAMPING/FAMCAMP: Holbrook Pond Recreation Area and Campground on post, year round, C-912-767-2717, D-312-870-2717, 20 camper spaces with W/E hookups, 20 camper spaces with W hookups.

SPACE-A: None. See Savannah IAP listing, C-912-964-1941, D-312-860-8210, Fax: C-912-966-8200.

LOGISTICAL SUPPORT:

Bank-368-3332	Barber Shop-876-0934
Beauty Shop-876-2663	Child Care-767-2311
Child Dev Center-767-3202	Commissary-767-1392
Conv Store-876-8434	Credit Union-876-2785
Dry Cleaner-876-7275	Education Office-767-8331
Exchange-876-2850	Gas Station-876-8434
Laundry-876-7275	Package Store-368-5080
Postal Service-368-3380	SATO-767-3642
Shoppette-876-2785	Snack Bar-876-2782
Visitor Center-767-5058	

ADMINISTRATIVE SUPPORT:

Fire Dept-767-1711/8118/8320/911	Housing Office-767-3280
ID Office-767-2277	Legal-767-8809
Locator-767-2862/5058	Pass/Permit Office-767-5032
Police-767-2822	Public Affairs-767-5457
SDO/NCO-767-8666	

HEALTH & WELFARE:

ACS/AER-767-5058/9	American Red Cross-767-2197
Chapel-767-8801	CHAMPUS-767-6015
Family Services-767-8549	Medical-767-5551
Retiree Services-767-5013	Central Appts-767-6609
TRICARE-767-6015	Emergency-767-6666
Veterinary Services-767-2842	Health Benefits-767-6015
	Hospital-767-6557

REST & RECREATION:

Arts & Crafts-368-9003	Archery/Rifle Range-ext 5032
Auto Hobby Shop-767-3527	Bowling-368-9832
Clubs	Community Center-767-2191
Consol-767-2837	Fitness Center-767-3031
Teen-ext 2815	Golf Course-368-2370
Gym-368-9074	ITT-767-4363
Library-767-2828	Music Center-ext 2180
Outdoor Rec-767-2717	Performing Arts-ext 3410
Rec Equip-ext 2988	Skeet-ext 3519
Swimming	Theater-767-7083
Indoor-ext 3034	Wood Hobby Shop-767-2515
Outdoor-ext 8575	Youth Center-767-4491
Youth Services-767-4491	

ATTRACTIONS: Tybee, Jekyll, and St Catherines Islands off coast of Georgia; fishing, beaches, and boating; Savannah and other historic sites; Cumberland Island National Seashore; Okefenokee Swamp National Wildlife Refuge. Hunting and fishing on Fort Stewart.

HUNTER ARMY AIRFIELD (GA10R1)

Army Community Services
ATTN: AFZP-GC, Building 1201
Hunter Army Airfield, GA 31409-5000

TELEPHONE NUMBER INFORMATION: Main installation numbers: C-912-352-5994, D-312-971-5994. E-mail: afzp-poh@stewart-emh4.army.mil.

LOCATION: From I-95 to GA-204 east for 13 miles to Savannah. Turn left onto Stephenson Avenue, to Wilson Avenue Gate to Installation. USMRA: Page 37 (H-7). NMC: Savannah, in southwest part of city.

GENERAL INFORMATION: Aviation Brigade, 3rd Infantry Division (Mechanized), 603rd Support Battalion (Aviation), 559th Quartermaster Battalion, 3/160th Special Operations Aviation Regiment, 1st Battalion, 1/75th Ranger Regiment, 260th Quartermaster Battalion, 224th Military Intelligence Battalion, USCG Air Station Savannah.

TEMPORARY MILITARY LODGING: Lodging office, Building 6010, Duncan & Leonard Street, 0730-2400 Mon-Fri, 0800-1700 Sat, Sun, Holidays, C-912-352-5910/5834, D-312-971-5910/5834, other hours, Building 1201, C-912-352-5140. All ranks. DV/VIP C-912-355-8610, D-312-870-8610.

RV, CAMPING/FAMCAMP: Lotts Island Army/Air Field Travel Camp on post year round, Community Recreation Division (AFZP-PAR), Outdoor Recreation, Building 8454, Hunter Army Airfield, Savannah, GA 31409-5000, C-912-352-5916, D-312-870-5722, 15 camper/tent spaces with W hookups.

SPACE-A: Very Limited. Army Ops, Hunter AAF, limited flights via executive aircraft, C-912-352-5030. Also, Savannah CGAS at Hunter AAF Ops, limited flights, C-912-352-6035.

LOGISTICAL SUPPORT:

Barber Shop-354-9214	Beauty Shop-354-9214
Carlson Wagonlit Travel-353-9295	Child Care-352-6064
Child Dev Center-352-6064	Class Six-354-8752
Commissary-352-5007	Conv Store-354-0075
Credit Union-354-6420	Dining Facility-352-6209
Dry Cleaner-352-5251	Education Office-352-6130
Exchange-352-5336	Laundry-352-5251
Postal Service-352-5587	Shoppette-354-0075

ADMINISTRATIVE SUPPORT:

CDO-352-5425	Fire Dept-352-5684
Housing Office-352-5268	Legal-352-5115
Locator-767-2862	Pass/ID Office-352-6133
Police-352-6133	Public Affairs-352-5994
SDO/NCO-352-5000	

HEALTH & WELFARE:

American Red Cross-352-5410	ACS-352-5259
Army Emergency Relief-352-5301	CHAMPUS-352-5552
Chapel-352-5111	Family Services-352-5259
Medical-352-5551	
Central Appts-352-6100	
Emergency-233-5700	

REST & RECREATION:

Auto Hobby Shop-352-6244	Bowling-352-6279
Combined Club-352-5270	Golf Course-352-5622
Gym-352-5078	ITT-353-9295
Marina-352-5722	Outdoor Rec-352-5722
Theater-352-5556	Youth Center-352-5864
Youth Services-352-2697	

ATTRACTIONS: Historic Savannah, period homes, General Sherman's headquarters, Cotton Exchange, Fort Pulaski and Fort McAllister.

KINGS BAY NAVAL SUBMARINE BASE (GA03R1)

1063 USS Tennessee Avenue
Kings Bay, GA 31547-2606

TELEPHONE NUMBER INFORMATION: Main installation numbers: C-912-673-2000, D-312-573-2111.

LOCATION: Off I-95 north of GA/FL border. Take Exit 1 which leads right into base, or Exits 2A or 2B, east to Kings Bay Road and follow the road north to base. USMRA: Page 37 (G-9). NMC: Jacksonville, FL, 40 miles south.

GEORGIA
Kings Bay Naval Submarine Base, continued

GENERAL INFORMATION: East Coast Submarine Base, Headquarters Submarine Squadron 20. Home of the East Coast Trident submarines and headquarters of Submarine Group 10 Commander.

TEMPORARY MILITARY LODGING: Lodging office, Building 1051-N, James Madison Road, 0800-1630 Mon-Fri, C-912-673-2163, D-312-573-2163. DV/VIP 912-673-2165, Fax: C-912-673-2752. Navy Lodge, Building 0158, C-912-882-6868.

RV, CAMPING/FAMCAMP: None. See Jacksonville NAS, FL listing, C-904-542-3227, D-312-942-3227.

SPACE-A: None. See Jacksonville NAS, FL listing, C-904-542-3956, D-312-942-3956, Fax: C-904-942-2514.

LOGISTICAL SUPPORT:

Cafeteria-882-6229	Child Care*-2043
Commissary-673-3310	Conv Store-882-6944
Exchange-882-6098	Gas Station-882-6945
Package Store*-3104	SATO*-2230
Snack Bar-882-6229	Visitor Center*-2272

ADMINISTRATIVE SUPPORT:

CDO/OOD-673-2020	Fire Dept-673-2263
Legal-673-2025	Locator*-3980
Police-673-2265	Public Affairs-673-4714

HEALTH & WELFARE:

CHAMPUS-673-2928-ext 4228	Chapel-673-4501
Dental-673-4262	Family Services-673-4512
Medical-673-4247/4215	Retiree Services*-4517
Emergency-673-4262	

REST & RECREATION:

Clubs	Golf Course*-8476
CPO*-8999	ITT*-2289
EM*-8999	MWR*-ext 2041
NCO*-ext 8999	Recreation*-8103
O*-8999	

Dial 673-2001 then the number listed.

ATTRACTIONS: Beautiful beaches, sport fishing, hunting, Cumberland Island, and Jekyll and St Simons Islands are one hour drives north.

LAKE ALLATOONA ARMY RECREATION AREA (GA05R1)

Army Recreation Area
40 Old Sandtown Road
Cartersville, GA 30121-5000

TELEPHONE NUMBER INFORMATION: Main installation numbers: C-404-464-3113, D-312-367-3113. Police for rec area, C-404-464-3712.

LOCATION: Located on 85 acre site at Lake Allatoona reservoir. From I-75 north of Atlanta, take exit 122 east. Follow signs for approximately three miles to entrance on left. USMRA: page 37 (B-3). NMC: Atlanta, 43 miles south. NMI: Dobbins ARB and Atlanta NAS, 15 miles south.

GENERAL INFORMATION: Full range of beach and water activities. Operated by Fort McPherson, off post year round. Military personnel active, retired, reserve, NG, and DoD civilians at Fort McPherson and Fort Gillem. Check in 1700 to closing. Reservations: Required for lodging. Active duty at Forts McPherson and Gillem have priority to make reservations during first 10 days of any month and three succeeding months; all others may make reservations for same period after 10th day. C-770-974-3413/9420, Fax: C-770-974-1278. Visa, MasterCard, American Express, Discover and Esprit accepted. No pets allowed. Motorcycles, minibikes, all-terrain vehicles and motor carts prohibited. Open fires within fire rings only. No firearms or fireworks. Fourteen day limit 1 Apr-31 Oct; cabin rentals - two day minimum on weekends (during peak season 1 Mar-30 Sep). Family members under 18 must be accompanied by authorized adult sponsor to use area. Personal VCRs are prohibited. No firearms allowed.

TEMPORARY MILITARY LODGING: Furnished three bedroom apartment, AC, microwave, cable TV, bed linens, pots, pans, dishes and kitchen utensils. Bring towels, extra blankets, can opener, soap, detergent, sharpened knives (3); furnished two bedroom, deluxe cabin, AC, microwave, cable TV, bed linens, pots, pans, dishes and kitchen utensils. Bring towels, extra blankets, can opener, soap, detergent, sharpened knives (5); furnished two bedroom cabin, AC, microwave, cable TV, bed linens, pots, pans, dishes and kitchen utensils. Bring towels, extra blankets, can opener, soap, detergent, sharpened knives (12); furnished one bedroom cabin, AC, microwave, cable TV, bed linens, pots, pans, dishes and kitchen utensils. Bring towels, extra blankets, can opener, soap, detergent, sharpened knives (8). Several two bedroom cabins, and the three bedroom apartments are handicap accessible. Rates: Apartment $75 daily; deluxe two bedroom cabin $63 daily; two bedroom cabin $57 daily; one bedroom cabin $48 daily. Off-season rates available 1 Oct-1 Mar.

RV, CAMPING/FAMCAMP: RV spaces with full hookups (12); tent spaces with W&E hookups (15). Rates: RV spaces $15 daily; tent spaces $10 daily. Off-season rates available 1 Oct-1 Mar.

OTHER SUPPORT & FACILITIES AVAILABLE: Basketball Court, Bath Houses*, Beach, Boat Launch, Fishing Piers, Game Room, Grills, Laundry, Marina, Miniature Golf, Pavilions, Picnic Area, Playgrounds, Restrooms, Sewage Dump, Showers, Trails, Volleyball-Sand Court.

** Handicap accessible.*

REST & RECREATION: Boating, Fishing/license, Horseshoes, Swimming.

ATTRACTIONS: Conveniently situated for sightseeing in Atlanta and surrounding area, including Stone Mountain Memorial State Park and Six Flags. Full range of support facilities available at Fort McPherson and Dobbins AFB in Atlanta.

MOODY AIR FORCE BASE (GA02R1)

5251 Berger Street, Suite 3
Moody Air Force Base, GA 31699-1795

TELEPHONE NUMBER INFORMATION: Main installation numbers: C-912-257-4211, D-312-460-1110.

LOCATION: On GA-125, 10 miles north of Valdosta. Also, can be reached from I-75, via GA-122. USMRA: Page 37 (D,E-9). NMC: Valdosta, 10 miles south.

GENERAL INFORMATION: Air Combat Command Base, 69th Fighter Squadron, 68th Fighter Squadron, 70th Fighter Squadron, 71st Air Control Squadron, 71st Reserve Squadron and 41st Reserve Squadron.

TEMPORARY MILITARY LODGING: Billeting Office, Building 3131, Cooney St, 24 hours daily, C-912-257-3893, D-312-460-3893. All ranks. DV/VIP 912-257-3480.

RV, CAMPING/FAMCAMP: Grassy Pond Rec Area off base, year round, C-912-559-5840, D-312-460-5840, 13 cabins, 18 camper spaces with full hookups, many tent spaces.

SPACE-A: Pax Term, Building 8153, 0700-2300 Mon-Fri, 0800-1600 Sat, Sun, Holidays, C-912-257-2465, D-312-460-2465, flights to CONUS locations. Also see Jacksonville NAS, FL listing.

LOGISTICAL SUPPORT:

Cafeteria-257-3031	Child Care-257-3935
Commissary-257-3365	Conv Store-257-3876
Exchange-257-3431	Gas Station-257-3451
Package Store-257-4166	SATO-257-3307
Snack Bar-257-3093	Theater-257-3557

GEORGIA
Moody Air Force Base, continued

ADMINISTRATIVE SUPPORT:
Command Post-257-3503
Locator-257-3585/3516
Legal-257-3414
Police-257-3200/3108

HEALTH & WELFARE:
CHAMPUS-257-3799
Family Services-257-3333
Retiree Services-257-3315
Chapel-257-3211/3646
Medical-257-2778
Central Appts-257-3816
Clinic-257-3232

REST & RECREATION:
Auto Hobby Shop-ext 3056
Ceramics-ext 3452
Fitness Center-ext 3348
Golf-ext 3297
Library-ext 3539
Swimming-ext 3560/3864
Youth Center-ext 3067
Bowling-ext 3872
Clubs
NCO-257-3794
O-251-3351
Rec Center-ext 3280
Wood Hobby Shop-ext 3452

ATTRACTIONS: Crystal Lake, 40 miles north.

ROBINS AIR FORCE BASE (GA14R1)

215 Page Road, Suite 106
Robins Air Force Base, GA 31098-1662

TELEPHONE NUMBER INFORMATION: Main installation numbers: C-912-926-1113, D-312-468-1001.

LOCATION: Off US-129 on GA-247 at Warner Robins. Access from I-75 S. USMRA: Page 37 (D-6). NMC: Macon, 18 miles northwest.

GENERAL INFORMATION: Air Force Materiel Command Base. Warner Robins Air Logistics Center and AFRC headquarters stationed here.

TEMPORARY MILITARY LODGING: Lodging office, Building 557, Club Drive, 24 hours daily, C-912-926-2100, D-312-468-2100. All ranks. DV/VIP 912-926-2761.

RV, CAMPING/FAMCAMP: FAMCAMP on base at Luna Lake, year round, C-912-926-4500, D-312-468-4500, 16 camper spaces with W/E hookups, 12 tent spaces.

SPACE-A: Pax Term/Lounge, Building 127, 0700-1700 hours daily, C-912-926-3166, D-312-468-3166 Fax: C-912-926-4355, flights to CONUS locations.

LOGISTICAL SUPPORT:
Barber Shop-923-7027
Cafeteria-922-8635
Child Dev Center-936-6349
Commissary-926-2126
Dining Facilities-328-3037
Gas Station-923-7292
Postal Service-936-2127
Shoppette-922-3851
Visitor Center-926-4208
Beauty Shop-923-7027
Child Care-923-6349
Class Six-923-5085
Conv Store-923-5085
Exchange-923-5536
Package Store-926-3142
Bay Area Travel-926-3101
Snack Bars
Bowling Center-936-5240
Rec Center-922-0136
19th Hole-923-1717

ADMINISTRATIVE SUPPORT:
Fire Dept-926-5323/911
Legal-926-3931
Pass Office-936-3583
Public Affairs-926-1748
Housing Office-936-5035
Locator-926-6027
Police-926-2187/1025

HEALTH & WELFARE:
Air Force Aid Society-936-1256
CHAMPUS-926-5004
Dental-936-2691
Medical
Central Appts-936-0195
Emergency-936-3845
Health Benefits-936-5004
American Red Cross-936-5493
Chapel-926-2821
Family Services-926-1256
Retiree Services-926-2019
TRICARE-936-5004
Veterinary Services-936-6116

REST & RECREATION:
Arts & Crafts-936-5282
Clubs
Aero-ext 4867
NCO-923-5581
O-922-3011
ITT-936-2945
MWR-927-0217
Swimming-ext 2105
Youth Center-936-2356
Bowling-936-2112
Community Center-ext 2105
Fitness Center-936-2208
Golf Course-926-4103
Indoor Rec-936-2208
Library-936-5378
Services-936-3135
Theater-926-2919

ATTRACTIONS: Macon, 4th largest city in Georgia, Andersonville Trail, Ocmulgee National Park, Robins AFB Museum of Aviation.

Other Installations in Georgia

Savannah International Airport (GA24R1), 165th (ANG)/P.O. Box 7568, Garden City, GA 31402-5000. Space-A: C-912-964-1941, D-312-860-8201, Fax: C-912-966-8200.

* * * * * *NOTES* * * * * *

HAWAII

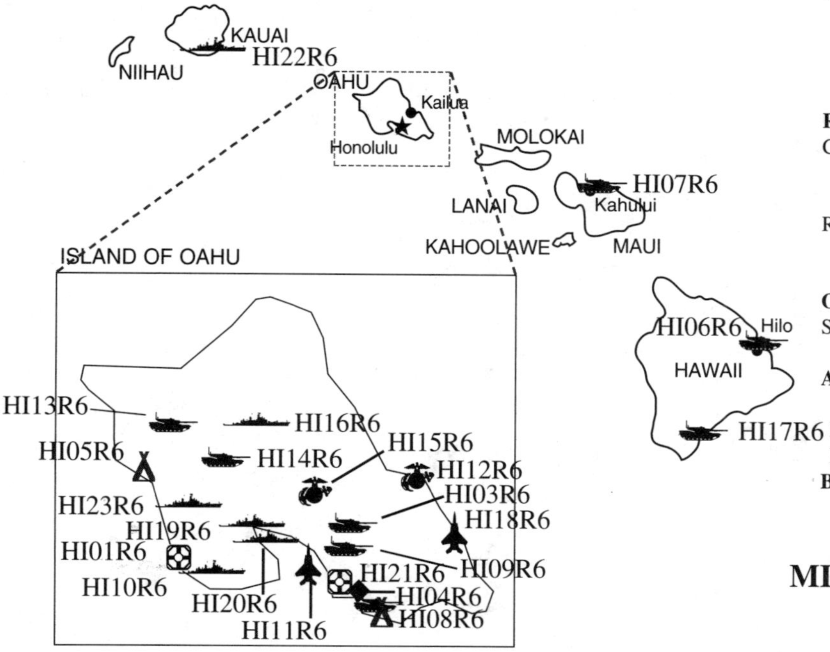

BARBERS POINT NAVAL AIR STATION (HI10R6)

Building 1
Barbers Point Naval Air Station, HI 96862-5050
Scheduled to close July 1999

TELEPHONE NUMBER INFORMATION: Main installation numbers: C-808-684-6266, D-315-484-6266.

LOCATION: Take H-1 west (toward Waianae) to Barbers Point NAS/Makakilo exit, south for a half mile to main gate. USMRA: Page 129 (C-7). NMC: Honolulu, 15 miles east.

GENERAL INFORMATION: Tactical naval aircraft squadrons, Coast Guard Air Station and support units.

TEMPORARY MILITARY LODGING: Lodging office, Building 1788, Bealleau Woods, off Enterprise, 24 hours daily, C-808-684-0687, D-315-484-0687. BEQ C-808-684-2290, D-315-484-2290, BOQ C-808-684-3191, D-315-484-3191, All ranks. DV/VIP: EM C-808-684-2290, Officers C-808-684-3191, Fax: C-808-684-0704.

RV, CAMPING/FAMCAMP: Recreation Area on base, year round, C-808-682-2019, 24 two-bedroom cottages, 21 camper spaces with water faucet only.

SPACE-A: None. See Hickam AFB listing, C-808-442-2729, D-315-449-1854, Fax: C-808-448-1503.

LOGISTICAL SUPPORT:

Child Care-682-0013	Commissary-684-0702
Conv Store-682-3074	Exchange-682-7330
Gas Station-682-3694	SATO-682-4551

ADMINISTRATIVE SUPPORT:

CDO/OOD-684-6266	OFC/CPO-682-4925
Fire Dept-471-7117	Legal-684-4202
Locator-684-1005	Police-684-6222
Public Affairs-684-7101	

HEALTH & WELFARE:

CHAMPUS-474-4406	Chapel-684-3111/3188
Family Services-684-7290	Medical
	Central Appts-684-6201
	Clinic-684-4300
	Emergency-684-8244

REST & RECREATION:

Clubs	Golf Course-682-3088
All Hands-682-4925	MWR-684-8283
Coast Guard Hideaway-682-2731	
Recreation-682-2010/19	
EM-682-5243	Rec Center 684-8281

OTHER FACILITIES AVAILABLE: Bowling, International Sports Shop, Fitness Center, Golf, Library, Picnic Area, Swimming, Tennis.

ATTRACTIONS: Honolulu, beaches, island tours.

Note: P-3 and Helicopter Squadrons will be transferred from Barbers Point Naval Station to Kaneohe Bay Marine Corps Base, HI in late 1999.

BARKING SANDS PACIFIC MISSILE RANGE FACILITY (HI22R6)

P.O. Box 128
Kekaha, Kauai, HI 96752-0128

TELEPHONE NUMBER INFORMATION: Main installation numbers: C-808-335-4254, D-315-471-6254.

LOCATION: Six miles west of Kekaha on Kaumualii Highway. USMRA: Page 129 (B-2). NMC: Lihue, 30 miles east.

GENERAL INFORMATION: Naval Base with the following tenant activities: 154th Composite Group, 115th Aircraft Warning Squadron Hawaii ANG, National Bureau of Standards, Naval Undersea Warfare Engineering Station, Sandia National Laboratories, Dept of Agriculture. Operations and maintenance.

TEMPORARY MILITARY LODGING: Lodging office, Building 1261, Tartar Drive, 0730-1600 daily, C-808-335-4383, D-315-471-6383, Fax: C-808-335-4304; Beach cottages C-808-335-4446.

RV, CAMPING/FAMCAMP: Beach cottages on base, year round, C-808-335-4255, D-312-471-6255, 10 two-bedroom cottages.

SPACE-A: Air Ops, Building 300, C-808-335-4310, D-315-471-6310.

LOGISTICAL SUPPORT:

Cafeteria-335-4249	Child Care-335-4453
Exchange-335-4300	Gas Station-335-4347
Package Store-335-4202	Snack Bar-335-4708
Visitor Center-335-4221	

ADMINISTRATIVE SUPPORT:

CDO/OOD-335-4254/4743	Fire Dept-335-4372
Legal-335-4732	Locator-335-4254
Police-335-4649/4523	Public Affairs-335-4740

HEALTH & WELFARE:

CHAMPUS Advisor-944-2281	Medical-335-4203
	Hospital-338-9431

REST & RECREATION:

Arts & Crafts 335-4303	Auto Hobby Shop-335-4439
Bowling-335-4379	Camping Equipment-335-4379
Ceramics-335-4303	Clubs
Gym-335-4379	Consol-335-4780/09
MWR-335-4446	O-335-4219
Racquetball/Tennis-335-4446	Recreation-335-4446

HAWAII
Barking Sands Pacific Missile Range Facility, continued

Recreation Equipment-335-4379	Rec Center-335-4379
Off-Post Camping 335-6061	Swimming335-4391
Theater-335-4210	Wood Hobby Shop-335-4438

ATTRACTIONS: Beaches, hiking and camping; beautiful countryside, views, sunsets, Kalalau Lookout..."Wettest spot on Earth,"..."The Garden Island."

BELLOWS AIR FORCE STATION (HI18R6)

220 Tinker Road
Waimanalo, HI 96795-1010

TELEPHONE NUMBER INFORMATION: Main installation numbers: C-808-259-8080.

LOCATION: On the eastern shore of Oahu. From Honolulu, take H-1 east to exit 21A Pali Highway (HI-61), go north. Take a right onto Kalanianaole (HI-72), south to AFS. Clearly marked. USMRA: Page 129 (E-7). NMC: Kaneohe, nine miles northwest.

GENERAL INFORMATION: Pacific Air Force Base, recreation center for uniformed services personnel and families, and Marine training area.

TEMPORARY MILITARY LODGING: Bellows Rec Center, 220 Tinker Road, From US mainland 1-800-437-2607, C-808-259-8080, Fax: C-808-259-4119.

RV, CAMPING/FAMCAMP: Beach cottages on base, year round, C-808-259-8080 or 1-800-437-2607, 97 cottages. Camping, year round, 52 sites, C-808-259-4121.

SPACE-A: None. See Hickam AFB listing, C-808-449-1515/1854, D-315-449-1515/1854, Fax: C-808-448-1503.

LOGISTICAL SUPPORT:

Class Six-259-5913	Dining Facilities-259-4110
Exchange-259-5913	Gas Station-259-5913
Shoppette-259-5913	

ADMINISTRATIVE SUPPORT:

Police-259-4200	Public Affairs-259-4210

HEALTH & WELFARE: None. See Kaneohe Bay MCB listing, C-808-257-2145.

REST & RECREATION:

Golf Driving Range-ext 4121	Indoor Rec-259-8080
Recreation-ext 4121	
Miniature Golf	
Equipment rental	

ATTRACTIONS: Great beaches on windward side of Island of Oahu. Watch out for the strong undertow. Blow Hole is nearby, and beautiful Kaneohe Bay.

CAMP H.M. SMITH MARINE CORPS BASE (HI15R6)

P.O. Box 64124, Building 1B
Camp H.M. Smith, HI 96861-5001

TELEPHONE NUMBER INFORMATION: Main installation numbers: C-808-477-6231/5052/6232, D-315-477-6231/5052/6232.

LOCATION: Off H-1 west in Halawa Heights. Take Halawa Heights Road. Clearly marked. USMRA: Page 129 (D-7), page 131 (C-1). NMI: Pearl Harbor Navy Navy Base, five miles southwest. NMC: Honolulu, 10 miles southeast.

GENERAL INFORMATION: Headquarters US Pacific Command, Headquarters Commander Marine Forces Pacific and support units.

TEMPORARY MILITARY LODGING: None, see Fort Shafter listing, C-808-839-2336, D-315-839-2336.

RV, CAMPING/FAMCAMP: Camp Hawkins Campground/Camp Smith Stables, year round, C-808-484-9417, Fax: C-808-477-0506. Twenty five units without hookups.

SPACE-A: None. See Hickam AFB listing, C-808-422-2729, D-315-449-1854, Fax: C-808-448-1503.

LOGISTICAL SUPPORT:

Bank-488-0676	Barber Shop-488-1234
Dry Cleaner-488-2163	Education Office-477-0412
Exchange-477-6302	Gas Station-488-1695
Postal Service-477-8408	SATO-487-1567
Snack Bar-477-6358	Travel Office-487-1567

ADMINISTRATIVE SUPPORT:

Housing Office-471-0167	Legal-477-8366
Locator-477-0344	OOD-477-5106
Pass/ID Office-477-0736	Police-477-0732
Public Affairs-477-8309	SDO/NCO-477-5106

HEALTH & WELFARE:

American Red Cross-422-9742	CHAMPUS-474-4406
Chapel-477-8529	Dental-477-6415
Medical-477-0636	N-MC Relief Society-422-9742
Clinic-477-0638	Retiree Services-471-3345
Emergency-477-0633	

REST & RECREATION:

Auto Hobby Shop-477-0500	Clubs
Fitness Center-477-6335	Combined-477-9322
Gym-477-5197	SNCO-484-9322
ITT-477-5143	Library-477-0514
MWR-477-0498	Pool-477-5059
Stables-477-5067	

ATTRACTIONS: Beautiful view of Honolulu and Pearl Harbor.

FORT DeRUSSY HALE KOA HOTEL ARMED FORCES RECREATION CENTER (HI08R6)

2055 Kalia Road
Honolulu, HI 96815-1998

TELEPHONE NUMBER INFORMATION: Main installation numbers: C-808-955-0555 (24 hours); 800-367-6027 from CONUS (0800-1600 hours daily HI time except holidays).

LOCATION: On Fort DeRussy at 2055 Kalia Road, Waikiki Beach, Oahu. Fort DeRussy is between Ala Moana Blvd, Kalakaua Avenue & Saratoga Road, nine miles east of Honolulu IAP. USMRA: Page 129 (D,E-7,8), page 131 (F-4). NMC: Honolulu, in city limits.

GENERAL INFORMATION: Hale Koa Hotel and Armed Forces Rec Center, Fort DeRussy Military Museum.

TEMPORARY MILITARY LODGING: The Hale Koa Hotel, two towers with 817 guest rooms, A/C and all modern resort hotel facilities. First class beachfront resort built by and run for active duty and retired uniformed personnel of all services. Rates from $53 to $142 per room per night, double occupancy. *For complete details on eligibility, rate structure and facilities, see Military Living's *"Temporary Military Lodging Around The World"* or *"Military RV, Camping & Rec Areas Around The World"*. Reservations may be made up to one year in advance.

HAWAII
Fort DeRussy Hale Koa Hotel Armed Forces Recreation Center, continued

LOGISTICAL SUPPORT: Exchange-955-0060

HEALTH & WELFARE: Chapel located on Fort DeRussy, one-half block from Hale Koa Hotel.

OTHER SUPPORT FACILITIES AVAILABLE: *For info call, 955-0555.* Coffee House, Dining Room, Lounge, Snack Bar, Activity Desk, Tour Office, Athletic Fields, Fitness Center, Handball, Racquetball, Swimming, Tennis, Volleyball.

ATTRACTIONS: Zoo, resort hotels, entertainment, beaches, water sports, military museum. Hale Koa Hotel entertainment includes: Magic Show with Mexican/Italian dinner buffet, Luau on the beach and Tama's Polynesian Revue.

FORT SHAFTER (HI09R6)

Building 5-380
ATTN: APVG-GF
Fort Shafter, HI 96858-5100

TELEPHONE NUMBER INFORMATION: Main installation numbers: C-808-471-7110, D-315-471-7110.

LOCATION: Take H-1 west, exit at Fort Shafter. Clearly marked. USMRA: Page 129 (D-7), page 131 (D,E-1,2). NMC: Honolulu, seven miles east.

GENERAL INFORMATION: US Army Pacific Command (USARPAC).

TEMPORARY MILITARY LODGING: Lodging office, Building 453B, Burr Road, 24 hours Mon-Fri, 0745-1145 Sat, Sun & holidays. C-808-839-2336, D-315-839-2336. All ranks. DV/VIP ext 1577.

RV, CAMPING/FAMCAMP: Off base. Waianae Army Rec Center, year round. C-1-800-333-4158, D-315-333-4158, 0900-1600 Mon-Fri. Studio, 2 and 3 bedroom beach cabins.

SPACE-A: None. See Hickam AFB listing, C-808-442-2729, D-315-449-1854, Fax: C-808-448-1503.

LOGISTICAL SUPPORT:

Barber Shop-847-3141	Beauty Shop-845-9666
Carlson Wagonlit Travel-847-0329	Child Care-438-7074
Child Dev Center-438-1960	Commissary-438-2903
Dry Cleaner-848-0466	Education Office-438-9217
Exchange-845-9626	Gas Station-848-0484
Laundry-848-0466	Package Store-845-9655
Shoppette-845-9621	Travel Office-438-9309
Visitor Center-438-6996	

ADMINISTRATIVE SUPPORT:

Fire Dept-471-7117	Housing Office-438-9205
Legal-438-2845	Locator-655-2299
Pass & ID Office-438-1757	Police-438-7114
Public Affairs-655-2918	

HEALTH & WELFARE:

American Red Cross-433-6631	ACS-438-9285
CHAMPUS-1-800-2929	Chapel-438-1939
Dental	Family Services-438-9285
Clinic-433-8903	Medical
Emergency-433-8814	Central Appts-433-2778
Retiree Services-438-2798	Emergency-433-8850
TRICARE-1-800-930-2929	Veterinary Services-438-2271

REST & RECREATION:

Arts & Crafts-438-1071	Auto Hobby Shop-438-9402
Bowling-438-6733	Com Club-438-1974
Fitness Center-438-1152	Golf Course-438-9587
Gym-438-1152	Indoor Rec-438-6733
ITR-438-1985	Library-438-9521
MWR-438-8768	Services-655-4806
Theater-438-4480	Wood Hobby Shop-438-1071
Youth Center-438-5401	Youth Services-438-1159

ATTRACTIONS: Honolulu, USS Arizona National Memorial, National Memorial Cemetery of the Pacific (Punch Bowl), Pearl Harbor.

HICKAM AIR FORCE BASE (HI11R6)

800 Scott Circle
Hickam Air Force Base, HI 96853-5328

TELEPHONE NUMBER INFORMATION: Main installation numbers: C-808-471-7110, D-315-471-7110.

LOCATION: Adjacent to the Honolulu IAP. Accessible from H-1 or Nimitz Highway. Clearly marked. USMRA: Page 129 (D-7), page 131 (B,C-2,3,4). NMC: Honolulu, six miles east.

GENERAL INFORMATION: Pacific Air Force Base. Headquarters PACAF, 65th Airlift Squadron, 15th Air Base Wing Support Units.

TEMPORARY MILITARY LODGING: Lodging office, Building 1153, 24 hours daily, C-808-449-2603, D-315-449-2603. All ranks.

RV, CAMPING/FAMCAMP: Hickam Harbor Recreation Area, on base year round, Recreation Services, 15 SVS/SVRO, 900 Hangar Avenue, Hickam AFB, HI 96853-5246, C-808-449-5215, D-312-430-5215. Day use (1000-2200) of Cabanas; no overnight facilities.

SPACE-A: Pax Term/Lounge, Building 2028, 24 hours daily, C-808-422-2729, D-315-449-1854, Fax: C-808-448-1503. Flights to CONUS and overseas locations.

LOGISTICAL SUPPORT:

Bank-422-2781	Barber Shop-422-4045
Beauty Shop-422-6121	Car Rental-422-6915
Class Six-422-4533	Commissary-449-7693
Credit Union-423-1391	Dining Facilities-449-1666
Dry Cleaner-422-5821	Education Office-449-6363
Exchange-422-1304	Gas Station-422-8744
Postal Service-422-6435	SATO-422-0548
Shoppette-422-8404	Snack Bar-422-8008
Travel Office-422-2729	Visitor Center-449-1083

ADMINISTRATIVE SUPPORT:

Fire Protection-449-7117	Housing Office-449-0317
Legal-449-1737	Locator-449-0165
Pass/ID Office-449-9394	Police-449-2200
Public Affairs-449-2490	

HEALTH & WELFARE:

Air Force Aid Society-449-2494	American Red Cross-449-1488
Chapel-449-1754	Dental-448-6371
Family Services-449-2494	Medical
Retiree Services-449-9896	Central Appts-448-6000
TRICARE-448-6124	Clinic-448-6110
Veterinary Services-449-6481	Emergency-448-6189

REST & RECREATION: Theater-449-2239

ATTRACTIONS: Honolulu, Waikiki Beaches and Pearl Harbor.

HONOLULU COAST GUARD BASE/ RED HILL COAST GUARD HOUSING (HI21R6)

400 Sand Island Parkway
Honolulu, HI 96819-4398

HAWAII
Honolulu Coast Guard Base/Red Hill Coast Guard Housing, continued

TELEPHONE NUMBER INFORMATION: Main installation numbers: C-808-541-2490/1, D-315-430-0111. NOTE: Prefix of 833 or 839 indicates activity is located at Red Hill.

LOCATION: Take H-1 and exit at HI-64 south to Sand Island Access Road to base. USMRA: Page 129 (D-7) Page 131 (C,D-1,2). NMC: Honolulu, in city limits.

GENERAL INFORMATION: The largest operating unit in the 14th Coast Guard District is located at Sand Island. Personnel perform all Coast Guard functions with the exception of ice-breaking.

TEMPORARY MILITARY LODGING: None. See Hickam Air Force Base listing, C-808-449-2603, D-315-449-2603.

RV, CAMPING/FAMCAMP: None. See Hickam AFB, C-808-449-5215, D-312-430-5215.

SPACE-A: None. See Hickam AFB listing, C-808-442-2729, D-315-449-1854, Fax: C-808-448-1503.

LOGISTICAL SUPPORT:

Exchange-541-2469	Gas Station-833-2448/72
Package Store-541-2499	SATO-541-2468

ADMINISTRATIVE SUPPORT: Public Affairs-541-2170

HEALTH & WELFARE: None. See Pearl Harbor Naval Base listing, C-808-471-9541.

REST & RECREATION:

Athletic Field-ext 2413	Auto Hobby Shop-ext 2416
Clubs	Gym/Weight Room-ext-2415
Consol-541-2475	Racquet Courts-833-9632
Teen-833-7850	Special Services-833-9632
Swimming-833-9632	Tennis-833-9632 or ext 2415
Tickets-ext 2413	

ATTRACTIONS: Honolulu, island tours, helicopter tours, USS Arizona Memorial and USS Bowfin Submarine Exhibit, Waikiki Beach, Diamond Head, National Memorial Cemetery of the Pacific.

KANEOHE BAY MARINE CORPS BASE (HI12R6)

4th Street, Building 216, Base Headquarters
Box 63002
Kaneohe Bay, HI 96863-3002

TELEPHONE NUMBER INFORMATION: Main installation numbers: C-808-471-7110, D-315-471-7110. E-mail: littlec@mfp.usmc.mil. HP: http://www.mcbh.usmc.mil.

LOCATION: At end of H-3 on the Windward side of Oahu. Off Mokapu Blvd and Kaneohe Bay Drive. Clearly marked. USMRA: Page 129 (E-6). NMC: Honolulu, 14 miles southwest.

GENERAL INFORMATION: 3rd Marine Regiment, Combat Service Support Group-3, 1st Marine Aircraft Wing, Aviation Support Element and other units.

TEMPORARY MILITARY LODGING: Lodging office, Building 3038, Box 63073, Kaneohe Bay, HI 96863-3037, 0630-1800 Mon-Fri, 0900-1800 Sat-Sun, Holidays, C-808-254-2716, Fax: C-808-254-2716. All ranks.

RV, CAMPING/FAMCAMP: Beach Cottages and Campsites on base, year round, C-808-254-7666 D-315-457-7666, 24 studio units, 11 cottages, four camper spaces with W hookups.

SPACE-A: Hangar 105, 0700-1500 Mon-Fri, C-808-257-2479/1622, D-315-457-2479/1622, Fax: C-808-257-9273.

LOGISTICAL SUPPORT:

Bank-254-1551	Barber Shop-254-6588/6586
Beauty Shop-254-6585	Book Store-254-7586
Car Rental-254-0808	Child Care-254-1593
Child Dev Center-257-1388	Commissary-257-1452
Conv Store-254-7644	Credit Union-254-3566
Dining Facilities-257-1004	Dry Cleaner-254-3392
Education Office-257-2158	Exchange-254-5871
Gas Station-254-7609	Laundry-254-3392
Package Store-254-7670	Postal Service-257-9933
Snack Bar-254-7585/7656	Travel Office-254-3581

ADMINISTRATIVE SUPPORT:

Fire Dept-257-2022	Housing Office-257-2705
Legal-257-0074/2110	Locator-257-1294
OOD-257-1824	Pass/ID Office-257-2047
Police-257-2103	Public Affairs-257-2728
SDO/NCO-257-2494	

HEALTH & WELFARE:

American Red Cross-257-3150	CHAMPUS-257-1701
Chapel-257-3552	Dental-257-3100
Family Services-257-1931	Medical-257-2145
N-MC Relief Society-254-1327	Central Appts-257-2131
Retiree Services-257-3135	Clinic-257-2145
TRICARE-257-1701	Emergency-254-3133
Veterinary Services-257-3643	Health Benefits-257-1701
	Information-257-2145

REST & RECREATION:

Auto Hobby Shop-254-7674	Bowling-254-7664
Clubs	Fitness Center-254-7659
EM-254-7660	Golf Course-254-1745
O-254-7649	Gym-254-7597
SNCO-254-5592	ITT-254-7562
Library-254-7623	Marina-254-7666
MWR-254-7515	Outdoor Rec-254-7695
Services-254-7501	Theater-254-7642
Youth Center-254-7610	Youth Services-254-7610

ATTRACTIONS: Kaneohe Bay, beaches, outdoor sports, historical sites, and wildlife refuges.

Note: P-3 and Helicopter Squadrons will be transferred from Barbers Point Naval Station to Kaneohe Bay in late 1999.

KILAUEA MILITARY CAMP JOINT SERVICES RECREATION CENTER (HI17R6)

Building 40
Hawaii National Park, HI 96718-5000

TELEPHONE NUMBER INFORMATION: Main installation number: C-808-967-7315.

LOCATION: On island of Hawaii, 216 air miles southeast of Honolulu, 32 miles from Hilo IAP. Scheduled bus transportation to camp: reservations required Hilo to KMC. USMRA: Page 129 (I,J-6,7). NMC: Hilo, 32 miles northeast.

GENERAL INFORMATION: Kilauea Military Camp (KMC) Joint Services Rec Center . A resort for uniformed services personnel, retirees, DoD civilians and their families.

TEMPORARY MILITARY LODGING: Lodging office, 0800-1630 Mon-Thu, 0800-1830 Fri, C-808-967-8333/34; direct from Oahu C-438-6707.

HAWAII
Kilauea Military Camp Joint Services Recreation Center, continued

All ranks. 62 cabins, six apartments and two dormitories (for large groups). Reservations required.

RV, CAMPING/FAMCAMP: Kilauea Military Camp AFRC, on post year round, 62 cabins, C-808-438-6707 (from Oahu), C-808-967-8333/34.

SPACE-A: None. See Hickam AFB listing, C-808-442-2729, D-315-449-1854, Fax: C-808-448-1503.

LOGISTICAL SUPPORT:
Cafeteria-967-8355
Country Store-967-8364
Gas Station-967-8362

ADMINISTRATIVE SUPPORT: SDO/NCOIC-967-7315

HEALTH & WELFARE: Medical Clinic-967-8368

REST & RECREATION: Tours—check with registration desk. Call C-438-6707/967-8333.

OTHER FACILITIES AVAILABLE: Bowling, Bicycle Rental, Golf, Mini Health Center, Multi-Purpose Court, Rental Equipment, Tennis.

ATTRACTIONS: Tours of the Big Island—Hawaii, Hilo, Black Sands Beach, Kona, Hawaii Volcanoes National Park, active lava flows. Hula shows. Helicopter rides.

LUALUALEI NAVAL MAGAZINE (HI23R6)

3 Constellation Street
Waianae, HI 96792-4301

TELEPHONE NUMBER INFORMATION: Main installation numbers: C-808-474-4340, D-315-474-4340.

LOCATION: Follow H-1 Freeway west towards Waianae to Ewa exit. Follow Fort Weaver Rd south to Iroquois Point Road. Turn left and travel to West Loch Branch gate. USMRA: Page 129 (B,C-7), page 131 (A,B-3,4). NMC: Honolulu, 20 miles southeast.

GENERAL INFORMATION: NUWES, SUBASE Pearl Harbor MK48 Torpedo Shop, USAO, DIO, Munitions Branch.

TEMPORARY MILITARY LODGING: Lodging office, Building 600, 0600-2200 hours daily, C-808-474-7908, D-315-474-7908, Fax: C-808-474-7919.

RV, CAMPING/FAMCAMP: None. See Barbers Point NAS listing, C-808-682-2019.

SPACE-A: None. See Hickam AFB listing, C-808-442-2729, D-315-449-1854, Fax: C-808-448-1503.

LOGISTICAL SUPPORT:
Exchange-668-3386 LB
Galley-474-7844
Snack Bar
LB-668-3586
WB-474-1381

Note: LB = Lualualei Branch, WB = West Loch Branch.

ADMINISTRATIVE SUPPORT:
CDO/OOD-474-4340
Fire Dept-474-7829
Police-668-3261 LB

HEALTH & WELFARE: Barbers Point Naval Branch Medical Clinic C-808-684-4300. Inpatient, see Tripler Medical Center listing, C-808-433-6661.

REST & RECREATION:
Auto Hobby Shop-499-2421
Camping Equip-ext 7933
CMO Club-474-7928
Rec Center-ext 7933
Swimming-ext 7933
Rec Equip-ext 7933
Special Services-ext 7933

ATTRACTIONS: Beaches, outdoor rec activities, tourist attractions.

PEARL HARBOR NAVAL BASE (HI19R6)

120 Minute Men Street, Suite E-133
Box 110
Pearl Harbor Naval Base, HI 96860-5020

TELEPHONE NUMBER INFORMATION: Main installation numbers: C-808-471-7110, D-315-430-0111.

LOCATION: Off H-1 adjacent to Honolulu IAP. Clearly marked. USMRA: Page 129 (C,D-7), page 131 (A-1,2,3; B-2,3; C-2). NMC: Honolulu, five miles east.

GENERAL INFORMATION: Headquarters Pacific Fleet, Headquarters Submarine Force Pacific, Naval Shipyard, support units and home port for approximately 40 ships.

TEMPORARY MILITARY LODGING: Lodging office, USS Arizona Hall, Building 1623, 24 hours daily, C-808-471-8053, D-315-474-5210. BEQ C-808-471-0148, D-315-474-5210, BOQ C-808-474-1201, D-315-474-5210, All ranks. DV/VIP 808-474-5210, Fax: C-808-423-1704.

RV, CAMPING/FAMCAMP: None. See Hickam AFB, C-808-449-5215, D-312-430-5215.

SPACE-A: None. See Hickam AFB listing, C-808-442-2729, D-315-449-1854, Fax: C-808-448-1503.

LOGISTICAL SUPPORT:
Child Care-422-7133
Conv Store-423-3217
Gas Station-423-3229
SATO-423-8770
Commissary-471-0263
Exchange-423-3344
Package Store-423-3254

ADMINISTRATIVE SUPPORT:
CDO/OOD-471-1222
Legal-471-3300
Public Affairs-471-0281
Fire Dept-471-7117
Police-471-7114

HEALTH & WELFARE:
ACS-471-9125
Family Services-474-4222
TRICARE-1-800-242-6788
Chapel-471-3971
Medical
Central Appts-471-9541
Clinic-471-1880
Emergency--471-7116

REST & RECREATION:
Athletic Fields-474-0786
Bowling-474-2162
Dependents Activities Center-471-0392
Gear Issue-474-1198
Golf Course-471-0142
ITT Office-474-1190
Recreation-474-1198
Swimming 471-5149
Theater-471-0726
Bloch Arena-474-0793
Clubs
All Hands (Banyans)-471-8455
All Hands (Palms)-474-7235
Club Pearl Admin-471-0841
MWR-471-0787
Special Services-471-1190
Tennis/Racquetball 471-0610

ATTRACTIONS: USS Arizona Memorial and Visitor Center, and USS Bowfin Submarine Exhibit.

PEARL HARBOR NAVAL STATION (HI20R6)

Bloch Arena, Building 161
Box 2093
Pearl Harbor, HI 96860-5000

HAWAII
Pearl Harbor Naval Station, station

TELEPHONE NUMBER INFORMATION: Main installation number: C-808-471-7110.

LOCATION: From Honolulu IAP, take Highway One west. Follow signs for Pearl Harbor/Hickam AFB. Take exit for Pearl Harbor and ask guard at Nimitz gate for further directions. USMRA: Page 129 (C-7). NMC: Honolulu five miles east.

GENERAL INFORMATION: Naval Logistics Support and Receiving Station.

TEMPORARY MILITARY LODGING: Building 1315, 0700-1600 daily, C-808-471-1226. BEQ C-808-471-9188, D-315-471-9188, BOQ C-808-471-0445, D-315-471-0445. DV/VIP C-808-422-9494, Fax: C-808-491-2944.

RV, CAMPING/FAMCAMP: None. See Barbers Point NAS listing, C-808-682-2019.

SPACE-A: None. See Hickam AFB listing, C-808-442-2729, D-315-449-1854, Fax: C-808-448-1503.

LOGISTICAL SUPPORT:

Child Care-422-7133	Commissary-471-0263
Conv Store-423-3250	Dining Facilities
Exchange-423-3344	Galley-474-8488
Gas Station-423-3229	Restaurant-471-0593
Package Store-423-3254	SATO-423-8770
Snack Bar-471-1746	Visitor Center-471-3627

ADMINISTRATIVE SUPPORT:

Legal-471-3300	Locator-471-7110
Police-474-7182	Public Affairs-471-0281
Quarterdeck-474-6249	

HEALTH & WELFARE:

Chapel-471-3971	Family Services-474-4222
Medical	Retiree Services-449-9896
Central Appts-471-9541	TRICARE-1-800-242-6788
Clinic-471-1880	
Emergency-471-7116	

REST & RECREATION:

Auto Hobby Shop-471-9072	Bowling-474-2162
Camping/Rec Equip-474-1198	Community Center-471-0392
Combined Club-471-8456/474-7235	Dive Shop-422-5551
Golf Course-471-0142	Gym-474-0793
ITT Office-474-6156	Library-471-8238
Marina-471-9680	MWR-471-0787
Swimming Pool-471-5149	Theater-471-0726
YMCA-471-3398	Youth Activities-474-3501/3071

ATTRACTIONS: Diamond Head, beaches, island tours, Polynesian Cultural Center.

SCHOFIELD BARRACKS (HI13R6)

25th Infantry Division (Light) & US Army, Hawaii
Building 580, Room 229
Schofield Barracks, HI 96857-6000

TELEPHONE NUMBER INFORMATION: Main installation numbers: C-808-471-7110, D-315-471-7110. E-mail; @schofield.emh2.army.mil. HP: http://www.usdr/dc.armh.mil.

LOCATION: Off H-2 or HI-99 in the center of the island of Oahu. Clearly marked. USMRA: Page 129 (C-6). NMC: Honolulu, 20 miles southeast.

GENERAL INFORMATION: 25th Infantry Division (Light) and US Army, Hawaii, US Army Garrison, Hawaii.

TEMPORARY MILITARY LODGING: Lodging office, Building 692, McCornack Road, 0730-1600 Mon-Fri, C-808-624-9877 All ranks. The Inn at Schofield Barracks C-808-624-9650, D-315-624-9650, Fax: C-808-624-5606, 24 hours daily, 190 guest rooms.

RV, CAMPING/FAMCAMP: None. See Barbers Point NAS listing, C-808-682-2019.

SPACE-A: None. See Hickam AFB listing, C-808-442-2729, D-315-449-1854, Fax: C-808-448-1503.

LOGISTICAL SUPPORT:

Bank-623-8616	Barber Shop-624-5541
Beauty Shop-624-5144	Carlson Wagonlit Travel-624-1700
Car Rental-624-2324	Child Care-656-6540
Child Dev Center-655-5314	Commissary-655-5066
Conv Store-624-3316	Dry Cleaner-621-8088
Education Office-655-4444	Exchange-622-1773
Gas Station-624-9857	Laundry-621-8088
Package Store-624-2692	Shoppette-624-9825
Travel Office-655-2248	Visitor Center-655-0216

ADMINISTRATIVE SUPPORT:

Fire Dept-471-7117	Housing Office-474-2343
Legal-655-4884	Locator-655-2299
Pass/ID Office-655-4104	Police-655-0911
Public Affairs-655-2918	

HEALTH & WELFARE:

American Red Cross-655-4927	ACS-656-1900
Army Emergency Relief-656-1900	CHAMPUS-1-800-930-2929
Chapel-655-9307	Dental
Family Services-656-1900	Clinic-433-8903
Medical	Emergency-433-8814
Central Appts-433-2778	Retiree Services-438-2798
Clinic-433-2778	TRICARE-1-800-930-2929
Emergency-433-8850	Veterinary Services-655-4041
Health Benefits-433-2778	
Hospital-433-6661	
Information-433-6661	

REST & RECREATION:

Arts & Crafts-655-4202	Athletic Fields-ext 0900
Auto Hobby Shop-655-9368	Bowling-655-0573
Clubs	Community Center-655-8522
Combined-624-5600	Fitness Center-655-0900
NCO-655-2251	Golf Course-655-9833
Sports Dome-624-2230	Gym-655-8007
Indoor Rec-655-8522	ITR-655-9971
Library-655-0145	MWR-655-0002
Outdoor Rec-655-0143	Rec Center-ext 0968
Rec Equip-ext 0143	Scuba-ext 0143
Services-655-4806	Swimming-655-9698
Tennis-ext 0852	Theater-251-4583
Wood Hobby Shop-655-4202	Youth Center-655-4641
Youth Services-655-4641	

ATTRACTIONS: Sugar cane and pineapple fields. Tropic Lightning Museum.

TRIPLER MEDICAL CENTER (HI03R6)

1 Jarrett White Road
Tripler Medical Center, HI 96859-5000

TELEPHONE NUMBER INFORMATION: Main installation numbers: C-808-433-6662, D-315-433-6662.

LOCATION: Take H-1 west from Honolulu to Tripler exit. Turn right on Jarrett White Road to Tripler Medical Center. USMRA: Page 129 (D-7), page 131 (D-1,2). NMC: Honolulu, three miles southeast.

HAWAII
Tripler Medical Center, continued

GENERAL INFORMATION: Tripler Medical Center is the largest military medical center in the Pacific area of operations. Tripler treats service members from all branches of the military.

TEMPORARY MILITARY LODGING: Lodging office, Building 228B, Jarrett White Road, 0630-2200 Mon-Fri, 24 hours daily, Sat-Sun, C-808-839-2336. All ranks. DV/VIP 433-2336.

RV, CAMPING/FAMCAMP: None. See Bellows AFS listing, C-808-259-8080 or 1-800-437-2607.

SPACE-A: None. See Hickam AFB listing, C-808-442-2729, D-315-449-1854, Fax: C-808-448-1503.

LOGISTICAL SUPPORT:
Carlson Wagonlit Travel-834-7499
Commissary-438-6164
Exchange-833-1267
Gas Station-833-1250
Snack Bar-833-1259

The Aliamanu Military Reservation, a nearby housing area, has a large Exchange/Shoppette 833-6997, and a Gas Station 833-6997.

ADMINISTRATIVE SUPPORT:
Legal-433-5311
AOD/SDNCO-433-6661

HEALTH & WELFARE:
CHAMPUS-1-800-242-6788
Chapel-433-5727
Medical-433-6661
Central Appts-433-2778
Emergency-433-6629
Patient Rep-433-6336

REST & RECREATION:
Gym-ext 6443
ITT-438-1985
Library-ext 6968
O'Club-833-1268
Racquet/Handball-ext 6443
Special Services-ext 5772
Swimming-ext 5257
Tennis-ext 6443

ATTRACTIONS: USS Arizona National Memorial, Pearl Harbor. Great view of Honolulu.

WAHIAWA NAVAL COMPUTER AND TELECOMMUNICATIONS AREA MASTER STATION, EASTERN PACIFIC [NCTAMS EASTPAC] (HI16R6)

500 Center Street
Wahiawa, HI 96786-3050

TELEPHONE NUMBER INFORMATION: Main installation numbers: C-808-653-5385, D-315-453-5385.

LOCATION: H-2 to Wahiawa, station is three miles north. USMRA: Page 129 (C-6). NMC: Honolulu, 20 miles southeast.

GENERAL INFORMATION: Naval Communications for Pacific area, provides operational direction and management to all Pacific Naval telecommunications system users.

TEMPORARY MILITARY LODGING: BEQ C-808-653-5367, D-315-453-5367, Fax: C-808-653-4600.

RV, CAMPING/FAMCAMP: None. See Waianae Army Rec Center listing, C-808-696-4158 (Oahu), 1-800-847-6771 (Outer Island), 1-800-333-4158 (Mainland).

SPACE-A: None. See Hickam AFB listing, C-808-442-2729, D-315-449-1854, Fax: C-808-448-1503.

LOGISTICAL SUPPORT:
Barber Shop-653-5527
Beauty Shop-653-5527
Child Care-653-5305
Education Office-653-7700
Exchange-653-5364
Gas Station-653-5451
Mini-Mart-653-5364
SATO-621-0733

ADMINISTRATIVE SUPPORT:
CDO/OOD-653-5385
Fire Dept-653-5479
Legal-653-5397
Locator-653-5385
Police-653-0234
Public Affairs-653-5569
Quarter Deck-653-5385

HEALTH & WELFARE:
CHAMPUS-474-4406
Chapel-653-5577
Dental-653-5475
Family Services-653-0203
Medical-653-5340

REST & RECREATION:
Arts & Crafts-653-5574
Auto Hobby Shop-653-5485
Bowling-653-5576
EM Club-653-5470
Gym-653-5542
Indoor Rec-653-5470
ITT Office-621-0733
Library-653-5420
MWR-653-5485
Racquet Sports-ext 5542
Rec Equip-ext 5542
Special Services-ext 0191
Swimming-ext 5306
Youth Center-653-0220
Youth Services-653-0220

ATTRACTIONS: Short drive to Honolulu, beach areas.

WAIANAE ARMY RECREATION CENTER (HI05R6)

85-010 Army Street
Waianae, HI 96792-5000

TELEPHONE NUMBER INFORMATION: Main installation numbers: C-808-471-7110, D-315-471-7110.

LOCATION: On west coast of Oahu. Take H1 west to HI-93 (Farrington Highway); north to Waianae. USMRA: page 129 (B-6). NMC: Honolulu, 35 miles southeast. NMI: Schofield Barracks, 20 miles northeast.

GENERAL INFORMATION: Located along beach of Pokai Bay in once-quiet fishing and plantation village. One of the favorite swimming and fishing spots on Oahu. The facility is one of the finest on the island. Operated by Fort Shafter, off post year round. Military personnel active, retired, reserve, DoD civilians, other federal employees. Reservations: Required with deposit: up to 90 days in advance for active duty Army; up to 80 days in advance for other active duty and retirees; up to 60 days in advance for reserve and DoD civilians; up to 30 days for other Federal Employees. C-808-696-4158, 800-333-4158 (from mainland), or 800-847-6771 (from outer islands), 0900-1600 M-F, Hawaiian time. No pets allowed. Twenty-one day limit.

TEMPORARY MILITARY LODGING: Deluxe two bedroom cabin, AC, kitchen, refrigerator, color TV, VCR, deck, grill; ocean front deluxe two bedroom cabin, AC, kitchen, refrigerator, color TV, VCR, deck, grill; ocean front deluxe three bedroom cabin, AC, kitchen, refrigerator, color TV, VCR, deck, grill; standard two bedroom cabin, AC, kitchen, refrigerator, color TV, VCR, deck, grill; ocean front standard two bedroom cabin, AC, kitchen, refrigerator, color TV, VCR, deck, grill; studio, AC, kitchen, refrigerator, color TV, VCR, deck, grill. Three cabins handicap accessible. Rates: deluxe two bedroom E1-E5 $65, E6-W3 $70, W4-W010 $75; ocean front deluxe two bedroom: E1-E5 $70, E6-W3 $75, W4-W010 $80; ocean front deluxe three bedroom: E1-E5 $75, E6-W3 $80, W4-W010 $85; standard two bedroom: E1-E5 $50, E6-W3 $55, W4-W010 $60; ocean front standard two bedroom: E1-E5 $55, E6-W3 $60, W4-W010 $65; studio: E1-E5 $40, E6-W3 $45, W4-W010 $50. Additional Fees: Cribs $5, Rollaways $10.

LOGISTICAL SUPPORT:
Package Store-696-2886
SATO-624-9513
WARC Manager-696-6026

HAWAII
Waianae Army Recreation Center, continued

ADMINISTRATIVE SUPPORT: Police-696-2811

HEALTH & WELFARE: CHAMPUS-433-6330

REST & RECREATION:
Beach Club-696-4778
ITT-655-9971
MWR-655-9971

OTHER SUPPORT & FACILITIES AVAILABLE: Beach, Club/all ranks, Convenience/Package Store, First Aid Station, Grills, Pavilions/fee, Picnic Area, Restrooms, Showers, Snack Bar, Snorkeling, Surfing, Swimming, Water Sports, Equipment Rental. Outdoor sports facilities, five minute walk from camp. Also, see Schofield Barracks listing, C-808-471-7110, D-315-471-7110.

ATTRACTIONS: Beautiful beaches. swimming, surfing, kayaking, snorkeling and fishing.

WHEELER ARMY AIRFIELD (HI14R6)

25th ID, Building 580, Room 229
Schofield Barracks, HI 96857-6000

TELEPHONE NUMBER INFORMATION: Main installation numbers: C-808-471-7110, D-315-471-7110.

LOCATION: Off H-2 or HI-99 in the center of the island of Oahu. Adjacent to Schofield Barracks. USMRA: Page 129 (C-6). NMC: Honolulu, 20 miles southeast.

GENERAL INFORMATION: Aviation Support for 25th INF DIV (Light), Air National Guard Aircraft Control and Warning Squadron and support units, Garrison Support Activities.

TEMPORARY MILITARY LODGING: None. See Schofield Barracks listing, the Inn at Schofield Barracks C-808-624-9650, D-315-624-9650.

RV, CAMPING/FAMCAMP: None. See Fort Shafter Listing, C1-800-333-4158, D-315-333-4158.

SPACE-A: None. See Hickam AFB listing, C-808-442-2729, D-315-449-1854, Fax: C-808-448-1503.

LOGISTICAL SUPPORT:
Bank-623-8616
Barber Shop-624-5818
Beauty Shop-624-5144
Car Rental-624-2324
Carlson Wagonlit Travel-624-1700
Child Care-656-1900
Child Dev Center-656-1900
Commissary-655-2360
Conv Store-624-9818
Dry Cleaner-624-3271
Education Office-655-0800
Exchange-624-9818
Gas Station-624-9825
Laundry-624-3271
Shoppette-624-9818
Snack Bar-656-1745
Travel Office-655-2248
Visitor Center-655-0216

ADMINISTRATIVE SUPPORT:
Fire Dept-471-7117
Housing Office-474-2343
Legal-655-4884
Locator-655-2299
Pass/ID Office-655-4104
Police-655-7114
Public Affairs-655-2918

HEALTH & WELFARE:
American Red Cross-655-4927
ACS-656-1900
Army Emergency Relief-656-1900
CHAMPUS-1-800-930-2929
Chapel-655-9207
Dental
  Clinic-433-8903
  Emergency-433-8814
Family Services-656-1900
Medical
  Central Appts-433-2778
  Emergency-433-8850
  Health Benefits-433-2778
  Hospital-433-2778
  Information-433-2778
Retiree Services-438-2798
TRICARE-1-800-930-2929
Veterinary Services-655-4041

REST & RECREATION:
Arts & Crafts-655-4202
Auto Hobby Shop-655-9368
Bowling-656-1745
Clubs
  Com-624-5600
  NCO-655-2251
Community Center-655-8522
Fitness Center-655-0900
Golf Course-655-9833
Gym-655-8007
Indoor Rec-655-8522
ITR-655-9971
Library-655-0145
MWR-438-8768
Outdoor Rec-655-0143
Services-655-4806
Theater-251-4583
Wood Hobby Shop-655-4202
Youth Center-656-1601
Youth Services-655-4641

ATTRACTIONS: Numerous activities on Oahu and other islands. Pineapple and sugar cane fields.

Other Installations in Hawaii

Aliamanu Military Reservation (HI04R6), 1875 Aliamanu Drive, Aliamanu, HI 96854-5000. USMRA: Page 131 (C-2). C-808-833-1185, MWR-836-0338, Service Station-833-6997.
Barbers Point Coast Guard Air Station (HI24R6), Barbers Point, HI 96862-5800, club facilities. USMRA: Page 129 (C-7). C-808-682-2614, Exchange-682-2731.
Hilo Big Island Exchange (HI06R6), 1300 Kekuanaoa Street, Building 505, Hilo, HI 96720-5000. USMRA: Page 129 (J-6). C-808-935-3449.
Maui Exchange (HI07R6), 1686 Kaahumanu Avenue, Wailuku, HI 96793-5000. USMRA: Page 129 (G-4). C-808-244-3006, Exchange-244-3006.

* * * * * ***N O T E S*** * * * * *

IDAHO

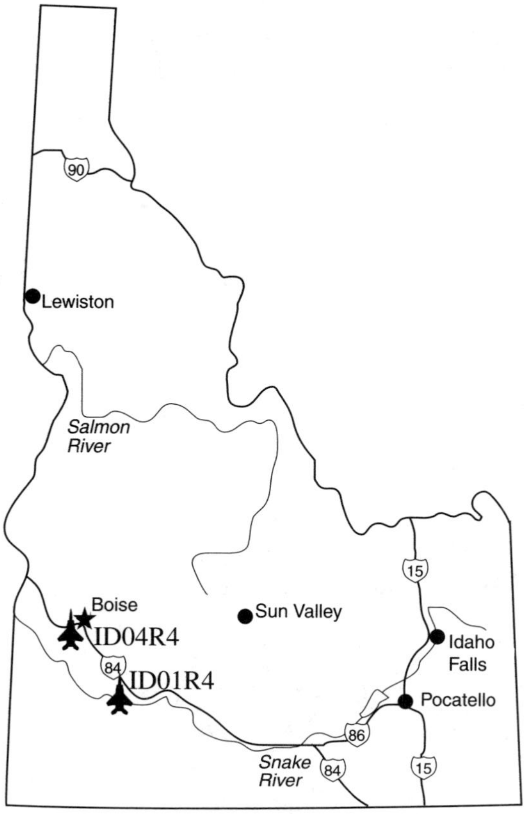

GOWEN FIELD (ID04R4)

P.O. Box 45
4040 Guard Street
Boise, ID 83705-5004

TELEPHONE NUMBER INFORMATION: Main installation numbers: C-208-422-5011, D-312-422-5011.

LOCATION: From I-84 west, take Orchard St exit (exit 52). Turn left and remain on road as it goes behind the airport. Watch for "Gowen Field" sign near tanks. Turn left into Main Gate. USMRA: Page 98 (B-8). NMC: Boise, five miles north.

GENERAL INFORMATION: Headquarters, Idaho Army and Air National Guard, US Naval , Marine and Army Reserves, Headquarters, 1/204th Regiment Armor Training, Headquarters, 2/204th Ordinance Training, 124th Fighter Wing, Headquarters, 321st Combat Engineer Battalion, Combat Vehicle Transition Training Team, 116th Cavalry Brigade.

TEMPORARY MILITARY LODGING: Lodging office, Building 669, 0800-1700 daily, C-208-422-6023, D-312-422-6023.

RV, CAMPING/FAMCAMP: None. See Mountain Home AFB listing, C-208-832-4661, D-312-728-6451, Fax C-208-828-4797.

SPACE-A: None. See Mountain Home AFB listing, C-208-828-2304, D-312-857-2304, Fax: C-208-828-4128.

LOGISTICAL SUPPORT:

Conv Store-422-5676	Exchange-422-5676
SATO-422-5000	Snack Bar-422-5674

ADMINISTRATIVE SUPPORT:

Fire Dept-422-5867	Legal-422-5474
Locator-422-5011	Police-422-5366
Public Affairs-422-5268	

HEALTH AND WELFARE:

CHAMPUS-422-5027	Chapel-422-6467/5394
Family Services-422-5067	Medical-422-5369
Retiree Services-422-5817	

REST & RECREATION:

Clubs	Fitness Center-422-6046
NCO-422-5674	MWR-422-6703
O-422-5667/5668	Recreation-422-5381
Swimming-422-5673	Theater-422-6245

ATTRACTIONS: Boise River: trout and bass fishing, swimming, waterskiing, windsurfing, skin diving, tubing, City of Trees, with five large parks along the river. Zoo, Rose Garden, State Historical Museum, Art Museum. Bogus Basin ski area (both nordic and alpine skiing), snowmobiling.

MOUNTAIN HOME AIR FORCE BASE (ID01R4)

366 Gunfighter Avenue, Suite 152
Mountain Home Air Force Base, ID 83648-5000

TELEPHONE NUMBER INFORMATION: Main installation numbers: C-208-828-2111, D-312-728-1110.

LOCATION: From Boise, take I-84 southeast, 39 miles to Mountain Home exit, follow road through town to Airbase Road, 10 miles to main gate. USMRA: Page 98 (C-9). NMC: Boise, 51 miles northwest.

GENERAL INFORMATION: Air Combat Command Base. B-1B, F-15C, F-15E, F-16, & KC-135R Air intervention aircraft composite wing. Air-to-ground and air-to-air combat.

TEMPORARY MILITARY LODGING: Lodging office, 366 SVS/SVMH, Building 2604, Falcon Street, 24 hours daily, C-208-828-6451, D-312-728-6451, Fax: C-208-828-2807, D-312-728-2807. All ranks. DV/VIP C-208-828-4536, D-312-728-4536.

RV, CAMPING/FAMCAMP: FAMCAMP on base, year round, 366 SVS/SVML, 445 Falcon Street, 24 hours daily, C-208-832-4661, D-312-728-6451, Fax: C-208-828-4797, D-312-728-4797, 22 camper spaces with full hookups, 10 tent spaces, Strike Dam Marina off base, C-208-828-6333, Marina only. Island Park Recreation Area off base, five travel trailers. Operates Grant's Village, Yellowstone National Park, WY, off base, 15 May-15 Sep, C-208-828-6333, D-312-728-6333, six travel trailers with full hookups.

SPACE-A: Pax Term/Lounge, Building 262, 0730-1630 Mon-Fri, C-208-828-2304, D-312-857-2304, Fax: C-208-828-4128, flights to CONUS locations. Also, Boise Air Terminal, limited Space-A, Reserve Units, C-208-389-5303, D-312-941-5303.

LOGISTICAL SUPPORT:

Bank-832-4202	Barber Shop-832-2105
Beauty Shop-832-4090	Child Care-828-2443
Child Dev Center-828-2443	Commissary-828-2286
Conv Store-828-6921	Credit Union-832-4675
Dining Facilities-828-6420	Dry Cleaner-832-7465
Education Office-828-6363	Exchange-832-4353
Gas Station-832-4459	Laundry-832-7893
N&N Travel-832-2276	Package Store-828-6291
Postal Service-828-6238	Shoppette-828-6921
Snack Bar-828-6546	

ADMINISTRATIVE SUPPORT:

Fire Dept-828-6292	Housing Office-828-2781
Legal-828-6060	Locator-828-1110

IDAHO
Mountain Home Air Force Base, continued

Pass & ID Office-828-2371
Public Affairs-828-6800
Police-828-2256
SDO/NCO-828-2071

HEALTH & WELFARE:
Air Force Aid Society-828-2458
CHAMPUS-828-7800
Dental-828-7300
Medical-828-7600
  Central Appts-828-2276
  Emergency-828-7100
American Red Cross-828-6622
Chapel-828-6417
Family Services-828-2964
Retiree Services-828-4878
TRICARE-828-7460
Veterinary Services-828-2221

REST & RECREATION:
Arts & Crafts-828-6229
Bowling-828-6329
Community Center-828-2246
Golf Course-828-6151
Gym-828-2381
Marinas-834-2723
Outdoor Recreation-828-6333
Rec Equip -ext 2237
Skeet/Trap-ext 6093
Swimming-ext 6620
Wood Hobby Shop-828-6338
Auto Hobby Shop-828-2295
Clubs
  Com-828-2105
  O-828-2597
Library-828-2326
MWR-828-2948
Rec Center-ext 2246
Services-828-6081
Stables-ext 4093
Theater-828-6184
Youth Center-828-2501

ATTRACTIONS: Snow skiing, hunting, and fishing. Boise, capital city of Idaho.

ILLINOIS

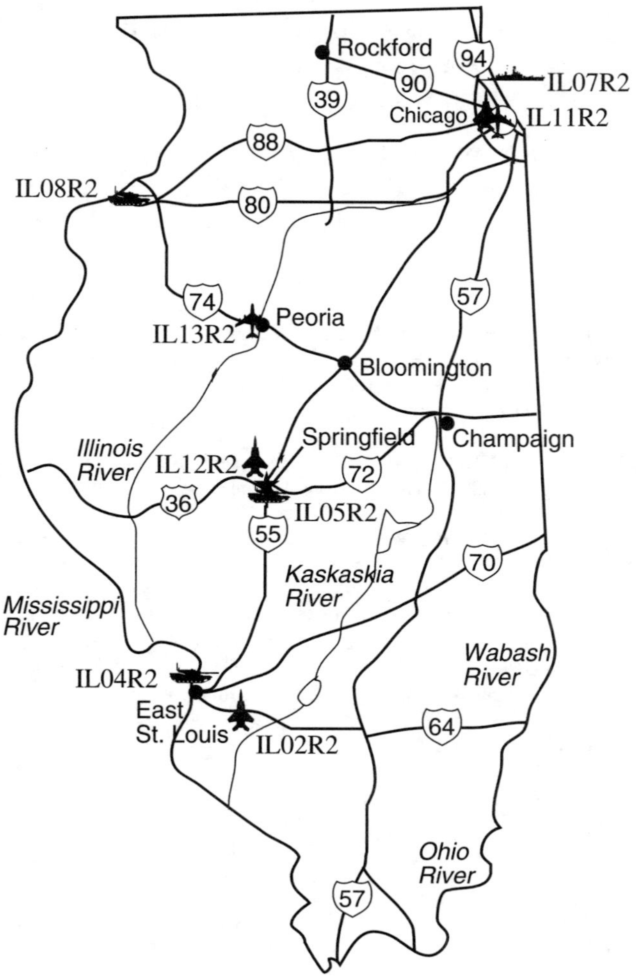

CHARLES MELVIN PRICE SUPPORT CENTER (IL04R2)

Research Management Division
Granite City, IL 62040-1801

TELEPHONE NUMBER INFORMATION: Main installation numbers: C-618-452-4212, D-892-4212.

LOCATION: From I-70 take McKinley Bridge exit, cross Mississippi River, follow signs to Center. From I-270, cross river bridges and take first Granite City exit (Route 3 south) to Center. USMRA: Page 64 (C,D-7). NMC: St Louis, seven miles west.

GENERAL INFORMATION: Army Area Support Center, Army Materiel Command aviation and other materiel procurement and logistical activities. Military Traffic Management Command POV processing center (nearby).

TEMPORARY MILITARY LODGING: Lodging office, Building 102, Niedringhaus Street, 0730-1615 daily, C-618-452-4287, D-312-892-4287. Other hours, Security Office, Building 221, C-618-452-4224. All ranks.

RV, CAMPING/FAMCAMP: None. See Scott AFB, IL, C-618-256-2056, D-312-576-2056.

SPACE-A: None. See Scott AFB listing, C-618-256-3017, D-312-576-3017, Fax: C-618-256-1948.

LOGISTICAL SUPPORT:

Child Care-452-4480	Commissary-452-4232
Exchange-452-5230	Package Store-452-6112
POV Center-452-4650/4651	SATO-452-4375

ADMINISTRATIVE SUPPORT: Police-452-4224

HEALTH & WELFARE:

ACS-452-4260	CHAMPUS-314-425-4851
Chapel-452-4277	Family Services-452-4260
Medical-331-4851	Retiree Services-452-4472

REST & RECREATION:

Auto Hobby-ext 4279	Bowling-ext 4319
Com Club-452-5595	Golf Course-ext 4444
Gym-ext 4209	Library-ext 4322
Rec Center-ext 4398	Swimming-ext 4221

ATTRACTIONS: Gateway Arch, Mississippi River Tours, St Louis, Lacledes Landing, Grants Farm, Busch Stadium, Six Flags, Kiel Aud, VP Fair (July), Fox Theater, Soulard Market area, museums, USS Inaugural Minesweeper.

GREAT LAKES NAVAL TRAINING CENTER (IL07R2)

2701 Sheridan Road
Great Lakes, IL 60088-5001

TELEPHONE NUMBER INFORMATION: Main installation numbers: C-847-688-3500, D-312-792-3500. E-mail: ntc-grl.n1c@smtp.cnet.navy.mil. HP: http://www.ntcpao.com.

LOCATION: From I-94 north or US-41 north of Chicago, exit to IL-137 east to Sheridan Road, turn right into the gate. Clearly marked. USMRA: Page 64 (G-1). NMC: Chicago, 30 miles south.

GENERAL INFORMATION: Naval Training Center, Service School Command, Recruit Training Command, Naval Hospital, Hospital Corps School, Hq US Military Entrance Processing Command, Personnel Support Activity.

TEMPORARY MILITARY LODGING: Lodging office, (BEQ) Building 834, 0700-1530 daily, C-847-688-2170, D-312-792-2710, Fax: C-847-688-4736. Navy Lodge, Building 2500, C-847-689-1485, Fax: C-708-689-1489. (BOQ) Building 62, 24 hours daily, C-847-688-3777, D-312-792-3777, Fax: C-847-688-5815.

RV, CAMPING/FAMCAMP: Great Lakes Naval Training Center, on base year round, 0800-1600 Tue-Sun, MWR, Building 160-NTC, C-847-688-5417, D-312-792-5417, Fax: C-847-688-5421, D-312-792-5421, eight camper spaces without hookups.

SPACE-A: None. See O'Hare IAP listing, C-773-825-6983, D-312-930-6983.

LOGISTICAL SUPPORT:

Barber Shop-578-6169	Beauty Shop-578-6211
Cafeteria-578-6120	Child Care-688-1291
Child Dev Center-688-2845	Commissary-688-2644
Conv Store-578-6247	Credit Union-578-7000
Dining Facilities-688-6946	Dry Cleaner-578-6218
Education Office-688-4681	Exchange-578-6100
Gas Station-578-6247	Laundry-578-6218
Package Store-578-6271	Postal Service-688-5392
SATO-689-1884	Snack Bar-578-6120
Travel Office-473-5775	Visitor Center-688-5670

ADMINISTRATIVE SUPPORT:

CDO/OOD-688-3939/3300	Fire Dept-688-3333
Housing Office-688-3391	Legal-688-3805
Locator-688-2445 (recruits)	Locator-688-3536 (service school)
Pass/ID Office-688-5550, ext 393	Police-688-3430
Public Affairs-688-2430	SDO/SNCO-688-3500

HEALTH & WELFARE:

American Red Cross-847-688-5676	CHAMPUS-688-5457

ILLINOIS
Great Lakes Naval Training Center, continued

Chapel-688-2384	Dental
Family Services-688-3603	Central Appts-688-2423
Medical-688-3444	Clinic-688-2424
Central Appts-688-5600	Emergency-688-2424
Clinic-688-5600	N-MC Relief Society-689-2228
Emergency-688-5618	Retiree Services-688-5434
Health Benefits-688-5457	Veterinary Services-688-5740
Hospital-688-4560	

REST & RECREATION:

Auto Hobby Shop-688-5612	Bowling-688-5612
Clubs	Fitness Center-688-3994
Com-688-6946	Golf Course-688-4593
EM-688-4641	Gym-688-3419
Indoor Rec-688-3419	ITT-688-3537
Library-688-4617	Marina-688-5417
Outdoor Rec-688-6978	Services-688-2110, ext 697
Theater-688-6763	Travel (TSG)-473-7045
Youth Center-688-5573	Youth Services-688-5581
Wood Crafts-688-4813	

ATTRACTIONS: Six Flags Great America, Gurnee Mills Shopping Mall, Milwaukee Zoo, Chicago Museum of Science and Industry. Excellent seasonal recreation available on Lake Michigan and in the Chain O'Lakes area.

ROCK ISLAND US ARMY ARMAMENT & CHEMICAL ACQUISITION & LOGISTICS ACTIVITY (IL08R2)

ATTN: AMSTA-AC-AP
Rock Island Arsenal, IL 61299-5000

TELEPHONE NUMBER INFORMATION: Main installation numbers: C-309-782-6001, D-312-793-6001.

LOCATION: From I-74 north in Moline exit to 3rd Avenue west and follow signs to Arsenal Island located in middle of Mississippi River. USMRA: Page 64 (C-2). NMC: Quad Cities of Rock Island, Moline, Davenport and Bettendorf.

GENERAL INFORMATION: Headquarters Rock Island Arsenal and Industrial Operations Command.

TEMPORARY MILITARY LODGING: Housing Office, Building 102, C-309-782-2376, D-312-793-2376, Fax: C-309-782-2550.

RV, CAMPING/FAMCAMP: None. See Great Lakes NTC listing, C-847-688-5417, D-312-792-5417, Fax: C-847-688-5421, D-312-792-5421.

SPACE-A: None. See O'Hare IAP listing, C-773-825-6983, D-312-930-6983.

LOGISTICAL SUPPORT:

Cafeteria-793-4337	Child Care-782-2828
Commissary-782-4798	Exchange-788-4940

ADMINISTRATIVE SUPPORT:

Legal-782-8432	Locator-782-3004
Police-782-2846	

HEALTH & WELFARE:

Chapel-782-4736	Family Services-782-3828
Medical-782-0805/0801	

REST & RECREATION:

Arsenal Club-788-4860	Auto Hobby Shop 782-4950
Fitness Center-782-6787	Gym-782-6787
Outdoor Rec-782-8630	Skeet-782-2014

ATTRACTIONS: Rock Island Arsenal Museum, National Cemetery, Confederate Cemetery, Colonel Davenport House.

SCOTT AIR FORCE BASE (IL02R2)

101 Heritage Drive, Room 28
Scott Air Force Base, IL 62225-5000

TELEPHONE NUMBER INFORMATION: Main installation numbers: C-618-256-1110, D-312-576-1110.

LOCATION: Off I-64, take exit 19 east or 19A west to IL-158 south, two miles and watch for signs to AFB entry. USMRA: Page 64 (D-8). NMC: St Louis, 25 miles west.

GENERAL INFORMATION: Headquarters for US Transportation Command; Air Mobility Command; Air Force Communications Agency; Air Weather Service; Defense Information Technology Contracting Office and USAF Medical Center Scott.

TEMPORARY MILITARY LODGING: Scott Inn, Building 1510, 24 hours daily, C-618-744-1200, D-312-576-1844. All ranks. DV/VIP ext 5555.

RV, CAMPING/FAMCAMP: FAMCAMP on base, year round, C-618-256-2056, D-312-576-2056, 24 camper spaces with W/E hookups.

SPACE-A: Pax Term, Building P-8, 0445-2400 daily, C-618-256-3017, D-312-576-3017, (Daily flight recording, C-618-256-1854, D-312-576-1874), Fax: C-618-256-1948, flights to CONUS, overseas flights board at Lambert-St Louis Airport AMC Counter C-314-263-6270. This facility will close October 1997.

LOGISTICAL SUPPORT:

Child Care-256-2669	Commissary-256-2783
Exchange-744-0888	Fire Dept-256-5130
Gas Station-746-2184	Rodgers Travel-256-5397
Package Store-256-5942	Snack Bar-744-1177

ADMINISTRATIVE SUPPORT:

Legal-256-2358	Locator-256-1841
Police-256-2223	Public Affairs-256-4241

HEALTH & WELFARE:

CHAMPUS-256-7521	Chapel-256-3303
Family Services-256-3616	Medical
Retiree Services-256-5092	Central Appts-256-1847
	Emergency-256-7595/911

REST & RECREATION:

Auto Hobby Shop-ext 4566	Bowling-256-4054
Clubs	Fitness Center-ext 4020
EM-744-1777	Golf Course-744-1400
O-744-1333	Gym-ext 4524
Library-ext 5100	Rec Equip-ext 2067
Skills Dev Center-ext 3839	Swimming-ext 2579
Theater-256-5177	Youth Center-ext 2115

ATTRACTIONS: St Louis nearby, Mississippi River.

Other Installations in Illinois

Camp Lincoln Exchange (IL05R2), Ima Building 10, North MacArthur Boulevard, Springfield, IL 62702-5000, Exchange-217-524-1758.
Capital Airport/Air National Guard Base (IL12R2), 183rd Fighter Wing (ANG), 3101 J. David Jones Parkway, Springfield, IL 63707-5000. From I-55 exit to Sangamon Ave, west on fifth street, approximately one-half mile and left to Browning Road, right on David Jones Parkway. Follow signs on the left. USMRA: Page 64 (D-5). NMC: Springfield, in city limits. C-217-753-8850, D-312-892-8210. Exchange-753-8394, Medical-753-8221/2.
Greater Peoria Regional Airport (IL13R2), 182nd Airlift Wing (ANG), Peoria, IL 61607-1498. Space-A: C-309-791-2282, D-312-724-2282.
O'Hare International Airport (IL11R2), Air National Guard, 6216 N Patton Road, O'Hare IAP, IL 60666-5018. Space-A C-773-825-6983, D-312-930-6983.

INDIANA

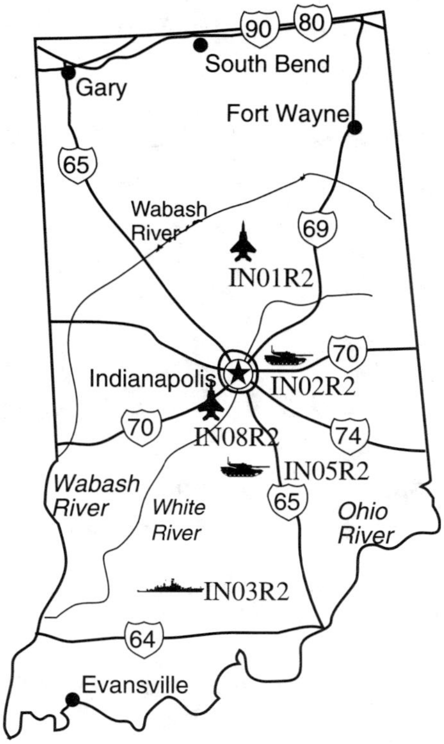

CAMP ATTERBURY (IN05R2)

Army National Guard
Building 708
Edinburg, IN 46124-1096

TELEPHONE NUMBER INFORMATION: Main installation numbers: C-812-526-9711, D-312-569-2499.

LOCATION: From I-65, take exit 76 (31 north), left at Hospital Road. Enter post on Eggleston Street at Main Gate. USMRA Page 65 (E-6,7). NMC: Indianapolis, 45 miles north.

GENERAL INFORMATION: Indiana Army National Guard Maneuver Training Center.

TEMPORARY MILITARY LODGING: Contract Quarters, Post Billeting Office, C-812-526-1128.

RV, CAMPING/FAMCAMP: Campgrounds, on post year round, Building 1, MWR, Camp Atterbury, C-812-526-1149, D-312-569-2149, 16 camper spaces with full hookups, unlimited tent spaces.

SPACE-A: None. See Scott AFB, IL listing, C-618-256-3017, D-312-576-3017, Fax: C-618-256-1948.

LOGISTICAL SUPPORT: Exchange-526-1140

ADMINISTRATIVE SUPPORT:

Pass/ID Office-526-1111	Public Affairs-526-1306

HEALTH & WELFARE: None. See Crane Division NSWC listing, C-812-854-1220.

REST & RECREATION:

Clubs	MWR-526-1101
Kings Hall-526-1141	
NCO-526-1143	
O-526-1141	

ATTRACTIONS: Indianapolis, 45 miles north, Camp Atterbury Veteran's Memorial Park, Camp Atterbury Prisoner of War Chapel.

CRANE DIVISION, NAVAL SURFACE WARFARE CENTER (IN03R2)

ATTN: N00164
300 Highway 361
Crane, IN 47522-5001

TELEPHONE NUMBER INFORMATION: Main installation numbers: C-812-854-1222, D-312-482-1222. E-mail: winklepleck_c@crane.navy.mil. HP: http://www.crane.navy.mil.

LOCATION: From Indianapolis, take Highway 465 south to 37 south to Bloomington, exit right on 45 south. Follow to Crane. USMRA: Page 65 (D-8). NMC: Bloomington, 30 miles northeast.

GENERAL INFORMATION: A major Naval Weapons and Ammunition Support Center, Army tenant located on station.

TEMPORARY MILITARY LODGING: Limited lodging, Building 2682, Code QL4, NAVSURFWARCEN Division, BEQ/BOQ/DV/VIP, C-812-854-1176, D-312-482-1176, Fax: C-812-854-4416, D-312-482-4416, 0700-1500 Mon-Fri. All ranks.

RV, CAMPING/FAMCAMP: Crane MWR Campgrounds on base, 1 April-31 Oct, MWR Campgrounds, NAVSURFWARCENDIV, C-812-854-1368, D-312-482-1368, 52 camper spaces with full hookups, 20 tent spaces.

SPACE-A: None. See Scott AFB, IL listing, C-618-256-3017, D-312-576-3017, Fax: C-618-256-1948.

LOGISTICAL SUPPORT:

Bank-854-1392	Barber Shop-584-1392
Cafeteria-854-1381	Commissary-854-1297
Conv Store-854-1392	Credit Union-854-3414
Dining Facilities	Education Office-854-3262
Consol Mess-854-3435	Exchange-854-1392
Gas Station-854-1864	Package Store-854-1392
Postal Service-854-3400	SATO-854-1244
Travel Office-854-1232	Visitor Center-854-4521

ADMINISTRATIVE SUPPORT:

CDO/OOD-854-1225	Fire Dept-854-5606
Housing Office-854-3510	Legal-854-1130
Locator-854-2511	Pass/ID Office-854-1213
Police-854-1640	Public Affairs-854-1640
Quarter Deck-854-1225	SDO/NCO-854-5621

HEALTH & WELFARE:

CHAMPUS-854-1220	Medical-854-4310
Retiree Services-854-1222	Emergency-854-1333

REST & RECREATION:

Bowling-854-1586	Community Center-854-1721
Fitness Center-854-1586	Golf Course-854-1242
Gym-854-1586	ITT-854-6059
Library-854-1526	Marinas-854-1368
MWR-854-2241	

ATTRACTIONS: Indiana University, Bloomington, Lake Greenwood Nature Trail.

Other Installations in Indiana

Benjamin Harrison Reserve Center (IN02R2), ATTN: ATZI-CDR, Indianapolis, IN 46216-5005. USMRA: Page 65 (E-5). C-317-542-2163, D-312-699-2163. Exchange-542-5698/2163, Commissary-549-5293, Customer Services-549-5293.

INDIANA

Grissom Air Reserve Base (IN01R2), Grissom ARB, IN 46971-5000. USMRA: Page 65 (E-3), C-765-688-5211, Com Club-689-9151, Shoppette-689-5270, Public Affairs-688-3348, Space-A 688-2861, TML-688-2844.

Stout Field (IN08R2), 2002 South Holt Road, Indianapolis, IN 46241-5000. C-800-237-2850 or C-317-247-3300, D-312-369-3278. From I-495 bypass northbound, exit at Airport Expressway, east approximately two miles, north on Holt Road to entrance. USMRA: Page 65 (E-6). NMC: Indianapolis, in city limits. Education Office-247-3224, SATO-247-3333, Pass/ID Office-247-3225, Public Affairs-247-3222.

IOWA

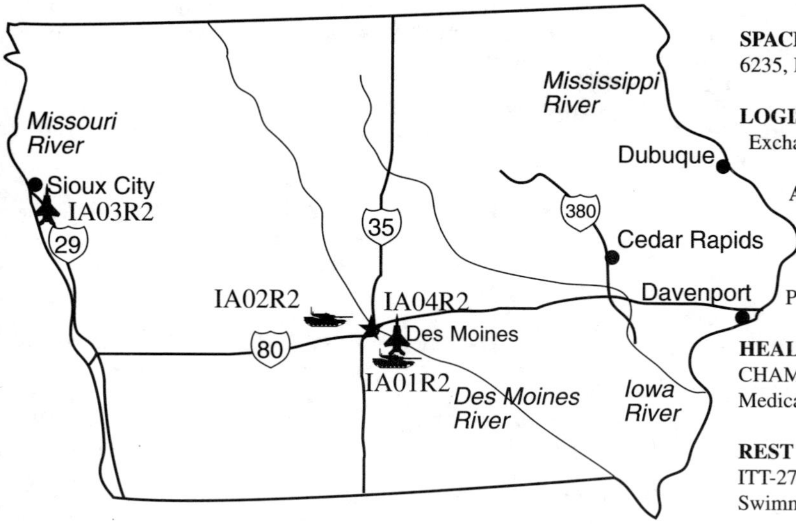

CAMP DODGE/IOWA NATIONAL GUARD BASE (IA02R2)

Headquarters, Iowa National Guard
7700 Northwest Beaver Drive
Johnston, IA 50131-1902

TELEPHONE NUMBER INFORMATION: Main installation numbers: C-515-252-4011, D-312-946-2011. HP: http://165.206.175.1.

LOCATION: From I-35/I-80, take Merle Hay/Camp Dodge exit (exit 131) north on Iowa 401 (Merle Hay Road) to NW Beaver Drive, left to Camp Dodge. Clearly marked. USMRA: Page 77 (E-5). NMC: Des Moines, eight miles southeast.

GENERAL INFORMATION: State Headquarters Iowa National Guard, Iowa Law Enforcement Academy, Iowa Communications Network, National Maintenance Training Center.

TEMPORARY MILITARY LODGING: Lodging office, Building A-8 (facilities), 7th Street and Des Moines Avenue, 24 hours daily, C-515-252-4238, D-312-946-2238. 1630-0800, call Security C-515-240-3742.

RV, CAMPING/FAMCAMP: None. See Offutt AFB, NE listing, C-402-294-2108, D-312-271-2108.

SPACE-A: None. See Offutt AFB, NE listing, C-402-294-6235, D-312-271-6235, Fax: C-402-294-4070.

LOGISTICAL SUPPORT:

Exchange-252-4382	SATO-270-2445

ADMINISTRATIVE SUPPORT:

Fire Dept-911	Housing Office-252-4238
Legal-252-4259	Locator-252-4413
Pass/ID Office-252-4413	Police-250-3742
Public Affairs-252-4582	SDO-252-4011

HEALTH AND WELFARE:

CHAMPUS-252-4679	Chapel-252-4378*
Medical-252-4265*	Retiree Services-252-4413

REST & RECREATION:

ITT-270-2445	Museum-252-4531*
Swimming 276-1106	

**These facilities are not manned by full-time personnel, call Public Affairs at 252-4582 for information.*

OTHER SUPPORT FACILITIES AVAILABLE: Class Six, Credit Union, Education Office, Ball Diamonds.

ATTRACTIONS: Camp Dodge is adjacent to the Saylorville Recreational Area, which provides boating, fishing, camping, hiking, and bicycling. Des Moines, with full cultural and entertainment activities. Adventureland Theme Park, White Water University Park, aquarium, zoo, State Fairgrounds.

Other Installations in Iowa

Fort Des Moines Exchange (IA01R2), Building 106, 217 E Army Post Road, Des Moines, IA 50315-5000. USMRA: Page 77 (E-5). Exchange C-515-287-7671.

Iowa Air National Guard Headquarters (IA04R2), 3100 McKinley Avenue, Des Moines, IA 50321-5000. USMRA: Page 77 (E-5). C-515-256-8210, Exchange-256-8550 (annex of Fort Des Moines Exchange).

Sioux City Gateway Airport (IA03R2), Building TI, 185th FG, Sergeant Bluff, IA 51054-1002. USMRA: Page 77 (A-4). C-712-233-0200, Exchange-277-2042, Medical-255-3511.

KANSAS

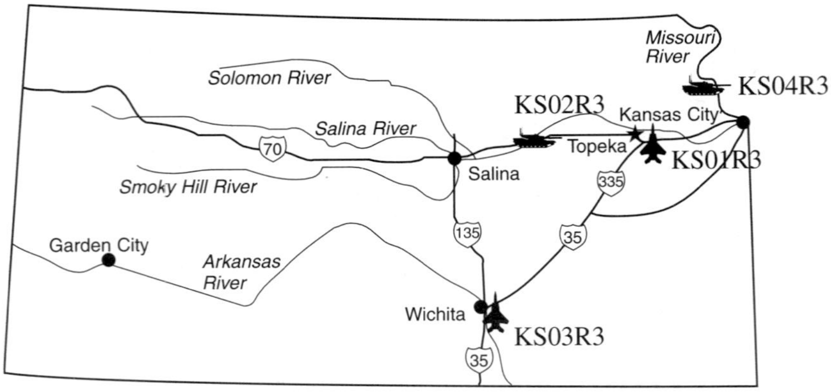

FORBES FIELD (KS01R3)

Forbes Field Air National Guard Base, 5920 SE Coyote Drive
Topeka, KS 66619-5370

TELEPHONE NUMBER INFORMATION: Main installation numbers: C-913-861-4210, D-312-720-4210.

LOCATION: From I-70, take Highway 75 south exit. Main gate located at second stoplight on Highway 75. USMRA: Page 78 (I-4). NMC: Topeka, three miles north.

GENERAL INFORMATION: 190th Air Refueling Wing, 117th Air Refueling Squadron, 127th Weather Flight.

TEMPORARY MILITARY LODGING: None. See Fort Riley listing, C-913-239-2830, D-312-856-2830.

RV, CAMPING/FAMCAMP: None. Nearest facility is over 100 miles away.

SPACE-A: Limited, infrequent flights. Call C-913-862-4210, D-312-720-4210, Fax: C-913-861-4555, D-312-720-4555.

LOGISTICAL SUPPORT: Exchange-861-4962

ADMINISTRATIVE SUPPORT:
Fire Dept-861-4501
Locator-861-4210
Public Affairs-861-4195
Legal-861-4002
Police-861-4080

HEALTH & WELFARE:
CHAMPUS-861-4130
Medical-861-4522
Chapel-861-4001

REST & RECREATION:
Museum 862-3303
MWR-861-4174

ATTRACTIONS: Combat Air Museum on post. Lake Shawnee, Topeka, Heartland Park Race Track, Kansas Expocenter, Topeka Zoo, Kansas Museum of History.

FORT LEAVENWORTH (KS04R3)

USACAC & Fort Leavenworth
ATTN: ATZL-GC
600 Thomas Avenue
Fort Leavenworth, KS 66027-1389

TELEPHONE NUMBER INFORMATION: Main installation numbers: C-913-684-4021, D-312-552-4021. HP: http://leav-www.army.mil.

LOCATION: From I-70, exit US-73 north to Leavenworth. From I-29, exit Highway 92 west to Leavenworth. Fort is adjacent to city of Leavenworth. USMRA: Page 78 (J-3). NMC: Kansas City, 30 miles southeast.

GENERAL INFORMATION: Combined Arms Center, US Disciplinary Barracks, Command and General Staff College, Headquarters 35th Infantry Division (Mech).

TEMPORARY MILITARY LODGING: Lodging office, Building 695, 214 Grant Avenue, 24 hours daily, C-913-684-4091, D-312-552-4091, Fax: C-913-684-4397. All ranks. DV/VIP C-913-684-4063.

RV, CAMPING/FAMCAMP: None. Nearest facility is over 100 miles away.

SPACE-A: Sherman Army Airfield, Pax Term/Lounge, Building 132, 0730-1630 Mon-Fri, C-913-684-2396, D-312-552-2396, flights to CONUS locations.

LOGISTICAL SUPPORT:
Bank-682-9090
Beauty Shop-651-6753
Cafeteria-651-6573
Child Care-684-2322
Commissary-651-4903
Credit Union-651-6555
Dry Cleaner-684-4679
Exchange-651-7271
Laundry-684-4679
Postal Service-682-0052
Snack Bar-651-6586
Barber Shop-651-3815
Book Store-651-6552
Carlson Wagonlit Travel-684-3236
Child Dev Center-684-9382
Conv Store-651-7186
Dining Facilities-684-6520
Education Office-684-2496
Gas Station-651-6541
Package Store-651-7183
SATO-684-3236

ADMINISTRATIVE SUPPORT:
Fire Dept-684-2341
Legal-684-4944
Pass/ID Office-684-4454
Public Affairs-684-5604
Housing Office-684-4921
Locator-684-3651
Police-684-2111
SDO/SNCO-684-2732

HEALTH & WELFARE:
American Red Cross-684-4843
Army Emergency Relief-684-2800
Chapel-684-2210
Family Services-684-4357
Medical
  Central Appts-684-6224
  Clinic/Emergency-684-1110
  Health Benefits-684-6210
  Information-684-6361
ACS-684-4357
CHAMPUS-684-6210
Dental
  Central Appts-684-5001
  Emergency-684-6110
Retiree Services-684-2425
TRICARE-684-6468
Veterinary Services-684-6510

REST & RECREATION:
Arts & Crafts-684-3377
Bowling-651-BOWL
Community Center-684-9350
Fitness Center-684-5120
Golf Course-651-7176
Gym-684-2188
ITR-684-2580
MWR-684-3479
Swimming-684-2187/3088/3998
Theater-684-4683
Youth Center-684-3850
Auto Hobby Shop-684-2767
Clubs
  Consol-651-7011
  Conf Center-651-7011
  EM-684-9383
  Flying-651-6808
Library-758-3101
Stables-651-7307
Tennis-684-3845
Wood Hobby Shop-684-3375
Youth Services-684-5121

ATTRACTIONS: Frontier Army Museum, Agriculture Hall of Fame in Bonner Springs, Harry S. Truman Library & Museum in Independence MO, Kansas City Royals, Kansas City Chiefs.

FORT RILEY (KS02R3)

1st Infantry Division (Mech) & Fort Riley
ATTN: AFZN-GC
Building 405
Fort Riley, KS 66442-5007

TELEPHONE NUMBER INFORMATION: Main installation numbers: C-913-239-3911, D-312-856-1110.

LOCATION: Clearly marked off I-70. USMRA: Page 78 (G,H-3,4). NMC: Topeka, 50 miles east.

GENERAL INFORMATION: Home of America's Army.

TEMPORARY MILITARY LODGING: Lodging office, Building 45, Barry Avenue, 24 hours daily, C-913-239-2830, D-312-856-2830. All ranks. DV/VIP C-913-239-3926/3037.

RV, CAMPING/FAMCAMP: None. Nearest facility is over 100 miles away.

SPACE-A: None. See Forbes Field listing, C-913-862-4210, D-312-720-4210, Fax: C-913-861-4555, D-312-720-4555.

LOGISTICAL SUPPORT:

Child Care-239-4497	Commissary-239-6621
Conv Store-784-6037	Exchange-784-4672
Gas Station-784-5081	Class Six-784-5182
Snack Bar-784-2231	Travel-239-2586
Visitor Center-239-2672	

ADMINISTRATIVE SUPPORT:

Fire Dept-239-4257	Legal-239-3117
Locator-239-9867/9868	Police-239-2431
Public Affairs-239-3032	SDO/EOC-239-2222

HEALTH & WELFARE:

ACS-239-9435	CHAMPUS-239-7727
Chapel-239-3359/2694	Family Services-239-9435
Medical-239-7777	Retiree Services-239-3667

REST & RECREATION:

Auto Hobby Shop-239-9764	Clubs
Crafts-239-9205	Leaders'-784-5999
Golf Course-239-5412	Riding-239-6651
Gyms-239- 3868/5562/5771/4683	ITR-239-5614
Library-239-5305	MWR-239-3467
Outdoor Rec-239-6363	Skating Rink-239-2243
Swimming-239-9441	Theater-239-9454
Wood Hobby Shop-239-9328	Youth Center-239-9224

ATTRACTIONS: Moon Lake Rec Area on post, 239-6189, no camping facilities. Custer House, US Cavalry Museum, and First Territorial Capitol.

McCONNELL AIR FORCE BASE (KS03R3)

57837 Coffeyville Street, Suite 240
McConnell Air Force Base, KS 67221-3504

TELEPHONE NUMBER INFORMATION: Main installation numbers: C-316-652-6100, D-312-743-1110.

LOCATION: Take I-35 to Wichita, exit at Kellogg Street (US-54) west to Rock Road south and McConnell AFB. USMRA: Page 78 (G-6). NMC: Wichita, six miles northwest.

GENERAL INFORMATION: Air Mobility Command Base, 22nd Air Refueling Wing.

TEMPORARY MILITARY LODGING: Lodging office, Building 193, Manhattan Street, 24 hours daily, C-316-683-7711, D-312-743-6500. All ranks. DV/VIP C-316-693-6500.

RV, CAMPING/FAMCAMP: None. Nearest facility is over 100 miles away.

SPACE-A: Pax Term/Lounge, Building 1112, 24 hours daily, C-316-652-3840, D-312-743-3840, Fax: C-316-652-4957, flights to CONUS, OCONUS and overseas via KC-135R aircraft.

LOGISTICAL SUPPORT:

Bank-652-5450	Child Care-652-4223
Class Six-652-5198	Clothing Store-652-4171
Commissary-652-5621	Credit Union-652-5457
Exchange-685-0231	Family Day Care-652-5783
Food Services-652-6185	Gas Station-652-5215
N & N Travel-652-5263	Shoppette-685-0291
Visitor Center-652-4713	

ADMINISTRATIVE SUPPORT:

Fire-117	Legal-652-3590
Locator-652-3555	Police-652-3976
Public Affairs-652-3141	

HEALTH & WELFARE:

CHAMPUS-652-5017	Chapel-652-3562
Family Services-652-3729	Family Support Center-652-6020
TRICARE-691-6300	

REST & RECREATION:

Arts & Crafts-652-4084	Bowling-652-6187
Clubs	Fitness Center-652-4009
EM-652-6184	Golf Course-652-4038
O-652-6182	Indoor Pool-652-6066
Library-652-4207	Rec Center-652-4432
Rec Equip-652-4432	Tickets & Tours-652-6038
Youth Center-652-4071	

ATTRACTIONS: Rebuilt downtown core area has resulted in an outstanding civic and cultural complex, Zoo, Museums of Art and History, Botanical Garden.

KENTUCKY

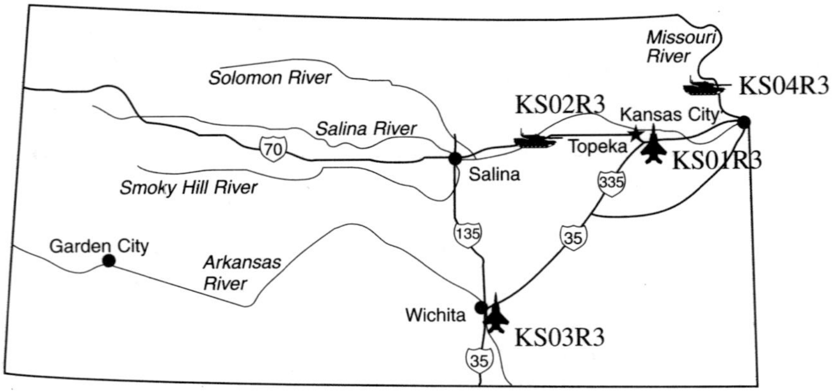

FORT CAMPBELL (KY02R2)

101st Airborne Division & Fort Campbell
ATTN: AFZB-GC
39 26th Street
Fort Campbell, KY 42223-5628

TELEPHONE NUMBER INFORMATION: Main installation numbers: C-502-798-2151, D-312-635-1110.

LOCATION: In the southwest part of Kentucky, four miles south of intersection of US-41A and I-24, 10 miles northwest of Clarksville, TN. USMRA: Page 40 (E,F-7). NMC: Hopkinsville, 15 miles north.

GENERAL INFORMATION: 101st Airborne Division (Air Assault), Air Assault School, 5th SFG (A), 101st Corps Support Group Regiment, 160th Special Operation Aviation Regiment.

TEMPORARY MILITARY LODGING: Lodging office, Building 1581, 26th & Indiana, C-502-798-5281/618. Reservations C-615-431-5107, D-312-635-2865, 0730-1600 Mon-Fri. All ranks. DV/VIP C-615-431-8924.

RV, CAMPING/FAMCAMP: Destiny Parks & Pavilion (Army Travel Camp) on post, year round, C-502-798-3126/5590 D-312-635-3126/5590, 75 camper spaces with W&E hookups, four cabins.

SPACE-A: Campbell Army Airfield, Pax Term, Zone H/I, 24 hours daily, C-502-798-2146, Fax: C-502-798-9288, flights via executive aircraft.

LOGISTICAL SUPPORT:
Cafeteria-631-3779
Commissary-798-2606
Exchange-439-1841
Package Store-431-3622
Snack Bar-431-6239
Child Care-798-2164
Conv Store-439-1914
Gas Station-439-1689
SATO-431-5660
Visitor Center-798-7463

ADMINISTRATIVE SUPPORT:
Fire Dept-798-7171
Locator-798-1110
Public Affairs-798-3025
Legal-798-5011
Police-798-7110
SDO/NCO-798-9793

HEALTH & WELFARE:
ACS-798-5127
Chapel-798-8464
Medical
  Central Appts-798-8287/439-8287
  Emergency-798-8000/8400
CHAMPUS-798-8280
Family Services-798-5127
Retiree Services-798-5680

REST & RECREATION:
Arts & Crafts-ext 6693
Bowling-ext 5887/4993
Golf Course-798-4906
Gym-ext 5894
ITT-798-7436
Library-ext 5729
Outdoor Rec-ext 3126/5590
Rec Center-ext 6383/4616/5818
Rec Equip-ext 3919/6806
Show Center-ext 6087
Swimming-ext 6290
Theater-798-2917
Auto Hobby Shop-ext 6317
Clubs
  EM-439-3897
  NCO-439-1772
  O-431-5603
MWR-798-2917
Recreation-798-7466
Stables-ext 2629/2487
Tennis-ext 6973/5225

ATTRACTIONS: A growing recreational area in Nashville..."Home of the Grand Ole Opry," Land Between the Lakes (170,000-acre national recreational and environmental education area).

FORT KNOX (KY01R2)

US Army Airmen Center & Fort Knox
ATTN: ATZK-GC
P.O. Box 995
Fort Knox, KY 40121-5000

TELEPHONE NUMBER INFORMATION: Main installation numbers: C-502-624-1181, D-312-464-1181.

LOCATION: From I-65 in Louisville, exit Gene Snyder Expressway west to US-31 west, go south to Fort Knox. From I-64, exit I-264 (Waterson Expressway west) to US-31 west, south to Fort Knox. From I-71, exit I-65 south to Gene Snyder Expressway to US-31 west then south to Fort Knox. USMRA: Page 40, 41 (H,I-3,4). NMC: Louisville, 25 miles north.

GENERAL INFORMATION: Army Armor Center, Training Brigades, HQ USAREC, and HQ, 2 ROTC Region.

TEMPORARY MILITARY LODGING: Lodging office, Building 4770 (Newgarden Tower), Dixie Highway 31 west, 24 hours daily, C-502-942-0490 or 502-943-1000, D-312-464-3491. All ranks. DV/VIP C-502-624-6951.

RV, CAMPING/FAMCAMP: Camp Carlson Army Travel Camp, on post, year round, C-502-624-4836, D-312-464-4836, seven camper spaces with W/E/S hookups, 18 camper spaces with W/E hookups, four family cabins, four youth cabins, 25 tent spaces.

SPACE-A: Godman Army Airfield, Pax Term, Building 5220, 24 hours daily, C-502-624-5545, D-312-464-5545, Fax: C-502-624-2421, flights via executive aircraft to CONUS locations.

LOGISTICAL SUPPORT:
Cafeteria-942-0805/0230
Commissary-624-5355
Exchange-942-0067/4300
Gas Station-942-4206
Package Store-942-4208
Shoppette-942-4262
Child Care-624-8320
Dining Facilities
  Burger King-942-4281
  Food Court-942-0744
SATO-942-2509

ADMINISTRATIVE SUPPORT:
Legal-624-2771
Police-624-2111/112
Locator-624-1141
SDO/NCO-624-4481/4421

HEALTH & WELFARE:
CHAMPUS-624-9050
Family Services-624-6291
Retiree Services-624-4315
Chapel-624-4524
Medical
  Central Appts-624-9148
  Emergency-624-9000

REST & RECREATION:
Arts & Crafts-624-4725/1552
Bowling-624-1651
Field House-624-2214
Golf Course-624-1548
Auto Hobby Shop-624-5410/5338
Clubs
  EM-942-0305
  NCO-942-0409

KENTUCKY
Fort Knox, continued

Gym-624-3316/3641
ITT-624-5030/8254
Outdoor Rec-624-7754
Rec Equip-624-2314
Swimming-624-6217
Theater-624-4284/3048
Youth Services-624-5128
O-942-0959
Library-624-1232/4723
Rec Center-624-8254
Skeet-624-7754
Tennis-624-2214/4033
Wood Hobby Shop-624-3540

ATTRACTIONS: Mammoth Cave, Louisville, Hodgenville..."Birthplace of Abraham Lincoln," and Bardstown...site of "My Old Kentucky Home," all within 50 miles. Patton Museum at Chaffee Avenue entrance to Fort Knox opens at 0900 to 1630 Mon-Fri year round, with special hours: 1 May through 30 Sept 1000-1800, 1000-1430 on Sat, Sun and holidays.

Other Installations in Kentucky

Blue Grass Army Depot (KY06R2), ATTN: SIOBG-CO, 209 Kingston Highway, Richmond, KY 40475-5001, USMRA: Page 41 (K-3), C-606-625-6246, D-312-745-6246. Exchange-293-1211.

Standiford Field Air National Guard Base (KY05R2), 123 Airlift, 1019 Grade Lane Louisville, KY 40213-2678, USMRA: Page 41 (I-3). C-502-364-9400, D-312-989-4400. HP: http://www.kyang.win.net. Space-A-C-502-364-9459, D-312-989-4459, Locator-364-9400, Exchange-364-9420.

LOUISIANA

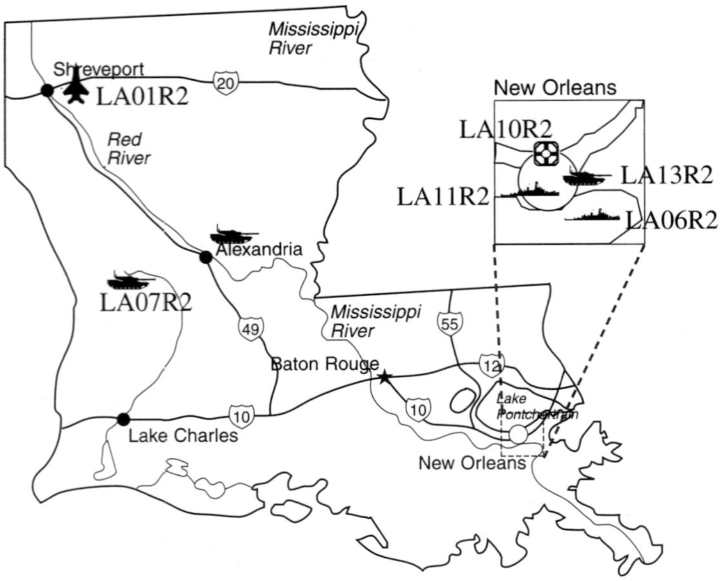

BARKSDALE AIR FORCE BASE (LA01R2)

841 Fairchild Avenue, Suite 103
Barksdale Air Force Base, LA 71110-2270

TELEPHONE NUMBER INFORMATION: Main installation numbers: C-318-456-1110, D-312-781-1110.

LOCATION: Exit I-20 at Airline Drive, go south to Old Minden Road (one quarter mile), left on Old Minden Road (one block), then right on North Gate Drive (one mile) to North Gate of AFB. USMRA: Page 79 (B-2). NMC: Shreveport, one mile west. Co-located with Bossier City and Shreveport.

GENERAL INFORMATION: Air Combat Command Base, Headquarters 8th Air Force, 2nd Bomb Wing, B-52, 917th Wing AFRES units with B52 and A-10.

TEMPORARY MILITARY LODGING: Building 5155, Davis Avenue, 24 hours daily, C-318-747-4708, D-312-781-3091. All ranks. DV/VIP C-318-456-2151.

RV, CAMPING/FAMCAMP: FAMCAMP on base, year round, C-318-456-2679, D-312-781-2679, 18 camper spaces with W&E hookups, four without hookups.

SPACE-A: Building 6448, C-318-456-3226/5630, D-312-781-3226/5630, Fax: C-318-456-4989/3800, D-312-781-4989/3800.

LOGISTICAL SUPPORT:

Bank-226-2722
Beauty Shop-746-5930
Child Dev Center-456-4139
Commissary-456-8263
Dining Facilities-456-8367
Exchange-746-2554
Gas Station-746-5662
SATO-741-3095
Travel Office-456-4901
Barber Shop-741-3114
Cafeteria-456-8367
Class Six-746-5662
Conv Store-746-5662
Dry Cleaner-742-0133
Education Office-456-2615
Postal Service-456-3950
Snack Bar-741-3394
Visitor Center-456-3587

ADMINISTRATIVE SUPPORT:

Fire Dept-117
Legal-456-2561
Pass/ID Office-456-4292
Public Affairs-456-3065
Housing Office-456-4740
Locator-456-3555
Police-456-2551

HEALTH & WELFARE:

AF Aid-456-8400
CHAMPUS-456-6572
Dental-456-4017
Medical
  Central Appts-456-6555
  Clinic-456-6538
  Emergency-911
  Health Benefits-456-6572
  Hospital-456-6111
  Information-456-6000
American Red Cross-456-8073
Chapel-456-2111
Family Services-456-8331
Retiree Services-456-4480
TRICARE-456-6572
Veterinary Services-456-4172

REST & RECREATION:

Arts & Crafts-456-3140
Bowling-456-4133
Community Center-456-8911
Fitness Center-456-4135
Golf Course-456-2263
Outdoor Rec-456-2679
Wood Hobby Shop-456-3409
Auto Hobby Shop-456-4695
Clubs
  EM-456-4467
  O-456-4926
Library-456-4101
Theater-456-3666
Youth Center-456-3448

ATTRACTIONS: Moderate climate. Great water sports. Horse racing (Louisiana Downs) Apr-Nov, NCAA sanctioned Independence Bowl late in December, Riverboard Casinos open 24 hours daily.

CAMP BEAUREGARD (LA12R2)

Training Site, Detachment 1 HQ STARC
409 F Street
Pineville, LA 71360-3737

TELEPHONE NUMBER INFORMATION: Main installation numbers: C-318-640-2080, D-312-485-8222.

LOCATION: Off US-165, nine miles south of Leesville. USMRA: Page 79 (D-4). NMC: Alexandria, five miles southwest.

GENERAL INFORMATION: National Guard Training Site with Modified Record Fire Range, M203 Range, 9MM Range. NGB Region VI NCO Academy at Camp Ball, five miles north of Camp Beauregard on US 165.

TEMPORARY MILITARY LODGING: Building 1111, 0730-1600, C-318-641-8269, D-312-485-8222, Fax: C-318-641-3341. After hours C-318-640-2080.

RV, CAMPING/FAMCAMP: Twin Lakes Recreation Area off base. C-318-640-2080 ext 269, 4 camper spaces with W&E hookups, 10 primitive sites with W hookups, 3 mobile homes.

SPACE-A: None. See Fort Polk listing, C-318-531-4831/7328, D-312-863-4831/7328.

LOGISTICAL SUPPORT:

Barber Shop-640-2938
Exchange-641-9661
Credit Union-641-8308
Tailor-641-1362

ADMINISTRATIVE SUPPORT:

Fire Dept-ext 2080
Locator-640-2080
Housing Office-641-8269
Police-641-8266

HEALTH & WELFARE: None. See Fort Polk listing, C-318-531-3118.

REST & RECREATION:

Clubs
  EM-640-8219
  O-641-8277
Gym/Pool-641-2080

OTHER SUPPORT AVAILABLE: Shoppette.

ATTRACTIONS: Alexandria Zoo, Kent House Plantation, Historic Natchatiches 50 miles north, Baton Rouge, state capital, approximately 100 miles southeast. New Orleans, approximately 150 miles southeast. Hunting and fishing opportunities available.

FORT POLK (LA07R2)

Joint Readiness Training Center & Fort Polk
ATTN: AFZX-GC
7073 Radio Road, Building 411
Fort Polk, LA 71459-5342

TELEPHONE NUMBER INFORMATION: Main installation numbers: C-318-531-2911, D-312-863-2911. E-mail: afzxpo@polk-emh2.army.mil. HP: http://www.jrtc-polk.army.mil.

LOCATION: Off US-171, nine miles south of Leesville. USMRA: Page 79 (C-4). NMC: Alexandria, 50 miles northeast.

GENERAL INFORMATION: Headquarters Joint Readiness Training Center, 2nd Armored Cavalry Regiment, Warrior Brigade and 519th Military Police Battalion.

TEMPORARY MILITARY LODGING: Lodging office, Magnolia House, Building 522, Utah Avenue, 24 hours daily, C-318-531-2941, D-312-863-2941, Fax: C-318-535-0968. All ranks.

RV, CAMPING/FAMCAMP: Toledo Bend Recreation Site off post, year round, C-318-531-1974, 15 camper spaces with W&E hookups, 12 mobile homes. South Fort RV Park on post, year round, C-318-531-2941/4822, 10 camper spaces with full hookups.

SPACE-A: Polk Army Airfield, Base Ops, 0700-2200 Mon-Fri, during JRTC rotations 24 hours a day. C-318-531-4831/7328, D-312-863-4831/7328.

LOGISTICAL SUPPORT:

Bank-537-3421	Barber Shop-537-7921
Beauty Shop-537-3102	Car Rental-537-8694
Carlson Wagonlit Travel-537-0658	Child Care-531-2149
Child Dev Center-531-2149	Class Six-535-0456
Commissary-531-2088	Credit Union-531-2991/2992
Exchange-537-1001	Dry Cleaner-537-2015
Education Office-531-5401	Gas Station-537-8269
Postal Service-531-2795/8676	Shoppette-537-1050
Snack Bar-537-0251	Travel-537-4120/4122
Visitor Center-531-6812/6339	

ADMINISTRATIVE SUPPORT:

Fire Dept-531-2026	Housing Office-531-2762
Legal-531-2580	Locator-531-1272/1273
Pass/ID Office-531-1839/1430	Police-531-2677
Public Affairs-531-2714	SDO-531-1726

HEALTH & WELFARE:

American Red Cross-531-1927/1929	ACS-531-2840
Army Emergency Relief-531-1957	CHAMPUS-531-3176
Chapel-531-4228/2332	Dental-531-2603/2327
Medical-531-3118	Retiree Services-531-4515
Central Appts-531-3000	TRICARE-1-800-406-2833
Emergency-531-3368/3361	Veterinary Services-531-1322

REST & RECREATION:

Arts & Crafts-531-1980	Auto Hobby Shop-531-6149
Bowling-531-6273	Combined Club-531-4440/6695
Fitness Center-531-6795	Golf Course-531-4661
ITR-531-1794	Library-531-1986/1987
Outdoor Rec-531-5332	Youth Services-531-6907/6917

ATTRACTIONS: Fort Polk Military Museum. Baton Rouge, state capital, 155 miles southeast. New Orleans, 232 miles southeast.

JACKSON BARRACKS (LA13R2)

Louisiana National Guard Base
6400 Dauphine Street
ATTN: PAO
New Orleans, LA 70146-0330

TELEPHONE NUMBER INFORMATION: Main installation numbers: C-504-271-6262, D-312-485-8210.

LOCATION: From Baton Rouge, take I-10 east to Claiborne exit; go straight, cross drawbridge; entrance to Jackson Barracks is after Caffin Avenue. USMRA: Page 90 (F-3,4). NMC: New Orleans, in city limits.

TEMPORARY MILITARY LODGING: Building 57, Area A, 0730-1600. C-504-278-8364, D-312-485-6207.

RV, CAMPING/FAMCAMP: None. See New Orleans NSA listing, Magnolia Shade RV Park, C-504-678-2527/2285, D-312-678-2527/2285.

SPACE-A: None. See New Orleans NAS listing, C-504-678-3213, D-312-678-3213, Fax: C-502-678-3734.

LOGISTICAL SUPPORT:

Carlson Wagonlit Travel-278-8409	Credit Union-278-8588
Exchange-278-8245	

ADMINISTRATIVE SUPPORT:

Police-278-8460	Public Affairs-278-8281
SDO-278-8460	

HEALTH & WELFARE: None. See New Orleans NSA listing, C-504-678-2670.

REST & RECREATION:
Clubs
EM-278-6490
NCO-278-6490 *(Only open drill weekends)*
O-*(Only open during special functions)*

OTHER SUPPORT FACILITIES AVAILABLE: Fitness Center, Gym, Basketball Court, Jogging Track, Picnic Area, Softball Field, Tennis Court, Volleyball Court, Weight Rooms, Military Library and Military Museum.

ATTRACTIONS: Officer quarters comprise largest collection of antebellum homes in the deep south. Nearby attractions include City of New Orleans, Superdome, New Orleans French Quarter, Riverwalk, IMAX Theatre, National Cemetery, Battlefield, Zoo, Aquarium, Audubon Park, Streetcars.

NEW ORLEANS COAST GUARD INTEGRATED SUPPORT COMMAND (LA10R2)

4640 Urquhart Street
New Orleans, LA 70117-4698

TELEPHONE NUMBER INFORMATION: Main installation number: C-504-942-3020.

LOCATION: From I-10 go south on Elysian Fields Avenue, left on Claiborne Avenue, right on Poland Street, left on Urquhart Street to main gate. USMRA: Page 79 (H-6,7) Page 90 (E-3). NMC: New Orleans, city limits.

GENERAL INFORMATION: Provides industrial and repair support to primarily the Eighth CG District. Host Command to many tenants, including CG Group New Orleans, CG Station and CG Aids to Navigation Team NOLA, and others.

TEMPORARY MILITARY LODGING: None. See Jackson Barracks listing, C-504-278-8364, D-312-485-6207.

LOUISIANA
New Orleans Coast Guard Integrated Support Command, continued

RV, CAMPING/FAMCAMP: None. See New Orleans NSA listing, Magnolia Shade RV Park, C-504-678-2527/2285, D-312-678-2527/2285.

SPACE-A: None. See New Orleans NAS listing, C-504-678-3213, D-312-678-3213, Fax: C-502-678-3734.

LOGISTICAL SUPPORT: Exchange-942-4537

ADMINISTRATIVE SUPPORT: CDO/OOD-942-3020

HEALTH & WELFARE: Medical
Emergency-911
Information-942-3021

REST & RECREATION: None. See Jackson Barracks/Louisiana National Guard Base listing, C-504-278-6490.

ATTRACTIONS: City of New Orleans, Superdome, Jefferson Downs Racetrack, Audubon Park, New Orleans Zoo, Bayou Segnette State Park.

NEW ORLEANS NAVAL AIR STATION/ JOINT RESERVE BASE (LA11R2)

400 Russell Avenue
New Orleans, LA 70143-5012

TELEPHONE NUMBER INFORMATION: Main installation numbers: C-504-678-3253, D-312-678-3253.

LOCATION: Off LA-23 in Belle Chasse. Clearly marked. USMRA: Page 79 (H-7), page 90 (F-6). NMC: New Orleans, 10 miles north.

GENERAL INFORMATION: Navy Fighter, Logistics, and Patrol Aircraft Squadrons, Coast Guard Air Station, Air Force Reserve and ANG units, US Customs Service and Marine Air Group Det 42.

TEMPORARY MILITARY LODGING: Lodging office, Building 21 (Olson Avenue) and Building 40 (Rinard Avenue), 24 hours daily, C-504-678-3841, D-312-678-3841. Fax: C-504-678-1959, DV/VIP C-504-678-3841.

RV, CAMPING/FAMCAMP: Campground on base, year round, C-504-678-3448, 17 camper spaces with full hookups, two camping trailers, one mobile home, 10 tent spaces.

SPACE-A: Pax Term/Lounge, Building 1, 0700-2300 hours daily, C-504-678-3213, D-312-678-3213, Fax: C-504-678-3734, Rec: C-504-678-3103, D-312-678-3103, flights to CONUS, OCONUS and overseas.

LOGISTICAL SUPPORT:
Child Care-678-3654
Exchange-678-3510
Package Store-678-3510
Snack Bar-678-3514
Conv Store-678-3506
Gas Station-678-3506
SATO-678-3625

ADMINISTRATIVE SUPPORT:
CDO/OOD-678-3253
Legal-678-3266
Police-678-3827
Fire Dept-678-3105
Locator-678-3253
Public Affairs-678-3260

HEALTH & WELFARE:
Chapel-678-3525
Retiree Services-678-2134
Medical-678-3660/1
TRICARE-678-2676

REST & RECREATION:
Auto Hobby Shop-678-3448
Clubs
Com-678-3509
EM-678-3509
NCO-678-3509
O-678-3844
Bowling-678-3514
Gym-678-3230
Golf Course-678-3453
ITT-678-3695
MWR-678-3231
Outdoor Rec-678-3230

ATTRACTIONS: New Orleans French Quarter, Mississippi River, New Orleans Zoo, Aquarium, Swamp Tours, River Boat Casinos.

NEW ORLEANS NAVAL SUPPORT ACTIVITY (LA06R2)

2300 General Meyer Avenue
New Orleans, LA 70142-5007

TELEPHONE NUMBER INFORMATION: Main installation numbers: C-504-678-5011, D-312-678-5011.

LOCATION: On the West bank of the Mississippi River. From I-10 east, take Mississippi River Bridge to the West bank. Take Gen DeGaulle east exit after passing over bridge and turn left at Shirley Drive which leads to NSA. USMRA: Page 90 (E,F-3,4). NMC: New Orleans, five miles east.

GENERAL INFORMATION: Headquarters for both the Naval and Marine Corps Reserve.

TEMPORARY MILITARY LODGING: Navy Lodge, Building 702, 0700-2000 daily, C-504-366-3266. BEQ, C-504-678-2220, D-312-678-2220, BOQ, C-504-678-2264, D-312-678-2264, DV/VIP C-504-678-2264, D-312-678-2264, Fax: C-504-678-2663. All ranks.

RV, CAMPING/FAMCAMP: Magnolia Shade RV Park on base, year round, C-504-678-2527/2285, D-312-678-2527/2285, 16 camper spaces with W&E hookups.

SPACE-A: None. See New Orleans NAS listing, C-504-678-3213, D-312-678-3213, Fax: C-502-678-3734.

LOGISTICAL SUPPORT:
Child Care-678-2450
Exchange-678-2702
Package Store-678-2749
Commissary-678-2182
Gas Station-678-2747
SATO-678-2330

ADMINISTRATIVE SUPPORT:
CDO/OOD-678-2655
Legal-678-2520
Public Affairs-678-2540
Locator-678-5011
Police-678-2570

HEALTH & WELFARE:
CHAMPUS-678-2675
Family Services-678-2647
Retiree Services-678-2134
Chapel-678-2244
Medical
Central Appts-678-2670
Clinic-678-2390
Emergency-911

REST & RECREATION:
Bowling-ext 2204
Courts-ext 2527
Hobby Shops-ext 2207
ITT-678-2208
MWR-678-2269
Swimming-ext 2654
Clubs
CPO-678-2218
EM-678-2219
O-678-2218
Rec Equipment-ext 2527

ATTRACTIONS: New Orleans French Quarter, Bourbon Street, Sports, New Orleans Zoo, River Boat Cruises, Aquarium, Superdome.

MAINE

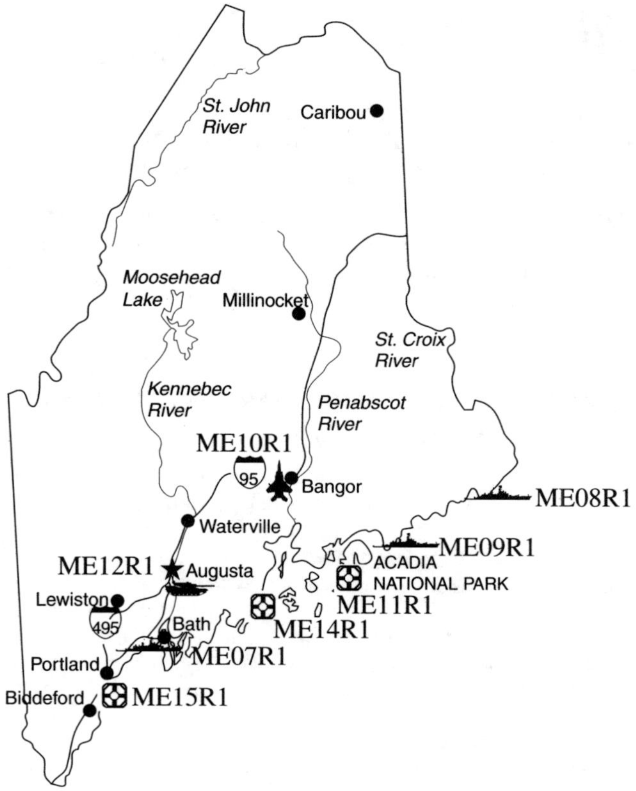

BANGOR AIR NATIONAL GUARD BASE (ME10R1)

103 Maineiac Avenue, Suite 505
Bangor, ME 04401-3099

TELEPHONE NUMBER INFORMATION: Main installation numbers: C-207-990-7700 (ask for extensions), D-312-698-7700.

LOCATION: Located in Bangor city limits. Northbound from I-95 take exit 47, Ohio Street, drive west two blocks and turn left, one block to right turn on Union Street (ME-222), pass Bangor IAP, turn left on Griffin Road, entrance is 300 yards on right. USMRA: Page 18 (E-6,7). NMC: Bangor, in city limits.

GENERAL INFORMATION: Air National Guard Air Refueling Wing with KC-135E aircraft, Over-the-Horizon Backscatter Radar Operations Center.

TEMPORARY MILITARY LODGING: The Army National Guard operates the "Pine Tree Inn," 24 hours daily, C-207-942-2081, D-312-698-7700. Located at 22 Cleveland Avenue on Bangor IAP adjacent to Bangor ANG Base. All ranks.

RV, CAMPING/FAMCAMP: None. See Winter Harbor NSGA listing, C-207-963-5537, D-312-476-9287/9288.

SPACE-A: Pax Term, Building 491, 0730-1600 Mon-Fri, C-207-990-7212/7247, D-312-698-7212/7247, Fax: C-207-990-7216. Flights to CONUS and overseas.

LOGISTICAL SUPPORT:

Child Care-941-0466	Commissary-990-7751
Exchange-990-7233	SATO-ext 355

ADMINISTRATIVE SUPPORT: Public Affairs-990-7228

HEALTH & WELFARE:

CHAMPUS-ext 458	Retiree Services-ext 458

REST & RECREATION: None. See Winter Harbor NSGA listing, C-207-963-5537/5534.

ATTRACTIONS: Lobster and other seafood, Penobscot Marine Museum in Searsport, Acadia National Park, Bar Harbor, Mt Desert Island, beaches, and boating.

BRUNSWICK NAVAL AIR STATION (ME07R1)

551 Fitch Avenue
Box 32
Brunswick Naval Air Station, ME 04011-5000

TELEPHONE NUMBER INFORMATION: Main installation numbers: C-207-921-1110, D-312-476-1110.

LOCATION: From I-95 north, exit Coastal Route 1 north. Take route 1 four miles to Cooks Corner. Turn right to main gate of Brunswick NAS. USMRA: Page 18 (C-9). NMC: Portland, 30 miles southwest.

GENERAL INFORMATION: Home to over 5,000 military personnel and six maritime patrol squadrons flying P-3 aircraft. The last active duty military airfield in the northeast.

TEMPORARY MILITARY LODGING: Lodging office, Building 512, Sewall Road, 24 hours daily, C-207-921-2245, D-312-476-2245, Fax: C-207-792-0232. Navy Lodge, Topsham Annex, 0730-2200 daily, C-207-921-2206. Note: located seven miles from base. Call for directions. All ranks. DV/VIP C-207-921-2214.

RV, CAMPING/FAMCAMP: None. See Winter Harbor NSGA listing, C-207-963-5537, D-312-476-9287/9288.

SPACE-A: Pax Term/Lounge, Building 200, 24 hours daily, C-207-921-2682/2689, D-312-476-2682/2689, limited flights to CONUS and overseas.

LOGISTICAL SUPPORT:

Cafeteria-921-2455	Child Care-921-2610
Commissary-921-2971*	Conv Store-921-2182
Exchange-921-2387	

**Located at Topsham Annex.*

ADMINISTRATIVE SUPPORT:

CDO/NCO-921-2214	Legal-921-2331
Locator-921-1110	Police-921-2585

HEALTH & WELFARE:

CHAMPUS-921-2901	Chapel-921-2231/2223
Family Services-921-2273	Medical
Retiree Services-921-2609	Central Appts-921-2243
	Emergency-921-2610

REST & RECREATION:

Arts & Crafts-ext 2168	Auto Hobby Shop-ext 2488
Bowling-ext 2145	EM Club-921-2121
Golf Course-ext 2155	Rec Equip-ext 2738
Ski Shop-ext 2488	

ATTRACTIONS: The last active-duty DoD airfield in the northeast is located on the coast of Maine, with skiing two hours north. Lobsters and other seafood. Maine Maritime Museum in Bath, Summer Music Theater in Brunswick. L. L. Bean eight minutes south.

CUTLER NAVAL COMPUTER & TELECOMMUNICATIONS STATION CENTER (ME08R1)

HC 69, Box 1198
Cutler, ME 04626-9603

TELEPHONE NUMBER INFORMATION: Main installation numbers: C-207-259-8203, D-312-476-7203. HP: http://www.ncts.cut.navy.mil.

LOCATION: From I-95 take Alt US-1 to Ellsworth ME, US-1 east to East Machias, right on ME-191 to base at Cutler. USMRA: Page 18 (G,H-7). NMC: Bangor, 100 miles west.

GENERAL INFORMATION: The world's most powerful transmitter. Provides fleet communications.

TEMPORARY MILITARY LODGING: BEQ/BOQ C-207-259-8201/8284, Fax: C-207-259-7231.

RV, CAMPING/FAMCAMP: Sprague's Neck on base, year round, C-207-259-8284, D-312-476-7284, one log cabin (Running water and indoor sanitary facilities 15 May-15 Sep), 10 camper spaces without hookups

SPACE-A: None. See Bangor ANGB listing, C-207-990-7212/7247, D-312-698-7212/7247, Fax: C-207-990-7216.

LOGISTICAL SUPPORT:
Cafeteria-259-8277
Commissary-259-8270
Exchange-259-8244
Snack Bar-259-8277

ADMINISTRATIVE SUPPORT:
CDO/OOD-259-8229/8226
Fire Dept-259-8260
Locator-259-8203
Police-259-8267

HEALTH & WELFARE:
CHAMPUS-259-8219/09
Chapel-259-8388
Medical
  Central Appts-259-8209/219
  Emergency, after hours-ext 226

REST & RECREATION:
Bowling-ext 275
Consol-259-8277
Hobby Shop-ext 285
ITT-259-8201
Rec Services-259-8284

ATTRACTIONS: Skiing, hiking.

SOUTH PORTLAND COAST GUARD BASE (ME11R1)

41 Mussey Street
South Portland, ME 04106-0007

TELEPHONE NUMBER INFORMATION: Main installation number: C-207-767-0320.

LOCATION: Exit I-95 to I-295 north, exit I-295 to Broadway, east to South Portland. Watch for signs to the base. USMRA: Page 18 (B,C-9). NMC: South Portland, in city limits.

GENERAL INFORMATION: Industrial Base/SAR Station.

TEMPORARY MILITARY LODGING: None. See Brunswick NAS listing, C-207-921-2245, D-312-476-2245, Fax: C-207-792-0232.

RV, CAMPING/FAMCAMP: None. See Winter Harbor NSGA listing, C-207-963-5537, D-312-476-9287/9288.

SPACE-A: None. See Brunswick NAS listing, C-207-921-2682/2689, D-312-476-2682/2689.

LOGISTICAL SUPPORT:
Exchange-767-4757
Package Store-767-4757

ADMINISTRATIVE SUPPORT:
CDO-767-0303
Housing Office-767-0390
Locator-767-0320
Public Affairs-767-0310

HEALTH & WELFARE:
Medical-767-0339

REST & RECREATION:
Consol Club-767-0374
MWR-767-0311

ATTRACTIONS: City of Portland.

WINTER HARBOR NAVAL SECURITY GROUP ACTIVITY (ME09R1)

10 Fabbri Green, Suite 10
Winter Harbor, ME 04693-7001

TELEPHONE NUMBER INFORMATION: Main installation numbers: C-207-963-5534/5535, (ask for extensions) D-312-476-9287.

LOCATION: From Ellsworth, take US-1 north to ME-186 east to Acadia National Park. Naval Security Station on Schoodic Point in the park. USMRA: Page 18 (F-8). NMC: Bangor, 45 miles northwest.

GENERAL INFORMATION: Provides communications security and performs other communications activities for Navy units.

TEMPORARY MILITARY LODGING: Lodging office, Building 84, 0730-2230 daily, C-207-963-5534 ext-223, D-312-476-9223. All ranks.

RV, CAMPING/FAMCAMP: Winter Harbor Recreation Area on base, 15 Apr-15 Oct, C-207-963-5537, D-312-476-9287/9288, five camper spaces with W&E hookups, one camper space without hookups, three tent spaces, six recreation cabins and five mobile homes.

SPACE-A: None. See Bangor ANG Base listing, C-207-990-7212/7247, D-312-698-7212/7247, Fax: C-207-990-7216.

LOGISTICAL SUPPORT:
Child Care-ext 265
Commissary-ext 259
Conv Store-ext 254
Exchange-ext 254
Gas Station-963-7391

ADMINISTRATIVE SUPPORT:
CDO/OOD-963-5534
Fire Dept-ext 229
Legal-ext -210
Locator-963-5534
Police-ext 225
Public Affairs-ext 224

HEALTH & WELFARE:
CHAMPUS-ext 297
Chapel-ext 279
Medical-963-7206 or 963-5534 ext 297

REST & RECREATION:
Auto Hobby Shop-963-5537
Bowling-963-5537
Club (all ranks) ext 283/4
Fitness Center-963-5537
MWR-963-5537/5534
Rec Equipment-963-5537
Recreation-ext 287

OTHER SUPPORT & FACILITIES AVAILABLE: Saunas, Racquetball and Tennis Courts, Hiking Trails, Car Wash, Child Dev Center.

ATTRACTIONS: Boating and fishing, hiking, swimming, golfing, fall foliage, downhill and cross-country skiing, fresh seafood, August blueberry harvest.

Other Installations in Maine

Camp Keyes (ME12R1), HQ MAINE NG, Building 7, Augusta, ME 04333-0033. USMRA: Page 18 (C-8). C-207-626-4390, D-312-476-4390, Exchange-626-4213. From I-95 take the Western Avenue Exit. Follow signs to Augusta Airport, continue past airport, veer right onto Winthrop Street. Camp Keyes entrance is on right.

Rockland Coast Guard Station (ME14R1), 54 Tillson Avenue, Rockland, ME 04841-3498. USMRA: Page 18 (D-8). C-207-596-6667, Exchange-594-7731.

Southwest Harbor Coast Guard Group (ME15R1), Clark Point Road, P.O. Box 5000, Southwest Harbor, ME 04679-5000. From Bangor, take Route 1A to Ellsworth, Route 3 to Mount Desert Island, Route 102 to downtown Southwest Harbor, second left onto Clark Point Road to end. USMRA: Page 18 (E,F-8). C-207-244-4213 Shoppette-244-5670, Exchange-244-5670, Medical (Corpsman)-244-4267.

MARYLAND

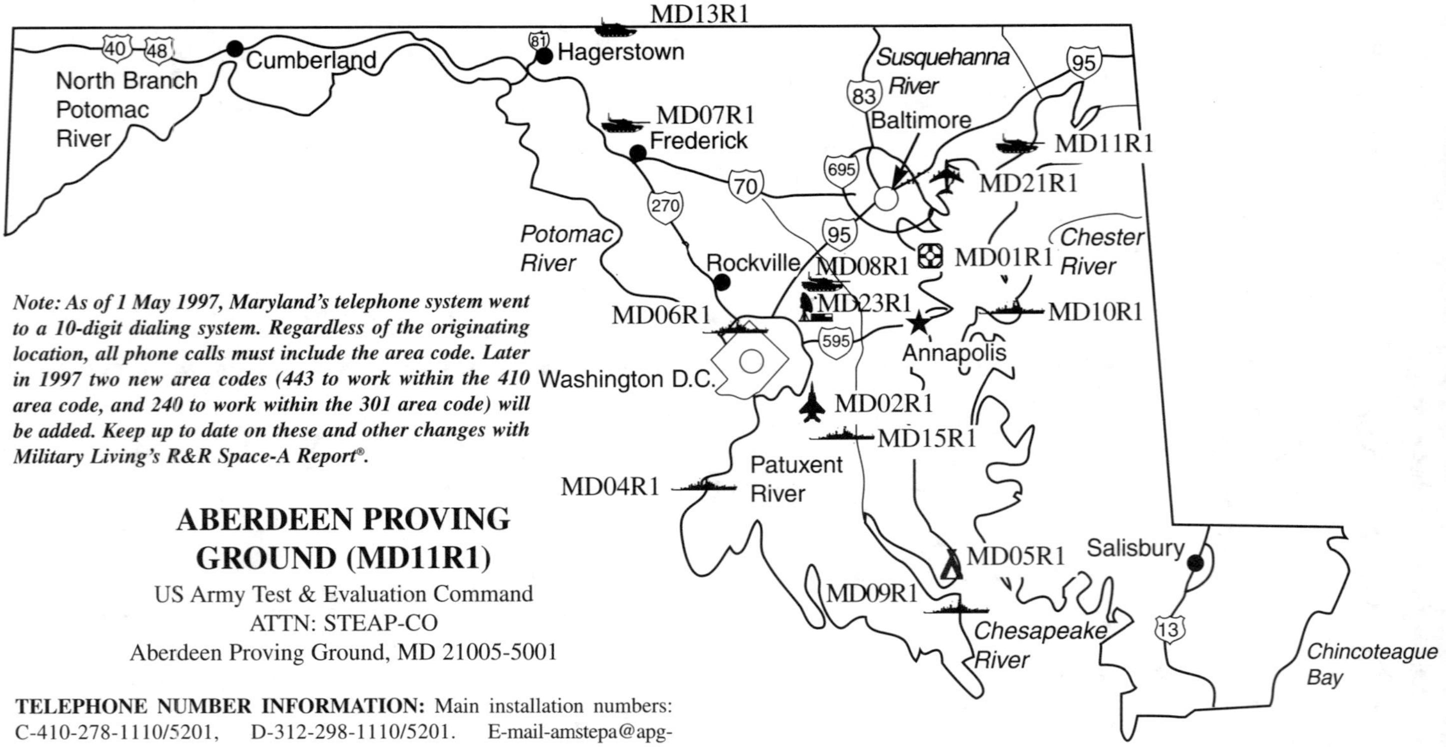

Note: As of 1 May 1997, Maryland's telephone system went to a 10-digit dialing system. Regardless of the originating location, all phone calls must include the area code. Later in 1997 two new area codes (443 to work within the 410 area code, and 240 to work within the 301 area code) will be added. Keep up to date on these and other changes with Military Living's R&R Space-A Report®.

ABERDEEN PROVING GROUND (MD11R1)

US Army Test & Evaluation Command
ATTN: STEAP-CO
Aberdeen Proving Ground, MD 21005-5001

TELEPHONE NUMBER INFORMATION: Main installation numbers: C-410-278-1110/5201, D-312-298-1110/5201. E-mail-amstepa@apg-9.apg.army.mil.

LOCATION: Aberdeen Area: From I-95, take exit 85 to MD-22 east for two miles to main gate. Edgewood Area: From I-95, take exit 77 to MD-24 east for two miles to main gate. Also, from US-40 right (if coming from Baltimore) on MD 755 (Edgewood Road) then right on US-24 to main gate. USMRA: Page 42 (G-2,3). NMC: Baltimore, 23 miles southwest.

GENERAL INFORMATION: US Army Test & Evaluation Command, Army Research Laboratory, US Army Ordnance Center & School, School of Military Packaging Technology, Army Environmental Center, 203rd Military Intelligence Battalion, US Army Center for Health Promotion and Preventive Medicine, Army Materiel Systems Analysis Activity, Chemical and Biological Defense Command, 389th Army Band, Aberdeen Test Center, Northeast Regional Civilian Personnel Operations Center.

TEMPORARY MILITARY LODGING: Aberdeen Area: Lodging office, Building 2207, Bel Air Street, 24 hours daily, C-410-278-5148, D-312-298-5148. All ranks. DV/VIP C-410-278-1038. Edgewood Area: Lodging office, C-410-671-3848.

RV, CAMPING/FAMCAMP: Skipper's Point Recreational Area on post, year round, C-410-278-5201, D-312-298-5201, six camper spaces without hookups, 15 tent spaces.

SPACE-A: None. See Andrews AFB listing, C-301-981-1854, D-312-858-1854, Fax: C-301-981-4241.

LOGISTICAL SUPPORT:

Bank-272-6907
Beauty Shop-272-6396
Child Care-278-7477
Child Dev Center-278-3487
Credit Union-272-4000
Dry Cleaner-272-5215
Exchange-272-6828
Shoppette-272-4646
Barber Shop-272-7886
Carlson Wagonlit Travel-273-1184 or 1-800-296-3074
Commissary-278-7561
Dining Facilities-278-2164/2059
Education Office-278-3385
Package Store-272-6269

ADMINISTRATIVE SUPPORT:

Fire Dept-278-3601
Legal-278-1107
Pass/ID Office-278-4631
Public Affairs-278-1142
Housing Office-278-2814
Locator-278-4357
Police-278-4007
SDO-278-4500

HEALTH & WELFARE:

American Red Cross-278-2088
Army Emergency Relief-278-2508
Chapel-278-4333
Medical
  Central Appts-278-1720
  Clinic-278-1725
  Emergency-911
ACS-278-7572
CHAMPUS-278-1719
Dental-278-1795
Retiree Services-278-4331 or 278-2649

REST & RECREATION:

Arts & Crafts-278-4207
Bowling-278-4041
Golf Course-278-4794/9994
Gym-278-5616
ITR-278-4011
MWR-278-7134
Youth Center-278-9059
Auto Hobby Shop-278-2884
Consolidated Club-278-3062
Fitness Center-278-9725
Indoor Rec-278-2621
Library-278-3417
Outdoor Rec-278-4124

Edgewood Area

LOGISTICAL SUPPORT:

Child Dev Center-671-2692
Education Office-671-2166
Credit Union-676-5700

ADMINISTRATIVE SUPPORT: Pass/ID Office-278-3360

HEALTH & WELFARE:

ACS-671-3362
Dental-671-3481
Chapel-671-4109
Medical-671-3001

REST & RECREATION:

Arts & Crafts-671-2153
Fitness Center-671-7134
Gym-671-3375
Library-671-3650
Consolidated Club-671-5400
Golf Course-671-2213
Indoor Rec-671-2713
Youth Center-671-2172

MARYLAND
Aberdeen Proving Ground, continued

OTHER SUPPORT FACILITIES AVAILABLE: Hunting and fishing programs, boat docks, Spesutie Island and Gunpowder Neck Boating Activities, swimming pools, parks and picnic areas, RV storage lots, instructional classes, Flying Activity and Saddle Activity.

ATTRACTIONS: Ordnance Museum. Baltimore a short drive away, one of the world's largest ports. Fort McHenry, where Francis Scott Key composed the "Star Spangled Banner."

ANDREWS AIR FORCE BASE (MD02R1)

1535 Command Drive
Andrews Air Force Base, MD 20762-5000

TELEPHONE NUMBER INFORMATION: Main installation numbers: C-301-981-1110, D-312-858-1110. HP: http://www.aon.af.mil.

LOCATION: From I-95 north (east portion of Capital Beltway, I-495), take exit 9; first traffic light after leaving exit ramp turn left. At next traffic light turn right into main gate of AFB. Also, from I-395 north, exit South Capitol Street, cross Anacostia River on South Capitol Street, bear left to Suitland Parkway east, exit Parkway at Morningside on Suitland Road east to main gate of AFB. From I-495 south, take exit 9; turn right, at stop sign turn right; turn right at next light onto Allentown Road; turn left into the main gate on Suitland Road. Clearly marked. USMRA: Page 42 (E-5), Page 55 (I,J-6,7). NMC: Washington, DC, 10 miles northwest.

GENERAL INFORMATION: Air Mobility Command Base. 89th Airlift Wing and support units, 459th Airlift Wing (AFRES), D.C. Air National Guard, Air National Guard Readiness Center, Naval Air Facility (USN), and Marine Aircraft Group-49 Detachment A.

TEMPORARY MILITARY LODGING: Lodging, The Gateway Inn, office, Building 1375, Arkansas Road, 24 hours daily, C-301-423-1412, D-312-858-4614.

RV, CAMPING/FAMCAMP: FAMCAMP on base, year round, C-301-981-4109, 11 camper spaces with full hookups.

SPACE-A: Pax Term/Lounge, Building 1245, 0600-2200 hours daily, C-301-981-1854, D-312-858-1854, Fax: C-301-981-4241, flights to CONUS locations.

LOGISTICAL SUPPORT:
Bank-735-8100
Beauty Shop-735-1988
Child Care-981-6927
Commissary-981-7106
Dining Facilities-981-3543/6548
Education Office-981-6377
Gas Station-735-0868
Postal Service-568-2218
Shoppette-568-2364
Snack Bar-568-2357
Visitor Center-981-0689
Barber Shop-420-9874
Cafeteria-568-2381
Child Dev Center-981-3035
Credit Union-702-5500
Dry Cleaner-568-7492
Exchange-568-1500
Laundry-420-9883
SATO
  Personal-817-2911
  Official-981-5362

ADMINISTRATIVE SUPPORT:
Fire Dept-981-4985
Legal-981-2042
Pass/ID Office-981-4640
Public Affairs-981-4424
Housing Office-981-5516
Locator-981-1110
Police-981-2001

HEALTH & WELFARE:
AF Aid-981-7088
Chapel-981-2111
Family Services-981-7087
Medical
  Central Appts-981-7511
American Red Cross-981-6008
Dental
  Central Appts-981-7560
  Clinic-981-2806
  Emergency-981-2806

Andrews Air Force Base

AAFES Army & Air Force Exchange Service

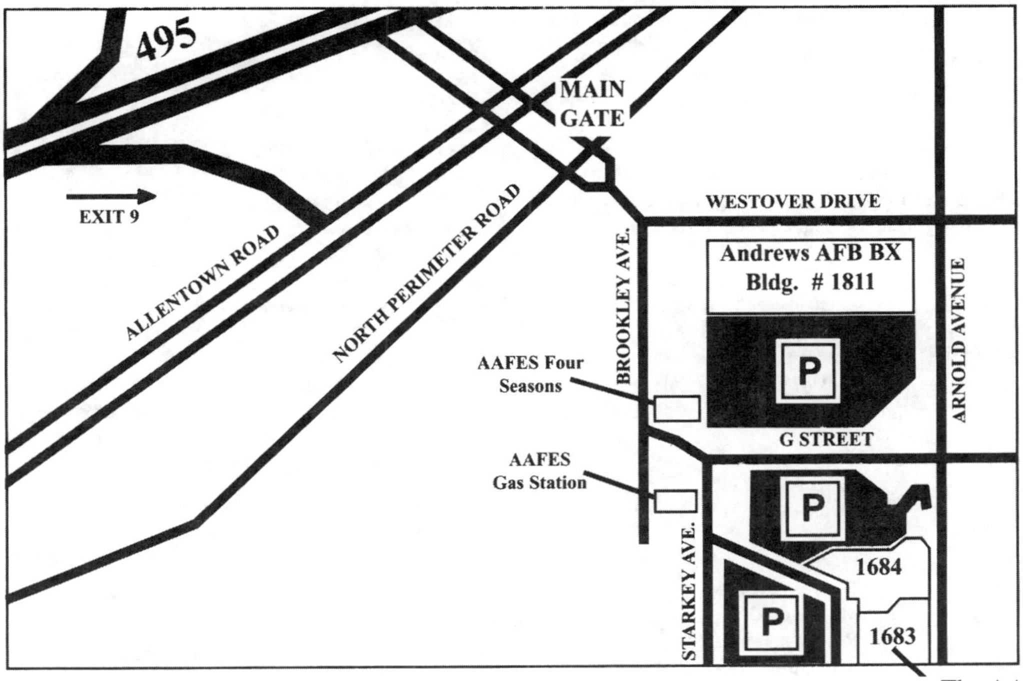

EASY ACCESS OFF BELTWAY

- From Outer Loop Take EXIT-9, Left at Light on ALLENTOWN ROAD to MAIN GATE.
- From Inner Loop Take EXIT-9, Right on FORESTVILLE ROAD, Right on ALLENTOWN ROAD to MAIN GATE.

MARYLAND
Andrews Air Force Base, continued

Clinic-981-6823	TRICARE-981-2475
Emergency-981-9911	Veterinary Services-981-2084
Health Benefits-981-5615	
Hospital-981-5911	

REST & RECREATION:

Auto Hobby Shop-981-3917	Bowling-981-6452
Clubs	Fitness Center-981-7101
NCO-568-3100	Golf Course-981-6300
O-420-4744	ITT-981-4413/4401
Library-981-6454	Outdoor Rec-981-4109/5663
Tennis Center-981-7101	Theater-981-6641
Youth Center-981-5637	

ATTRACTIONS: Aerial gateway to Washington, DC, home of "Air Force One," the President's aircraft. Monuments, White House, parks, and museums.

CURTIS BAY COAST GUARD YARD (MD01R1)

2401 Hawkins Point Road
Baltimore, MD 21226-1797

TELEPHONE NUMBER INFORMATION: Main installation number: C-410-789-1600.

LOCATION: Take I-695 to exit 1, bear to your right, right on Hawkins Point Road, left into Coast Guard Yard. USMRA: Page 42 (F-3) Page 49 (C-4). NMC: Baltimore, two miles north.

GENERAL INFORMATION: The Coast Guard's only shipbuilding and repair facility. Curtis Bay Station, CG Activities Baltimore, CG Engineering Logistics Center, two homeported ships.

TEMPORARY MILITARY LODGING: No central lodging office, CGES office, Building 28A (BOQ), C-410-636-7373; Transient Family Lodging, Guest Housing Manager, C-410-636-4187, 0900-1500 Mon-Fri, other hours, OOD/JOOD, Building 33, C-410-636-7493. All ranks. Space available.

RV, CAMPING/FAMCAMP: None. See Aberdeen Proving Ground listing, Skippers Point Rec Area, C-410-278-5201, D-312-298-5201.

SPACE-A: None. See Martin State Airport/Warfield ANG listing, C-410-780-8551, D-312-780-2346, flights to CONUS, OCONUS and overseas locations. This organization is not staffed to process requests for Space-A travel on a regular basis.

LOGISTICAL SUPPORT: Exchange-636-4198

ADMINISTRATIVE SUPPORT:

Legal-636-7250	OOD/JOOD-636-7493
Police-636-3695	

HEALTH & WELFARE:

CHAMPUS-636-3144	Chapel-636-7715
Family Services-636-3159	Medical-636-3144

REST & RECREATION:

Auto Hobby Shop-ext 3785	Bowling-ext 3968
Clubs	Marina-ext 2656
Drydock-636-7382	Rec Center-ext 7494
O-636-7356	Services-ext 7494
Swimming-ext 7494	

ATTRACTIONS: Oriole Park at Camden Yards, Inner Harbor (Aquarium, Science Center, Baltimore Zoo) maritime and streetcar museums, Baltimore Arena, Fort McHenry, World Trade Center.

FORT DETRICK ARMY GARRISON (MD07R1)

ATTN: MCHD-ZA
Building 810
Fort Detrick, MD 21702-5000

TELEPHONE NUMBER INFORMATION: Main installation numbers: C-301-619-8000, D-312-343-8000.

LOCATION: From Washington, DC, take I-270 north to US-15 north. From Baltimore, take I-70 west to US-15 north. From US-15 north, in Frederick, exit Seventh Street to post. Clearly marked. USMRA: Page 42 (D-2). NMC: Baltimore, 50 miles east and Washington, DC, 50 miles southeast.

GENERAL INFORMATION: US Army Medical Research and Materiel Command, US Army Medical Research Institute of Infectious Diseases, 1110th Signal Battalion Telecommunications Center, Quad-Service Medical Logistics.

TEMPORARY MILITARY LODGING: Lodging office, Building 810, Schreider Street, 0745-1630 Mon-Fri, C-301-619-2154, D-312-343-2154. All ranks. DV/VIP C-301-619-7114.

RV, CAMPING/FAMCAMP: None. See Aberdeen Proving Ground listing, Skippers Point Rec Area, C-410-278-5201, D-312-298-5201.

SPACE-A: None. See Andrews AFB listing, C-301-981-1854, D-312-858-1854, Fax: C-301-981-4241.

LOGISTICAL SUPPORT:

Child Care-619-3300	Commissary-619-2521
Exchange-619-2262	Gas Station-662-7777
Travel-631-2073	

ADMINISTRATIVE SUPPORT:

Fire Dept-619-7318	Legal-619-2221
Locator-619-8000/1110	Police-619-7114
Public Affairs-619-2018	SDO/NCO-619-7114

HEALTH & WELFARE:

ACS-619-2197	CHAMPUS-619-7175
Chapel-619-7371	Family Services-619-2197
Medical-619-7175	

REST & RECREATION:

Arts & Crafts-ext 2292	Auto Hobby Shop-ext 2759
Bowling-ext 2816	Community Center-619-2823
Driving Range-ext 2964	Field House/Gym-ext 2498
Fishing-ext 2498	Fitness Center-ext 2374
Library-ext 7519	Recreation-619-2711
Skeet/3D Archery Range-ext 2823	Swimming-ext 2374
Tennis-ext 2498	Youth Center-ext 2901

ATTRACTIONS: Baltimore, Washington, and Gettysburg are easy drives. Near snow ski resorts. Quaint shops and excellent restaurants in Historic Frederick.

FORT GEORGE G. MEADE (MD08R1)

ATTN: ANME-CD
HQ, Building 4551, Llewelyn Avenue
Fort George G. Meade, MD 20755-5000

TELEPHONE NUMBER INFORMATION: Main installation numbers: C-301-677-6261, D-312-923-6261. HP:http://www.mdw.army.mil/meade:HTM.

LOCATION: Off Baltimore-Washington Parkway, I-295, exit MD-198 east, Fort Meade Road. Clearly marked. USMRA: Page 42 (E,F-4). NMC: Baltimore, 15 miles north.

GENERAL INFORMATION: Headquarters First Army (East), National Security Agency, 694th Intelligence Group, Naval Security Group Activities,

MARYLAND
Fort George G. Meade, continued

Defense Information School, Army Field Band, Defense Courier Service, 1st Rctg Bde (NE), 902nd MI Grp, 704th MI Bde.

TEMPORARY MILITARY LODGING: Lodging office, Building 4707, Ruffner Road, Brett Hall, 24 hours daily, C-301-677-6529/5884, D-312-923-6529/5884, Fax: C-301-677-4704, D-312-923-4704.

RV, CAMPING/FAMCAMP: Building 2724, Ernie Pyle Street, 0700-1630. C-301-677-3810/3825, D-312-923-3810-3825. Fax: C-301-677-5616, D-312-923-5616.

SPACE-A: None. See Andrews AFB listing, C-301-981-1854, D-312-858-1854, Fax: C-301-981-4241.

LOGISTICAL SUPPORT: ***Note: All numbers with 677 prefix are Area Code 301. All other prefixes are Area Code 410.***

Bank-551-5300	Barber Shop-551-2053
Beauty Shop-674-2262	Carlson Wagonlit Travel-674-7325
Child Care-677-7712	Child Dev Center-677-5201/6002
Class Six-674-7170	Commissary-677-7463
Conv Store-674-7170/6026 or 672-3287/2121	Credit Union-551-5800
	Dining Facilities-677-0864
Dry Cleaner-519-0003	Education Office-677-6842/6421
Exchange-674-7170	Gas Station-672-3238
Laundry-519-0003	Leisure Travel Office-677-7354
Postal Service-551-0848 or 677-4660	SATO-677-6477/3869

ADMINISTRATIVE SUPPORT:

CPAC-677-6846/2867/3106	Fire Dept-674-2117
Housing Office-677-2413/5816	Legal-677-9504/9536
Locator	Pass/ID Office-677-2558/6031/6032
Army-677-4547	Police-677-6622
Navy-677-6217	Public Affairs-677-1361/62
AF-677-2414/3298	SDO-677-4805
Marines-677-5266/4506	

HEALTH & WELFARE:

American Red Cross-677-2141	ACS-677-5590/3418
CHAMPUS-677-8982	Chapel-677-7959/5673
Dental-677-7903/8960/6078	Emergency Relief-677-5662
Family Services-677-6113/3586	Medical
Navy-MC Relief-677-0219	Central Appts-677-8151
Retiree Services-677-7433/7685	Health Benefits-677-8982
TRICARE-677-8675	Information-677-8392
Veterinary Services-677-1300	

REST & RECREATION:

Arts & Crafts-677-7809	Auto Hobby Shop-677-5542
Bowling-677-5541	Golf Course-677-5326
Gym-677-3716/3042	ITT-677-7354
Library-677-5522	MWR-677-2988
O'Club-677-5298	Outdoor Rec-677-3810
Theater-677-4620	Wood Hobby Shop-677-7809
Youth Center-677-1437	Youth Services-677-1437

ATTRACTIONS: Museum on post, horse races at Laurel.

INDIAN HEAD DIVISION, NAVAL SURFACE WARFARE CENTER (MD04R1)

101 Strauss Avenue
Indian Head, MD 20640-5000

TELEPHONE NUMBER INFORMATION: Main installation numbers: C-301-743-4000, D-312-354-4000.

LOCATION: Take I-495 (Capital Beltway) east, exit to MD-210 south for 25 miles to station. USMRA: Page 42 (D-5,6). NMC: Washington, DC, 25 miles north.

GENERAL INFORMATION: Naval Explosive Ordnance Disposal Technology Center.

TEMPORARY MILITARY LODGING: BEQ/BOQ, Building 901, C-301-743-4845, D-312-354-4845. Fax: C-301-743-4486.

RV, CAMPING/FAMCAMP: None. See Patuxent River NAS listing, Goose Creek/West Basin Rec Area, C-301-342-3508, D-312-342-3508, Fax: C-301-342-3232.

SPACE-A: None. See Andrews AFB listing, C-301-981-1854, D-312-858-1854, Fax: C-301-981-4241.

LOGISTICAL SUPPORT:

Child Care-743-4458	Exchange-743-4851
SATO-743-7116	

ADMINISTRATIVE SUPPORT:

CDO/OOD-743-4845	Fire Dept-743-4370
Legal-743-6668	Locator-743-4000
Police-743-4381	SDO/NCO-743-4438

HEALTH & WELFARE:

CHAMPUS-743-4601	Chapel-743-3183
Family Services-743-5180	Medical-743-4601

REST & RECREATION:

Auto Hobby Shop-ext 6314	Bowling-ext 4761
Combined Club-743-4648	Golf Course-743-4662
Gym-ext 4850	ITT-743-4875
Library-ext 4747	Outdoor Rec-ext 4850/4761
Racquetball-ext 1396	Weight Room-ext 1396/4661

ATTRACTIONS: New amphitheater alongside the Potomac River has summer concerts and special events. The Potomac River and Washington, DC, 28 miles north.

NATIONAL NAVAL MEDICAL CENTER (MD06R1)

8901 Wisconsin Avenue
Bethesda, MD 20889-5600

TELEPHONE NUMBER INFORMATION: Main installation numbers: C-301-295-4611, D-312-295-4611.

LOCATION: From VA: I-495 N to Wisconsin Avenue exit. Stay in left lane through two lights to NNMC entrance on left. From MD: I-95 S to I-495 W to Connecticut Avenue exit. Stay in center lane to light, turn left onto Connecticut Avenue. At next light turn right onto Jones Bridge Road, right on Wisconsin Avenue, right at next light into NNMC. USMRA: Page 55 (D,E-1). NMC: Washington, DC, one mile southeast.

GENERAL INFORMATION: The Navy's largest and most advanced medical center, Uniformed Services University of the Health Sciences.

TEMPORARY MILITARY LODGING: BEQ/BOQ/DV/VIP 0800-1630 daily, C-301-295-5855/1111. D-312-295-0321/0307. Navy Lodge, Building 52, 0800-2200 daily, C-301-654-1795, for reservations call 1-800-NAVY-INN, Fax: C-301-295-5955. All ranks.

RV, CAMPING/FAMCAMP: None. See Andrews AFB listing, C-301-981-4109.

SPACE-A: None. See Andrews AFB listing, C-301-981-1854, D-312-858-1854, Fax: C-301-981-4241.

MARYLAND
National Naval Medical Center, continued

LOGISTICAL SUPPORT:

Barber Shop-295-6390	Beauty Shop-530-1624
Cafeteria-295-5367	Child Care-295-0167/5475
Child Dev Center-295-0167/5475	Conv Store-295-6129
Credit Union-295-5555	Dry Cleaner-295-6358
Education Office-295-1150	Exchange-295-0871/6362
Gas Station-295-2665	Package Store-295-6382
Postal Service-295-0162	SATO-295-5101
Shoppette-295-2665	

ADMINISTRATIVE SUPPORT:

CDO-295-4611	Fire Dept-295-0043
Housing Office-295-1138	Legal-295-6052
Locator-BUPERS 703-614-3158	Pass/ID Office-295-1246/7
Public Affairs-295-5727	Police-295-1246

HEALTH & WELFARE:

American Red Cross-295-1538	CHAMPUS-295-5143/5144
Chapel-295-1510	Dental
Family Services-Anacostia 202-433-6289	Central Appts-295-4339
Medical	Information-295-1126
Information-295-4611	N-MC Relief-295-1207
Sick Call-295-1093	

REST & RECREATION:

Bowling-295-2034/2060	Combined Club-652-6318
Fitness Center-295-0030/31/32	MWR-295-0030/31/32
ITT-295-0030	

OTHER FACILITIES AVAILABLE: Library, Marina.

ATTRACTIONS: National Zoo in nearby Rock Creek Park. Wisconsin Avenue S ends in the Georgetown section of Washington, DC. Washington National Cathedral is off Wisconsin Avenue at Massachusetts Avenue.

PATUXENT RIVER NAVAL AIR STATION (MD09R1)

Building 440
Patuxent River, MD 20670-5409

TELEPHONE NUMBER INFORMATION: Main installation numbers: C-301-342-3000/1000, D-312-342-3000.

LOCATION: From I-95 (east portion of Capital Beltway, I-495) take exit 7A to Branch Avenue (MD-5) south. Follow MD-5 until it becomes MD-235 near Oraville, on to Lexington Park, and the NAWC. Main gate is on MD-235 and MD-246 (Cedar Point Road). USMRA: Page 42 (F-6,7). NMC: Washington, DC, 65 miles northwest.

GENERAL INFORMATION: Naval Air Warfare Center Aircraft Division and Naval Air Station.

TEMPORARY MILITARY LODGING: Lodging Office C-301-863-9343, D-312-342-3601 BOQ C-301-863-9343, DV/VIP C-301-342-1108, Navy Lodge C-301-737-2400, 1-800-NAVY-INN. Housing Welcome Center Building 2371, C-301-342-3847, D-312-342-3847 All ranks.

RV, CAMPING/FAMCAMP: Goose Creek/West Basin Recreation Area on base, Feb-Nov, C-301-342-3508, D-312-342-3508, Fax: C-301-342-3232, 14 camper spaces with W&E hookups, 46 camper/tent spaces without hookups.

SPACE-A: Pax Term/Lounge, Building 103, 24 hours daily, C-301-342-3836/7, D-312-342-3836/7, flights to CONUS locations.

LOGISTICAL SUPPORT:

Child Care-342-7639	Commissary-342-3789
Conv Store-342-8715	Exchange-342-7483
Gas Station-342-5828	Package Store-342-9315
SATO-342-1051 ext 115	Snack Bar-342-5608
Theater-342-3572	Visitor Center-342-3231

ADMINISTRATIVE SUPPORT:

CDO/OOD-342-1095	Command Post-342-1418
Fire Dept-342-3333	Legal-342-1045/1046
Locator-342-3000	Police-342-3277
Public Affairs-342-7512	

HEALTH & WELFARE:

CHAMPUS-342-1457	Chapel-342-3812
Family Services-342-4911	Medical
Retiree Services-342-4911	Central Appts-342-1500
	Emergency-342-1422

REST & RECREATION:

Arts & Crafts-ext 3160	Auto Hobby Shop-ext 3507
Bowling-ext 3994	Clubs
Golf Course-342-3597	CPO-342-3657/3685
Gym-ext 3519/3508	EM-342-3657/3685
ITT-342-3508	O-342-3656
Library-ext 1927	Marina-ext 3573
MWR-342-3510	Rec equipment-ext 3519
Recreation-342-3510/3521	Stables-ext 3296
Swimming-ext 4225/5960	Wood Hobby Shop-ext 3569
Youth Center-ext 3329	

ATTRACTIONS: Calvert Cliffs Nuclear Power Plant Museum, Calvert Marine Museum, Naval Air Test & Evaluation Museum, Potomac River-St Clement's Island Museum, St Mary's City, Sotterley Plantation, Cecil's Mill, Point Lookout State Park, Seafood Festivals.

SOLOMONS NAVY RECREATION CENTER (MD05R1)

P.O. Box 147
Solomons, MD 20688-0147

TELEPHONE NUMBER INFORMATION: Main installation numbers: C-410-326-1260, DC Metro: 1-800-NAVY-230.

LOCATION: On the Patuxent River. From US-301 take MD-4 southeast to Solomons; *OR* take MD-5 southeast to MD-235, then MD-4 northeast to Solomons. USMRA: page 42 (F-6). NMC: Washington DC, 65 miles northwest. NMI: Patuxent River NAS, 10 miles south.

GENERAL INFORMATION: Located in southern Maryland on the delta where the Patuxent River meets the Chesapeake Bay. Rustic and relaxing area that has retained its natural beauty. Campground and facilities encompass approximately 260 acres with extensive frontage on river. Only Navy facility dedicated solely to recreation. Historic waterfront community. Operated/managed by the Navy, on base year round. Military personnel active, retired, reserve and DoD civilians. Reservations: Required with payment in full. Reservation procedures depend on branch of service and status. Camping reservations processed by lottery system. For specific information contact C-410-326-1260; DC, Maryland and Virginia: 800-NAVY-230. Fax: C-410-326-4280. Visa, MasterCard, American Express, and Discover accepted. Pets are not allowed in lodging units; must have proof of shots and be registered at Reservation and Information Center; must be on leash and under positive control. 1 Apr-15 Oct: seven day limit to include only one holiday weekend. Open fires prohibited except in group site areas where fire rings are provided. DoD Civilians can make reservations.

TEMPORARY MILITARY LODGING: Apartments, Bungalows and Cottages, AC, bath, kitchen, utensils, picnic tables, grill, rental linens; no TV or telephones. Waterfront cottages are not heated. 19 cottages handicap accessible. Rates: One bedroom: E1-E5 $34-$40, E6-E9 $41-$48.50, Officers $49.50-$59,

DoD $62-$75; two bedroom: E1-E5 $37-$44, E6-E9 $44-$52.50, Officers $52.50-$63, DoD $66-$79; three bedroom: E1-E5 $32-$47.50, E6-E9 $39.50-$56, Officers $48.50-$66, DoD $61-$82; four bedroom: E1-E5 $35-$51.50, E6-E9 $41.50-$60, Officers $51.50-$70, DoD $65-$86; five bedroom: E1-E5 $45-$56, E6-E9 $52.50-$64, Officers $61-$75, DoD $76-$90. Higher rate includes Leisure Value Package; monthly rates available.

RV, CAMPING/FAMCAMP: Camper spaces with full hookups (146); camper spaces with W&E hookups (151); camper spaces with E hookups (7); camper/tent spaces with no hookups (56); group tent spaces with no hookups (15). Rates: Camper spaces with full hookups: $20-$25 daily, $312.50-$360 monthly; camper spaces with W&E hookups: $18-$23.50 daily, $260-$312.50 monthly; camper spaces with E hookup: $15-$19 daily, $239-$291.50 monthly; camper/tent spaces with no hookups: $11-$13 daily, $155-$207.50 monthly; tent spaces with no hookups: $3.25-$3.75 person daily, $32.50-$37.50 minimum daily. Depending on status. Includes up to four leisure passes per individual campsite. Also available without leisure passes.

ADMINISTRATIVE SUPPORT: Security-326-2436

REST & RECREATION: Basketball, Bicycling, Boating, Crabbing, Duck Hunting, Fishing/license, Horseshoes, Special Events, Swimming, Volleyball, Windsurfing.

OTHER SUPPORT & FACILITIES AVAILABLE: ATM Machine, Bait/Tackle, Ball Fields, Basketball, Beach, Boat Launch, Boat Rental, Boat Slip Rental, Camper Rental, Campers' Store (summer season), Camping Equipment, Fish/Crab Pier, Gazebo, Gear Issue, Grills, Horse shoes, Ice, Laundry, Marina, Miniature Golf, Movies, Party Pavilions, Picnic Area, Playground, Racquetball Court, Restrooms, RV Storage, Sewage Dump, Showers, Softball Field, Sports Equipment, Swimming Pools, Tennis Courts, Video Arcade, Volleyball. Also see Patuxent River Naval Air Station listing, C-301-342-3000/1000, D-312-342-3000.

ATTRACTIONS: Local points of interest include Calvert Marine Museum, Cliffs of Calvert, Oyster Fleet, St Mary's City, Battle Creek Cypress Swamp, Naval Air Test & Evaluation Museum, area festivals, Point Lookout State Park, Solomons Island area and many other historical sites. Excellent area for crabbing, fishing, sailing and boating.

UNITED STATES NAVAL ACADEMY/ ANNAPOLIS NAVAL STATION (MD10R1)

330 Kinkaid Road
Annapolis, MD 21402-5071

TELEPHONE NUMBER INFORMATION: Main installation numbers: C-410-293-1000, D-312-281-1000.

LOCATION: Off US-50/301, clearly marked. Naval Station is off US-50/301 east, clearly marked. USMRA: Page 42 (F-4), page 48 (D,E,F,G-1,2,3). NMC: Annapolis, within city limits.

GENERAL INFORMATION: Navy education facility for officers and support personnel.

TEMPORARY MILITARY LODGING: BOQ, Building 2, 0800-1600 daily, C-410-293-3906, D-312-281-3906, Fax: C-410-293-2444, D-312-281-2444.

RV, CAMPING/FAMCAMP: FAMCAMP on base, year round. Address, MWR Department, Bennion Road, Annapolis, MD 21402-5058, Mon-Fri 0645-2200, Sat 0900-2100, Sun 1200-2100, C-410-293-9200, D-312-281-9200, Fax: C-410-239-3034, D-312-281-3034 14 camper spaces with W&E hookups.

SPACE-A: None. See Andrews AFB listing, C-301-981-1854, D-312-858-1854, Fax: C-301-981-4241.

LOGISTICAL SUPPORT:

Barber Shop-757-0005	Beauty Shop-757-3101
Cafeteria-293-2873	Child Care-293-9395
Commissary-293-2494	Conv Store-757-2120
Credit Union-266-1167/757-0700	Dry Cleaner-757-0005
Exchange-757-0005	Gas Station-349-0226
Package Store-757-2120	Postal Service-293-3787
SATO-268-7203	Visitor Center-263-6933

ADMINISTRATIVE SUPPORT:

CDO/OOD-293-2584	Fire Dept-293-3333
Housing Office-293-2192	Legal-293-9025
Locator-293-2385	OOD-293-2701
Pass/ID Office-293-5762	Police-293-9300
Public Affairs-293-2291	Quarter Deck-293-2385

HEALTH & WELFARE:

CHAMPUS-293-2276	Chapel-293-1100/9100
Dental	Family Services-293-2641
Central Appts-293-3788	Medical
Clinic-293-3921	Central Appts-293-2061
N-MC Relief-293-9220	Clinic-293-1758/4400
Retiree Services-293-2641	Health Benefits-293-2276
Veterinary Services-677-1300	Information-293-1330

REST & RECREATION:

Auto Hobby Shop-293-3859	Fitness Center-293-9200
Golf Course-757-2022	ITT-293-9200
Library-ext 2311	Marinas-293-3731
MWR-293-9200/9201	O'Club-293-2611
Outdoor Rec-293-9200	Rec Center-ext 2518/3691
Swimming-ext 2082/3033	Theater-293-9200
Youth Center-293-4997	

ATTRACTIONS: Walking tour of the Naval Academy, museum, tour of historic Annapolis, city dock area, and the Maryland Capitol building.

Other Installations in Maryland

Cheltenham Naval Communications Detachment (MD15R1), Washington, DC 20397-5310. USMRA: Page 42 (E-5). C-301-394-0385 (Security), Package Store-394-0406. *Note: Facility has decreased tremendously due to downsizing. Although not on the BRAC, future is uncertain.*

Fort Ritchie (MD13R1), 343 Banfill Avenue, Fort Ritchie, MD 21719-5010. USMRA: Page 42 (C,D-1). Main installation numbers: C-301-878-1300, D-312-277-1300. Fort Ritchie is **scheduled to close in October 1998,** however, the fort is under an accelerated closure plan and is consolidating rapidly; call ahead to verify facility availability.

Goddard Space Flight Center NASA (MD23R1), Visitor Center, Greenbelt, MD 20771. USMRA: Page 42 (E-4). Visitor Center C-301-286-8981.

Martin State Airport/Warfield Air National Guard (MD21R1), Building 1110, 2701 Eastern Boulevard, Baltimore, MD 21220-2899. USMRA: Page 42 (F,G-3). C-410-780-8210, Exchange 780-8443, Space-A-780-8551, DSN-312-780-2346.

MASSACHUSETTS

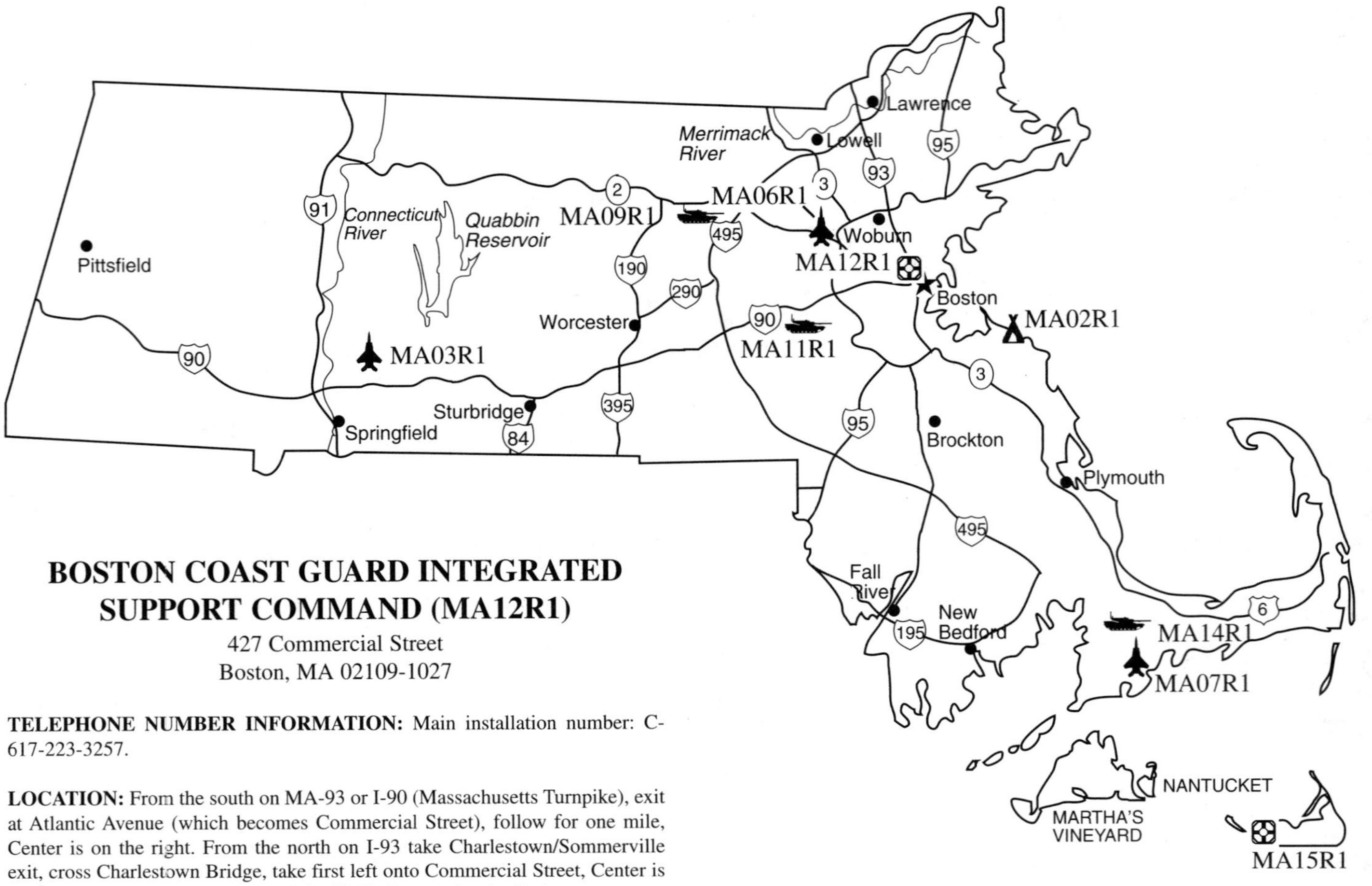

BOSTON COAST GUARD INTEGRATED SUPPORT COMMAND (MA12R1)

427 Commercial Street
Boston, MA 02109-1027

TELEPHONE NUMBER INFORMATION: Main installation number: C-617-223-3257.

LOCATION: From the south on MA-93 or I-90 (Massachusetts Turnpike), exit at Atlantic Avenue (which becomes Commercial Street), follow for one mile, Center is on the right. From the north on I-93 take Charlestown/Sommerville exit, cross Charlestown Bridge, take first left onto Commercial Street, Center is on the left. USMRA: Page 24 (E-4,5). NMC: Boston, in city limits.

GENERAL INFORMATION: Logistic support for major cutters homeported here. Tenant Commands include Marine Safety Office, Group Boston, Naval Engineering Support Unit, Electronic Systems Support Unit.

TEMPORARY MILITARY LODGING: MAA office, Building 4, 427 Commercial Street, 0730-1500 Mon-Fri, C-617-223-3171.

RV, CAMPING/FAMCAMP: None. See Fourth Cliff Rec Area listing, C-617-837-9269, 800-468-9547.

SPACE-A: None. See Hanscom AFB listing, C-617-377-11433, D-312-478-11433, Fax: C-617-377-2383.

LOGISTICAL SUPPORT:
Exchange-223-3133/67 Galley-223-3267

ADMINISTRATIVE SUPPORT: CDO/OOD-223-3313

HEALTH & WELFARE:
CHAMPUS-223-3250 Chapel-223-3164
Medical
Clinic-223-3250
Hospital-782-3400

REST & RECREATION:
Consolidated Club-223-3265 Gym-ext 3125
Rec Equipment-ext 3125

ATTRACTIONS: City of Boston: Fenway Park, JFK Library and Museum, Blue Hills Reservation, Prospect Hill Ski Area, many universities, Aquarium, Franklin Park Zoo, "Boston Pops," Museum of Science, Celtics, Bruins, Patriots, Red Sox.

FOURTH CLIFF FAMILY RECREATION AREA (MA02R1)

348 Central Avenue
P.O. Box 479
Humarock, MA 02047-5000

TELEPHONE NUMBER INFORMATION: Main installation numbers: C-617-377-4441, D-312-478-4441. Police for rec area, C-617-545-1212 (local police).

LOCATION: Off base. I-95 or I-93 to MA-3, approximately 10 miles south of Boston; south to exit 12; MA-139 east to Marshfield. One-and-a-half miles to Furnace Street; turn left. Continue to "T" intersection; turn left on Ferry Street. Stay on Ferry Street to Sea Street; right over South River Bridge; left on Central Avenue, bear left at fork. (Do not go straight up hill on Cliff Road.) Proceed to gate. USMRA: Page 17 (M-4). NMC: Boston, 30 miles north. NMI: Hanscom AFB, 55 miles northwest.

GENERAL INFORMATION: Rec area is 56-acre seaside resort situated high on a cliff on the tip of a small peninsula overlooking the Atlantic Ocean on one side and scenic North River on the other. Operated by Hanscom Air Force Base, off base, 16 units: Memorial Day-Columbus Day; 13 units: year round; self-contained trailers can be accommodated year round. Military personnel active, retired, 100% DAV, reserve, and DoD civilians. Check in at Fourth Cliff Recreation Hall, Building 7, 1200 daily, check out 1100. Call desk clerk at 617-837-6785 (before 1400 on weekdays and 1000 on Sundays and holidays) to make arrangements for other hours to check in or out and for off-season hours. No checking in after 2300. Reservations: Required on credit card or with one night's deposit. (Ask for map; check on refund policy.) Reservation procedure based on status of sponsor. C-617-837-9269, 800-468-9547 (0900-1630 Mon-Fri). Visa and MasterCard accepted. Pets are not allowed inside any cabins or on the porches. In other areas, they must be leashed or tied at all times and must not annoy others. No open fires. Firearms and/or hunting equipment are not allowed. Children may not be left unattended. Wildlife may not be captured, killed or harassed in any way. Visitor information display for local sights and attractions. Discount passes and season tickets may be available.

TEMPORARY MILITARY LODGING: Three bedroom cottage with closed porch (1); two bedroom townhouse, furnished, color TV, microwave, crib, highchair, linens, pots, pans, dishes, bring toiletries (2); two bedroom chalets, furnished, color TV, microwave, crib, highchair, linens, pots, pans, dishes, bring toiletries (11); furnished one-three bedroom cabins, color TV, microwave, crib, highchair, linens, pots, pans, dishes, bring toiletries (2). Rates: In season: cottage $90 daily, townhouse $65 daily, chalets $75, cabins $45; Off season: cottage $65, townhouse $45, chalets $50. Folding cots may also be rented. Cabins available in season only.

RV, CAMPING/FAMCAMP: Concrete camper spaces with full hookups (11); tent spaces with no hookups. Rates: camper spaces $12 daily; tent spaces $8. Other vehicles used as sleeping quarters and parked overnight $10. Tent spaces available in season only.

ADMINISTRATIVE SUPPORT: Police-545-1212 (local police)

REST & RECREATION: Fishing, Horseshoes, Rec Equipment. Summer and fall programs available.

OTHER SUPPORT & FACILITIES AVAILABLE: Beach, Dishwashing Facility, Grills, Ice, Laundry/summer, Picnic Area, Pay Telephone, Playground, Pavilion*, Rec Hall/summer, Restrooms, Sewage Dump, Showers, Snack Bar. Also, see Hanscom Air Force Base listing, C-617-377-4441, D-312-478-4441.

*May be rented for group picnics; reservation required.

ATTRACTIONS: Easy access to Boston, Cape Cod, Martha's Vineyard, Nantucket Islands and a host of recreational activities.

HANSCOM AIR FORCE BASE (MA06R1)

Electronics Systems Center/Public Affairs
9 Eglin Street
Hanscom Air Force Base, MA 01731-2118

TELEPHONE NUMBER INFORMATION: Main installation numbers: C-617-377-4441, D-312-478-4441.

LOCATION: From I-95 south, take exit 30B (MA-2A) west for two miles then turn right at the Hanscom Field Sign. From I-95 north, take exit 31B, keep to right, follow signs to base; two miles. USMRA: Page 17 (J-3), page 24 (A-2). NMC: Boston, 17 miles southeast.

GENERAL INFORMATION: Air Force Materiel Command Base. Hq, Electronics Systems Center.

TEMPORARY MILITARY LODGING: Lodging office, Building 1427, 24 hours daily, C-617-377-2112, D-312-478-2112. All ranks. DV/VIP ext 5151.

RV, CAMPING/FAMCAMP: FAMCAMP off base, year round, C-617-377-4670, 35 camper spaces with full hookups, 21 camper spaces with W&E, 10 tent spaces. Operates Fourth Cliff Rec Area off base, 55 miles southeast of post. See Fourth Cliff Rec Area listing for more information.

SPACE-A: Pax Term, Building 1714, Mon-Fri: 0730-1600, C-617-377-1143, D-312-478-1143, (Daily flight recording C-617-377-3333, D-312-478-3333) Fax: C-617-377-2383, flights to Andrews AFB, MD and other East Coast locations. Uses runways of Lawrence G. Hanscom Field adjoining the base.

LOGISTICAL SUPPORT:
Cafeteria-377-2189
Child Care-377-2858
Commissary-377-2544
Conv Store-274-3675
Exchange-377-5258
Gas Station-377-5155
Package Store-377-3675
SATO-377-2631
Snack Bar-377-2395

ADMINISTRATIVE SUPPORT:
SDO/NCO-377-5144
Legal-377-2362
Locator-377-5111/4441
Police-377-4357/2314
Public Affairs-377-5191

HEALTH & WELFARE:
CHAMPUS-377-4701
Chapel-377-3538
Family Services-377-3436
Medical
  Central Appts-377-4706
  Emergency-377-2333
Retiree Services-377-2476

REST & RECREATION:
Activity Schedule-ext 2687
Auto Hobby Shop-ext 2612
Bowling-ext 2237
Clubs
  Aero-ext 5160
  NCO-377-2123
  O-377-5740
  Services-ext 2610
Gym-ext 3435/3639
ITT -377-3262
Library-ext 2177
Rec Center-ext 2610
Rec Equipment-ext 3348
Rec Services-ext 3901
Swimming-ext 2455
Theater-377-5200

ATTRACTIONS: The Bedford flag..."Oldest flag in America." Concord, North Bridge, Lexington, historic sites and taverns.

NATICK SOLDIER SYSTEMS COMMAND (MA11R1)

15 Kansas Street
Natick, MA 01760-5000

TELEPHONE NUMBER INFORMATION: Main installation numbers: C-508-233-4001, D-312-256-4001.

LOCATION: Exit from I-90 (Massachusetts Pike), exit 13, Natick to MA-30 east to MA-27 south. Or exit MA-9 west for six miles to MA-27 south. Watch for signs to the Center's main entrance off Kansas Street. USMRA: Page 17 (J-4). NMC: Boston, 25 miles east.

GENERAL INFORMATION: Natick is a US Army AMC Research, Development and Engineering Center.

TEMPORARY MILITARY LODGING: None. See Hanscom AFB listing, C-617-377-2112, D-312-478-2112.

RV, CAMPING/FAMCAMP: None. See Hanscom AFB listing, C-617-377-4670.

SPACE-A: None. See Hanscom AFB listing, C-617-377-1143, D-312-478-1143, Fax: C-617-377-2383.

LOGISTICAL SUPPORT:
Exchange-651-4765
SATO-233-4299

ADMINISTRATIVE SUPPORT:
Legal 233-4322
Locator-233-4001
Police-233-4201

HEALTH & WELFARE:
ACS-233-4798
Family Services-233-4798
Medical-651-4155

REST & RECREATION:
Clubs
  NCO-233-5583
  O-233-4791
MWR-233-4960
Sailing-ext 4960

MASSACHUSETTS
Natick Soldier Systems Command, continued

OTHER FACILITIES AVAILABLE: Auto Hobby Shop, Weight Room, Rec Services, Swimming.

ATTRACTIONS: Cities of Boston and Cambridge, Boston National Historical Park, *USS Constitution* and Museum, many other historical sites and museums.

OTIS AIR NATIONAL GUARD BASE/ CAPE COD COAST GUARD AIR STATION (MA07R1)

102nd Fighter Wing (ANG)
Otis Air National Guard Base, MA 02542-5024

TELEPHONE NUMBER INFORMATION: Main installation numbers: C-508-968-1000, D-557-1000.

LOCATION: Off MA-28 at the base of Cape Cod. USMRA: Page 17 (M-7). NMC: Boston, 70 miles northwest.

GENERAL INFORMATION: Air Force Air National Guard, Army National Guard, Coast Guard Air Station, Marines, Dept of Agriculture.

TEMPORARY MILITARY LODGING: Temporary quarters, Building 5204, C-508-968-6461.

RV, CAMPING/FAMCAMP: Cape Cod Vacation Apartments on base, year round, 12 town house apartments, 18 suites, two single rooms, C-508-968-6461. Also Cuttyhunk Island Rec Facility off base on Cuttyhunk Island, year round, two apartments. All apartments furnished. Reservations by application are required. More requests are received for the Cuttyhunk apartments than can be approved, C-617-223-8047/8375. See Military Living's *Military RV, Camping & Rec Areas Around the World* for additional information.

SPACE-A: AF/ARNG, 0800-1600 Mon-Fri (weekend hours vary), C-508-968-4831, D-312-557-4831, CONUS flights.

LOGISTICAL SUPPORT:

Beauty Shop-563-6535	Child Care-968-6450
Conv Store-564-5486	Dry Cleaners-563-5412
Exchange-968-2518	Gas Station-564-5486
Grocery Annex-563-2587	Package Store-564-5486
Post Office-563-7336	

ADMINISTRATIVE SUPPORT:

Commander
- 102d Air National Guard-968-4106
- Army National Guard-968-5885
- CG Air Station-968-6300
- Marines-968-7169

HEALTH & WELFARE:

CHAMPUS-968-6570	Chapel-968-4901
Medical-968-6570	

REST & RECREATION:

Auto Hobby Shop-968-6516	Golf Course (9 hole)-968-6454/6453
Gym-968-5985	Library-968-6456
Rec Equipment-968-6447/6448	Theater-968-6452
Youth Center-968-6451	

OTHER FACILITIES AVAILABLE: Tennis, Stables, Racquetball, Consignment Shop 968-6682.

ATTRACTIONS: Beautiful Cape Cod, near Plymouth and other historic towns. Beaches and water sports.

WESTOVER AIR RESERVE BASE (MA03R1)

439 Airlift Wing (AFRES)
Westover Air Reserve Base, MA 01022-5000

TELEPHONE NUMBER INFORMATION: Main installation numbers: C-413-557-1110, D-312-589-1110.

LOCATION: Take exit 5 off I-90 (Massachusetts Turnpike) in Chicopee. Westover is on MA-33, north of I-90; signs mark way to base. USMRA: Page 16 (F-4). NMC: Springfield, eight miles south.

GENERAL INFORMATION: Air Force Reserve Base. 439th Airlift Wing, Army Reserve, Navy Reserve, Marine Corps Reserve, and Air Force Reserve units.

TEMPORARY MILITARY LODGING: Lodging office, Building 2200, Outer Drive. (VOQ) C-413-557-2700, D-312-589-2700, 24 hours daily. SDO, 557-3557. All ranks. DV/VIP C-413-557-3478.

RV, CAMPING/FAMCAMP: None. See Hanscom AFB listing, C-617-377-4670.

SPACE-A: Very limited. Pax Term, Building 7075, Base Ops, 0700-2300 daily, C-413-557-2951, D-312-589-2951, flight information C 413-557-2549, D-312-589-2549, flight sign-up C-413-557-2622, D-312-589-2549, flights to CONUS and OCONUS locations on transient aircraft.

LOGISTICAL SUPPORT:

Commissary-593-3288	Exchange-593-5941/5413
Gas Station-593-3288	Shoppette-593-3288
Snack Bar-557-3896	

ADMINISTRATIVE SUPPORT:

Fire Dept-557-3818	Legal-557-3513
Locator-557-3874	Police-557-3557
Public Affairs-557-2020	SDO/NCO-557-3571

HEALTH & WELFARE:

CHAMPUS-557-3918	Chapel-557-3031
Medical-557-3565	Retiree Services-557-3918

REST & RECREATION:

Bowling-ext 3010	Consol-593-5531
Gym-ext 3958	MWR-557-3958

ATTRACTIONS: Springfield, Mt Tom Snow Ski Resort, Holyoke. Basketball Hall of Fame in Springfield.

Other Installations in Massachusetts

Camp Edwards (MA14R1), Building 3468 Camp Edwards, MA 02542-5003. USMRA: Page 17 (M-6,7). C-508-968-5887, Exchange-772-4825, TML-968-5916. Gas Station, Shoppette, Golf Course.

Devens Reserve Forces Training Center (MA09R1), ATTN: AFRTC-FMD-CO, Building 679, Quebec Street, Devens, MA 01433-5010. USMRA: Page 17 (I-2,3). C-508-796-2107, D-312-256-2107. Locator-796-7954, Police-772-7200, Medical-796-2577 (Apr-Sept only), TML-772-4300/0188.

Nantucket Coast Guard LORAN Station (MA15R1), Natick, MA 01760-5000. USMRA: Page 17 (O-9). C-508-257-6302 or C-508-228-0388.

MICHIGAN

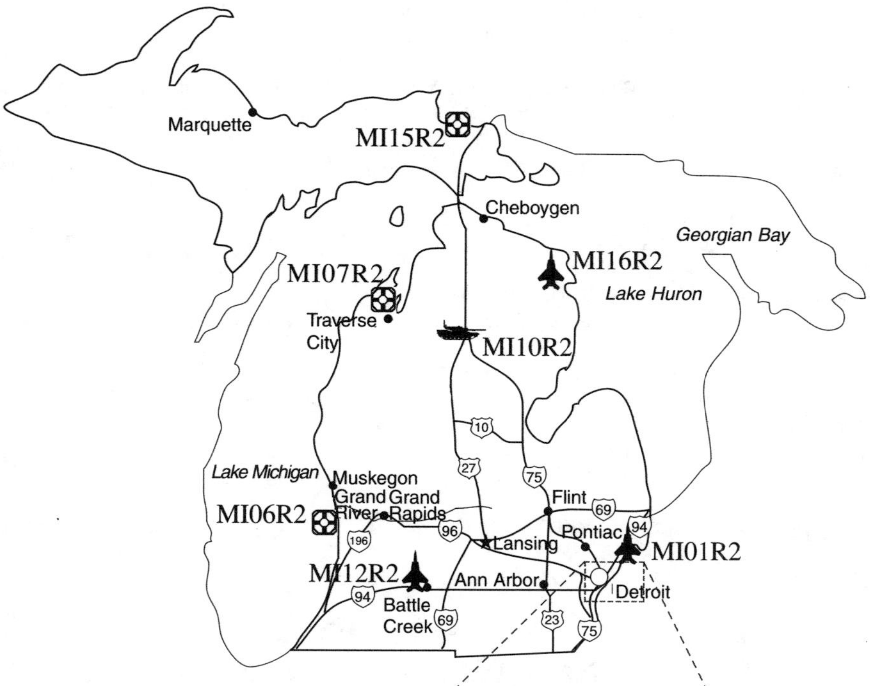

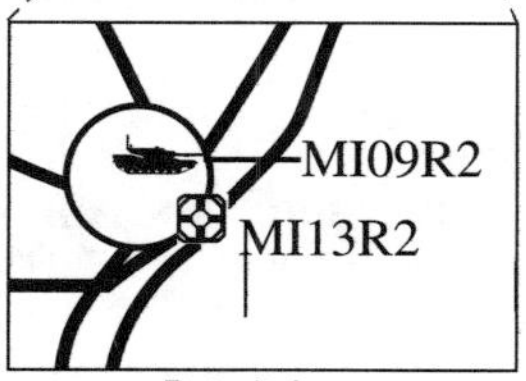

Detroit Area

ALPENA COMBAT READINESS TRAINING CENTER (MI16R2)

5884 A Street
Alpena, MI 49707-8125

TELEPHONE NUMBER INFORMATION: Main installation numbers: C-517-354-6291, D-312-741-3291.

LOCATION: Five miles west of Alpena on M-32. USMRA: Page 66 (F-4). NMC: Alpena, five miles west.

GENERAL INFORMATION: Air National Guard Training Base.

TEMPORARY MILITARY LODGING: None. See Camp Grayling MTC listing, C-517-348-3661, D-312-623-3661, Fax: C-517-348-3844.

RV, CAMPING/FAMCAMP: None. See Camp Grayling MTC listing, C-517-348-7621 ext 3389, Fax: C-517-348-9033.

SPACE-A: Building 10, C-517-354-6305, D-312-741-3305.

LOGISTICAL SUPPORT:

Exchange-354-6272	SATO-354-6290

ADMINISTRATIVE SUPPORT:	Police-354-6210

HEALTH & WELFARE: None. See Traverse City CGAS listing, C-616-922-8282.

REST & RECREATION: None. See Camp Grayling Maneuver Training Center listing, C-517-348-9033.

ATTRACTIONS: Lake Huron shore, fishing, hunting, and camping.

CAMP GRAYLING MANEUVER TRAINING CENTER (MI10R2)

ATTN: PAO
Grayling, MI 49739-0001

TELEPHONE NUMBER INFORMATION: Main installation numbers: C-517-348-3611. D-312-623-3601, Fax: C-517-348-3855, D-312-623-3855.

LOCATION: Located three miles west of city of Grayling, just off of I-75. USMRA: Page 66 (D-5). NMC: Grayling, three miles east.

GENERAL INFORMATION: Guard and reserve training center with approximately 147,000 acres of prime infantry, tank, helicopter, artillery, mortar and A/G training area.

TEMPORARY MILITARY LODGING: Lodging office, Building 560, 0700-1700 daily, C-517-348-3661, D-312-623-3661, Fax: C-517-348-3844.

RV, CAMPING/FAMCAMP: Camp Grayling Trailer Park on post, 15 May-15 Sep, C-517-348-7621 ext 3225, Fax: C-517-348-9033, 70 camper spaces with full hookups, 10 tent spaces.

SPACE-A: None. See Alpena Combat Readiness Training Center listing, C-517-354-6305, D-312-741-3305.

LOGISTICAL SUPPORT:

Cafeteria-348-3662 ext 3286	Exchange-348-3662 ext 3285

ADMINISTRATIVE SUPPORT:

Locator-348-3611	Police-ext 3764
Public Affairs-348-3855	

HEALTH AND WELFARE:	Chapel-348-3699
REST & RECREATION:	Clubs EM-ext 3229 NCO-ext 3305 O-348-9033

ATTRACTIONS: Lake Margrethe, boat launch and beach area, nearby. Huron National Forest, Lake Michigan, Lake Huron, skiing, water recreation. Upper Peninsula 90 miles north, Canada 130 miles north, Traverse City 55 miles west.

DETROIT COAST GUARD GROUP (MI13R2)

110 Mount Elliott Avenue
Detroit, MI 48207-4380

TELEPHONE NUMBER INFORMATION: Main installation number: C-313-568-9525.

LOCATION: From 94 east or west, take the Mt Elliott exit and travel east. The base is located at 110 Mt Elliott Avenue. USMRA: Page 70 (E-4) NMC: Detroit, in city limits.

GENERAL INFORMATION: Host unit for Group Detroit Offices, Aids to Navigation Detroit, Marine Safety Office Detroit, USCGG Bristol Bay, and the entire Coast Guard Team (Reserves and auxiliary).

TEMPORARY MILITARY LODGING: None. See Selfridge ANGB listing, C-810-307-4062, D-312-273-4062.

RV, CAMPING/FAMCAMP: None. Nearest facility is over 100 miles away.

SPACE-A: None. See Selfridge ANGB listing, C-810-307-5884, D-312-273-5884.

MICHIGAN
Detroit Coast Guard Group, continued

LOGISTICAL SUPPORT: Exchange-259-6217

ADMINISTRATIVE SUPPORT: None. See Selfridge ANGB listing, C-810-307-4021.

HEALTH & WELFARE:
CHAMPUS-568-9526 Medical-568-9526/7

REST & RECREATION: None. See Selfridge ANGB listing.

ATTRACTIONS: Pontiac Silverdome (Lions), the Palace (Pistons), Joe Louis Arena.

GRAND HAVEN COAST GUARD GROUP (MI06R2)

650 Harbor Avenue
Grand Haven, MI 49417-1762

TELEPHONE NUMBER INFORMATION: Main installation number: C-616-847-4501.

LOCATION: From I-96 east, to US-31 south in Grand Haven, west on Jackson Street and follow it along the waterfront to the Group Office. From US-31 north, go west on Franklin Street to Harbor Drive, turn left and follow the road to the Group Office. USMRA: Page 66 (B-8). NMC: Muskegon, 12 miles north.

GENERAL INFORMATION: The center of Coast Guard operations for the western shore of Lake Michigan from Michigan City, IN to Frankfort, MI.

TEMPORARY MILITARY LODGING: None. See Camp Grayling MTC listing, C-517-348-3661, D-312-623-3661, Fax: C-517-348-3844.

RV, CAMPING/FAMCAMP: Operates Point Betsie Recreation Cottage in Frankfort, C-616-847-4510.

SPACE-A: None. See Selfridge ANGB listing, C-810-307-5884, D-312-273-5884.

LOGISTICAL SUPPORT:
Exchange-846-0490 Package Store-846-0490

ADMINISTRATIVE SUPPORT:
CDO/OOD-847-4501 Admin (Gen)-847-4517

HEALTH & WELFARE:
CHAMPUS-847-4520 Family Services-847-4503

REST & RECREATION: Downhill skiing, cross country skiing, ice skating, boating, fishing, golf, beaches, indoor swimming, tennis courts, YMCA programs, trap/skeet shooting, bicycling, canoeing.

ATTRACTIONS: Grand Haven State Park, world's largest musical fountain, Annual Coast Guard Anniversary Festival (city has been recognized by Congress as Coast Guard City, USA).

SAULT STE MARIE COAST GUARD GROUP/MARINE SAFETY OFFICE (MI15R2)

337 Water Street
Sault Ste Marie, MI 49783-9501

TELEPHONE NUMBER INFORMATION: Main installation number: C-906-635-3217. E-mail: Admin/Grusault01@cgsmtp.uscg.mil.

LOCATION: Take I-75 north to exit 392, merge onto I-75 Business Spur/Ashmun Street Follow Ashmun Street until it ends at St Mary's River. Turn right on Water Street, base is three blocks on left. USMRA: Page 66 (E-1,2). NMC: Detroit, 350 miles south.

GENERAL INFORMATION: Vessel Traffic Safety Search Rescue Group, Group Sault Radio telecommunications, Captain of the Port-marine safety, environmental pollution, general administration, ID card issuing activity, ATON/STA small boat stations.

TEMPORARY MILITARY LODGING: None. Nearest facility is more than 100 miles away.

RV, CAMPING/FAMCAMP: None. Nearest facility is more than 100 miles away.

SPACE-A: None. See Alpena CRTC listing, C-517-354-6305, D-312-741-3305.

LOGISTICAL SUPPORT:
Cafeteria-635-3267 Exchange-635-3275/3276

ADMINISTRATIVE SUPPORT:
Quarterdeck-635-3229 SDO/NCO-635-3233

HEALTH & WELFARE:
CHAMPUS-635-3225 Medical-635-3226

REST & RECREATION: None. Nearest facility is more than 100 miles away.

ATTRACTIONS: Hunting and fishing.

SELFRIDGE AIR NATIONAL GUARD BASE (MI01R2)

29423 George Avenue
Selfridge Air National Guard Base, MI 48045-5029

TELEPHONE NUMBER INFORMATION: Main installation numbers: C-810-307-4011, D-312-273-4011.

LOCATION: Take I-94 north from Detroit to Selfridge exit, then east on MI-59 to main gate of base. USMRA: Page 66 (G-9), page 70 (G-1). NMC: Detroit, 10 miles southwest.

GENERAL INFORMATION: Air National Guard units, Reserve units of Air Force, Navy, Marine Corps and Army. Coast Guard Air Station Detroit.

TEMPORARY MILITARY LODGING: Lodging office, Building 410, George Avenue, 24 hours daily, C-810-307-4062, D-312-273-4062. DV/VIP C-810-307-4062. All ranks.

RV, CAMPING/FAMCAMP: None. Nearest facility is more than 100 miles away.

SPACE-A: Information, C-810-307-5884, D-312-273-5884.

LOGISTICAL SUPPORT:
Child Care-307-4711 Commissary-307-5570
Conv Store-307-4256 Exchange-307-5789
Gas Station-307-4256 Package Store-307-5072
SATO-307-7651 Snack Bar-307-4397

ADMINISTRATIVE SUPPORT:
Locator-307-4021 Police-307-4673
SDO/NCO-307-4011

HEALTH & WELFARE:
CHAMPUS-307-5261 Chapel-307-4761
Family Services-307-5903 Medical
Central Appts-307-4650
Emergency-911 or 307-5000

REST & RECREATION:
Arts & Crafts-ext 5155 Auto Hobby Shop-ext 4535
Bowling-ext 5941 Golf Course-ext 4344
O'Club-307-4785 Outdoor Rec-ext 4344
Picnic Area 463-3070 Rec Center-ext 4524/4564

MICHIGAN
Selfridge Air National Guard Base, continued

Swimming/Tennis-ext 5765	Wood Hobby Shop-ext 4535
Youth Services-ext 4524/4564	

OTHER SUPPORT FACILITIES AVAILABLE: Selfridge Outdoor Rec Area, on base, Apr-Sep, C-810-463-3070, D-312-273-3070, marina only, no camping.

ATTRACTIONS: Air Museum, Detroit, Canadian cities of Windsor and Sarnia.

TRAVERSE CITY COAST GUARD AIR STATION (MI07R2)

1175 Airport Access Road
Traverse City, MI 49686-3586

TELEPHONE NUMBER INFORMATION: Main installation number: C-616-922-8300.

LOCATION: Located across from Cherry Capital Airport. From US-31 north go south on Airport Access Road. Air Station will be on the left. USMRA: Page 66 (C-5). NMC: Traverse City, in city limits.

GENERAL INFORMATION: A large rescue air station covering the northern Great Lakes area.

TEMPORARY MILITARY LODGING: None. See Camp Grayling MTC listing, C-517-348-3661, D-312-722-3661, Fax: C-517-348-3844.

RV, CAMPING/FAMCAMP: None. See Grand Haven CGG listing, Point Betsie Rec Cottage, C-616-847-4510.

SPACE-A: None. See Alpena CRTC, C-517-354-6305, D-312-741-3305.

LOGISTICAL SUPPORT:

Dining Facilities-922-8311	Education Office-922-8230
Exchange-922-8330	Package Store-947-5790

ADMINISTRATIVE SUPPORT:

Housing Office-922-8321	Pass/ID Office-922-8228
Operations-922-8211	Public Affairs-922-8218

HEALTH & WELFARE:

CHAMPUS-922-8281	Dental-922-8282
Medical-922-8282	

REST & RECREATION: None. See Camp Grayling MTC listing, C-517-348-9033.

ATTRACTIONS: Fresh water lakes, local golf courses, ski areas nearby. Sleeping Bear Dunes National Lakeshore, Peshawbetown Indian Village, Old Mission Lighthouse, Manistee National Forest.

Other Installations in Michigan

Detroit Arsenal, US Army Tank-Automotive & Armaments Command (MI09R2), Warren, MI 48397-5000. USMRA: Page 70 (E-2). C-810-574-5000, Medical-574-5771.
Michigan Air National Guard Base (MI12R2), 110 Fighter Wing, 3545 Mustang Avenue, Battle Creek, MI 49015-5509. USMRA: Page 66 (D-9). C-616-969-3400, D-312-580-3400. Exchange-969-3372, All Ranks Club open irregular hours, call 969-3374.

MINNESOTA

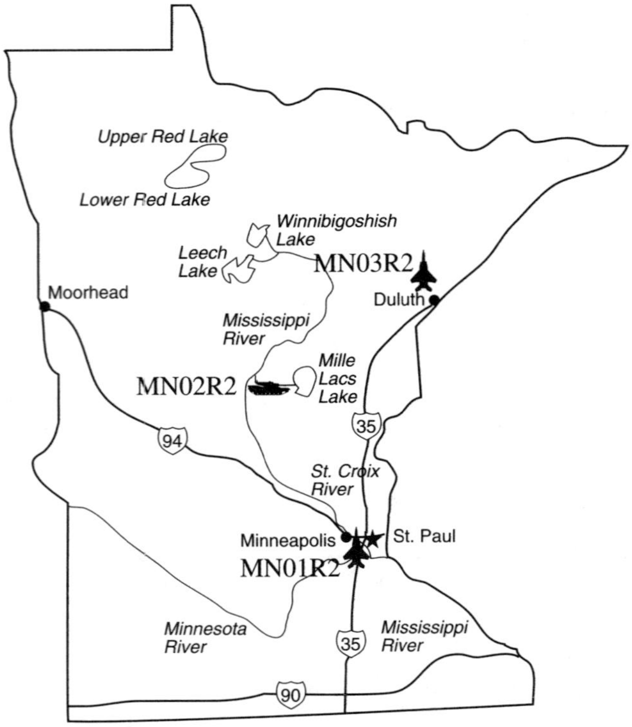

CAMP RIPLEY (MN02R2)

P.O. Box 150
Little Falls, MN 56345-5000

TELEPHONE NUMBER INFORMATION: Main installation number: C-320-632-7000, D-312-871-7000.

LOCATION: Clearly marked off Highway 371. USMRA: Page 80 (C,D-6), NMC: Little Falls, seven miles south.

TEMPORARY MILITARY LODGING: BOQ when available. C-320-632-7378, D-312-871-7378.

RV, CAMPING/FAMCAMP: Policy being developed; camping to be available in 1998.

SPACE-A: None. See Minneapolis-St Paul IAP/ARS listing, C-612-713-1719/1741/2450, D-312-783-1719/1741/2450.

LOGISTICAL SUPPORT:
Exchange-632-7382 — SATO-632-7465
Snack Bar-632-7412

ADMINISTRATIVE SUPPORT: Police-632-7665

HEALTH & WELFARE:
Family Services-632-7296 — Medical-632-7378

REST & RECREATION: Clubs
NCO-632-7255
O-632-7239

ATTRACTIONS: Hunting, fishing and camping, military museum, Mississippi Headwaters, Charles Lindberg home.

MINNEAPOLIS-ST PAUL INTERNATIONAL AIRPORT/AIR RESERVE STATION (MN01R2)

760 Military Highway
Minneapolis, MN 55450-2000

TELEPHONE NUMBER INFORMATION: Main installation numbers: C-612-713-1110, D-312-783-1110.

LOCATION: From I-35 E or MN-55 S to crosstown MN-62, exit at 34th Avenue and entrance. USMRA: Page 89 (C-3,4). NMC: Minneapolis-St Paul, in city limits.

GENERAL INFORMATION: Air Reserve Station, co-located Air Force Reserve Wing, and ANG Airlift Wing, Navy, Marine Corps and other reserve units.

TEMPORARY MILITARY LODGING: Lodging office, Building 711, 0700-2200 hours Mon-Fri, 0630-1700 Sat, C-612-713-1983, D-312-83-1983. All ranks.

RV, CAMPING/FAMCAMP: None. Nearest facility is more than 100 miles away.

SPACE-A: Base Ops, Building 821, 0730-1600 daily, C-612-713-1719/1741, D-312-783-1719/1741, and ANGB Ops Building 684, C-612-713-2450, D-312-783-2450. Flights to CONUS and OCONUS locations, mostly training flights on weekends.

LOGISTICAL SUPPORT:
Exchange-726-9023 — Omega Travel-726-1995

ADMINISTRATIVE SUPPORT:
Police-713-1102 — Public Affairs-713-1217

HEALTH & WELFARE: Family Services-713-1516

REST & RECREATION:
Clubs — Recreation-713-1128
NCO-713-1655
O-713-3678

ATTRACTIONS: Minneapolis-St Paul (Twin Cities) on the Mississippi and Minnesota Rivers. Many lakes within the cities with walking and bicycling trails.

Other Installations in Minnesota

Duluth Air National Guard (MN03R2), 4680 Viper Street, Duluth, MN 55811-6031. USMRA: Page 80 (F-5). C-218-727-6886, Exchange-727-8365.

MISSISSIPPI

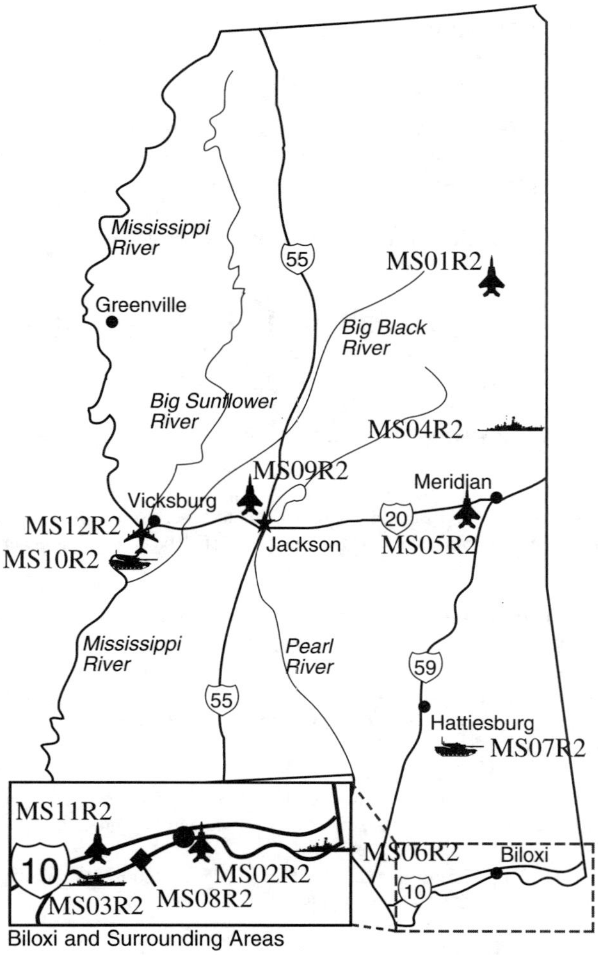

CAMP SHELBY TRAINING CAMP (MS07R2)

1001 Lee Avenue
Camp Shelby, MS 39407-5500

TELEPHONE NUMBER INFORMATION: Main installation numbers: C-601-558-2000, D-312-921-2540.

LOCATION: From Hattiesburg, take Highway 49 south, follow signs. USMRA: Page 43 (F-8). NMC: Hattiesburg, 10 miles north.

GENERAL INFORMATION: Training Site Headquarters, Regional School Support Detachment, Mississippi Military Academy.

TEMPORARY MILITARY LODGING: Building 6606, 0730-1600 daily, C-601-558-2540, D-312-921-2540. All ranks.

RV, CAMPING/FAMCAMP: Lake Walker Family Campground on post, year round, C-601-558-2397, D-312-921-2397, eight cabins and 25 camper spaces with full hookups.

SPACE-A: None. See Meridian NAS listing, C-601-679-2505, D-312-637-2505, Fax: C-601-637-2038.

LOGISTICAL SUPPORT: Exchange-558-2349

ADMINISTRATIVE SUPPORT: Locator-558-2000

HEALTH & WELFARE:
Chapel-558-2378
Medical-558-2805

REST & RECREATION:
Clubs
NCO-558-2427
O-558-2749
Museum-558-2757
Rec Center-ext 2397
Services-ext 2397

OTHER SUPPORT FACILITIES AVAILABLE: Swimming Softball, Tennis, and Basketball.

ATTRACTIONS: Kamper Park and Zoo, Hattiesburg Historical Society, Paul B. Johnson State Park, Armed Forces Museum.

COLUMBUS AIR FORCE BASE (MS01R2)

14th FTW/Public Affairs
Columbus Air Force Base, MS 39710-5000

TELEPHONE NUMBER INFORMATION: Main installation numbers: C-601-434-7322, D-312-742-1110. HP: http://www.col.aetc.af.mil.

LOCATION: Clearly marked off US-45. USMRA: Page 43 (G-3). NMC: Columbus, 10 miles south.

GENERAL INFORMATION: Air Education and Training Command Base, Specialized undergraduate pilot training.

TEMPORARY MILITARY LODGING: Lodging office, Building 956, B Street, 24 hours daily, C-601-434-2548, D-312-742-2548. All ranks. DV/VIP 601-434-7024.

RV, CAMPING/FAMCAMP: None. Nearest facility is over 100 miles away.

SPACE-A: Limited. See Meridian NAS listing, C-601-679-2505, D-312-778-2505, Fax: C-601-637-2038.

LOGISTICAL SUPPORT:
Child Care-434-2479
Conv Store-434-6026
Gas Station-434-6026
SATO-434-2669
Commissary-434-7103
Exchange-434-6013
Package Store-434-6026
Snack Bar-434-6498

ADMINISTRATIVE SUPPORT:
Fire Dept-434-2263
Locator-434-2620
Public Affairs-434-7067
Legal-434-7030
Police-434-7129
SDO/NCO-434-7020

HEALTH & WELFARE:
CHAMPUS-434-2132
Family Services-434-2790
Retiree Services-434-2790
Chapel-434-2500
Medical
Central Appts-434-2847
Emergency-434-2101

REST & RECREATION:
Auto Hobby Shop-434-7842
Clubs
EM-434-7927
O-434-2489
Library-434-2934
Services-434-7437/2316
Theater-434-2930
Youth Center-434-2504
Bowling-434-2426
Community Center-434-7858
Golf Course-434-7932
Gym-434-2722
Rec Equipment-434-2507
Skills Development Center-434-7836
Wood Hobby Shop-434-7837

ATTRACTIONS: Period historic homes, Columbus, and northeast Mississippi.

GULFPORT NAVAL CONSTRUCTION BATTALION CENTER (MS03R2)

5200 Construction Battalion Center 2nd Street
Gulfport, MS 39501-5001

TELEPHONE NUMBER INFORMATION: Main installation numbers: C-601-871-2555, D-312-868-2555.

MISSISSIPPI
Gulfport Naval Construction Battalion Center, continued

LOCATION: Take US-49 south to Gulfport. Follow signs to Center. From US-90 exit to Broad Avenue From I-10 exit to US-49. USMRA: Page 43 (F-10). NMC: New Orleans, 70 miles west.

GENERAL INFORMATION: Naval Construction Training Center, 20th Naval Construction Regiment and Construction Battalions.

TEMPORARY MILITARY LODGING: Lodging office, 0700-1600 daily. Building 314 BOQ, C-601-871-2505, 1-800-628-9466, D-312-868-2505. Building 317 BEQ, C-601-871-2506, D-312-868-2505. Navy Lodge, C-601-864-3101. DV/VIP C-601-865-2202, D-312-363-2205, Fax: C-601-871-2130.

RV, CAMPING/FAMCAMP: None. See Keesler AFB listing, C-601-377-3160, D-312-597-3160.

SPACE-A: None. See Keesler AFB listing, C-601-377-4538, D-312-597-4538.

LOGISTICAL SUPPORT:

Child Care-871-2323	Commissary-871-2040
Conv Store-863-4506	Exchange-871-2619
Gas Station-864-5527	Package Store-864-5527
SATO-864-9219	Visitor Center-871-3164

ADMINISTRATIVE SUPPORT:

Fire Dept-871-2333	Housing Office-871-2586
Legal-871-2626	Locator-871-2555
Police-871-2433	Public Affairs-871-2393
SDO/NCO-871-2555	

HEALTH & WELFARE:

Chapel-871-2454	Family Services-871-2581
Medical	Retiree Services-871-2647
Central appts-871-2806	TRICARE-871-2821
Emergency-871-2809	

REST & RECREATION:

Arts & Crafts-ext-2560	Auto Crafts-ext 2804
Bowling-ext 2739	Clubs
Gym-ext 2353/2668	Anchors & Eagles-871-2616
Golf Course-871-2494	Stingers-871-2396
ITT-871-2231	Library-ext 2409
MWR-871-2538	Racquetball-ext 2668
Recreation-871-2696	Swimming-ext 2768
Theater-871-2489	Youth Center-ext 2251

ATTRACTIONS: Gulf Coast, beaches, and water sports. Cities of Mobile and New Orleans, short drives.

JACKSON IAP/THOMPSON FIELD (MS09R2)

172nd AW
141 Military Drive, Building 129
Jackson, MS 39208-8881

TELEPHONE NUMBER INFORMATION: Main installation numbers: C-601-936-3633, D-312-731-9210.

LOCATION: Off I-20 and US-49, clearly marked. USMRA: Page 43 (D-6). NMC: Jackson, five miles west.

GENERAL INFORMATION: Mississippi Air National Guard, 172nd Airlift Group.

TEMPORARY MILITARY LODGING: None. See Meridian NAS listing, C-601-679-2186, D-312-637-2186, Fax: C-601-679-2745.

RV, CAMPING/FAMCAMP: None. Nearest facility is more than 100 miles away.

SPACE-A: Pax Term Info, C-601-936-8761, D-312-731-9761, Fax: C-601-936-8509, D-312-731-9509.

LOGISTICAL SUPPORT: Exchange-932-3930

ADMINISTRATIVE SUPPORT: Fire Dept-731-9411

HEALTH & WELFARE: Medical-936-8351

REST & RECREATION: Combined Club-936-8468

ATTRACTIONS: Historic Homes, Vicksburg National Battlefield Park 30 miles west.

KEESLER AIR FORCE BASE (MS02R2)

720 Chappie James Avenue, Room 106
Keesler Air Force Base, MS 39534-2603

TELEPHONE NUMBER INFORMATION: Main installation numbers: C-601-377-1110, D-312-597-1110.

LOCATION: From I-10 exit 46, follow signs to base. From US-90, north on White Avenue to main gate. USMRA: Page 43 (F-10). NMC: Biloxi, in city limits.

GENERAL INFORMATION: Air Education and Training Command Base, Training Wing, USAF Medical Center, and AFRES units.

TEMPORARY MILITARY LODGING: Lodging office, Larcher Boulevard, 24 hours daily Building 2101, Muse Manor, 0715-1600 Mon-Fri, C-601-377-2631/3663, All ranks.

RV, CAMPING/FAMCAMP: Keesler FAMCAMP on base, year round, C-601-377-3160, D-312-597-3160, 20 camper spaces with full hookups.

SPACE-A: Pax Term/Lounge, Building 0233, 0600-2300 daily, C-601-377-4538, D-312-597-4538, flights to CONUS locations.

LOGISTICAL SUPPORT:

Bank-374-4285	Barber Shop-377-2221/3200
Child Dev Center-377-3324/2211	Class Six-432-2367
Commissary-377-2830	Credit Union-385-5583
Dry Cleaner-374-6994/6996	Education Office-377-2323
Exchange-435-2216	Gas Station-432-2404
Laundry-374-6994/6996	Package Store-436-3683
Postal Service-377-2289	SATO-377-2230
Shoppette-432-2367	Sub Shop-436-3124
Visitor Center-377-3844	

ADMINISTRATIVE SUPPORT:

Fire Dept-377-3441	Housing Office-377-3014
Legal-377-3510	Locator-377-3988
Pass/ID Office-377-3893	Police-377-2878
Public Affairs-377-2783	Quarter Deck-377-9067
SDO/NCO-377-1110	

HEALTH & WELFARE:

AF Aid-377-2179	American Red Cross-377-3030
CHAMPUS-377-6001	Chapel-377-8633
Dental	Family Services-377-4293
Central Appts-377-4510	Medical
General-377-5130	Central Appts-377-2530
Retiree Services-377-3871	Emergency-911 or 377-0500
TRICARE-377-7685	Information-377-6550

REST & RECREATION:

Arts & Crafts-377-2821	Auto Hobby Shop-377-3872
Bowling-377-2817	Clubs
Community Center-377-3708	NCO-377-3439
Golf Course-377-3832	O-377-2219
Gym-377-4385/2907	Library-377-2181

MISSISSIPPI
Keesler Air Force Base, continued

Marinas-377-3160	Outdoor Rec-377-3160
Theater-377-4281	Wood Hobby Shop-377-3078
Youth Center-377-3349	

ATTRACTIONS: Gulf Coast beaches, seafood, Pensacola, FL, New Orleans, LA, and Mobile, AL, all within easy driving distance.

KEY FIELD (MS05R2)

186th ARW
6255 M Street
Meridian, MS 39307-7112

TELEPHONE NUMBER INFORMATION: Main installation numbers: C-601-484-9000, D-312-778-9210.

LOCATION: From 20 West, take 11 South, Air National Guard signs clearly marked. USMRA: Page 43 (F-6). NMC: Meridian, within the city limits.

GENERAL INFORMATION: Mississippi Air National Guard.

TEMPORARY MILITARY LODGING: None. See Meridian NAS listing, C-601-679-2186, D-312-637-2186, Fax: C-601-679-2745.

RV, CAMPING/FAMCAMP: None. Nearest facility is more than 100 miles away.

SPACE-A: Very limited, C-601-484-9726, D-312-778-9210.

LOGISTICAL SUPPORT: Exchange-485-3072

ADMINISTRATIVE SUPPORT: None. See Meridian NAS listing, C-601-679-2602

HEALTH & WELFARE: Medical-484-9206

REST & RECREATION: None. See Meridian NAS listing, C-601-679-2551.

ATTRACTIONS: Historic Homes, Vicksburg National Battlefield Park 120 miles west.

MERIDIAN NAVAL AIR STATION (MS04R2)

1155 Rosenbaum Avenue, Suite 13
Meridian Naval Air Station, MS 39309-5003

TELEPHONE NUMBER INFORMATION: Main installation numbers: C-601-679-2211, D-312-637-2211.

LOCATION: Take MS-39 north from Meridian, for 12 miles to four-lane access road. Clearly marked. Right for three miles to NAS main gate. USMRA: Page 43 (G-6). NMC: Meridian, 15 miles southwest.

GENERAL INFORMATION: Naval Air Training Wing, Naval Technical Training Center, Marine Aviation Training Support Group and Regional Counterdrug Training Academy.

TEMPORARY MILITARY LODGING: Lodging office, 24 hours daily. Building 218 (CBQ), Fuller Road, BEQ C-601-679-2186, D-312-637-2186, Fax: C-601-679-2745.

RV, CAMPING/FAMCAMP: None. Nearest facility is more than 100 miles away.

SPACE-A: Pax Terminal, Building 1, 1400-0300 Mon-Thu, 1400-2200 Fri, C-601-679-2505, D-312-637-2505, Fax: C-601-637-2038. Flights to CONUS destinations via Admin Aircraft.

LOGISTICAL SUPPORT:

Bank-679-2585	Barber Shop-679-2641
Beauty Shop-679-8411	Book Store-679-2568
Child Care-679-2362	Child Dev Center-679-2652
Commissary-679-2554	Conv Store-679-2568
Credit Union-693-8569	Dining Facilities-679-2634
Dry Cleaner-679-3430	Education Office-679-2671
Exchange-679-8461	Gas Station-679-8553
Laundry-679-3430	Package Store-679-2653
Postal Service-679-2580	SATO-679-2346
Snack Bar-679-2780	

ADMINISTRATIVE SUPPORT:

CDO-679-2528	Fire Dept-679-2336
Housing Office-679-2555	Legal-679-2590
Locator-679-2301	Pass/ID Office-679-2302
Police-679-2601	Public Affairs-679-2602
Quarter Deck-679-2528	

HEALTH & WELFARE:

American Red Cross-679-2679	Chapel-679-2139
Dental	Family Services-679-2360
Central Appts-679-2682	Medical-679-2633
Clinic-679-2383	Navy-MC Relief-679-2504
Emergency-679-2501	

REST & RECREATION:

Auto Hobby Shop-679-2609	Bowling-679-2651
Fitness Center-679-2379	Golf Course-679-2526
Gym-679-2379	ITT-679-2636
Library-679-2623	MWR-679-2551
Outdoor Rec 679-2731	Rec Center-679-2640
Swimming-ext 3470/3402	Wood Hobby Shop-679- 2609
Youth Center-679-2687	

ATTRACTIONS: Lake Okatibbee, 10 miles west, Jimmie Rodgers Museum, Monument and annual music festival in Meridian, Meridian Breakmen Professional Baseball Club (Independent-Big South League), Meridian Little Theatre, Meridian Art Museum, Meridian Symphony Orchestra, Mississippi State Games, Dunn's Falls water park, 11 miles south.

PASCAGOULA NAVAL STATION (MS06R2)

Building 10
Pascagoula, MS 39595-5000

TELEPHONE NUMBER INFORMATION: Main installation numbers: C-601-761-2140, D-312-358-2140.

LOCATION: From I-10 east, exit 69, four miles south to Highway 90, four miles west to Ingalls Access Road, one mile to Naval Station Causeway, three miles to the gate. USMRA: Page 43 (G-10). NMC: Pascagoula two miles east.

GENERAL INFORMATION: Shore Intermediate Maintenance Activity, Fleet Industrial Supply Center Detachment, Branch Medical Clinic, Branch Dental Clinic, Personnel Support Detachment (until 10/1/97).

TEMPORARY MILITARY LODGING: A 154-person combined Bachelor Quarters is sometimes used as temporary lodging. C-601-761-2182, D-312-358-2182. Also see Keesler AFB listing, C-601-377-2631/3663.

RV, CAMPING/FAMCAMP: None. See Keesler AFB listing, C-601-377-3160, D-312-597-3160.

SPACE-A: None. See Keesler AFB listing, C-601-377-4538, D-312-597-4538.

LOGISTICAL SUPPORT: Exchange-761-5133

ADMINISTRATIVE SUPPORT:

CDO/OOD-761-2020	Fire Dept-761-2028
Legal-761-2372	Locator-761-2017

MISSISSIPPI
Pascagoula Naval Station, continued

HEALTH & WELFARE:

CHAMPUS-761-2365	Chaplain-761-2010
Dental-761-2395	Family Services-761-4281
Medical-761-2222	TRICARE-761-2365

REST & RECREATION: MWR-761-2134

OTHER FACILITIES AVAILABLE: Fitness Center, Ball fields, Tennis Courts.

ATTRACTIONS: Gulf Islands National Seashore, Sheppard State Park, and beautiful beaches.

WATERWAYS EXPERIMENT STATION (MS10R2)

3909 Halls Ferry Road
Vicksburg, MS 39180-5000

TELEPHONE NUMBER INFORMATION: Main installation number: C-601-636-3111.

LOCATION: From I-20, exit 1-C, one mile south. USMRA: Page 43 (C-6). NMC: Vicksburg, five miles west.

TEMPORARY MILITARY LODGING: None. Nearest facility is more than 100 miles away.

RV, CAMPING/FAMCAMP: None. Nearest facility is more than 100 miles away.

SPACE-A: None. See Vicksburg Municipal Airport listing, C-601-638-6550, or Jackson IAP listing, C-601-936-8761, D-312-731-9761.

LOGISTICAL SUPPORT:

Cafeteria-634-2560	Exchange-634-2136

ADMINISTRATIVE SUPPORT: SDO/NCO-634-2513

HEALTH AND WELFARE: CHAMPUS-634-5790

REST & RECREATION: Fitness Center on base.

ATTRACTIONS: Visitors facility, self-guided tours. City of Vicksburg: historic tours, National Military Park, toy soldiers museum, houses of the Old South, and riverboat casino gambling.

Other Installations in Mississippi

Gulfport-Biloxi Regional Airport/ANGB (MS11R2), 4715 Hewes Avenue, Building 1, Gulfport, MS 39507-4324. USMRA: Page 43 (F-10), C-601-868-6200, D-312-363-8200, Exchange-868-6200.
US Naval Home (MS08R2), 1800 Beach Drive, Gulfport, MS 39507-1597. USMRA: Page 43 (F-10), C-1-800-332-3527, 601-897-4000, Exchange-897-4000.
Vicksburg Municipal Airport (MS12R2), Reserve Center, 386th Transportation Co., 1000 Lee Street, Vicksburg, MS 39180-9616. USMRA: Page 43 (C-6), C-601-638-6550, Space-A-638-6550.

MISSOURI

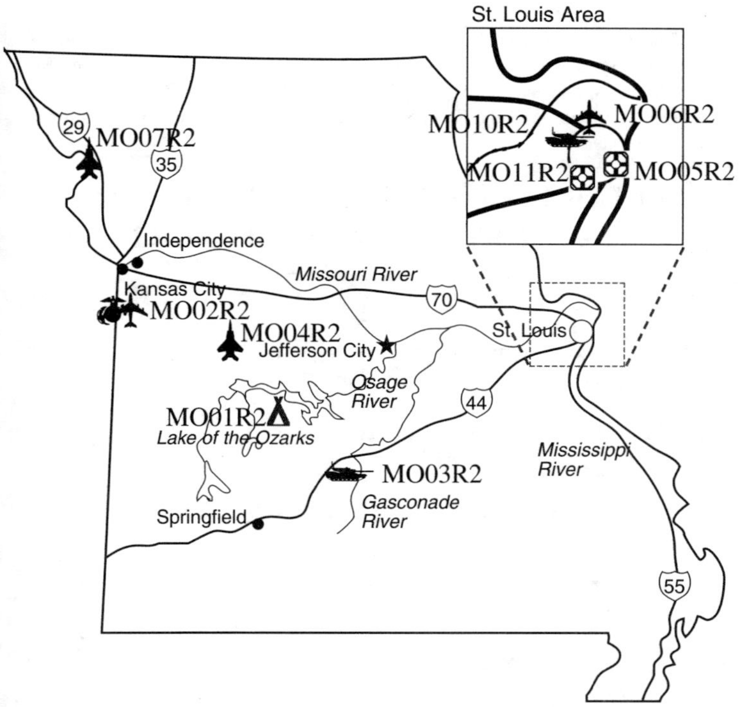

FORT LEONARD WOOD (MO03R2)

US Army Engineering Center & Fort Leonard Wood
ATTN: ATZT-GC
Hodge Hall, Building 3200
Fort Leonard Wood, MO 65473-5000

TELEPHONE NUMBER INFORMATION: Main installation numbers: C-573-596-0131, D-312-581-0110.

LOCATION: Two miles south of I-44, adjacent to St Robert & Waynesville, at Fort Leonard Wood exit. USMRA: Page 81 (E-6). NMC: Springfield, 85 miles southwest.

GENERAL INFORMATION: Basic Training installation and Army, Navy, Marines, Air Force Training Center for Engineer Corps personnel.

TEMPORARY MILITARY LODGING: Lodging office, Building 470, Missouri Avenue, 24 hours daily, C-573-596-0999, or 1-800-677-8356.

RV, CAMPING/FAMCAMP: Operates Lake of the Ozarks Recreation Area off post, 60 miles northwest of post. See Lake of the Ozarks Recreation Area listing for more information.

SPACE-A: Forney Army Airfield, Base Ops, 24 hours daily, C-573-596-0165/4819, D-312-581-0165, Fax: C-573-596-0166, flights to CONUS.

LOGISTICAL SUPPORT:

Bank-329-2000/3151	Barber Shop-329-3655
Beauty Shop-329-2212	Book Store-329-6034
Cafeteria-329-3601	Car Rental-329-2200
Carlson Wagonlit Travel-329-3231	Child Care-596-1028
Child Dev Center-596-0197	Class Six-329-6333
Commissary-596-0689	Conv Store-329-2777
Credit Union-329-3151	Dining Facilities-596-6533
Dry Cleaner-329-3490	Exchange-329-2200
Gas Station-329-3373	Package Store-329-6333
Postal Service-329-2717	Shoppette-329-2777/6200
Snack Bar-329-5677	Visitor Center-596-8015

ADMINISTRATIVE SUPPORT:

Fire Dept-596-0965	Housing Office-596-0965
Legal-596-0629	Locator-596-0677
Pass/ID Office-596-0744	Police-596-6141
Public Affairs-563-4015	SDO-563-6126

HEALTH & WELFARE:

American Red Cross-596-4151	ACS-596-0186
Army Emergency Relief-596-0186	CHAMPUS-596-9427
Chapel-596-0309	Dental-596-0364
Family Services-596-0195	Medical
Retiree Services-596-0947	Central Appts-596-1490
TRICARE-596-0552	Emergency-596-0456/2157
Veterinary Services-596-0094	Information-596-0094

REST & RECREATION:

Arts & Crafts-596-0242	Auto Hobby Shop-596-0243
Bowling-596-1498	Clubs
Fitness Center-596-4359	EM-329-6000
Golf Course-596-4770	NCO-329-6533
Gym-596-4359	O-329-6500
Library-563-4113	Marinas-346-5640
MWR-329-3300	Outdoor Rec-596-4223
Theater-596-1267/2531	Wood Hobby Shop-596-0242
Youth Center-596-2559	

ATTRACTIONS: Near Lake of the Ozarks recreational areas.

Note: Fort Leonard Wood will receive the US Army Military Police and US Army Chemical schools in late 1999 from Fort McClellan, Alabama.

LAKE OF THE OZARKS RECREATION AREA (MO01R2)

Route 1, Box 380
Linn Creek, MO 65052-5000

TELEPHONE NUMBER INFORMATION: Main installation numbers: C-573-596-0131, D-312-581-0110. Police for rec area, C-573-346-3693.

LOCATION: Located on Grand Glaize Arm of the Lake of the Ozarks in the center of a State Wildlife Refuge. From I-70, take Highway 63 to Jefferson City, then take US 54 to Linn Creek area; left at State Road A for six miles to Freedom; left on Lake Road A-33 for approximately five miles to travel camp. From I-44 northeast of Springfield, MO-7 northwest to Richland; right on State Road A and travel approximately 20 miles to Freedom; right on Lake Road A-33 approximately five miles to travel camp. USMRA: page 81 (D-6). NMC: Jefferson City, 40 miles northeast. NMI: Fort Leonard Wood, 60 miles southeast.

GENERAL INFORMATION: Situated on 360-acre reserve with excellent fishing and beautiful scenery. Operated by Fort Leonard Wood, off post 4 Apr-26 Oct (full season 23 May-1 Sep). Military personnel active, retired, NG, Reserve, DoD and NAF employees. Check in at Rental Office, Building 528, after 1500, check out Fri, Sat, Sun 1100. Reservations: Required by phone or in person at the Lake of the Ozarks Recreation Area office, Building 528 (3 Mar-23 May, 0900-1700 Mon-Wed; 24 May-1 Sep, 0900-1700 Mon-Fri), with full advance payment. Single night reservations will not be made more than five days in advance for weekends or holidays. No mail reservations. C-573-346-5640. Discounts to holders of Golden Age Passports for hookup camping only. Pets must be on leash or under voice control and have all shots (tags displayed); owner responsible for damage caused by pet. No open fires. No swimming except in beach area.

TEMPORARY MILITARY LODGING: Two bedroom duplex, AC, kitchen, private bath, color TV, sofa bed, furnished, except cleaning supplies, linens, including towels (2); cabins, AC, kitchen, private bath, color TV, sofa bed, furnished, except cleaning supplies, linens, including towels (3); Mobile homes: three bedroom deluxe, AC, kitchen, private bath, color TV, sofa bed, furnished, except cleaning supplies, linens, excluding towels (17); three bedroom, AC, kitchen, private bath, color TV, sofa bed, furnished, except cleaning supplies, linens, excluding towels (6); two bedroom, AC, kitchen, private bath, color TV, sofa bed, furnished, except cleaning supplies, linens, excluding towels (4). Rates: duplex $49-$76 daily; three bedroom deluxe mobile home $41-$66; three bedroom mobile home $33-$59; two bedroom mobile home $25-$48 daily.

RV, CAMPING/FAMCAMP: Hardstand camper spaces with W&E hookups (16); hardstand camper/tent spaces with no hookups (21). Rates: with hookups $10 daily; with no hookups $9 daily.

ADMINISTRATIVE SUPPORT: Police-346-3693

REST & RECREATION: Boating, Fishing/license, Hiking, Jet Skiing, Special Events, Swimming, Water Skiing.

OTHER SUPPORT & FACILITIES AVAILABLE: Beach, Boat Rental, Boat/RV Storage*, Country Store, Grills, Laundry, Marina, Party Barges, Pavilion/fee, Picnic Area, Playground, Restrooms, Sewage Dump, Showers, Ski Boats, Water Sports Equipment Rental. Also, see Fort Leonard Wood listing, C-573-596-0131, D-312-581-0110.

** By reservation*

ATTRACTIONS: Nearby attractions include Osage Beach, Ozark Caverns, musical shows, theme park, water slides, helicopter rides, etc. Historical and recreational points of interest surround the area.

MARINE CORPS ACTIVITIES AT RICHARDS-GEBAUR MEMORIAL AIRPORT (MO02R2)

15424 Andrews Road
Kansas City, MO 64147-1219

TELEPHONE NUMBER INFORMATION: Main installation number: C-816-843-3800.

LOCATION: From US-71 south, take Belton Richards-Gebaur Memorial Airport exit, west on County Line Road (or 155th Street) to former base. Between Grandview & Belton. USMRA: Page 81 (B-5), page 89 (B-5). NMC: Kansas City, 10 miles north.

GENERAL INFORMATION: Marine Corps Support Activity, Marine Corps Reserve Support Command, 24th Marine Regiment, 9th Marine District.

TEMPORARY MILITARY LODGING: Lodging office, 15820 Elmwood, Kansas City, MO 64147. 0630-2345 Mon-Fri, 0730-2345 Sat-Sun, C-816-843-3855/3850, D-312-894-3855/3850, Fax: C-816-843-3857, D-312-894-3857.

RV, CAMPING/FAMCAMP: None. See Lake of the Ozarks Rec Area listing, C-573-346-5640.

SPACE-A: None. See Rosecrans Memorial Airport/ANG listing, C-816-236-3260.

LOGISTICAL SUPPORT:
Barber Shop (part-time)-843-3713
Credit Union-331-6600
Exchange-331-2019
SATO-843-3404/6

ADMINISTRATIVE SUPPORT:
Housing Office-843-3860/1
Pass/ID Office-843-3816
Public Affairs-843-3051

HEALTH & WELFARE:
CHAMPUS-843-3816
Dental-843-3670/1/2
Family Services-843-3650
Medical
  Clinic-843-3665/6/7
  Health Benefits-843-3816

REST & RECREATION:
Consol-843-3840/1
MWR-843-3870/1

ATTRACTIONS: Kansas City, the city of fountains. Harry S. Truman Library and home in Independence, a short drive away; KC Royals, KC Blades and KC Chiefs pro sports teams; Worlds of Fun; Oceans of Fun; Swope Park Zoo; Starlight (outdoor theater); Plaza Shopping (and Christmas lighting); Hallmark Crown Center.

ST LOUIS COAST GUARD INTEGRATED SUPPORT COMMAND (MO05R2)

1222 Spruce Street
St Louis, MO 63103-5000

TELEPHONE NUMBER INFORMATION: Main installation number: C-314-539-3900, ext 350.

LOCATION: Take I-70 west, exit Bircher Boulevard USMRA: Page 81 (G-5), page 91 (B-3,4). NMC: St Louis, in city limits.

GENERAL INFORMATION: Three WLR Class Buoy Tenders, two Reserve Units.

TEMPORARY MILITARY LODGING: None. See Scott AFB, IL listing, C-618-744-1200, D-312-576-1844.

RV, CAMPING/FAMCAMP: None. See Lake of the Ozarks Rec Area listing, C-573-346-5640.

SPACE-A: None. See Scott AFB, IL listing, C-618-256-3017, D-312-576-3017, Fax: C-618-256-1948.

LOGISTICAL SUPPORT:
Carlson Wagonlit Travel-421-0500
Exchange-845-2467/9303

ADMINISTRATIVE SUPPORT: Locator-832-5941

HEALTH & WELFARE: AF Aid-618-256-1110

REST & RECREATION: EM Club-832-5021

ATTRACTIONS: St Louis, Gateway Arch, *USS Inaugural* Minesweeper, planetarium, Ulysses S. Grant's farm.

WHITEMAN AIR FORCE BASE (MO04R2)

509 Spirit Boulevard, Suite 111
Whiteman Air Force Base, MO 65305-5097

TELEPHONE NUMBER INFORMATION: Main installation numbers: C-816-687-1110, D-312-975-1110.

LOCATION: From I-70 east exit to US-13 south to US-50 east for 10 miles, Highway 23 (south) which leads to AFB. USMRA: Page 81 (C-5). NMC: Kansas City, 60 miles northwest.

GENERAL INFORMATION: Air Combat Command Base. 509th Bomb Wing and Air Force Reserve 442nd Fighter Wing, and the Missouri Army National Guard.

TEMPORARY MILITARY LODGING: Lodging office, Building 3200, Spirit Boulevard, 24 hours daily, C-816-687-1844, D-312-975-1844, DV/VIP C-816-687-6543. All ranks.

RV, CAMPING/FAMCAMP: None. See Lake of the Ozarks Rec Area listing, C-573-346-5640.

SPACE-A: Base Ops, C-816-687-3101, D-312-975-3101, flights to CONUS locations.

MISSOURI
Whiteman Air Force Base, continued

LOGISTICAL SUPPORT:
Child Care-687-5592
Conv Store-563-5445
Food Court-563-3167
Package Store-563-5445
Commissary-687-5655
Exchange-563-3003
Gas Station-687-5445
Travel Office-563-4120

ADMINISTRATIVE SUPPORT:
Legal-687-6809
Police-687-3700
Locator-687-1841

HEALTH & WELFARE:
Chapel-687-3652
Medical
Central Appts-687-2273
or 1-800-537-7405 within 816 area code
Family Services-687-3660
Retiree Services-687-6457
TRICARE-687-2242

REST & RECREATION:
Auto Hobby Shop-ext 5689
Community Center-ext 5617
Bowling-ext 5114
Fitness Center-ext 5496
Golf Course-ext 5572
MWR-687-5617
Theater-687-5110
Youth Center-ext 5586
Library-ext 5614
Swimming-ext 5502
The Club-687-2273

ATTRACTIONS: Outdoor sports, Lake of the Ozarks region, Kansas City.

Other Installations in Missouri

Lambert-St Louis IAP (MO06R2), St Louis, MO 63145-0305. USMRA: Page 81 (G-5) Page 91 (A-1,2). C-314-263-6400, Space-A-263-6270. ***Scheduled to close October 1997.***
Louis-Page Exchange (MO10R2), Building 101, 9700 Page Boulevard, St Louis, MO 63132-5000. USMRA: Page 91 (A-2). C-314-427-8188, Exchange-427-8188 open 0800-1400 Mon-Fri.
Rosecrans Memorial Airport/ANG (MO07R2), 705 Memorial Drive, St Joseph, MO 64503-9307. USMRA: Page 81 (B-3). C-816-236-3300, Space-A-236-3260.
St Louis Coast Guard Exchange (MO11R2), 96 Worth Road, St Louis, MO 63125-9998. USMRA: Page 91 (B-4). C-314-845-2467, Exchange-845-2467.

MONTANA

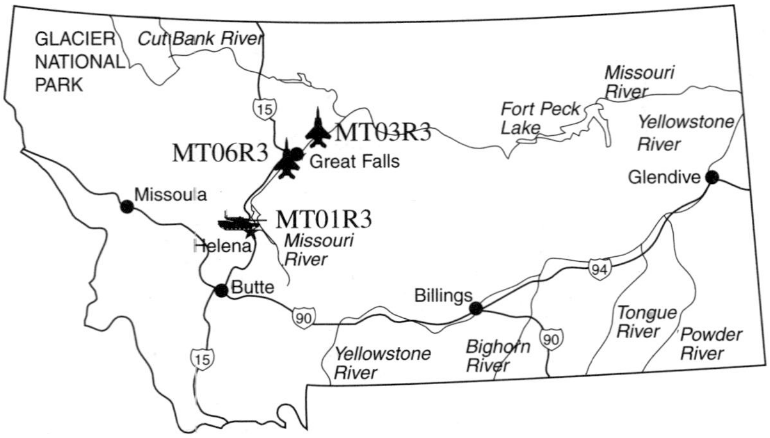

MALMSTROM AIR FORCE BASE (MT03R3)

21, 77th Street North
Malmstrom Air Force Base, MT 59402-5000

TELEPHONE NUMBER INFORMATION: Main installation numbers: C-406-731-1110, D-312-632-1110.

LOCATION: From I-15 take 10th Avenue south, exit to AFB. From the east take Malmstrom exit off US-87/89 to AFB. Clearly marked. USMRA: Page 99 (D,E-4). NMC: Great Falls, one mile west.

GENERAL INFORMATION: Air Force Space Command Base and 341st Missile Wing (AFSPC).

TEMPORARY MILITARY LODGING: Lodging office, Building 1680, 24 hours daily C-406-727-8600.

RV, CAMPING/FAMCAMP: FAMCAMP on base, May-Oct, C-406-731-3263, D-312-632-3263, 25 camper spaces with full hookups, five camper/tent spaces without hookups. Duval's RV and Bike Park off base, May-Sep, C-406-731-3263, D-312-632-3263, seven trailers.

SPACE-A: None. (Recently shut down.) Nearest facility is more than 100 miles away.

LOGISTICAL SUPPORT:

Cafeteria-731-4607	Child Care-731-2417
Commissary-731-3675	Conv Store-761-8004
Exchange-761-8004	Gas Station-761-7333
Package Store-761-8004	Snack Bar-761-8004/3194
Travel-731-2934	Visitor Center-731-3892

ADMINISTRATIVE SUPPORT:

Fire Dept-911	Legal-731-2878
Locator-731-4121/ after hours-727-3895	Police-911
	Public Affairs-731-4044

HEALTH & WELFARE:

Chapel-731-3721	Family Services-731-4900
Medical	Retiree Services-731-4142
Central Appts-731-3425	TRICARE-731-4396
Emergency-731-1110 ext 118	

REST & RECREATION:

Arts & Crafts-ext 3691	Auto Hobby Shop-ext 3777
Bowling-ext 2494	Club Malmstrom-761-6430
Community Center-731-4633	ITT-731-4634
Library-ext 2748	MWR-731-3263
Outdoor Rec-ext 3263	Rec Center-ext 2248
Recreation-731-3691	Sports Arena-ext 3621
Theater-731-3236	Wood Hobby Shop-ext 3232
Youth Center-ext 2422	

ATTRACTIONS: Big Sky Country, snow skiing, wildlife, fish and game.

MONTANA AIR NATIONAL GUARD BASE (MT06R3)

120th Fighter Wing
2800 Airport Avenue B
Great Falls, MT 59404-5570

TELEPHONE NUMBER INFORMATION: Main installation numbers: C-406-791-6220, D-312-279-2220, Fax: C-406-791-6488.

LOCATION: Great Falls International Airport. Airport exit is off I-15, and is one mile south of the 10th Avenue S exit. USMRA: Page 99 (D-4). NMC: Great Falls, one mile.

GENERAL INFORMATION: Montana Air National Guard, 120th Fighter Wing.

TEMPORARY MILITARY LODGING: None. See Malmstrom AFB listing, C-406-727-8600.

RV, CAMPING/FAMCAMP: None. See Malmstrom AFB listing, C-406-731-3263, D-312-632-3263.

SPACE-A: None. Nearest facility is more than 100 miles away.

LOGISTICAL SUPPORT:

Credit Union-ext 2306	Dining Facilities-ext 2259
Exchange-791-6299	Shoppette-ext 2299
Snack Bar-791-6224	Travel Office- ext 6277

ADMINISTRATIVE SUPPORT:

Fire Dept-ext 2232	Legal-ext 2180
Pass/ID Office- ext 2337	Police-ext 2336
Public Affairs-ext 2228	

HEALTH & WELFARE: Chapel-ext 2300

REST & RECREATION: None. See Malmstrom AFB listing, C-406-731-3263.

ATTRACTIONS: C.M. Russel Museum, Paris Gibson Art Gallery, Malmstrom Aircraft Museum, Heritage Park, Giant Springs State Park.

Other Installations in Montana

Fort Harrison Site (MT01R3), P.O. Box 4789, Building 40, Helena, MT 59604-4789. USMRA: Page 99 (D-5). C-406-444-6910, Exchange-444-7910.

NEBRASKA

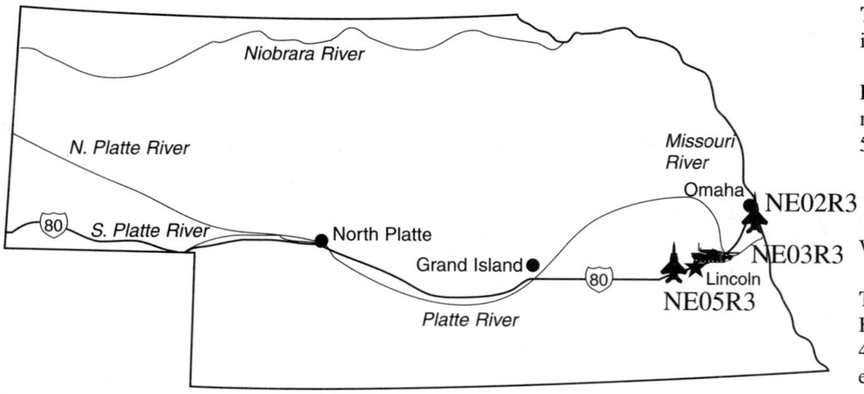

NEBRASKA AIR NATIONAL GUARD BASE (NE05R3)

155 Air Refueling Wing
2420 West Butler Avenue
Lincoln, NE 68524-1897

TELEPHONE NUMBER INFORMATION: Main installation numbers: C-402-458-1110, D-312-946-1110.

LOCATION: Adjacent to Lincoln Municipal Airport, right on I-80. USMRA: Page 82 (I-5). NMC: Lincoln, two miles southeast.

GENERAL INFORMATION: 155th Air Refueling Wing, Air National Guard.

TEMPORARY MILITARY LODGING: None. See Offutt AFB listing, C-402-294-3671/9000, D-312-271-3671/9000.

RV, CAMPING/FAMCAMP: None. See Offutt AFB listing, C-402-294-2108, D-312-271-2108.

SPACE-A: Pax terminal C-402-458-1248.

LOGISTICAL SUPPORT: Exchange-474-3454

ADMINISTRATIVE SUPPORT:
Fire Dept-458-1500
Police-458-1563
Legal-458-1122
SDO/NCO-458-1266

HEALTH & WELFARE: Chapel-458-1121

REST & RECREATION: None. See Offutt AFB listing, C-402-294-1110, D-312-271-1110.

OTHER FACILITIES AVAILABLE: Running track, softball diamond.

ATTRACTIONS: Home of state government, University of Nebraska, Elephant Hall at University of Nebraska, Nebraska State Historical Society Museum, and Lincoln Children's Zoo. Many fine restaurants, hotels/motels and area lakes with camping. "The Clean City."

OFFUTT AIR FORCE BASE (NE02R3)

906 SAC Boulevard, Suite 1
Offutt Air Force Base, NE 68113-5000

TELEPHONE NUMBER INFORMATION: Main installation numbers: C-402-294-1110, D-312-271-1110.

LOCATION: From I-80 exit to US-75 south to AFB exit, 6.5 miles south of I-80/US-75 interchange. USMRA: Page 82 (I,J-5). NMC: Omaha, eight miles north.

GENERAL INFORMATION: Air Combat Command Base. 55th Wing, Headquarters US STRATCOM, Air Force Global Weather Center, and other support units.

TEMPORARY MILITARY LODGING: Lodging office, Building 44, Grants Pass Street, 24 hours daily, C-402-294-3671/9000, D-312-271-3671/9000. All ranks. DV/VIP ext 4461.

RV, CAMPING/FAMCAMP: FAMCAMP on base, year round, C-402-294-2108, D-312-271-2108, 10 camper spaces with full hookups.

SPACE-A: Pax Term/Lounge, Building T-47, 0500-2100 Mon-Fri, 0700-1900 Sat-Sun, C-402-294-6235, D-312-271-6235, Fax: C-402-294-4070, flights to CONUS and OCONUS locations.

LOGISTICAL SUPPORT:
Cafeteria-291-9596
Commissary-294-5920
Exchange-291-9100
Package Store-292-7097
Child Care-294-2203
Conv Store-292-0218
Gas Station-291-8745

ADMINISTRATIVE SUPPORT:
Legal-294-3732
Police-294-6110
Locator-294-5125

HEALTH & WELFARE:
Chapel-294-6244/6051
Family Services-294-3111
Retiree Services-294-7693
CHAMPUS-294-7424
Medical
  Central Appts AD-294-6477
    Dependents-292-5510
  Emergency-294-7334

REST & RECREATION:
Arts & Crafts-ext 3872
Bowling-ext 2514
Golf Course-ext 3362/292-1680
Gym-ext 5904
Library-ext 2533
Photo Hobby-ext 3872
Rec Center-ext 6247
Theater-294-5951
Youth Center-ext 5152
Auto Hobby Shop-ext 5564
Clubs
  Aero-ext 3503
  EM-291-6785
  NCO-292-1600
  O-292-1560
Swimming-ext 2274/3593/6466
Wood Hobby Shop-ext 3318

ATTRACTIONS: City of Omaha, Old Market area, Boys Town.

Other Installations in Nebraska

Camp Ashland (NE03R3), RR 1, Box 160 C, Ashland, NE 68003-9801. USMRA: Page 82 (I-5). NMC: Omaha, 25 miles northeast. C-402-944-2110, TML and RV-944-2110, Shoppette-944-2750, Public Affairs-471-7352. From I-80 exit 432, Highway 31, north one quarter mile to Highway 5, east four-and-a-half miles to Highway 53 north, one half mile to Camp.

NEVADA

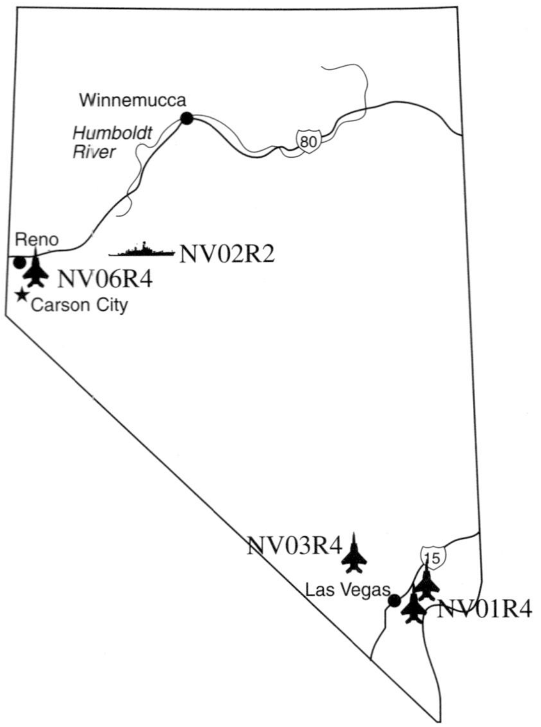

FALLON NAVAL AIR STATION (NV02R4)

4755 Pasture Road
Fallon Naval Air Station, NV 89496-5000

TELEPHONE NUMBER INFORMATION: Main installation numbers: C-702-426-5161, D-312-890-5161.

LOCATION: From Reno take US Highway 80 to Femley (exit 48). Go to stop light and turn left onto US Highway alternate 50 to Fallon. Once through Fallon turn right on Crook Road then left on Wildes Road then right on Pasture Road to main gate. USMRA: Page 113 (C-4). NMC: Reno, 72 miles west.

GENERAL INFORMATION: Naval Strike & Air Warfare Center, Construction Battalion Unit 416, Strike Fighter Wing Detachment, VFC-13, Naval Air Station.

TEMPORARY MILITARY LODGING: Lodging office, 24 hours daily, BOQ C-702-428-3003, BEQ C-702-426-2515, D-312-890-2515. All ranks. DV/VIP C-702-428-2859, Fax: C-702-426-2408.

RV, CAMPING/FAMCAMP: Fallon RV Park and Recreation Area on base, year round, C-702-426-2598, D-312-890-2598, 16 camper spaces with W&E hookups.

SPACE-A: Pax Term, hangar 7, Call for hours, C-702-426-3415, D-312-890-3415, flights to CONUS and OCONUS locations.

LOGISTICAL SUPPORT:

Barber Shop-426-2547
Cafeteria-426-2501
Child Care-423-5808
Commissary-426-3420
Credit Union-426-2500
Dry Cleaner-426-2484
Gas Station-426-2853
Postal Service-426-2738
Travel Office-426-2865
Beauty Shop-426-2547
Car Rental-426-2592
Child Dev Center-423-5808
Conv Store-426-2583
Dining Facilities-426-2520
Exchange-426-2400
Laundry-426-2484
Snack Bar-426-3660

ADMINISTRATIVE SUPPORT:

CDO-426-2715
Housing Office-426-2788
Locator-426-5161
Police-426-2853 (non emergency)
Fire Dept-911
Legal-426-2711
Pass/ID Office-426-2856
Public Affairs-426-2880

HEALTH & WELFARE:

CHAMPUS-426-3102
Dental-426-3333
Medical
  Central Appts-426-3110
  Emergency-911
  Health Benefits-426-3102
Chapel-426-2813
Family Services-426-3333
Navy-MC Relief-426-2739

REST & RECREATION:

Arts & Crafts-ext 3425
Bowling-ext 2451
Fitness Center-ext 2251
Gym-ext 2949
ITT-ext 2865
Library-ext 2599
Outdoor Rec-ext 2437/2279
Youth Center-423-4004
Auto Hobby Shop-ext 2575
Clubs
  CPO-ext 2483
  EM-ext 2445
  O-ext 2841/2625
MWR-ext 2819
Theater-ext 2580

ATTRACTIONS: Reno, Carson City, Virginia City, and Lake Tahoe nearby.

INDIAN SPRINGS AIR FORCE AUXILIARY FIELD (NV03R4)

3770 Duffer Drive
Indian Springs, NV 89018-5000

TELEPHONE NUMBER INFORMATION: Main installation numbers: C-702-652-0201, D-312-682-0201.

LOCATION: Off US-95, 47 miles northwest Nellis AFB. USMRA: Page 113 (F-8). NMC: Las Vegas, 45 miles southeast.

GENERAL INFORMATION: Forward operating location and emergency landing airfield for Nellis AFB.

TEMPORARY MILITARY LODGING: None. See Nellis AFB listing, C-702-643-2710, D-312-682-2711, DV/VIP C-702-643-2987.

RV, CAMPING/FAMCAMP: None. See Nellis AFB listing, Lucky Seven FAMCAMP, C-702-643-3060.

SPACE-A: None. See Nellis AFB listing, C-702-652-1854, D-312-682-1854, Fax: C-702-652-1561.

LOGISTICAL SUPPORT: Exchange-652-0326

ADMINISTRATIVE SUPPORT: None. See Nellis AFB listing, C-702-652-2750.

HEALTH & WELFARE: Medical-652-0286

REST & RECREATION: None. See Nellis AFB listing, C-702-652-4891.

ATTRACTIONS: Desert area, Tolyabe National Forest and Lee Canyon ski area, south of US-95, nearby.

NELLIS AIR FORCE BASE (NV01R4)

4370 N Washington Boulevard
Nellis Air Force Base, NV 89191-5000

TELEPHONE NUMBER INFORMATION: Main installation numbers: C-702-652-1110, D-312-682-1110.

NEVADA
Nellis Air Force Base, continued

LOCATION: Off I-15. Also, accessible from US-91/93. Clearly marked. USMRA: Page 113 (G-9). NMC: Las Vegas, eight miles southwest.

GENERAL INFORMATION: Air Combat Command Base. Air Warfare Center, Combat Fighter units. USAF Air Demonstration Squadron, "The Thunderbirds."

TEMPORARY MILITARY LODGING: Lodging office, Building 780, 5990 Fitzgerald Boulevard, Nellis AFB NV 89191-6514, 24 hours daily, C-702-643-2710, D-312-682-2711. All ranks. DV/VIP C-702-652-2987.

RV, CAMPING/FAMCAMP: Lucky Seven FAMCAMP off base, year round, C-702-643-3060.

SPACE-A: Pax Term/Lounge, Building 1044, 6255 Depot Road, Nellis AFB NV 89191-7224, 0730-1630 daily, C-702-652-1854, D-312-682-1854, Fax: C-702-652-1561, flights to CONUS locations.

LOGISTICAL SUPPORT:

Bank-385-8160	Barber Shop-643-9556
Beauty Shop-644-5558	Car Rental-644-5567
Child Care-652-4241	Child Dev Center-652-9730
Commissary-643-7919	Conv Store-644-6375
Credit Union-457-1000	Education Office-652-5280
Exchange-644-2044	Gas Station-643-1686
Package Store-644-1433	Post Office-652-2769
SATO-644-5400	Visitor Center-652-3216

ADMINISTRATIVE SUPPORT:

Fire Dept-652-9630	Housing Office-652-1840
Legal-652-9188	Locator-652-8134
Pass/ID Office-652-1845	Police-652-2311
Public Affairs-652-2750	SDO/NCO-652-2638

HEALTH & WELFARE:

CHAMPUS-653-2500	Chapel-652-2950
Family Services-652-6070	Medical
Retiree Services-652-8712	Central Appts-653-2778
	Emergency-653-2343
	Health Benefits-653-2500

REST & RECREATION:

Arts & Crafts-ext 4021	Auto Hobby Shop-ext 2284
Bowling-ext 2170	Clubs
Fitness Center-ext 6433	EM-652-9733
Golf Course-652-2602	O-652-9188
Gym-652-4891	Library-ext 9210
Theater-652-5020	Youth Center-ext 5015

ATTRACTIONS: Las Vegas, Lake Mead National Recreation Area, Mt. Charleston, Hoover Dam, Red Rock Canyon, Spring Mountain Ranch, Valley of Fire, beautiful deserts.

NEVADA AIR NATIONAL GUARD BASE (NV06R4)

1776 National Guard Way
Reno, NV 89502-5000

TELEPHONE NUMBER INFORMATION: Main installation numbers: C-702-788-4500, D-312-830-4500.

LOCATION: Reno-Cannon International Airport exit off I-395. Co-located at the IAP. USMRA: Page 113 (B-4). NMC: Reno, within city limits.

GENERAL INFORMATION: Air National Guard activities, Airlift Wing.

TEMPORARY MILITARY LODGING: None. See Fallon NAS listing, C-703-423-3003/2515, D-312-830-3003/2515, Fax: C-702-426-2408.

RV, CAMPING/FAMCAMP: None. See Fallon NAS listing, Fallon RV Park and Rec Area, C-702-426-2598, D-312-830-2598.

SPACE-A: None. See Fallon NAS listing, C-702-426-3415, D-312-830-3415.

LOGISTICAL SUPPORT: SATO-788-4667

ADMINISTRATIVE SUPPORT:

Police-788-4549	SDO/NCO-788-4550

HEALTH & WELFARE:

CHAMPUS-788-4510	Medical-786-7200

Chapel serving all faiths one weekend per month (during Guard drills).

REST & RECREATION: Combined Club-788-4570

ATTRACTIONS: Lake Tahoe, skiing. casinos, gambling, fishing, historic sites, Virginia City, Pyramid Lake.

NEW HAMPSHIRE

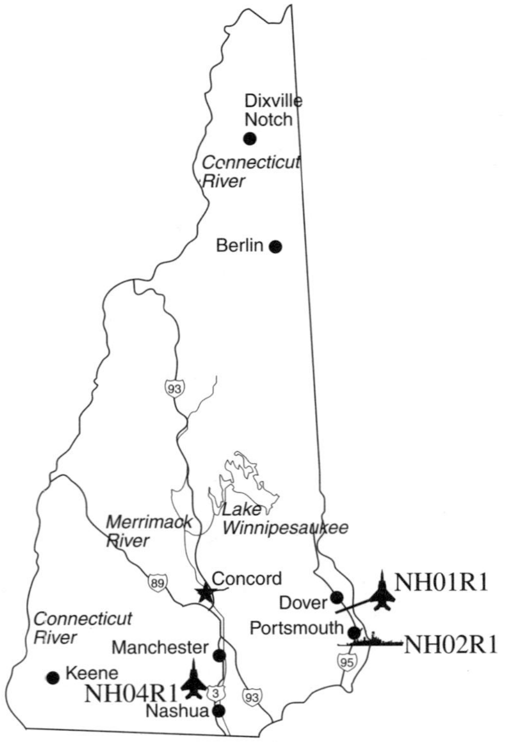

NEW BOSTON AIR STATION (NH04R1)

23rd Space Operations Squadron
317 Chestnut Hill Road
Amherst, NH 03031-1514

TELEPHONE NUMBER INFORMATION: Main installation number: C-603-471-2000, D-312-489-2000.

LOCATION: From I-93 north, take I-293 west to Route 101 west to Route 114 north to New Boston Road. USMRA: Page 23 (F-10). NMC: Manchester, eight miles northeast.

TEMPORARY MILITARY LODGING: None. See Hanscom AFB, MA listing, C-617-377-2112, D-312-478-2112.

RV, CAMPING/FAMCAMP: New Boston Recreation Area on base, June-Sep, C-603-471-2452/2234, D-312-489-2452/2234, three mobile homes, 12 camper spaces with W&E hookups, 42 camper/tent spaces without hookups.

SPACE-A: None. See Hanscom AFB, MA listing, C-617-377-1143, D-312-478-1143.

LOGISTICAL SUPPORT: None. See Pease ANGB listing, C-603-436-0302.

ADMINISTRATIVE SUPPORT:

Fire Dept-471-2470	Pass/ID Office-471-2379
Police-471-2450	Public Affairs-471-2211

HEALTH & WELFARE: None. See Hanscom AFB, MA listing, C-617-377-4706.

REST & RECREATION:

Auto Hobby Shop-471-2469	Combined Club-471-2323
Fitness Center-471-2215	MWR-471-2452/2234
Outdoor Rec-471-2452/2234	

ATTRACTIONS: Snow Skiing, hiking.

PEASE AIR NATIONAL GUARD BASE (NH01R1)

157th Air Refueling Wing
302 Newington Street
Pease ANGB, NH 03803-0157

TELEPHONE NUMBER INFORMATION: Main installation numbers: C-603-430-2453, D-312-852-2453.

LOCATION: From I-95 north to Spaulding Turnpike, then follow signs. Base is at intersection of Spaulding Turnpike & Gosling Road. USMRA: Page 23 (H-9). NMC: Portsmouth, three miles northeast.

GENERAL INFORMATION: 157th Air Refueling Wing, New Hampshire Air National Guard.

TEMPORARY MILITARY LODGING: None. See Portsmouth Naval Shipyard listing, C-207-438-1513, D-312-684-1513, Fax: C-207-438-3580.

RV, CAMPING/FAMCAMP: None. See New Boston AS listing, C-603-471-2452/2234, D-312-489-2452/2234.

SPACE-A: Pax Term/Lounge, Building 257, C-603-430-3323, D-312-852-3323, flights to CONUS, OCONUS and overseas.

LOGISTICAL SUPPORT: Exchange-436-0302

ADMINISTRATIVE SUPPORT: Public Affairs-430-3413

HEALTH & WELFARE: None. See Portsmouth Naval Shipyard listing, C-207-438-1799.

REST & RECREATION: None. See Portsmouth NS listing, C-207-738-2351.

ATTRACTIONS: City of Portsmouth, harbor, beaches, skiing in White Mountains is a one hour drive.

PORTSMOUTH NAVAL SHIPYARD (NH02R1)

ATTN: Code 100
Portsmouth Naval Shipyard, NH 03801-5000

TELEPHONE NUMBER INFORMATION: Main installation numbers: C-207-438-1000, D-312-684-1000.

LOCATION: From I-95 north, cross Piscataqua River Bridge into Maine. Take exit 2 to US-236 to US-1 south to US-203, left onto Walker Street to gate 1. From I-95 south, take exit 2, follow above directions. Located on an island on Piscataqua River between Portsmouth and Kittery, ME. USMRA: Page 23 (H-9). NMC: Portsmouth, in city limits.

GENERAL INFORMATION: A Naval Shipyard and Repair Facility.

TEMPORARY MILITARY LODGING: Lodging office, C-207-438-1513, D-312-684-1513, Fax: C-207-438-3580.

RV, CAMPING/FAMCAMP: None. See New Boston AS listing, C-603-471-2452/2234, D-312-489-2452/2234.

SPACE-A: None. See Pease ANGB listing, C-603-430-3323, D-312-852-3323.

LOGISTICAL SUPPORT:

Child Care-438-3804	Commissary-438-5532
Exchange-438-2341	Pizza Parlor-438-3536
Visitor Center-438-3550	

ADMINISTRATIVE SUPPORT:

Legal-438-2703	Locator-438-2436
Police-438-2002	Public Affairs-438-1525
Emergency-438-2444	SDO/NCO-438-2200

NEW HAMPSHIRE
Portsmouth Naval Shipyard, continued

HEALTH & WELFARE:
CHAMPUS-438-3862
Chapel-438-1970
Medical
Central Appts-438-1799
Emergency-438-4940

REST & RECREATION:
Auto Hobby Shop-ext 2981
Bowling-ext 2404
Clubs
CPO-438-2455
O-438-2269
ITT-438-2351
Marina 438-1583
Rec Equipment-ext 1514
Tennis-ext 2404
Fitness Center-ext 2402
Gym-ext 2360
Handball/Racquetball-ext 2404
Library-ext 2769
MWR-438-2351
Sailing/Boat Rental-ext 1514
Wood Hobby Shop-ext 1820

ATTRACTIONS: Beaches, snow skiing nearby.

MILITARY Living's™ **Ann & Roy**

NEW RV, CAMPING & REC AREA IN TEXAS

Bird Watcher's Paradise

The NASKING Recreation FamCamp is located on the Naval Air Station Kingsville, TX, which is located on the world-famous King Ranch. It will be in full operation by October 1997. The rec area is located less than a mile from the front gate and about 1/2 mile from the Navy Exchange and commissary. Of special interest to campers will be the ceramics shop, auto hobby shop and wood shop which are within a stone's throw of the campsites. This might be just the place to take up a hobby!

The Naval Air Station is very close to Site 89 of the South Texas birding trail. This area of Texas is known to have more than 250 different species of birds which can be observed. If you are not into birding, you probably will be by the time you leave the area.

The almost-extinct whooping cranes can be seen during the winter at Aransas Pass which is about an hour or so away. In the spring the whooping cranes migrate back to Canada where their nesting location is almost unreachable. If you cannot go by air, you might well not be able to see them in Canada. This makes birding in Texas even more meaningful!

The new NASKING Rec Area is open year-round and will soon have five RV sites with water and electricity with 30 amps. The rate is $8 daily. There are also 10 sites with water only at $5 a day; tent camping space is $3 a day. There is a dump station on the rec area.

You don't have to have your own RV or tents. Outdoor Rec, located next door, will rent them to you for nominal fees. There is a full range of camping equipment for rent as well. Therefore, you can just make a reservation for an 18' camper at $30 daily or a 16' one at $25 daily. Just show up in your vehicle and you can try out the outdoor life before making a big investment! Only things missing are sheets, blankets and cookware; so bring them! Or, you can buy them at the exchange. By the way, pets are allowed on a leash.

There are two fresh-water ponds on base stocked with catfish, bass and other fish. You can get a Texas fishing license at the nearby Walmart; you will also need a station permit which can be obtained at Outdoor Rec located next to the campsite. You can also rent boats with motor and trailers at the same place. Bicycles are also available for rent at Outdoor Rec. There are miles and miles of roads on the station to enjoy them.
Needed info: Outdoor Rec, 3765 Nimitz Ave, Naval Air Station, Kingsville, TX 78363. Phone 512-516-6443.
This feature is based on info from our book, ***Military RV, Camping, and Rec Areas Around the World***

* This excerpt was taken from *Military Living's R&R Space-A Report*®.
For more info, please call the number above.

NEW JERSEY

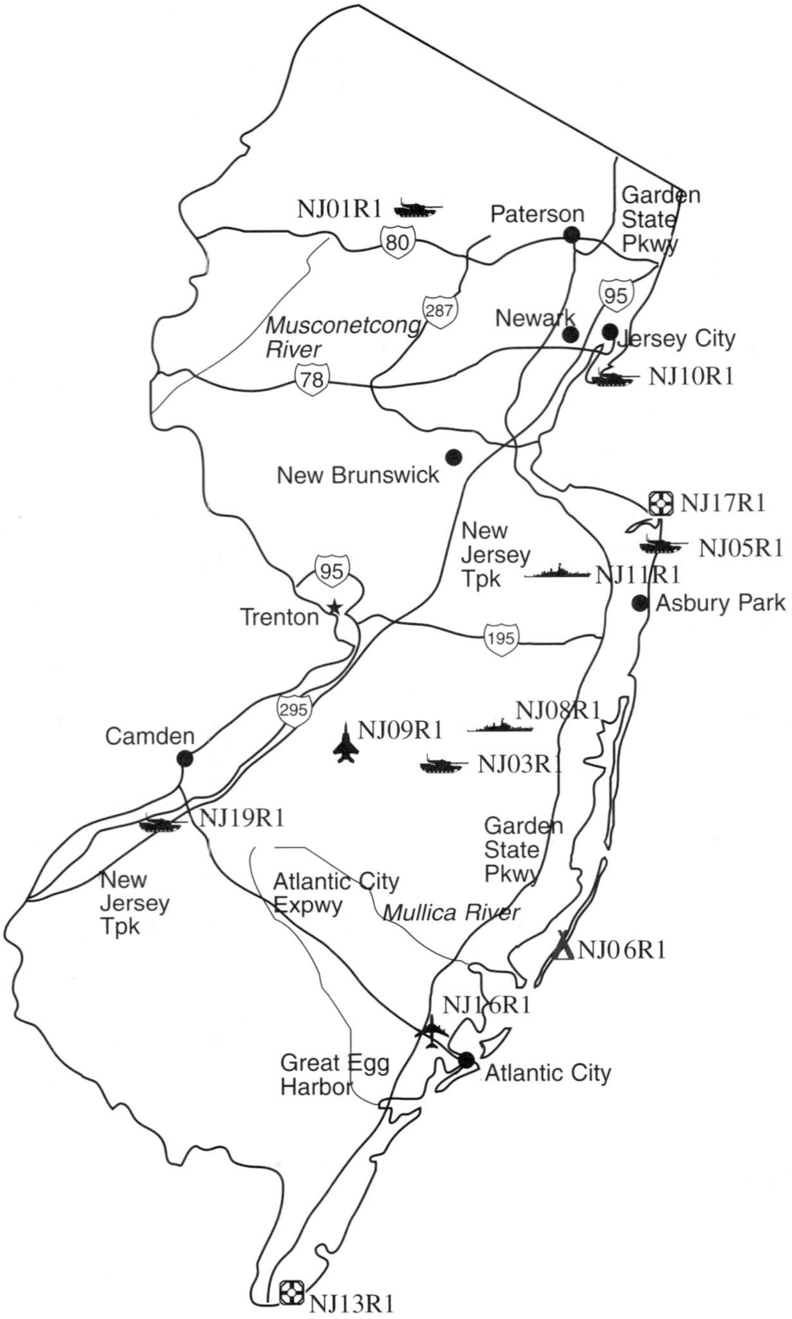

BARNEGAT RECREATION COTTAGE (NJ06R1)

Caretaker Barnegat Recreation Cottage
Barnegat Light, NJ 08006-9999

TELEPHONE NUMBER INFORMATION: Main installation number: C-212-668-7116.

LOCATION: On northern tip of Long Beach Island, NJ. Take exit 63 off Garden State Parkway; NJ-72 east to Long Beach Blvd. Left on Long Beach to right on 7th Street. USMRA: page 19 (F-8). NMC: Camden, 65 miles west. NMI: Fort Dix and McGuire AFB, 40 miles northwest.

GENERAL INFORMATION: Converted Coast Guard lighthouse near beautiful beach between Barnegat Bay and Atlantic Ocean. Season of operation: year round. Military personnel active, retired, reserve, government civilian employees. Check in with caretaker after 1300, check out 1200. Reservations: Required, *by application only*, with payment in full, starting mid-April. Address: Maintenance & Logistics Command Atlantic, 300 E. Main Street, Suite 900, Norfolk, VA 23510-9108. C-757-628-4490. Fax: C-757-628-4511. (*For information only:* address above, C-609-494-9800.) No pets allowed. Up to two apartments may be reserved for up to seven nights. Campers/trailers and motor homes are permitted on Long Beach Island as long as they are used for transportation purposes only.

TEMPORARY MILITARY LODGING: Apartment beach house, community kitchen and dining room; fully furnished except bed linens, blankets and towels. Rates: $40-65 daily.

OTHER SUPPORT & FACILITIES AVAILABLE: Beach, Laundry, Picnic Area. Also, see McGuire Air Force Base listing, C-609-724-1100, D-312-440-1110.

REST & RECREATION: Fishing and Swimming.

ATTRACTIONS: Sand, surf and sun.

BAYONNE MILITARY OCEAN TERMINAL (NJ10R1)

Foot of 32nd Street
Bayonne, NJ 07002-5302
Scheduled to close July 2001

TELEPHONE NUMBER INFORMATION: Main installation numbers: C-201-823-5111, D-312-247-5111.

LOCATION: From New Jersey Turnpike, exit 14A to NJ-169 east to main gate. Follow green and white signs. USMRA: Page 26 (C-5,6). NMC: New York City, 10 miles northeast.

GENERAL INFORMATION: An activity of the Military Traffic Management Command, Eastern Area, whose headquarters is co-located at terminal.

TEMPORARY MILITARY LODGING: Liberty Lodge, C-201-823-8700.

RV, CAMPING/FAMCAMP: None. See Picatinny Arsenal listing, Lake Denmark Rec Area, C-201-724-4014, D-312-880-4014.

SPACE-A: None. See McGuire AFB listing, C-609-724-3078, D-312-440-3078, Fax: C-609-724-4621.

LOGISTICAL SUPPORT:

Child Care-823-5980	Exchange-339-4520

ADMINISTRATIVE SUPPORT:

Legal-823-7122	Locator-823-5111/0111
Police-823-6666/6000	SDO/NCO-823-7207

HEALTH & WELFARE:

ACS-823-7737	Chapel-823-7265
Medical	
AD-447-3010	
Clinic-823-7371	
Dependents-823-5643	

REST & RECREATION:

Community Club-823-7603	Community Rec-ext 5672
ITR-ext 5319	Sports/Fitness Center-ext 7767

ATTRACTIONS: New York City, Atlantic City, Liberty State Park with ferries to Statue of Liberty, Jersey Shore.

NEW JERSEY

CAPE MAY COAST GUARD TRAINING CENTER (NJ13R1)

1 Munro Avenue
Cape May, NJ 08204-5002

TELEPHONE NUMBER INFORMATION: Main installation number: C-609-898-6900.

LOCATION: Take Garden State Parkway or US-9 to Cape May. In Cape May, take Pittsburgh Avenue to Pennsylvania Avenue to main gate of Center. USMRA: Page 19 (D-10). NMC: Atlantic City, 45 miles northeast.

GENERAL INFORMATION: Coast Guard Training Center for Recruits, Center, Cape May Air Station, several Coast Guard ships.

TEMPORARY MILITARY LODGING: Housing office, 0800-1630 hours daily, C-609-898-6922. All ranks.

RV, CAMPING/FAMCAMP: USCG Townsends Inlet Rec Facility, Apr-Oct, C-609-263-3722. A four apartment coastal cottage.

SPACE-A: None. See McGuire AFB listing, C-609-724-3078, D-312-440-3078, Fax: C-609-724-4621.

LOGISTICAL SUPPORT:
Child Care-898-6922
Exchange-898-6940
SATO-884-3197
Commissary-898-6940
Package Store-898-6940
Visitor Center-898-6922

ADMINISTRATIVE SUPPORT:
Legal-898-6902
Police-898-6225
SDO/NCO-898-6915
Locator-898-6900
Public Affairs-898-6969

HEALTH & WELFARE:
CHAMPUS-898-6966
Family Services-898-6925
Chapel-898-6974
Medical
Central Appts-898-6959
Emergency-898-6959

REST & RECREATION:
Clubs
Com-898-6937
CPO-898-6344
Recreation-898-6922
Theater-898-6922
Gym-ext 6973
ITT-898-6989
MWR-898-6922
Swimming-ext 6973

ATTRACTIONS: Beaches, Atlantic City Resort. Auto/Passenger ferry from Cape May to Lewes, DE, operates year round.

EARLE NAVAL WEAPONS STATION (NJ11R1)

ATTN: PAO
201 State Highway, 34 South
Colts Neck, NJ 07722-5007

TELEPHONE NUMBER INFORMATION: Main installation numbers: C-732-866-2000, D-312-449-2000.

LOCATION: From New Jersey Turnpike (I-95), exit 8 to NJ-33, east through Freehold to NJ-34, north to main gate. Or exit Garden State Parkway to NJ-33, west to NJ-34, north to Station. USMRA: Page 19 (F,G-5). NMC: Newark, 50 miles north.

GENERAL INFORMATION: Naval Ammunition, Storage and Transshipment site with loading facilities near Sandy Hook at Leonardo.

TEMPORARY MILITARY LODGING: Very limited in bachelor-type quarters. Officers C-732-866-2167, EM C-732-866-2121, Fax: C-732-866-1068.

RV, CAMPING/FAMCAMP: None. See Fort Dix AG listing, Brindle Lake Travel Camp, C-609-562-6667, D-312-944-6667, Fax: C-609-562-2354.

SPACE-A: None. See McGuire AFB listing, C-609-724-3078, D-312-440-3078, Fax: C-609-724-4621.

LOGISTICAL SUPPORT:
Child Care-866-2518
Package Store-866-2417
Exchange-866-2349

ADMINISTRATIVE SUPPORT:
CDO/OOD-866-2500
Legal-866-2066
Public Affairs-866-2171
Fire Dept-866-2260
Police-866-2069
SDO/NCO-866-2500

HEALTH & WELFARE:
CHAMPUS-866-2303
Family Services-866-2115
Retiree Services-866-2115
Chapel-866-2405
Medical-866-2300

REST & RECREATION:
Auto Hobby Shop-866-2105
Clubs
All Hands-866-2438
Consol-866-2436
Library-866-2167
Recreation-866-2351
Youth Activities-866-2148
Bowling-866-2394
Gym-866-2119
Hobby Shops-866-2105
ITT-866-2167
MWR-866-2350
Special Services-ext 2350/2389

ATTRACTIONS: The New Jersey Shore nearby. New York City, Atlantic City, Six Flags Great Adventure Theme Park.

FORT DIX ARMY GARRISON (NJ03R1)

ATTN: AFZT-PAZ
Fort Dix, NJ 08640-5075

TELEPHONE NUMBER INFORMATION: Main installation numbers: C-609-562-1011, D-312-944-1011. HP: http://www.dix-emh5.army.mil.

LOCATION: From NJ Turnpike (I-95), exit 7, right onto NJ-206, short distance left on NJ-68, continue to General Circle & main gate. USMRA: Page 19 (E,F-6). NMC: Trenton, 17 miles northwest.

GENERAL INFORMATION: Regional Reserve Training Center.

TEMPORARY MILITARY LODGING: Lodging office, Building 5255, Maryland Avenue & First St, 24 hours daily, C-609-562-4849, D-312-944-4849. All ranks. DV/VIP C-609-562-5059/6293.

RV, CAMPING/FAMCAMP: Brindle Lake Travel Camp on post, year round, C-609-562-6667, D-312-944-6667, Fax: C-609-562-2354 10 spaces without hookups.

SPACE-A: None. See McGuire AFB listing, C-609-724-3078, D-312-440-3078, Fax: C-609-724-4621.

LOGISTICAL SUPPORT:
Bank-723-3235
Beauty Shop-723-7377
Child Dev Center-723-1009
Commissary-724-4154
Dry Cleaner-723-6446
Exchange-723-6100
Laundry-723-6446
SATO-723-3426
Barber Shop-723-5190
Cafeteria-723-2671
Class Six-723-0464
Conv Store-723-0464
Education Office-562-5001
Gas Station-723-0464
Postal Service-723-2089
Shoppette-723-2980

NEW JERSEY
Fort Dix Army Garrison, continued

ADMINISTRATIVE SUPPORT:
Fire Dept-562-5484
Legal-562-2497
Police-562-6001
Housing Office-562-5847
Locator-562-6051
Public Affairs-562-4034

HEALTH & WELFARE:
American Red Cross-562-2258
Army Emergency Relief-562-4245
Medical-562-3142
Veterinary Services-562-4992
ACS-562-2767
Chapel-562-5751
Retiree Services-562-2666

REST & RECREATION:
Arts & Crafts-562-5691
Bowling-562-6895
Fitness Center-562-3961
Golf Course-562-5443
ITT-562-4848
MWR-562-6772
Swimming-562-2863
Youth Activities-652-5061
Auto Hobby Shop-562-6762
Clubs
Club Dix-723-3272
Rod/Gun-652-4676
Library-652-3587
Outdoor Rec-562-6667
Theater-562-3986

ATTRACTIONS: Atlantic City and Philadelphia, short drives.

FORT MONMOUTH (NJ05R1)

ATTN: PAO/SELFM-CO
Fort Monmouth, NJ 07703-5016

TELEPHONE NUMBER INFORMATION: Main installation numbers: C-908-532-9000, D-312-992-9000.

LOCATION: Take New Jersey Turnpike to Garden State Parkway, exit 105 for Eatontown, NJ-35 north to main gate. USMRA: Page 19 (G-5). NMC: New Brunswick, 23 miles northwest.

GENERAL INFORMATION: Army Communications-Electronics Command, other supporting electronics organizations, US Military Academy Preparatory School.

TEMPORARY MILITARY LODGING: Lodging office, Building 270, Allen & Barton Avenue, 0745-2400 daily, C-908-532-1635/1092, D-312-992-1635. All ranks. DV/VIP C-908-532-1635.

RV, CAMPING/FAMCAMP: None. See Fort Dix AG listing, Brindle Lake Travel Camp, C-609-562-6667, D-312-944-6667, Fax: C-609-562-2354.

SPACE-A: None. See McGuire AFB listing, C-609-724-3078, D-312-440-3078, Fax: C-609-724-4621.

LOGISTICAL SUPPORT:
Child Care-532-8069
Conv Store-542-5353
Gas Station-542-7417
Visitor Center-532-6078
Commissary-532-1260
Exchange-542-7235
Package Store-532-5353

ADMINISTRATIVE SUPPORT:
CDO/OOD-532-1100
Legal-532-4371
Ombudsman-532-6078
Public Affairs-532-1258
Fire Dept-532-1265
Locator-532-1492
Police-532-1112/911
SDO/NCO-532-1100

HEALTH & WELFARE:
ACS-532-2076
Chapel-532-2066
Medical-532-3851
CHAMPUS-532-3203
Family Services-532-2076
Retiree Services-532-4673

REST & RECREATION:
Arts & Crafts-ext 3159
Auto Hobby Shop-ext 3301
Bowling-ext 3805
Community Center-ext 2695
Fitness Center-ext 2848
Golf Course-532-4307
ITR-532-3892
MWR-532-7810
Photo Hobby-ext 3159
Theater-542-4317
Clubs
All Hands-532-3892
EM-532-3892
O-532-4561
Library-ext 3172
Outdoor Rec-532-2374
Swimming-ext 3275

ATTRACTIONS: New Jersey beaches nearby, Monmouth Park Racetrack, New York City, Atlantic City.

LAKEHURST NAVAL AIR ENGINEERING STATION (NJ08R1)

Code 75000B/150-2
Highway 547
Lakehurst, NJ 08733-5041

TELEPHONE NUMBER INFORMATION: Main installation numbers: C-732-323-2011, D-312-624-1110. HP: http://www.lakehurst.navy.mil.

LOCATION: Take the Garden State Parkway south to NJ-70, west to junction of NJ-547, turn right and proceed one mile to base. USMRA: Page 19 (F-6). NMC: Trenton, 30 miles northwest.

GENERAL INFORMATION: Naval Air Warfare Center Aircraft Division, Naval Air Engineering Station.

TEMPORARY MILITARY LODGING: Lodging office, Building 480-481, 24 hours daily, BEQ/BOQ/DV/VIP C-732-323-2266, D-312-624-2266, Fax: C-732-323-2269. All ranks.

RV, CAMPING/FAMCAMP: None. See Fort Dix AG listing, Brindle Lake Travel Camp, C-609-562-6667, D-312-944-6667, Fax: C-609-562-2354.

SPACE-A: Pax Terminal C-732-323-2438, D-312-624-2438, Fax: C-732-323-7802.

LOGISTICAL SUPPORT:
Child Care-323-2406/2034
Conv Store-323-2909
Galley-323-2554
Commissary-323-2516
Exchange-323-7680/7683

ADMINISTRATIVE SUPPORT:
COM-323-2340
Pass/ID Office-323-2693
Public Affairs-323-2620
Legal-323-2571/2170
Police-323-2457/2332

HEALTH & WELFARE:
Chapel-323-2272/2539
Medical-323-1223/4
Family Services-323-1223/4

REST & RECREATION:
Auto Hobby Shop-ext 2468
Golf Course-ext 7483
Library-ext 2468
Rec Equipment-ext 2468
Theater-ext 2468
Bowling-ext 2027
Gym-ext 2468
Picnic Area-ext 2468
Swimming-ext 2468

ATTRACTIONS: Atlantic City, New Jersey beaches, Six Flags Great Adventure Theme Park, Manhattan, Philadelphia.

McGUIRE AIR FORCE BASE (NJ09R1)

2901 Falcon Lane
McGuire Air Force Base, NJ 08641-5000

TELEPHONE NUMBER INFORMATION: Main installation numbers: C-609-724-1100, D-312-440-1110.

NEW JERSEY
McGuire Air Force Base, continued

LOCATION: From New Jersey Turnpike (I-95), exit 7 to NJ-206 southeast to AFB. Adjacent to Fort Dix. Clearly marked. USMRA: Page 19 (E-6). NMC: Trenton, 18 miles northwest.

GENERAL INFORMATION: Air Mobility Command base. Air Mobility Wing, East Coast Mobility Center, ANG and AFRES units.

TEMPORARY MILITARY LODGING: Lodging office, Building 2717, 24 hours daily, C-609-724-2954, D-312-440-2954. All ranks. DV/VIP C-609-724-2405.

RV, CAMPING/FAMCAMP: None. See Fort Dix AG listing, Brindle Lake Travel Camp, C-609-562-6667, D-312-944-6667, Fax: C-609-562-2354.

SPACE-A: Pax Term/Lounge, Building 1706, C-609-724-3078, D-312-440-3078, Fax: C-609-724-4621, flights to CONUS and overseas.

LOGISTICAL SUPPORT:

Cafeteria-723-5056	Child Care-724-3806
Commissary-724-4155	Conv Store-723-3933
Exchange-723-6100	Gas Station-724-4608
Package Store-724-3888	SATO-724-3131
Visitor Center-724-3154	

ADMINISTRATIVE SUPPORT:

Legal-724-4601	Locator-724-2345
Police-724-2001	Public Affairs-724-2104
SDO/NCO-724-3935	

HEALTH & WELFARE:

CHAMPUS-562-4040	Chapel-724-3811
Family Services-724-3294	Medical-724-5509
Retiree Services-724-2459	

REST & RECREATION:

Bowling-724-3345	Clubs
Golf Course-724-4814	NCO-724-2396
Gym-724-4645	O-724-3297
ITT-723-3111	MWR-724-3737
Theater-724-3240	Youth Center-724-2050

ATTRACTIONS: New Jersey Shore, Atlantic City and Philadelphia nearby.

PICATINNY ARSENAL (NJ01R1)

US Army Tank-Automotive and Armaments Command
Armaments, Research, Development and Engineering Center
Building 1
Picatinny Arsenal, NJ 07806-5000

TELEPHONE NUMBER INFORMATION: Main installation numbers: C-201-724-4021, 800-831-2759, D-312-880-4021.

LOCATION: Take I-80 west, exit 34B to Route 15 north, follow signs to Center, one mile north. From I-80 east, exit 34 to Route 15 follow signs to Center. USMRA: Page 19 (E-2). NMC: Newark, 30 miles east.

GENERAL INFORMATION: US Army Tank-automotive and Armaments Command Armament Research, Development and Engineering Center located at Picatinny Arsenal.

TEMPORARY MILITARY LODGING: Lodging office, Building 3359, Lower Belt Road, 0800-1630 Mon-Fri, C-201-724-2633/3506, D-312-880-2633/3506. All ranks. DV/VIP ext 7026.

RV, CAMPING/FAMCAMP: Lake Denmark Rec Area on post, late June-Sep, C-201-724-4014, D-312-880-4014, 12 mobile homes, three camper spaces with W&E hookups, 15 camper spaces without hookups, and 16 tent spaces.
SPACE-A: None. See Philadelphia IAP/ARS, PA, C-215-897-5600, D-312-443-5600, Fax: C-215-897-5647, D-312-443-5647.

LOGISTICAL SUPPORT:

Barber Shop-724-7157	Beauty Shop-724-7157
Cafeteria-734-5649	Child Care-724-4994
Commissary-724-2918	Credit Union-724-5532
Exchange-724-2518	SATO-724-0525
Snack Bar-724-2405	

ADMINISTRATIVE SUPPORT:

Fire Dept-724-4544	Legal-724-6598
Locator-724-2852	Police-724-6666
Public Affairs-724-6364	

HEALTH & WELFARE:

CHAMPUS-724-2113	Chapel-724-4139
Family Services-724-7247	Medical
	Central Appts-724-2113
	Emergency-724-4611

REST & RECREATION:

Arts & Crafts-ext 4014	Clubs
Equipment Rental-ext 4016	NCO-724-2639
Golf Course-724-4430	O-989-2460
Gymnasium-724-4835	Rod/Gun-ext 2598
ITT-724-4186	Ski-ext 4014
Recreation-724-4186	

ATTRACTIONS: Lake Country, skiing, New York City nearby.

Other Installations in New Jersey

Atlantic City International Airport/Air National Guard (NJ16R1), 177th FW, 400 Langley Road, Egg Harbor Township NJ 08234-9500. USMRA: Page 19 (E-8). C-609-645-6000, Exchange-485-5115.
Pedricktown Support Installation Exchange (NJ19R1), Scheduled to close under the 1995 BRAC. No closure date has been established, Building 328, Route 130 Pedricktown, NJ 08067-5000. USMRA: Page 19 (C-7). C-609-299-4303.
Sandy Hook Coast Guard Exchange (NJ17R1), c/o US Coast Guard Group, P.O. Box 87, Sandy Hook, NJ 07732-4999. USMRA: Page 19 (G-4). C-908-872-3450.

NEW MEXICO

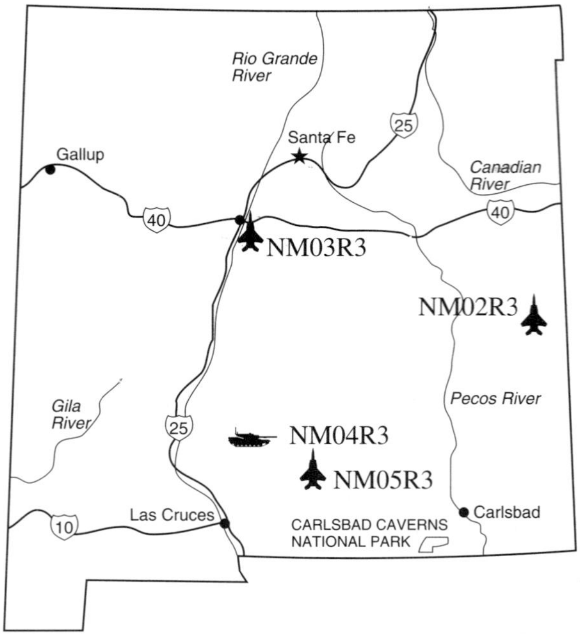

CANNON AIR FORCE BASE (NM02R3)

100 S DL Ingram Boulevard, Suite 204
Cannon Air Force Base, NM 88103-5216

TELEPHONE NUMBER INFORMATION: Main installation numbers: C-505-784-3311, D-312-681-1110. HP: http://cannon.af.mil.

LOCATION: From Clovis, west on US-60/84 to AFB. From NM-467 enter the Portales gate. USMRA: Page 114 (H-5). NMC: Clovis, seven miles east.

GENERAL INFORMATION: Home of the 27th Fighter Wing, "America's Go-To Wing." An Air Combat Command installation. Base provides superior air combat power through F-16 and EF-111A operations.

TEMPORARY MILITARY LODGING: Lodging office, Caprock Inn, Building 1801, 401 S Olympic Boulevard, 24 hours daily, C-505-784-2935, D-312-681-2935, Fax: C-505-784-4833, D-312-681-4833. All ranks. DV/VIP C-505-784-2727. Advance reservations C-505-784-2935, Fax: C-505-784-4833.

RV, CAMPING/FAMCAMP: None. Nearest facility is more than 100 miles away.

SPACE-A: Extremely limited Space-A. Base Operations/Lounge, Building 135, 0700-2300 Mon-Fri, 0800-1600 weekends, closed holidays, C-505-784-2802, D-312-681-2802, Fax: C-505-681-4658, D-312-681-4658, flights to CONUS. Extremely limited.

LOGISTICAL SUPPORT:

Bank-784-2500
Commissary-784-2160
Dining Facility
  Pecos Trail-784-2420
Exchange-784-3387
Package Store-784-3421
Shoppette-784-3421
Travel Office-784-2304
Visitor Center-784-2400
Child Dev Center-784-2704/6259
Credit Union-791-3353
Dry Cleaner-784-5347
Education Office-784-4184
Gas Station-784-3421
SATO-784-2304
Snack Bar
  Bowling Alley-784-2280
  Golf Course-784-2312
  Sports Lounge-784-2448

ADMINISTRATIVE SUPPORT:

Fire Dept-784-2577
Legal-784-2211
Pass/ID Office-784-2362
Public Affairs-784-4131
Housing Office-784-2982
Locator-784-4636
Police-784-4111
Command Post-784-2253

HEALTH & WELFARE:

Air Force Aid Society-784-4228
CHAMPUS-784-4085
Dental
  Clinic-784-4041
  Emergency-784-4033
Retiree Services-784-4865
TRICARE-784-6251
Veterinary Services-784-4098
American Red Cross-784-2023
Chapel-784-2507
Family Services-784-2452
Medical
  Central Appts-784-2778
  Emergency-784-4033
  Health Benefits Advisor-784-4085
  Hospital-784-4582
  Information-784-4021

REST & RECREATION:

Auto Hobby Shop-784-2170
Clubs
  Afterburner-784-2826
  Consol-784-2853
ITT-784-2536
Outdoor Rec-784-27734
Theater-784-2582
Bowling-784-2280
Community Center-784-2819
Fitness Center-784-2466
Golf Course-784-2800
Library-784-2786
Services-784-2374
Youth Center-784-2747

OTHER SUPPORT AVAILABLE: Barber shop, Beauty Shop, Commissary, Postal Service and Hospital.

ATTRACTIONS: Blackwater Draw Archeological Site and Museum, Billy the Kid's Grave and Museum, Hillcrest Park Zoo and Ned Houk Memorial Park.

HOLLOMAN AIR FORCE BASE (NM05R3)

490 First Street, Suite 2800
Holloman Air Force Base, NM 88330-8287

TELEPHONE NUMBER INFORMATION: Main installation numbers: C-505-475-6511, D-312-687-6511.

LOCATION: Exit US-70/82, eight miles southwest of Alamogordo. Route to AFB clearly marked. USMRA: Page 114 (D,E-7). NMC: Las Cruces, 50 miles southwest.

GENERAL INFORMATION: Air Combat Command Base. Headquarters Fighter Wing, and many support activities.

TEMPORARY MILITARY LODGING: Billeting Office, Building 583, W New Mexico Avenue, 24 hours daily, C-505-475-6123, D-312-867-3311. All ranks. DV/VIP C-505-475-5573/5574.

RV, CAMPING/FAMCAMP: FAMCAMP on base, year round, C-505-475-5369, D-312-867-5369, 12 camper spaces with full hookups.

SPACE-A: Pax Term/Lounge, Building 571, 24 hours daily, C-505-475-5411, D-312-867-5411, limited flights to CONUS locations.

LOGISTICAL SUPPORT:

Cafeteria-479-2698
Commissary-475-5127
Exchange-479-6164
Package Store-479-2201
Shoppette-479-2381
Visitor Center-475-5920
Child Care-475-7505
Conv Store-479-2381
Gas Station-479-6004
SATO-475-3245
Snack Bar-479-2779

ADMINISTRATIVE SUPPORT:

Legal-475-7216
Police-475-7171
SDO/NCO-475-7575
Locator-475-7510
Public Affairs-475-5406

HEALTH & WELFARE:

CHAMPUS-475-7700
Dental-475-3742
Medical-475-3260
  Appointment-475-2778
  Emergency-475-3268
Chapel-475-7211/7024
Family Services-475-3944

NEW MEXICO
Holloman Air Force Base, continued

REST & RECREATION:

Arts & Crafts-475-3970
Bowling-ext 7378
Consol Hobby-ext 3760
Fitness center-ext 3229
Golf course-ext 3574
Library-ext 3939
Rec Supply-ext 5369
Swimming-ext 3639
Youth Center-ext 3753
Auto Hobby Shop-475-7438
Clubs
  Aero-475-3752
  NCO-475-3226
  O-475-3611
Rec Equipment-ext 7328
Stables-ext 3848
Theater-475-3286

ATTRACTIONS: Sierra Blanca ski area. El Paso TX and Ciudad Juarez, Mexico easy drive south. International Space Hall of Fame and White Sands National Monument in Alamogordo; Horse Racing, Ruidoso; Carlsbad Caverns, Whites City.

KIRTLAND AIR FORCE BASE (NM03R3)

2000 Wyoming Boulevard SE
Kirtland Air Force Base, NM 87117-5606

TELEPHONE NUMBER INFORMATION: Main installation numbers: C-505-846-0011, D-312-246-0011. E-mail: pam@commgate.kirtland.af.mil.

LOCATION: From I-40 E, exit on Wyoming Boulevard, south for two miles to Wyoming gate to AFB. USMRA: Page 114 (D-4). NMC: Albuquerque, one mile northeast.

GENERAL INFORMATION: Air Force Materiel Command Base. Air Force Operational Test and Evaluation Center, Phillips Lab, Field Command Defense Special Weapons Agency, ANG and AFRES units and other units.

TEMPORARY MILITARY LODGING: Lodging office, Building 22016, Club Drive, 24 hours daily, C-505-846-9652, D-312-246-9652. All ranks. DV/VIP C-505-846-4119.

RV, CAMPING/FAMCAMP: Kirtland FAMCAMP, on base year round, C-505-846-0337, D-312-246-0337, Fax: C-505-846-7084, D312-246-7084, 0800-1600 hours. Twenty-nine camper spaces with full hookups, 29 camper spaces, no hookups.

SPACE-A: Pax Term/Lounge, Building 333, 0715-1600 Mon-Fri, C-505-846-1652, D-312-246-1652, Recorded flight information, C-505-846-0785, flights to CONUS locations.

LOGISTICAL SUPPORT:

Child Care-846-1103
Conv Store 265-7552
Education Office 846-8955
Gas Station
  265-9093
  846-9268
  265-7552
Commissary-846-9588
Dining Facility 846-1516
Exchange-846-9642
Package Store-265-7301
SATO
  military-846-7171
  leisure-846-2914

ADMINISTRATIVE SUPPORT:

Fire Dept-846-8069
Legal-846-4217
Pass/ID Office-846-6429
Public Affairs-846-5991
Housing Office-846-8217
Locator-846-0011
Police-846-7913

HEALTH & WELFARE:

Air Force Aid Society-846-0741
Chapel-846-5691
Family Services-846-6359
Retiree Services-846-1536
Veterinary Services-846-4276
CHAMPUS-846-3335/6
Dental-846-3027
Medical
  Central Appts-846-3200
  Emergency-846-3730
  Information-846-0011

REST & RECREATION:

Arts & Crafts-846-1070
Bowling-846-1156
Community Center-846-2059
Fitness Center
  East-846-1102
  West-846-1068
Golf Course-846-1169
Library-846-1071
Recreation-846-4123/4124
Theater-846-SHOW(7649)
Youth Center-853-KIDS (5437)
Auto Hobby Shop-846-1104
Clubs
  CPO-265-6791
  O-846-5165
  NCO-846-1467
  Sandia Skeet-846-0196
ITT-846-2924
Outdoor Rec-846-1275
Services-846-1827
Wood Hobby Shop-846-1861

OTHER SUPPORT AVAILABLE: Bank, Barber Shop, Beauty Shop, Credit Union, Dry Cleaner, Postal Service and Shoppette.

ATTRACTIONS: National Atomic Museum, Albuquerque, world's longest free span tram, Old Town founded in 1706, variety of Indian Pueblos, Albuquerque International Hot Air Balloon Fiesta each October, State Fair each September "4th largest in US," ski resorts, Santa Fe, Indian cliff dwellings, Santa Fe Opera.

WHITE SANDS MISSILE RANGE (NM04R3)

Building 122 Augusta Street
White Sands Missile Range, NM 88002-5047

TELEPHONE NUMBER INFORMATION: Main installation numbers: C-505-678-2121, D-312-258-2211.

LOCATION: From US-70, follow signs to White Sands Missile Range, (WSMR). Clearly marked. USMRA: Page 114 (D-6,7,8). NMC: El Paso TX, 45 miles south.

GENERAL INFORMATION: Army Test and Evaluation Command, NASA, and other tenants and support activities.

TEMPORARY MILITARY LODGING: Billeting Office, 0745-1530 daily, C-505-678-4559, D-312-258-4559. All ranks. DV/VIP C-505-678-1028.

RV, CAMPING/FAMCAMP: Volunteer Park Travel Camp Site on post, year round, C-505-678-1713, D-312-258-1713, eight camper spaces with full hookups.

SPACE-A: None. See the Fort Bliss, TX listing, C-915-568-8097, D-312-978-0897.

LOGISTICAL SUPPORT:

Cafeteria-678-2081
Commissary-678-2358
Exchange-678-2072
Package Store-678-2072
Visitor Center-678-8824
Child Care-678-7882
Conv Store-678-2072
Gas Station-678-4877
SATO-678-4778

ADMINISTRATIVE SUPPORT:

Fire Dept-117
Locator-678-1630
Public Affairs-678-1134
Legal-678-1263
Police-678-1234
SDO/NCO-678-2031

HEALTH & WELFARE:

ACS-678-6767
Chapel-678-2615/2031
Medical-678-1231
  Emergency-678-2882
  Information-678-1231
CHAMPUS-678-3099
Family Services-678-1663
Retiree Services-678-3221

REST & RECREATION:

Arts & Crafts-ext 5321
Bowling-ext 3465
Golf Course-ext 1759
ITT-678-1111
Library-ext 5820
Rec Center-ext 4134
Swimming-ext 3870
Auto Hobby Shop-ext 5800
Community Club-678-2057
Gym-ext 3374
ITR-678-4134
MWR-678-1256
Rec Equipment-ext 1713
Theater-678-2483

ATTRACTIONS: White Sands National Monument and Space Center.

NEW YORK

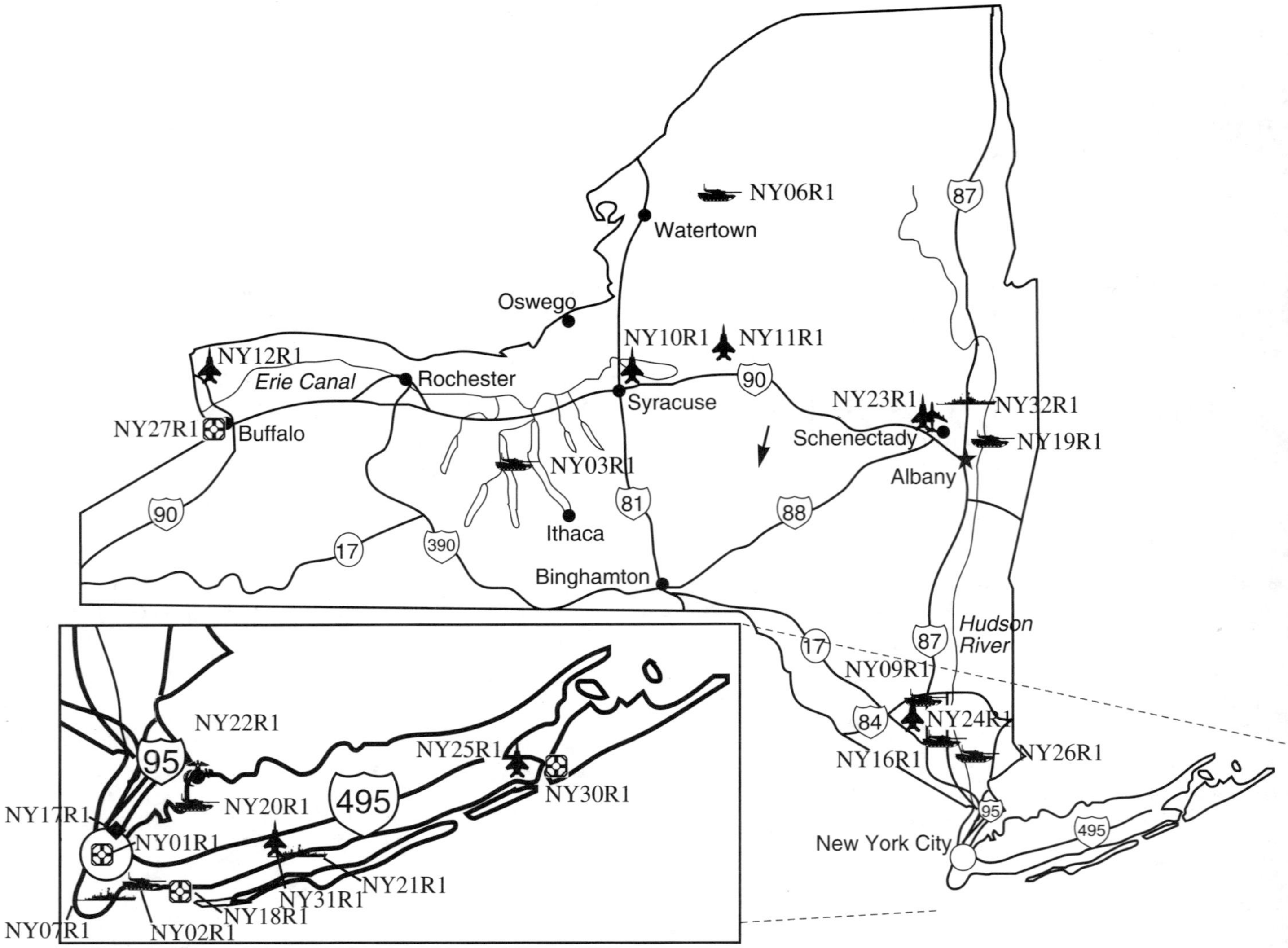

New York City, Long Island and Surrounding Areas

BROOKLYN COAST GUARD AIR STATION (NY18R1)

Floyd Bennett Field, Building 90
Brooklyn, NY 11234-7097

TELEPHONE NUMBER INFORMATION: Main installation numbers: C-718-615-2422.

LOCATION: Take Belt Parkway to exit 11, south to Flatbush Avenue. Watch for main entrance on the left. USMRA: Page 26 (F-7). NMC: Brooklyn, in city limits.

GENERAL INFORMATION: US Coast Guard Helicopter Base located in a National Park.

TEMPORARY MILITARY LODGING: Extremely limited transient quarters. Call main number for information.

RV, CAMPING/FAMCAMP: None. See USMA, West Point listing, Round Pond Rec Area, C-914-938-2503, D-312-688-2503, Fax: C-914-446-5503.

SPACE-A: Limited, via helicopter, C-718-615-2410. See McGuire AFB, NJ C-609-724-3078, D-312-440-3078, Fax: C-609-724-4621

LOGISTICAL SUPPORT:

Cafeteria-615-2456	Conv Store-615-2469
Exchange-377-0380/91	Package Store-615-2469
Snack Bar-615-2469	Travel-703-9548
Visitor Center-338-5799	

ADMINISTRATIVE SUPPORT:

Locator-615-2420	Police-692-1220
Public Affairs-615-2406	SDO/NCO-615-2410/9

HEALTH & WELFARE: Medical-615-2457

REST & RECREATION:

Clubs	MWR-615-2457
All Hands-615-2480	Recreation-615-2535
O-615-2476	Rec Services-ext 2453

OTHER FACILITIES AVAILABLE: Archery, Auto Hobby Shop, Baseball, Boat Ramp, Camping, Model Plane Field, Picnic Area, Putting Green, Pool, Volleyball, Wood Hobby Shop.

ATTRACTIONS: City of New York with its many restaurants, shows and museums, including the *Intrepid* Sea-Air-Space Museum.

NEW YORK

BUFFALO COAST GUARD GROUP (NY27R1)

1 Furhman Boulevard
Buffalo, NY 14203-3189

TELEPHONE NUMBER INFORMATION: Main installation number: C-716-843-9503. E-mail: comms/grubuffalo@cgsmtp.uscg.gov.mil.

LOCATION: From Route 5 Skyway toward Buffalo. Take exit marked Buffalo Coast Guard. USMRA: Page 20 (D-6). NMC: Buffalo, in city limits.

GENERAL INFORMATION: Operational Commander for 10 stations in Ohio, Pennsylvania and New York.

TEMPORARY MILITARY LODGING: None. See Niagara Falls ARS listing, C-716-236-2014, 800-456-4990, D-312-238-2014, Fax: C-716-236-6348, D-312-238-6348.

RV, CAMPING/FAMCAMP: None. Nearest facility is more than 100 miles away.

SPACE-A: None. See Niagara Falls ARS listing, C-716-236-2175, D-312-238-2175.

LOGISTICAL SUPPORT: None. See Niagara Falls ARS listing, C-716-236-2100.

ADMINISTRATIVE SUPPORT: CDO/OOD-843-9527

HEALTH & WELFARE: Benefits Advisor-843-9515

REST & RECREATION: None. See Niagara Falls ARS listing, C-716-236-2101.

OTHER SUPPORT AVAILABLE: Package Store, Shoppette

ATTRACTIONS: Niagara Falls.

FORT DRUM (NY06R1)

10th Mountain Division (Light)
ATTN: AFZS-GC
Fort Drum, NY 13602-5046

TELEPHONE NUMBER INFORMATION: Main installation numbers: C-315-772-6011, D-312-341-6011.

LOCATION: From Syracuse, take I-81 north to exit 48 (past Watertown), and follow signs to Fort Drum. USMRA: Page 21 (J-3). NMC: Watertown, eight miles southwest.

GENERAL INFORMATION: Home for the 10th Mountain Division (Light Infantry), and the largest reserve component training and mobilization center in the northeastern United States.

TEMPORARY MILITARY LODGING: Lodging office, Building T-2227, 24 hours daily, C-315-772-5435, D-312-341-5435. All ranks. DV/VIP C-315-772-5010. Also, The Inn at Fort Drum at 4205 Po Valley Road, C-315-773-7777.

RV, CAMPING/FAMCAMP: Remington Pond Recreational Area, on post, Apr 1-Oct-15, C-315-772-5169, D-312-341-5169. six camper/tent spaces with no hookups.

SPACE-A: Wheeler-Sack Army Airfield, Building P-2065, 0700-1730 hours, C-315-772-5681, D-312-341-5681, limited flights via executive aircraft to primarily east coast CONUS locations.

LOGISTICAL SUPPORT:

Bank
  772-7881
  773-0155
Car Care Center-773-8025/6
Child Care
  772-7105
  772-8672
Credit Union-772-5244
Dry Cleaner-772-4977
Education Office
  772-6878
  772-3286
Shoppette-773-1005

Barber shop-772-3498
Beauty shop-772-4422
Cafeteria-772-5164
Carlson Wagonlit Travel-772-8066/7
Class Six-772-6989
Commissary-772-7457
Conv Store-773-4149
Dining Facilities-772-3295
  Food Court-773-0065
Exchange-773-0061
Laundry-772-4977
Postal Service-772-5220
Travel Office-772-5750

ADMINISTRATIVE SUPPORT:

Fire Dept-772-4131
Legal-772-5261
Pass/ID Office-772-8939
Public Affairs-772-5461
Housing Office-772-5435
Locator-772-5869/9183
Police-772-5156/7
SDO/SNCO-772-5647/8

HEALTH & WELFARE:

American Red Cross-772-6561
Army Emergency Relief-772-6560
Chapel-772-5591
Family Services-772-6799
Medical
  Central Appts-772-8162
  Specialty Clinic-772-4350
  Emergency-911 or 772-5236
  Health Benefits-772-4855
  Information-722-8175
ACS-772-7618
CHAMPUS-772-5111
Dental
  Central Appts-772-8891
  Clinic-772-4614
  Emergency-772-5236
Retiree Services-772-6434
TRICARE-772-4312
Veterinary Services-772-4265

REST & RECREATION:

Arts & Crafts-772-6857/5606
Bowling-772-6601
Fitness Center-772-4806
Gym-772-9670
Indoor Rec-772-6857/5606
ITR-772-8222/3
Library-772-5929
MWR-772-5001
Outdoor Rec-772-5169
Youth Center-772-6717
Youth Services-772-6719
Auto Hobby Shop-772-5785/7902
Clubs
  Benway's Tavern-772-2736
  Christie's-772-2734
  Commons-772-6222
  Pennants-773-8003
  Spinners-773-8005
  Winner's Circle-772-7673
Wood Hobby Shop
  772-5606
  772-6857

ATTRACTIONS: Sackets Harbor Battlefield (site of War of 1812 battle), Thousand Islands and St Lawrence River, New York Finger Lakes, Lake Ontario, Adirondack Park and Lake Placid and Canada (Toronto, Kingston, Montreal and Ottawa) nearby.

FORT HAMILTON (NY02R1)

Headquarters New York Area Command & Fort Hamilton
ATTN: AFZT-FHZ
Brooklyn, NY 11252-5700

TELEPHONE NUMBER INFORMATION: Main installation numbers: C-718-630-4101, D-312-232-4101.

LOCATION: From Belt Parkway, exit 2 (Fort Hamilton Parkway) to 100th Street, right to Fort Hamilton Parkway, right to main gate. USMRA: Page 26 (D-7). NMC: New York, in city limits.

GENERAL INFORMATION: New York Area Command providing facilities and support for Army and DoD activities in the New York City metro area.

TEMPORARY MILITARY LODGING: Lodging office, Building 109, 0800-1630 hours daily, C-718-630-4564, D-312-232-4564. All ranks. DV/VIP C-716-630-4324.

RV, CAMPING/FAMCAMP: None. See USMA, West Point listing, Round Pond Rec Area, C-914-938-2503, D-312-688-2503, Fax: C-914-446-5503.

NEW YORK
Fort Hamilton, continued

SPACE-A: None. See Stewart IAP/ANGB, C-914-563-2965/3298/2226, D-312-247-2965/3298/2226.

LOGISTICAL SUPPORT:

Child Care-630-4040	Commissary-921-4007
Exchange-748-3440	Gas Station-680-2773
Package Store-680-7093	SATO-230-2706
Snack Bar-748-3440	

ADMINISTRATIVE SUPPORT:

Legal-630-4024	Locator-630-4958
Police-630-4445	Public Affairs-630-4820

HEALTH & WELFARE:

ACS-630-4754	CHAMPUS-630-4754
Chapel-630-4969	Family Services-630-4332
Medical-630-4036	Retiree Services-630-4930
Central Appts-630-4268	
Emergency-630-4555	
Hospital-390-6000	

REST & RECREATION:

Arts & Crafts-ext 4942	Auto Hobby Shop-ext 4150
Bowling-ext 4440	Community Club-630-4903
ITT-630-4911	Library-ext 4875
Museum-ext 4349	MWR-630-4778
Rec Center-ext 4476	Sports-ext 4793
Theater-748-3440	Youth Activities-ext 4123

ATTRACTIONS: Historic fort, New York City nearby, Harbor Defense Museum.

FORT TOTTEN (NY20R1)

Ernie Pyle Army Reserve Center
Fort Totten, NY 11359-1016
This base is scheduled to close under the 1995 BRAC. No closure date has been established.

TELEPHONE NUMBER INFORMATION: Main installation numbers: C-718-352-5700, D-312-456-0700.

LOCATION: From Manhattan: Whitestone Bridge to Cross Island Parkway. Take Bell Boulevard exit and follow signs to fort. From Long Island: Take Cross Island Parkway to Bell Boulevard exit and proceed to fort. USMRA: Page 26 (G-3). NMC: New York City, in city limits.

GENERAL INFORMATION: Headquarters of the 77th Regional Support Command.

TEMPORARY MILITARY LODGING: None. See Fort Hamilton listing, C-718-630-4564, D-312-232-4564.

RV, CAMPING/FAMCAMP: None. Nearest facility is more than 100 miles away.

SPACE-A: None. See McGuire AFB, NJ listing, C-609-724-3078, D-312-440-3078, Fax: C-609-724-4621.

LOGISTICAL SUPPORT: Exchange-352-8314

ADMINISTRATIVE SUPPORT:

Police-352-5793	Public Affairs-352-5657
SDO/NCO-352-5804	

HEALTH & WELFARE: None. See Fort Hamilton listing, C-718-630-4268.

REST & RECREATION: None. See Fort hamilton Listing, C-718-630-4778.

ATTRACTIONS: New York City. Fort has been in existence since 1857.

MITCHEL COMPLEX (NY21R1)

82B Mitchel Avenue
East Meadow, NY 11554-5000

TELEPHONE NUMBER INFORMATION: Main installation numbers: C-516-483-3405.

LOCATION: From the north: Northern State Parkway to Meadowbrook Parkway (exit 29B) south to right at Merrick Avenue, right on Front Street, left at Mitchel Avenue. From the south: Verrazano Bridge to east on Belt Parkway, stay left to Southern State Parkway to Meadowbrook Parkway (exit 22) north to exit M3 (Stewart Avenue) west on Stewart to left at second light. At next light turn left at Garden City Center Building Go one block, turn right (Mitchel Field is on the left, West Road). USMRA: Page 26 (I,J-4). NMC: New York City, 27 miles west.

GENERAL INFORMATION: Mitchel Field and Mitchel Manor Housing Areas with supporting facilities. The two areas are approximately five miles apart on Long Island, New York. It is a joint services community (Army, Air Force, Navy, Marines and Coast guard): Mostly recruiters assigned throughout the New York area.

TEMPORARY MILITARY LODGING: None. See Fort Hamilton listing, C-718-630-4564, D-312-232-4564.

RV, CAMPING/FAMCAMP: None. Nearest facility is more than 100 miles away.

SPACE-A: None. See Suffolk County ANGB/Francis Gabreski ANGS listing, C-516-288-7416, D-312-456-7416.

LOGISTICAL SUPPORT:

Child Care-483-3106	Class Six-222-1293/4
Commissary-222-0880	Exchange-222-1293

ADMINISTRATIVE SUPPORT:

Housing Office-486-2022	Police-222-1285
SDO/NCO-222-1285	

HEALTH & WELFARE:

CHAMPUS-222-0228	Family Services-486-1922
Medical-222-0228	Retiree Services-222-1282

REST & RECREATION:

Community Center-ext 0282	Gym-222-0340
MWR-483-3106	Rec Equipment-ext-1611
Swimming Pool-222-0340	Theater-222-1610
Youth Services-483-3106	

ATTRACTIONS: New York City Cradle of Aviation Museum on base (hangar 384), Nassau Veterans Memorial Coliseum, Jones Beach State Park, New York City and Garden city's Children's Museum. Departure site for Charles Lindbergh's first nonstop, solo transatlantic flight.

NEW YORK COAST GUARD ACTIVITIES (NY01R1)

Commander
Fort Wadsworth
Staten Island, NY 10004-5000
Activities are in the process of moving from Governors Island to Staten Island. Completion was set for June 1997, however at press time only the numbers listed below were available.

TELEPHONE NUMBER INFORMATION: C-(Public Affairs) 212-618-7114.

LOCATION: From I-278 to Bay Street Exit (last exit before Verranzo Bridge). (If entering from the east, follow ramp to the right). Turn left at light, half mile to next light, turn right, entrance straight ahead. USMRA: Page 26 (D-5). NMC: New York, one mile northwest.

GENERAL INFORMATION: Coast Guard Activities New York.

TEMPORARY MILITARY LODGING: None. See Staten Island Navy Lodge, C-1-800-NAVY-INN or C-718-442-0413, Fax: C-718-816-0830.

RV, CAMPING/FAMCAMP: None. Nearest facility is more than 100 miles away.

SPACE-A: None. See McGuire AFB, NJ listing, 609-724-3078, D-312-440-3078, Fax: C-609-724-4621.

LOGISTICAL SUPPORT: Exchange-718-816-7920

ADMINISTRATIVE SUPPORT: Housing office-718-390-1756

HEALTH & WELFARE: Chapel-718-390-1376

REST & RECREATION: Fitness Center-718-390-1760

ATTRACTIONS: New York City.

NIAGARA FALLS AIR RESERVE STATION (NY12R1)

914th AW/Public Affairs
2720 Kirkbridge Drive
Niagara Falls ARS, NY 14304-5001

TELEPHONE NUMBER INFORMATION: Main installation numbers: C-716-236-2000, D-312-238-2000.

LOCATION: Take I-190 to Niagara Falls, exit Porter Packard Road. Turn right onto Porter Packard and stay on it until it becomes Lockport. Turn right at main gate. USMRA: Page 20 (D-6). NMC: Niagara Falls, six miles west.

GENERAL INFORMATION: 914th Airlift Wing (AFRES), 107th Air Refueling Group (NYANG).

TEMPORARY MILITARY LODGING: 10780 Kinross Street, 0700-2300 daily, C-716-236-2014, 800-456-4990, D-312-238-2014, Fax: C-716-236-6348, D-312-238-6348. All ranks. DV/VIP C-716-236-2136/2139.

RV, CAMPING/FAMCAMP: None. Nearest facility is more than 100 miles away.

SPACE-A: Pax Term/Lounge, Building 807, 0715-1600 Mon-Fri, C-716-236-2175, D-312-238-2175, Fax: C-716-236-2380, D-312-238-2380 flights to CONUS and overseas via AFRES aircraft.

LOGISTICAL SUPPORT:
Class Six-236-2100
Credit Union-236-2085
Exchange-236-2100
Snack Bar-236-2329
Travel Office-236-6392

ADMINISTRATIVE SUPPORT:
Fire Dept-236-2086
Legal-236-2133
Pass/ID Office-236-2197/2280
Police-236-2280
Public Affairs-236-2136/7

HEALTH & WELFARE:
Chapel-236-2382
Family Services-236-2097
Medical-236-2301

REST & RECREATION:
Bowling-236-2329
Consolidated Club-236-2027
Fitness Center-236-2101

ATTRACTIONS: Niagara Falls, Canada.

SENECA ARMY DEPOT ACTIVITY (NY03R1)

ATTN: SIOSE-CO
5786 State Route 96
Romulus, NY 14541-5001
Scheduled to close July 2001

TELEPHONE NUMBER INFORMATION: Main installation numbers: C-607-869-1110, D-312-489-5110. E-mail: siose-co@seneca-emh.army.mil.

LOCATION: Fifty-five miles southeast of Rochester, 12 miles south of Geneva, on NY-96A. USMRA: Page 20 (H-7). NMC: Geneva, 12 miles north, Rochester, 55 miles northwest.

GENERAL INFORMATION: Coast Guard Loran Station.

TEMPORARY MILITARY LODGING: None. See Niagara Falls ARS listing, C-716-236-2014, 800-456-4990, D-312-238-2014, Fax: C-716-236-6348, D-312-238-6348.

RV, CAMPING/FAMCAMP: None. Nearest facility is more than 100 miles away.

SPACE-A: None. See Niagara Falls ARS listing, C-716-236-2175, D-312-489-2175.

LOGISTICAL SUPPORT: Police-869-1366

ADMINISTRATIVE SUPPORT:
Fire Dept-869-1313
Legal-869-1447
Public Affairs-869-1353

HEALTH & WELFARE: CHAMPUS-869-1243

REST & RECREATION: Clubs
NCO-869-1438
O-869-1666

ATTRACTIONS: Finger Lakes region of NY, wineries and Womens' Rights National Park.

SOLDIERS', SAILORS', MARINES' & AIRMEN'S CLUB (NY17R1)

283 Lexington Avenue
New York, NY 10016-3540

TELEPHONE NUMBER INFORMATION: Main installation numbers: C-212-683-4353, Fax: C-212-683-4374, Reservations 1-800-678-TGIF (8443).

LOCATION: Midtown Manhattan, on Lexington Avenue between 36th and 37th Streets; five blocks from Grand Central Terminal at 42nd Street and Lexington Avenue. USMRA: Page 26 (E-4). NMC: New York, in city limits.

AUTHOR'S NOTE: The **Soldiers', Sailors', Marines' and Airmen's Club** is a tax exempt, not-for-profit organization founded in 1919 to serve the needs of service personnel while visiting New York City. **This club is not US Military/Government lodging.**

OFFICE: Check in and out at the lobby desk, 24 hours daily. Check in 1430 hours, check out 1030 hours. Call the numbers listed above for reservations and information on lodging and related club activities.

The USO of Metropolitan New York is now located at the Soldiers', Sailors', Marines' and Airmen's Club.

NEW YORK

STEWART ARMY SUBPOST (NY09R1)

United States Military Academy West Point
P.O. Box 9000
New Windsor, NY 12553-9000

TELEPHONE NUMBER INFORMATION: Main installation numbers: C-914-563-3323, D-312-688-1110.

LOCATION: From I-87 take Newburgh exit to Union Avenue, south to NY-207. Follow signs to Stewart Airport and Subpost. USMRA: Page 21 (M-10). NMC: New York City, 60 miles south.

GENERAL INFORMATION: Support activity for US Military Academy, West Point.

TEMPORARY MILITARY LODGING: Lodging office, Building 2605, 6th and D Streets, Five Star Inn, 24 hours daily, C-914-563-3311, D-312-220-3311/3524. All ranks.

RV, CAMPING/FAMCAMP: None. See USMA, West Point listing, Round Pond Rec Area, C-914-938-2503, D-312-688-2503, Fax: C-914-446-5503.

SPACE-A: None. See Stewart IAP/ANGB, C-914-563-2965/3298/2226, D-312-247-2965/3298/2226.

LOGISTICAL SUPPORT:
Barber Shop-567-0150
Commissary-938-3663
Credit Union-564-7860
Exchange-564-7601
Shoppette-564-7600/7601
Child Dev Center-563-3522
Conv Store-564-7601
Dry Cleaner-563-3481
Laundry-563-3481

ADMINISTRATIVE SUPPORT:
Fire Dept-564-7033
Public Affairs (West Point)-938-3808
Police-567-6031

HEALTH & WELFARE:
ACS-563-3257
Dental-563-3438
Medical-563-2113
Chapel-564-3310
Family Services-563-3485
N-MC Relief Society-563-3203

REST & RECREATION:
Arts & Crafts-563-3584
Bowling-563-3447
Gym-563-3565
Library-563-3501
MWR-563-3485
Auto Hobby Shop-563-3420
Clubs
  Community-564-6661
  Wings-564-7590
Youth Services-563-3544

ATTRACTIONS: Historic USMA, West Point, and Hudson River Valley.

SUFFOLK COUNTY AIR NATIONAL GUARD BASE/FRANCIS GABRESKI AIR NATIONAL GUARD STATION (NY25R1)

150 Riverhead Road
Westhampton Beach, NY 11978-1294

TELEPHONE NUMBER INFORMATION: Main installation numbers: C-516-288-7471, D-312-456-7471.

LOCATION: Two miles south of Sunrise Highway. USMRA: Page 20 (F-2). NMC: Westhampton Beach, in city limits.

GENERAL INFORMATION: Air National Guard Base.

TEMPORARY MILITARY LODGING: None. Nearest facility is more than 100 miles away. Military rates available at surrounding commercial motels.

RV, CAMPING/FAMCAMP: None. Nearest facility is more than 100 miles away.

SPACE-A: Pax Term, Building 369, Monday through Friday 0730-1600, C-516-288-7416, D-312-456-7416.

LOGISTICAL SUPPORT:
Exchange-288-7557
Package Store-288-7557

ADMINISTRATIVE SUPPORT:
CDO/OOD-288-7416
Legal-288-7587
Police-288-7478
Fire Dept-288-7534
Pass/ID Office-288-7571
Public Affairs-288-7400

HEALTH & WELFARE:
Chapel-288-7566
Medical-288-7447

REST & RECREATION:
Clubs
  EM-288-7481
  O-288-7481

ATTRACTIONS: Beaches nearby, gateway to "The Hamptons," New York City, with its many attractions, is just 70 miles east.

UNITED STATES MILITARY ACADEMY, WEST POINT (NY16R1)

Building 600, Room A
West Point, NY 10996-5000

TELEPHONE NUMBER INFORMATION: Main installation numbers: C-914-938-4011, D-312-688-1110.

LOCATION: Off I-87 or US-9 west. Clearly marked. USMRA: Page 21 (M, N-10), page 28 (D-3). NMC: New York City, 50 miles south.

GENERAL INFORMATION: Military Educational Institution, Corps of Cadets and support units.

TEMPORARY MILITARY LODGING: Hotel Thayer, Building 674, 24 hours daily, C-914-446-4731, D-312-688-2632 or 1-800-247-5047. All ranks. DV/VIP C-914-938-4315/4316, Five Star Inn C-914-563-3311.

RV, CAMPING/FAMCAMP: Round Pond Recreation Area, off base, April 15-Nov 15, C-914-938-2503, D-312-688-2503. Twenty-six camper spaces with W & E hookups, 26 tent spaces without hookups.

SPACE-A: None. See Stewart IAP/ANGB, C-914-563-2965/3298/2226, D-312-247-2965/3298/2226.

LOGISTICAL SUPPORT:
Child Care-938-4523
Conv Store-938-3035
Gas Station-446-5556
Visitor Center-938-2638
Commissary-938-3663
Exchange-446-5406
SATO-446-6400

ADMINISTRATIVE SUPPORT:
Legal-938-4541
Police-938-3312
SDO/NCO-938-3500
Locator-938-4412
Public Affairs-938-2006

HEALTH & WELFARE:
CHAMPUS-938-4838
Family Services-938-2023
Retiree Services-938-4217
Chapel-938-3412
Medical-938-5169
  Emergency-938-4004
  Information-938-5169

REST & RECREATION:
Arts & Crafts-ext 4812/2074
Clubs
  Com-938-5120
Bowling-ext 2140
Golf Course-ext 2435
Gym-ext 2338

NEW YORK
United States Military Academy, West Point, continued

West Point-446-5506	ITR-938-2070
Library-ext 2974	Lodge-ext 4335
Rec Center-ext 3601/2070	Rec Office-ext 3809/4455
Rental-ext 2503	Ski Slope-ext 3726
Swimming-ext 2946/5158	Tate Skating Rink-ext 2991
Theater-938-4159	Youth Center-ext 3208

ATTRACTIONS: Tours of historic USMA, West Point. Hudson River Valley.

WATERVLIET ARSENAL (NY19R1)

ATTN: SIOWV-CO
Building 10
Watervliet, NY 12189-4050

TELEPHONE NUMBER INFORMATION: Main installation numbers: C-518-266-5111, D-312-974-6111.

LOCATION: Take I-787 to exit 6 to 19th Street. Watch for signs to the arsenal. USMRA: Page 21 (N-7). NMC: Albany, six miles south.

GENERAL INFORMATION: Watervliet is an Army R&D and artillery/cannon production facility. Oldest continually active arsenal in the US.

TEMPORARY MILITARY LODGING: None. See Westover ARB, MA listing C-413-557-2700, D-312-589-2700.

RV, CAMPING/FAMCAMP: None. Nearest facility is more than 100 miles away.

SPACE-A: None. See Stewart IAP/ANGB, C-914-563-2965/3298/2226, D-312-247-2965/3298/2226.

LOGISTICAL SUPPORT:

Cafeteria-266-5473	Exchange-266-5371

ADMINISTRATIVE SUPPORT:

Legal-266-5298	Police-266-4334
Public Affairs-266-5090/5418	

HEALTH & WELFARE:

ACS-266-5103	Family Services-266-5920
Medical-266-4195	

REST & RECREATION: Com Club-266-5971

OTHER FACILITIES AVAILABLE: Pitch and Putt Golf Course, Tennis, Swimming, Racquetball Court, Health Facility.

ATTRACTIONS: Albany (New York's Capital), Rivers Park (Industrial Heritage Tour), Saratoga Race Track, Saratoga Performing Arts Center, State Museum, Peebles Island State Park, Watervliet Arsenal Museum.

Other Installations in New York

Camp Smith (NY26R1), Building 501, Peekskill, NY 10566-5000. USMRA: Page 28 (D,E-5,6). Billeting-914-734-7395. Police-914-734-7397. *At press time, restructuring was taking place.*

Hancock Field Air National Guard Base (NY10R1), 174th FW, 6001 E Malloy Road, Syracuse, NY 13211-7099. USMRA: Page 21 (I-6). C-800-982-3696, Exchange-454-6440, Consol Club-454-6200

Roslyn Air National Guard Station (NY31R1), 209 Harbor Hill Road, Roslyn, NY 11576-2345. ***Scheduled to close September 1998.*** USMRA: Page 26 (I-4). C-516-299-5229, Exchange-299-5310 and 625-6946. Cafeteria, Class Six, Conv Store, NCO and Community Clubs, and Fitness Center available.

Schenectady County Airport/National Guard Base (NY23R1), 109th Airlift Wing, 1 Air National Guard Road, Stratton ANGB, Scotia, NY 12302-9460. USMRA: Page 21 (M,N-6). C-518-344-2400. Space-A-344-2401/2420.

Scotia Navy Administration Unit (NY32R1), 1 Amsterdam Road, Scotia, NY 12302-9460. USMRA: Page 21 (M,N-6). C-518-395-3600. Commissary-370-5935, Exchange-377-6440.

Shinnecock Coast Guard Station (NY30R1), Foster Avenue, Hampton Bays, NY 11946-3298. USMRA: Page 20 (G-2). C-516-728-0343, Exchange-728-4350.

Staten Island Navy Lodge (NY07R1), Building 408 N Path Road, Staten Island, NY 10305-5000. USMRA: Page 26 (C-7). Navy Lodge C-718-442-0413, 800-NAVY-INN. Take I-95 N to Elizabeth, NJ, I-278 to Staten Island. Last exit before Verrazano bridge, Bay Street exit, follow signs. USMRA: Page 26 (C-7).

Stewart International Airport/Air National Guard Base (NY24R1), 218 Militia Way, Newburg, NY 12550-5043. USMRA: Page 21 (M-10). C-914-563-2285/6, D-312-636-2285/6. HP: http://132.24.33.177, Group Tours-563-2007, Public Affairs-563-2031/2040, Space-A-None. See Stewart IAP/ANGB, C-914-563-2965/3298/2226, D-312-247-2965/3298/2226.

United States Merchant Marine Academy (NY22R1), Steamboat Road, Kings Point, NY 11024-1699. C-516-773-5000. Take the Long Island Expressway to exit 33. Follow Community Drive, East Shore Road, Hicks Lane (road changes names) to Middle Neck Road. Right onto Middle Neck Road to Steamboat Road. USMRA: Page 26 (H-3). NMC: New York city, in city limits. Federal Academy operated by the Maritime Administration of the US Department of Transportation. Emergency-ext 5911, Museum-773-5515, Chapel Library, Swimming and Theater. ATTRACTIONS: Waterfront activities, cultural events, The Schulyer Otis Bland Memorial Library and the American Merchant Marine Museum.

NORTH CAROLINA

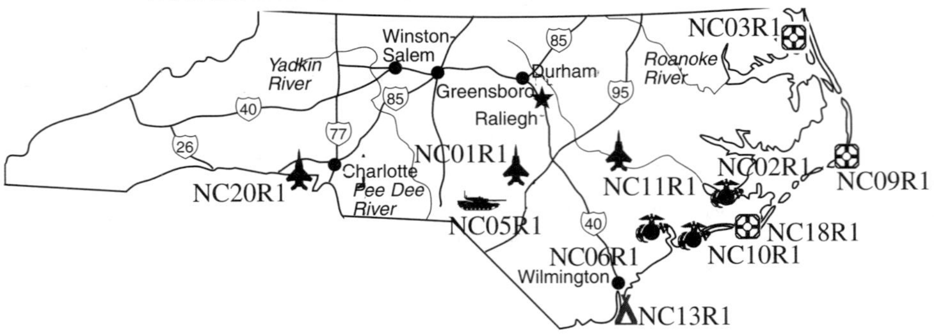

CAMP LEJEUNE MARINE CORPS BASE (NC10R1)

ATTN: PAO
Box 20004
Camp Lejeune Marine Corps Base, NC 28542-0004

TELEPHONE NUMBER INFORMATION: Main installation numbers: C-910-451-1113, D-312-484-1113.

LOCATION: Main gate is six miles east of junction of US-17 and NC-24, off NC-24. USMRA: Page 45 (L,M-5). NMC: Jacksonville, three miles northwest.

GENERAL INFORMATION: USMC Forces Atlantic, II MEF. 2nd Marine Division, 2nd Force Service Support Group.

TEMPORARY MILITARY LODGING: Lodging office, Building 2617, 24 hours daily, C-910-451-1385/2146, D-312-484-1385/2146. Hostess House, C-910-451-3041. DV/VIP C-910-451-2523.

RV, CAMPING/FAMCAMP: Onslow Beach Campsites and Rec Area, on base, year round, C-910-451-7473/7502, D-312-484-7473/7502.

SPACE-A: None. See Cherry Point MCAS listing, C-919-466-3225/2379, D-312-582-3225/2379.

LOGISTICAL SUPPORT:

Commissary-451-2172	Dining Facilities
Conv Store-451-5491	Food Court-451-5776
Exchange-451-5030	Mess Halls-451-1567
Gas Station-451-2443	Omega Travel-451-3788
SATO-451-2192/5889	

ADMINISTRATIVE SUPPORT:

CDO-451-2414/3031	Legal-451-1903
Locator-451-3074	Police-451-2555
Public Affairs-451-5655	SDO/NCO-451-2528

HEALTH & WELFARE:

CHAMPUS-451-4150	Chapel-451-5775/5646/5342
Family Services-451-5340	Medical-451-4300
Retiree Services-451-5927	

REST & RECREATION:

Clubs	Golf Course-451-5445
CPO-451-2839	ITT-451-5380
EM-451-2872	Recreation-451-2108
O-451-2465	Theater-451-1759
SNCO-451-2839	Visitor Center-451-1821

ATTRACTIONS: Raleigh, NC, state capital, 116 miles northeast. Wilmington, 45 miles south. Both offer many museums, historical areas and gardens. Beaches on base.

CAPE HATTERAS COAST GUARD STATION (NC09R1)

P.O. Box 604
Old Lighthouse Road
Buxton, NC 27920-0604

TELEPHONE NUMBER INFORMATION: Main installation number: C-919-995-6408. E-mail: gruchops@pinn.net.

LOCATION: From US-158 or US-64, take NC-12 to Buxton (approximately 50 miles south of Nags Head). East on Old Lighthouse Road, one half mile to base. USMRA: Page 45 (P-3). NMC: Elizabeth City, 110 miles northwest.

GENERAL INFORMATION: Coast Guard Group.

TEMPORARY MILITARY LODGING: Recreational Quarters, C-919-995-3676, Fax: C-919-995-6416. Six units that sleep four, one suite that sleeps six and one suite that sleeps seven.

RV, CAMPING/FAMCAMP: None. See Cherry Point MCAS listing, C-919-466-2197/2172, D-312-582-2197/2172.

SPACE-A: None. See Cherry Point MCAS listing, C-919-466-3225/2379, D-312-582-3225/2379.

LOGISTICAL SUPPORT:

Dining Facilities-995-6484	Exchange-995-3747
Package Store-995-3747	

ADMINISTRATIVE SUPPORT:

Housing Service-995-6458	OOD-995-6408
Public Affairs-995-6442	

HEALTH & WELFARE: Medical-995-6427

REST & RECREATION: Fitness Center available

OTHER SUPPORT AVAILABLE: Gas Station.

ATTRACTIONS: Within walking distance of the historic Cape Hatteras Lighthouse. Excellent beaches, fishing, and wind surfing.

CHARLOTTE DOUGLAS INTERNATIONAL AIRPORT/NORTH CAROLINA AIR NATIONAL GUARD BASE (NC20R1)

5225 Morris Field Drive
Charlotte, NC 28208-5797

TELEPHONE NUMBER INFORMATION: Main installation numbers: C-704-391-4100, D-312-583-9210.

LOCATION: From I-77 take exit 6 A/B to Billy Graham Parkway (US-521) north to Morris Field Drive (three-and-a-half miles), turn left. Base is on your right. From I-85 take Billy Graham Parkway Exit south to Morris Field Drive, turn right. USMRA: Page 44 (G-4). NMC: Charlotte, three miles east.

GENERAL INFORMATION: Headquarters of the North Carolina Air National Guard.

TEMPORARY MILITARY LODGING: None. See Fort Bragg listing, C-910-436-2211, D-312-236-5575

RV, CAMPING/FAMCAMP: None. See Fort Bragg listing, Smith Lake Army Travel Campground, C-919-396-5979, D-312-236-5979.

NORTH CAROLINA
Charlotte Douglas International Airport/North Carolina Air National Guard Base, continued

SPACE-A: Base Operations C-704-391-4177, D-312-583-9177, Fax: C-704-391-4322. Unscheduled flights to CONUS and overseas.

LOGISTICAL SUPPORT:
SATO-391-4163

ADMINISTRATIVE SUPPORT:
Fire Department-391-4206
Police-391-4152
Legal-391-4260
Public Affairs-391-4141

HEALTH & WELFARE:
Chapel-391-4179

REST & RECREATION:
Clubs
EM-391-4426
O-39104427

ATTRACTIONS: City of Charlotte, NC.

CHERRY POINT MARINE CORPS AIR STATION (NC02R1)

PSC Box 8003
Cherry Point, NC 28533-0003

TELEPHONE NUMBER INFORMATION: Main installation numbers: C-919-466-2811, D-312-582-1110.

LOCATION: On NC-101 between New Bern and Morehead City. US-70 connects with NC-101 at Havelock. USMRA: Page 45 (N-4). NMC: New Bern, 17 miles north.

GENERAL INFORMATION: Second Marine Aircraft Wing, Naval Aviation Depot, Naval Hospital and Defense Distribution Depot.

TEMPORARY MILITARY LODGING: Lodging office, 24 hours daily, Building 3673 (EM), 24 hours daily, C-919-466-3060, D-312-582-3060. DV/VIP C-919-466-5169, 24 hours daily.

RV, CAMPING/FAMCAMP: MWR FAMCAMP on base, year round, C-919-466-2197/2172, D-312-582-2197, 15 camper spaces with full hookups.

SPACE-A: Pax Term/Lounge, Building 199, 0600-2300 daily, C-919-466-3225/2379, D-312-582-3225/2379, flights to CONUS and overseas.

LOGISTICAL SUPPORT:
Bank-447-2077
Beauty Shop-447-1857
Child Dev Center-446-3782
Commissary-447-2061
Dining Facilities-466-4209
Education Office-466-3500
Gas Station-447-2402
Package Store-447-7041
Snack Bar-447-7041
Visitor Center-466-5921
Barber Shop-447-7041
Child Care-466-3783
Conv Store-447-7041
Credit Union-447-0692
Dry Cleaner-447-2130
Exchange-447-7041
Laundry-447-2603
Postal Service-466-2496
Travel Office-466-5813

ADMINISTRATIVE SUPPORT:
Fire Dept-466-2241
Housing Office-466-4345
Locator-466-2109/2811
Police-466-4366
SDO/NCO-466-2848
CDO/OOD-466-5236/4388
Legal-466-2310
Pass/ID Office-466-4687
Public Affairs-466-4241

HEALTH & WELFARE:
American Red Cross-466-3641
Chapel-466-4000
Family Services-466-4401
Medical
Central Appts-800-263-4323
Emergency-466-0255/0256
Health Benefits-466-0122
Information-466-0266
CHAMPUS-466-0122
Dental
Central Appts-466-0400
Clinic-466-0438
N-MC Relief Society-466-2031
Retiree Services-466-4401
Veterinary services-466-2166

REST & RECREATION:
Arts & Crafts-ext 3965
Boat Docks-ext 5812
Clubs
O-447-2395
SNCO-466-3087
Indoor Rec-466-4232
Library-ext 3552
MWR-466-2431
Picnic Area-ext 2197
Swimming-ext 2277/2168
Wood Hobby Shop-466-3965
Auto Hobby Shop-466-2352
Bowling-ext 3910
Fitness Center-466-2713
Golf Course-466-3044
Gym-466-2566
ITT-466-2197
Marinas-466-5812
Outdoor Rec-466-2197
Recreation-466-4232/2197
Theater-466-3850/3884
Youth Center-466-3861

ATTRACTIONS: Outer Banks of NC, hunting, fishing, swimming, beaches and outdoor recreation of all types. New Bern, first colonial capital of NC, 17 miles north. Morehead City, 19 miles southeast, is a large commercial fishing port.

ELIZABETH CITY COAST GUARD SUPPORT CENTER (NC03R1)

Building 47
Elizabeth City, NC 27909-5000

TELEPHONE NUMBER INFORMATION: Main installation numbers: C-919-335-6379.

LOCATION: Take I-64 E to VA-104, south to US-17, south to Elizabeth City, left on Halstead Boulevard, three miles to main gate of Center. USMRA: Page 45 (O-1). NMC: Elizabeth City, in city limits.

GENERAL INFORMATION: Air Station, Aviation Technical Training and Repair Center for the Coast Guard, Station Elizabeth City.

TEMPORARY MILITARY LODGING: Lodging office, Building 5, 0800-1630 daily, C-919-335-6397. Six two-bedroom trailers, reservations required, C-919-335-6397. All ranks.

RV, CAMPING/FAMCAMP: Weeksville Campsites on base, year round, C-919-335-6597, six mobile homes and four camper spaces with full hookups.

SPACE-A: Coast Guard Air Station, Air Ops Center, 0800-1600 Mon-Fri, C-919-335-6333, D-312-935-1520, flights to CONUS and overseas.

LOGISTICAL SUPPORT:
Barber Shop-335-6403
Conv Store-335-6187
Dining Facilities-335-6193
Education Office-335-6370
Gas Station-335-6187
Package Store-335-6187
Shoppette-335-6187
Beauty Shop-335-6382
Credit Union-338-1681
Dry Cleaner-335-6207
Exchange-335-6469
Laundry-335-6207
SATO-(AAA)335-6321/2855

ADMINISTRATIVE SUPPORT:
Fire Dept-335-6257
Pass/ID Office-335-6379
Public Affairs- 335-6540
OOD-335-6130
Police-335-6398

HEALTH & WELFARE:
CHAMPUS-335-6460
Dental-335-6375
Chapel-335-6202
Medical
Central Appts-335-6460
Emergency-335-6460
Clinic-335-6460

NORTH CAROLINA
Elizabeth City Coast Guard Support Center, continued

REST & RECREATION:
Clubs
EM-335-6389
Consol-335-6301
O-335-6226
Gym-335-6397

OTHER SUPPORT AVAILABLE: Auto hobby, Boat Ramp, Gym, Swimming Pool (Apr-Sep, weekends only), Racquet Ball and Tennis.

ATTRACTIONS: Outer Banks of North Carolina, fresh seafood, beaches.

FORT BRAGG (NC05R1)

XVIII Airborne Corps & Fort Bragg
ATTN: AGZA-GC
Building I-1326
Fort Bragg, NC 28307-5000

TELEPHONE NUMBER INFORMATION: Main installation numbers: C-910-396-0011, D-312-236-0011.

LOCATION: Take I-95, exit to NC-24 west for 15 miles. NC-24 runs through Post as Bragg Boulevard. From US-401 (Fayetteville Bypass) exit to All American Expressway, five miles to Fort. USMRA: Page 45 (I,J-4). NMC: Fayetteville, 10 miles southeast.

GENERAL INFORMATION: XVIII Airborne Corps, Airborne Division, Army Special Operations Command, Field Artillery Brigade, Corps Support Command, Joint Special Operations Command, other support units.

TEMPORARY MILITARY LODGING: Lodging office, Building D-3601 (Moon Hall), Room 101, 24 hours daily, C-910-436-2211, D-312-236-5575. All ranks. DV/VIP C-910-436-2804.

RV, CAMPING/FAMCAMP: Smith Lake Army Travel Campground on Post, year round, C-910-396-5979, D-312-236-5979, on post, year round, 13 camper spaces with full hookups, 11 camper spaces with W/E hookups.

SPACE-A: None. See Pope AFB, NC listing, C-910-394-4429/2803, D-312-486-4429/2803, Fax: C-910-394-2474.

LOGISTICAL SUPPORT:
Cafeteria-436-4901
Commissary-396-2428
Exchange-436-4888
Package Store-436-0404
Visitor Center-396-2815
Child Care-396-6979
Conv Store-436-0800/4600
Gas Station-497-3985
SATO-436-5808

ADMINISTRATIVE SUPPORT:
Fire Dept-396-1504
Locator-396-3601
Police-396-0391
Legal-396-1445
Public Affairs-396-5600
SDO/NCO-396-6100

HEALTH & WELFARE
ACS-396-8682
Chapel-396-1121
Medical
Central Appts-432-1351
Emergency-432-0301/2
CHAMPUS-432-4424/2741
Family Services-396-6316
Retiree Services-396-5304

REST & RECREATION:
Auto Hobby Shop
-ext 4397
432-5696
497-1257
Field House/Swimming
-ext 4468/2231
432-6489/3573
Bowling
436-1432
497-3428
Clubs
EM-436-3200
Green Beret Parachute-436-4056
NCO-436-4200
432-6493/1712
432-1031
Golf Course
436-3811
497-1752
436-3390
Music Center-ext 4373
Rec Equipment-ext 1065/1340
Theater-436-5323
O-436-0111
Rod/Gun-436-3323
Sport Parachute- 436-5858
ITT-396-1278
Library-ext 3526
MWR-396-2077
Recreation-396-2077
Stables 497-1257
Youth Center-ext 1278

ATTRACTIONS: Pinehurst Resort is nearby. JFK Special Warfare Museum and 82nd Airborne Division Museum on Post.

FORT FISHER AIR FORCE RECREATION AREA (NC13R1)

118 River Front Road
Kure Beach, NC 28449-5000

TELEPHONE NUMBER INFORMATION: Main installation numbers: C-919-736-5400, D-312-488-1110.

LOCATION: Fort Fisher is located on Pleasure Island between Cape Fear River and Atlantic Ocean. On US-421 south of Wilmington NC, go through Carolina and Kure Beaches to Fort Fisher AF Rec Area. USMRA: page 45 (L-6). NMC: Wilmington NC, 20 miles northwest. NMI: Camp Lejeune, 70 miles northeast.

DESCRIPTION OF AREA: Its history predates Civil War. Beaches within walking distance. Operated by Seymour Johnson Air Force Base, off base year round. Military personnel active, retired, reserve, NG, DoD civilians. Check in 1600 at Reception Center, check out 1100. Reservations: Accepted with advance payment or confirmation with major credit card. May be made up to 90 days in advance for active duty Air Force; up to 85 days for all other active duty; up to 75 days for retired military; up to 60 days for all others. C-910-458-6546/6549. Reservations for groups are welcomed during non-peak use periods. Visa, MasterCard, American Express and Seymour Johnson Club Card accepted. No pets allowed in accommodations. Pets allowed on leash in designated areas only; owner must clean up after pet; kennel available. No children under 12 in executive quarters.

TEMPORARY MILITARY LODGING: Beach cottages, sleeps 12, CATV, washer/dryer (4); sleeps six-eight, CATV, washer/dryer (18); Executive cottage, sleeps 6, CATV, washer/dryer (4); Mobile home, sleeps eight (6); River Marsh landing executive suites (2); executive rooms (6); Lodge suites, shared bath, sleeps four (6); shared bath sleeps six (7); Lodge rooms, shared bath sleeps two (27). Rates: Beach cottage sleeps 12 $70-$135 daily; sleeps six-eight $50-$125 daily; executive cottage $70-$135 daily; mobile home $60-$125 daily; River Marsh Landing executive suites $40-$75 daily; executive rooms $30-$60 daily. Lodge suites sleeps four $30-$50; sleeps six $35-$60; sleeps two $15-$30. Rates vary depending on season and day of week; additional charge for extra person.

RV, CAMPING/FAMCAMP: Hardstand camper spaces with full hookups (16); tent spaces with no hookups (20). Rates: camper spaces $12-$20 daily; tent spaces $10-$15 daily. Rates vary depending on season and day of week; additional charge for extra person.

REST & RECREATION: Beach, Boating, Canoeing, Clamming, Fishing, Rec Equipment, Sailing, Sightseeing, Swimming.

OTHER SUPPORT & FACILITIES AVAILABLE: Beach, Boat Ramp, Camping Equipment, Exercise/Weight Room, General Store, Gift/Beach Shop, Jacuzzi, Kennel (fee), Laundry, Restaurant, Rec Center, Rec Equipment, Restrooms, Sauna, Sewage Dump, Showers, Sports Fields, Swimming Pool, Tennis Courts. Also, see Camp Lejeune Marine Corps Base listing, C-910-451-1113, D-312-484-1113.

ATTRACTIONS: Numerous local attractions: NC Aquarium at Fort Fisher; parks, fishing and museums nearby.

NORTH CAROLINA

FORT MACON COAST GUARD BASE (NC18R1)

P.O. Box 237
End of Fort Macon Road (East)
Atlantic Beach, NC 28512-0237

TELEPHONE NUMBER INFORMATION: Main installation numbers: C-919-247-4598, D-312-247-4698/4570/4544.

LOCATION: Take US-70 to Atlantic Beach/Morehead City Bridge. Left at traffic light in Atlantic Beach onto NC-58 (Fort Macon Road). Proceed to entrance at end of road on left. USMRA: Page 45 (N-5). NMC: New Bern, 30 miles northwest.

GENERAL INFORMATION: Homeport of USCGC's *Primrose, Block Island, Staten Island, Gentian*, and *ANT Primrose*.

TEMPORARY MILITARY LODGING: None. See Camp Lejeune listing, C-910-451-1385/2146, D-312-484-1385/2146.

RV, CAMPING/FAMCAMP: None. See Cherry Point MCAS listing, C-919-466-2197/2172, D-312-582-2197/2172.

SPACE-A: None. See Cherry Point MCAS listing, C-919-466-3225/2379, D-312-582-3225/2379.

LOGISTICAL SUPPORT:
Cafeteria-247-8390
Exchange-247-9442
Dining Facilities-240-8390
Postal service-247-9442

ADMINISTRATIVE SUPPORT:
CDO/OOD-247-4598/4570/4698
Pass/ID Office-247-4594
SDO/NCO-247-4598
Locator-247-4590
Public Affairs-247-4571

HEALTH & WELFARE:
CHAMPUS-247-4551
TRICARE-247-4551
Medical-247-4551

REST & RECREATION: Rec Equipment-ext 4598

OTHER SUPPORT AVAILABLE: Housing Office, Package Store.

ATTRACTIONS: Resort town of Atlantic Beach, beaches, fishing, Fort Macon State Park, Cape Lookout National Seashore.

NEW RIVER MARINE CORPS AIR STATION (NC06R1)

PSC Box 21002
Jacksonville, NC 28545-1002

TELEPHONE NUMBER INFORMATION: Main installation numbers: C-910-451-1113/1115, D-312-484-1113/1115.

LOCATION: Off US-17, two miles south of Jacksonville. Clearly marked. USMRA: Page 45 (L,M-5). NMC: Jacksonville, two miles northeast.

GENERAL INFORMATION: Marine Aircraft Groups, Marine Air Traffic Control Squadron, and Marine Wing Support Squadron, Headquarters Squadron.

TEMPORARY MILITARY LODGING: Lodging office, Building 705, duty hours, C-910-451-6621, D-312-484-6568. All ranks. DV/VIP C-910-451-6621.

RV, CAMPING/FAMCAMP: Marina on base, year round, C-910-451-6578, D-312-484-6578. Six camper spaces without hookups.

SPACE-A: Limited. Helicopter aircraft here. See Cherry Point MCAS listing, C-919-466-3225/2379, D-312-582-3225/2379, Fax: C-919-466-4518/6526.

LOGISTICAL SUPPORT:
Bank-451-2492
Child Care-451-6712
Conv Store-451-0539
Gas Station-451-6092
Barber Shop-451-0593
Commissary-451-6395
Exchange-451-0539
Package Store-451-0539

ADMINISTRATIVE SUPPORT:
CDO/OOD-451-6305
Legal-451-6160
Police-451-6111
Fire Dept-451-6620
Locator-451-6568
Public Affairs-451-6196

HEALTH & WELFARE:
CHAMPUS-451-4152
Family Services-451-6110
Chapel-451-6801
Medical/Emergency-451-6511

REST & RECREATION:
Arts & Crafts-ext 6711
Bowling-ext 6582
Clubs
EM-451-0589
O-451-6409
MWR-451-6573
Rec Equipment-ext 6387
Theater-451-6292
Auto Hobby Shop -ext 6709
Ceramics-ext 6711
Gym-ext 6714
Library-ext 6942
Marina-ext 6578
Recreation-451-6410
Swimming-ext 6436
Wood Hobby Shop-ext 6690

ATTRACTIONS: Great North Carolina beaches. Cape Lookout National Seashore to the northeast.

POPE AIR FORCE BASE (NC01R1)

259 Maynard Street
Pope Air Force Base, NC 28308-2391

TELEPHONE NUMBER INFORMATION: Main installation numbers: C-910-394-0001, D-312-4824-1110.

LOCATION: Take I-95, exit 55 to NC-87/24 W. Follow signs to Pope AFB and Fort Bragg. USMRA: Page 45 (J-4). NMC: Fayetteville, 12 miles southeast.

GENERAL INFORMATION: Transferred to Air Mobility Command Base April 1997. 23rd Wing. 624th Air Mobility Support Group; 23rd Aeromedical Evacuation Squadron; 21st Special Tactics Squadron (AFSOC); 3rd Aerial Port Squadron.

TEMPORARY MILITARY LODGING: Lodging office, 302 Ethridge Street, 24 hours daily, C-910-394-4131, D-312-424-4131. All ranks. DV/VIP C-910-394-4739.

RV, CAMPING/FAMCAMP: None. See Fort Bragg listing, Smith Lake Army Travel Campground, C-919-396-5979, D-312-236-5979.

SPACE-A: Pax Term/Lounge, 1427 Surveyor Street, 24 hours daily, C-910-394-4429/2803, D-312-424-4429/2803, Fax: C-910-394-2474, flights to CONUS and OCONUS locations.

LOGISTICAL SUPPORT:
Child Care-394-4323
Exchange-436-4888
Package Store-497-8181
Visitor Center-394-4616
Commissary-497-6777
Gas Station-497-6615
SATO-436-4700

ADMINISTRATIVE SUPPORT:
Fire Dept-394-2464
Locator-394-4822
Public Affairs-394-4183
Legal-394-2341
Police-394-2808

HEALTH & WELFARE:
CHAMPUS-394-2182
Family Services-394-2119
Retiree Services-394-2174
Chapel-394-2676/7
Medical-394-2278
Emergency -394-2232

NORTH CAROLINA
Pope Air Force Base, continued

REST & RECREATION:

Auto Hobby Shop-ext 2293	Bowling-ext 2891
Consol Club-394-2154	Golf Course-ext 2325
Library-ext 2791	MWR-394-2145
Recreation-394-2779	Rec Equipment-ext 4730
Theater-394-2679	

ATTRACTIONS: Raleigh, Durham, and Chapel Hill are easy drives. Myrtle Beach, SC is two-and-a-half hours southeast. Mountains three hours west. Great hunting and fishing areas.

SEYMOUR JOHNSON AIR FORCE BASE (NC11R1)

1510 Wright Brothers Avenue
Seymour Johnson Air Force Base, NC 27531-2468

TELEPHONE NUMBER INFORMATION: Main installation numbers: C-919-736-5400, D-312-488-1110.

LOCATION: From US-70 Bypass, take Seymour Johnson AFB exit onto Berkeley Boulevard to main gate. Clearly marked. USMRA: Page 45 (L-3). NMC: Raleigh, 50 miles west.

GENERAL INFORMATION: Air Combat Command Base.

TEMPORARY MILITARY LODGING: Lodging office, Building 3804, 24 hours daily, Wright Brothers Avenue, C-919-736-6705, D-312-488-6705. All ranks. DV/VIP call Billeting.

RV, CAMPING/FAMCAMP: FAMCAMP on Base, year round, C-919-736-5405, D-312-488-5405, eight camper spaces with full hookups. Rogers Bay Family Campway off base, year round, C-919-736-5405, D-312-488-5405, three travel trailers. Also operates Fort Fisher Air Force Recreation Area off base. See Fisher Air Force Recreation Area listing for more information.

SPACE-A: Building 4012, 0800-1600 Mon-Fri, C-919-736-6568, D-312-488-6568, flights to CONUS and overseas.

LOGISTICAL SUPPORT:

Child Care-736-6289	Commissary-736-6183
Exchange-735-9786	Gas Station-734-7358
Package Store-734-2948	Shoppette-735-9364
Welcome Center-736-6237	

ADMINISTRATIVE SUPPORT:

Legal-736-6256	Locator-736-5584
Police-736-6413/5473	Public Affairs-736-6352

HEALTH & WELFARE:

CHAMPUS-736-5650	Chapel-736-5211
Family Services-736-5404	Medical-736-2778
Retiree Services-736-6377	Clinic-736-5577

REST & RECREATION:

Arts & Crafts-ext 5423	Auto Hobby Shop-ext 5284
Bowling-ext 6669	Clubs
Community Center-ext 6745	EM-734-2757
Golf Course-ext 6249	O-735-8546
Gym-ext 6643	Library-ext 5739
Outdoor Rec-ext 5405	Theater-736-6164

ATTRACTIONS: NC Research Triangle of Raleigh, Durham and Chapel Hill.

Another Attractive Military Hotel in Hawaii

Article by Ann Crawford

Hawaii is fun! That's why so many military members and their families want to go there on leave or vacation. Hawaii offers such prime vacation spots as the Hale Koa, Waianae Army Recreation Center and Bellows (Air Force) Recreation Area. These all have ocean-front rooms or cottages.

Sometimes you may find that you cannot obtain reservations for all the nights of your stay at these locations. If that happens to you, consider the new Inn at Schofield Barracks to fill in the missing nights. This hotel is so nice that you might choose to stay there your whole vacation!

The Inn at Schofield Barracks sits right amidst this historic military installation next door to Division Headquarters. It offers 192 air-conditioned, beautifully appointed rooms with private bath, color TV, VCR, microwave, and refrigerator. Other amenities include coin-operated washer/dryers and ice machines.

Rates are reasonable for Hawaii - single rooms are $68.50; two adults with one or two queen-sized beds - $95; one or two adults with one bed and a sleeper sofa - $100. There is no extra charge for children using the same accommodations until age 16. Taxes are extra.

At Schofield Barracks, you can do all those fun things you enjoy at your home military installation - golf, swimming, bowling, etc. In addition, you can visit historic spots on the installation and actually see bullet holes in some walls from the Japanese attack on Hawaii before WWII.

If you are a "romantic" who enjoys movies, you might wish to see if you can recognize where some scenes were filmed in "From Here To Eternity."

Staying on a military installation offers a sense of home and good security not always found outside the gates. The Inn at Schofield caters to the special needs of the military and its staff wants to show you how well they are prepared to make your stay pleasant.

Military Living's book, *Temporary Military Lodging Around the World* offers full details on the Inn at Schofield Barracks as well as hundreds of other world-wide locations. Look for it at your nearest military exchange. The book has a blue cover with photos from the Hale Koa Hotel in Hawaii.

You may also contact the Inn at Schofield Barracks at 563 Kolekole Avenue, Wahiawa, Hawaii 96786-6000 or phone for reservations at 1-800-490-9638; DSN: (315) 455-5036. Their local phone number is (808) 490-9638 and FAX (808) 490-9638. E-mail: theinn@aloha.com. Look for their handsome home page on the internet at this address: http://www.innatschofield.com.

* This excerpt was taken from Military Living Magazine Volume 29, No. 1. For more info on Schofield Barracks, see page 76 of this book.

NORTH DAKOTA

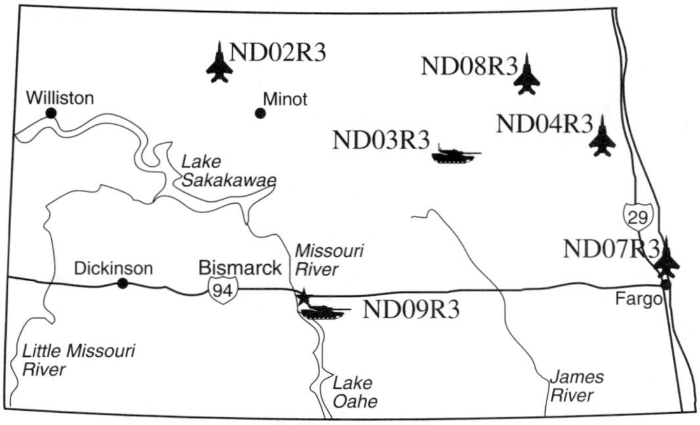

CAMP GILBERT C. GRAFTON ARMY NATIONAL GUARD TRAINING SITE (ND03R3)

Rural Route 5, Box 278A
Devils Lake, ND 58301-9235

TELEPHONE NUMBER INFORMATION: Main installation numbers: C-701-662-0200, D-312-344-5226.

LOCATION: From Highway 2 at Devils Lake go to Highway 20-S, entrance is four miles on right. USMRA: Page 83 (G-3). NMC: Devils Lake, four miles north.

GENERAL INFORMATION: Army National Guard Training Site for National Guard reserve and Active Duty units. Home to the 136th Quarter Master Battalion, 3662nd Maintenance Company and the North Dakota Regional Training Institute.

TEMPORARY MILITARY LODGING: Billeting, C-701-662-0239, Fax: C-701-662-0597, 0700-1600 hours Mon-Thu, 0600-2300 hours Fri-Sun. Nineteen double wide trailers for retirees and military members in non-duty status.

RV, CAMPING/FAMCAMP: None. See Grand Forks AFB listing, C-701-747-3688.

SPACE-A: None. See Grand Forks AFB listing, C-701-747-4376/4409, D-312-362-4376/4409, Fax: C-701-747-6540.

LOGISTICAL SUPPORT:

Exchange-662-0314	Shoppette-662-0314
Snack Bar-662-0285	

ADMINISTRATIVE SUPPORT:

Locator-662-0200	Police-662-5323

HEALTH & WELFARE: Medical-662-5323

REST & RECREATION:

Consol Clubs-662-0221	Indoor Rec-662-0285

OTHER SUPPORT & FACILITIES AVAILABLE: Barber Shop, Boat Rental, Community/Combined Club and Golf Course.

ATTRACTIONS: Base has shoreline with Devils Lake, an excellent site for hunting and fishing.

CAVALIER AIR STATION (ND08R3)

HCR 3, Box 260, Building 830
Cavalier AS, ND 58220-9314

TELEPHONE NUMBER INFORMATION: Main installation numbers: C-701-993-3292, D-312-330-3292.

LOCATION: North on I-29. Take Highway 5, Cavalier exit. Go west 18 miles to town of Cavalier, through town continuing west on Highway 5 another 16 miles to site, on left side of road. USMRA: Page 83 (I-2). NMC: Grand Forks, 75 miles south.

GENERAL INFORMATION: 10th Space Warning Squadron.

TEMPORARY MILITARY LODGING: None. See Grand Forks listing, C-701-747-7051, D-312-362-7051.

RV, CAMPING/FAMCAMP: None. See Grand Forks AFB listing, C-701-747-3688.

SPACE-A: None. See Grand Forks AFB listing, C-701-747-4376/4409, D-312-362-4376/4409, Fax: C-701-747-6540.

LOGISTICAL SUPPORT:

Exchange-993-3224	Snack Bar-993-3228

ADMINISTRATIVE SUPPORT:

Fire Dept-993-3671	Police-993-3365
SDO/NCO-993-3292	

HEALTH & WELFARE: None. See Grand Forks AFB listing, C-701-747-5468.

REST & RECREATION:

Bowling-ext 3229	Gym-ext 3376
MWR-ext 3201	Recreation-ext 3201

ATTRACTIONS: Icelandic State Park, Pembina gorge, and Frost Fire mountain. The Red River Valley is one of the most fertile areas of the Midwest. Very good fishing, hunting, skiing and camping. Close to major cultural center in Winnipeg.

GRAND FORKS AIR FORCE BASE (ND04R3)

460 Steen Boulevard
Grand Forks Air Force Base, ND 58205-6231

TELEPHONE NUMBER INFORMATION: Main installation numbers: C-701-747-3000, D-312-362-3000.

LOCATION: From I-29, take US-2 west exit for 14 miles to Grand Forks, County Road B-3 (Emerado/Air Base) one mile to AFB. USMRA: Page 83 (I-3). NMC: Grand Forks, 15 miles east.

GENERAL INFORMATION: Air Mobility Command Base. 319th Air Refueling Wing and 321st Missile Group.

TEMPORARY MILITARY LODGING: Lodging office, 632 Holzapple Street, 24 hours daily, C-701-747-7051, D-312-362-7051. All ranks. DV/VIP C-701-747-4513.

RV, CAMPING/FAMCAMP: FAMCAMP, on base, 1 May-1 Oct, C-701-747-3688, 21 camper spaces with full hookups.

SPACE-A: Pax Term/Lounge, Building 528, 24 hours daily, C-701-747-4409/4410, D-312-362-4409/4410, Fax: C-701-747-6540. Flights to CONUS, OCONUS and overseas.

LOGISTICAL SUPPORT:

Child Care-747-3042	Commissary-747-3090
Exchange-594-5542	Gas Station-594-5951
Package Store-594-5206	SATO-594-5141
Snack Bar-594-2695	Theater-747-3101
Visitor Center-747-4283	

NORTH DAKOTA
Grand Forks Air Force Base, continued

ADMINISTRATIVE SUPPORT:
Community Services-747-3112
Legal-747-3606
Police-747-5351
Fire Dept-747-6304
Locator-747-3344
Public Affairs-747-5016

HEALTH & WELFARE:
CHAMPUS-747-5323
Family Services-747-3240
Retiree Services-747-6197
Chapel-747-3074/6
Medical-747-5468
Central Appts-747-3000

REST & RECREATION:
Arts & Crafts-747-3481
Bowling-747-3050
Golf Course-747-4279
Library-747-3046
Rec Center-747-3112
Auto Hobby Shop-ext 3394
Clubs
EM-747-3392
O-747-3131

ATTRACTIONS: Outdoor sports and recreation. Canada is 140 miles north of the base on I-29.

MINOT AIR FORCE BASE (ND02R3)

201 Summit Drive, Unit 4
Minot Air Force Base, ND 58705-5000

TELEPHONE NUMBER INFORMATION: Main installation numbers: C-701-723-1110, D-312-453-1110. HP: http://www.minot.af.mil.

LOCATION: On US-83, north of Minot. USMRA: Page 83 (D-2). NMC: Minot, 13 miles south.

GENERAL INFORMATION: Air Combat Command Base, 5th Bomb Wing (B-52) host; 91st Missile Wing (Minuteman III) Associate Wing.

TEMPORARY MILITARY LODGING: Lodging office, Building 173. C-701-723-2184, D-312-453-2184, Fax: C-701-723-1844, D-312-453-1844, 24 hours. All ranks. DV/VIP C-701-723-3474.

RV, CAMPING/FAMCAMP: 315 Bomber Boulevard, Building 510/511On base, 15 May-15 Oct, C-701-723-3648, D-312-453-3648. Fax: C-701-723-2175, first-come, first-served basis. Six camper spaces with W & E hookups.

SPACE-A: Pax Term/Lounge, Building 746, Base Ops, 24 hours daily, C-701-723-2348/1854, D-312-453-2348/1854, flights to CONUS and overseas.

LOGISTICAL SUPPORT:
Bank-727-4523
Beauty Shop-727-9799
Child Dev Center-723-3750
Class Six-727-4973
Conv Store-727-4973
Dining Facilities-723-2359
Education Office-723-2772
Gas Station-727-4876
Shoppette-727-4973
Visitor Center-723-3093
Barber Shop-727-4868
Cafeteria-727-4625
Child Care-723-3750
Commissary-723-4559
Credit Union-727-6111
Dry Cleaner-727-6800
Exchange-727-4717
SATO-723-5575
Snack Bar-727-9132

ADMINISTRATIVE SUPPORT:
Fire Dept-723-2461
Legal-723-3026
Pass/ID Office-723-4066
Public Affairs-723-6212
Housing Office-723-2461
Locator-723-4653
Police-723-3096
SDO/NCO-723-3102

HEALTH & WELFARE:
Air Force Aid Society-723-2865
CHAMPUS-723-5176
Dental-723-5565
American Red Cross-723-1855
Chapel-723-2456
Family Services-723-1818
Medical
Central Appts-723-5000
Emergency-723-5633
Retiree Services-723-4365
TRICARE-723-5174
Veterinary Services-723-6449

REST & RECREATION:
Arts & Crafts-ext 3640
Bowling-ext 2610
Golf Course-ext 3164
Gym-ext 3174/2124
ITT-727-6171
Library-ext 3344
Recreation-723-4670
Rec Equipment-ext 2175
Tennis-ext 2786
Tickets-ext 4670
Auto Hobby Shop-ext 2127
Clubs
EM-727-3806
NCO-727-6157
O-723-3731
Outdoor Rec-ext 3648
Rec Center-ext 4670
Swimming (Summer only)-ext 3388
Theater-723-3802
Youth Center-723-2838

ATTRACTIONS: Trestle Valley Ski Area, outdoor recreation. Canada easy drive north via US-83.

NORTH DAKOTA AIR NATIONAL GUARD BASE (ND07R3)

119th FW
1400 28th Avenue N
Fargo, ND 58102-1031

TELEPHONE NUMBER INFORMATION: Main installation numbers: C-701-241-7102, D-312-362-8102. HP: http://rrnet.com/ hooligan.

LOCATION: From I-29 to 19th street exit to University Drive N to Hector Field on left. USMRA: Page 83 (J-5). NMC: Fargo, in city limits.

GENERAL INFORMATION: Air National Guard Base.

TEMPORARY MILITARY LODGING: None. See Grand Forks listing, C-701-747-7051, D-312-362-7051.

RV, CAMPING/FAMCAMP: None. See Grand Forks AFB listing, C-701-747-3688.

SPACE-A: None. See Grand Forks AFB listing, C-701-747-4376/4409, D-312-362-4376/4409, Fax: C-701-747-6540.

LOGISTICAL SUPPORT:
Credit Union-232-0828
Shoppette-241-7184
SATO-241-7370

ADMINISTRATIVE SUPPORT:
Fire Dept-241-7220
Police-241-7288
Pass/ID Office-241-7288

HEALTH & WELFARE: None. See Grand Forks AFB listing, C-701-747-5468.

REST & RECREATION: None. See Grand Forks AFB listing, C-701-747-3112

ATTRACTIONS: Bonanzaville USA Historic Village & Museum, Hjemkomst Heritage Interpretive Center and the Fargo Dome.

Other Installations in North Dakota

Fraine Barracks ND ANG HQ (ND06R3), Office of the Adjutant General, 030 Fraine Barracks, P.O. Box 5511, Bismarck, ND 58506-5511. USMRA: Page 83 (E-5,6). C-701-224-5100, D-312-344-5100, Exchange-224-5119/5168, Legal-224-5194, Public Affairs-224-5106, Retiree Services-224-5134, SATO-224-8615.

OHIO

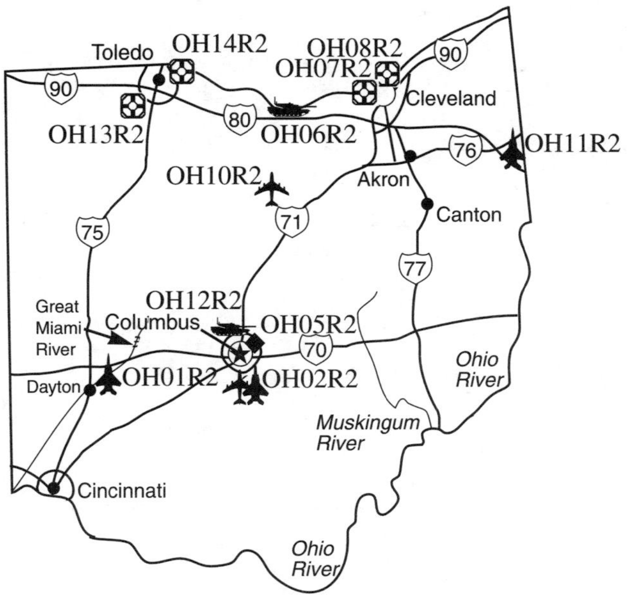

CLEVELAND COAST GUARD MARINE SAFETY OFFICE (OH07R2)

1055 East 9th Street
Cleveland, OH 44114-1092

TELEPHONE NUMBER INFORMATION: Main installation numbers: C-216-522-4404.

LOCATION: Take I-71 north or I-90 east to OH-2 west. Exit at East 9th Street and travel north towards Lake Erie on East 9th Street From I-77 north, also exit onto East 9th Street USMRA: Page 67 (F-3). NMC: Cleveland, in city limits.

GENERAL INFORMATION: *USCG Cutter Neah Bay*, Electronics Support Detachment, USCG Station Cleveland Harbor, Coast Guard Club and Coast Guard Exchange Satellite.

TEMPORARY MILITARY LODGING: None. See Camp Perry Training Site listing, C-419-635-4114, D-312-346-4114.

RV, CAMPING/FAMCAMP: None. Nearest facility is more than 100 miles away.

SPACE-A: None. See Wright-Patterson AFB, listing, C-513-257-7741, D-312-787-7741, Fax: C-513-476-1580.

LOGISTICAL SUPPORT:
Exchange*-671-3500/3267 Package Store-687-1756

* The Exchange is about a 10 minute drive from CGMSO at 13920 West Parkway Drive, C-216-671-3500. It has exchange items and some uniform items for the five armed services.

ADMINISTRATIVE SUPPORT: Public Affairs-522-4404

HEALTH & WELFARE:
CHAMPUS-522-73925 Hospital-281-2500
Medical-363-2353

REST & RECREATION: Coast Guard Club-687-1755

ATTRACTIONS: Rock and Roll Hall of Fame and Museum, Great Lakes Science Center. Major League baseball, soccer, and basketball teams, Great Lakes, NASA Lewis Research Center, West Side Market, world-class symphony orchestra, ballet and opera.

COLUMBUS DEFENSE SUPPLY CENTER (OH05R2)

P.O. Box 3990
3990 East Broad Street
Columbus, OH 43216-5000

TELEPHONE NUMBER INFORMATION: Main installation numbers: C-614-692-3131, D-312-850-3131.

LOCATION: From I-270 (Beltway) take exit 39 to Broad Street west, main gate at 3990 Broad Street. USMRA: Page 67 (D-6). NMC: Columbus, in city limits.

GENERAL INFORMATION: Logistical Support for construction supplies, weapons systems, and equipment for DoD.

TEMPORARY MILITARY LODGING: Limited facility near O'Club, C-614-692-4758.

RV, CAMPING/FAMCAMP: None. See Wright-Patterson AFB listing, C-513-257-9889, D-312-787-9889.

SPACE-A: None. See Wright-Patterson AFB listing, C-512-257-7741, D-312-787-7741, Fax: C-513-476-1580.

LOGISTICAL SUPPORT:
Cafeteria-692-1423 Exchange-231-0976
SATO-692-1447

ADMINISTRATIVE SUPPORT:
CDO/OOD-692-2166 Fire Dept-692-2026
Legal-692-3284 Locator-692-3131
Police-692-3722 Public Affairs-692-2328

HEALTH & WELFARE:
CHAMPUS-692-2227 Medical-692-2227
Retiree Services-692-4165 Inpatient-257-2969

REST & RECREATION:
Golf Course-239-6669 ITR-692-1111
MWR-692-2011 O'Club-239-0482
Recreation-692-3084 RV/Camping-692-1111

OTHER FACILITIES AVAILABLE: Golf Course with Driving Range, Gym, Pool and Racquetball.

ATTRACTIONS: State Fairgrounds, Ohio Historical Center, Franklin Park Conservatory, Ohio State University, Center of Science and Industry, Palace Theatre, German Village, Brewery District, and Columbus Museum of Art.

WRIGHT-PATTERSON AIR FORCE BASE (OH01R2)

1865 Fourth Street, Suite 15
Wright-Patterson Air Force Base, OH 45433-5542

TELEPHONE NUMBER INFORMATION: Main installation numbers: C-937-257-1110, D-312-787-1110. HP: http://www.wpafb.af.mil.

LOCATION: South of I-70, off I-675 at Fairborn. Also, access from OH-4. AFB clearly marked. USMRA: Page 67 (B-7). NMC: Dayton, 10 miles southwest.

GENERAL INFORMATION: Air Force Materiel Command Base. Air Force Institute of Technology, USAF Medical Center, Aeronautical Systems Center and National Air Intelligence Center, 88th Air Base Wing and Crew Systems Directorate of Armstrong Laboratory, 445th Airlift Wing (Reserve).

OHIO
Wright-Patterson Air Force Base, continued

TEMPORARY MILITARY LODGING: Lodging office, Building 825, Schlatter Drive & Childlaw Road, 24 hours daily, C-937-257-3451, D-312-787-3451. All ranks. DV/VIP C-937-257-3110.

RV, CAMPING/FAMCAMP: FAMCAMP, on base, year round, C-513-257-9889, D-312-787-9889, 16-20 camper spaces with W/E hookups (no water in winter).

SPACE-A: Pax Term/Lounge, Building 206, Area C, Skeel Avenue, 0530-2000 Mon-Fri, other days 0800-1600, C-937-257-7741, D-312-787-7741, Fax: C-513-476-1580, flights to CONUS and OCONUS locations.

LOGISTICAL SUPPORT:

Child Care-257-2173	Commissary-257-7420
Day Care Center-257-3107	Exchange-293-7296
Gas Station-257-3760	Package Store-278-1060
Snack Bar-879-4317	

ADMINISTRATIVE SUPPORT:

Legal-257-6142	Locator-257-3231
Police-257-6516	Public Affairs-255-3334

HEALTH & WELFARE:

Chapel-257-7941	Family Services-257-3592
Medical-257-2969	

REST & RECREATION:

Arts & Crafts-ext 7025	Auto Hobby Shop-257-3310
Bowling-ext 7796	Clubs
Fishing/Hunting-257-9889	Aero-257-7714
Gym-ext 4225/3607	NCO-257-7292
Library-ext 4815	O-257-9762
Picnic Area-257-9889	Rec Center-ext 2001
Rec Equipment-257-9889	Stables-257-7790
Swimming-257-2977	Tennis-ext 7248
Theater-257-4697	Youth Center-ext 55053

ATTRACTIONS: Air Force Museum on base. Wright Brothers Memorial, Dayton. Other aviation attractions in Dayton area.

YOUNGSTOWN AIR RESERVE STATION (OH11R2)

ATTN: 910 AW/PA
3976 King Graves Road
Vienna, OH 44473-0910

TELEPHONE NUMBER INFORMATION: Main installation numbers: C-330-609-1000 or 1-800-278-7046 (press 2, then 1000), D-312-346-1000.

LOCATION: From OH-193 N or S, exit to King Graves Road W at signs pointing to base, main gate left one mile. Base is clearly marked. USMRA: Page 67 (H-3). NMC: Youngstown, three miles south.

TEMPORARY MILITARY LODGING: Eagles Nest Inn, C-330-609-1268, D-312-346-1268, Fax: C-330-609-1120, D-312-346-1120.

RV, CAMPING/FAMCAMP: None. Nearest facility is more than 100 miles away.

SPACE-A: Pax Term, C-330-609-1082, D-312-346-1082, Fax: C-330-609-1161, D-312-346-1161.

LOGISTICAL SUPPORT:

Exchange-609-1395	MWR-609-1295

ADMINISTRATIVE SUPPORT:

Fire Dept-609-1117	Legal-609-1292
Police-609-1277	Public Affairs-609-1236

HEALTH & WELFARE:

Chapel-609-1393	Family Readiness-609-1201

REST & RECREATION: Consol Club-609-1295

ATTRACTIONS: Geauga Lake amusement park and Sea World.

Other Installations in Ohio

Beichtler Armory Air National Guard (OH12R2), Building 2825 W Dublin Granville Road, Columbus, OH 43085-5000. USMRA: Page 67 (D-6). C-614-889-0258, D-312-273-7000. E-mail: paooh@oh-ngnet.army.mil. HP: http://www.state.oh.us/ohguard/. Exchange-889-0258.

Camp Perry Training Site (OH06R2), Building 600, Port Clinton, OH 43452-9578. USMRA: Page 67 (D-3). C-419-635-4114, Exchange-635-4116, TML-635-4114.

Cleveland North Coast Guard Exchange (OH08R2), 13920 West Parkway, Cleveland, OH 44135-5000. USMRA: Page 67 (F-3). C-216-671-3500.

Mansfield-Lahm Airport (OH10R2), 179th Airlift Wing, 1947 Harrington Memorial Road, Mansfield, OH 44903-0179. USMRA: Page 67 (E-4,5). C-419-521-0124, Exchange-526-5358, Space-A-521-0124.

Rickenbacker IAP/Air National Guard Base (OH02R2), 7556 South Perimeter Road, Rickenbacker ANGB, OH 43217-5910. USMRA: Page 67 (D-7). C-614-492-4223, Space-A-492-4595.

Swanton Coast Guard Exchange (OH13R2), 180th Fighter Wing, 2660 S Eber Road, Swanton, OH 43558-5000. USMRA: Page 67 (B,C-3). C-419-867-9939, Police-868-4099.

Toledo Coast Guard Station (OH14R2), Bay View Park, 3900 N Summit Street, Toledo, OH 43611-5000. USMRA: Page 67 (C-3). C-419-729-2034, Exchange-729-5911.

OKLAHOMA

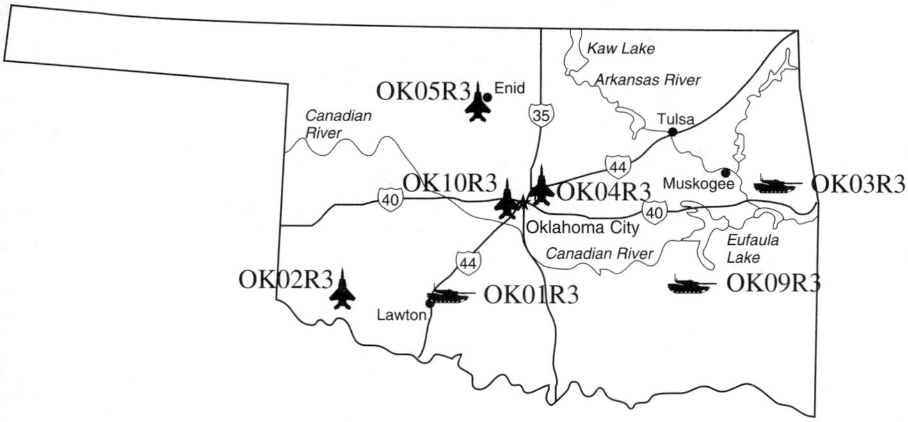

ALTUS AIR FORCE BASE (OK02R3)

100 Inez Boulevard
Altus Air Force Base, OK 73523-5047

TELEPHONE NUMBER INFORMATION: Main installation numbers: C-405-482-8100, D-312-866-1110.

LOCATION: From US-62 traveling west from Lawton, turn right at first traffic light in Altus and follow the road to the main gate on Falcon Road. USMRA: Page 84 (E-5). NMC: Lawton, 56 miles east.

GENERAL INFORMATION: Air Education and Training Command Base. C-141, C-5, C-17 and KC-135 aircrew training missions. Worldwide Air Refueling and Airlifting Mission.

TEMPORARY MILITARY LODGING: Billeting Office, Building 82, 24 hours daily, C-405-481-7356, D-312-866-7356, also 1-800-528-1218. All ranks. DV/VIP C-405-481-7044.

RV, CAMPING/FAMCAMP: FAMCAMP, on base, year round, C-405-481-6704, D-312-866-6704, four camper spaces with full hookups, three camper spaces with E hookups.

SPACE-A: Pax Term/Lounge, Building 178, 0730-1630 hours Mon-Fri, C-405-481-6350/6428, D-312-866-6350/6428, Fax: C-405-481-5065, flights to CONUS and overseas.

LOGISTICAL SUPPORT:
Child Care-481-7502
Conv Store-481-7095
Gas Station-482-7002
SATO-481-6466
Commissary-481-6529
Exchange-481-7441
Package Store-481-6276

ADMINISTRATIVE SUPPORT:
Fire Dept-481-6333
Locator-481-7250
Public Affairs-481-7700
Legal-481-7294
Police-481-7444

HEALTH & WELFARE:
CHAMPUS-481-5313
Family Services-481-7460
Retiree Services-481-5671
Chapel-481-7485
Medical-482-5222
Central Appts-481-5970
Emergency-482-5222

REST & RECREATION:
Arts & Crafts-ext 7048
Bowling-ext 6420
Golf Course-ext 7207
Gym-ext 7153
Library-ext 6302
Pools
Base Pool-ext 6377
EM Club Pool-ext 5106
O'Club Pool-ext 6281
Auto Hobby Shop-ext 6326
Clubs
EM-481-7034
O-481-6224
MWR-481-7731
Recreation-481-6600
RV/Camping-481-7646
Theater-481-7341

ATTRACTIONS: Western prairie country. Lake Altus, 15 miles north. Outdoor sports.

CAMP GRUBER (OK03R3)

P.O. Box 29
Building 154
Braggs, OK 74423-0029

TELEPHONE NUMBER INFORMATION: Main installation numbers: C-918-487-6001.

LOCATION: Exit I-40 at Webber Falls (exit 287), take Highway 64 to Gore, take state highway 10 to Braggs. First entrance to camp after passing through Braggs. USMRA: Page 84 (I-4). NMC: Muskogee, 12 miles north.

GENERAL INFORMATION: Camp Gruber is an Army National Guard Training Site.

TEMPORARY MILITARY LODGING: Lodging office, Building 155, 4th Street and Anzio Drive, 0730-1600 Mon-Fri, C-918-487-6067, Fax: C-918-487-6135.

RV, CAMPING/FAMCAMP: Blackhawk Recreational Vehicle Park, on base year round, ATTN: Billeting Office, P.O. Box 29, C-918-487-6065, Fax: C-918-487-6135. Twelve camper spaces with W/S/E hookups

SPACE-A: None. See Tinker AFB listing, C-405-739-4339, D-312-339-4339, Fax: C-405-739-3826, D-312-339-3826.

LOGISTICAL SUPPORT:
Exchange-487-5643
Package Store-487-5643

ADMINISTRATIVE SUPPORT:
Fire Dept-487-6071
Locator-487-6062
Public Affairs-425-8212
Housing Office-487-6065
Police-487-6021

HEALTH & WELFARE:
American Red Cross-682-1366
Medical-683-3261

REST & RECREATION:
Fitness Center-487-6065

OTHER SUPPORT & FACILITIES AVAILABLE: Barber Shop, Convenience Store, Laundry, Marinas, Gas Station, Golf Course, Package Store, Postal Service, Shoppette, Snack Bar.

ATTRACTIONS: Located in western edge of Ozark Mountains. Rolling hills, lakes, fishing and water recreation, Native American culture, Cherokee Heritage Center, Trail of Tears dramatization, all short drives.

FORT SILL (OK01R3)

US Army Field Artillery Center
ATTN: ATZR-CS
Building 455
Fort Sill, OK 73503-5001

TELEPHONE NUMBER INFORMATION: Main installation numbers: C-405-442-8111, D-312-639-7090.

LOCATION: From Lawton, take I-44 north to Key Gate exit. Clearly marked. USMRA: Page 84 (E, F-5). NMC: Lawton, on the northern border.

OKLAHOMA
Fort Sill, continued

GENERAL INFORMATION: Headquarters, US Army Field Artillery Center, US Army Field Artillery School, Headquarters III Corps Artillery and support units.

TEMPORARY MILITARY LODGING: Billeting Office, Building 5676, Fergusson Road, 24 hours daily, C-405-442-5000/353-5007, D-312-639-5000, Fax: C-405-442-7033.

RV, CAMPING/FAMCAMP: DCA, ATTN: ATZR-PN, Fort Sill, OK 73503, 0700-1600 hours daily. C-405-442-4522, D-312-639-4522, Fax: C-405-442-2549.

SPACE-A: None. See Will Rogers ANGB listing, C-405-686-5550, D-312-940-5550.

LOGISTICAL SUPPORT:

Bank-357-9880	Barber Shop-353-5697
Beauty Shop-353-6104	Car Rental-355-9010
Carlson Wagonlit Travel-357-6616	Child Care-442-3927
Class Six-355-4088	Commissary-442-2305
Credit Union-353-2124	Exchange-248-7506
Family Services-442-5018	Gas Station-357-0786
Laundry-248-2255	Postal Service-442-6172
Shoppette-357-7601	

ADMINISTRATIVE SUPPORT:

Fire Dept-442-6010	Housing Office-442-2813
Legal-442-2685	Locator-442-3693
Pass/ID Office-442-5010	Police-442-2101
Public Affairs-442-4500	SDO/NCO-442-4912

HEALTH & WELFARE:

American Red Cross-442-2426/2586	ACS-442-4337
Army Emergency Relief-442-2946	CHAMPUS-458-2484
Chapel-442-3319	Dental-442-5223
Medical-458-2500/2800	Emergency-442-5566/4263
Emergency-458-2770/2033	Retiree Services-442-5963/4009
TRICARE-458-2102	Veterinary Services-442-3416/4951

REST & RECREATION:

Arts & Crafts-442-4824/5687	Auto Hobby Shop-442-4147/2549
Bowling-442-2882	Clubs
Fitness Center-442-6652	EM-355-3021/357-4380
Golf Course-442-2723	O-355-9112
Gym-ext 6652/6712	ITR-442-6211
Library-442-3806	MWR-442-4522
Outdoor Rec-355-8270	Rec Center-442-5623
Theater-353-5623	Youth Services-442-6745

OTHER SUPPORT AVAILABLE: Child Development Center, Dental and Medical Clinics and Education Office.

ATTRACTIONS: Geronimo's burial place in post's Apache Cemetery, Fort Sill Museum, Wichita Mountains Wildlife Refuge and Lake Latonka.

McALESTER ARMY AMMUNITION PLANT (OK09R3)

ATTN: SIOMC-CO
1 C Tree Road
McAlester, OK 74501-9002

TELEPHONE NUMBER INFORMATION: Main installation numbers: C-918-421-3490, D-312-956-7490.

LOCATION: Off Indian Nation Turnpike, west of US-69. The southeast Oklahoma area is mostly rolling pasture with timber-covered hills and creek bottoms. USMRA: Page 84 (I-5). NMC: Tulsa, 90 miles north.

GENERAL INFORMATION: Produces, stores, renovates, and issues ammunition, explosives, and ordnance items to all branches of the Armed Forces.

TEMPORARY MILITARY LODGING: None. See Tinker AFB listing, Indian Hills Inn, C-405-734-2822/5095, D-312-884-2822/5095.

RV, CAMPING/FAMCAMP: Murphy's Meadow on base, year round, C-918-421-3484/2673, D-312-956-3484/2673, 34 camper spaces with W/E hookups.

SPACE-A: None. See Tinker AFB listing, C-405-739-4339, D-312-339-4339, Fax: C-405-739-4317/3826, D-312-339-3826.

LOGISTICAL SUPPORT:

Child Care-421-2204	Exchange-421-2388
Package Store-421-2388	Snack Bar-421-2384

ADMINISTRATIVE SUPPORT:

Fire Dept-421-2221	Legal-421-2439
Police-421-3370	Public Affairs-421-2591
SDO/NCO-421-2642	

HEALTH & WELFARE:

ACS-421-3490	CHAMPUS-421-2496
Family Services-421-3490	Medical-421-2495/6

REST & RECREATION:

Com Club-421-3587	ITT-421-2418
MWR-421-3262	Recreation-421-3262

OTHER FACILITIES AVAILABLE: Auto Hobby Shop, Boat Rental, Bowling, Gym, Library, Pool, Rec Center, Rec Equipment, Tennis and Youth Activities.

ATTRACTIONS: Lake Eufaula.

TINKER AIR FORCE BASE (OK04R3)

3001 Staff Drive, Suite 1AG78A
Tinker Air Force Base, OK 73145-3010

TELEPHONE NUMBER INFORMATION: Main installation numbers: C-405-732-2456, D-312-334-2456. HP: http://www1.tinker.af.mil.

LOCATION: Southeast Oklahoma City, off I-40. Use Tinker gate off Air Depot Boulevard. Clearly marked. USMRA: Page 84 (G-4). NMC: Oklahoma City, 12 miles northwest.

GENERAL INFORMATION: Air Force Materiel Command Base. Major Logistics Center for the Air Force. Navy Stratcom E-6 Wing. AWACS E-3 Sentry Wing. AFRES Tanker Wing.

TEMPORARY MILITARY LODGING: Indian Hills Inn, 72nd SPTG/SVML, 4002 Mitchell Avenue, Tinker AFB, OK 73145-8101. C-405-734-2822/5095, D-312-884-2822/5095. Fax: C-405-734-7426, D-312-884-7426, 24 hours daily.

RV, CAMPING/FAMCAMP: FAMCAMP, 72D SPTG/SV, 6120 Arnold, Tinker AFB, OK 73145-8101, off base, year round, C-405-734-2289, D-312-884-2289. Twenty-nine camper spaces with W/E hookups and five tent spaces without hookups.

SPACE-A: Pax Term/Lounge, Building 268, C-405-739-4339, D-312-339-4339. Fax: C-405-739-3826, D-312-339-3826, Mon-Fri 0715-1800 hours. Off schedule show times, weekends and holidays closed. Flights to CONUS and overseas locations.

LOGISTICAL SUPPORT:

Barber Shop-732-5032	Beauty Shop-737-6509
Cafeteria-734-3884	Child Care-734-3116
Commissary-734-5212	Conv Store-733-3445
Credit Union-734-7888	Dining Facilities-734-2918

OKLAHOMA
Tinker Air Force Base, continued

Dry Cleaner-737-5225	Education Office-739-7408
Exchange-734-3035	Laundry-737-5225
Gas Station-734-3040	Package Store-734-3466
Postal Service-734-3538	SATO-739-5057
Shoppette-733-3445	Snack Bar-739-0340
Travel Office-739-5057	

ADMINISTRATIVE SUPPORT:

Fire Dept-734-7964	Housing Office-734-2821
Legal-739-5811	Locator-734-2456
Pass/ID Office-734-2605	Police-734-3737
Public Affairs-739-2026	Quarter Deck-739-3044

HEALTH & WELFARE:

Air Force Aid Society-739-2747	American Red Cross-734-3030
CHAMPUS-734-2615	Chapel-734-2111
Dental-736-2074	Family Services-739-2505
Medical	Retiree Services-739-2795
Central Appts-734-2778	TRICARE-1-800-406-2832
Clinic-734-2778	Veterinary Services-734-5780
Emergency-736-2184/6	
Health Benefits-734-2614	
Hospital-732-7321	

REST & RECREATION:

Arts & Crafts-734-5615	Auto Hobby Shop-734-5616
Boat Rental-734-2289	Bowling-734-3484
Clubs	Fishing-734-2289
NCO-734-3435	Fitness Center-734-3651
O-734-3418	Golf Course-734-2909
Gym-734-5657	Handball-734-5607
Library-734-7837	Outdoor Rec-734-2289
Riding Club-737-4775	Swimming-734-5607
Theater-734-3400	Wood Hobby Shop-734-5616
Youth Center-734-7866	

ATTRACTIONS: Oklahoma City (the capital), Kirkpatrick Planetarium, Oklahoma Air Space Museum, Omniplex Science Museum, National Cowboy Hall of Fame and Western Heritage Center, Oklahoma City Zoo, Remington Park Racetrack, arts and entertainment.

VANCE AIR FORCE BASE (OK05R3)

246 Brown Parkway
Vance Air Force Base, OK 73705-5015

TELEPHONE NUMBER INFORMATION: Main installation numbers: C-405-213-5000, D-312-448-7110.

LOCATION: Off of US-81 south of Enid. Clearly marked. USMRA: Page 84 (F-3). NMC: Oklahoma City, 90 miles southeast.

GENERAL INFORMATION: Air Education and Training Command Base. Flying Training Wing, Undergraduate Pilot Training.

TEMPORARY MILITARY LODGING: Lodging office, Building 714, Williams Road, 24 hours daily, C-405-213-7358, D-312-448-7358. All ranks.

RV, CAMPING/FAMCAMP: None. See Altus AFB listing, C-405-481-6704, D-312-866-6704.

SPACE-A: Base Ops, C-405-237-2121/7424, D-312-448-2121/7424.

LOGISTICAL SUPPORT:

Child Care-213-7310	Commissary-213-7788
Exchange-237-6765	Gas Station-237-7445
Package Store-237-6765	

ADMINISTRATIVE SUPPORT:

Legal-213-7404	Locator-213-7791/7358
Police-213-7476	

HEALTH & WELFARE:

CHAMPUS-249-7746	Chapel-213-7211
Family Services-249-7322	Medical-213-7416
Retiree Services-249-7421	Central Appts-237-7416
	Inpatient-734-6841
	Emergency-237-6117

REST & RECREATION:

Arts & Crafts-ext 7402	Auto Hobby Shop-ext 7508
Bowling-ext 7331	Clubs
Gym-ext 7830/7670	NCO-237-7311
Library-ext 7368	O-237-2326
Youth Center-ext 7474	

ATTRACTIONS: National Cowboy Hall of Fame, Kirkpatrick Planetarium, National Softball Hall of Fame, Humphrey Heritage Village/Museum of the Cherokee Strip, Railroad Museum of Oakland, Midgley Museum, Leonardo's Discovery Warehouse, George's Museum of Antique Cars, the Zoo, and Frontier City.

Other Installations in Oklahoma

Will Rogers Air National Guard Base (OK10R3), 137 th TAW/DOO (ANG), Will Rogers ANGB, OK 73169-1040, C-405-686-5210, D-312-940-5210. From I-40 west, exit I44 south to airport. USMRA: Page 84 (G-4). NMC: Oklahoma City, seven miles northeast. NCO Club-686-5279, Space-A-686-5550, Police-686-5300.

OREGON

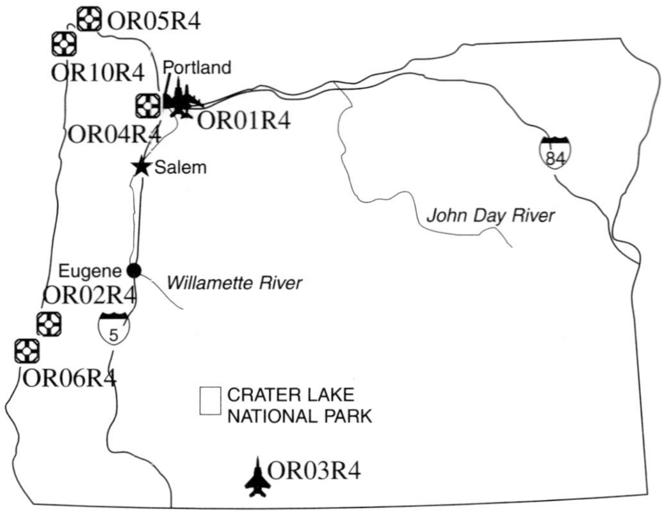

ASTORIA COAST GUARD GROUP/ AIR STATION (OR05R4)

2185 SE, 12th Place
Warrenton, OR 97146-5000

TELEPHONE NUMBER INFORMATION: Main installation number: C-503-861-6192.

LOCATION: Take highway 30 from Portland west to Astoria. Go through Astoria and across the Young River Bridge. Follow signs, plainly marked. USMRA: Page 100 (B-1). NMC: Portland, 100 miles east.

GENERAL INFORMATION: Coast Guard Group is based in Astoria, The Coast Guard Air Station is based in Warrenton.

TEMPORARY MILITARY LODGING: None. See Camp Rilea AFTC listing, C-503-861-4018, Fax: C-503-861-4050.

RV, CAMPING/FAMCAMP: None. See Camp Rilea AFTC listing, C-503-861-4018, Fax: C-503-861-4050.

SPACE-A: None. See Portland IAP/ANGB listing, C-503-335-4390, D-312-638-4390, Fax: C-503-335-5098.

LOGISTICAL SUPPORT:

Barber Shop-861-6175	Commissary-325-0108
Conv Store-861-3350	Education Office-861-6231
Exchange-325-0108 ext 13	Gas Station-325-0108

ADMINISTRATIVE SUPPORT:

CDO/OOD-861-6211/2	Housing Office-861-6193
Pass/ID Office-861-6130	Public Affairs-861-6123

HEALTH & WELFARE:

Chapel-861-6229	Dental-861-6240
Medical-861-6240	

REST & RECREATION:

Gym-861-6349	MWR-861-6237

ATTRACTIONS: The Columbia River. Minutes from: Washington State, Saddle Mountain State Park, and Clatsop and Tillamook National Forests.

KINGSLEY FIELD (OR03R4)

302 Vandenberg Drive, Suite 38
Klamath Falls, OR 97603-0400

TELEPHONE NUMBER INFORMATION: Main installation numbers: C-541-885-6350, D-312-830-6110.

LOCATION: Take I-5 through Medford to highway 140E to south side bypass. Go East approximately four-and-a-half miles to the airport. USMRA: Page 100 (D-8). NMC: Medford, 80 miles west.

GENERAL INFORMATION: Near the Oregon/California border, Southern Oregon's only military installation.

TEMPORARY MILITARY LODGING: Billeting Office, Kingsley Lodge, Building 208, McConnell Circle, 0800-1600 Mon-Fri (closed 1200-1300), C-541-885-6365.

RV, CAMPING/FAMCAMP: None. Nearest facility is more than 100 miles away.

SPACE-A: Limited. C-541-885-6686, D-312-830-6686.

LOGISTICAL SUPPORT:

Barber Shop-885-6370	Class Six-885-6371
Credit Union-885-6410	Dry Cleaner-885-6371
Exchange-885-6371	

ADMINISTRATIVE SUPPORT:

Pass/ID Office-885-6142	Police-885-6647

HEALTH & WELFARE: Medical-885-6312

REST & RECREATION: Consol Club-885-6484

OTHER SUPPORT AVAILABLE: Bank and Fire Department.

ATTRACTIONS: Crater Lake, Lava Beds, Oregon Caves, Freemont National Forest, Rogue River National Forest, Winema National Forest.

NORTH BEND COAST GUARD GROUP (OR02R4)

2000 Connecticut Avenue
North Bend, OR 97459-2399

TELEPHONE NUMBER INFORMATION: Main installation numbers: C-541-756-9210/9220.

LOCATION: Take US-101 to Virginia Street, west one mile to Connecticut, turn right, two blocks (follow signs). USMRA: Page 100 (A-5,6). NMC: Eugene, 80 miles northeast.

GENERAL INFORMATION: Coast Guard Group.

TEMPORARY MILITARY LODGING: None. Nearest facility is more than 100 miles away.

RV, CAMPING/FAMCAMP: None. Nearest facility is more than 100 miles away.

SPACE A: None. See Portland IAP/ANGB listing, C-541-335-4390, D-312-638-4390, Fax: C-541-335-5098.

LOGISTICAL SUPPORT: Exchange-888-5285

ADMINISTRATIVE SUPPORT:

Public Affairs-756-9669	SDO/NCO-756-9210

HEALTH & WELFARE:

CHAMPUS-756-9234	Family Services-756-9234
Medical-756-9234	

REST & RECREATION: MWR-756-9282

OREGON
North Bend Coast Guard Group, continued

ATTRACTIONS: Oregon Dunes National Recreation Area.

PORTLAND IAP/AIR NATIONAL GUARD BASE (OR01R4)

6801 NE Cornfoot Road
Portland, OR 97218-2797

TELEPHONE NUMBER INFORMATION: Main installation number: C-503-335-4000.

LOCATION: Go south on I-205 to NE Airport Way exit, west on NE Airport Way to Alderwood, south on Alderwood to Cornfoot Road. Co-located with Portland International Airport. USMRA: Page 100 (C-2), page 103 (C-1). NMC: Portland, in city limits.

GENERAL INFORMATION: Oregon Air National Guard, 142nd Fighter Wing, 244th and 272nd Combat Communications Squadrons, 939th Rescue Wing and 304th Air Rescue Squadrons, Civil Air Patrol.

TEMPORARY MILITARY LODGING: None. See Camp Rilea AFTC listing, C-503-861-4018, Fax: C-503-861-4050.

RV, CAMPING/FAMCAMP: None. See Camp Rilea AFTC listing, C-503-861-4018, Fax: C-503-861-4050.

SPACE-A: Portland IAP/ANG Ops, 24 hours daily, C-503-335-4390, D-312-638-4390, Fax: C-503-335-5098, transit aircraft.

LOGISTICAL SUPPORT:
Exchange-249-0997 Travel-335-4265

ADMINISTRATIVE SUPPORT:
Fire Dept-335-4889 Police-335-4752
Public Affairs-335-4104

HEALTH & WELFARE:
Chapel-335-4449 Medical-335-4757
Retiree Services-335-4945

REST & RECREATION:
Camping Equipment-335-4748 Consol Club-335-5151
MWR-335-4176 Rec Center 335-4748

ATTRACTIONS: Greater Portland area.

Other Installations in Oregon

Camp Rilea Armed Forces Training Center (OR07R4), Route 2, Box 497-E, Warrenton, OR 97146-9711. C-503-861-4000, D-312-355-3974. Exchange-861-4231, TML-861-1018.
Coos Bay Coast Guard Exchange (OR06R4), 1684 Ocean Boulevard, Coos Bay, OR 97420-5000. USMRA: Page 100 (A-6). C-541-888-5285, Exchange-888-5285.
Portland Coast Guard Marine Safety Office/Group (OR04R4), 6767 N. Basin Avenue, Portland, OR 97217-3929. USMRA: Page 100 (C-2), page 103 (B-2). C-503-240-9310, Exchange-286-3510.
Warrenton Coast Guard Exchange (OR08R4), 1240 W Marine Drive, Astoria, OR 97103-5612. C-503-861-3350.

PENNSYLVANIA

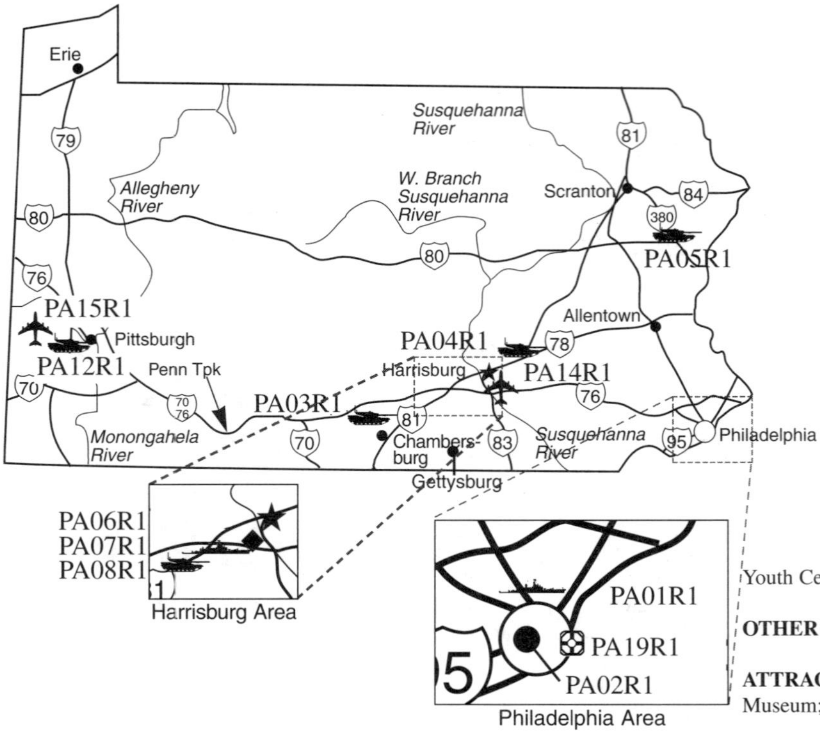

CARLISLE BARRACKS (PA08R1)

US Army War College
ATTN: ATZE-GC
122 Forbes Avenue
Carlisle Barracks, PA 17013-5050

TELEPHONE NUMBER INFORMATION: Main installation numbers: C-717-245-3131, D-312-242-3131. E-mail: awcci@carlisle-emh.a.army.mil. HP: http://carlisle-www.army.mil/.

LOCATION: From I-81 exit 17 to US-11, two miles southwest to Carlisle, signs clearly marked to Barracks and Army War College. USMRA: Page 22 (F-6). NMC: Harrisburg, 18 miles northeast.

GENERAL INFORMATION: Army War College and Army Military History Institute, Center for Strategic Leadership, Army Physical Fitness Center

TEMPORARY MILITARY LODGING: Lodging office, Building 7, 0700-1800 Mon-Fri, 0800-1600 Sat-Sun and holidays, C-717-245-4245, D-312-242-4245. All other times C-717-245-4115. All ranks. DV/VIP C-717-245-4818.

RV, CAMPING/FAMCAMP: None. See Letterkenny Army Depot listing, C-717-267-9494/9620, D-312-570-9494/9620.

SPACE-A: None. See Fort Indiantown Gap listing, Muir Army Airfield, C-717-861-2000, D-312491-2000.

LOGISTICAL SUPPORT:

Barber Shop-249-4958	Beauty Shop-258-4700
Book Store-258-3326	Carlson Wagonlit Travel-245-9891
Child Care-245-3701	Child Dev Center-245-3701
Class Six-245-2275	Commissary-245-3105
Credit Union-243-3900	Dry Cleaner-258-1856
Education Office-245-3943	Exchange-243-2463
Postal Service-258-1930	SATO-245-3158
Snack Bar-245-4883	

ADMINISTRATIVE SUPPORT:

Fire Dept-245-4419	Housing Office-245-4017
Legal-245-4940	Locator-245-3131
Police-245-4115	Public Affairs-245-4101
SDO/NCO-245-4342	

HEALTH & WELFARE:

ACS-245-4357	CHAMPUS-245-4112
Chapel-245-3318	Dental-245-4542
Family Services-245-4357	Medical
Retiree Services-245-4501	Central Appts-245-3400
Veterinary services-245-3430	Clinic-245-3915

REST & RECREATION:

Arts & Crafts-245-3319	Auto Hobby Shop-245-3913
Bowling-245-4109	Com Support Center-245-3215
Fitness Center-245-3228	Golf Course-243-3262
Gym	ITR-245-3309
245-3418 (Building 23)	ITT-245-3309
245-4375 (Building 120)	Library
Outdoor Rec-245-4935	245-4300 (Building 122)
Sports Office-245-4343	245-3718 (Building 46)
Theater-245-4108	Wood Hobby Shop-245-3466
Youth Center-245-3354	Youth Services-245-3354

OTHER SUPPORT AVAILABLE: Army Emergency Relief.

ATTRACTIONS: Hessian Powder Magazine Museum and Omar N. Bradley Museum; Amish Country and Gettysburg Battlefield nearby.

CHARLES E. KELLY SUPPORT FACILITY (PA12R1)

6 Lobaugh Street
Oakdale, PA 15071-5000

TELEPHONE NUMBER INFORMATION: Main installation numbers: C-412-693-1844/5.

LOCATION: From I-279 take I-79 south to Carnegie exit (exit 13). Bear right (left if coming from the south) on Nobblestown Road and travel approximately two-and-a-half miles through town of Rennerdale. Follow signs. USMRA: Page 22 (A-6). NMC: Pittsburgh, 13 miles east.

GENERAL INFORMATION: Location of 99th Reserve Support Command. A local area Army Support Center.

TEMPORARY MILITARY LODGING: None. See Pittsburgh IAP/ARS listing, C-412-474-8230, D-312-277-8230.

RV, CAMPING/FAMCAMP: None. Nearest facility is more than 100 miles away.

SPACE-A: None. See Pittsburgh IAP/ARS listing, C-412-474-8163/8147, D-312-277-8163/8147.

LOGISTICAL SUPPORT:

Carlson Wagonlit Travel-693-8710/1/2	Commissary-693-2471/2463
Exchange-693-2434	Four Seasons-693-2426
Package Store-693-2436	Snack Bar-693-2437

ADMINISTRATIVE SUPPORT: Pass/ID Office-693-2475

HEALTH & WELFARE:

CHAMPUS-693-2475/6	Medical
Retiree Services-693-2186	Emergency- 693-2476

REST & RECREATION:

Community Center-ext 1858	Fitness Center-ext 1860
Recreation-693-1858/1860	

ATTRACTIONS: City of Pittsburgh, The Shops at Station Square, Carnegie Science Center, the Boardwalk, the Gateway Clipper Fleet boats and a magnificent view of the city atop Mount Washington. Pittsburgh Pirates baseball, Penguins hockey, and Steelers football.

DEFENSE DISTRIBUTION REGION EAST (PA06R1)

14 Dedication Drive
New Cumberland, PA 17070-5001

TELEPHONE NUMBER INFORMATION: Main installation numbers: C-717-770-6011, D-312-977-6011.

LOCATION: From I-83, exit 18 to PA-114, east for one mile to Old York Road, left three-quarters-of-a-mile to Ross Avenue, right for one mile to main gate of depot. USMRA: Page 22 (G-6). NMC: Harrisburg, seven miles northeast.

GENERAL INFORMATION: Defense Logistics Agency.

TEMPORARY MILITARY LODGING: Lodging office, Building 268, J Avenue, 0700-1700 hours daily, C-717-770-7035, D-312-977-7035. All ranks. DV/VIP C-717-770-7192.

RV, CAMPING/FAMCAMP: None. See Letterkenny Army Depot listing, C-717-267-9494/9620, D-312-570-9494/9620.

SPACE-A: None. See Philadelphia IAP/ARS listing, C-215-897-5600, D-312-443-5600, Fax: C-215-897-5647, D-312-443-5647.

LOGISTICAL SUPPORT:

Cafeteria-770-7165/6973	Child Care-770-7360
Commissary-770-6540	Conv Store-774-4482
Exchange-774-4482	Gas Station-774-4066
Package Store-774-4482	SATO-770-6468
Snack Bar-770-5125	

ADMINISTRATIVE SUPPORT:

Fire Dept-770-6632	Legal-770-6310
Locator-770-6770	Police-770-6222
Public Affairs-770-6223	

HEALTH & WELFARE:

CHAMPUS-770-7281	Family Services-770-6203
Medical-782-7281	

REST & RECREATION:

Auto Hobby Shop-ext 6664	Bowling-ext 7325
Consol Club-770-7802	Fitness Center-ext 6428
Golf Course-ext 5199	Gym-ext 6428
ITR-770-7670	MWR-770-6118
Outdoor Recreation-ext 7718	Recreation-770-7718
Rec Center-ext 7625	Rec Equipment-ext 7625
Swimming-ext 6476	Youth Center-ext 4413

ATTRACTIONS: State Capitol in Harrisburg, Harley Davidson Plant (York, PA), Hershey Park, Gettysburg Battlefield, Pennsylvania Dutch Country.

DEFENSE PERSONNEL SUPPORT CENTER (PA02R1)

2800 South 20th Street,
Philadelphia, PA 19145-5099
Scheduled to relocate June 1999

TELEPHONE NUMBER INFORMATION: Main installation numbers: C-215-737-2411, D-312-444-2411. E-mail: fjohnson@dpsc.dla.mil. HP: http://www.dpsc.dla.mil. *(Military Personnel may call C-215-737-2390.)*

LOCATION: From I-95 take Broad Street exit, go two miles to intersection of 20th Street and Oregon Avenue, follow signs. USMRA: Page 27 (D-6). NMC: Philadelphia, within city limits.

GENERAL INFORMATION: Provides defense personnel and their eligible dependents with $3 billion worth of food, clothing and textiles, medicines, and medical equipment.

TEMPORARY MILITARY LODGING: None. See Willow Grove NAS/JRB listing, C-215-442-5800, D-312-991-5800, DV/VIP C-215-443-1776.

RV, CAMPING/FAMCAMP: None. See Fort Dix AG, NJ listing, Brindle Lake Travel Camp, C-609-562-6667, D-312-944-6667, Fax: C-609-562-2354.

SPACE-A: None. See Philadelphia IAP/ARS listing, C-215-897-5600, D-312-443-5600, Fax: C-215-897-5647, D-312-443-5647.

LOGISTICAL SUPPORT:

Cafeteria-737-3932	Exchange-737-3925
Snack Bar-737-3933	Travel Office-467-5925 (official) 467-5945 (Leisure)

ADMINISTRATIVE SUPPORT:

CDO/OOD-737-2341	Locator-737-2411
Police-737-2222	Public Affairs-737-2311

HEALTH & WELFARE:

CHAMPUS-737-2324	Medical-737-2251
Retiree Services-737-2429	

REST & RECREATION:

Fitness Center-ext 3936	MWR-737-3932
O-737-3939	Recreation-737-3936
Rec Services-ext 3936	

ATTRACTIONS: Independence Hall, Betsy Ross House, Liberty Bell Pavilion. Edgar Allen Poe National Historic Site. Museums, professional sports, tours.

FORT INDIANTOWN GAP (PA04R1)

ATTN: AFZS-FIG-GC
1 Garrison Road, Room 19
Fort Indiantown Gap, PA 17003-5040
Pennsylvania National Guard will assume command of Fort Indiantown Gap in October of 1998.

TELEPHONE NUMBER INFORMATION: Main installation numbers: C-717-861-2000, D-312-491-2000. E-mail: pao@indgap-emhl.army.mil. HP: www.indgap.army.mil.

LOCATION: From I-81 take exit 29 B, north on PA-934 to post. USMRA: Page 22 (G-6). NMC: Harrisburg, eight miles southwest.

GENERAL INFORMATION: US Army Garrison, Pennsylvania Department of Military Affairs, Reserve Component training and area support.

TEMPORARY MILITARY LODGING: Lodging office, Building T-0-1, 0800-2330 daily, C-717-861-2512, D-312-491-2512. All ranks. DV/VIP C-717-861-2552.

RV, CAMPING/FAMCAMP: None. See Letterkenny Army Depot listing, C-717-267-9494/9620, D-312-570-9494/9620.

SPACE-A: Muir Army Airfield, C-717-861-2000, D-312-491-2000.

LOGISTICAL SUPPORT:

Barber Shop-861-2853	Carlson Wagonlit Travel-865-1073 or 865-1068
Child Care-861-8351	Credit Union-865-6641
Class Six-861-2058	Exchange-861-2058
Education Office-861-2513	Laundry-861-2058
Gas Station-865-6938	

PENNSYLVANIA
Fort Indiantown Gap, continued

Shoppette-865-6938	Snack Bar-865-2044
Travel Office-865-2311	

ADMINISTRATIVE SUPPORT:

Fire Dept-861-2349	Locator-861-2000
Police-861-2160	Public Affairs-861-2193
SDO/NCO-861-2160	

HEALTH & WELFARE:

ACS-861-2610	Chapel-861-2241
Medical-861-2091	

REST & RECREATION:

Auto Hobby Shop-861-2477	Bowling-861-2061
Clubs	Flying Activity-861-2813
Com-861-2173	Gym 861-2860
NCO-861-2450	ITR-861-2622
Library-861-2030	MWR-861-2060
Outdoor Rec-861-2622	Swimming-ext 2656

ATTRACTIONS: Hershey Amusement Park, Pennsylvania Dutch Country, Lebanon and origin of Lebanon Bologna.

LETTERKENNY ARMY DEPOT (PA03R1)

ATTN: SIOLE-CO
1 Overcash Avenue
Chambersburg, PA 17201-4150
This base is scheduled to downsize in 1999 under the 1995 BRAC.

TELEPHONE NUMBER INFORMATION: Main installation numbers: C-717-267-8111, D-312-570-5110. E-mail: letterkenny-emh1.army.mil. HP: http://www.letterkenny.army.mi.

LOCATION: From I-81 exit 8 to PA-997 N left, enter depot at gate 6. USMRA: Page 22 (E-7). NMC: Harrisburg, 55 miles northeast.

GENERAL INFORMATION: Army Depot that maintains Army materiel and ammunition. DoD tactical missile maintenance center.

TEMPORARY MILITARY LODGING: Lodging office, Building 663, 0730-1615 Mon-Fri, C-717-267-8890, D-312-570-8890. All ranks.

RV, CAMPING/FAMCAMP: Army Travel Camp on post, 1 Apr-31 Oct, C-717-267-9494/9620, D-312-570-9494/9620, eight camper spaces, with W/E hookups.

SPACE-A: None. See Philadelphia IAP/ARS listing, C-215-897-5600, D-312-443-5600, Fax: C-215-897-5647, D-312-443-5647.

LOGISTICAL SUPPORT:

Barber Shop-267-8685	Cafeteria-264-1321
Carlson Wagonlit Travel-267-1316	Child Care-267-8846
Class Six-264-1713	Credit Union-263-4444
Exchange-264-1713	Travel-267-1315

ADMINISTRATIVE SUPPORT:

Fire Dept-267-9101	Housing Office-267-8890
Legal-267-9889	Locator-267-8111
Pass/ID Office-267-9754	Police-267-8800
Public Affairs-267-5102	

HEALTH & WELFARE:

Medical-267-8805	Retiree Services-267-9725

REST & RECREATION:

Community Center-267-8478	Com Club-267-8478
Gym-ext 9383	

ATTRACTIONS: Gettysburg Battlefield, Hershey Park, Potomac C&O Canal, Carlisle Barracks and War College.

MECHANICSBURG NAVAL INVENTORY CONTROL POINT (PA07R1)

P.O. Box 2020
5450 Carlisle Pike
Mechanicsburg, PA 17055-0788

TELEPHONE NUMBER INFORMATION: Main installation numbers: C-717-790-2000, D-312-430-2000.

LOCATION: From I-83 exit 20 to US-11, four miles. Or from PA Turnpike (I-76), exit 16 (Carlisle), eight miles to Center. USMRA: Page 22 (F,G-6). NMC: Harrisburg, 10 miles northeast.

GENERAL INFORMATION: Logistics Support Activity for Naval ships parts.

TEMPORARY MILITARY LODGING: None. See Carlisle Barracks listing, C-717-245-4245, D-312-242-4245.

RV, CAMPING/FAMCAMP: None. See Letterkenny Army Depot listing, C-717-267-9494/9620, D-312-570-9494/9620.

SPACE-A: None. See Philadelphia IAP/ARS listing, C-215-897-5600, D-312-443-5600, Fax: C-215-897-5647, D-312-443-5647.

LOGISTICAL SUPPORT:

Barber Shop-790-4344	Cafeteria-790-3537
Child Dev Center-790-5683	Credit Union-790-3596
Exchange-790-2608	Package Store-790-2608
SATO-1-800-949-7286	

ADMINISTRATIVE SUPPORT:

CDO-790-4444	Fire Dept-790-3467
Housing Office-790-2900	Legal-790-2424
Pass/ID Office-790-3795	Police-790-3351
Public Affairs-790-3338	SDO/NCO-790-4444

HEALTH & WELFARE: Medical-790-3409/2636

REST & RECREATION:

Auto Hobby Shop-790-4338	Bowling-790-3948
O' Club-790-3505	Fitness Center-790-3948
Golf Course-790-1610	Gym-790-3948
MWR-790-1610	

ATTRACTIONS: Gettysburg National Battlefield Park and Pennsylvania State capital, Harrisburg.

PHILADELPHIA COAST GUARD MARINE SAFETY OFFICE/GROUP (PA19R1)

1 Washington Avenue, Box 18
Philadelphia, PA 19147-4395

TELEPHONE NUMBER INFORMATION: Main installation number: C-215-271-4800, Fax: C-215-271-4919. E-mail: cgphilly@pond.com. HP:http://www.dot.gov/dotinfo/uscg.

LOCATION: Exit 16 off I-95. Follow signs. USMRA: Page 27 (D,E-6). NMC: Philadelphia, within city limits.

TEMPORARY MILITARY LODGING: None. See Willow Grove NAS/JRB listing, C-215-442-5800, D-312-991-5800, DV/VIP C-215-443-1776.

RV, CAMPING/FAMCAMP: None. See Fort Dix AG, NJ listing, Brindle Lake Travel Camp, C-609-562-6667, D-312-944-6667, Fax: C-609-562-2354.

SPACE-A: None. See Philadelphia IAP/ARS listing, C-215-897-5600, D-312-443-5600, Fax: C-215-897-5647, D-312-443-5647.

LOGISTICAL SUPPORT: Exchange-271-4921

ADMINISTRATIVE SUPPORT:
CDO/OOD-271-4800
Police-271-4971
Fire Dept-271-4927/4940
Public Affairs Office-271-4889

HEALTH & WELFARE: Medical-271-4816

OTHER SUPPORT & FACILITIES AVAILABLE: Fitness Room, Galley, Outdoor Baseball and Weight Room.

ATTRACTIONS: Independence Hall, Betsy Ross House, Liberty Bell Pavilion. Edgar Allen Poe National Historic Site. Museums, professional sports, tours.

PITTSBURGH IAP/ AIR RESERVE STATION (PA15R1)

911 Airlift Wing/PA
2475 Defense Avenue, Suite 218
Coraopolis, PA 15108-4403

TELEPHONE NUMBER INFORMATION: Main installation numbers: C-412-474-8000, D-312-277-8000.

LOCATION: Take I-279 W which merges into PA-60 (Airport Parkway) take Exit 3 Business Route 60 to Thorn Run Interchange, follow signs. USMRA: Page 22 (A-5,6). NMC: Pittsburgh, 15 miles southeast.

TEMPORARY MILITARY LODGING: 316 Defense Avenue, 0700-2400, C-412-474-8230, D-312-277-8230, Fax: C-412-474-8752, D-312-277-8752.

RV, CAMPING/FAMCAMP: None. Nearest facility is more than 100 miles away.

SPACE-A: Pax Term Building 419, 0730-1600, C-412-474-8163/8147, D-312-277-8163/8147, Fax: C-412-474-8156, D-312-277-8156.

LOGISTICAL SUPPORT:
Credit Union-474-8208
Exchange-424-8207
Travel Office-474-8197
Education Office-474-8519
Snack Bar-474-8737

ADMINISTRATIVE SUPPORT:
Fire Dept-911
Pass/ID Office-474-8274
Public Affairs-474-8750
Legal-474-8265
Police-474-8255

HEALTH & WELFARE:
Chapel-474-8204
Retiree Services-474-8558
Family Services-474-8544

REST & RECREATION:
Consolidated Mess-474-8227
Gym-474-8245
Fitness Center-474-8245
Services-474-8241

ATTRACTIONS: City of Pittsburgh, The Shops at Station Square, Carnegie Science Center, Carnegie Museum, The Boardwalk, the Gateway Clipper Fleetboats and a magnificent view of the city atop Mount Washington. Pittsburgh Pirates baseball, Penguins hockey, and Steelers football.

TOBYHANNA ARMY DEPOT (PA05R1)

ATTN: SIOTY-C
11 Hap Arnold Boulevard
Tobyhanna, PA 18466-5000

TELEPHONE NUMBER INFORMATION: Main installation numbers: C-717-895-7000, D-312-795-7000.

LOCATION: Take I-80 to I-380 west, exit 7 to depot. USMRA: Page 22 (I-4). NMC: Scranton, 24 miles northwest.

GENERAL INFORMATION: The Defense Department's largest facility for the repair, overhaul and fabrication of communications-electronics systems and equipment, including radio, radar and satellite communications systems.

TEMPORARY MILITARY LODGING: Lodging office, Building 1001, Admin Loop, 0800-1630 daily, C-717-895-7970, D-312-795-7970. All ranks. DV/VIP 717-895- 6223.

RV, CAMPING/FAMCAMP: None. See ARD&EC, Picatinny Arsenal, NJ listing, Lake Denmark Rec Area, C-201-724-4014, D-312-880-4014 or C-201-724-4484, D-312-880-4484.

SPACE-A: Army flights C-717-895-7000. Also see McGuire AFB, NJ listing, C-609-724-3078, D-312-440-3078, Fax: C-609-724-4623.

LOGISTICAL SUPPORT:
Barber Shop-895-7695
Carlson Wagonlit Travel-894-8025
Child Dev Center-895-6148
Commissary-895-7628
Dining Facilities-895-7045
Exchange-895-7716/7030
Snack Bar-895-7030
Cafeteria-895-7998
Child Care-895-6148
Class Six-895-7030
Credit Union-895-7368
Education Office-895-7697
Gas Station-895-7401

ADMINISTRATIVE SUPPORT:
Fire Dept-895-7300
Legal-895-7210
Pass/ID Office-895-7409
Public Affairs-895-7308
Housing Office-895-7970
Locator-895-7409
Police-895-7550

HEALTH & WELFARE:
ACS-895-7069
CHAMPUS-895-7225
Family Services-895-7069
Retiree Services-895-7019
Veterinary Services-895-7950
Army Emergency Relief-895-6128
Chapel-895-6397
Medical-895-7225
Clinic-895-7121
Emergency-911

REST & RECREATION:
Arts & Crafts-895-7634
Com Club-895-7045
Gym-895-7583
Library-895-7316
Outdoor Rec-895-7092
Youth Center-895-6156
Auto Hobby Shop-895-6609
Fitness Center-895-7583
ITT-895-7584
MWR-895-7584
Wood Hobby Shop-895-7650

ATTRACTIONS: Located in the Pocono Mountains of northeastern Pennsylvania. The Poconos are a four-season tourist and resort area.

WILLOW GROVE NAVAL AIR STATION/ JOINT RESERVE BASE (PA01R1)

ATTN: PAO
Willow Grove, PA 19090-5000

TELEPHONE NUMBER INFORMATION: Main installation numbers: C-215-443-1000, D-312-991-1000.

LOCATION: PA Turnpike, exit 27, to NAS. USMRA: Page 22 (I,J-6). NMC: Philadelphia, 21 miles south.

GENERAL INFORMATION: Naval Air Reserve Unit training.

TEMPORARY MILITARY LODGING: Lodging office, Building 609, 24 hours daily, C-215-442-5800, D-312-991-5800, Fax: C-215-442-5817. All ranks. DV/VIP 215-443-1776.

PENNSYLVANIA
Willow Grove Naval Air Station/Joint Reserve Base, continued

RV, CAMPING/FAMCAMP: Operates Lake Laurie Campground, NJ, C-215-443-6082, D-312-991-6082, two campers with full hookups.

SPACE-A: Pax Term/Lounge, Hangar 80, 0730-1600 Wed-Sun, C-215-433-6216/7, D-312-991-6216, Fax: C-215-443-6188, flights to CONUS and overseas.

LOGISTICAL SUPPORT:
Barber Shop-443-6030
Child Care-443-6080
Credit Union-674-1772
Exchange-443-6031
Postal Service-443-6023
Visitor Center-443-6033
Cafeteria-443-6282
Conv Store-443-6078
Dining Facilities-443-6282
Package Store-443-6078
Travel Office-443-6867

ADMINISTRATIVE SUPPORT:
CDO/OOD-443-6454
Housing Office-773-2114/6
Locator-443-1000
Police-443-6067
Quarter Deck-443-6454
Fire Dept-443-6198
Legal-443-6056
Pass/ID Office-443-1776
Public Affairs-443-1766
SDO-443-6454

HEALTH & WELFARE:
CHAMPUS-443-6351
Dental-443-6379
Chapel-443-6002
Family Services-443-6033
Medical
Central Appts-443-6372/3
Clinic-443-6360
Emergency-443-1600
Health Benefits-443-6351
Information-443-6360
N-MC Relief Society-443-6002
Retiree Services-443-6033
TRICARE-443-6351

REST & RECREATION:
Auto Hobby Shop-443-6087
Clubs
EM-443-6089
O-443-6081
Library-443-6095
Rec Equipment-ext 6066
Swimming-ext 6079
Bowling-ext 6092
Fitness Center-ext 6066
Gym-ext 6066
ITT-443-6082
MWR-443-6072/3
Services-443-6082

ATTRACTIONS: New Jersey beaches are a one and a half hour drive; Pocono Mountain resorts, a one hour drive.

Other Installations in Pennsylvania

Harrisburg International Airport (PA14R1), Middletown, PA 17057-5086. USMRA: Page 22 (G-6). C-717-948-2200. Exchange-948-2415, Medical-948-2234.
Philadelphia International Airport (PA16R1), 305th APS/Det 1, (AMC), Terminal D, Philadelphia, PA 19153-3701. Space-A: C-215-897-5600, D-312-443-5600, Fax: C-215-897-5647, D-312-443-5647.

RHODE ISLAND

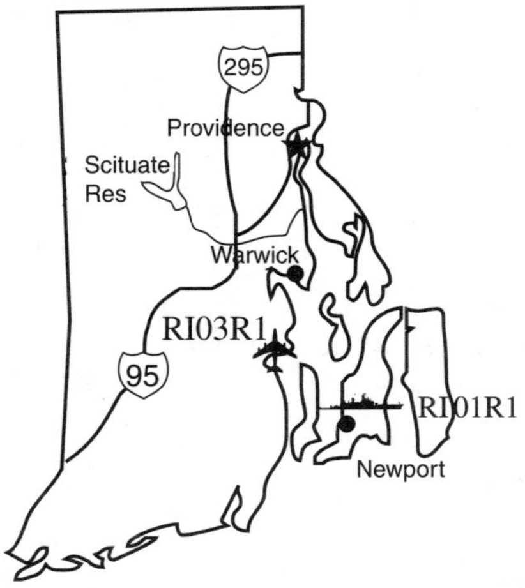

NEWPORT NAVAL EDUCATION AND TRAINING CENTER (RI01R1)

61 Capodanno Drive
Newport, RI 02841-1513

TELEPHONE NUMBER INFORMATION: Main installation numbers: C-401-841-2311, D-312-948-2311. HP: http://netc-nep.13f@smtp.cnet.navy.mil.

LOCATION: From US-1 exit to RI-138 east over Jamestown/Newport bridge (toll) to Newport. Follow signs to Navy Base, gate 1. USMRA: Page 17 (J-8), page 25 (B,C-1,2,3). NMC: Newport, adjacent.

GENERAL INFORMATION: Naval War College, Surface Warfare Officers School, Naval Justice School, Naval Hospital, Naval Undersea Warfare Center, other training and support activities.

TEMPORARY MILITARY LODGING: Lodging office, 24 hours daily; Building 684 (Officers) C-401-841-3156; Building 447 (EM), C-401-841-4410. Navy Lodge, Building 685, 0700-2300 daily, C-401-849-4500. All ranks. DV/VIP C-401-841-3715, Fax: C-401-849-3906.

RV, CAMPING/FAMCAMP: Carr Point Recreation Area, off base, Memorial Day Weekend-30 Sep, 656 Whipple Street, C-401-841-3116. Fax: C-401-841-4500. Six sites with W & E hookups.

SPACE-A: None. See Quonset State Airport listing, 0800-1600 Mon-Fri, C-401-866-1420.

LOGISTICAL SUPPORT:

Cafeteria-841-4445	Child Care-841-4562
Commissary-841-2111	Conv Store-846-2831
Exchange-841-1399	Package Store-846-3080
SATO-841-3710	SDO/NCO-841-3456
Snack Bar-846-7671/814	

ADMINISTRATIVE SUPPORT:

Legal-841-3766	Locator-841-3456
Police-841-3241/3242	Public Affairs-841-3538

HEALTH & WELFARE:

CHAMPUS-841-4309	Chapel-841-2234
Family Services-841-2283	Medical-841-7100
Retiree Services-841-4089	Emergency-841-3111

REST & RECREATION:

Auto Hobby Shop-ext 3026	Clubs
Gym-ext 3154	CPO-841-6160
ITT-841-3116	EM-841-3054
MWR-841-2643	O-846-2515
Rec Center-ext 4293	Rec Equipment-ext 2568
Swimming-ext 3957	Yacht Club-ext 3283

ATTRACTIONS: Beaches, Newport Music Festivals, Tennis Hall of Fame, mansion tours.

Other Installations in Rhode Island

Quonset Point State Airport (RI03R1), 1 Minuteman Way, North Kingstown, RI 02852-7502. USMRA: Page 17 (J-7). C-401-886-1420, NCO-886-1143, Space-A-886-1420.

SOUTH CAROLINA

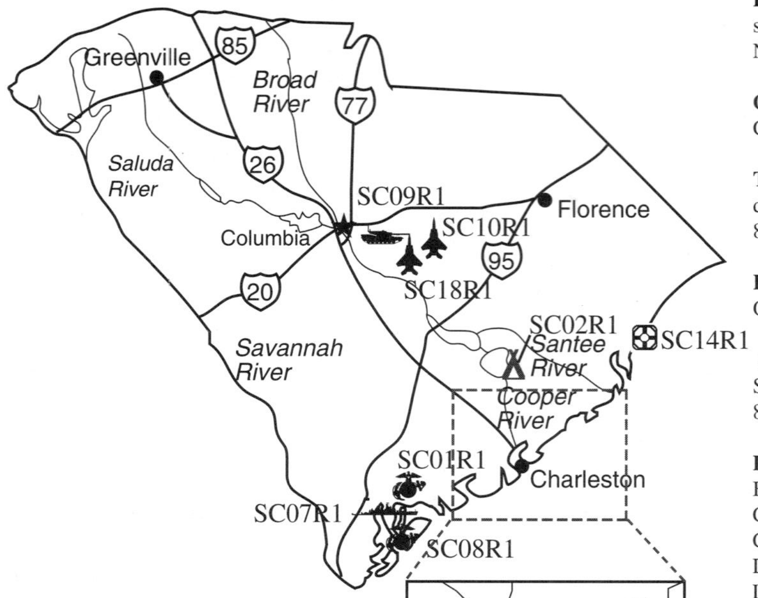

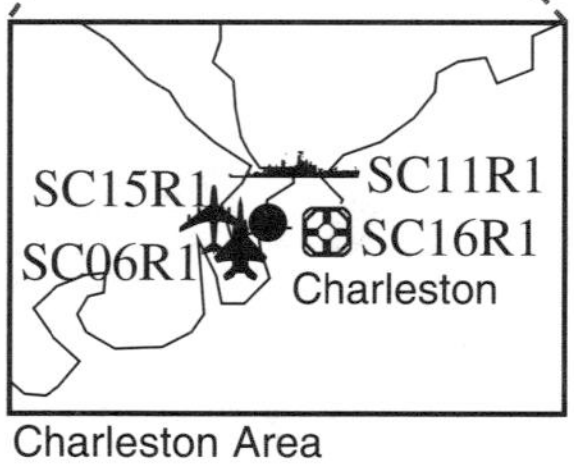

BEAUFORT NAVAL HOSPITAL (SC07R1)

1 Pinckney Boulevard
Beaufort, SC 29902-6148

TELEPHONE NUMBER INFORMATION: Main installation numbers: C-803-525-5600, D-312-832-5600.

LOCATION: From I-95, take any Beaufort exit and follow signs. USMRA: Page 44 (G-9). NMC: Savannah, 40 miles south.

TEMPORARY MILITARY LODGING: BEQ C-803-525-5418/9, D-312-832-5419, Fax: C-525-5320.

RV, CAMPING/FAMCAMP: None. See Charleston AFB listing, Shady Oaks Family Campground, C-803-566-5270, D-312-673-5270.

SPACE-A: None. See Beaufort MCAS listing, C-803-522-7110/7143, D-312-832-7110/7143, Fax: C-803-522-7221.

LOGISTICAL SUPPORT:
Exchange-525-5483
Mini Mart-525-5488

ADMINISTRATIVE SUPPORT: None. See Beaufort MCAS listing, C-803-522-7201.

HEALTH & WARFARE: Medical-525-5600

REST & RECREATION: None. See Beaufort MCAS listing, C-803-522-7400.

ATTRACTIONS: Beaches, seafood, period homes, Savannah, Charleston.

BEAUFORT MARINE CORPS AIR STATION (SC01R1)

P.O. Box 55001, Giger Boulevard
Beaufort Marine Corps Air Station, SC 29904-5001

TELEPHONE NUMBER INFORMATION: Main installation numbers: C-803-522-7023, D-312-832-7023.

LOCATION: From I-95 take Beaufort exit (SC-21 southeast) and follow signs. Sixteen miles to MCAS. Clearly marked. USMRA: Page 44 (G-9). NMC: Savannah, GA, 40 miles south.

GENERAL INFORMATION: Marine Aircraft Group-31, Marine Air Control Squadron-2, Marine Corps Support Squadron-273.

TEMPORARY MILITARY LODGING: BOQ, Building 431, 24 hours daily, C-803-522-7676/7658, D-312-832-7676/7658. All ranks. DV/VIP C-803-522-7158. DeTreville House 522-1663.

RV, CAMPING/FAMCAMP: None. See Charleston AFB listing, Shady Oaks Family Campground, C-803-566-5270, D-312-673-5270.

SPACE-A: Pax Term/Lounge, Building 860, 0700-2300 Mon-Fri, 1000-1800 Sat, 1200-2000 Sun, C-803-522-7110/7143, D-312-832-7110/7143, Fax: C-803-522-7221, flights to CONUS and OCONUS locations.

LOGISTICAL SUPPORT:
Barber shop-522-6130
Cafeteria-522-7895
Conv Store-522-7615
Dry Cleaner-522-6107
Laundry-522-6107
Gas Station-522-7727
Postal Service
  Mil-522-6053/7220
  US-522-7003
Beauty Shop-522-6130
Child Care-522-7290
Credit Union-522-7751/7652
Exchange-522-7627
Education Office-522-7754
Package Store-522-7627
Snack Bar-522-7895
Travel Office-522-7820

ADMINISTRATIVE SUPPORT:
Fire Dept-7293
Legal-522-7330
OOD-522-7017
Police-522-7373/7589
SDO-522-7121
Housing Office-522-7065
Locator-522-7100
Pass/ID Office-522-7750/7941
Public Affairs-522-7201

HEALTH & WELFARE:
CHAMPUS-525-5343/9415
Dental-522-7512
Medical-522-7495
  Emergency-522-7311
Chapel-522-7775
Family Services-522-7353

REST & RECREATION:
Auto Hobby Shop-522-7586
Gym-522-7192
ITT-522-6375/6377/7340
Library-522-7682
Marina-522-7472
Picnic Area-522-6099
Stables-846-2644
Theater-522-7183
Clubs
  NCO-522-7543/7726
  O-522-7541/7561
  The Club-522-7534/7726
MWR-522-7400
RV Rental-522-7472
Swimming-522-7524

ATTRACTIONS: Beaches, seafood, period homes, Savannah, Charleston.

CHARLESTON AIR FORCE BASE (SC06R1)

102 East Hill Boulevard, Room 223
Charleston Air Force Base, SC 29404-5154

TELEPHONE NUMBER INFORMATION: Main installation numbers: C-803-566-6000, D-312-673-6000. E-mail: @charleston.af.mil.

LOCATION: From I-26 East, exit to West Aviation Avenue to traffic light, continue through light to second light right, follow road around end of runway to gate 2 (Rivers Gate). USMRA: Page 44 (H-8,9). NMC: Charleston, 10 miles southeast.

GENERAL INFORMATION: Air Mobility Command Base. Active Duty Airlift Wing, Air Force Reserve Airlift Wing and Air National Guard Fighter Detachment.

SOUTH CAROLINA
Charleston Air Force Base, continued

TEMPORARY MILITARY LODGING: Lodging office, Building 322, Simpson Street & Davis Drive, 24 hours daily, C-803-556-3806, (552-9900-room number after duty hours) D-312-673-3806. All ranks.

RV, CAMPING/FAMCAMP: Shady Oaks Family Campground on base, year round, C-803-566-5270, D-312-673-5270, 23 camper spaces with W/E hookups.

SPACE-A: Pax Term/Lounge, Building 164, 0500-2300 daily, C-803-566-3082, D-312-673-3082, Fax: C-803-566-3060, flights to CONUS and overseas.

LOGISTICAL SUPPORT:
Child Care-566-4366
Exchange-552-5000
Package Store-767-4594
Travel-566-3091
Commissary-566-5709/5696
Gas Station-767-4594
Shoppette-767-4594

ADMINISTRATIVE SUPPORT:
Fire Dept-566-3118/3777
Legal-566-5502
Pass/ID Office-566-4514
Public Affairs-566-5608
Housing Office-566-3859
Locator-566-3282
Police-566-3600

HEALTH & WELFARE:
Air Force Aid Society-566-4414
Chapel-566-2536
Family services-566-4406
Medical-566-6750
Central Appts-743-3709
Emergency-743-7011
Health Benefits-566-3971
American Red Cross-566-3377
Dental-566-6892
Retiree Services-566-2228
TRICARE-566-6706
Veterinary Services-566-4264

REST & RECREATION:
Arts & Crafts-ext 4936
Bowling-ext 3315
Golf Course-566-4174
MWR-566-3800
Swimming-ext 5271
Theater-566-3333
Auto Hobby Shop-ext 4942
Fitness Center-ext 3347
Library-ext 3320
O'Club-566-3920
Tennis-ext 3347
Youth Center-ext 5684

ATTRACTIONS: Beautiful sandy beaches, period homes, gardens.

CHARLESTON COAST GUARD BASE (SC16R1)

196 Tradd Street
Charleston, SC 29401-1899

TELEPHONE NUMBER INFORMATION: Main installation numbers: C-803-724-7600/723-9378, D-312-794-2086/563-2086.

LOCATION: In downtown Charleston. USMRA: Page 44 (H-9). NMC: Charleston, in city limits.

GENERAL INFORMATION: Performs search-and-rescue operations.

TEMPORARY MILITARY LODGING: None. See Charleston AFB listing, C-803-556-3806, D-312-673-3806.

RV, CAMPING/FAMCAMP: None. See Charleston AFB listing, Shady Oaks Family Campground, C-803-566-5270, D-312-673-5270.

SPACE-A: None. See Charleston AFB listing, C-803-803-566-3082, D-312-673-3082, Fax: C-803-566-3060.

LOGISTICAL SUPPORT:
Exchange-722-8817/8421
Package Store-722-8817

ADMINISTRATIVE SUPPORT:
CDO/OOD-724-7619/76
Locator-724-7608

HEALTH & WELFARE:
CHAMPUS-724-7653
Medical-724-7653
Chapel-720-7723

REST & RECREATION:
Clubs
EM-724-7674
NCO-724-7674

ATTRACTIONS: Charleston "One of America's most historic cities" features miles of beautiful, sandy beaches, gardens, fresh water lakes, great fishing.

CHARLESTON NAVAL WEAPONS STATION (SC11R1)

2316 Red Bank Road, Suite 100
Goose Creek, SC 29445-8601

TELEPHONE NUMBER INFORMATION: Main installation numbers: C-803-764-7901, D-312-794-7901.

LOCATION: Exit 205 off I-26, east on US-78, to US-52, to SC-37 E (Red Bank Road) to main gate. USMRA: Page 44 (H-8,9). NMC: Charleston, 25 miles south.

GENERAL INFORMATION: Provides materiel and technical support for ammunition and assigned weapons and weapon systems. It operates an explosive ordnance out-loading facility. Manages Navy family housing for Charleston area.

TEMPORARY MILITARY LODGING: BEQ/BOQ C-803-764-7646. Also, see Charleston Air Force Base listing, C-803-556-3806, D-312-673-3806.

RV, CAMPING/FAMCAMP: None. See Charleston AFB listing, Shady Oaks Family Campground, C-803-566-5270, D-312-673-5270.

SPACE-A: None. See Charleston AFB listing, C-803-566-3082, D-312-673-3082, Fax: C-803-566-3060.

LOGISTICAL SUPPORT:
Child Care-764-7408
Exchange-764-7042
Package Store-764-7314
Commissary-764-7015
Gas Station-764-7573

ADMINISTRATIVE SUPPORT:
Police-764-7771

HEALTH & WELFARE:
Chapel-764-7222
Medical
Clinic-764-7634
Hospital-525-7000
Family Services-764-7294

REST & RECREATION:
Gym/Fitness Center-764-7530
MWR-764-7601

OTHER FACILITIES AVAILABLE: Bowling, Golf course, Hunting/fishing, Picnic Area, Racquetball, Swimming and Theater.

ATTRACTIONS: Historic Charleston (25 miles south), and scenic Myrtle Beach (100 miles northeast).

FORT JACKSON (SC09R1)

US Army Training Center & Fort Jackson
ATTN: ATZJ-GC
Percival Road
Fort Jackson, SC 29207-5060

SOUTH CAROLINA
Fort Jackson, continued

TELEPHONE NUMBER INFORMATION: Main installation numbers: C-803-751-7511, D-312-734-1117. E-mail: pao@jackson-emhl.army.mil.

LOCATION: Exit from I-20 north of fort, or from US-76/378 at the main gate. From I-20 and I-77 interchange take newly constructed Beltway to Percival Road, right onto Percival Road to Gate 2. USMRA: Page 44 (G-6). NMC: Columbia, 12 miles southwest.

GENERAL INFORMATION: Two Training Brigades for training recruits, one Combat Service Support Training (AIT) Brigade, Army Reception Station, and Reserve Command, US Army Soldier Support Institute, US Army Chaplain Center and School.

TEMPORARY MILITARY LODGING: Kennedy Hall, Building 2785, Semmes & Lee Rd, 24 hours daily, C-803-751-6223/6149, D-312-734-6223/6149. Palmetto Lodge, Building 6000 C-803-751-5205/4429, D-312-734-5205/4429. All ranks. DV/VIP C-803-751-6618, D-312-734-5218.

RV, CAMPING/FAMCAMP: Weston Lake Recreation Area & Travel Camp on post, year round, C-803-751-5253, D-312-734-5253, 13 camper spaces with full hookups, five camper spaces with W/E, 10 tent spaces with W/E, seven cabins.

SPACE-A: None. See Charleston AFB listing, C-803-566-3082, D-312-673-3082, Fax: C-803-566-3060.

LOGISTICAL SUPPORT:

Child Care-751-6222/6221	Commissary-751-2789
Conv Store-782-0590	Exchange-787-1950
Gas Station-782-1639	Package Store-782-1601
Retiree Services-751-6715	SDO/NCO-751-7611
Snack Bar-751-4759	Travel-782-5121

ADMINISTRATIVE SUPPORT:

Fire Dept-751-7217	Housing Office-751-5306
Legal-751-4287	Locator-751-7671
Pass/ID Office-751-6020	Police-751-3113
Public Affairs-751-6719	

HEALTH & WELFARE:

American Red Cross-751-4329	ACS-751-5256
Army Emergency Relief-751-4518	CHAMPUS-751-2425
Chapel-751-3121	Dental-751-6625
Family Services-751-5256	Medical
Retiree Services-751-6652	Clinic-751-4733
TRICARE-751-CARE	Emergency-751-2169
Veterinary Services-751-4390	Hospital-751-2117
	Information-751-5308

REST & RECREATION:

Arts & Crafts-ext 6359	Auto Hobby Shop-ext 5755
Bowling-ext 4656	Clubs
Fitness Center-751-5896	NCO-782-1932
Golf course-ext 4344	O-787-4906
Gym-ext 6258	Riding-ext 6357
Indoor Rec-751-4057	ITT-751-6219
Library-ext 5589	Marinas-751-7865
MWR-782-8876	Outdoor Rec-ext 4948
Picnic Area-ext 6606/4215	Rec Center-ext 5743/4057
Rec Equipment-ext 5481	Rifle Range-ext 6954
Swimming-ext 4796/7472/7084	Theater-751-7488
Wood Hobby Shop-751-3910	Youth Center-751-6387
Youth Services-751-5040	

ATTRACTIONS: Outdoor sports and recreation. Columbia, the state capital. Ernie Pyle Media Center located on Fort Jackson, a memorial to the slain World War II correspondent, Finance Corps Museum, Adjunct General Corps Museum. Museum traces South Carolina and Fort Jackson history.

McENTIRE AIR NATIONAL GUARD BASE (SC18R1)

1325 South Carolina Road
Eastover, SC 29044-5017

TELEPHONE NUMBER INFORMATION: Main installation number: C-803-776-5121, D-312-583-8301.

LOCATION: On SC highway 378 between Sumter and Columbia. USMRA: Page 44 (G-6,7). NMC: Columbia, 15 miles west.

GENERAL INFORMATION: 169th Tactical Fighter Group, 240th Combat Communications Squadron.

TEMPORARY MILITARY LODGING: None. See Shaw Air Force Base listing, C-803-668-3210, or 1-800-769-7429.

RV, CAMPING/FAMCAMP: None. See Fort Jackson, Weston Lake Rec Area and Travel Camp listing, C-803-751-5253, D-312-734-5253.

SPACE-A: C-803-695-6210, D-312-583-8210.

LOGISTICAL SUPPORT: Exchange-695-6517

ADMINISTRATIVE SUPPORT:

Fire Dept-695-6287	Legal-695-6210
Public Affairs-695-6208	Police-695-6284

HEALTH & WELFARE:

Chapel-695-6265	Medical-695-6296

REST & RECREATION:

Clubs
EM-695-6326
NCO-695-6326
O-695-6326

ATTRACTIONS: Charleston, Myrtle Beach 100 miles., Columbia: State Capital, State Fairgrounds, gardens, zoo.

PARRIS ISLAND MARINE CORPS RECRUIT DEPOT (SC08R1)

ATTN: PAO
Building 283, Boulevard De France
Parris Island, SC 29905-0059

TELEPHONE NUMBER INFORMATION: Main installation numbers: C-803-525-2111, D-312-832-2111.

LOCATION: From I-95 south, exit at Beaufort to SC-170 or US-21, both east to SC-280 to SC-281 which leads to main gate of depot. USMRA: Page 44 (G-10). NMC: Savannah, GA 43 miles southwest.

GENERAL INFORMATION: Recruit Depot for USMC male recruits east of Mississippi and all female recruits.

TEMPORARY MILITARY LODGING: Billeting, 24 hours daily, C-803-525-2976/3460, D-312-832-2976/3460: Building 200 (Hostess House), Building 254 (TLQ), Building 331 (BEQ), Building 289 (BOQ). All ranks. DV/VIP C-803-525-2594.

RV, CAMPING/FAMCAMP: None. See Charleston AFB listing, Shady Oaks Family Campground, C-803-566-5270, D-312-673-5270.

SPACE-A: None. See Beaufort MCAS listing, C-803-522-7110/7143, D-312-832-7110/7143, Fax: C-803-522-7221.

LOGISTICAL SUPPORT: *Note: in order to access an extension for any of the following numbers, you must first dial 525-3302.*

Bank-525-1161	Barber Shop-525-3550

SOUTH CAROLINA
Parris Island Marine Corps Recruit Depot, continued

Beauty Shop-525-3270
Commissary-525-2679
Credit Union-525-3801
Exchange-525-3301
Package Store-525-3611
SATO-525-2627
Travel Office-525-2410
Child Care-525-3514
Conv Store-ext 7351
Dry Cleaner-ext 7320
Gas Station-ext 7351
Postal Service-525-2812
Snack Bar-525-4578
Visitor Center-525-3650

ADMINISTRATIVE SUPPORT:
Fire Dept-525-3637
Legal-525-2559
Pass/ID Office-525-2478
Public Affairs-525-3276
Housing Office-525-2853
Locator-525-3358
Police-525-2478
SDO-525-3712

HEALTH & WELFARE:
CHAMPUS-525-5343
Dental-525-3725
Medical
Clinic-525-2617
Emergency-525-3351
Hospital-525-5301
Chapel-522-3533
Family Services-525-3791
Veterinary Services-525-3317

REST & RECREATION:
Auto Hobby Shop-ext 7321
Clubs
Com-525-3302
E-ext 7367
SNCO-ext 7344
O-525-2905
Rod/Gun-525-3635
MWR-525-3302
Swimming-ext 7339/6/7
Bowling-ext 7324
Ceramics Hobby Shop-ext-7322
Fitness Center-ext 7360
Golf Course-525-2240
ITT-525-3302 ext 7341
Library-ext 7327
Marinas-ext 7370
Special Services-525-3301
Theater-525-3302 ext 7325

ATTRACTIONS: Weekly recruit graduations at 9:15 AM most Fridays. Museum on base. Visitors Center Building 283.

SHAW AIR FORCE BASE (SC10R1)

205th Fighter Wing/PA
517 Lance Avenue
Shaw Air Force Base, SC 29152-5000

TELEPHONE NUMBER INFORMATION: Main installation numbers: C-803-668-8110, D-312-965-1110. HP: http://www.shaw.af.mil.

LOCATION: Off US-76/378, eight miles west of Sumter. Clearly marked. USMRA: Page 44 (H-6). NMC: Columbia, 35 miles west.

GENERAL INFORMATION: Air Combat Command. 9th Air Force Headquarters, 20th Fighter Wing.

TEMPORARY MILITARY LODGING: Lodging office, Building 471, Myers Street, 24 hours daily, C-803-668-3210, D-312-965-3210. Switchboard, C-803-666-3658, D-312-965-3210. All ranks. DV/VIP C-803-668-3210.

RV, CAMPING/FAMCAMP: Operates Wateree Recreation Area off base, 39 miles west of post. See Wateree Recreation Area listing for more information.

SPACE-A: Building 1578, Base Ops, 0800-1500 daily, C-803-668-3818, D-312-965-3818, Fax: C-803-668-4156, D-312-965-2796, infrequent flights to CONUS locations.

LOGISTICAL SUPPORT:
Child Care-668-2305
Conv Store-666-3215
Gas Station-666-3140
SATO-668-3644/3293
Commissary-668-3207
Exchange-666-3481
Package Store-666-3167
Snack Bar-666-2115

ADMINISTRATIVE SUPPORT:
CDO/OOD-668-3330
Locator-668-2811
Public Affairs-668-3621
Legal-668-2505
Police-668-3200

HEALTH & WELFARE:
CHAMPUS-668-2589
Family Services-668-3533
Retiree Services-668-3036
Chapel-668-3224
Medical-668-2571
Central Appts-668-2778
Emergency-668-2571

REST & RECREATION:
Arts & Crafts-ext 2362
Bowling-ext 3553
Fitness Center-ext 2941
Golf course-ext 3950
Library-ext 3084
Rec Center-ext 2205
Rod/Gun Club-ext 2492
Theater-668-3914
Auto Hobby Shop-ext 2929
Clubs
Aero-ext 2057
EM/NCO-666-3651
O-666-3661
Rec Equip-ext 2204
Swimming-ext 3520
Youth Center-ext 5420

ATTRACTIONS: Sumter Iris Gardens. Columbia is an easy drive. Myrtle Beach is a one-and-a-half hour drive. Outdoor sports and recreation.

SHORT STAY NAVY OUTDOOR RECREATION AREA (SC02R1)

211 Short Stay Road
Moncks Corner, SC 29461-5000

TELEPHONE NUMBER INFORMATION: Main installation numbers: 1-800-447-2178, C-803-761-8353, 803-743-1366.

LOCATION: On Lake Moultrie. Take US-52 north from Charleston. Follow the signs. USMRA: page 44 (H-8). NMI: Charleston Naval Station, 35 miles south. NMC: Charleston, 30 miles south.

DESCRIPTION OF AREA: Situated on a 55-acre peninsula at southern tip of Lake Moultrie. Excellent freshwater fishing. Family programs and activities during summer months. Season of Operation: year round. Military personnel active, retired, reserve and DoD civilians. Check in 1500, check out 1100. Reservations: Accepted (minimum age 21). Write for brochure. No pets allowed in villas or cabins; allowed on leash in campground. Admission fee for day users.

TEMPORARY MILITARY LODGING: Villas: three bedroom, sleeps six, fully equipped, including kitchen, private bath, cable TV. Soap and other personal items are not provided (12), two bedroom, sleeps four, fully equipped, including kitchen, private bath, cable TV. Soap and other personal items are not provided (24); Cabins, two bedroom, sleeps four, fully equipped, including kitchen, private bath, cable TV. Soap and other personal items are not provided (6); Log cabins, sleeps two, AC/heated, outdoor cooking grill and picnic table is provided, public bath and restroom facilities(5). Two two-bedroom villas and one cabin are equipped for the physically challenged. Rates: Villas: three bedroom $51-$62 daily, two bedroom $40-$50 daily; cabins $55-$66 daily; log cabins $18-$22 daily. Rates vary depending on status of sponsor and season; weekly and monthly rates.

RV, CAMPING/FAMCAMP: Waterfront RV/Camper spaces with W&E hookups (13); wooded camper spaces with W&E hookups (70); primitive camper/tent spaces with no hookups (25). Rates: waterfront $9-$15 daily; wooded $5-$12 daily; primitive $2.50-$9 daily. Rates vary depending on status of sponsor and season; weekly and monthly rates.

REST & RECREATION: Boating, Fishing, Horseshoes, Swimming, Volleyball.

OTHER SUPPORT & FACILITIES AVAILABLE: Bait/Fishing Tackle, Beach, Boat Rental, Conference Center*, Convenience Store, Fishing License Sales, Fishing Pier, Game Room, Gas, Laundry, Marina, Miniature Golf,

SOUTH CAROLINA
Short Stay Navy Outdoor Recreation Area, continued

Pavilions*, Picnic Areas, Playground, Sewage Dump, Showers, Snack Bar. Also, see Charleston Naval Weapons Station, C-803-764-7901, D-312-794-7901.

** Conference Room/seats 200; four Pavilions/seat 200-375*

ATTRACTIONS: Freshwater fishing, boating, sun and fun.

WATEREE RECREATION AREA (SC05R1)

Highway 97
Camden, SC 29020-5000

TELEPHONE NUMBER INFORMATION: Main installation numbers: C-803-668-8110, D-312-965-1110.

LOCATION: On Hwy 97. USMRA: page 44 (G-5). NMC: Columbia, 35 miles south. NMI: Shaw AFB, 39 miles east.

GENERAL INFORMATION: Situated in peaceful, quiet, 24-acre, wooded area bordering Lake Wateree. Operated by Shaw Air Force Base, off base year round. Military personnel active, retired, ANG, reserves and DoD civilians. Check in at Shaw AFB Outdoor Recreation 0800-1800 Sun-Thu, 0800-1900 Sat-Sun and holidays. Site office closed 2200-0600. Reservations: For cabins, available up to 60 days in advance for AD stationed at Shaw AFB. Reservation must be made in person. All others, up to 45 days in advance and by phone. Address: Outdoor Recreation, P.O. Box 52696, Shaw AFB, SC 29152-5000. C-803-668-3245/2204, D-312-965-3245. (Wateree Rec Area phone number is C-803-432-7976). Visa and MasterCard accepted. Restrictions: No pets allowed in cabins or on decks. Pets allowed on leash in camping area. Roped-off swimming area with sandy beach. Firearms allowed only during hunting season with notification of Site Manager at area.

TEMPORARY MILITARY LODGING: Cabins: two bedroom, fully equipped, including TV/VCR, linens, dishes, pots & pans, and microwave (11-eight small, three large); three bedroom, fully equipped, including TV/VCR, linens, dishes, pots & pans, and microwave (1). Handicap accessible. Rates: two bedroom $50 daily (small), $55 daily large; three bedroom $75 daily.

RV, CAMPING/FAMCAMP: Camper Spaces with W&E hookups (15); tent spaces with no hookups (unlimited). Rates: camper spaces $10; tent spaces $5.

REST & RECREATION: Fishing/license, Swimming, Water Skiing.

OTHER SUPPORT & FACILITIES AVAILABLE: Bait/Retail, Bathhouse, Boat Launch, Boat Rental, Boat Storage, Boat Tie-up Docks, Check-out Store, Grills, Ice, Fishing, Marina, Pavilions, Picnic Area, Playground, Pontoon Boat/Rental, Rec Room (New), Restrooms, Sewage Dump, Showers, Ski Rental, Water Sports Equipment Rental. Also, see Shaw Air Force Base listing, C-803-668-8110, D-312-965-1110.

ATTRACTIONS: Peaceful, back to nature surroundings.

Other Installations in South Carolina

Charleston International Airport (SC15R1), Suite 124, 5500 International Boulevard, Charleston, SC 29418-6924. USMRA: Page 44. (H-9). C-803-566-5794/5, Space A-566-5794/5795.
Georgetown Coast Guard Station Exchange (SC14R1), 355 Marina Drive, Georgetown, SC 29440-2412. USMRA: Page 45 (J-7). C-803-520-4116.

SOUTH DAKOTA

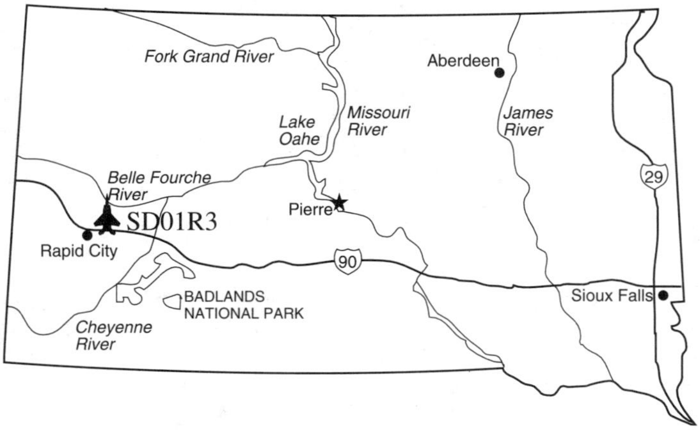

ELLSWORTH AIR FORCE BASE (SD01R3)

1958 Scott Drive, Suite 1
Ellsworth Air Force Base, SD 57706-4710

TELEPHONE NUMBER INFORMATION: Main installation numbers: C-605-385-1000, D-312-675-1000.

LOCATION: Two miles north of I-90, exit 66. Seven miles east of Rapid City. Clearly marked. USMRA: Page 85 (B-5). NMC: Rapid City, 7 miles west.

GENERAL INFORMATION: Air Combat Command Base, 28th Bomb Wing, B-1B base.

TEMPORARY MILITARY LODGING: Billeting Office, Building 1103, Risner Drive, 24 hours daily, C-605-385-2844, D-312-675-2844. All ranks. DV/VIP C-605-385-1205, D-312-675-1205.

RV, CAMPING/FAMCAMP: FAMCAMP on base, 15 May-15 Oct, C-605-385-2997/9, D-312-675-2997/9, 24 camper spaces with full hookups, 12 camper spaces with E hookups, 12 tent spaces.

SPACE-A: Pax Term/Lounge, Building 7510, 0700-1630 hours C-605-385-1181, D-312-675-1181, Fax: C-605-385-2161, flights to CONUS, OCONUS and overseas locations.

LOGISTICAL SUPPORT:

Cafeteria-923-1623	Child Care-385-2488
Commissary-385-4364	Conv Store-923-5231
Exchange-923-4774	Gas Station-923-1489
Package Store-923-6220	SATO-923-1466
Theater-385-1684/1685	Visitor Center-385-2894

ADMINISTRATIVE SUPPORT:

Legal-385-2329	Locator-385-1379
Police-385-4001	Public Affairs-385-5056

HEALTH & WELFARE:

CHAMPUS-385-3259	Chapel-385-1597/7630
Family Services-385-1348	Medical-385-7630
Retiree Services-385-5050	Central Appts-385-3333

REST & RECREATION:

Arts & Crafts 385-2899	Auto Hobby Shop-ext 2900
Bowling-ext 2536	Consolidated Club-385-1764
Fitness Center-ext 2266	Golf Course-923-4999
Library-ext 1686	MWR-385-1315
Recreation-385-1613	Rec Center-ext 1613

ATTRACTIONS: Air and Space Museum, and three small fishing lakes on base, Black Hills, Badlands, Deadwood (Casinos), and Mt Rushmore nearby. An outdoor sports and recreation paradise.

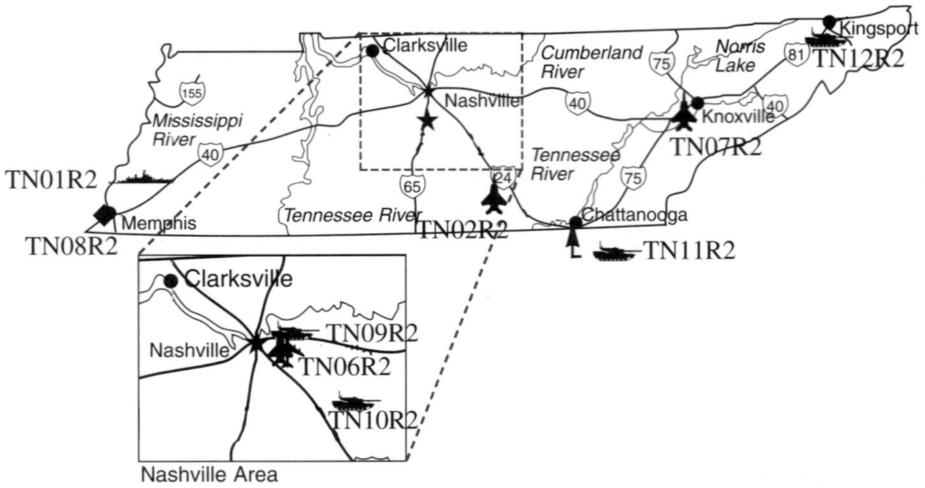

TENNESSEE

ARNOLD AIR FORCE BASE (TN02R2)

100 Kindel Drive, Suite B213
Arnold Air Force Base, TN 37389-2213

TELEPHONE NUMBER INFORMATION: Main installation numbers: C-615-454-3000, D-312-340-5011.

LOCATION: From US-231 north of Huntsville, take TN-55 east to AEDC access highway in Tullahoma. From I-24 take AEDC exit 117, four miles south of Manchester. Clearly marked. USMRA: Page 41 (I-9). NMC: Chattanooga, 65 miles southeast; Nashville, 65 miles northwest.

GENERAL INFORMATION: Air Force Materiel Command. Arnold Engineering Development Center, nation's largest complex of wind tunnels, altitude rocket test cells, space environment chambers, and other related R&D test and evaluation facilities.

TEMPORARY MILITARY LODGING: Lodging office, Building 3027, 0600-2200 Mon-Fri, 1000-2000 Sat, 1200-2200 Sun, C-615-454-3099, D-312-340-3099. All ranks.

RV, CAMPING/FAMCAMP: FAMCAMP on base, 1 Apr-1 Oct, C-615-454-6084, D-312-340-6084, 26 camper spaces with W/E hookups, 57 tent spaces.

SPACE-A: None. See Nashville IAP/Tennessee ANGB listing, C-615-399-6581, D-312-340-6581.

LOGISTICAL SUPPORT:
Commissary-455-7249
Travel-454-4798
Exchange-455-7153

ADMINISTRATIVE SUPPORT:
Fire Dept-454-56548
Locator-454-3000
Public Affairs-454-5586
Legal-454-7153/7814
Police-454-5222
SDO/NCO-454-7752

HEALTH & WELFARE:
CHAMPUS-454-5351
Medical-454-5351
Chapel-454-3470
Retiree Services-454-4574

REST & RECREATION:
All Ranks Club-454-3090
Boat Rental-ext 6084
Golf Course-455-5870
Sailing-ext 6084
Arts & Crafts-ext 6084
Fitness Center-454-6440
ITT-454-3128
Tennis-ext 6084

ATTRACTIONS: Chattanooga and Lookout Mountains are an easy drive southeast. Home of Grand Ole Opry, Opryland, Nashville.

MEMPHIS NAVAL SUPPORT ACTIVITY (TN01R2)

7800 Third Avenue
Millington, TN 38054-5045

TELEPHONE NUMBER INFORMATION: Main installation numbers: C-901-874-5111, D-312-882-5111.

LOCATION: From US-51 N, follow signs. USMRA: Page 40 (B-9,10). NMC: Memphis, 11 miles southwest.

GENERAL INFORMATION: Support Facility Providing Logistical Support to Approximately 30 Tenant Commands (Army, Navy, Air Force).

TEMPORARY MILITARY LODGING: Lodging office, 24 hours daily, C-901-874-7082, D-312-882-7082. Reservations: BOQ C-901-874-5345 or 901-872-6317, BEQ C-901-874-5459. All ranks. DV/VIP, C-901-874-5101. Navy Lodge, Building N-931, all ranks. Reservations 1-800-NAVY-INN. Lodge number is C-901-872-0121, Fax: C-901-873-1695.

RV, CAMPING/FAMCAMP: Navy Lake Recreational Area, on base, year round, MWR Dept, Memphis NAS, P.O. Box 54278, 7800 Third Avenue, Millington, TN 38054-0278, C-901-872-5151/3660, D-312-882-5163, Fax: C-901-874-5690, D-312-882-5690. E-mail: mwrfun@vantek.net. Twelve camper spaces with full hookups, some tent space.

SPACE-A: Limited. C-901-874-5111, D-312-966-5111.

LOGISTICAL SUPPORT:
Barber Shop-872-2191
Child Care-874-5745/5786
Commissary-872-5122
Credit Union-873-2300
Dry Cleaner-872-7259
Exchange-872-7716/0138
Gas Station-872-2610
Package Store-872-1660
SATO-872-0104
Beauty Shop-873-4962
Child Dev Center-874-5745
Conv Store-872-1334
Dining Facilities-874-5132
Education Office-874-5109
Family Services-874-5075
Laundry-872-7259
Postal Service-874-5577
Travel Office-874-5303

ADMINISTRATIVE SUPPORT:
Fire Dept-874-5580
Legal-874-5251
OOD-874-5509
Police-874-5533
Quarter Deck-874-5509
Housing Office-874-5547
Locator-874-5111
Pass/ID Office-874-5783
Public Affairs-874-5761

HEALTH & WELFARE
American Red Cross-874-5607
Chapel-874-5341
Family Services-874-5075
Medical
  Clinic-874-5204
  Health Benefits-874-5824
  Information-1-800-700-8607
TRICARE-1-800-700-8607
CHAMPUS-874-5824
Dental-874-5363
  Central Appts-874-5361
  Clinic-874-5363
  Emergency-481-4520
N-MC Relief Society-872-7266
Retiree Services-874-5195
Veterinary services-874-5858

REST & RECREATION:
Arts & Crafts-874-5507
Bowling-ext 5779
Golf course-ext 5168
Gym-ext 5383
Auto Hobby Shop-874-5675
Clubs-874-5132
  Consol-874-5132
  Rod/Gun-ext 5665

ITT-874-5303	Library-ext 5683
MWR-874-5136	Outdoor Rec-874-5163
Stables-ext 5301	Swimming-ext 5187
Tennis-ext 5163	Youth Center-874-5155

ATTRACTIONS: Graceland, Peabody Hotel, Mud Island, Libertyland, The Orpheum, Overton Square, Memphis Zoo, and historic Beale Street..."Home of the Blues."

TENNESSEE NATIONAL GUARD ARMORY, HOUSTON BARRACKS (TN09R2)

P.O. Box 41502
3041 Sidco Drive
Nashville, TN 37204-1502

TELEPHONE NUMBER INFORMATION: Main installation numbers: C-615-513-0662, D-312-683-0662. E-mail: paotn@tn-mgnet.army.mil. HP: http://www.state.tn.us/military.

LOCATION: I-65 south, to Armory Drive exit, USMRA: Page 40 (G,H-8). NMC: Nashville, four miles northwest.

GENERAL INFORMATION: Headquarters Tennessee Army National Guard and Tennessee Air National Guard.

TEMPORARY MILITARY LODGING: None. See Fort Campbell, KY listing, C-502-798-5281/618. Reservations C-615-431-5107, D-312-635-2865.

RV, CAMPING/FAMCAMP: None. See Fort Campbell, KY listing, Destiny Parks and Pavilions (Army Travel Camp), C-502-798-3126/5590, D-312-635-3126/5590.

SPACE-A: None. See Nashville IAP/Tennessee ANGB listing, C-615-399-6581, D-312-340-6581.

LOGISTICAL SUPPORT:

Carlson Wagonlit Travel-313-0556	Exchange-313-0531

ADMINISTRATIVE SUPPORT: Legal-313-0659

HEALTH & WELFARE: Family Services-313-0541

REST & RECREATION: None. See Fort Campbell, KY listing, C-502-798-2917.

ATTRACTIONS: Opryland, Grand Ole Opry, The Hermitage (home of Andy Jackson) and "The District."

Other Installations in Tennessee

Chattanooga Armory Exchange (TN11R2), 1801 Holtz Claw Avenue, Chattanooga, TN 37404-5000. USMRA: Page 41 (J-10). C-423-265-8941.
Defense Distribution Region Central (TN08R2), 2163 Airways Boulevard, Memphis, TN 38114-5210. USMRA: Page 40 (A-10), page 51 (B-3). C-901-775-6011, Consol Club-775-2440, Exchange-775-2343. Golf Shop, Post Office.
Kingsport Site Exchange (TN12R2), 4401 W Stone Drive, Kingsport, TN 37660-1050. USMRA: Page 41 (O-7). C-423-247-8721.
McGhee Tyson Air National Guard Base (TN07R2), 134th Air Refueling Wing, 134 Briscoe Drive, McGhee Tyson ANGB, TN 37777-6200. C-423-985-3210, D-312-588-3210. From US-129, take McGhee Tyson Airport exit. Clearly Marked. USMRA: Page 41 (L-8). NMC: Knoxville, 10 miles north. Exchange-985-3400, Space-A-985-4403/4419, TML-985-3300.
Nashville IAP/Tennessee ANGB (TN06R2), 240 Knapp Boulevard, Nashville, TN 37217-2538. USMRA: Page 40 (G, H-8). C-615-399-6000/6532, D-312-778-6532, Exchange-399-5638, Pass/ID Office-399-5516, Police-399-5854, Public Affairs-399-5532, SATO-800-641-2968, Space-A-399-6581.
Smyrna Exchange (TN10R2), Building 607, A Street, Smyrna, TN 37167-5000. USMRA: Page 40 (H-8). Exchange-615-355-3616.

TEXAS

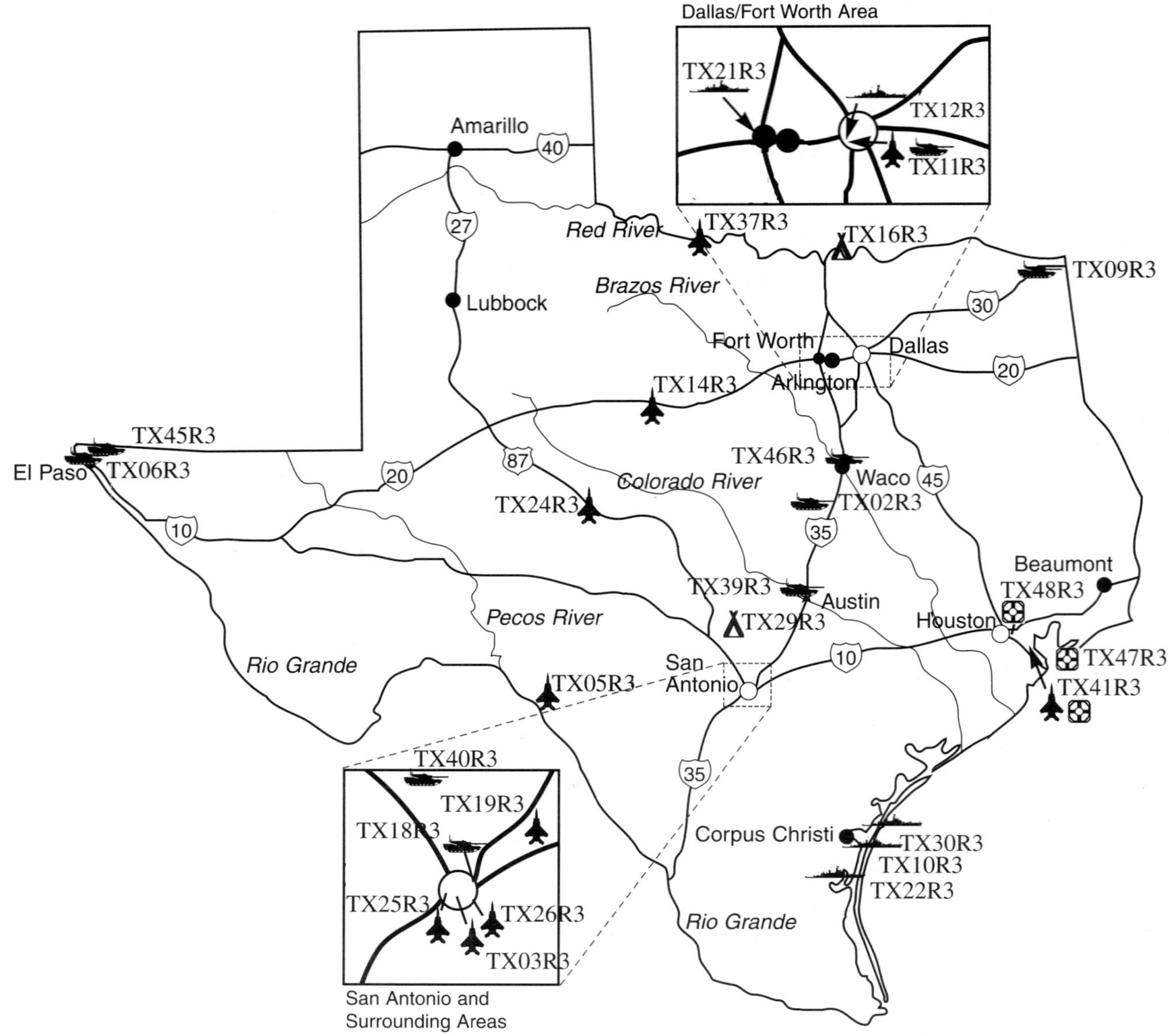

BROOKS AIR FORCE BASE (TX26R3)

HSC/PAS
2510 Kennedy Circle, Room 130
Brooks Air Force Base, TX 78235-5120

TELEPHONE NUMBER INFORMATION: Main installation numbers: C-210-536-1110, D-312-240-1110.

LOCATION: At the intersection of I-37 and Military Drive (Loop 13). USMRA: Page 91 (C-4). NMC: San Antonio, five miles northwest.

GENERAL INFORMATION: Air Force Materiel Command base. Human Systems Center, research laboratories, USAF School of Aerospace Medicine and support units.

TEMPORARY MILITARY LODGING: Lodging office, Building 214, 24 hours daily, C-210-536-1844, D-312-240-1844. All ranks. DV/VIP C-210-536-3238.

RV, CAMPING/FAMCAMP: FAMCAMP on base, year round, 70 SVS/SVRO, ATTN: Lodging Office/Innkeeper, 2804 5th Street, C-210-536-1844, D-312-240-1844, seven camper spaces with full hookups, eight camper spaces with W/E hookups.

SPACE-A: None. See Kelly AFB listing, C-210-925-8714/5, D-312-945-8714/5.

LOGISTICAL SUPPORT:

Child Care-536-2736	Commissary-536-2727
Conv Store-533-9161	Exchange-533-9161
Gas Station-532-2191	SATO-536-1800/3230
Snack Bar-536-2671/2140	

ADMINISTRATIVE SUPPORT:

Legal-536-3301	Locator-536-1841
Police-536-2851	Public Affairs-536-3234
SDO/NCO-536-3278	

HEALTH & WELFARE:

CHAMPUS-536-2928	Chapel-536-3824
Family Services-536-2531	Medical-536-1847
Retiree Services-536-2116	Emergency-911
Veterinary Services-536-2723	

REST & RECREATION:

Auto Hobby Shop-ext 2624	Bowling-ext 3763
Brooks Club-536-3782	Ceramics-ext 2120
Community Center-ext 2847	Fitness Center-ext 2342
Golf course-ext 2636	ITT-536-2077

Library-ext 2634	Picnic Area-ext 2881
Services-ext 3691	Swimming-ext 3744
Wood Hobby Shop-ext 2120	Youth Center-ext 2515

ATTRACTIONS: Close to San Antonio, Sea World of Texas, museums, missions, The Alamo, San Antonio Zoo, Sea World, Fiesta Texas.

CAMP MABRY (TX39R3)

2210 West 35th Street
Austin, TX 78703-5218

TELEPHONE NUMBER INFORMATION: Main installation numbers: C-512-465-5001, D-312-954-5001.

LOCATION: From Dallas, take I-35 to Austin, right onto 38 1/2 Street exit (turns onto 35th Street West). Cross over Loop 1, installation is on the right. USMRA: Page 87 (K-5). NMC: Austin, in city limits.

GENERAL INFORMATION: Texas National Guard Headquarters.

TEMPORARY MILITARY LODGING: Lodging office, C-512-465-5500.

RV, CAMPING/FAMCAMP: None. See Randolph AFB listing, C-210-652-3702.

SPACE-A: Robert Gray Army Airfield, Building 13, 0800-1700 Mon-Fri, C-817-288-9281, D-312-738-9281, Fax: C-817-288-1930, occasional flights available within US, C-817-288-9718 after 1800 hours.

LOGISTICAL SUPPORT:

Barber Shop-454-6363	Beauty Shop-323-0762
Cafeteria-706-6720	Carlson Wagonlit Travel-452-5222
Class Six-465-5120	Credit Union-453-6263
Dry Cleaner-371-1844	Education Office-465-5515
Postal Service-465-5195	Snack Bar-706-6720

ADMINISTRATIVE SUPPORT:

Legal-465-5057	Police-465-5004
Public Affairs-465-5059	SDO-465-5001

HEALTH & WELFARE:

CHAMPUS-465-5239	Chapel-465-5069
Family Services-465-5000	Retiree Services-465-5090

REST & RECREATION: Outdoor Rec-465-5001

ATTRACTIONS: The city of Austin.

CANYON LAKE RECREATION AREA (TX29R3)

Canyon Lake, TX 78133-5000

TELEPHONE NUMBER INFORMATION: Main installation numbers: C-210-221-1211.

LOCATION: Take I-35 to Canyon Lake exit 191. Turn west onto FM 306, and drive approximately 16 miles to Canyon City. Continue another 1.5 miles past the blinking light in Canyon City to Jacob Creek Park Road. Turn left, and the recreation area will be on the right. USMRA: page 87 (J-6). NMC: San Antonio, 48 miles south. NMI: Randolph AFB, 35 miles south.

GENERAL INFORMATION: Nestled in the scenic hill country between San Antonio and Austin, Canyon Lake's 80 miles of shoreline shimmer with a singular beauty found only in central Texas. The Canyon Lake Recreation Area includes 300 feet of well-maintained sandy beach and 1/4-acre marina. Operated by Fort Sam Houston, off post year round, (closed Christmas and New Year's Day). Military personnel active, retired, reserve, NG, DoD civilians and foreign military. Check in at office 1600-2000, check out 1200. Reservations: Required for mobile homes and cabanas; reservations may be made up to one year in advance. No advance reservations for camping areas and RV spots. Address: ITR, Building 124, Stanley Road, Fort Sam Houston, TX 78234-5000. C-1-888-882-9878 or 210-964-3318, D-312-471-3318, 0800-1630 Mon-Fri, 0800-1600 Sat. "Snowbirds" welcome year round. Discounts available for entrance fee only to holders of Golden Age, Golden Access and Golden Eagle Passports. Visa, MasterCard, American Express, Discover and Diners accepted. Pets allowed on leash. Open fires in designated areas only. Nominal entrance fee into park ($4 per vehicle/annual permit $30). No firearms are allowed.

TEMPORARY MILITARY LODGING: Mobile homes, three bedroom, furnished except towels and soap (32). Rates: $25-$35 daily, vary depending on seasons/days.

RV, CAMPING/FAMCAMP: Screened Shelters, bunk beds with W&E hookups (10); hardstand camper spaces with W&E hookups (32); open tent spaces with no hookups. Rates: screened shelters $35-$45 daily, vary depending on seasons/days.; camper spaces $10 daily; tent spaces $8 daily.

REST & RECREATION: Boating, Fishing, Hiking, Jet Skiing, Sand Volleyball, Swimming, Water Skiing.

OTHER SUPPORT & FACILITIES AVAILABLE: Beach, Boat Launch, Boat Rental, Boat Slip, Cabanas/fee, Fishing Pier, Fishing Tackle, Grills, Laundry, Marina, MWR, NAF Store, Party Boat, Pavilion, Picnic Areas*/**, Playgrounds, Rec Equipment, Restrooms*, Sewage Dump, Shelters/screened, Showers*, TV Room, TV/VCR Rental. Also, see Fort Sam Houston listing, C-210-221-1211.

** Handicap accessible.*
*** Group picnic area available by reservation.*

ATTRACTIONS: Mild winter temperatures make this natural haven a year-round attraction for fishing, camping, boating and picnicking.

CORPUS CHRISTI NAVAL AIR STATION (TX10R3)

11001 D Street, Suite 143
Corpus Christi Naval Air Station, TX 78419-5021

TELEPHONE NUMBER INFORMATION: Main installation numbers: C-512-939-2811, D-312-861-1110. E-mail: nascc-pao-at-nas-cc@navdafgw.navy.mil.

LOCATION: From San Antonio, take Interstate 37 south to Highway 357 east. USMRA: Page 87 (K-8). NMI: Naval Station Ingleside, 37 miles northeast. NMC: Corpus Christi, 10 miles west.

GENERAL INFORMATION: Naval Air Training Command, Coast Guard Air Station, and Corpus Christi Army Depot, Tenant Commands, Training Squadrons 27, 38 and 31, Surveillance Support Center, Training Air Wing Four, Commander Mine Warfare Command, US Coast Guard Group/Air Station, HM 15, Marine Corps Reserve Training Center, CNATRA.

TEMPORARY MILITARY LODGING: Lodging office, 24 hours daily, Building 1281, Ocean Drive C-512-939-2388/89 D-312-861-2388/89, Fax: C-512-939-3275. Navy Lodge, Building 1281, 0800-1800 Mon-Fri, 0900-1800 Sat-Sun, C-512-937-6361. All ranks. DV/VIP C-512-939-2388/89, Fax: C-512-939-3275.

RV, CAMPING/FAMCAMP: Shields Park NAS Recreation Area, on base year round, Outdoor Recreation, Building 39, Code 22, C-512-937-5071, 24 camper spaces with W/E, seven tent spaces with W.

SPACE-A: Pax Term, Hangar 58, 0700-2300 Mon-Fri, C-512-939-2505, D-312-861-2505, Fax: C-512-939-3774, flights to CONUS locations.

LOGISTICAL SUPPORT:

Barber Shop-939-7981	Beauty Shop-939-7032

TEXAS
Corpus Christi Naval Air Station, continued

Child Care-939-8702	Child Dev Center-939-8702
Commissary-939-3177	Credit Union-986-4500
Education Office-939-7910	Exchange-939-2166
Gas Station-939-7910	Package Store-939-2166
Postal Service-939-2984	SATO-937-8806
Visitor Center-939-3722	

ADMINISTRATIVE SUPPORT:

CDO/OOD-939-2383	Fire Dept-939-3492
Housing Office-939-3336	Legal-939-3568
Locator-939-3841 (navy mil)	Pass/ID Office-939-2282
Police-939-2282	Public Affairs-939-3420

HEALTH & WELFARE:

American Red Cross-939-2180	CHAMPUS-939-3238
Chapel-939-3751	Dental-939-2466
Family Services-939-3722	Central Appts-939-2485
Medical-939-2994	Clinic-939-3838
Central Appts-939-3157	Emergency-939-2688
Emergency-939-3577	N-MC Relief Society-939-3482
Health Benefits-939-3238	Retiree Services-939-3113
Hospital-939-2688	TRICARE-939-6610
Information-939-2688	Veterinary Services-939-2031

REST & RECREATION:

Arts & Crafts-ext 3169	Auto Hobby Shop-939-3470
Bowling-939-3805	Camping Equip-937-5071
Fitness Center-939-3164	Gym-939-2401
Golf Course-939-3250	Library-939-3574
ITT-939-3637	Marinas-937-5071
MWR-939-2267	O' Club-939-2541
Party House-ext 2444	Picnic Area-ext 2444
Skeet Range-ext 2444	Theater-939-3497
Youth Center-939-2355	Youth Services-939-2355

ATTRACTIONS: Bay and gulf water sports. Also, symphony, museums, and historical homes.

DYESS AIR FORCE BASE (TX14R3)

650 Second Street
Dyess Air Force Base, TX 79607-1960

TELEPHONE NUMBER INFORMATION: Main installation numbers: C-915-696-0212, D-312-461-3113.

LOCATION: Main gate is three miles east of I-20 and US-277. USMRA: Page 87 (I-3). NMC: Abilene, six miles northeast.

GENERAL INFORMATION: Air Combat Command Base and most tenant units, 7th Wing/Airlift Group and support units.

TEMPORARY MILITARY LODGING: Lodging office, 441 Fifth Street, Dyess Inn, 24 hours daily, C-915-696-2861, D-312-461-2861. All ranks. DV/VIP C-915-696-5610.

RV, CAMPING/FAMCAMP: None. Nearest facility is more than 100 miles away.

SPACE-A: Pax Term/Lounge, 674 Alert Avenue, 24 hours daily, C-915-696-3108/2237, D-312-461-3108/2237, flights to CONUS, OCONUS and foreign locations.

LOGISTICAL SUPPORT:

Cafeteria-698-1720	Child Care-696-4337
Commissary-696-2434	Conv Store-692-4771
Exchange-692-8976	Gas Station-692-6721
Package Store-696-3497	SATO-696-4743

ADMINISTRATIVE SUPPORT:

Legal-696-3305	Locator-696-3098
Police-696-2131	Public Affairs-696-2862

HEALTH & WELFARE:

CHAMPUS-696-5114	Chapel-696-4224
Medical-696-4677	
Emergency-696-2334	

REST & RECREATION:

Arts & Crafts-ext 4175	Auto Hobby Shop-ext 4179
Bowling-ext 4166	Clubs
Golf course-ext 5067	Consol-696-4311
Gym-ext 4306	O-696-2405
Library-ext 2618	Rec Center-ext 4305
Rec Equip-ext 2402	Stables-ext 3471
Swimming-ext 3346	Theater-696-4320
Youth Center-696-4797	

ATTRACTIONS: Abilene, outdoor sports, Abilene Zoo, and Dyess Linear Air Park.

FORT BLISS (TX06R3)

US Army Air Defense Artillery Center and School & Fort Bliss
1733 Pleasonton Road, Building 15
Fort Bliss, TX 79916-6816

TELEPHONE NUMBER INFORMATION: Main installation numbers: C-915-568-2121, D-312-978-2121.

LOCATION: Accessible from I-10 or US-54. USMRA: Page 86 (B,C-5,6). NMC: El Paso, within city limits.

GENERAL INFORMATION: Air Defense Artillery Center and School, Sergeants Major Academy, 11th Air Defense Artillery Brigade, 6th Air Defense Artillery Brigade, 108th Air Defense Artillery Brigade, 31st Air Defense Artillery Brigade, 35th Air Defense Artillery Brigade, Range Command, 1st Combined Arms Support Battalion, William Beaumont Army Medical Center, and other units.

TEMPORARY MILITARY LODGING: Lodging office, Building 251, Club Road, 24 hours daily, C-915-568-4888, D-312-978-4888. All ranks. DV/VIP C-915-568-5319/5225. New YMCA Residence Center on William Beaumont Medical Center, C-915-562-8461. The Inn at Fort Bliss, C-915-565-7777.

RV, CAMPING/FAMCAMP: Fort Bliss RV Park, on post year round, Outdoor Recreation Branch, Building 1986, C-915-568-4693, D-312-978-4693/0106, Fax: C-915-568-2028, D-312-978-2028, 73 camper spaces with full hookups, eight tent spaces without hookups.

SPACE-A: Biggs Army Airfield, Building 11210, 0600-2200 Mon-Fri, 0800-1600 Sat-Sun, C-915-568-8097, D-312-978-8097, limited CONUS flights.

LOGISTICAL SUPPORT:

Carlson Wagonlit Travel-562-2340	Child Care-562-3843
Commissary-568-4022	Conv Store-562-3774
Exchange-562-7200	Gas Station-562-2353
Package Store-566-8371	

ADMINISTRATIVE SUPPORT:

Legal-568-6513	Locator-568-1113
Police-568-2115/6	Public Affairs-568-4505
SDO/NCO-568-4233/1501	

HEALTH & WELFARE:

CHAMPUS-569-2536	Chapel-568-5992
Family Service-568-4614	Medical-569-2450
Retiree Services-568-2632	Emergency-568-3194

TEXAS
Fort Bliss, continued

REST & RECREATION:

Auto Hobby Shop-ext 7280/1172	Bowling-ext 6272/1685
Clubs	Golf Course-562-1273/2066
NCO-562-5969	Gym-ext 6281
O-568-2738	ITR-568-7506
Rod/Gun-ext 2983	Library-ext 2489
Saddle-ext 8648	Music-ext 2595/7427
Picnic Area-ext 6097	Rec Center-ext 3881/8276
Rec Equip-ext 7705	Swimming-ext 7431
Theater-ext 2595/7427	Tickets-ext 6498/5210
Youth Center-ext 5437	

ATTRACTIONS: Four museums (Fort Bliss, Air Defense Artillery, and Noncommissioned Officer) on post, Carlsbad Caverns National Park, White Sands National Monument, Ciudad Juarez. El Paso Symphony, El Paso Diablos (minor league baseball, Double-A), and Tigua Indian Reservation.

FORT HOOD (TX02R3)

III Corps & Fort Hood
ATTN: AFZF-PO
Fort Hood, TX 76544-5000

TELEPHONE NUMBER INFORMATION: Main installation numbers: C-817-287/288-1110, D-312-737/738-1110.

LOCATION: From I-35 north, exit to US-190 west, nine miles to Killeen. Main gate is clearly marked. USMRA: Page 87 (K-4,5). NMC: Killeen, at main entrance.

GENERAL INFORMATION: Armored Corps Headquarters, and headquarters for 1st Cavalry Division and 4th Infantry Division (Mechanized), 6th Cavalry Brigade, 13th Corps Support Command, 3rd Signal Brigade, 89th Military Police Brigade, 504th Military Intelligence Group, 3rd Air Support Group (AF), Medical Activity, Dental Activity, and TEXCOM (Test Activity) and the Combat Aviation Training Brigade.

TEMPORARY MILITARY LODGING: Lodging office, Building 36006, Wratten Drive, 24 hours daily, C-817-287-5001/27008, D-312-738-5001/27008, Fax: C-817-288-7604. DV/VIP C-817-287-5001.

RV, CAMPING/FAMCAMP: West Fort Hood Travel Camp on post year round, AFZF-CA-BOD-WFHTC, Building 70004, Clarke Road, P.O. Box K, C-817-288-9926, D-312-738-9926, 64 camper spaces with full hookups, 20 tent spaces. Belton Lake Recreation Area on post year round, Business Operations Division, AFZF-CA-BOD-OR-BLORA, C-817-287-2523, D-312-737-2523, 10 cottages, 11 camper spaces with full hookups, 48 camper spaces with W/E hookups, 22 tent spaces with W/E hookups, 60 tent spaces without hookups.

SPACE-A: Robert Gray Army Airfield, Building 13, 0800-1700 Mon-Fri, C-817-288-1432, D-312-738-1432, Fax: C-817-288-1930, occasional flights available within US. Hood Airfield C-817-287-7585.

LOGISTICAL SUPPORT:

Child Care-287-5448	Commissary-287-5943
Conv Store-532-3089	Exchange-287-3228
Gas Station-532-8464	Package Store-532-5239
SATO-532-8955	Snack Bar-532-5779
Visitor Center-287-4936/288-2865	

ADMINISTRATIVE SUPPORT:

CDO/OOD-287-2520/2506	Legal-287-9726
Locator-287-2137	Police-287-2176
Public Affairs-287-0103	SDO/NCO-287-2624

HEALTH & WELFARE:

ACS-287-3071	CHAMPUS-288-8155
Chapel-288-8849	Chaplain-287-1625
Family Services-287-4031	Medical-288-8000
Retiree Services-287-6125	Emergency-288-8113
	Central Appts-288-8888

REST & RECREATION:

Arts & Crafts-288-2970	Archery-532-4552
Auto Hobby Shop-287 5595/0011	Boat Rental-287-5526
Clubs	Bowling-287-3424/2281
Dirt Riders-532-4552	Golf Course-287-3466
EM-287-6737	Hunting/Fishing-287-5841
Hunt/Saddle-287-5847	ITR-287-7310
NCO-532-5816	Library-288-9520
O-532-5073	Marina-287-5526
Riding-287-5847	Music Center-287-6116
Rod/Gun-287-5847	MWR-287-4339
Sport Parachute-532-4552	Pool-287-4648
Recreation-287-7803	Rec Center- 288-9828/0353
Rec Equip-287-1853	Skating Center-287-5623
Swimming/Beach-287-6644	Theater-287-2998
Youth Activities-287-9833	

ATTRACTIONS: State capital, Austin. Hunting and fishing.

FORT SAM HOUSTON (TX18R3)

ATTN: AFZG-CO
1212 Stanley Road, Building 124
Fort Sam Houston, TX 78234-5000

TELEPHONE NUMBER INFORMATION: Main installation number: C-210-221-1211.

LOCATION: Accessible from I-410 or I-35. USMRA: Page 91 (C,D-2,3). NMC: San Antonio, in city limits.

GENERAL INFORMATION: Headquarters 5th Army, Headquarters 90th Army Reserve Command, Headquarters US Army Medical Command, US Army Medical Dept and School, Brooke Army Medical Center, US Army Dental Command, US Army Veterinary Command, 41st Combat Support Hospital, 147th Medical Logistics Battalion, 5th Recruiting Brigade.

TEMPORARY MILITARY LODGING: Lodging office, Building 592, Dickman Road, 24 hours daily, C-210-221-6125/6262, D-312-471-6125/6262, Fax: C-210-221-6275. All ranks.

RV, CAMPING/FAMCAMP: Operates Canyon Lake Army Recreation Area off post. See Canyon Lake Army Recreation Area listing for more information.

SPACE-A: None. See Kelly AFB listing, C-210-925-8714/5, D-312-945-8714/5.

LOGISTICAL SUPPORT:

Carlson Wagonlit Travel-225-5261	Child Care-221-5002
Commissary-221-5626	Conv Store-225-0216
Exchange-225-5566	Gas Station-228-9001
Package Store-223-3427	Snack Bar-228-9071

ADMINISTRATIVE SUPPORT:

Fire Dept-221-2727	Legal-221-2353
Locator-221-3315	Police-221-0463
SDO/NCO-221-2810	

HEALTH & WELFARE:

ACS-221-2705	CHAMPUS-916-9989
Chapel-221-9680	Family Services-221-2705
Medical-916-6141	Retiree Services-221-5958
Central Appts-916-6770	
Emergency-221-6466	

REST & RECREATION:

Arts & Craft-ext 7125	Auto Hobby Shop-224-7046

TEXAS
Fort Sam Houston, continued

Bowling-ext 3683
Golf Course-222-9386
Gym-ext 2593
Hunting/Fishing-ext 7367
ITR-221-2333
Library-ext 3702
Outdoor Rec-224-7162
Stables-224-7207
Theater-ext 2186
Youth Center-ext 7882
Clubs
EM-224-2721
NCO-224-2721
O-224-4211
ITT-221-0703
Music-ext 2186
Rec Center-ext 4829/2892
Swimming-ext 3290/5993
Theater (Plays)- ext 5953

ATTRACTIONS: San Antonio, Botanical Gardens. Gulf Coast and Mexico nearby, Natural Bridge Caverns. Sea World, Fiesta Texas Amusement Park, Historic Fort Sam Houston, The Alamo, San Antonio Riverwalk.

FORT WORTH NAVAL AIR STATION/ JOINT RESERVE BASE (TX21R3)

12151 Depot Avenue, Building 1215
Fort Worth Naval Air Station/Joint Reserve Base, TX 76127-5000

TELEPHONE NUMBER INFORMATION: Main installation numbers: C-817-782-5000, D-312-739-5000.

LOCATION: On TX-183. From Fort Worth, west on I-30, exit at Carswell AFB/Horne Street Follow signs to main gate. USMRA: Page 88 (A-3). NMC: Fort Worth, seven miles east.

GENERAL INFORMATION: Air Combat Command Base. Bomb Wing and AFRES units.

TEMPORARY MILITARY LODGING: Lodging office, Building 1324 Military Parkway, 24 hours daily, C-817-782-5393, Fax: C-817-782-5391. All ranks. DV/VIP C-817-782-7614.

RV, CAMPING/FAMCAMP: None. Nearest facility is over 100 miles away.

SPACE-A: Pax Term/Lounge, Building 1423, 0730-1630 Mon-Fri, C-817-782-5649/7513, D-312-739-5649/7513, flights to CONUS, OCONUS and foreign locations.

LOGISTICAL SUPPORT:
BX-Mart-737-1213
Conv Store-731-4187
Gas Station-738-1002
SATO-782-5579
Snack Bar-731-2075
Child Care-782-5753
Exchange-738-1943
Package Store-738-0462
Shoppette-731-4187

ADMINISTRATIVE SUPPORT:
Legal-782-7595
Police-782-5200
Locator-782-7082/5000
SDO/NCO-782-5555

HEALTH & WELFARE:
CHAMPUS-782-4827
Family Services-782-7877
Retiree Services-782-5661
Chapel-782-7301
Medical-782-4000
Central Appts-782-4500
Emergency-782-4050

REST & RECREATION:
Arts & Crafts-ext 7114
Bowling-ext 5505
Fitness Center-ext 7770
Golf course 738-8402
Library-ext 5230
MWR-ext 5411
Rec Equip-ext 7972
Tennis-ext 7770
Youth Center-ext 5498
Auto Hobby Shop-ext 7114
Clubs
EM-782-5293
O-782-5631
Marina-ext 7972
Rec Center-ext 7077
Swimming-ext 7770/7869
Theater-782-5450

ATTRACTIONS: Zoo, Fort Worth Botanic Gardens, Museum of Science and History. Dallas, Six Flags over Texas.

GALVESTON COAST GUARD BASE (TX47R3)

P.O. Box 1912
End of Ferry Road, Galveston
TX 77553-1912

TELEPHONE NUMBER INFORMATION: Main installation numbers: C-409-766-5620/1 or 800-742-8917.

LOCATION: Take I-45 S to Island, changes to Broadway, at the seawall go northeast, follow signs to base. USMRA: Page 87 (N-6). NMC: Galveston, three miles south.

GENERAL INFORMATION: Coast Guard Base.

TEMPORARY MILITARY LODGING: None. Nearest facility is more than 100 miles away.

RV, CAMPING/FAMCAMP: None. Nearest facility is more than 100 miles away.

SPACE-A: None. See Ellington ANGB/Houston CGAS listing, C-713-481-0025, D-312-929-2316.

LOGISTICAL SUPPORT:
Exchange-766-5673

ADMINISTRATIVE SUPPORT:
CDO/OOD-766-5641
Public Affairs-766-5603

HEALTH & WELFARE:
Chapel-766-5667
Medical-766-5661
Family Services-766-4751

REST & RECREATION: None. Nearest facility is more than 100 miles away.

GOODFELLOW AIR FORCE BASE (TX24R3)

184 Lancaster Avenue, Suite J
Goodfellow Air Force Base, TX 76908-4410

TELEPHONE NUMBER INFORMATION: Main installation numbers: C-915-654-3231, D-312-477-3217.

LOCATION: Off US-87 or US-277. Clearly marked. USMRA: Page 86 (H-6,7). NMC: San Angelo, two miles southeast.

GENERAL INFORMATION: Air Education and Training Command.

TEMPORARY MILITARY LODGING: Lodging office, Building 3305, Kearney Boulevard, 24 hours daily, C-915-654-3332/3206, D-312-477-3332/3206. All ranks.

RV, CAMPING/FAMCAMP: Lake Nasworthy Recreation Camp off base, year round: Thu-Mon, 1950 S. Concho Drive, San Angelo, TX 76504-5000, C-915-944-1012, D-312-477-3217 (ask operator to ring 944-1012), 20 camper spaces with full hookups.

SPACE-A: None. See Dyess AFB listing, C-915-696-3108/2237, D-312-461-3108/2237.

LOGISTICAL SUPPORT:
Bank-659-6922
Beauty Shop-655-5024
Child Care-654-3241
Class Six-654-3249
Conv Store-655-5794
Dining Facilities-654-3153
Education Office-654-3317
Gas Station-655-5793
Barber Shop-653-8637
Car Rental-655-0546
Child Dev Center-654-3240
Commissary-653-2441
Credit Union-653-1465
Dry Cleaner-653-1210
Exchange-655-3361
Laundry-653-1210

Postal Service-654-3466
Shoppette-654-3363
Travel Office-654-5139
SATO-654-3328
Snack Bar-654-3361

ADMINISTRATIVE SUPPORT:
Fire Dept-654-3532
Legal-654-3203
Pass/ID Office-654-3264
Public Affairs-654-3876
Quarter Deck-654-3668
Housing Office-654-3694
Locator-654-3410
Police-654-3511
SDO/NCO-654-3044

HEALTH & WELFARE:
American Red Cross-655-7539
CHAMPUS-654-3276
Dental-654-3050
Medical-654-3135
TRICARE-481-3600
Air Force Aid Society-654-3263
Chapel-654-3424
Family Service-654-3893
Retiree Services-654-5388
Veterinary Services-654-3251

REST & RECREATION:
Arts & Crafts-654-3236
Bowling-654-3227
Community Center-654-3247
Fitness Center-654-3242
Gym-654-5127
MWR-654-3254
Swimming-ext 3226
Wood Hobby Shop-654-5643
Auto Hobby Shop-654-3233
Clubs
  Goodfellow-654-5327
  Oasis-655-3256
Library-654-3232
Rec Center-ext 3247
Theater-654-3206
Youth Center-654-3211

ATTRACTIONS: Lakes, Fort Concho and city of San Angelo.

INGLESIDE NAVAL STATION (TX30R3)

1455 Ticonderoga Road, Suite W123
Ingleside, TX 78362-5001

TELEPHONE NUMBER INFORMATION: Main installation numbers: C-512-776-4201, D-312-776-4201.

LOCATION: I-37 south to Route 361 to Route 1069. USMRA: Page 87 (K,L-8). NMC: Corpus Christi, 37 miles south

GENERAL INFORMATION: Navy's designated "Mine Warfare Center of Excellence," home port to 12 mine countermeasures ships (MCM), nine coastal mine hunters (MHC) and the Mine Countermeasures Command, Control and Support Ship, the *USS Inchon*.

TEMPORARY MILITARY LODGING: Lodging office, BEQ, C-512-776-4420, D-312-776-4420, Fax: C-512-776-4519.

RV, CAMPING/FAMCAMP: None. See Corpus Christi NAS listing, C-512-937-5071.

SPACE-A: None. See Corpus Christi NAS listing, C-512-939-2505, D-312-861-2505.

LOGISTICAL SUPPORT:
Barber Shop-776-4115
Exchange-776-4100
SATO-776-4216
Dining Facilities-776-4424
Postal Service-776-4256
Snack Bar-776-4777

ADMINISTRATIVE SUPPORT:
Fire Dept-776-4294
Legal-776-4122
Police-776-4238
Housing Office-776-4562
Pass/ID Office-776-5854
Public Affairs-776-4206

HEALTH & WELFARE:
Dental-776-4587
  Central Appts-776-4581
  Clinic-776-4581
  Emergency-776-4581
N-MC Relief Society-776-4564
TRICARE-1-800-406-2823
Family Services-776-4551
Medical-776-4580
  Central Appts-776-4585
  Health Benefits-776-4575
Retiree Services-776-4551

REST & RECREATION:
Auto Hobby Shop-776-4299
Gym-776-4601
Marinas-758-0350
Fitness Center-776-4601
ITT-776-4227
MWR-776-4631

ATTRACTIONS: Bay and gulf water sports. Also, symphony, museums, and historical homes.

KELLY AIR FORCE BASE (TX03R3)

807 Buckner Drive, Suite 1
Kelly Air Force Base, TX 78241-5842

TELEPHONE NUMBER INFORMATION: Main installation numbers: C-210-925-1110, D-312-945-1110.

LOCATION: All of the following, I-10, I-35, I-37, I-410 intersect with US-90. From US-90 take either the Gen Hudnell or Gen McMullen exit and go south to AFB. USMRA: Page 91 (B-3,4). NMC: San Antonio, seven miles northeast.

GENERAL INFORMATION: Air Force Materiel Command Base. San Antonio Air Logistics Center, Air Intelligence Agency, Electronic Warfare Center, Air Force News Agency, AFRES and ANG units.

TEMPORARY MILITARY LODGING: Lodging office, Building 1650, 24 hours daily, C-210-925-1844/924-7201, D-312-945-1844. All ranks. DV/VIP 210-925-7678.

RV, CAMPING/FAMCAMP: On base, year round, C-210-925-5725. Thirty paved camper spaces with W/S/E hookups and many tent spaces without hookups.

SPACE-A: Pax Term/Lounge, Building 1614, 0700-1800 Mon-Fri, 0800-1600 Sat-Sun, C-210-925-8714/8715, D-312-945-8714/5, flights to CONUS, OCONUS and foreign locations.

LOGISTICAL SUPPORT:
Cafeteria-925-4990
Commissary-925-6991
Gas Station-924-2960
Visitor Center-925-5551
Child Care-925-5747
Exchange-924-9247
SATO-925-7371

ADMINISTRATIVE SUPPORT:
Fire Dept-925-5526
Locator-925-1841
Public Affairs-925-7951
Legal-925-3095
Police-925-6811
SDO/NCO-925-6906

HEALTH & WELFARE:
CHAMPUS-925-8206
Family Services-925-4181
Retiree Services-925-9314
Chapel-925-7874
Medical-925-6333
  Emergency-925-4544
  Appointments-925-8811

REST & RECREATION:
Arts & Crafts-925-8346
Bowling-925-5933/ 5480
Golf Course-925-4006
Gym-925-4846
ITT-925-4584
MWR-925-7144
Youth Center-925-8100
Auto Hobby Shop-925-3872
Clubs
  NCO-924-8354
  O-924-8254
Library-925-4116
Pool-925-4846

ATTRACTIONS: The Alamo, River Walk, Tower of the Americas, San Antonio Zoo, Institute of Texas Cultures, McNay Art Museum, Six Flags Fiesta Texas and Sea World.

TEXAS

KINGSVILLE NAVAL AIR STATION (TX22R3)

554 McCain Street, Suite 309
Kingsville, TX 78363-5054

TELEPHONE NUMBER INFORMATION: Main installation numbers: C-512-516-6136, D-312-861-6136.

LOCATION: Off US-77 south, exit to TX-425 southeast to main gate. USMRA: Page 87 (K-9). NMC: Corpus Christi, 50 miles northeast.

GENERAL INFORMATION: Training Air Wing # 2, two squadrons, and support units.

TEMPORARY MILITARY LODGING: Lodging office, Building 3729, duty hours, C-512-516-6321/6309, D-312-861-6321/6309, Fax: C-512-516-6428. All ranks. DV/VIP C-512-516-6136/6321.

RV, CAMPING/FAMCAMP: Nasking Recreation FAMCAMP, on base year round, Outdoor Recreation, 3765 Nimitz Avenue, C-512-516-6443, D-312-861-6443, four campers for rent with W/E hookups, five camper spaces with W/E hookups, 10 camper spaces with W hookups.

SPACE-A: Very limited, C-512-516-6108, D-312-861-6108. Also see Corpus Christi NAS listing.

LOGISTICAL SUPPORT:
Child Care-516-6176
Conv Store-516-6106
Gas Station-516-6106
Commissary-516-6241
Exchange-516-6361
Package Store-516-6473

ADMINISTRATIVE SUPPORT:
Legal-516-6426
SDO/NCO-516-6136
Police-516-6217

HEALTH & WELFARE:
CHAMPUS-516-6238
Family Services-516-6333
Retiree Services-516-6333
Chapel-516-6331
Medical-516-6305
  Central Appts-516-6342
  Emergency-516-6911

REST & RECREATION:
Arts & Crafts-ext 6171/2
Bowling-ext 6171/2
Gym-ext 6171/2
ITT-516-6449
Nautilus Center-ext 6171/2
Picnic Area-ext 6171/2
Tennis-ext 6171/2
Auto Hobby Shop-ext 6171/2
Clubs
  CPO-516-6121
  EM-516-6121
  O-516-6121
Swimming-ext 6171/2

ATTRACTIONS: Gulf Coast, Corpus Christi, King Ranch, and fishing in Baffin Bay.

LACKLAND AIR FORCE BASE (TX25R3)

1701 Kenly Avenue, Suite 220
Lackland Air Force Base, TX 78236-5110

TELEPHONE NUMBER INFORMATION: Main installation numbers: C-210-671-1110, D-312-473-1110.

LOCATION: Off US-90 south. Loop 13 (Military Drive) bisects Lackland AFB. USMRA: Page 87 (J-6,7), page 91 (A,B-3). NMC: San Antonio, six miles northeast.

GENERAL INFORMATION: Air Training Command Installation, Host: 37th Training Wing, Basic and technical Education and training, Defense Language Institute English Language Center, Inter-American Air Forces Academy, Tenant: 59th Medical Wing (Wilford Hall Medical Center).

TEMPORARY MILITARY LODGING: Lodging office, Building 10203, 24 hours daily, C-210-671-2556. All ranks. DV/VIP C-210-671-3622.

RV, CAMPING/FAMCAMP: FAMCAMP on base, year round, C-210-671-3106, D-312-473-3106, 24 camper spaces with full hookups.

SPACE-A: None. See Kelly AFB listing, C-210-925-8714/8715, D-312-945-8714/8715.

LOGISTICAL SUPPORT:
Bank-674-6266
Beauty Shop-674-1341
Child Care-671-3168
Commissary-671-2830
Credit Union-673-5610
Dry Cleaner-674-8943
Exchange-674-8965
Package Store-674-0848
SATO-673-9057
Snack Bar-671-4047
Barber Shop-673-5252
Car Rental-670-4232
Child Dev Center-671-2830
Conv Store-674-0848
Dining Facilities-671-3901
Education Office-671-2895
Gas Station-673-0848
Postal Office-671-1101
Shoppette-674-0848
Visitor Center-671-3024

ADMINISTRATIVE SUPPORT:
CDO/OOD-671-4225
Fire Dept-671-2921
Legal-671-3361
Pass/ID Office-671-3594
Public Affairs-671-2907
Command Post-671-4225
Housing Office-671-1840
Locator-671-1841
Police-671-2018

HEALTH & WELFARE:
American Red Cross-671-1855
CHAMPUS-670-2832
Dental-670-6379
Medical-670-7100
  Emergency-670-7331
  Health Benefits-1-800-406-2832
  Hospital-670-5392
Air Force Aid Society-670-1666
Chapel-671-4104
Family Services-671-3609
Retiree Services-671-2728
Veterinary Services-671-3354

REST & RECREATION:
Arts & Crafts-671-2515
Bowling-671-2271
Community Center-671-2619
Fitness Center-671-2751
Golf Course-671-3466
Indoor Rec-671-4269
Library-ext 2678
Outdoor Rec-671-3106
Rec Equip-ext 3106
Swimming-ext 3445
Youth Center-671-2388
Auto Hobby Shop-671-3549
Clubs
  NCO-671-2110
  O-673-5881
  Rod/Gun-674-7831
ITT-671-3133
MWR-671-3906
Rec Center-ext 2619
Services-671-3395
Theater-673-3985

ATTRACTIONS: City of San Antonio, Zoo, River Walk, The Alamo, El Mercado La Villita, Institute of Texan Cultures, Spanish missions, McNay Art Institute, Sea World of Texas, Fiesta Texas.

LAUGHLIN AIR FORCE BASE (TX05R3)

47FTW/PA
561 Liberty Drive, Suite 3
Laughlin Air Force Base, TX 78843-5227

TELEPHONE NUMBER INFORMATION: Main installation numbers: C-210-298-3511, D-312-732-1110. HP: http://www.lau1.aetc.af.mil/.

LOCATION: Take US-90 west from San Antonio, 150 miles or US-277 south from San Angelo, 150 miles to Del Rio area. The AFB is clearly marked off US-90. USMRA: Page 86 (H-9). NMC: Del Rio, six miles northwest.

GENERAL INFORMATION: Air Education and Training Command Base. Home of the 47th Flying Training Wing, Specialized Undergraduate Pilot Training.

TEMPORARY MILITARY LODGING: Lodging office, 416 Liberty Drive, 24 hours daily, C-210-298-5731, D-312-732-5731. All ranks. DV/VIP C-210-298-5041.

RV, CAMPING/FAMCAMP: FAMCAMP on base year round, Recreation Services, 47 SPTG/SVRO, 416 Liberty Drive, C-210-298-5474, D-312-732-5474, Fax: C-210-298-5554, D-312-732-5554, 15 camper spaces with full hookups. Also operates South Winds on Lake Amistad, off base year round, HCR #3, Box 37J, Del Rio, TX 78840-5000, C-210-775-5971, D-312-732-5971, Fax: C-210-298-5554, 11 camper spaces with hookups.

SPACE-A: Limited. Building 306, C-210-298-5308/5309, D-312-732-5308/5309.

LOGISTICAL SUPPORT:
Bank-774-6861
Barber Shop-298-3289
Beauty Shop-298-3224
Child Care-298-5419
Child Dev Center-298-5419
Class Six-298-2111
Commissary-298-5815
Conv Store-298-3867
Credit Union-774-3503
Dining Facilities-298-5295
Dry Cleaner-298-2111
Education Office-298-5545
Exchange-298-3627
Gas Station-298-3867
Package Store-298-2111
Postal Service-298-5417
SATO-298-5205
Shoppette-298-2111
Snack Bar-298-3001

ADMINISTRATIVE SUPPORT:
CDO/OOD-298-5167
Fire Dept-298-5034
Housing Office-298-5904
Legal-298-5172
Locator-298-3511
Pass/ID Office-298-5295
Police-298-5100
Public Affairs-298-5988
SDO/NCO-298-5167

HEALTH & WELFARE:
Air Force Aid Society-298-5324
American Red Cross-298-5125
CHAMPUS-298-6350
Chapel-298-5111
Dental-298-6331
Family Services-298-5620
Medical-298-3578
  Emergency-911
  Health Benefits-298-6350
TRICARE-298-6350
Veterinary Services-298-5500

REST & RECREATION:
Auto Hobby Shop-298-5844
Bowling-298-5526
Clubs
  EM-298-5346
  O-298-5134
Community Center-298-5474
Fitness Center-298-5326
Library-298-5119
Marina-775-5971
Outdoor Rec-775-5971
Rec Center-ext 5474
Services-298-5810
Skeet Range-ext 5830
Stables-ext 5830
Theater-298-5144
Youth Center-298-5343
Youth Services-298-5343
Wood Hobby Shop-298-5153

ATTRACTIONS: On the Mexican border at Ciudad Acuna, Mexico. Lake Amistad, Alamo Village.

RANDOLPH AIR FORCE BASE (TX19R3)

1 Washington Circle, Suite 4
Randolph Air Force Base, TX 78150-4562

TELEPHONE NUMBER INFORMATION: Main installation numbers: C-210-652-1110, D-312-487-1110. HP: http://www.rnd.aetc.af.mil.

LOCATION: From I-35, Pat Booker Road exit. USMRA: Page 91 (E-2). NMC: San Antonio, five miles southwest.

GENERAL INFORMATION: Air Education and Training Command Base. 12th Flying Training Wing, Headquarters Air Education and Training Command, Air Force Personnel Center, Air Force Recruiting Service, Headquarters 19th Air Force, Air Force Center for Quality and Management Innovation, Air Force Occupational Measurement Squadron, Air Force Services Agency, Air Force Security Assistance Training Squadron and support units.

TEMPORARY MILITARY LODGING: Lodging office, Building 118, 24 hours daily, C-210-652-1844, D-312-487-1844. All ranks. DV/VIP 652-4126.

RV, CAMPING/FAMCAMP: Randolph Off Base Recreation Area year round (marina closed Mon-Tue), Outdoor Recreation Resource Center, 415 B Street East, C-210-652-3702, six camper spaces with W/E hookups, 45 tent spaces without hookups, 11 primitive shelters with E hookups.

SPACE-A: Pax Term/Lounge, Hangar 7, east side, 0600-1800 Mon-Fri, Sat and Sun as required, C-210-652-1854/3725, D-312-487-1854/3725, Fax: C-210-652-5618, flights to CONUS locations.

LOGISTICAL SUPPORT:
Child Care-652-4946
Commissary-652-6545
Exchange-652-2301
Gas Station-658-1515
Package Store-658-4544
SATO-658-3585
Shoppette-658-1717
Snack Bar-659-5898

ADMINISTRATIVE SUPPORT:
Legal-652-6781
Locator-652-1841
Police-652-5700
Public Affairs-652-4410
SDO/NCO-652-1859

HEALTH & WELFARE:
Chapel-652-6121/4659
Family Services-652-3060
Medical
  Central Appts-652-2273
  Clinic-652-4373
Retiree Services-652-6880
TRICARE-652-5524

REST & RECREATION:
Art/Crafts-652-2788
Auto Hobby Shop-652-2952
Bowling-652-6271
Clubs
  EM-658-3557
  Hunt/Saddle-652-2346
  O-658-7445
Golf Course-652-4570
Gym 652-2955/5955
ITT-652-2301
Library 652-2617
MWR Office-652-5971
Rec Equip-652-3702
Skeet Range-652-2064
Theater-652-3278
Youth Activities-652-3298

ATTRACTIONS: San Antonio, New Braunfels and Canyon Lake. Rec areas are nearby.

RED RIVER ARMY DEPOT (TX09R3)

Building 15, Main Street
Texarkana, TX 75507-5000
Scheduled for realignment by 1999

TELEPHONE NUMBER INFORMATION: Main installation numbers: C-903-334-2141, D-312-829-2141.

LOCATION: Off I-30, take Red River Army Depot exit #206. Route clearly marked. USMRA: Page 87 (N-2). NMC: Texarkana, 18 miles east.

GENERAL INFORMATION: Army Depot Activity for maintenance for armored vehicles, ammunition, and missiles.

TEMPORARY MILITARY LODGING: Lodging office, Building 228, 0745-1645 daily, C-903-334-3976/3227, D-312-829-3976/3227. All ranks. DV/VIP C-903-334-2316.

RV, CAMPING/FAMCAMP: Elliott Lake Recreation Area, on post year round, Community Recreation Branch, Building 12, ATTN: SDSRR-U, C-903-334-2254, D-312-829-2254, Fax: C-903-334-3290, 16 camper spaces with full hookups, 16 camper spaces with W/E, 16 rental log cabins, 20 tent spaces, five wooded screen shelters.

TEXAS
Red River Army Depot, continued

SPACE-A: None. See Barksdale AFB, LA listing, C-318-456-3226/5630, D-312-781-3226/5630.

LOGISTICAL SUPPORT:

Child Care-ext 2466	Credit Union-832-8858
Exchange-334-2396	Package Store-ext 2396
Shoppette-ext 2396	Visitor Center-ext 3151

ADMINISTRATIVE SUPPORT:

Fire Dept-ext 3627	Housing Office-ext 3976
Legal-334-3258	Locator-ext 3617
Pass/ID Office-ext 3151	Police-334-2911
Public Affairs-ext 3143	SDO/NCO-334-2911

HEALTH & WELFARE:

American Red Cross-793-5602	ACS-ext 2466
Army Emergency Relief-ext 2466	CHAMPUS-334-2155
Family Services-334-2466	Medical-334-2155
Retiree Services-334-2726	TRICARE-ext 2155

REST & RECREATION:

Clubs	Fitness Center-ext 2733
Com-334-2350	Golf Course-ext 2359
Rod/Gun-ext 2379/4868	Gym-ext 2733
MWR-ext 3606	Outdoor Rec-ext 2254
Rec Services-ext 3506	Youth Services-ext 2466

ATTRACTIONS: Near Texarkana, TX/AR, outdoor sports and recreation.

SHEPPARD AIR FORCE BASE (TX37R3)

82 TRW/PA
419 G Avenue, Suite 3
Sheppard Air Force Base, TX 76311-2943

TELEPHONE NUMBER INFORMATION: Main installation numbers: C-817-676-2511, D-312-736-2511. HP: http://www.spd.aetc.af.mil.

LOCATION: Take US-281 north from Wichita Falls, exit to TX-325 which leads to main gate. Clearly marked. USMRA: Page 87 (J-1). NMC: Wichita Falls, five miles southwest.

GENERAL INFORMATION: Air Education and Training Command. Sheppard Training Center, 80th Flying Training Wing & support units. 82nd Training, Logistics, Support, and Medical Groups. 782nd Training Group, 882nd Training Group, and 982nd Training Group.

TEMPORARY MILITARY LODGING: Lodging office, Building 1600, Avenue J, 24 hours daily, C-817-855-7370, D-312-736-2631 Fax: C-817-676-7434, D-312-736-7434. All ranks. DV/VIP C-817-855-2123.

RV, CAMPING/FAMCAMP: Operates Sheppard AFB Recreation Annex off base. See Sheppard AFB Recreation Annex listing for more information.

SPACE-A: Pax Term/Lounge, Building 1360, duty hours, C-817-676-2180/6474, D-312-736-2180/6474, flights to CONUS locations.

LOGISTICAL SUPPORT:

Bank-855-2321	Barber Shop-855-2211
Beauty Shop-855-2087	Child Care-676-2038
Child Dev Center-676-2038	Class Six-855-6502
Commissary-676-7269	Conv Store-855-4341
Credit Union-720-8000	Dining Facilities-676-2080
Dry Cleaner-855-2880	Education Office-676-6231
Exchange-855-4318	Gas Station-855-4341
Laundry-855-2880	Package Store-855-6502
Postal Service-855-3319	SATO-676-4267
Snack Bar-855-5451	Travel Office-676-2302
Visitor Center-676-7441	

ADMINISTRATIVE SUPPORT:

Fire Dept-911	Housing Office-676-4364
Legal-676-6760	Locator-676-1841
Pass/ID Office-676-1853	Police-676-4522
Public Affairs-676-7250	SDO/NCO-676-2621

HEALTH & WELFARE:

Air Force Aid Society-676-4358	American Red Cross-676-2308
Chapel-676-6348	Dental-676-1846
Family Services-676-2300	Medical-676-1847
Retiree Services-676-5088	TRICARE-676-1847
Veterinary Services-676-6883	

REST & RECREATION:

Arts & Crafts-676-2870	Auto Hobby Shop-676-2249
Bowling-676-7174/4806	Clubs
Community Center-676-6210	EM-676-2083
Fitness Center-676-6336	NCO-676-6427
Golf Course-676-6369	O-676-6460
Gym-676-6133	ITT-676-2302
Library-676-6152	MWR-676-2089
Outdoor Rec-676-4141	Picnic Area-ext 2876
Rec Center-676-6210	Services-676-2745
Skeet/Trap Range-ext 6852	Swimming-ext 6494
Theater-676-4427	Youth Center-676-5437

ATTRACTIONS: Wichita Falls and outdoor sports.

SHEPPARD AIR FORCE BASE RECREATION ANNEX (TX16R3)

Route 3, Box 151
Whitesboro, TX 76273-5000

TELEPHONE NUMBER INFORMATION: Main installation numbers: C-817-676-2511, D-312-736-2511.

LOCATION: Located approximately 120 miles east of base at Wichita Falls, near the Texas/Oklahoma line. From US-82 east of Gainesville, take US-377 north approximately 11 miles (pass Gordonville exit) to TX FM-901 and turn left. (Just prior to this exit is a green SAFB Annex sign.) Go two miles; turn right at SAFB Annex sign. Follow signs approximately five miles to recreation annex. Rec area is located on Texas side of Lake Texoma. USMRA: page 87 (K-1,2). NMC: Dallas, 95 miles south. NMI: Dallas NAS, 95 miles south.

GENERAL INFORMATION: One of the largest, most popular inland lakes in the area. Some of the best fishing is available as well as a variety of other water sports. Operated by Sheppard Air Force Base, off base year round. Military personnel active, retired, dependents, guard, reserve and federal civilian employees. Check in at main lodge, 1500, check out 1300. Reservations: Accepted. C-903-523-4613 (0800-1700 daily). Visa and MasterCard accepted. No pets allowed in cabins; allowed on leash in other areas; proof of current rabies vaccination required. No fireworks. Hunting firearms only and must be registered at lodge. No hunting permitted on the annex.

TEMPORARY MILITARY LODGING: Cabins: two bedroom, AC, private bath, TV; furnished except towels, personal items (1), sleeps four, AC, private bath, TV; furnished except towels, personal items (1), sleeps four-six, AC, private bath, TV; furnished except towels, personal items (41); Mobile home, sleeps six, AC, private bath, TV; furnished except towels, personal items (1). Rates: Cabins: two bedroom $40 daily, sleeps four $40 daily, sleeps four-six $25-$30 daily; mobile home $40 daily.

RV, CAMPING/FAMCAMP: Camper spaces with full hookups (8); camper spaces with W&E hookups (16); tent spaces with no hookups. Rates: camper spaces with full hookups $10 daily, weekly/monthly rates available; camper spaces with W&E hookups $8, weekly/monthly rates available; tent spaces $0. Dry Boat Storage $18-$25 monthly; Day Act slips (30) $3 daily.

ADMINISTRATIVE SUPPORT: Police-893-4388

REST & RECREATION: Basketball, Driving Range, Fishing, Hiking, Holiday Specials, Horseshoes, Volleyball, Water Skiing, Softball, Swimming.

OTHER SUPPORT & FACILITIES AVAILABLE: Airstrip/grass, Bait, Beach, Boat Launch, Boat Rental, Boat Slips, Convenience Store, "Crappie" House, Fitness Center, Gas, Grills, Laundry, Movies, Multi-Purpose Court, Pavilions, Picnic Area, Playgrounds, Rec Equipment, Rec Room/TV, Restrooms, Sewage Dump, Showers, Snack Bar*, Trails, Vending Machine, Video Rental. Also, see Fort Worth Naval Air Station/Joint Reserve Base listing, C-817-782-5000, D-312-739-5000.

*Open on Saturdays & Sundays from Memorial Day through Labor Day.

ATTRACTIONS: Great fishing, various water sports, sun and fun.

Other Installations in Texas

Biggs Field (TX45R3), 11210 CSM E Slewitzke Street, Biggs AAF, TX 79908-0053. USMRA: Page 86 (B-6). C-915-568-2121, Gas Station-562-8442, Exchange-562-7200, Space A-568-8097.

Camp Bullis (TX40R3), Fort Sam Houston Training Site, TX 78234-5066. Off of I-10, northwest of San Antonio. USMRA: Page 87 (J-6); Page 91 (B,C-1). C-210-698-1246. Exchange-698-1183.

Dallas Naval Air Station (TX12R3), 8100 West Jefferson Boulevard, Dallas Naval Air Station, TX 75211-9501. ***Scheduled to close September 1998. Facilities are moving to Fort Worth NAS/JRB. Call PAO at Fort Worth for more information; C-817-782-7815/7816.*** Main installation numbers: C-972-266-6111, D-312-874-6111. Exit from I-30 at loop 12, west of Dallas, go south on loop 12 to Jefferson Avenue exit, NAS on left (south) side of Avenue. Near Grand Prairie. USMRA: Page 88 (E-3). NMC: Dallas, 15 miles northeast. Exchange-266-6411, Police-266-6139, Gym-266-6108.

Ellington Field ANGB/Houston CGAS (TX41R3), 14657 Sneider Street, Houston, TX 77034-5586. USMRA: Page 89 (D-4,5). C-281-929-2222, Exchange-929-4321. Space-A-481-0025.

Headquarters Army & Air Force Exchange Service (TX11R3), 3911 South Walton Walker Boulevard, Dallas, TX 75236-1598. USMRA: Page 88 (F-4). C-214-312-2011, D-312-967-2011. HP: http://www.aafes.com. Exchange-312-2011.

Houston CG Marine Safety Office (TX48R3), 9640 Clinton Drive, Galena Park, TX 77547-0446. USMRA: Page 89 (C-3). C-713-671-5100, Exchange-678-4573.

Waco Shoppette (TX46R3), 1801 Exchange Parkway, Waco, TX 76712-5000. USMRA: Page 87 (K-4). C-817-666-8309, Exchange-666-8309.

UTAH

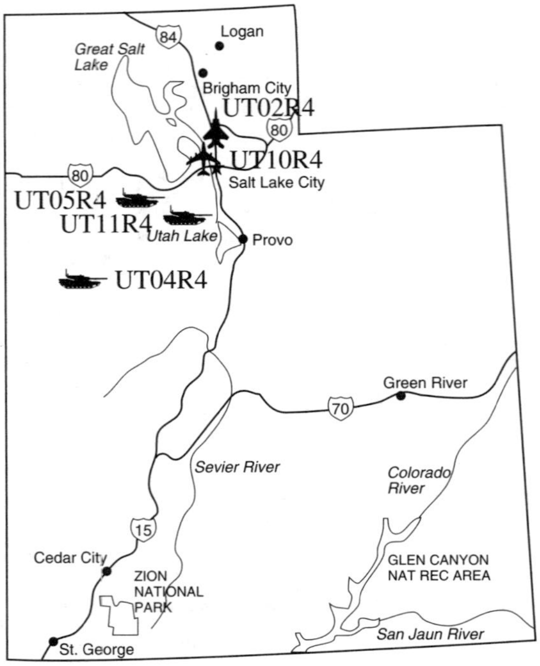

CAMP W.G. WILLIAMS (UT11R4)

17800 South Camp Williams Road
Riverton, UT 84065-4999

TELEPHONE NUMBER INFORMATION: Main installation numbers: C-801-253-5402, D-312-766-5402.

LOCATION: From I-15 take exit 296 (Draper/Riverton), turn west onto highway 111. Turn left at third traffic light, drive approximately seven miles, and Camp Williams is on the left. USMRA: Page 112 (D-4). NMC: Salt Lake City, 25 miles north.

GENERAL INFORMATION: Utah Regional Training Academy. Camp Williams is a National Guard training base.

TEMPORARY MILITARY LODGING: Lodging office, Building 802, 1000-1700 Mon-Fri, 1000-1400 Sat-Sun. C-801-253-5410, D-312-766-5410, Fax: C-801-253-9543.

RV, CAMPING/FAMCAMP: None. See Hill AFB listing, C-801-777-3250, D-312-458-3250.

SPACE-A: None. See Hill AFB listing, C-801-777-1854/2887, D-312-458-1854/2887, Fax: C-801-777-3249.

LOGISTICAL SUPPORT:

Cafeteria-254-2819	Exchange-576-3815*

ADMINISTRATIVE SUPPORT:

Locator-253-5455	Police-253-5455

HEALTH & WELFARE:	Medical-576-3871*

REST & RECREATION:

Clubs	MWR-253-5401
NCO-254-2819	Rec Equipment-253-5425
O-254-7623	

* Phone numbers will be changing. Call main installation number for further information.

OTHER FACILITIES AVAILABLE: Fitness Center.

ATTRACTIONS: Salt Lake City: Temple Square, planetarium, Hogle Zoo, Trolley Square for shopping, Delta Center for pro sports. Close to skiing and hiking.

DUGWAY PROVING GROUND (UT04R4)

ATTN: STEDP-CO
Building 4142
Dugway Proving Ground, UT 84022-5000

TELEPHONE NUMBER INFORMATION: Main installation numbers: C-801-831-2151, D-312-789-2151. **NOTE:** When calling from Salt Lake City the prefix is 522 instead of 831.

LOCATION: Isolated but can be reached from I-80. Take Skull Valley Road (exit 77) for 40 miles south. USMRA: Page 112 (B,C-4,5). NMC: Salt Lake City, 80 miles northeast.

GENERAL INFORMATION: Major Army Test and Evaluation Command. Range and evaluation units.

TEMPORARY MILITARY LODGING: Lodging office, Building 5228, Valdez Circle, 0730-1845 Mon-Thu, 0700-1545 Fri. C-801-831-2333, D-312-789-2333. All ranks. DV/VIP C-801-831-2020.

RV, CAMPING/FAMCAMP: None. See Tooele Army Depot listing, Oquirrh Hills Travel Camp, C-801-833-3129, D-312-790-3129.

SPACE-A: None. See Salt Lake City IAP, C-801-595-2274 D-312-790-9274, Fax: C-801-595-2271. Flights to CONUS and OCONUS locations.

LOGISTICAL SUPPORT:

Child Care-831-3345	Commissary-831-2164
Conv Store-831-4773	Exchange-831-4491
Gas Station-831-4773	Package Store-831-4491
SATO-831-2131	

ADMINISTRATIVE SUPPORT:

Legal-831-3716	Locator-831-3545/1110
Police-831-5161	SDO/NCO-831-3870

HEALTH & WELFARE:

CHAMPUS-831-3311	Chapel-831-2431
Family Services-831-2278	Medical-831-2222

REST & RECREATION:

Bowling-ext 2687	Com Club-831-2901
Fitness Center-ext 2705	Library-ext 2178
Outdoor Rec-ext 2318	Youth Center-ext 2177

ATTRACTIONS: Great Salt Lake, Salt Lake City, historic Church of Jesus Christ of Latter Day Saints, museums, and skiing. Four national parks within a day's drive.

HILL AIR FORCE BASE (UT02R4)

7981 Georgia Street
Hill Air Force Base, UT 84056-5824

TELEPHONE NUMBER INFORMATION: Main installation numbers: C-801-777-7221, D-312-777-7221 (Operator assistance), C-801-777-1411, D-312-777-1411.

LOCATION: Adjacent to I-15 between Ogden and Salt Lake City. Take exit 336, east on UT-193 to south gate *OR* exit 338 west to west gate. USMRA: Page 112 (D-3). NMI: Tooele Army Depot, 60 miles southwest. NMC: Ogden, eight miles north.

UTAH
Hill Air Force Base, continued

GENERAL INFORMATION: Air Force Materiel Command Base, Headquarters Ogden Air Logistics Center and 75th Air Base Wing. Provides engineering and logistics for F-16 Fighting Falcon and C-130 Hercules and Minuteman and Peacekeeper missiles, overhauls and repairs landing gear, brakes, struts and wheels for Air Force Aircraft. Also, 388 FW (ACC) and 419 FW (AFRES), both flying F-16.

TEMPORARY MILITARY LODGING: Lodging office, Building 146, D Street, 24 hours daily, C-801-777-1844/2601, D-312-777-1844/2601. All ranks.

RV, CAMPING/FAMCAMP: Carter Creek Camp, off base weekends prior to Jul 4-Oct 31, Outdoor Recreation, Building 402, C-801-777-2225/9666, six cabins, four trailers, four camper spaces with W/E hookups, three tent spaces. Hill FAMCAMP, on base year round, Outdoor Recreation, 75 Services, C-801-777-3250, D-312-458-3250. Hillhaus Lodge, off base year round, reservations not handled by Hill AFB, call for information C-801-621-2202, D-312-458-3525.

SPACE-A: Pax Term/Lounge, Building 900, C-801-777-1854 (recording) C-801-777-2887, D-312-458-1854/2887, Fax: C-801-775-3249. Flights to CONUS locations.

LOGISTICAL SUPPORT:

Child Dev Center-777-6321	Commissary-777-2300
EXA Travel-777-4677	Exchange-773-1207
Gas Station-773-3600	Package Store-777-2169
Restaurants-777-2043	Shoppette-773-4673

ADMINISTRATIVE SUPPORT:

Legal-777-6756	Locator-777-1841
Police-777-3056	Public Affairs-777-5201

HEALTH & WELFARE:

CHAMPUS-777-6206	Chapel-777-2106
Family Services-777-4044	Medical
Retiree Services-777-5735	Central Appts-777-4061 (AD)
	777-1847 (Dep)
	Emergency-777-5285
	Hospital-777-6298

REST & RECREATION:

Arts & Crafts-777-2649	Auto Hobby Shop-777-3476
Bowling-777-6565	Clubs
Golf Course-777-3272	EM-773-3166
Hess Fitness Center-777-2762	O-773-2809
777-8360 (West Area)	Rod/Gun-777-6767
Library-777-3833	Theater-777-2328
Thornton Rec Center-777-3525	Tickets & Tours-777-2892
Outdoor Rec-777-9666	Youth Center-777-2419

ATTRACTIONS: Hill Aerospace Museum, Great Salt Lake and Antelope Island, Bear River Bird Refuge and Golden Spike National Historic Site, Lagoon Amusement Park, Nature trail, dinosaur park, Union Station, Temple Square, museums, Utah Jazz basketball, planetarium, zoo, Salt Lake City, snow skiing. Park City, Temple Square.

TOOELE ARMY DEPOT (UT05R4)

ATTN: SIOTE-CO
Building 1
Tooele, UT 84074-5008

TELEPHONE NUMBER INFORMATION: Main installation numbers: C-801-833-3211, D-312-790-1110.

LOCATION: From west I-80, exit 99, to UT-36 south for about 15 miles to main entrance. USMRA: Page 112 (C-4). NMC: Salt Lake City, 40 miles northeast.

GENERAL INFORMATION: There are three main missions at Tooele Army Depot (TEAD), a subordinate of the Industrial Operations command in Rock Island, Illinois. These include Ammunition Operations, Ammunition Equipment Design and Development and Rail Shop Maintenance and on-site support. Additionally the depot provides base operations support to various activities and tenants.

TEMPORARY MILITARY LODGING: Lodging office, Building 1, Hq Loop, 0630-1700 daily, C-801-833-2124, D-312-790-2124. All ranks.

RV, CAMPING/FAMCAMP: Oquirrh Hills Travel Camp on post, May-Oct, Community and Family Activities, Building 1011, C-801-833-3129, D-312-790-3129, 14 camper spaces with W/E hookups, eight tent spaces.

SPACE-A: None. See Hill AFB listing, C-801-777-1854/2887, D-312-458-1854/2887, Fax: C-801-777-3249.

LOGISTICAL SUPPORT:

Exchange-833-2394	Package Store-833-2394
SATO-833-3251	

ADMINISTRATIVE SUPPORT:

Fire Dept-833-2015	Legal-833-2536
Locator-833-2094	Police-833-2559
Public Affairs-833-3216	SDO/SNCO-833-2304

HEALTH & WELFARE:

ACS-833-2852	CHAMPUS-1-800-842-4333
Family Services-833-2852	Medical-833-2572
Retiree Services-833-2249	Emergency-833-2666

REST & RECREATION:

Arts & Crafts-ext 2940	Auto Hobby Shop-ext 2873
Bowling-882-9922	Com Club-833-2582
Gym-ext 3189	ITT-833-3129
MWR-833-2039	Recreation-833-2039
Sports-ext 2005	Sports Rental-ext 2107
Stables-ext 3345	Swimming-ext 3189
Theater-833-2582	

ATTRACTIONS: Salt Lake City nearby, Utah desert, and mountains are available for rock climbing, exploration, camping, motorcycling, hiking, and/or sightseeing.

Other Installations in Utah

Salt Lake City International Airport (UT10R4), Salt Lake City, UT 84116-5000. USMRA: Page 112 (D-3); Page 116 (B-2). C-801-595-2200, Exchange-355-1923, Medical-595-2337, Space-A-595-2274.

VERMONT

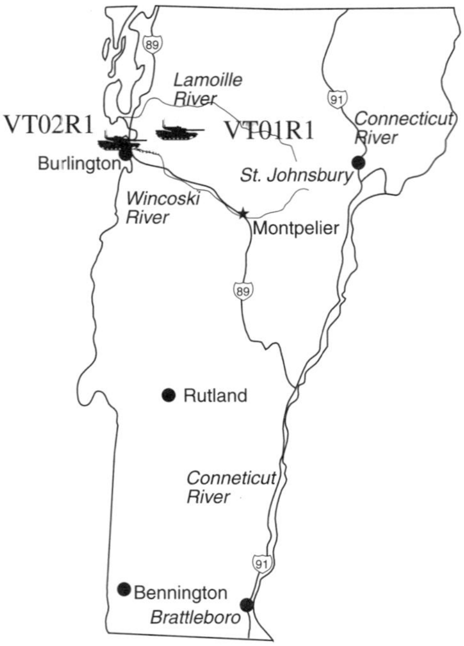

Other Installations in Vermont

Camp Johnson (VT01R1), Building 17 Colchester, VT 05446-5000. USMRA: Page 23 (A-4). C-802-655-3030, Exchange-655-3030.

Ethan Allen Firing Range (VT02R1), Rural Route 1, Box 57, Jericho, VT 05465-9706. USMRA: Page 23 (B-4). C-802-899-2811, Exchange (only open when units are in field for annual training - approximately eight to 10 weeks a year)-899-2811.

VIRGINIA

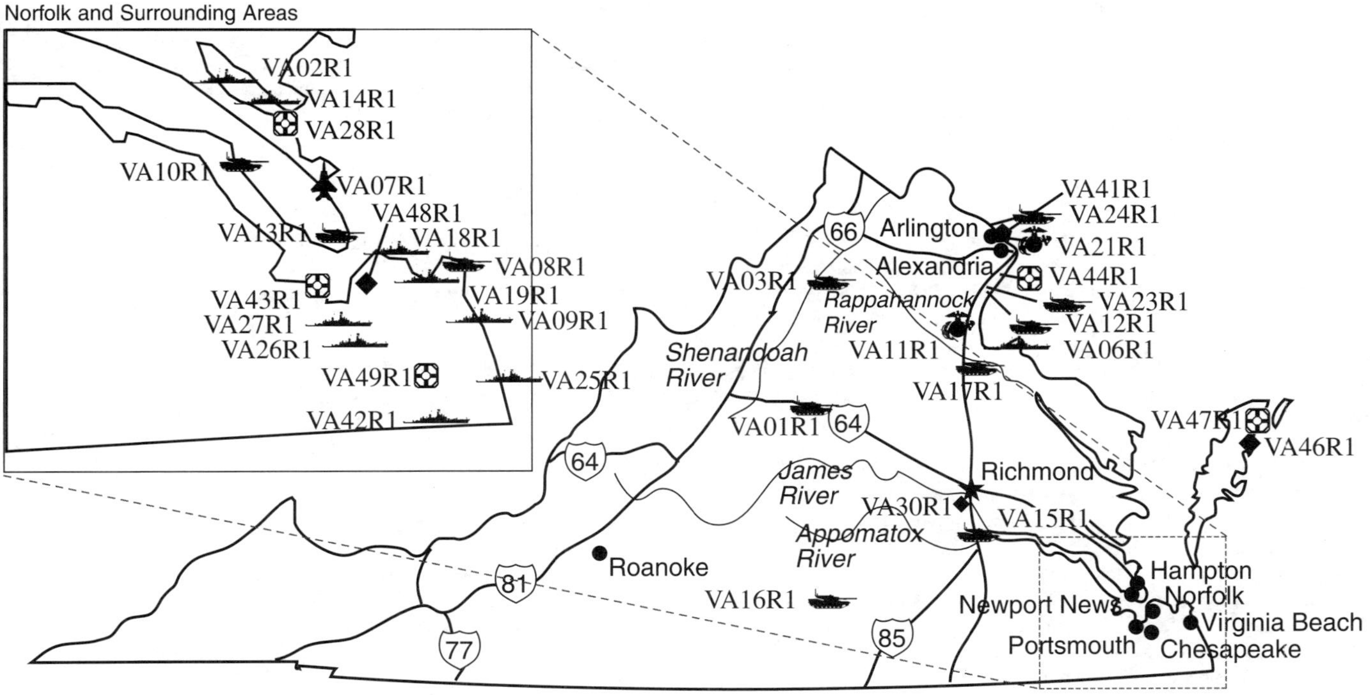

ALEXANDRIA COAST GUARD TELECOMMUNICATION AND INFORMATION SYSTEMS COMMAND (VA44R1)

7323 Telegraph Road
Alexandria, VA 22310-3999

TELEPHONE NUMBER INFORMATION: Main installation number: C-703-313-5400.

LOCATION: Take I-95 to Telegraph Rd exit. Travel south on Telegraph Road four miles to Base on left. USMRA: Page 47 (M-5). NMC: Washington, DC, 15 miles northeast.

GENERAL INFORMATION: TISCOM, Ceremonial Honor Guard, Navigation Systems Center.

TEMPORARY MILITARY LODGING: None. See Fort Belvoir listing, C-703-805-2333 or 1-800-295-9750.

RV, CAMPING/FAMCAMP: None. See Quantico MCB listing, Lunga Park, C-703-784-5270, D-312-278-5270.

SPACE-A: None. See Andrews AFB, MD listing, C-301-981-1854, D-312-858-1854, Fax: C-301-981-4241.

LOGISTICAL SUPPORT:	Exchange-313-5992/5734
ADMINISTRATIVE SUPPORT:	Public Affairs-313-5555
HEALTH & WELFARE:	Medical-313-5446

REST & RECREATION:

Anchorage Club-313-5990	Auto Hobby Shop-ext 5994
Picnic Grounds-ext 5987	Rec Equipment-ext 5797

ATTRACTIONS: Mount Vernon, Old Town Alexandria, Washington, DC.

ARMED FORCES STAFF COLLEGE (VA48R1)

7800 Hampton Boulevard
Norfolk, VA 23511-5000

TELEPHONE NUMBER INFORMATION: Main installation numbers: (Quarterdeck 24-hours) C-757-444-5150, D-312-564-5150.

LOCATION: From I-64 east to I-564 to Terminal Boulevard. Armed Forces Staff College will be on the corner of Terminal and Hampton Boulevard. USMRA: Page 52 (F-6). NMC: Norfolk, in city limits.

GENERAL INFORMATION: Armed Forces Staff College.

TEMPORARY MILITARY LODGING: Building SC 407. C-757-444-5311, D-312-564-5311. Officers only.

RV, CAMPING/FAMCAMP: None. See Little Creek NAB listing, C-757-464-7516, D-312-680-7516.

SPACE-A: None. See Norfolk NB listing, C-757-444-4118/4148/3947 or 445-6538, D-312-564-4118/4148/3947 or 565-6538, Fax: C-757-445-7501, D-312-565-7501.

LOGISTICAL SUPPORT:	Exchange-440-2000 (Marianas Hall)-440-2070
ADMINISTRATIVE SUPPORT:	Police-444-5255

HEALTH & WELFARE:

Chapel-444-5183	Family Services-444-5183

REST & RECREATION:

Fitness Center-ext 1198	Library-ext 5155
O'Club-423-4713	Rec Equip Rental-ext 5443
Youth Activities-ext 5443	

ATTRACTIONS: Virginia Beach nearby, entertainment and restaurants.

VIRGINIA

CAPE HENRY INN (VA51R1)

Building 1116
Fort Story, VA 23459-5034

TELEPHONE NUMBER INFORMATION: Main installation numbers: C-757-422-7305, D-312-438-7305.

LOCATION: From North, take I95-S to I295-E around Richmond to I64-E. Exit on13N-Northampton Boulevard. Then exit on Shore Drive (last exit before Bay Bridge-Tunnel). Follow Shore Drive east to Fort Story entrance on left. Inn is first left turn after the gate. OR take 13S through Delaware, Maryland, and Virginia across the Chesapeake Bay Bridge-Tunnel. Exit east on Shore Drive and proceed to Fort Story. From South, take I95-N to 58E to 64W. Exit 13E Northampton Boulevard. Exit on Shore Drive east and proceed to Fort Story. USMRA: page 47 (O-9), page 52 (I,J-5,6). NMC: Virginia Beach, three miles south.

GENERAL INFORMATION: Located between Seashore State Park and the Virginia Beach oceanfront on the environmentally protected dunes overlooking the Chesapeake Bay. A variety of wildlife, including red fox, make their home in the dunes, and wildflowers are abundant. Operated by Fort Story, on post year round. Military personnel active, retired, reserve and DoD civilians. Reservations: Accepted up to a year in advance, after October 1997, up to six months in advance. One night deposit required, seven-day cancellation policy. C-757-422-8818. Fax: C-757-422-6397. MasterCard accepted. Pets and smoking allowed in bungalows only. No grills allowed.

TEMPORARY MILITARY LIVING: Sandpiper, one room, two full beds, 5 cf refrigerator, sleeps four (10); Dune, sleeping area, two full beds, separated sitting area with pull-out couch and kitchenette, sleeps six (30); Pelican, queen-sized bed and kitchenette, sleeps two (10); Chesapeake, full kitchen and living room with pull out couch, two bedrooms, sleeps six (12); Tidewater, full kitchen and living room with pull out couch (6); Bungalow, eat-in kitchen or dining room, two bedrooms and living room with pull out couch, no voice mail or long distance capability(8). One Pelican unit and one Chesapeake unit are handicap accessible. Bungalows near Fort Story center, built in 1942, spacious; most have 2 TVs, screened-in front/back porches, most are close to the fishing beach, but no water view, ground level. Rates: Sandpiper $29-$45 daily; Dune $39-$55 daily; Pelican $39-$55 daily; Chesapeake $60-$70 daily; Tidewater $65-$75 daily; Bungalow $60-$70 daily. Also, Cape Henry Travel Camp, on post, year round, ATTN: Travel Camp, Fort Story, VA 23459-5034, C-757-422-7601, D-312-438-7601, 13 log cabins, three Kamping Kabins.

REST & RECREATION: Beaches, Dolphin watching, Sightseeing, Swimming.

OTHER SUPPORT & FACILITIES AVAILABLE: CATV, Modems*, Refrigerators, Restaurants nearby, Telephones with voice mail. Also, see Fort Story listing, C-757-422-7305, D-312-438-7305.

** Limited number of rooms with modems available.*

ATTRACTIONS: Williamsburg, Jamestown, Yorktown, Norfolk.

CHEATHAM ANNEX FLEET AND INDUSTRIAL SUPPLY CENTER (VA02R1)

108 Sanda Avenue
Williamsburg, VA 23187-8792

TELEPHONE NUMBER INFORMATION: Main installation numbers: C-757-887-4000, D-312-953-4000.

VIRGINIA
Cheatham Annex Fleet and Industrial Supply Center, continued

LOCATION: From I-64 take exit 242B to US-199 East to main gate of Cheatham Annex. USMRA: Page 47 (N-8). NMC: Williamsburg, six miles west.

GENERAL INFORMATION: Annex of Norfolk Fleet and Industrial Supply Center, Depot activity for Naval supplies and other special programs.

TEMPORARY MILITARY LODGING: Lodging office, MWR, Building 284, 0700-1530 Mon-Fri, C-757-887-7224/7101, D-312-953-7224/7101. All ranks. DV/VIP C-757-887-7108.

RV, CAMPING/FAMCAMP: Recreation Cabins and RV Park, on base, year round, 108 Sanda Avenue, Williamsburg, VA 23185-8792, C-757-887-7224, D-312-953-7224. Nineteen camper spaces with full hookups, 12 cabins.

SPACE-A: None. See Norfolk NB listing, C-757-444-4118/4148/3947 or 445-6538, D-312-564-4118/4148/3947 or 565-6538, Fax: C-757-445-7501, D-312-565-7501.

LOGISTICAL SUPPORT:
Conv Store-887-3582
Gas Station-887-3582
Exchange-887-3582

ADMINISTRATIVE SUPPORT:
Police-887-7222
SDO/NCO-887-7222

HEALTH & WELFARE:
Medical-887-7222

REST & RECREATION:
Auto Hobby Shop-ext 7418
ITT-887-7101
Swimming-ext 7102
Golf Course-887-7159
MWR-887-7101

ATTRACTIONS: Historic Williamsburg, Jamestown, and Yorktown are nearby. Water Country USA, Busch Gardens, Mariners' Museum, and Virginia Living Museum within 30 minutes. Paramount's King's Dominion is 75 minutes away.

CHESAPEAKE NAVAL SECURITY GROUP ACTIVITY, NORTHWEST (VA42R1)

1320 Northwest Boulevard, Suite 100
Chesapeake, VA 23322-4094

TELEPHONE NUMBER INFORMATION: Main installation numbers: C-757-421-8000, D-312-564-1336.

LOCATION: Five miles west of VA-168 at NC/VA border, turn right onto Ballahack Road, and follow to base gate (a left on Relay Road). Located between Moyock, NC and Great Bridge, VA. USMRA: Page 47 (N,O-10). NMC: Norfolk, 35 miles north.

GENERAL INFORMATION: Naval Security Group and Communications Activity.

TEMPORARY MILITARY LODGING: BEQ/BOQ C-757-421-8331, D-312-564-1336, DV/VIP C-757-421-8331, D-312-564-1336, Fax: C-757-421-8235.

RV, CAMPING/FAMCAMP: Stewart Campground, on base, 1 May-1 Dec, C-757-421-8262, Fax: C-757-421-8785. Eighteen camper spaces with E hookups.

SPACE-A: None. See Norfolk NB listing, C-757-444-4118/4148/3947 or 445-6538, D-312-564-4118/4148/3947 or 565-6538, Fax: C-757-445-7501, D-312-565-7501.

LOGISTICAL SUPPORT:
Child Care-421-8266
Dining Facilities
  Galley-421-8276
  Snack Bar-421-8250
Conv Store-421-8254
Exchange-421-8254
Gas Station-421-8252
Package Store-421-8252

ADMINISTRATIVE SUPPORT:
CDO/OOD-421-8000
Legal-421-8375
Public Affairs-421-8328
Fire Dept-421-8243
Police-421-8334

HEALTH & WELFARE:
Chapel-421-8204
Family Services-421-8770
Dental-421-8225
Medical-421-8220

REST & RECREATION:
Clubs
  CPO-421-8290
  EM-421-8250
  O-421-8285
Gym-421-8303
Fitness Center-421-8263
MWR-421-8260

ATTRACTIONS: Casemate Museum at Fort Monroe, Portsmouth Naval Shipyard Museum, Mariners' Museum, Nauticus Marine Museum, and Busch Gardens and Williamsburg are nearby.

DAHLGREN NAVAL SURFACE WARFARE CENTER (VA06R1)

17320 Dahlgren Road
Dahlgren, VA 22448-5100

TELEPHONE NUMBER INFORMATION: Main installation numbers: C-540-653-8291, D-312-249-8291.

LOCATION: From I-95 in Fredericksburg, east on VA-3 to VA-206 (17 miles), left at Arnolds Corner, east to Dahlgren (11 miles). Also, US-301 south to VA-206, east to main gate of Center. USMRA: Page 47 (M-6). NMC: Washington, DC, 38 miles north.

GENERAL INFORMATION: Naval Surface Weapons RDT&E Center.

TEMPORARY MILITARY LODGING: Lodging office, Building 960, 24 hours daily, C-540-653-7671, D-312-249-7671. All ranks. DV/VIP C-540-653-8153.

RV, CAMPING/FAMCAMP: None. See Fort A.P. Hill Recreation Facilities, C-804-633-8219, D-312-934-8219.

SPACE-A: None. See Andrews AFB, MD listing, C-301-981-1854, D-312-858-1854, Fax: C-301-981-4241.

LOGISTICAL SUPPORT:
Cafeteria-653-3841
Commissary-653-7318
Gas Station-653-2050
SATO-653-0074
Child Care-653-4994
Exchange-653-2121
Gen Mess-653-8277
Snack Bar-653-2720

ADMINISTRATIVE SUPPORT:
Fire Dept-911
Locator-653-8216
Public Affairs-653-8153
Legal-653-7121
Police-653-8500
SDO/NCO-653-8531

HEALTH & WELFARE:
CHAMPUS-653-8241
Family Services-653-1839
Retiree Services-653-1839
Chapel-653-8297
Medical-653-8241

REST & RECREATION:
Bowling-653-7327
Golf Course-653-3002
Gym-653-8580
ITT-653-8785
MWR-653-7777
Rec Equip-653-8585
Tennis-653-8580
Clubs
  EM-653-8785
  O-653-1916
Library-653-7474
Recreation-653-7777
Swimming-653-8088
Theater-653-7777

ATTRACTIONS: Center is on the Potomac River. Washington, DC, easy drive.

VIRGINIA

DAM NECK FLEET COMBAT TRAINING CENTER, ATLANTIC (VA25R1)

1912 Regulus Avenue
Virginia Beach, VA 23461-2098

TELEPHONE NUMBER INFORMATION: Main installation numbers: C-757-433-2000, D-312-433-2000. E-mail: fctclant.n1@netpmsa.cnet.navy.mil.

LOCATION: On ocean front, off Oceana Boulevard. USMRA: Page 47 (O-9,10) page 52 (J-7,8). NMC: Virginia Beach, two miles northeast.

GENERAL INFORMATION: Fleet Combat Training Center with major tenant commands. Navy and Marine Corps Intelligence Training Center, Naval Surface Warfare Center, Port Hueneme Division, East Coast Office, Naval Processing Facility.

TEMPORARY MILITARY LODGING: Lodging office, Building 566, BEQ C-757-491-2449; Building 241 BOQ, C-757-433-7013. All ranks. DV/VIP C-757-433-6542.

RV, CAMPING/FAMCAMP: None. See Chesapeake NSGA, NW, Stewart Campground, C-757-421-8262, Fax: C-757-421-8785.

SPACE-A: None. See Oceana NAS listing, C-757-433-2903/2260, D-312-433-2903/2260.

LOGISTICAL SUPPORT:

Child Care-433-8638	Conv Store-433-7754
Exchange-433-6496	Gas Station-433-7794

ADMINISTRATIVE SUPPORT:

CDO-433-6234	Housing Office-433-2195
Locator-433-6000	Police-433-6186

HEALTH & WELFARE:

Chapel-433-6602	Medical-433-6327

REST & RECREATION:

Beaches-433-7208	Bowling-ext 7208
Golf-ext 2866	Gym-ext 7483
Library-ext 6565	O'Club-433-6141
Swimming-ext 6551	

ATTRACTIONS: Virginia Beach, water sports. Close to Norfolk, Williamsburg.

DEFENSE SUPPLY CENTER (VA30R1)

8000 Jefferson Davis Highway
Richmond, VA 23297-5100

TELEPHONE NUMBER INFORMATION: Main installation numbers: C-804-279-3861, D-312-695-3861.

LOCATION: From I-95 (Richmond-Petersburg Turnpike) exit 64 or 67 to US-1/301. Clearly marked on US-1/301. USMRA: Page 47 (L-8). NMC: Richmond, eight miles north.

GENERAL INFORMATION: A Defense Logistics Agency Field Level Activity.

TEMPORARY MILITARY LODGING: C-804-279-3371, D-312-695-4198, Fax: C-804-279-6419, D-312-695-6419.

RV, CAMPING/FAMCAMP: None. See Fort Pickett listing, C-804-292-2443, D-312-438-2443.

SPACE-A: None. See Langley AFB listing, C-757-764-4698/4311, D-312-574-4698/4311, Fax: C-757-764-5941.

LOGISTICAL SUPPORT:

Barber Shop-279-3553	Cafeteria-271-9497
Child Care-279-6694	Commissary-279-3904
Exchange-279-2654	Gas Station-279-1478
Package Store-279-1498	Postal Service-279-3013
SATO-279-5774	Shoppette-279-3904
Snack Bar-279-3572	Travel Office-279-3747

ADMINISTRATIVE SUPPORT:

Fire Dept-279-3630	Housing office-279-5411
Legal-279-4811	Locator-279-3861
OOD-279-3803	Pass/ID Office-279-4888
Police-279-4888	Public Affairs-279-3139
SDO/NCO-279-3805	

HEALTH & WELFARE:

CHAMPUS-279-3821	Medical-279-3821

REST & RECREATION:

Fitness Center-279-6992	Gym-279-6992
Indoor Rec-279-6982	O'Club-279-3772
Outdoor Rec-279-6982	

OTHER SUPPORT AVAILABLE: Education Office, Visitors Center.

ATTRACTIONS: Historic Richmond short drive north, Edgar Allen Poe Museum, First White House of the Confederacy. Museum of the Confederacy, Virginia Museum of Fine Arts, Science Museum of Virginia, St John's Church, King's Dominion and Busch Gardens amusement parks, and various Civil War battlefields.

FORT A.P. HILL (VA17R1)

ATTN: AFKA-FHA-PA
Bowling Green, VA 22427-5000

TELEPHONE NUMBER INFORMATION: Main installation numbers: C-804-633-8760, D-312-934-8760.

LOCATION: From I-95, take Bowling Green/Fort A.P. Hill exit, US-17 (bypass) east to VA-2 south to Bowling Green, take VA-301 northeast to main gate. Also, exit I-95 to VA-207 north to VA-301 north and to main gate. USMRA: Page 47 (L,M-6,7). NMC: Fredericksburg, 14 miles northwest.

GENERAL INFORMATION: Army Active, Reserve and ANG Training Center, Marine, Navy, Air Force Reserve Officer Training Corps, and other Civilian Organizations.

TEMPORARY MILITARY LODGING: Lodging office, Building TT-0142, 0800-1630 Sat-Thu, 0800-2300 Fri. C-804-633-8335, D-312-578-8335. All ranks. DV/VIP C-804-633-8205.

RV, CAMPING/FAMCAMP: A.P. Hill Recreation Facilities, on post year round, Commander, US Army Garrison, ATTN: Morale Support Activities Division, C-804-633-8219, D-312-934-8219, *The Lodge,* four log cabins.

SPACE-A: Extremely limited. C-804-633-8335.

LOGISTICAL SUPPORT:

Exchange-633-8690	Snack Bar-633-8690

ADMINISTRATIVE SUPPORT:

CDO/OOD-633-8206	Fire Dept-633-8317
Locator-633-8372	Police-633-8425
Public Affairs-633-8324/8120	SDO/NCO-633-8201

HEALTH & WELFARE:

Chaplain-633-8311	Medical-633-8339

REST & RECREATION:

EM/Com Club-633-8378	MWR-633-8219
Recreation-633-8219	Theater-633-8375/8219

OTHER FACILITIES AVAILABLE: Rec Center, Pool, Hunting, Skeet Range, Fishing, Golf driving range.

ATTRACTIONS: Nearby historic Fredericksburg and Civil War battlefields.

FORT BELVOIR (VA12R1)

ATTN: ANFB-GC
9820 Flagler, Suite 201
Fort Belvoir, VA 22060-5984

TELEPHONE NUMBER INFORMATION: Main installation numbers: C-703-545-6700, D-312-227-0101.

LOCATION: From I-95 S or US-1 S take Fort Belvoir exits. Signs clearly mark support facilities. USMRA: Page 47 (L,M-5), page 55 (B,C-8). NMC: Washington, 10 miles northeast.

GENERAL INFORMATION: Defense Systems Management College, Defense Mapping School, Army Management Staff College and support units.

TEMPORARY MILITARY LODGING: Lodging office, Building 470, 24 hours daily, C-703-805-2333 or 1-800-295-9750, D-312-665-9750, Fax: C-703-805-3566. All ranks. DV/VIP C-703-805-2333.

RV, CAMPING/FAMCAMP: None. Large Rec area planned for the future. See Andrews Air Force Base, MD, C-301-981-4109.

SPACE-A: Davison Army Airfield, Building 1327, 0730-1600 daily, C-703-806-7546, D-312-656-7546, Fax: C-703-806-7297, flights to CONUS locations.

LOGISTICAL SUPPORT:

Child Care-806-4344/6540	Commissary-781-0536
Conv Store-805-5155	Exchange-806-5800/01/02
Food Court-806-5808	Gas Station-806-4581
Gas Station North-806-5488	SATO-799-5680/3400
Shoppette	Snack Bar-805-3069
North Post (Class VI)-806-5263	
South Post-805-5154	

ADMINISTRATIVE SUPPORT:

Fire Dept-805-1107	Legal-805-4018
Locator-805-2043/3758	Police-806-3104
Public Affairs-805-5001	SDO/NCO-805-3101

HEALTH & WELFARE:

ACS-805-2277/4590	CHAMPUS-805-0644/0542
Chapel-806-3177/4316	Exchange-781-7070
Family Services-805-2908	Medical-805-0824
Retiree Services-805-3673	Emergency-805-0510

REST & RECREATION:

Arts & Crafts-806-4143/5803	Auto Hobby Shop-806-4655
Bowling-805-3068	Clubs
Golf Course	EM-780-0962
806-6016	NCO-780-0962
806-4043	O-780-0930
806-5892	Gym-805-3594
ITR-806-5532	Library-805-3323
Marina-781-8282	MWR-805-4137
Picnic Area-805-3781	Rec Center-805-3714
Rec Equip-805-2378	Swimming-805-2620
Tennis-805-2538	Theater-806-5237
Wildlife Refuge-806-4007	Youth Center-805-4605

ATTRACTIONS: Washington, DC, Smithsonian Institution.

FORT EUSTIS (VA10R1)

ATTN: ATZF-GC
Building 213
Fort Eustis, VA 23604-5015

TELEPHONE NUMBER INFORMATION: Main installation numbers: C-757-878-1110, D-312-927-1110.

LOCATION: From I-64, exit 250A to VA-105, west to Fort Eustis. USMRA: Page 47 (N-9), page 52 (B,C-2,3). NMC: Newport News, 13 miles southwest.

GENERAL INFORMATION: Army Transportation Center.

TEMPORARY MILITARY LODGING: Lodging office, Building 2110, Pershing Avenue, 24 hours daily, C-757-878-5807, D-312-927-5807. All ranks. DV/VIP C-757-878-6030.

RV, CAMPING/FAMCAMP: None. See Langley AFB listing, Bethel Park Rec Area, C-757-764-7170, D-312-574-7170.

SPACE-A: None. See Langley AFB listing, C-757-764-4698/4311, D-312-574-4698/4311, Fax: C-757-764-3577, D-312-754-3577.

LOGISTICAL SUPPORT:

Child Care-878-3794	Commissary-878-5966
Conv Store-887-0882	Exchange-887-0293
Gas Station-887-0392	Package Store-887-0882
Snack Bar-887-0494	Travel-878-5577

ADMINISTRATIVE SUPPORT:

Fire Dept-878-4281	Legal-878-2205
Locator-878-5215	Police-878-4554
Public Affairs-878-4920	SDO/NCO-878-5050

HEALTH & WELFARE:

ACS-878-3638	CHAMPUS-878-7861
Chapel-878-1304/1317	Family Services-878-3638
Medical-878-7511	Retiree Services-878-2953
Emergency-878-7675	TRICARE-677-6000

REST & RECREATION:

Auto Hobby Shop-ext 5440	Bowling-ext 5482
Clubs	Go-Cart Track-ext 5883
Consol-887-5700	Golf Course-878-2965
Flying-ext 3722	Gym-ext 4380
Saddle-ext 2835	ITT-878-3694
Library-ext 5017	Marina-ext 2610
MWR-878-5031	Skeet Range-ext 5822
Swimming-ext 5544	Tennis-ext 2097
Theater-878-3436	Youth Activities-ext 4448

ATTRACTIONS: On the James River, historic Williamsburg nearby, Busch Gardens, Water Country USA, US Transportation Museum (free), Mariners' Museum, Nauticus, and the Virginia Air & Space Center.

FORT LEE (VA15R1)

USACASCOM & Fort Lee
ATTN: ATZM-G
1100 Lee Avenue
Fort Lee, VA 23801-1720

TELEPHONE NUMBER INFORMATION: Main installation numbers: C-804-765-3000, D-312-539-3000.

LOCATION: From 1-95 take Fort Lee/Hopewell exit, and follow VA-36 to main gate. USMRA: Page 47 (L-8). NMC: Petersburg, three miles west.

VIRGINIA
Fort Lee, continued

GENERAL INFORMATION: Combined Arms Support Command, Quartermaster Center and School, Defense Commissary Agency, Army Logistics Management College, Army Information Systems Software Development Center-Lee, and reserve units.

TEMPORARY MILITARY LODGING: Lodging office, Building P-8025, Mahone Avenue, 24 hours daily, C-804-733-4100, D-312-687-6698. All ranks. DV/VIP C-804-733-4293.

RV, CAMPING/FAMCAMP: None. See Fort Pickett listing, C-804-292-2443, D-312-438-2443.

SPACE-A: None. See Langley AFB listing, C-757-764-4698/4311, D-312-574-4698/4311, Fax: C-757-764-3577, D-312-574-3577.

LOGISTICAL SUPPORT:

Cafeteria-861-6480	Carlson Wagonlit Travel-733-1460
Child Care-765-3765	Commissary-765-2260
Conv Store-861-3297	Exchange-861-5970
Gas Station-861-6621	Package Store-861-3297
Snack Bar-734-6861	

ADMINISTRATIVE SUPPORT:

Fire Dept-734-7031	Legal-765-1500
Locator-734-6855	Police-765-3988
Public Affairs-765-3100	SDO/NCO-734-7993

HEALTH & WELFARE:

ACS-734-6388	CHAMPUS-734-9448
Chapel-734-1187	Family Services-734-7967
Medical-734-9000	Retiree Services-734-6973
Central Appts-765-3400/734-9166	
Emergency-734-9269	

REST & RECREATION:

Arts & Crafts-734-6858	Auto Hobby Shop-734-6859
Bowling-734-6860	Clubs
Fitness Center-765-3070	Leisure-765-2651
Golf Course-734-1228/2899	O-734-7545
Gym-734-3070	Rod/Gun-765-2210
ITR-734-6622	Library-734-6846
Live Theater-734-6630/2611	MWR-734-6629
Music Center-734-6623	Recreation-765-2212
Rec Equip-734-2212	Riding Club-734-6396
Swimming-734-6747	Youth Center-765-3763

ATTRACTIONS: Quartermaster Museum, Petersburg National Battlefield Park, Colonial Williamsburg, Richmond's Virginia and Poe Museums and Monument Avenue; Petersburg's Blandford Church and Cemetery and Trapezium House, Colonial Heights' Lee Headquarters (Violet Bank), and Hopewell's Appomattox Manor.

FORT MONROE (VA13R1)

ATTN: ATZG-CO
Headquarters, Building 77
Fort Monroe, VA 23651-6000

TELEPHONE NUMBER INFORMATION: Main installation numbers: C-757-727-2111, D-312-680-2111. E-mail: userid@emhio,monroe,army.mil. HP: http://www-tradoc.monroe.mil.

LOCATION: From I-64 exit at Hampton and follow tour signs through Phoebus to fort. USMRA: Page 47 (N-9), page 52 (F-4). NMC: Hampton, one mile north.

GENERAL INFORMATION: Headquarters Army Training & Doctrine Command, US Army Reserve Officers' Training Corps (ROTC) Cadet Command, Joint Warfighting Center, Mobility Concepts Agency, Naval Surface Weapons Center, Continental Army Band, and support units.

TEMPORARY MILITARY LODGING: Lodging office, Building 80, Ingalls Road, 0800-1645, Mon-Fri, C-757-727-2128, D-312-680-2128. All ranks. DV/VIP C-757-727-3596.

RV, CAMPING/FAMCAMP: "The Colonies" Travel Park on post, year round, ATTN: MCECC, P.O. Box 51106, Fenwick Road, Fort Monroe, VA 23651-6144, C-757-727-2384, D-312-680-2384, 13 camper spaces with full hookups.

SPACE-A: None. See Langley AFB listing, C-757-764-4698/4311, D-312-574-4698/4311, Fax: C-757-764-3577, D-312-574-3577.

LOGISTICAL SUPPORT:

Bank-727-3495, 728-1272	Barber Shop-722-3604
Beauty Shop-722-3714	Car Rental-727-0427
Carlson Wagonlit Travel-727-0427	Child Care-727-2855
Class Six-727-2487	Commissary-727-3326/4178
Credit Union-722-1626	Dining Facilities-727-2334
Dry Cleaner-723-9285	Education Office-728-5853
Exchange-722-0794	Postal Service-722-6267
Snack Bar-727-2089	

ADMINISTRATIVE SUPPORT:

Fire Dept-727-2422	Housing Office-727-2127/2129
Legal-727-3616	Locator-727-2000
OOD-727-2238	Pass/ID Office-727-2391
Police-727-2238	Public Affairs-727-3205
SDO/NCO-727-2256	

HEALTH & WELFARE:

American Red Cross-764-2652	ACS-727-3878
Army Emergency Relief-727-4132	CHAMPUS-727-2701
Chapel-727-2611/4157	Dental-727-2367/2835
Family Services-727-3993	Medical
Retiree Services-727-2093	Central Appts-677-6000
TRICARE-677-6000	Clinic-727-3305
Veterinary services-727-2623	Emergency-727-2840
	Health Benefits-727-2701
	Information-727-3305

REST & RECREATION:

Arts & Crafts-727-2728	Auto Hobby Shop 727-2311
Bowling-727-2939	Fishing/Boating-727-4308
Fitness Center-727-3090	Gym-727-2783
Library-727-2909	Marinas-727-4308
MWR-727-3737	O'Club-727-2406/2432
Outdoor Rec-727-4305	Services-727-2650
Swimming-727-4181	Theater-727-2793/2004
Wood Hobby Shop-727-3594	Youth Center-727-3957
Youth Services-727-3957	

ATTRACTIONS: Williamsburg, Jamestown, Norfolk, Casemate Museum.

FORT MYER (VA24R1)

ATTN: ANMY-GC
Building 59
Fort Myer, VA 22211-5050

TELEPHONE NUMBER INFORMATION: Main installation numbers: C-703-545-6700, D-312-222-0101.

LOCATION: Adjacent to Arlington National Cemetery. Take Fort Myer exit from Washington Boulevard, at 2nd St, or enter from US-50 (Arlington Boulevard) first gate. Also, exit from Boundary Drive to 12th Street North entrance near the Iwo Jima Memorial. USMRA: Page 54 (E-5). NMC: Washington, DC, one mile northeast.

VIRGINIA
Fort Myer, continued

GENERAL INFORMATION: Headquarters Command Fort Myer, Headquarters 3rd Infantry (Old Guard), Headquarters US Army Band, and support units.

TEMPORARY MILITARY LODGING: Lodging office, Building T-49, Jackson Street, 24 hours daily, C-703-696-3576, D-312-226-3576. All ranks. DV/VIP C-703-696-7051.

RV, CAMPING/FAMCAMP: None. See Quantico MCB listing, Lunga Park, C-703-784-5270, D-312-278-5270.

SPACE-A: None. See Andrews AFB, MD listing, C-301-981-1854, D-312-858-1854, Fax: C-301-981-4241.

LOGISTICAL SUPPORT:
Child Care-696-3095
Consol Club-527-1300
Gas Station-522-2584
Commissary-696-3674
Exchange-696-7201
Snack Bar-528-4766

ADMINISTRATIVE SUPPORT:
Fire Dept-911
Locator-475-2005
Public Affairs-696-3944
Legal-696-0761
Police-696-3089
SDO/NCO-696-3250

HEALTH & WELFARE:
ACS-696-3510
Chapel-545-3532/3535
Retiree Services-696-5948
CHAMPUS-696-3656
Medical-696-3466
Central Appts -545-3464/3078
Emergency-545-3628

REST & RECREATION:
Arts & Crafts-696-3385
Bowling-696-3567
Community Center-696-3470
Fitness Center-696-0649
Gym-696-9655
MWR-696-8864
Recreation-696-8849
Swimming-696-3226
Auto Hobby Shop-696-3387
Clubs
NCO-527-1300
O-524-3037
Library-696-3608
Museum-696-6670
Rec Center-696-3470
Youth Activities-696-3199

ATTRACTIONS: Arlington National Cemetery, Tomb of the Unknown Soldier, barracks and activities of the Old Guard, Old Guard Museum, Iwo Jima Memorial, Netherlands Carillon, Washington, DC.

FORT PICKETT (VA16R1)

ATTN: AFRC-FMP-C
Building 472, Military Road
Blackstone, VA 23824-5000

NOTE: Under BRAC 1995, Virginia Army National Guard will assume command of Fort Pickett 1 October 1997. Services and activities will be changing. Call ahead for information.

TELEPHONE NUMBER INFORMATION: Main installation numbers: C-804-292-8621, D-312-438-8621.

LOCATION: On US-460, one mile from Blackstone. Clearly marked. USMRA: Page 47 (K-9). NMI: Fort Lee, 45 mile northeast. NMC: Petersburg, 40 miles northeast.

GENERAL INFORMATION: Provides and maintains maneuver and training areas that reflect current doctrine of the active and reserve components of the Army and other military services.

TEMPORARY MILITARY LODGING: Lodging office, Building T-469, Military Road, 0730-1600 duty days, C-804-292-2443, D-312-438-2443. All ranks.

RV, CAMPING/FAMCAMP: Pickett Travel Camp, on post year round, Commander, US Army Garrison, ATTN: AFRC-FMP-PW-H, Building T-469, Military Road, Fort Pickett, Blackstone, VA 23824-5000, C-804-292-2443, D-312-438-2443, Fax: C-804-292-8617, 15 Pegram camper spaces with full hookups, six tent spaces.

SPACE-A: None. See Langley AFB listing, C-757-764-4698/4311, D-312-574-4698/4311, Fax: C-757-764-5941.

LOGISTICAL SUPPORT:
Barber Shop-292-2783
Gas Station-292-5537
Postal Service-292-2266
SATO-292-2303/8340
Exchange-292-5489
Package Store-292-5489
Snack Bar-292-8518

ADMINISTRATIVE SUPPORT:
Fire Dept-292-2217
Legal-292-2168
Pass/ID Office-292-2306
Housing Office-292-2999
Locator-292-2266
Police-292-8444

HEALTH & WELFARE:
ACS-292-2233
Chapel-292-2601
Retiree Services-292-2306
CHAMPUS-292-2528
Medical-292-2528
Emergency-292-2211

REST & RECREATION:
Auto Hobby Shop-292-2616
Com Club-292-2336
Gym-292-8626
MWR-292-2613
Sports-ext 8626
Theater-292-8466
Bowling-292-8518
Crafts-ext 2616
Hunting/Fishing-ext 2618
Outdoor Rec-292-2618
Swimming-ext 8538

OTHER FACILITIES AVAILABLE: Racquetball Courts.

ATTRACTIONS: Dollhouse Museum, Petersburg Civil War Battlefields, Appomattox Court House National Historic Park.

FORT STORY (VA08R1)

ATTN: ATZF-FS
Building 300
Fort Story, VA 23459-5001

TELEPHONE NUMBER INFORMATION: Main installation numbers: C-757-422-7305, D-312-438-7305.

LOCATION: From the south exit of Chesapeake Bay Bridge Tunnel (US-13), east on US-60 (Atlantic Avenue) to Fort Story. Clearly marked. From I-64 take US-60 east. From VA-44 (Norfolk-VA Beach Expressway) exit US-58, turn left, N. Atlantic Avenue (US-60) to 89th St to Fort Story. USMRA: Page 47 (O-9); Page 52 (I,J-5,6). NMC: Virginia Beach, three miles south.

GENERAL INFORMATION: Sub-Installation of Fort Eustis. Army Transportation Units, Test Activity, Army Logistics, and Over-the-Shore Training & Test Site.

TEMPORARY MILITARY LODGING: Lodging office, Atlantic Avenue, 0730-2330 daily, C-757-422-7321, D-312-927-9321. All ranks. DV/VIP, Fort Eustis, C-757-878-5206, D-312-927-5206/5207.

RV, CAMPING/FAMCAMP: Operates Cape Henry Inn on post. See Cape Henry Inn listing for more information.

SPACE-A: None. See Norfolk NB listing, C-757-444-4118/4148/3947 or 445-6538, D-312-564-4118/4148/3947 or 565-6538, Fax: C-757-445-7501, D-312-565-7501.

LOGISTICAL SUPPORT:
Barber Shop-422-7027
Child Dev Center-422-7413
Child Care-422-7413
Class Six-422-7863

VIRGINIA
Fort Story, continued

Conv Store-428-7071	Credit Union-422-7874
Dry Cleaner-422-7622	Exchange-422-7858
Gas Station-428-7071	Package Store-422-7869
Postal Service-422-7816	Shoppette-422-7071
Snack Bar-422-7458	Travel Office-422-7712/7752

ADMINISTRATIVE SUPPORT:

Fire Dept-422-7456	Housing Office-442-7510
Legal-878-3031	Locator-422-7682
Pass/ID Office-422-7834	Police-422-7141
Public Affairs-422-7755	SDO/SNO-422-7454/7482

HEALTH & WELFARE:

American Red Cross-446-7754	ACS-422-7311
Army Emergency Relief-442-7311	CHAMPUS-1-800-990-8272
Chapel-422-7552/7665	Family Services-422-7311
Medical-422-7822/7851	TRICARE-1-800-990-8272
Veterinary Services-422-7734	

REST & RECREATION:

Auto Hobby Shop-ext 7713	Bowling-ext 7458
Community Center-422-7558	Fort Story Club-425-6631
Gym-422-7975/7053	Indoor Rec-422-7472
ITR-422-7712	ITT-422-7472
Library-422-7458	MWR-878-3102
Outdoor Rec-422-7601	Rec Center-ext 7472
Rec Equip-ext 7472	Sports-ext 7052
Tennis-ext 7975	Theater-422-7472
Youth Center-422-7714	

ATTRACTIONS: City of Virginia Beach and resort beaches nearby. See the Cross at Cape Henry (located on Fort Story), site of the first stop of English settlers in the USA, and the Old Cape Henry Lighthouse, a registered Historical Landmark.

HENDERSON HALL USMC (VA21R1)

1555 South Southgate Road, Building 29
Arlington, VA 22214-5000

TELEPHONE NUMBER INFORMATION: Main installation numbers: C-703-694-1235, D-312-224-1235.

LOCATION: From Columbia Pike, VA-244, exit to South Orme Street, Sheraton National Hotel at corner, west to dead end, right to second gate left. Also, from Memorial Drive (VA-27) exit to Columbia Pike, first traffic light right onto Southgate Road, enter first gate on right. Across Southgate Road from Navy Annex. USMRA: Page 54 (E-5). NMC: Washington, DC, one mile northeast.

GENERAL INFORMATION: Headquarters Battalion USMC, HQMC and support units. Provides support to personnel at HQMC (Navy Annex across the street).

TEMPORARY MILITARY LODGING: None. See Fort Myer listing, C-703-696-3576, D-312-226-3576.

RV, CAMPING/FAMCAMP: None. See Andrews AFB, MD listing, C-301-981-4109.

SPACE-A: None. See Andrews AFB, MD listing, C-301-981-1854, D-312-858-1854, Fax: C-301-981-4241.

LOGISTICAL SUPPORT:

Child Care-607-8459	Exchange-979-8420
Package Store-979-8420	

ADMINISTRATIVE SUPPORT:

Legal-614-3800	Pass/ID Office-614-2013
Police-614-2200	Public Affairs-614-8958
Relocation Assistance-614-7202	SDO/NCO-746-0950

HEALTH & WELFARE:

Chapel-614-9280	Family Services-614-7200/01
Medical-614-1229	

REST & RECREATION:

EM Club-614-2125	Gym-614-2969
ITT-979-8420 ext 116	Racquetball-727-2706
Rec Equip-727-2706	Swimming-695-4431

ATTRACTIONS: Adjacent to Arlington National Cemetery and Pentagon. Iwo Jima Memorial, Netherlands Carillon, Kennedy Center for the Performing Arts, Lincoln Memorial, Washington DC with its many sights, museums and galleries.

JUDGE ADVOCATE GENERAL'S SCHOOL (VA01R1)

600 Massie Road
Charlottesville, VA 22903-1781

TELEPHONE NUMBER INFORMATION: Main installation numbers: C-804-972-6300, D-312-274-7115, ext 300.

LOCATION: Take Route 29 to Arlington Street to Massie Road, located on University of Virginia. USMRA: Page 47 (J-7). NMC: Charlottesville, in city limits.

GENERAL INFORMATION: Army Judge Advocate General's School.

TEMPORARY MILITARY LODGING: Lodging office, room 156, 0750-1650 Mon-Fri, C-804-972-6450.

RV, CAMPING/FAMCAMP: None. See Fort A.P. Hill listing, C-804-633-8219, D-312-934-8219.

SPACE-A: None. See Andrews AFB, MD listing, C-301-981-1854, D-312-858-1854, Fax: C-301-981-4241.

LOGISTICAL SUPPORT:

Exchange-972-6324	Snack Bar-972-6324

ADMINISTRATIVE SUPPORT:

Housing Office-972-6334	Locator-972-6325
Pass/ID Office-972-6300	SDO-972-6300

HEALTH & WELFARE: CHAMPUS-972-6336

REST & RECREATION: All the facilities of the University of Virginia, with special permission.

ATTRACTIONS: Historic University of Virginia, and city of Charlottesville.

LANGLEY AIR FORCE BASE (VA07R1)

159 Sweeney Boulevard, Suite 100
Langley Air Force Base, VA 23665-2292

TELEPHONE NUMBER INFORMATION: Main installation numbers: C-757-764-9990, D-312-574-1110.

LOCATION: From I-64 E in Hampton take Armistead Avenue exit, keep right to stop light; right onto LaSalle Avenue and enter AFB. USMRA: Page 47 (N-9), page 52 (E-3). NMC: Hampton, one mile west.

GENERAL INFORMATION: Air Combat Command Base. Headquarters Air Combat Command, Headquarters Air Division Air Combat Command, 1st Fighter Wing, and support units.

VIRGINIA
Langley Air Force Base, continued

TEMPORARY MILITARY LODGING: Lodging office, Building 75, Nealy Avenue, 24 hours daily, C-757-764-4051, D-312-574-4051. All ranks. DV/VIP C-757-764-3467.

RV, CAMPING/FAMCAMP: Bethel Park Rec Area, off base, 1 Apr-31 Oct, Outdoor Recreational Office, SVS/SVRO, 52 Willow Street, Suite 101, C-757-764-7170, D-312-574-7170, new camper spaces now available.

SPACE-A: Pax Term/Lounge, Building 754B, 0600-1800 Mon-Fri. C-757-764-4698/4311, D-312-574-4698/4311, Fax: C-757-764-5941, flights to CONUS locations.

LOGISTICAL SUPPORT:

Bank-873-7816	Barber Shop-766-1805
Beauty Shop-766-1283	Child Care-764-3449
Child Dev Center-764-3585	Class Six-766-1330
Commissary-766-1304	Conv Store-766-1249
Credit Union-827-7200	Dining Facilities-764-3694
Dry Cleaner-766-1287	Education Office-764-2962
Exchange-766-1253	Gas Station-766-1286
Laundry-766-1288	Postal Service-764-3136
SATO-766-5890	Shoppette-766-1249
Travel Office-764-2292	Visitor Center-764-4169

ADMINISTRATIVE SUPPORT:

Fire Dept-764-7717	Housing Office-764-5048
Legal-764-3277	Locator-764-5615
Pass/ID Office-764-7770	Police-764-2000
Public Affairs-764-2018	

HEALTH & WELFARE:

Air Force Aid Society-764-3990	American Red Cross-764-2652
CHAMPUS-764-6987	Chapel-764-7847
Dental-764-7611	Family Services-764-3390
Medical	Retiree Services-764-7386
Central Appts-677-6000	TRICARE-677-6000
Emergency-764-6801	Veterinary Services-764-5678
Health Benefits-764-6987	
Hospital-764-6833	
Information-764-6833	

REST & RECREATION:

Arts & Crafts-764-4647	Auto Hobby Shop-764-4607
Bowling-7642433	Clubs
Eagle Park-764-5792	Flying-764-7486
Golf Course-764-4547	NCO-766-3550
Gym-764-5791	O-766-1361
ITT-764-2983	Rifle-764-2312
Library-865-2906	Scuba-764-2312
Marinas-764-7220	Skeet-764-3769
MWR-764-3999	Outdoor Rec-764-7170
Rec Center-764-7175	Rec Equip-764-4616
Services-764-7881	Swimming-764-5791
Theater-764-2580	Wood Hobby Shop-764-3978
Youth Center-764-2300	Youth Services-764-4343

ATTRACTIONS: Virginia Tidewater Area, Norfolk nearby. Great fishing, beaches, and water sports.

LITTLE CREEK NAVAL AMPHIBIOUS BASE (VA19R1)

2600 Tarawa Court, Suite 107
Norfolk, VA 23521-2438

TELEPHONE NUMBER INFORMATION: Main installation numbers: C-757-444-0000, D-312-680-7000.

LOCATION: From I-64 south to Northampton Boulevard exit to base, exit VA-225. From Chesapeake Bay Bridge/Tunnel US-60 west to base. USMRA: Page 47 (N,O-9); Page 52 (G,H-5,6). NMC: Norfolk, 11 miles southwest.

GENERAL INFORMATION: Expeditionary Warfare Training Group Atlantic, Special Warfare Group Atlantic, and homeport for approximately 30 ships.

TEMPORARY MILITARY LODGING: Lodging office, 24 hours daily, Building 3408 (BOQ) C-757-464-7522/3; Building 3601 (BEQ) C-757-464-7577/8601. Navy Lodge, Building 3531, C-757-464-1194. All ranks. DV/VIP C-757-464-5901, Fax: C-757-464-8635.

RV, CAMPING/FAMCAMP: MWR RV Park on base, year round, C-757-464-7516, D-312-680-7516, 45 camper spaces with W/E hookups, 6 tent spaces.

SPACE-A: None See Norfolk NAS listing, C-757-444-4118/4148, D-312-564-4118/4148, Fax: C-757-445-6563.

LOGISTICAL SUPPORT:

Child Care-464-7868	Commissary-464-3561
Conv Store-464-3090	Credit Union-480-1777
Exchange-363-3218	
Galley-464-7546	Gas Station-363-3119
SATO-464-2392	Snack Bar-464-2663

ADMINISTRATIVE SUPPORT:

Legal-464-7331	Locator-464-7226
Police-464-7438	Public Affairs-464-7923
SDO/NCO-464-7385	

HEALTH & WELFARE:

CHAMPUS-464-8189	Chapel-464-7427/9
Family Services-464-7563	Medical-464-7850/7793
	Central Appts-399-1100
	Emergency-464-7850

REST & RECREATION:

Auto Hobby Shop-ext 7339	Ballet/Slimnastic Classes-ext 7665
Boats/Campers-ext 7516	Bowling-ext 7952
Clubs	Ceramics Hobby-ext 7998
CPO-464-7789	Fishing Boat (Gator III)-ext 7140
EM-464-7949	Golf-ext 8526
O-460-1111	Gym-ext 4821
ITT-464-7665	Library-ext 7998
MWR Dir-ext 7905	Picnic Area-ext 7369
Rec Equip-ext 7735	Swimming-ext 8139
Tennis-ext 8118	Wood Hobby Shop-ext 7605

ATTRACTIONS: Water sports, beaches, fishing, Norfolk.

NORFOLK NAVAL BASE (VA18R1)

1530 Gilbert Street, Suite 2200
Norfolk, VA 23511-5000

TELEPHONE NUMBER INFORMATION: Main installation numbers: C-757-444-0000, D-312-564-0000.

LOCATION: Take I-64 west, Naval Base exit I-564, follow signs. USMRA: Page 52 (F-5,6). NMC: Norfolk, in city limits.

GENERAL INFORMATION: CINC Atlantic Fleet, SACLANT (NATO), FMF Atlantic, Surface and Submarine Forces Atlantic, Air Forces Atlantic, Armed Forces Staff College, and the world's largest Naval Base comprised of Norfolk NAS, Norfolk Naval Station, Naval Computer and Telecommunications Area Master Station Atlantic, Fleet Industrial Supply Center, and Camp Elmore Marine Corps Base.

TEMPORARY MILITARY LODGING: Lodging office, Building R-63 (BEH), 0730-1600 Mon-Fri, C-757-444-4425, Fax: C-757-444-0797. Building A-128 (BOH), 24 hours daily, C-757-402-4444, Fax: C-757-445-9888. Navy

VIRGINIA
Norfolk Naval Base, continued

Lodge, 24 hours daily, C-757-489-2656. All ranks. DV/VIP C-757-444-6323, Navy C-757-402-4401.

RV, CAMPING/FAMCAMP: None. See Little Creek NAB listing, C-757-464-7516, D-312-680-7516.

SPACE-A: Norfolk Naval Air Station, Naval Air Terminal, Code 053, 8449 Air Cargo Road, Bldg LP-84, Norfolk Naval Air Station, VA 23511-4497. C-757-444-4118/4148/3947 or 445-6538, D-312-564-4118/4148/3947 or 565-6538, Fax: C-757-445-7501, D-312-565-7501. AMC Term is three miles from Gate 4 off Patrol Road on A-Term Road, Bldg LP-84, flights to CONUS, OCONUS and foreign locations.

LOGISTICAL SUPPORT:

Cafeteria-440-2243	Child Care-444-3379
Commissary-423-8286	Conv Store-440-2321
Exchange-440-2214	Gas Station-440-2269
Package Store-440-2119	SATO-440-0621
Snack Bar-440-2114	

ADMINISTRATIVE SUPPORT:

CDO/OOD-322-2866	Fire Dept-444-3333
Legal-444-4497	Locator-444-0000
Police-444-2324	Public Affairs-322-2853
Quarter Deck-322-2866	SDO/NCO-322-2866

HEALTH & WELFARE:

Chapel-444-7361	Family Services-444-2102
Medical-677-6291	N-MC Relief Society-423-8830
Central Appts-667-6000	Retiree Services-444-2102
Emergency-677-6290	TRICARE-677-6000

REST & RECREATION:

Arts & Crafts-ext 3846	Auto Hobby Shop-ext 8383
Bowling-ext 7908	Clubs
Fishing-ext 4392	CPO-ext 360
Golf Course-ext 5572/5267	EM-440-5483
Gym-ext 2276/7218	O-444-0773
ITT-445-6663	Library-ext 2888
MWR-444-3670	Rec Center-ext 0897
Rec Equip-ext 5448	Rec Office-ext 7218/2276
Rec Park-ext 2536	RV/Camping-444-4388
Sailing-ext 2918	Theater-440-5304

ATTRACTIONS: Largest naval base in the world. Local attractions include: Hampton Roads Naval Museum, Gardens by the Sea, MacArthur Memorial, Williamsburg, City of Norfolk, and Waterside Downtown Norfolk.

NORFOLK NAVAL SHIPYARD (VA26R1)

Code 1160, Building 5000
Portsmouth, VA 23709-5000

TELEPHONE NUMBER INFORMATION: Main installation numbers: C-757-496-3000, D-312-961-0111.

LOCATION: From I-264 in Portsmouth exit on Effingham Street south to enter the Shipyard. USMRA: Page 52 (F-7). NMC: Portsmouth, in city limits.

GENERAL INFORMATION: World's largest shipyard devoted exclusively to warship repair work.

TEMPORARY MILITARY LODGING: Lodging office, 24 hours daily, Building 1504A, C-757-396-4449, D-312-961-4449, Fax: C-757-396-4968. All ranks. Chesapeake Inn, Building 1530, C-757-398-8500. DV/VIP C-757-396-8605.

RV, CAMPING/FAMCAMP: None. See Chesapeake NSGA, NW, C-757-421-8262, Fax: C-757-421-8785.

SPACE-A: None. See Norfolk NB listing, C-757-444-4118/4148/3947 or 445-6538, D-312-564-4118/4148/3947 or 565-6538, Fax: C-757-445-7501, D-312-565-7501.

LOGISTICAL SUPPORT:

Child Care-396-5863	Commissary-393-6309
Exchange-397-2220	Gas Station-397-4319
Package Store-399-6673	SATO-398-0636
Snack Bar-397-2220	

ADMINISTRATIVE SUPPORT:

Legal-396-8625	Locator-396-3000
Police-396-7266	Public Affairs-396-9550
SDO/NCO-396-3221	

HEALTH & WELFARE:

CHAMPUS-398-5100	Chapel-396-5021
Medical-398-3226	Retiree Services-396-4484
Ambulance-396-3678	
Central Appts-396-3226	

REST & RECREATION:

Athletic Facilities-396-3845/3835	Bowling-396-3808/7051
Consol Club-396-5054	Gym-396-3845
ITT-396-7639	Library-444-1571
MWR Office-396-3835	Pool Tables-396-3835
Swimming-396-3835.	

ATTRACTIONS: Virginia Beach nearby. Tidewater outdoor sports. Naval Shipyard Museum, Mariners' Museum, college sports, Triple-A baseball.

OCEANA NAVAL AIR STATION (VA09R1)

ATTN: PAO
Virginia Beach, VA 23460-5120

TELEPHONE NUMBER INFORMATION: Main installation numbers: C-757-444-0000, D-312-433-2000.

LOCATION: From I-64 exit to Norfolk-Virginia Beach Expressway (VA-44 E), east on Virginia Beach Boulevard. Bordered by Oceana Boulevard (VA-615) and London Bridge Rd. Also bordered by Potters and Harpers Roads. USMRA: Page 47 (O-9); Page 52 (I,J-7). NMC: Virginia Beach, in city limits.

GENERAL INFORMATION: Home to all F-14 Tomcats and A-6 Intruders on the East Coast. Headquarters for Commander Fighter Wing, US Atlantic Fleet, and Commander Attack Wing, US Atlantic Fleet.

TEMPORARY MILITARY LODGING: Lodging office, Building 460, 24 hours daily, C-757-425-0500 ext 168/171/172, D-312-423-3293, Fax: C-757-422-0173.

RV, CAMPING/FAMCAMP: None. See Chesapeake NSGA, NW, C-757-421-8262, Fax: C-757-421-8785.

SPACE-A: Pax Term/Lounge, Building 100, 24 hours daily, C-757-433-2903/2260, D-312-433-2902/2260, flights to CONUS and OCONUS locations.

LOGISTICAL SUPPORT:

Child Care-433-3164	Commissary-428-2931
Conv Store-491-4267	Credit Union-491-2354
Exchange-491-4260	Gas Station-491-4283
Package Store-433-2840	SATO-422-0487

ADMINISTRATIVE SUPPORT:

Legal-433-3116	Locator-433-2366
Police-433-3123	Public Affairs-433-3131
SDO/NCO-433-2366	

HEALTH & WELFARE:

CHAMPUS-433-3328	Chapel-433-2871

VIRGINIA
Oceana Naval Air Station, continued

Family Services-433-2912
Medical-677-7000
Central Appts C-433-2336/2151
Emergency-433-2221

REST & RECREATION:
Athletic/Rec Office-ext 2695
Bowling-ext 2167
Fishing Boat/Campers-ext 3215
Golf-ext 2866
Gym-ext 2695
Library-ext 2401
Rifle/Pistol-ext 2875
Spec Services-ext 3381
Swimming Office-ext-3285
Auto Hobby Shop-ext 3403
Clubs
EM-433-2453 or ext 2825
NCO-433-2637
O-428-0036
Picnic Area-ext 3381
Skeet/Trap-ext 2875
Stables-ext 3266

ATTRACTIONS: Virginia Beach, resort beaches, and entertainment nearby.

PENTAGON (VA41R1)

Room 2E 765
Washington, DC 20301-5000

TELEPHONE NUMBER INFORMATION: Main installation numbers: C-703-545-6700, D-312-227-0101.

LOCATION: From I-395 S, exit to South Parking or from Columbia Pike (VA-244) exit to South Parking. North Parking accessible from Boundary Channel Drive, exit from I-395 S. Visitor parking entrance is from Boundary Channel Drive and is paid parking. Due to tightened security the River and Mall entrances are accessible only by walking from other parking areas. Bus, METRO, and taxi service from Concourse. Concourse and all entrances have directions posted to support activities/facilities. USMRA: Page 54 (E-5), page 55 (B-4). NMC: Washington, DC, adjacent.

GENERAL INFORMATION: Headquarters Department of Defense, Joint Chiefs of Staff and the military departments. The world's largest office building, 17.5 miles of corridors, employing about 27,000 people.

TEMPORARY MILITARY LODGING: None. See Fort Myer listing, C-703-696-3576, D-312-226-3576, DV/VIP C-703-696-7091.

RV, CAMPING/FAMCAMP: None. See Quantico MCB listing, Lunga Park, C-703-784-5270, D-312-278-5270.

SPACE-A: None. See Andrews AFB, MD listing, C-301-981-1854, D-312-858-1854, Fax: C-301-981-4241.

LOGISTICAL SUPPORT:
Carlson Wagonlit Travel 979-5500
MCSS-695-7637

ADMINISTRATIVE SUPPORT:
Legal-AF-695-2450
Legal-NA-695-1332
Legal-AR-697-3170

HEALTH & WELFARE:
CHAMPUS-695-3597
Medical
Clinic AF-697-4598
Clinic AR-697-6594
Chapel-695-3336

REST & RECREATION:
Athletic Center 521-5020
Library 695-5346
MWR-695-5338
Rec Services
USA-697-3816
USAF 697-9866
ITT
AF-697-9866
AR-697-3816
Ski Club 697-9866

OTHER SUPPORT AVAILABLE: Armed Forces Hostesses Association, Room 1A736, 697-6857/3180, volunteers, info on the area.

ATTRACTIONS: The Pentagon guided one-hour tour is an exciting tourist attraction (office on Concourse). Free tours leave approximately every 30 minutes, 695-1776. Great military art on the corridor walls and in Hall of Heroes (Medal of Honor winners).

PORTSMOUTH COAST GUARD INTEGRATED SUPPORT COMMAND (VA43R1)

4000 Coast Guard Boulevard
Portsmouth, VA 23703-2199

TELEPHONE NUMBER INFORMATION: Main installation numbers: C-757-483-8586, D-312-483-8532.

LOCATION: From I-664 exit to High Street through Churchland, left on Cedar Lane, right on West Norfolk Boulevard, left on Coast Guard Boulevard to gate. USMRA: Page 47 (N-9), page 52 (E-6). NMC: Norfolk eight miles southeast.

TEMPORARY MILITARY LODGING: None. See Norfolk NB listing, (BEH) C-757-444-2839, Fax: C-757-444-0797; (BOQ) C-757-402-4444, Fax: C-757-445-9888. Navy Lodge, C-757-489-2656. Reservations: C-1-800-NAVY-INN. DV/VIP, C-757-402-4401.

RV, CAMPING/FAMCAMP: None. See Little Creek NAB listing, C-757-464-7516, D-312-680-7516.

SPACE-A: None. See Norfolk NB listing, C-757-444-4118/4148/3947 or 445-6538, D-312-564-4118/4148/3947 or 565-6538, Fax: C-757-445-7501, D-312-565-7501.

LOGISTICAL SUPPORT:
Barber Shop-483-8614
Credit Union-483-6393
Dry Cleaner-483-8576
SATO-686-3010
Conv Store-483-8615
Dining Facilities-483-8539
Exchange-483-8618/8612

ADMINISTRATIVE SUPPORT:
CDO/OOD-483-8428
Public Affairs-483-4020
Police-483-8586

HEALTH & WELFARE:
CHAMPUS-483-8462
Medical-483-8596
Chapel-483-8699

REST & RECREATION:
All Hands Club-483-8536
Gym-483-8532
Recreation-483-8671
Auto Hobby Shop-483-8685
MWR-483-8670

OTHER FACILITIES AVAILABLE: Pool, Tennis Court

ATTRACTIONS: Tours: Portsmouth Harbor, MacArthur Memorial, Naval Museums.

PORTSMOUTH NAVAL MEDICAL CENTER (VA27R1)

620 John Paul Jones Circle
Portsmouth, VA 23708-5100

TELEPHONE NUMBER INFORMATION: Main installation numbers: C-757-398-5008, D-312-564-0111. HP: http://164.167.49.97.

LOCATION: Off I-264 in Portsmouth, take Effingham Street exit to medical center. USMRA: Page 52 (F-7). NMC: Norfolk, two miles north.

GENERAL INFORMATION: The oldest medical center in the Navy; providing continuous medical care since 1830. One of four major teaching hospitals in the Navy. Supports the entire Tidewater area. Undergoing major

VIRGINIA
Portsmouth Naval Medical Center, continued

construction/renovation project through year 2003 to add parking garage, support facilities, BEQs, and large replacement hospital.

TEMPORARY MILITARY LODGING: None. See Norfolk NB listing, Building I-A, BEH, C-757-444-2839, Fax: C-757-444-0797, 0730-1530 hours; Building A128, BOH C-757-402-4444, Fax: C-757-445-9888, 24 hours daily. Navy Lodge, Building SDA-314, C-757-489-2656, Fax: C-757-489-9621, 24 hours. Reservations: C-1-800-NAVY-INN. DV/VIP C-757-402-4401.

RV, CAMPING/FAMCAMP: None. See Little Creek NAB listing, C-757-464-7516, D-312-680-7516.

SPACE-A: None. See Norfolk NB listing, C-757-444-4118/4148/3947 or 445-6538, D-312-564-4118/4148/3947 or 565-6538, Fax: C-757-445-7501, D-312-565-7501.

LOGISTICAL SUPPORT:
Exchange-397-5857
SATO-396-0640
Package Store-397-5857

ADMINISTRATIVE SUPPORT:
CDO/OOD-398-5008
Legal-398-5452
Locator-398-5624
Police-398-5224
Quarter Deck-398-5007
Fire Dept-398-5444
  Emergency-398-5777
Pass/ID Office-398-6950
Public Affairs-398-7986/7422

HEALTH & WELFARE:
American Red Cross-398-5435
Chapel-398-5550
Family Services-398-7801
N-MC Relief Society-398-5956
Retiree Services-398-7689
TRICARE-677-6000
CHAMPUS-398-7377/87
Dental-398-5325/24
Medical-398-5064
  Central Appts-399-1100
  Emergency-398-5064

REST & RECREATION:
Com Club-398-5017
Gym-398-7024/25
ITT-398-5439
MWR-398-5094
Theater-398-5858
Fitness Center-398-5094
Indoor Rec-398-5095
Library-ext 5384
Services-ext 5094/5

ATTRACTIONS: Tours: Portsmouth Harbor, MacArthur Memorial, Naval Museums.

QUANTICO MARINE CORPS BASE (VA11R1)

Marine Corps Combat Development Command
Building 3098
Quantico, VA 22134-5001

TELEPHONE NUMBER INFORMATION: Main installation numbers: C-703-784-2121, D-312-278-2121.

LOCATION: From I-95 take exit 150A (Quantico/Triangle). US-1 is adjacent to the base. Directions to the base are clearly marked. USMRA: Page 47 (L-5,6). NMC: Washington, DC, 30 miles north.

GENERAL INFORMATION: Home to the Marine Corps Combat Development Command and various tenant commands.

TEMPORARY MILITARY LODGING: Hostess House, Building 3072, C-703-784-2983, D-312-278-2983, All ranks. DV/VIP C-703-784-4477.

RV, CAMPING/FAMCAMP: Lunga Park, c/o Recreational Branch, P.O. Box 186, on base, year round, C-703-784-5270, D-312-278-5270, 13 camper spaces with full hookups, six camper spaces with W/E hookups, 12 tent spaces.

SPACE-A: None. See Andrews AFB, MD listing, C-301-981-1854, D-312-858-1854, Fax: C-301-981-4241.

LOGISTICAL SUPPORT:
Bank-640-9220/9200
Beauty Shop-640-6600
Commissary-784-2476/2230
Credit Union-640-7505/7181
Dry Cleaner-640-6902
Exchange-640-8800
Package Store-221-4553
Snack Bar-784-5943/5942
  Golf Course-784-2426
Barber Shop-784-6497/7900/7501
Child Care-784-2716/4322/4470
Conv Store-640-6615
Dining Facilities-640-0965
Education Office-784-3308/4309
Gas Station-640-7400/8816
Postal Service-784-4293
Pro Travel Corp-784-7101
Visitor Center-784-2506

ADMINISTRATIVE SUPPORT:
CDO/OOD-784-2707
Housing Office-784-2711
Locator-784-2048/9
Public Affairs-784-3341
Fire Dept-640-2224
Legal-784-3122/3
Police-784-2251/2/3

HEALTH & WELFARE:
American Red Cross-784-3113
Chapel-784-2035/2512
Family Services-784-2650/2659
Medical
  Clinic-784-2708/2796
  Information-784-2525
Veterinary Services-784-2770/9
CHAMPUS-784-2491
Dental
  Central Appts-784-2802/3/4
  Clinic-784-2803
N-MC Relief Society-640-7136
Retiree Services-784-2511

REST & RECREATION:
Auto Hobby Shop-784-2729
Clubs
  Aero-640-6596
  EM-784-2676/5223/5595
  O-784-2676
  Rifle/Pistol-640-6336
  SNCO-784-2676
  Special Interest-784-3196
  TBSO/Hawkins Bar-784-5238/5283
Stables-784-2930
Theater-784-2638
Youth Services-784-2305/2014
Bowling-784-2210
Golf Course-784-2424/2463
Gym-784-2003
ITR-784-2002
ITT-784-2789
Library-784-2240/2248
Marinas-784-2359
MWR-784-3007
Recreation-784-2014
Swimming-784-2973
Youth Center-784-2249

ATTRACTIONS: Borders Potomac River, near historic Fredericksburg, VA and Washington, DC.

WALLOPS ISLAND AEGIS COMBAT SYSTEMS CENTER (VA46R1)

Building R-30
Wallops Island, VA 23337-5000

TELEPHONE NUMBER INFORMATION: Main installation number: C-757-824-1979/1692. HP: http://www.navy.mil.

LOCATION: From the south: Take Chesapeake Bay Bridge-Tunnel north, stay on US Route 13, to Route 175 (a right at T's Corner) for five miles, a left at Route 798 (Ocean Deli). BQ facilities will be on right. From the north: Take Route 13 south, five miles over MD/VA line to Route 175, same directions as above. USMRA: Page 47 (P-7). NMC: Norfolk, VA 100 miles south.

GENERAL INFORMATION: Aegis Combat Systems Center is a tenant of NASA, Goddard Space Flight Center, Wallops Flight Facility.

TEMPORARY MILITARY LODGING: Lodging office, Building R-20, Route 798. 24 hours daily, BEQ C-757-824-2064, BOQ C-757-824-2355, Fax: C-757-824-1764. All ranks.

RV, CAMPING/FAMCAMP: None. Nearest facility is more than 100 miles away.

SPACE-A: None. See Dover AFB, DE listing, C-302-677-4090, D-312-445-2854, Fax: C-302-677-2953.

LOGISTICAL SUPPORT:
Exchange-824-5434 Galley-824-1009

ADMINISTRATIVE SUPPORT:
CDO/OOD-824-2058 Locator-824-2079
Police-824-2037 Public Affairs-824-1692

HEALTH & WELFARE:
CHAMPUS-824-2130 Medical-824-2130
Emergency-546-6400

REST & RECREATION: MWR-824-1836

ATTRACTIONS: NASA/Wallops Visitor Center. Close to beaches, boating, fishing. Assateague and Chincoteague Island, with wild horse populations.

YORKTOWN COAST GUARD RESERVE TRAINING CENTER (VA28R1)

ATTN: PAO
Yorktown, VA 23690-5002

TELEPHONE NUMBER INFORMATION: Main installation numbers: C-757-898-3500, D-312-827-3500.

LOCATION: From I-64 exit 25D, follow signs to Highway 17. Left on Highway 17, then right at second light onto Cook Road. Follow this until road ends, then take a right. This will lead to the base. USMRA: Page 47 (N-8,9); Page 52 (D-1). NMC: Newport News, 15 miles southeast.

GENERAL INFORMATION: Coast Guard Training Schools.

TEMPORARY MILITARY LODGING: Lodging Office, C-757-898-2378, D-312-827-2378, Fax: C-757-890-0406. DV/VIP C-757-898-2212, D-312-827-2212.

RV, CAMPING/FAMCAMP: Yorktown CG Campground, on base, year round, C-757-898-2128. Nine camper spaces and five tent spaces available.

SPACE-A: None. See Langley AFB listing, C-757-764-4698/4311, D-312-574-4698/4311, Fax: C-757-764-5941.

LOGISTICAL SUPPORT:
Exchange-898-2153/2115 Gas Station-898-2156
Package Store-898-2156

ADMINISTRATIVE SUPPORT:
CDO/OOD-898-2354 Legal-898-2374
Locator-898-3500 Police-898-3500

HEALTH & WELFARE:
Chapel-898-2245 Medical-898-2230

REST & RECREATION:
Auto Hobby Shop-898-2279 Clubs
Gym-898-2128 EM-898-2141
Library-898-2396 O-898-2108/2286

ATTRACTIONS: Historic Yorktown, Jamestown, and Williamsburg nearby. Busch Gardens, Water Country USA.

YORKTOWN NAVAL WEAPONS STATION (VA14R1)

P.O. Drawer 160
Yorktown, VA 23691-0160

TELEPHONE NUMBER INFORMATION: Main installation numbers: C-757-887-4545, D-312-953-4545.

LOCATION: From I-64 W exit 247, left on US-143, five miles to US-238 left, five miles to Gate 3, Skiffes Creek. USMRA: Page 47 (N-8), page 52 (B,C-1). NMC: Newport News, 15 miles southeast.

GENERAL INFORMATION: Naval Ordnance Center Atlantic Division and Support Units.

TEMPORARY MILITARY LODGING: Lodging office, Building 704, 0800-1530 Mon-Fri, BEQ/BOQ/DV/VIP C-757-887-7621, D-312-953-7631, Fax: C-757-887-4340. All ranks.

RV, CAMPING/FAMCAMP: None. See Yorktown CGRTC listing, C-757-898-2128.

SPACE-A: None. See Langley AFB listing, C-757-764-4698/4311, D-312-574-4698/4311, Fax: C-757-764-5941.

LOGISTICAL SUPPORT:
Child Care-887-4734 Conv Store-887-2307
Exchange-887-2307 SATO-887-1422

ADMINISTRATIVE SUPPORT:
CDO/OOD-887-4545 Fire Dept-887-7343
Legal-887-7641 Police-887-7103
Public Affairs-887-4939

HEALTH & WELFARE:
Chapel-887-4711 Family Services-887-4606
Medical
Central Appts-887-7255
Emergency-887-7404

REST & RECREATION:
Auto Hobby Shop-ext 7294 Boats/Motors-ext 4601
Bowling-ext 4207 Clubs
Golf-ext 4323 EM-887-4555
Gym-ext 4918 O-887-4272
Handball/Racquetball-ext 4278 ITT-887-4609
Library-ext 4720/4726 MWR-887-4234
Picnic Area-ext 4601 Recreation-887-4233
Swimming-ext 4601 Tickets-ext 4609
Youth Center-ext 4824

ATTRACTIONS: Historic Yorktown, Jamestown and Williamsburg nearby, Busch Gardens, and Water Country USA.

Other Installations in Virginia

Chesapeake Coast Guard Exchange (VA49R1), 1430A Kristina Way, Chesapeake, VA 23326-1000. USMRA: Page 52 (G-8). C-757-523-6028/6002.
Chincoteague Coast Guard Group - Eastern Shore (VA47R1), 3823 S Main Street, Chincoteague, VA 23336-1510. USMRA: Page 47 (P-7), C-804-336-6511, CDO/OOD-336-2840, Exchange-336-2848.
Davison Army Airfield (VA23R1), 6970 Britten Drive, Fort Belvoir, VA 22060-5133. USMRA: Page 47 (L,M-5). C-703-806-7225, D-312-656-7225, Space-A C-703-806-7225, D-312-656-7225.
Vint Hill Farms Station (VA03R1), ATTN: PAO, Warrenton, VA 20187-5010. ***Scheduled to close September 1997.*** C-540-349-6000, D-312-229-6000. From Washington, DC, area, take I-66 to VA-29/211 South, proceed four miles to VA-215 (Mitchell Road), left for two miles to Station main gate. USMRA: Page 47 (L-5). NMC: Washington, DC, 35 miles northeast. CECOM Signal's Warfare Directorate, Intelligence Materiel Management Center. Conv Store-349-1870, Shoppette-349-1870, Police-349-6236/7800, ACS-349-5917, Family Services-349-5032, Gym-ext 5895, Swimming-ext 6793/6794, Theater-349-6086.

WASHINGTON

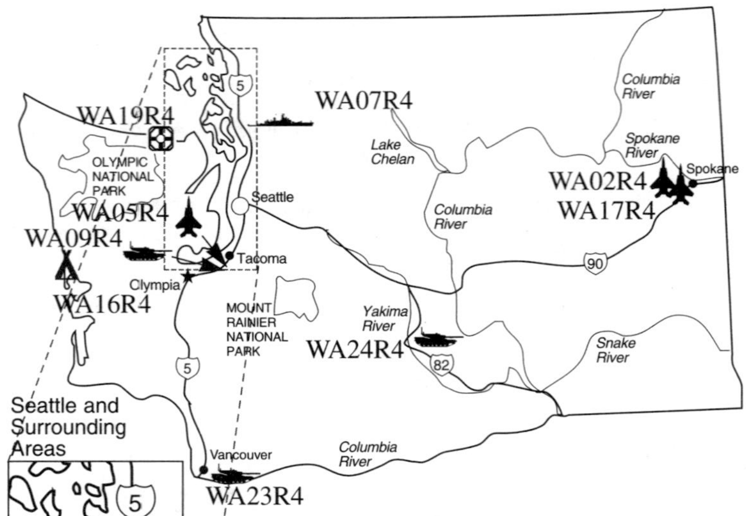

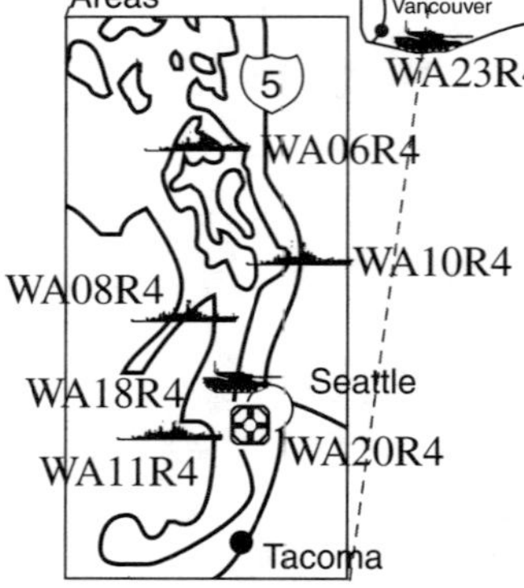

BANGOR NAVAL SUBMARINE BASE (WA08R4)

1100 Hunley Road
Silverdale, WA 98315-1199

TELEPHONE NUMBER INFORMATION: Main installation numbers: C-360-396-6111, D-312-744-6111. HP: http://www.nsb.navy. mil.

LOCATION: Approximately 15 miles north of Bremerton, on WA-3, exits to base clearly marked. USMRA: Page 103 (A-1,2). NMC: Tacoma, 40 miles southeast.

GENERAL INFORMATION: Ohio-class (TRIDENT) Submarines, Commander Submarine Group 9, Commander, Naval Base Seattle, Submarine Squadron 17, Trident Training Facility, Strategic Weapons Facility (Pacific), Trident Refit Facility, Marine Corps Security Force Company, Personnel Support Activity, Puget Sound.

TEMPORARY MILITARY LODGING: Lodging office, Building 2300, Scorpion Street, 24 hours daily, BEQ/BOQ/DV/VIP C-360-396-4046/6581, D-312-744-4046/6581, Fax: C-360-396-6032. Navy Lodge C-360-779-9100.

RV, CAMPING/FAMCAMP: None. See Whidbey Island NAS listing, C-360-257-2434, D-312-820-2434.

SPACE-A: None. See McChord AFB listing, C-206-984-2657/5327, D-312-984-2657/5327, Fax: C-206-984-5659.

LOGISTICAL SUPPORT:

Child Care-779-4066
Conv Store-697-8727
Gas Station-697-8711
Post Office-396-6141
Snack Bar-779-9907
Commissary-396-6025
Exchange-697-8703
Package Store-697-8727
SATO-779-1458
Visitor Center-396-4665

ADMINISTRATIVE SUPPORT:

CDO/OOD-396-4800
Legal-396-6157
Police-396-4312
SDO/NCO-396-4800
Fire Dept-396-4333
Locator-396-5733
Public Affairs-396-4843

HEALTH & WELFARE:

CHAMPUS-396-4391
Family Hotline-396-6310
Chapel-396-6005
Family Services-396-4115
Medical
  Central Appts-396-4391
  Emergency-396-4222
Retiree Services-396-4115

REST & RECREATION:

Arts & Crafts-779-3815
Bowling-779-2838
Golf Course-779-4852
Gym-779-4852
ITT-396-4026
Library-779-9724
Rec Center-779-3815
Theater-779-3668
Auto Hobby Shop-779-3596
Clubs
  CPO-697-8033
  EM-697-8039
  O-697-8033
MWR-697-8000
Swimming-779-4817
Wood Hobby Shop-ext 2264

ATTRACTIONS: Kitsap and Olympic Peninsulas, Hood Canal, Puget Sound, Poulsbo, and the Seattle/Tacoma area.

EVERETT NAVAL STATION (WA10R4)

2000 West Marine View Drive
Everett, WA 98207-5001

TELEPHONE NUMBER INFORMATION: Main installation numbers: C-206-304-3000, D-312-727-3000. E-mail: kitchens@everett.navy.mil.

LOCATION: Take I-5 north, exit 193 to Pacific Avenue. Turn right onto West Marine View Drive, base is on the left. USMRA: Page 101 (D-3), page 103 (C-2). NMC: Seattle, 25 miles south.

GENERAL INFORMATION: Support Activity for the Navy in the Seattle area.

TEMPORARY MILITARY LODGING: BOQ C-206-304-4860, BEQ C-206-304-3111/3112. Navy Lodge 1-800-NAVY-INN.

RV, CAMPING/FAMCAMP: Operates Pacific Beach Resort & Conference Center off base. See Pacific Beach Resort & Conference Center listing for more information. Also, see Jim Creek NRS listing, C-360-435-7335, D-312-727-5315, Fax: C-360-435-7433.

SPACE-A: None. See McChord AFB listing, C-206-984-2657/5327, D-312-984-2657/5327, Fax: C-206-984-5659.

LOGISTICAL SUPPORT:

Bank-304-4110
Beauty Shop-304-4965
Commissary-304-3411
Dining Facilities-304-3169
Education Office-304-3159
Package Store-527-7858
Barber Shop-304-4968
Child Care-304-3640
Conv Store-304-4453
Dry Cleaner-304-4447
Exchange-304-4455
SATO-304-4001

ADMINISTRATIVE SUPPORT:

CDO/OOD-304-3366
Housing Office-1-800-972-3372
Locator-304-3000
Police-304-3446
Quarter Deck-304-3366
Fire Dept-911
Legal-304-4551
Pass/ID Office-304-3260
Public Affairs-304-3201
SDO/NCO-304-3366

HEALTH & WELFARE:

American Red Cross-304-4476
Chapel-304-3342
Family Services-304-3367
N-MC Relief Society-304-3203
TRICARE-1-800-404-4506
CHAMPUS-304-4057
Dental-304-4092
Medical-304-4062
  Central Appts-800-404-4506

REST & RECREATION:

Arts & Crafts-304-3531
Com Club-304-3912
Gym-304-3912
ITT-304-3167
Auto Hobby Shop-304-3583
Fitness Center-304-3912
Indoor Rec-304-3912
Library-304-3912

Marina-304-3336
Outdoor Rec-304-3336
Services-304-3167
MWR-304-3912
Recreation-304-5967

ATTRACTIONS: Seattle and the Puget Sound area, hiking, camping, fishing and skiing.

FAIRCHILD AIR FORCE BASE (WA02R4)

1 East Bong Street, Suite 103
Fairchild Air Force Base, WA 99011-5000

TELEPHONE NUMBER INFORMATION: Main installation numbers: C-509-247-1212, D-312-657-1110.

LOCATION: Take US-2 exit from I-90 west of Spokane. Follow US-2 through Airway Heights, after two miles turn left to base main gate and visitors' control center. USMRA: Page 101 (I-4). NMC: Spokane, 12 miles east.

GENERAL INFORMATION: Air Mobility Command, 92nd Air Refueling Wing, 141st ANG Air Refueling Wing, USAF Survival School, and support units.

TEMPORARY MILITARY LODGING: Lodging office, Building 2392, Short St, 24 hours daily, C-509-247-5519, 509-244-2290, D-312-657-5519, Fax: C-509-247-2307.

RV, CAMPING/FAMCAMP: On base, year round, C-509-247-2511/5366, D-312-657-2511, Fax: C-509-247-4495. Sixteen camper spaces with W/S/E hookups.

SPACE-A: Pax Term/Lounge, Building 1, 24 hours daily, C-509-247-5435, D-312-657-5435, Fax: C-509-247-4909, flights to CONUS and overseas.

LOGISTICAL SUPPORT:
Child Care-247-2403/2408
Conv Store-244-5095
Gas Station-244-5095
Snack Bar-244-2022
Visitor Center-247-5495
Commissary-244-5591
Exchange-244-2832
Package Store-244-2601
Travel Office-247-5069

ADMINISTRATIVE SUPPORT:
Fire Dept-247-2389
Locator-247-5875
Public Affairs-247-5704
Legal-247-2838
Police-247-5493

HEALTH & WELFARE:
CHAMPUS-247-2672
Family Services-247-5154
Retiree Services-247-5359
Chapel-247-2264
Medical
  Appointments-247-2361
  Emergency-247-5661

REST & RECREATION:
Arts & Crafts-247-2810/5189
Bowling-247-2422
Gym-247-2791
Library-247-5556
Pool-247-2242
Rec Center-247-5649
Youth Center-ext 5601
Auto Hobby Shop-247-2310
Clubs
  NCO-244-3622
  O-244-3622
Recreation-247-2511/2240
Theater-244-5600

ATTRACTIONS: Spokane, parks, EXPO site, theater, nightlife.

FORT LEWIS (WA09R4)

I Corps & Fort Lewis
ATTN: AFZH-GC
Building 5025, Liggett Avenue
Fort Lewis, WA 98433-9500

TELEPHONE NUMBER INFORMATION: Main installation numbers: C-253-967-1110, D-312-357-1110.

LOCATION: On I-5 in Puget Sound area, 14 miles north of Olympia. Exits clearly marked. USMRA: Page 101 (C-5), page 103 (A,B-7). NMC: Tacoma, 12 miles north.

GENERAL INFORMATION: I Corps Headquarters, and ROTC Region Headquarters.

TEMPORARY MILITARY LODGING: Lodging office, Building 2111, between Utah and Pendleton Streets, 24 hours daily, C-253-967-2815, D-312-357-2815. All ranks.

RV, CAMPING/FAMCAMP: Travel Camp on post, year round, C-253-967-7744, D-312-357-7744, 24 camper spaces with full hookups, six camper spaces with E hookups, five tent spaces. Also, Westport Rec Park, operated by USCG Station, Grays Harbor, Westport, Mar-Oct, C-360-268-0121, six camper spaces with W/E hookups, six tent spaces.

SPACE-A: Gray Army Airfield, Building 3082, 0730-1700 Mon-Fri, C-253-967-6628/5998, D-312-357-6628/5998, OSA-253-967-2414, flights to West Coast and Midwest locations.

LOGISTICAL SUPPORT:
Bank-593-5219
Beauty Shop-964-3252
Car Rental-964-1331
Child Care-967-3056
Class Six-964-4128
Conv Store-964-5459
Dining Facilities
  Burger King-964-8998
Exchange-964-3161
Laundry-964-1250
Postal Service-471-6133
Shoppette-964-5459
Barber Shop-964-9600
Book Store-964-3749
Carlson Wagonlit Travel-964-0424
Child Dev Center-967-3506
Commissary-967-3142
Credit Union-967-6685
Dry Cleaner-964-5872
Education Office-967-7175
Gas Station-964-5459
Package Store-964-4128
SATO-967-5099
Visitor Center-967-4873

ADMINISTRATIVE SUPPORT:
Fire Dept-967-4479
Legal-967-0701
Pass/ID Office-967-5065
Public Affairs-967-0156
Housing Office-967-4512
Locator-967-6221
Police-967-3107
SDO/SNO-967-0015

HEALTH & WELFARE:
American Red Cross-967-7686
Army Emergency Relief-967-7166
Chapel-967-8489
Family Services-967-7166
Retiree Services-967-4424
Veterinary Services-967-6410
ACS-967-7166
CHAMPUS-968-2165
Dental-968-1240
Medical-964-7136
TRICARE-964-7136

REST & RECREATION:
Archery-ext 6263
Auto Hobby Shop-967-3728
Clubs
  EM-964-0473
  Flying-964-4932
  NCO-964-2555
  O-967-4986
  Parachute-ext 3906
  Riding-964-2318
Marina-967-7788
Outdoor Rec-967-7788
Rec Equip-ext 5415
Swimming-ext 2490
Youth Center-967-4441
Arts & Crafts-967-5746
Bowling-967-6761
Fitness Center-967-3508
Golf Course-967-6522
Gym-967-4771
Handball-ext 3694
Hunting/Fishing-ext 6263
ITT-967-3085
Library-967-2824
MWR-967-2539
Rec Center-ext 2539
Stadium-ext 2912
Theater-967-5976
Youth Services-967-4441

ATTRACTIONS: Military Museum, Tacoma, Olympia and Seattle nearby.

WASHINGTON

JIM CREEK NAVAL RADIO STATION (WA07R4)

Jim Creek Wilderness Recreation Area
21027 Jim Creek Road
Arlington, WA 98223-8599

TELEPHONE NUMBER INFORMATION: Main installation numbers: C-206-304-5316, D-312-727-5316.

LOCATION: Take I-5, take exit 208 east towards Arlington. Proceed three miles through Arlington, cross bridge, continue for three more miles and take a right on Jim Creek Road. Proceed for eight miles to front gate. USMRA: Page 101 (D-3). NMC: Everett, 30 miles south.

TEMPORARY MILITARY LODGING: Completion date scheduled for Fall of 1997, C-360-435-7335, Fax: C-360-435-7433.

RV, CAMPING/FAMCAMP: Jim Creek Regional Outdoor Recreation Area, on base year round, Outdoor Recreation Area, Jim Creek NRS (T), C-360-435-7335, D-312-727-5315, Fax: C-360-435-7433, two camper spaces with W/E/S hookups, 23 campsites, two group campsites, two log cabins, and one group picnic area.

SPACE-A: None. See McChord AFB listing, C-206-984-2657/5327, D-312-984-2657/5327, Fax: C-206-984-5659.

LOGISTICAL SUPPORT:
Snack Bar-304-5315
Visitor Center*-304-5315
*Completion date scheduled for Fall of 1997.

ADMINISTRATIVE SUPPORT: Police-304-5314

HEALTH & WELFARE: None. See Everett NS listing, C-206-304-4044/4045.

REST & RECREATION:
Fitness Center-435-7335
Indoor Rec-435-7335
MWR-435-7335
Gym-435-7335
Marina-435-7335

ATTRACTIONS: Beautiful mountains and wilderness, lakes for fishing and canoeing, mountain bike/hiking trails.

McCHORD AIR FORCE BASE (WA05R4)

100 Main Street
McChord Air Force Base, WA 98438-1109

TELEPHONE NUMBER INFORMATION: Main installation numbers: C-206-984-1910, D-312-984-1110.

LOCATION: From I-5 take exit 125. Clearly marked. USMRA: Page 101 (C-5), page 103 (B-7). NMC: Tacoma, eight miles north.

GENERAL INFORMATION: Air Mobility Command Base. 62nd Airlift Wing, 446th AFRES units, 22nd Special Tactics Squadron, WADS and other support activities.

TEMPORARY MILITARY LODGING: Lodging office, Building 166, Main Street, 24 hours daily, C-206-584-1471, D-312-984-5613. All ranks. DV/VIP C-208-584-2621.

RV, CAMPING/FAMCAMP: Holiday Park FAMCAMP on base year round, Holiday Park FAMCAMP, c/o Adventures Unlimited, 62 SVS/SVRO, Building 739, C-206-984-5488, 18 camper spaces with full hookups, 18 camper spaces with W/E, 20 camper spaces without hookups, 20 tent spaces.

SPACE-A: Pax Term/Lounge, Building 1179, 24 hours daily, C-206-984-2657/5327, D-312-984-2657/5327, Fax: C-206-984-5659, flights to CONUS and foreign locations.

LOGISTICAL SUPPORT:
Bank-593-5772
Beauty Shop-584-1595
Child Dev Center-984-2958
Commissary-984-3285
Dining Facilities-984-2145
Education Office-984-5695
Gas Station-584-4807
Postal Service-984-5198
Snack Bar-584-5145
Visitor Center-984-2119
Barber Shop-588-2345
Child Care-984-2958
Class Six-589-4734
Credit Union-584-6413
Dry Cleaner-584-7038
Exchange-582-9451
Package Store-588-2527
Shoppette-582-0788
Travel Office-984-3521

ADMINISTRATIVE SUPPORT:
Fire Dept-984-2603
Legal-984-5512
Pass/ID Office-984-2256
Public Affairs-984-5637
Housing Office-984-5514
Locator-984-1110
Police-984-5624

HEALTH & WELFARE:
Air Force Aid Society-984-2695
ACS-984-2813
Chapel-984-5556
Family Services-984-2535
Retiree Services-984-3214
TRICARE-581-0818
Veterinary Services-984-3951
American Red Cross-984-5577
CHAMPUS-984-2257
Dental-984-5505
Medical
  Central Appts-1-800-404-4506
  Emergency-984-5458/911
  Health Benefits-984-2476

REST & RECREATION:
Arts & Crafts-984-2816
Bowling-984-5954
Health & Wellness Center-984-2393
Gym-984-5666
MWR-984-5836
Rec Equip-ext 2206
Theater-984-5836
Wood Hobby Shop-984-2816
Auto Hobby Shop-984-2407
Combined Clubs-984-5581
Golf Course-984-2053
Library-984-3454
Rec Center-ext 2068
Swimming-ext 2807
Tickets-ext 2216
Youth Center-984-2203

ATTRACTIONS: Tacoma and Puget Sound area.

PACIFIC BEACH RESORT AND CONFERENCE CENTER (WA16R4)

P.O. Box O
108 First Street
Pacific Beach, WA 98571-1700

TELEPHONE NUMBER INFORMATION: Main installation numbers: C-206-304-3000, D-312-727-3000. Police for center, C-911.

LOCATION: From I-5 at Olympia, take exit 104 (Aberdeen/Port Angeles); west on US-8 and US-12 through Aberdeen to Hoquiam. Follow US-101 north approximately four miles to sign indicating Ocean Beaches; turn left and continue on Ocean Beach Road through Copalis Crossing, Carlisle and Aloha to Pacific Beach. Follow Main Street to entrance to Pacific Beach Recreation and Conference Center. Watch for signs to office. USMRA: page 101 (A-4,5). NMC: Aberdeen, 25 miles southeast. NMI: Fort Lewis, 115 miles northeast.

GENERAL INFORMATION: Situated on Olympic Peninsula, overlooking Pacific Ocean, providing starting point for exploring the Peninsula with its spectacular rain forest, Quinalt Indian Reservation and Ocean Shores area. It also offers steelhead and salmon fishing. Operated by Everett Naval Station off base year round. Military personnel active, retired, guard, reserve, DoD civilians and 100% DAV. Check in 1600-2000, check out 1100 (1300 for RV/tent spaces). Reservations; Recommended for RV park, studios and motel units; required for cabins and suites; with deposit: up to 90 days in advance for active duty, up to 60 days in advance for retired and reserve, up to 30 days in advance for all others. (Make checks payable to "Pacific Beach.") C-1-800-626-4414, 360-276-

4414, Fax: 360-276-4615 (Mon-Fri 0800-1600, Sat-Sun 0800-1600). For information, C-206-304-3122. Visa, MasterCard and American Express accepted. Pets allowed on leash and must be registered; owner must clean up after pet. No open fires except in covered picnic area, in grills and camp stoves; must not be left unattended at any time. Two night minimum; three night minimum on holiday weekends (Fri-Mon); 14 day limit. No cooking in studios and family units; no children, pets nor smoking in suites. Any excess cleaning/repair will be billed to patron. Sponsor must accompany guest during stay. Quiet hours 1000-0700. No RV/camper parking at beach houses. Hunting rifles must be declared, no other firearms are allowed.

TEMPORARY MILITARY LODGING: Beach houses: three bedroom, fully equipped (23), four bedroom, fully equipped (5); Suites (adults only), fully equipped (6); Studios, fully equipped (15); Family units (12). Rates: three bedroom $40-$60 daily; four bedroom $45-$65 daily; suites $35-$55 daily; studios $15-$25 daily; family units $20-$30 daily. Rates vary depending on rank, days of week, and season. Oceanview with fireplace, $10 additional daily. $5 additional daily for units with wood stoves. Cribs (no linens), $5 per visit.

RV, CAMPING/FAMCAMP: Hardstand RV spaces with W&E hookups (43); camper/tent spaces with no hookups (125). Rates: RV spaces $7-$11 daily; camper/tent spaces $5 daily. 25 camper/tent spaces upgraded with fire pits, private parking, shower facilities, and restrooms. $1 additional daily for 33 RV spaces with cable TV; weekly and monthly rates available.

REST & RECREATION: Beachcombing, Bingo, Card Tournament, Clamming, Crabbing, Dancing, Fishing, Group Activities, Hiking, Hunting, Kiddie Bingo, Weekly Events. Scheduled activities for all ages.

OTHER SUPPORT & FACILITIES AVAILABLE: Basketball/1 on 1, Bowling, Cable TV, Conference Facility, Exercise Room, Hot Tubs/Spa, Laundry, Lounge, Meeting Rooms, Pay Telephones, Restaurant, Restrooms, Sewage Dump, Showers, Social Room, Weight Room. Most restrooms and buildings are handicapped accessible. Also, see Fort Lewis listing, C-253-967-1110, D-312-357-1110.

ATTRACTIONS: Rain forest, Quinalt Indian Reservation and Ocean Shores.

PORT ANGELES COAST GUARD GROUP/ AIR STATION (WA19R4)

Commander US Coast Guard Group
Eniz Hook Road
Port Angeles, WA 98362-0159

TELEPHONE NUMBER INFORMATION: Main installation numbers: C-360-457-2206, D-312-744-6431.

LOCATION: Take I-5 north to Tacoma, 16 north to Bremerton, 3 to Hood Canal Bridge, 104 to 101 west to Port Angeles. USMRA: Page 101 (B-3). NMC: Bremerton, 50 miles.

GENERAL INFORMATION: Coast Guard Air Station and Group.

TEMPORARY MILITARY LODGING: None. See Whidbey Island NAS listing, C-360-257-2529, D-312-820-2529.

RV, CAMPING/FAMCAMP: None. See Pacific Beach Resort and Conference Center listing, C-800-626-4414, 360-276-4414, Fax: C-360-276-4615.

SPACE-A: None. See McChord AFB listing, C-360-984-2657/5327, D-312-984-2657/5327, Fax: C-206-984-5659.

LOGISTICAL SUPPORT:
Barber Shop-457-2288
Exchange-457-2285

ADMINISTRATIVE SUPPORT:
Legal-457-2212
Locator-457-2226
Housing Office-457-2219
OOD-457-2226
Public Affairs-457-2228
SDO/NCO-457-2226

HEALTH & WELFARE:
CHAMPUS-457-2275
Dental-457-2275
Medical-457-2275
Retiree Services-457-2275
  Central Appts-457-2777
  Emergency-457-8513

REST & RECREATION:
Gym-ext 399

ATTRACTIONS: Olympic National Park, great hunting, fishing. hiking. Port Angeles only 18 miles south of Victoria, BC, and 87 miles west of Seattle (two hour drive with ferry ride).

PUGET SOUND NAVAL SHIPYARD (WA11R4)

1400 Farragut Avenue
Bremerton, WA 98314-5001

TELEPHONE NUMBER INFORMATION: Main installation numbers: C-360-476-3711, D-312-439-3711.

LOCATION: Take I-5 north to highway 16 exit (Bremerton). The 24-hour gate is at Naval Avenue. Also, can be reached via a one hour ferry ride from Seattle. USMRA: Page 101 (C-4), page 103 (A-3). NMC: Bremerton, in city limits.

GENERAL INFORMATION: Homeport for ships undergoing repair and other ships.

TEMPORARY MILITARY LODGING: Lodging office, Building 865, BEQ C-360-476-7619, D-312-439-7619, BOQ C-360-476-2840, D-312-439-2840.

RV, CAMPING/FAMCAMP: None. See Whidbey Island NAS listing, C-360-257-2434, D-312-820-2434.

SPACE-A: None. See McChord AFB listing, C-206-984-2657/5327, D-312-984-2657/5327, Fax: C-206-984-5659.

LOGISTICAL SUPPORT:
Bank-478-2240
Barber Shop-478-5513
Beauty Shop-478-5515
Cafeteria-476-2527
Child Care-476-1152
Child Dev Center-476-1152
Class Six-377-8434
Commissary-405-1971
Conv Store-478-5540
Credit Union-478-2240
Dining Facilities-476-2527
Dry Cleaner-478-5522
Education Office-476-4282
Exchange-478-5570
Laundry-478-5522
Package Store-478-5522
Postal Service-478-5522
SATO-476-5417 (official)
  476-2044 (leisure)
Shoppette-478-5527
Snack Bar-476-5756/5529

ADMINISTRATIVE SUPPORT:
CDO/OOD-476-2335
Fire Dept-476-2796
Housing Office-476-2363
Legal-476-2156
Locator-476-7210
Pass/ID Office-476-4883
Police-476-2515
Public Affairs-476-7111
Quarter Deck-476-2335

HEALTH & WELFARE:
American Red Cross-478-9341
ACS-377-0602
CHAMPUS-478-9386
Chapel-476-2183
Dental-476-2211
Family Services-476-5113
Medical-479-6600
N-MC Relief Society-377-0602
  Central Appts-1-800-404-4506
Retiree Services-476-5113
  Emergency-478-9286
TRICARE-478-9651
  Health Benefits-478-9201
  Hospital-479-6600
  Information-479-6600

REST & RECREATION:
Auto Hobby Shop-476-2778
Bowling-476-2990

WASHINGTON
Puget Sound Naval Shipyard, continued

Clubs
CPO-476-3391
EM-476-2546
O-373-5014
MWR-476-8188
Wood Hobby Shop-476-2778
Youth Services-476-6405
Fitness Center-476-2331
Gym-476-2231
ITT-476-7576
Library-476-3178
Outdoor Rec-476-3428
Youth Center-476-6405

OTHER FACILITIES AVAILABLE: Swimming, Tennis, Picnic Area.

ATTRACTIONS: Puget Sound and Seattle/Tacoma area.

SEATTLE COAST GUARD INTEGRATED SUPPORT COMMAND (WA20R4)

1519 Alaskan Way, South
Seattle, WA 98134-1192

TELEPHONE NUMBER INFORMATION: Main installation number: C-206-217-6400.

LOCATION: From the south, take I-5 north to King Dome exit. Take a right onto 4th Avenue, turn right on Royal Brougham. Turn left onto Alaskan Way South, Pier 36 will be on your right about one-quarter of a mile down. From the north, take I-5 south to Airport Way/4th Avenue exit, make a right onto 4th Avenue. Take right on Royal Brougham then left onto Alaskan Way South. USMRA: Page 103 (C-3). NMC: Seattle, in city limits.

GENERAL INFORMATION: Coast Guard Cutters: Bayberry, Mariposa, Mellon, Midgett, Polar Sea, and Polar Star. Units: Naval Engineering Support Unit Seattle, Electronic Support Unit Seattle, Marine Safety Office Puget Sound, Vessel Traffic Service Puget Sound, Group Seattle, and Station Seattle.

TEMPORARY MILITARY LODGING: BEQ, 1519 Alaskan Way South, 0730-1600 daily, C-206-217-6410. Transient enlisted only (Active or Reserve in Drill Status).

RV, CAMPING/FAMCAMP: None. See Whidbey Island NAS listing, C-360-257-2434, D-312-820-2434.

SPACE-A: None. See McChord AFB listing, C-206-984-2657/5327, D-312-984-2657/5327, Fax: C-206-984-5659.

LOGISTICAL SUPPORT:
Barber Shop-622-1579
Dining Facilities-217-6416
Package Store-587-0307
Cafeteria-217-6416
Exchange-587-0307
Visitor Center-217-6993

ADMINISTRATIVE SUPPORT:
CDO-217-6410
Legal-220-7110
Police-217-6990
SDO/NCO-217-6410
Housing Office-217-6480
Pass/ID Office-217-6510
Public Affairs-217-6408

HEALTH & WELFARE:
CHAMPUS-217-6430
Dental-217-6430
Medical-217-6430
TRICARE-217-6430
Chaplain-217-6995
Family Services-217-6999
Retiree Services-217-6430

REST & RECREATION:
Fitness Center-217-6358
MWR-217-6357
Rec Center-ext 6410
Gym-217-6358
Museum-217-9993

ATTRACTIONS: Space Needle, Pike Place Market, Seattle Zoo (Woodland Park), Puget Sound, Olympic and Mt. Rainier National Parks, Seattle King Dome, Seattle Aquarium, Museum of Flight, Boeing and Microsoft, Crystal Mountain, Mount Baker-Snoqualmie National Forest and Tillicum Village.

WHIDBEY ISLAND NAVAL AIR STATION (WA06R4)

3730 N Charles Porter Avenue, B-385, Room 219
Oak Harbor, WA 98278-5100

TELEPHONE NUMBER INFORMATION: Main installation numbers: C-360-257-22111, D-312-820-2211. HP: http://www.naswi.navy.mil.

LOCATION: Take WA-20 to Whidbey Island, three miles west of WA-20 on Ault Field Road. USMRA: Page 101 (C-2,3). NMC: Seattle, 80 miles southeast.

GENERAL INFORMATION: Commander, Electronic Combat Wing, US Pacific Fleet (COMVAQWINGPAC), Marine Aviation Training Support Group (MASTG), Naval Air Maintenance Training Group Detachment (NAMTRAGRUDET), Commander, Patrol Wing Ten, US Pacific Fleet (COMPATWING-10).

TEMPORARY MILITARY LODGING: Lodging office: Buildings 973, McCormick Lodger, Midway Boulevard, C-360-257-2529. Navy Lodge, Building 2125 N Coral Sea Avenue, Oak Harbor, WA 98278, C-800-NAVY-INN, C-360-675-0633. DV/VIP C-360-257-2037. All ranks.

RV, CAMPING/FAMCAMP: Cliffside RV Park on base, year round, Outdoor Recreation Center, 1130 W Storm Lane, C-360-257-2434, D-312-820-2434, 20 camper spaces with W/E hookups, six tent spaces without hookups. Rocky Point RV Park, off base year round, Gallery Golf Course, 1130 W Storm Lane, C-360-257-2178, 23 RV spaces, self contained, with no hookups.

SPACE-A: Pax Term/Lounge, Building 2734, 0730-1900 daily, C-360-257-2604, D-312-820-2604, Fax: C-360-257-1942, flights to CONUS locations.

LOGISTICAL SUPPORT:
Bank-675-0764
Beauty Shop-257-0530
Child Dev Center-257-3302
Dining Facilities-257-2715
Education Office-257-2284
Gas Station-257-2829
Package Store-257-0574
SATO-679-4415
Barber Shop-257-0511
Child Care-257-3302
Commissary-257-3318
Dry Cleaner-257-0522
Exchange-257-0600
Laundry-257-0522
Postal Service-257-2060
Travel Office-257-6437
MWR Leisure Travel-679-3461

ADMINISTRATIVE SUPPORT:
CDO/OOD-257-2631
Housing Office-257-3331
Locator-257-8787
Police-257-3122
Quarter Deck-257-2631
Fire Dept-257-2533
Legal-257-2126
Pass/ID Office-257-5620
Public Affairs-257-2286

HEALTH & WELFARE:
CHAMPUS-257-9542
Dental-257-2106
Central Appts-257-2301
N-MC Relief Society-257-2728
TRICARE-257-9542
Chapel-257-2414
Family Services-257-2902
Medical-257-9547
Retiree Services-257-8054
Veterinary Services-257-2001

REST & RECREATION:
Arts & Crafts-257-2173
Bowling-257-1567
Fitness Center-257-2420
Golf Course-257-2178
Gym-257-2420
Library-257-2702
Marina-679-2628
MWR-257-2432
Outdoor Rec-257-5281
Theater-257-2427
Youth Center-257-3150
Auto Hobby Shop-257-4841
Clubs
Archery-ext 9723
CPO-257-2892
EM-257-3308
Flying-679-4359
O-257-2521
Rod/Gun-ext 5539
Sailing-ext 2432
Wood Hobby Shop-257-2427

WASHINGTON
Whidbey Island Naval Air Station, continued

OTHER SUPPORT & FACILITIES AVAILABLE: American Red Cross, Indoor Rec, Services.

ATTRACTIONS: Outdoor sports (mostly water), fishing, great seafood.

Other Installations in Washington

Fort Lawton 70th Regional Support Command (WA18R4), 4575 36th Avenue West, Fort Lawton, WA 98199-5000, USMRA: Page 101 (C-4), page 103 (B,C-2), C-800-347-2735, Family Services-800-677-3980/206-281-3131, Public Affairs-281-3026, Exchange-217-9213, Retiree Services-281-299.

USAF Survival School (WA17R4), 336 TRG/CCE, 811 W Los Angeles Avenue, Suite 103, Fairchild AFB, WA 99011-8648. USMRA: Page 101 (I,J-4) NMC: Spokane, 12 miles east. C-509-247-2691, D-312-657-2691. E-mail: jenkins@336server.fairchild. af.mil. HP: http://131.35.201.50/public/336_trgl. Dining Facilities-247-5553, Fitness Center-247-2991, Library-247-2597, Shoppette-244-9615.

Vancouver Barracks Exchange (WA23R4), Building 752, Hathaway Road, Vancouver, WA 98661-3826. USMRA: Page 101 (C-8). C-360-695-8749.

Yakima Training Center (WA24R4), Building T-1, Yakima, WA 98901-9399. USMRA: Page 101 (F-5,6). C-509-577-3000, Consol Club-577-3415, Medical-577-3251, Exchange-577-3416 or 452-7356, Gym-577-3209, Rec Equipment-577-3271.

WEST VIRGINIA

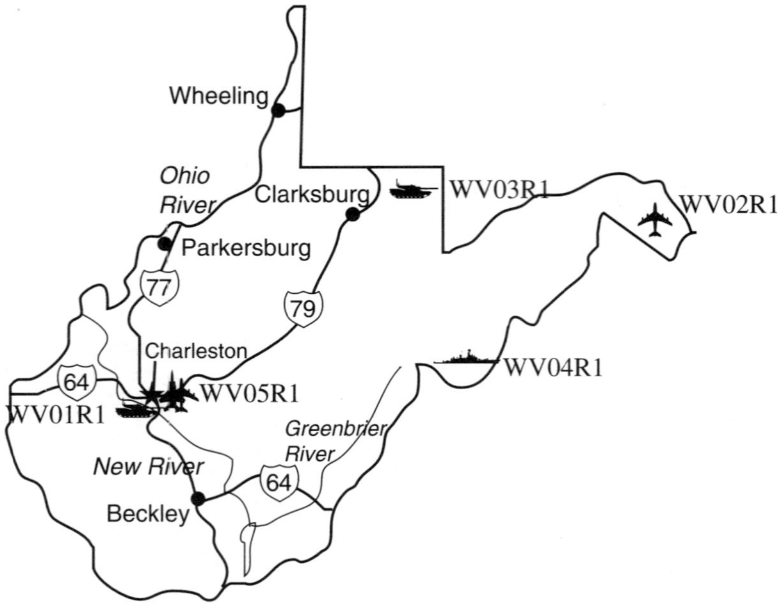

EASTERN WEST VIRGINIA REGIONAL AIRPORT (WV02R1)

167th Airlift Wing (ANG)
Martinsburg, WV 25401-0204

TELEPHONE NUMBER INFORMATION: Main installation numbers: C-304-262-5100, D-312-242-3210.

LOCATION: From I-81, take exit 12 east, right to route 11, south for four miles, left to Paynes Ford Road. Airport is approximately one mile on the right. USMRA: Page 47 (K-3,4). NMC: Hagerstown, MD, 15 miles north.

GENERAL INFORMATION: 167th Air National Guard Unit, C-130s.

TEMPORARY MILITARY LODGING: Very limited, C-304-262-5174.

RV, CAMPING/FAMCAMP: None. See Quantico MCB, VA listing, C-703-784-5270, D-312-278-5270.

SPACE-A: C-304-262-5250. Flights to CONUS and OCONUS locations.

LOGISTICAL SUPPORT:
Credit Union-262-5262
Exchange-262-5204
Education Office-262-5208
Travel Office-262-5216

ADMINISTRATIVE SUPPORT:
Fire Dept-262-5277
Police-262-5300
Pass/ID Office-262-5276

HEALTH & WELFARE:
Medical-262-5244

REST & RECREATION:
Consol Club-262-5298
Services-267-5174

ATTRACTIONS: Beautiful Shenandoah Valley 20 miles south.

SUGAR GROVE NAVAL SECURITY GROUP ACTIVITY (WV04R1)

ATTN: PAO
Sugar Grove, WV 26815-9700

TELEPHONE NUMBER INFORMATION: Main installation numbers: C-304-249-6304, D-312-564-7276 ext 6304.

LOCATION: From I-81 in VA take Route 33 west from Harrisonburg VA, to Brandywine, WV. Left on Sugar Grove Road, approximately seven miles on the right. USMRA: Page 47 (I-6). NMC: Harrisonburg, VA, 36 miles east.

GENERAL INFORMATION: Naval Radio Station, Naval Security Group Detachment, Customer Service Desk, and branch medical clinic.

TEMPORARY MILITARY LODGING: Lodging office, Building 63, 0730-1600 daily, C-304-249-6350, D-312-564-7276, Fax: C-304-249-6307.

RV, CAMPING/FAMCAMP: Sugar Grove Cabins, on base, year round, C-304-249-6309, D-312-564-7276, Fax: C-304-249-6385.

SPACE-A: None. See Eastern West Virginia Regional Airport listing, C-304-267-5250, D-312-249-9250, Fax: C-304-267-5144.

LOGISTICAL SUPPORT:
Barber Shop-249-6355
Child Care-249-6309
Education Office-249-6374
Cafeteria-249-6350
Exchange-249-6355

ADMINISTRATIVE SUPPORT:
CDO/OOD-249-6310
Police-249-6310
Fire Dept-249-6390
Public Affairs-249-6304

HEALTH & WELFARE:
CHAMPUS-249-6380
Medical-249-6380
Emergency-249-6390
TRICARE-249-6380
Family Services-249-6354
N-MC Relief Society-249-6375
Retiree Services-249-6304

REST & RECREATION:
Auto Hobby Shop-249-6367
Community Center-249-6362
ITT-249-6360
Library-249-6360
MWR-249-6366
Outdoor Recreation-249-6367
Wood Hobby Shop-249-6367
Clubs
CPO-249-6362
EM-249-6362
NCO-249-6362
O-249-6362
Theater-249-6362
Youth Services-249-6309

ATTRACTIONS: Excellent hunting and fishing area.

Other Installations in West Virginia

Camp Dawson Army Training Site (WV03R1), 240 Army Road, Kingwood, WV 26537-1092. USMRA: Page 46 (H-3). C-304-329-4334, D-312-366-6552. Exchange-329-4469, Snack Bar-329-4383, TML-329-4420.
Charleston Armory Exchange (WV01R1), 1679 Coonskin Drive, Charleston, WV 25311-1085. USMRA: Page 46 (E-6). C-304-346-4957. HP: http://www.newwave.net/-wvarng/.
Yeager Airport/ Air National Guard Base (WV05R1), 1679 Coonskin Drive, Charleston, WV 25311-1085. C-304-341-6000, D-312-366-6100. From I-77, take exit 102, follow signs to airport. USMRA: Page 46 (E-6). NMC: Charleston four miles southwest. 130th Airlift Wing, Air National Guard C-130H. Space-A-341-6185/6240. Unscheduled flights to CONUS and OCONUS locations. Exchange-341-4957, Medical-341-6252.

WISCONSIN

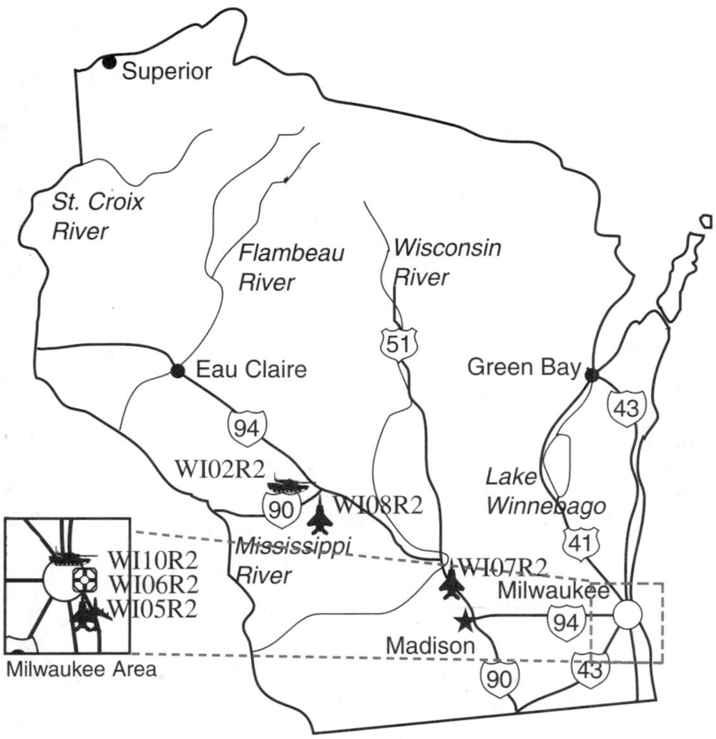

FORT McCOY(WI02R2)

ATTN: AFRC-FM-CO
100 E Headquarters Road
Fort McCoy, WI 54656-5263

TELEPHONE NUMBER INFORMATION: Main installation numbers: C-608-388-2222, D-312-280-1110. E-mail: tcc@mccoy-emhl.army.mil.

LOCATION: From I-90, to WI-21 northeast to fort. USMRA: Page 68 (C,D-7). NMC: La Crosse, 35 miles southwest.

GENERAL INFORMATION: Army Reserve Readiness Training Center, 2nd Brigade (Field Exercise) 85th Division, Readiness Group-McCoy, 88th Explosive Ordnance Company, Wisconsin Nation Guard Mobilization and Training Equipment Site and Military Academy, Region E, Tradoc Regional Coordinating Element and Naval Mobile Construction Battalion 25.

TEMPORARY MILITARY LODGING: Lodging office, Building 2168, South 8th Street, 24 hours daily, C-608-388-2107, D-312-280-2107, Fax: C-608-388-3946. All ranks. DV/VIP C-608-388-3607, D-312-280-3607.

RV, CAMPING/FAMCAMP: Pine View Recreation Area, on post 18 Apr-30 Nov, DPCA, 1439 South M Street, ATTN: Pine View Recreation Area, C-608-388-3517, D-312-280-3517, two duplexes, two cabins, 35 camper spaces with full hookups, 70 camper spaces with E hookup, 32 tent/camper spaces.

SPACE-A: None. See Volk Field/ ANGB, C-608-427-1210, D-312-798-3210, flights via transient ANG aircraft.

LOGISTICAL SUPPORT:

Barber Shop-338-3960	Beauty Shop-338-3690
Cafeteria-269-4865	Car Rental-269-7692
Child Care-388-4124	Child Dev Center-388-2238
Class Six-388-4134	Commissary-388-3542
Conv Store-269-5364	Credit Union-388-2171
Dining Facilities-388-2642	Education Office-338-3656
Exchange-269-4860	Gas Station-388-5364
Package Store-269-4860	Postal Service-388-3825
Shoppette-269-5364	Snack Bar-388-4968

ADMINISTRATIVE SUPPORT:

Fire Dept-388-2508	Housing Office-388-2804
Legal-388-2165	Locator-388-2225
Pass/ID Office-388-4563	Police-388-4116
Public Affairs-388-2407	SDO/NCO-388-2216

HEALTH & WELFARE:

ACS-388-3505	Army Emergency Relief-388-3505
CHAMPUS-388-2246	Chapel-388-4203
Dental	Family Services-388-2919
Central Appts-372-1720 ext 6720	Medical-388-3025
Clinic-388-2245	Health Benefits-388-2246
Retiree Services-388-3716	

REST & RECREATION:

Arts & Crafts-388-4353	Auto Hobby Shop-388-3013
Bowling-388-2065	Com Club-388-2065
Community Center-388-2065	Fishing/Hunting-ext 3337
Fitness Center-388-2290	Gym-388-2290
ITT-388-3505	Library-388-2410
MWR-388-4375	Outdoor Rec-388-3360
Rec Center-ext 3213	Rec Equip-ext 2619
Swimming-ext 2290	Tennis-ext 2290
Theater-388-4968	Wood Hobby Shop-388-2516
Youth Services-388-4373	

ATTRACTIONS: Historical Center, La Crosse, Sparta, and Tomah. Outdoor sports and recreation.

GENERAL MITCHELL INTERNATIONAL AIRPORT/AIR RESERVE STATION (WI05R2)

300 East College Avenue
Milwaukee, WI 53207-6299

TELEPHONE NUMBER INFORMATION: Main installation numbers: C-414-482-5000 (AFRES), 414-747-4420 (ANG), D-312-950-5000 (AFRES), 312-550-8420 (ANG).

LOCATION: From I-94 take the 318 East exit to the airport. USMRA: Page 68 (G-9). NMC: Milwaukee, three miles north.

GENERAL INFORMATION: Units at General Mitchell IAP include the 128th Air Refueling Group (ANG) and the 440th Airlift Wing (AFRES).

TEMPORARY MILITARY LODGING: None. See Great Lakes NTC, IL listing, C-847-688-2170, D-312-792-2710.

RV, CAMPING/FAMCAMP: None. See Milwaukee CGG listing, Rawley Point Cottage and Sherwood Point Cottage, C-414-747-7185.

SPACE-A: 440 AW (AFRES), 0700-1700, C-414-482-5918, D-312-950-5918. Flights to CONUS, OCONUS, and foreign locations.

LOGISTICAL SUPPORT:

Exchange-744-1207	SATO-482-5799

ADMINISTRATIVE SUPPORT:

Fire Dept-482-5000	Legal-482-5214
Police-482-5375	Public Affairs-482-5481

HEALTH & WELFARE: Family Services-482-5424

REST & RECREATION:

Consol Club-482-5711	MWR-482-5706

ATTRACTIONS: City of Milwaukee, Summerfest, Wisconsin State Fairgrounds, Lake Michigan.

WISCONSIN

MILWAUKEE COAST GUARD GROUP (WI06R2)

2420 South Lincoln Memorial Drive
Milwaukee, WI 53207-1997

TELEPHONE NUMBER INFORMATION: Main installation numbers: C-414-747-7100.

LOCATION: Take I-94 west to Milwaukee to I-794 east. Proceed over Hoan Bridge on I-794 to stop sign. Turn left, office is one-quarter mile. USMRA: Page 68 (G-9). NMC: Milwaukee, in city limits.

GENERAL INFORMATION: USCG Group/Base, Marine Safety Office.

TEMPORARY MILITARY LODGING: None. See Great Lakes NTC, IL listing, C-847-688-2170, D-312-792-2710.

RV, CAMPING/FAMCAMP: Rawley Point Cottage, off base year round, Commander, Group Milwaukee USCG, C-414-747-7185. Sherwood Point Cottage, off base year round, Commander, Coast Guard Group Morale Fund, C-414-747-7185.

SPACE-A: None. See General Mitchell IAP/ARS listing, C-414-482-5918, D-312-950-5918.

LOGISTICAL SUPPORT: Exchange-747-1466

ADMINISTRATIVE SUPPORT: SDO/NCO-747-7266

HEALTH & WELFARE: None. See Great Lakes NTC, IL, C-847-688-5600.

REST & RECREATION: RV/Camping-747-7185

ATTRACTIONS: City of Milwaukee. Lake Michigan, lakefront festivals, recreational boating and charter fishing. Wisconsin farmland to the south, west, and north. All professional sports.

TRUAX FIELD (WI07R2)

115 Fighter Wing
3110 Mitchell Street, Building 500
Madison, WI 53704-2591

TELEPHONE NUMBER INFORMATION: Main installation numbers: C-608-245-4500, D-312-724-8395. E-mail: eehlers@wimsn.ang.af.mil.

LOCATION: From I-90/94 exit west on Highway 151. North on Highway 151 for one and a half miles, take a left on Persdorf then a left on Mitchell Street, two blocks to front gate. USMRA: Page 68 (E-8). NMC: Madison, in city limits.

GENERAL INFORMATION: 115 Fighter Wing.

TEMPORARY MILITARY LODGING: None. See Great Lakes NTC, IL listing, C-847-688-2170, D-312-792-2710.

RV, CAMPING/FAMCAMP: None. See Milwaukee CGG listing, Rawley Point Cottage and Sherwood Point Cottage, C-414-747-7185.

SPACE-A: None. See General Mitchell IAP/ARS listing, C-414-482-5918, D-312-950-5918.

LOGISTICAL SUPPORT:
Credit Union-245-4599 | Exchange-249-5229
SATO-245-4573

ADMINISTRATIVE SUPPORT:
Fire Dept-245-4340 | Legal-245-4396
Pass/ID Office-245-4468 | Police-245-4560
Public Affairs-245-4395

HEALTH & WELFARE: Medical-245-4567

REST & RECREATION: Com Club-249-6201.

ATTRACTIONS: State Capitol, state parks, University Wisconsin-Madison campus, State Guard headquarters, Milwaukee.

Other Installations in Wisconsin

Milwaukee Post Exchange (WI10R2), 4828 W Silver Springs Drive, Building 304, Milwaukee, WI 53218-5000. USMRA: Page 68 (G-8). C-414-527-4552.
Volk Field/Air National Guard Base (WI08R2), Combat Readiness Training Center, 100 Independence Drive, Camp Douglas, WI 54618-5001. C-608-427-1210, D-312-946-3210. From Madison, take I-90/94 north west 85 miles to Camp Douglas exit. From Lacrosse, take I-90 east to I-94 south 55 miles. USMRA: Page 68 (D-7). NMI: Fort McCoy, 25 miles northwest. NMC: La Cross, 55 miles west. One of four ANG Combat Readiness Training Centers (CRTCs), manages 10,000 acres including Hardwood Air to Ground Range and 4,000 square miles of Airspace. Hosts units deployed for inspections, exercises and field training. Space-A-C-608-427-1210, D-312-427-1210, Fax: C-608-427-1266; Fire Dept-ext 1317, Pass/ID Office-ext 1236, Police-ext 1236, Public Affairs- ext 1202.

WYOMING

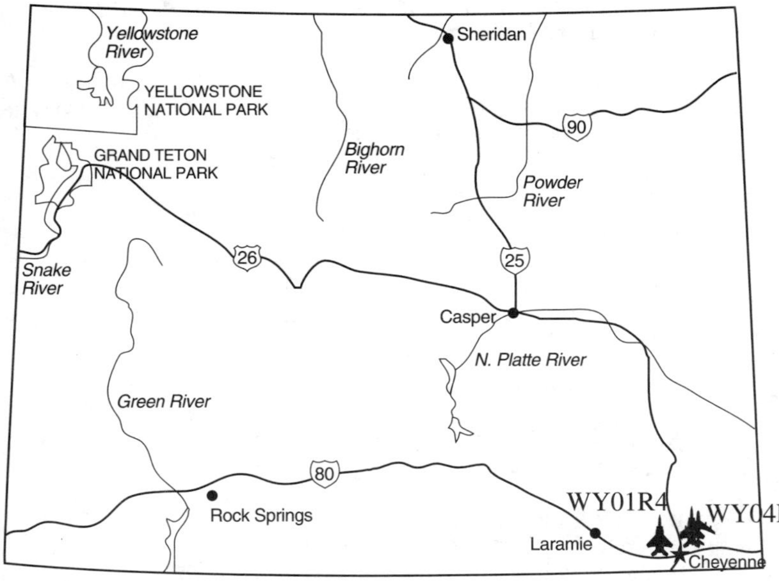

FRANCIS E. WARREN AIR FORCE BASE (WY01R4)

5305 Randall Avenue
Francis E. Warren Air Force Base, WY 82005-2266

TELEPHONE NUMBER INFORMATION: Main installation numbers: C-307-773-1110, D-312-481-1110.

LOCATION: Off I-25, Exit #11, two miles north of I-80. Clearly marked. USMRA: Page 102 (I-8). NMC: Cheyenne, adjacent to city.

GENERAL INFORMATION: Air Force Space Command base, 90th Missile Wing, 20th Air Force support units.

TEMPORARY MILITARY LODGING: Lodging Office, Building 216, 7103 Randall Avenue, 24 hours daily, C-307-773-1844, D-312-481-1844. All ranks. DV/VIP C-307-773-3434.

RV, CAMPING/FAMCAMP: FAMCAMP on base, May-Labor Day, Outdoor Recreation, 7103 Randall Avenue, C-307-773-2988, D-312-481-2988, 40 camper spaces with W/E hookups, 10 tent spaces.

SPACE-A: Limited. Base Ops C-307-773-1110, D-312-481-1110. Also, see Cheyenne Municipal Airport listing, C-307-772-6132, D-312-943-6132, Fax: C-307-772-6000.

LOGISTICAL SUPPORT:

American Express Travel-634-2948

Child Care-773-2639	Class Six-773-3008
Commissary-773-2427	Exchange-634-1593
Gas Station-634-7432	Shoppette-634-7432
Visitor Center-773-3694	

ADMINISTRATIVE SUPPORT:

Fire Dept-773-2931	Legal-773-2256
Locator-773-1841	Police-773-3501
Public Affairs-773-3381	SDO/NCO-775-3921

HEALTH & WELFARE:

Chapel-773-3434	Family Services-773-3739
Medical	Retiree Services-773-2309

Health Benefits Advisor-773-2620
TRICARE-772-4020
Information-773-2273

REST & RECREATION:

Bowling-773-2210	Consol Club-773-3024/3048
Community Center-773-2446	Golf Course-773-3556
Gym-773-2304	ITT-773-2988
Library-773-3416	Outdoor Rec-773-2988
Rec Equip-773-2988	Services-773-2858
Theater-773-2345	Youth Center-773-2564

ATTRACTIONS: Cheyenne, historic Governor's Mansion, National First Day Cover Museum, State Capital.

Other Installations in Wyoming

Cheyenne Municipal Airport/ANGB (WY04R3), 217 Dell Range Boulevard, Cheyenne, WY 82009-4799. USMRA: Page 102 (I-8). C-307-772-6110, D-312-943-6110, Space-A-772-6132.

UNITED STATES POSSESSIONS

AMERICAN SAMOA

PAGO PAGO INTERNATIONAL AIRPORT (AS01R8), PPG/Pago Pago International Airport, P.O. Box 280, Pago Pago, American Samoa 96799-5000, C-011-684-699-1515. On the south coast of the Island of Tutuila in American Samoa. Approximately 2,630 miles southwest of Honolulu, HI, and 2,660 miles northeast of Christchurch, NZ. NMC: Village of Utulei, main US Government offices, nine miles from IAP. American Red Cross-633-5222, Exchange-699-2241, Police-699-9101, Space-A-699-1515.

GUAM

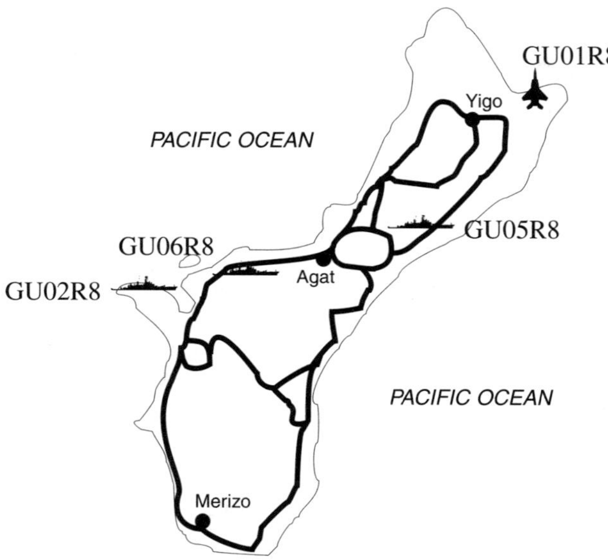

ANDERSEN AIR FORCE BASE (GU01R8)

Unit 14003, Box 25
APO AP 96543-4003

TELEPHONE NUMBER INFORMATION: Main installation numbers: C-671-366-1110, D-315-366-1110.

LOCATION: On the north end of the island, accessible from Marine Drive which extends the entire length of the island of Guam. USMRA: Page 130 (E,F-1,2). NMC: Agana, 15 miles south.

GENERAL INFORMATION: Pacific Air Forces. Air Base Wing, AMC Squadron and other support units.

TEMPORARY MILITARY LODGING: Lodging office, Building 27006, 4th & Caroline Streets, 24 hours daily, C-671-366-8201/8144, D-315-366-8201/8144. All ranks. DV/VIP C-671-651-4228.

RV, CAMPING/FAMCAMP: Outdoor Recreation Services, off base, year round, Guam Naval Activities MWR Office, PSC 455, Box 169, FPO 96540-4153, C-671-564-1847/81, D-315-564-4153, Fax: C-671-564-1853. Camping is allowed on some beaches, no hookups, no fees.

SPACE-A: Pax Term/Lounge, Building 17002, 24 hours daily, C-671-366-2096/2097, D-315-366-5165, Fax: C-671-366-2079, flights to CONUS, OCONUS and foreign locations.

LOGISTICAL SUPPORT:

Cafeteria-362-3247	Car Rental-653-6945
Child Care-362-6280	Commissary-366-2264
Conv Store-653-8143	Exchange-653-1141
Gas Station-653-4677	Package Store-653-8143/4
SATO-653-8945	Snack Bar-366-8283
Visitor Center-366-4230	

ADMINISTRATIVE SUPPORT:

Fire Dept-911 or 366-5268	Legal-366-2937
Locator-366-3247	Police-911 or 366-2913
Public Affairs-366-4202	SDO/NCO-363-2981

HEALTH & WELFARE:

CHAMPUS-366-6547	Chapel-366-6139
Family Services-366-8136	Medical-366-2978
Retiree Services-366-4315	Emergency-366-4267

REST & RECREATION:

Arts & Crafts 366-5214	Auto Hobby Shop-366-1258
Bowling-366-2695	Consol Clubs
Fitness Center-366-6100	366-6166
Golf Course-362-4653	653-9810/1
Gym-366-6100	Library-366-4294
MWR-366-4221	Recreation-366-2209
Rec Equip-ext 5197	Theater-653-7450/1334
Youth Center 362-2137	

ATTRACTIONS: Great beaches, scuba diving, snorkeling, and many other popular water sports.

GUAM NAVAL ACTIVITIES (GU02R8)

Building 100, Johnson Road
PSC 455, Box 1157
FPO AP 96540-1157

TELEPHONE NUMBER INFORMATION: Main installation numbers: C-671-351-1110, D-315-355-1110.

LOCATION: South on Marine Drive. Clearly marked. USMRA: Page 130 (C-3). NMC: Agana, 10 miles north.

GENERAL INFORMATION: Headquarters Commander US Naval Forces Marianas; Naval Hospital; Camp Covington (Seabees); Naval Activities; Naval Pacific and Meterological Oceanography Center/Joint Typhoon Warning Center (NAVCMETOCCENT/JTWC); Marianas Section Coast Guard; Naval Computer & Telecommunications Area Master Station Western Pacific (NAVCAMS WESTPAC).

TEMPORARY MILITARY LODGING: Centralized lodging office, 24 hours daily, C-671-339-5259, D-315-339-5139, Fax: C-671-339-6250. All ranks.

RV, CAMPING/FAMCAMP: Outdoor Recreation Services, on base, year round, Guam Naval Activities MWR Office, PSC 455, Box 169, FPO 96540-4153, C-671-564-1847/81, D-315-564-4153, Fax: C-671-564-1853. Camping is allowed on some beaches, no hookups, no fees.

SPACE-A: None. See Andersen AFB listing, C-671-366-2096/2095, D-315-366-2096/2095, Fax: C-671-366-2079.

GUAM
Guam Naval Activities, continued

LOGISTICAL SUPPORT:
Cafeteria-564-3124
Conv Store-564-3285
Exchange-564-3177
Navy Campus-339-8291/2
Snack Bar-564-3124
Commissary-339-5177
Credit Union-477-1055
Garage-564-3191
SATO-564-1636

ADMINISTRATIVE SUPPORT:
Legal-333-2061
Police-333-2989
Locator-355-1110
SDO-349-5235

HEALTH & WELFARE:
Chapel-339-2126
344-9745
355-5415
Family Services-343-2981
Medical-344-9202
Central Appts-344-9326/7
Emergency-344-9314

REST & RECREATION:
Beach-564-1823
Clubs
Consol-564-1834/5
O-472-4607/6/7
Library-564-1836
Rec Center-564-1847
Theater-564-1830
Bowling-564-1828
Golf-734-1124
Gym-564-1824
Hobby Complex-564-1826
MWR-564-1847
Swimming-564-1822

ATTRACTIONS: Great beaches, water sports, hiking, historical landmarks, miniature submarine tour, boat tours, Cocos Island.

PUERTO RICO

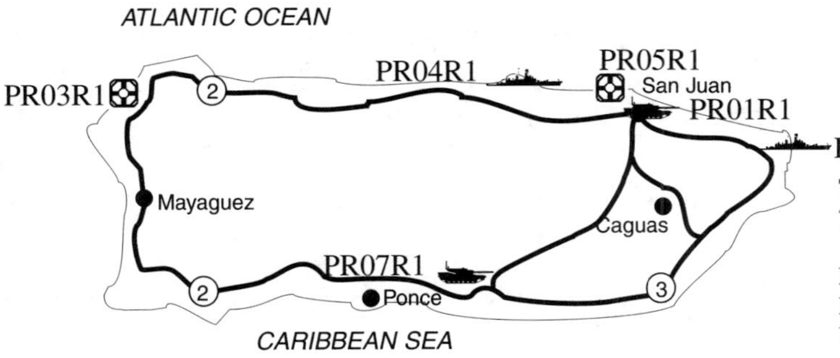

BORINQUEN COAST GUARD AIR STATION (PR03R1)

ATTN: Special Services
Aguadilla, PR 00604-9999

TELEPHONE NUMBER INFORMATION: Main installation numbers: C-787-890-8400, D-312-831-3392-3399.

LOCATION: At the old Ramey AFB, north of Aguadilla. Take PR-2 west from San Juan or north from Mayaguez to PR-110 north to CGAS. USMRA: Page 130 (B,C-2). NMC: San Juan, 65 miles east.

GENERAL INFORMATION: Coast Guard Air Station for the Puerto Rico area.

TEMPORARY MILITARY LODGING: Lodging office, La Plaza, Room 26. 0800-1600 Mon-Fri, C-787-890-8492. All ranks.

RV, CAMPING/FAMCAMP: Recreation Area off base, year round, C-787-890-8492, 16 guest houses and two apartments.

SPACE-A: Pax Term/Lounge, CG Hangar, 0730-1530 Mon-Fri, C-787-890-8423, weekends, C-787-890-8421, unscheduled flights to Puerto Rico and CONUS.

LOGISTICAL SUPPORT:
Barber Shop-ext 8484
Child Care-890-8494
Exchange-890-3127/7272
or 890-8400 ext 870
Shoppette-890-8701
Beauty Shop-ext 8484
Conv Store-890-8701
Package Store-890-8701
SATO-890-8975

ADMINISTRATIVE SUPPORT:
Housing Office-890-8470
OPS/OOD-890-8421
SDO/NCO-890-8421
Locator-882-8400
Police-890-8472

HEALTH & WELFARE:
CHAMPUS-ext 1500
Medical-890-8485
Emergency-890-8477
Chapel-890-8486

REST & RECREATION:
Clubs
CG-890-2581
CPO-8499
EM-890-8729
NCO-890-2581
MWR-890-8492

OTHER FACILITIES AVAILABLE: Fitness center, Golf Course, Gym, Indoor Rec (Racquetball), Library, Outdoor Recreation (Basketball, Tennis, Volleyball), Swimming Pool and Theater.

ATTRACTIONS: Local beaches and restaurants, excellent surfing during winter months, 18-hole golf course, excellent snorkeling and scuba diving, whale watching during migratory season.

FORT BUCHANAN (PR01R1)

ATTN: AFZK-B-PO
Fort Buchanan, PR 00934-5065

TELEPHONE NUMBER INFORMATION: Main installation numbers: C-787-273-3400, D-313-740-3400. E-mail: ortizi@ftmcphsnemh2.army.mil.

LOCATION: From San Juan IAP toward San Juan, exit Caguas/Bayamon to PR-18, exit Bayamon right to PR-22, one-and-a-half miles to fort on left. USMRA: Page 130 (E-2). NMC: San Juan, six miles southwest.

GENERAL INFORMATION: The major US Army Post in Puerto Rico providing support to National Guard and Reserve units.

TEMPORARY MILITARY LODGING: Lodging office, Building 556, 0700-1600 daily, C-787-273-3821, D-313-740-7289/3256. All ranks. DV/VIP C-787-273-3240.

RV, CAMPING/FAMCAMP: None. See Borinquen CGAS listing, C-787-890-8492.

SPACE-A: None. See Roosevelt Roads NS listing, C-787-865-4383, D-313-831-4383/3257, Fax: C-787-865-4208.

LOGISTICAL SUPPORT:
Child Care-273-3280
Conv Store-273-8046
Exchange-792-2066
Gas Station-792-4297
Travel Office-273-3915
Commissary-273-2078
Credit Union-273-1307
Food Court-792-4049
Package Store-793-1984
Visitor Center-273-3714

ADMINISTRATIVE SUPPORT:
CPO/OOD-273-3773
Legal-273-3345
Police-273-3913
Fire Dept-273-3917
Locator-273-2424
Public Affairs-273-3205

PUERTO RICO
Fort Buchanan, continued

HEALTH & WELFARE:
ACS-273-3292
Chapel-273-3336
Medical-273-2043
Central Appts-783-2424
Emergency-783-2424
CHAMPUS-273-3339
Family Services-273-3332
Retiree Services-273-3877

REST & RECREATION:
Auto Hobby Shop-ext 8172
Clubs
EM-273-3535
NCO-273-3535
O-273-3535
Recreation-273-3301
Rec Services-ext 2101
Swimming-ext 8182
Wood Hobby Shop-ext 8160
Ceramics-ext 7172
Golf Course-273-3980
Health Club-ext 7167
Library-ext 3208
MWR-273-3301
Rec Equip-ext 7134
Scuba-ext 8280
Tennis/Racquetball Court-ext 7134
Youth Center-ext 7187

ATTRACTIONS: San Juan is the oldest city under the American flag. 16th-Century Spanish architecture, fortresses. Largest shopping center in the Caribbean. Rain forest. Beaches. Luxury hotels and casinos. Water sports, deep sea fishing. World's largest radio telescope.

ROOSEVELT ROADS NAVAL STATION (PR02R1)

COMFAIR CARIB, ATTN: PAO
Building 92202, Langley Drive
PSC 1008, Box 3591
FPO AA 34051-3591

TELEPHONE NUMBER INFORMATION: Main installation numbers: C-787-865-2000, D-313-831-2000/4311, Fax: C-787-831-2000. E-mail: sepulveda@apollo.netspr.navy.mil/.

LOCATION: From Luis Munoz IAP, San Juan left (east) onto PR-3 for 45 miles, sign on right indicating exit to Naval Station. USMRA: Page 130 (F-2,3). NMC: San Juan, 50 miles northwest.

GENERAL INFORMATION: Fleet Air Caribbean, Atlantic Fleet Weapons Training Facility, Marine Corps Security Force Company, Naval Air Station, and support units.

TEMPORARY MILITARY LODGING: Lodging office, Buildings 1688 (officers) and 1708 (enlisted), C-787-865-3490 ext 4334/3364 (officers), C-787-865-2000 ext 4145/4147 (enlisted). Navy Lodge C-787-865-8283.

RV, CAMPING/FAMCAMP: None. See Borinquen CGAS listing, C-787-890-8492.

SPACE-A: Pax Term/Lounge, Air Ops Building, STOP 23, 0700-1600 Mon-Sat, Sun for flights only, C-787-865-4383, D-313-831-4383/3257, Fax: C-787-865-4208, flights to CONUS, OCONUS and foreign locations.

LOGISTICAL SUPPORT:
Child Care-865-4699/4504/3359
Conv Store-865-4868
EXA Travel-865-2130/2150
Gas Station-865-4609
SATO-865-1539/1570
Commissary-865-4287/5361/4295
Deli-865-3509/4045
Exchange-865-3252
Package Store-865-7140

ADMINISTRATIVE SUPPORT:
CDO/JOOD-865-4311/4352
Locator-865-2000
Legal-865-4315/4320
Police-865-4195/4106

HEALTH & WELFARE:
American Red Cross-865-3428
Chapel-865-4326/4328
CHAMPUS-865-7133
Dental-865-4090
Family Services-865-3369/4091/97
Retiree Services-865-4091
Veterinary Services-865-3438/2150
Medical-865-4133/7133
Ambulance-865-4144/4123
Health Benefits Advisor-865-5913
Information-865-4133/7133

REST & RECREATION:
Auto Hobby Shop-865-4773
Beach-865-4865
Com Center-865-4854
Fitness Center-865-4033
Golf Course-865-4751
ITT-865-4757/5354
Library-865-4353
Outdoor Rec-865-4839/4565
Stables-865-3345
Theater-865-4380
Yacht Club-865-4537
Bowling-865-4524/4482
Clubs
CPO-865-5279
EM-865-5288/4142
Flying-865-3023
O-865-7200/3342
Petty O-865-4142
Marina-865-3297
Swimming-865-4033
Wood Hobby Shop-865-4839/4947
Youth Center-865-3560/4926

ATTRACTIONS: El Yunque rain forest with waterfalls, hiking trails, and restaurants. Vieques Island with beaches, restaurants and guest houses.

SABANA SECA NAVAL SECURITY GROUP ACTIVITY (PR04R1)

PSC 1009, Box 1
FPO AA 34053-1000

TELEPHONE NUMBER INFORMATION: Main installation numbers: C-787-795-2255/2399, D-313-831-7202.

LOCATION: From San Juan IAP, take Route 26 west to Bayamon exit to PR-22 west to PR-886 north (Las Arenas exit) to base. *OR,* take Interstate 22 west (toward Arecibo), get off exit La Arena. At the next intersection turn left, the base will be located on the left. USMRA: Page 130 (D,E-2). NMC: San Juan, 14 miles east.

GENERAL INFORMATION: Naval Security Group Activity for the Caribbean.

TEMPORARY MILITARY LODGING: None. See Fort Buchanan listing, C-787-273-3821, D-313-740-7289/3256.

RV, CAMPING/FAMCAMP: None. See Borinquen CGAS listing, C-787-890-8492.

SPACE-A: None. See Roosevelt Roads NS listing, C-787-865-4383, D-313-831-4383/3257, Fax: C-787-865-4208.

LOGISTICAL SUPPORT:
Barber Shop-261-8376
Dining Facilities-261-8417/8421
Gas Station-261-8403
Postal Service-261-8313
Travel Office-261-8313
Child Dev Center-261-8451
Education Office-261-8466/8
Mini-Mart-261-8367/9
Snack Bar-795-8429

ADMINISTRATIVE SUPPORT:
Fire Dept-784-8385
Legal-261-8398
Police-261-8395
Quarter Deck-261-8300
Housing Office-261-8330/8357
Pass/ID Office-261-8395
Public Affairs-261-8307

HEALTH & WELFARE:
Chapel-261-8386
Medical-795-8755
Dental-8384

REST & RECREATION:
Auto Hobby Shop-261-8372
Com Club-261-8425
Gym-261-8386
Library-261-8312
Bowling-261-8429
Fitness Center-261-8386
ITT-261-8313
MWR-261-8368

ATTRACTIONS: Great beaches, El Yunque Rain Forest, El Morro Fort and Casinos.

Other Installations in Puerto Rico

Camp Santiago Training Site (PR07R1), P.O. Box 1166, Salinas, PR 00751-1166. C-787-824-7400, Fax: C-787-824-7477. PR Route 52 (exit 68) from San Juan to Ponce and south area of Puerto Rico. Camp Santiago is at the town of Salinas, right of the exit of route 52. USMRA: Page 130 (D,E-3). NMC: Ponce, 25 miles. Puerto Rico National Guard. 201st Evac Hospital, Troop E 192nd Cavalry, and other units. Cafeteria-824-7662, Clubs: EM-824-7662 and O-824-7521, Exchange-824-4270, Package Store-824-2562.
San Juan Coast Guard Base (PR05R1), P.O. Box S-2029, Old San Juan Station, San Juan, PR 00902-2029, C-787-729-6800. From San Juan airport take Castro Avenue, pass Condado Lagoon to Munoz Rivera, bear right to old San Juan and CGB gate. USMRA: Page 130 (E-2). NMC: San Juan, in city limits. Exchange-722-9497, Medical 729-6800 ext 230, Public Affairs-729-6800 ext 121.

VIRGIN ISLANDS

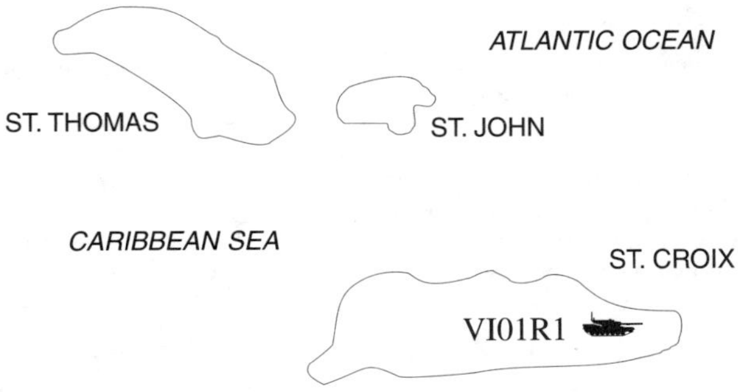

Other Installations in Virgin Islands

Virgin Islands National Guard Headquarters (VI01R1), 4031 La Grande Princesse, Lot B, St Croix, USVI 00820-4353. USMRA: Page 130 (H-4). C-340-712-7728/7732, Fax: C-340-712-7754, Carlson Wagonlit Travel-778-8998, Exchange-773-5000, SATO-772-7836, Space-A-778-2165, Space-A Fax: C-340-778-9261.

APPENDIX A
GENERAL ABBREVIATIONS USED IN THIS BOOK

This appendix contains general abbreviations used in this book. Commonly understood abbreviations and standard abbreviations found in addresses have not been included in order to save space.

A
AAF - Army Airfield
AAFES - Army Air Force Exchange Service
AC - Air Conditioning
ACS - Army Community Services
AD - Active Duty
Admin - Administration
AF - Air Force
AFAF - Air Force Auxiliary Field
AFB - Air Force Base
AFRC - Armed Forces Reserve Center
AFRC - Armed Forces Recreation Center
AFS - Air Force Station
AMC - Air Mobility Command
ANG - Air National Guard
ANGB - Air National Guard Base
ANGS - Air National Guard Station
APG - Army Proving Ground
Appts - Appointments
ARB - Air Reserve Base
ARD&EC - Armament, Research, Development and Engineering Center
ARNG - Army National Guard
ARS - Air Reserve Station
ARW - Air Refueling Wing
ASU - Arizona State University
ATM - Automated Teller Machine
ATTN - Attention

B
BEQ - Bachelor Enlisted Quarters
BOQ - Bachelor Officers' Quarters
BQ - Bachelors' Quarters
BRAC - Base Realignment and Closure
BX - Base Exchange

C
C - Commercial
CATV - Cable Television
CBQ - Combined Bachelors Quarters
CDO - Command Duty Officer
CEC - Combat Engineering Command
cf - cubic feet
CG - Coast Guard
CGAS - Coast Guard Air Station
CGB - Coast Guard Base
CGG - Coast Guard Group
CGMSO - Coast Guard Marine Safety Office
Civ - Civilian
Com - Community/Combined
Conf - Conference
Consol - Consolidated
CONUS - Continental United States
Conv - Convenience
CPO - Chief Petty Officer
CRTC - Combat Readiness Training Center
CSS - Coastal Systems Station

D
D - Defense Switched Network
DAV - Disabled American Veteran
DDRW - Defense Distribution Region West
Dep -Dependent
Dept - Department
Det - Detachment
Dev - Development
Dir - Director
DoD - Department of Defense
DSN - Defense Switched Network
DV - Distinguished Visitors
DVQ - Distinguished Visitors' Quarters

E
E - Electric
EM - Enlisted Members
ER - emergency room
Ext - extension

F
FAMCAMP - Family Campground
FG - Fighter Group
FW - Fighter Wing

H
HP - Home Page
Hq - Headquarters

I
I - Interstate
IAP - International Airport
ID - Identification
INF - Infantry
ISC - Integrated Support Command
ITR - Information, Ticketing and Registration
ITT - Information, Tickets and Tours

J

L

M
MCAS - Marine Corps Air Station
MCB - Marine Corps Base
MCLB - Marine Corps Logistics Base
MCRD - Marine Corps Recruiting Depot
Mil - Military
MLB - Major League Baseball
MSO- Marine Safety Office
MWR - Morale, Welfare and Recreation
Mt - Mount

N
NAF - Naval Air Facility
NARS - Naval Air Reserve Station
NAS - Naval Air Station
NAWC - Naval Air Weapons Center
NAWS - Naval Air Weapons Station
NB - Naval Base
NCAA - National Collegiate Athletic Association
NCO - Noncommissioned Officers'
NCS - Naval Communications Station
NETC - Naval Education Training Center
NFL - National Football League
NG - National Guard
NGB - National Guard Base
NHL - National Hockey League
NMC - Nearest Major City
NMI - Nearest Major Installation
NNMC - National Naval Medical Center
NRS - Naval Reserve Station
NSA - Naval Support Activity
NSB - Naval Submarine Base
NSGA - Naval Security Group Activity
NSWC - Naval Surface Weapons Center
NTC - Naval Training Center
NTTC - Naval Technical Training Center
NWC - Naval Weapons Center

O
O - Officers'
OCONUS - Outside Continental United States
OD - Officer of the Day
OOD - Officer of the Day/on Deck/on Duty
Ops - Operations

P
PA - Public Affairs
PAO - Public Affairs Office
Pax - Passenger
PCS - Permanent Change of Station
PGA - Professional Golf Association
PX - Post Exchange

R
Rec - Recreation
RV - Recreational Vehicle
RVC - Recreational Vehicle Camping

S
S - Sewer
SATO - Scheduled Airlines Ticket Office
SDO - Staff Duty Officer
SNCO - Senior Noncommissioned Officer
Space-A - Space Available
St - Saint

T
TDY - Temporary Duty
Term - Terminal
TLQ - Temporary Living Quarters
TML - Temporary Military Lodging
TV - Television

U
USA - United States of America
USAF - United States Air Force
USCG - United States Coast Guard
USCGG - United States Coast Guard Group
USMA - United States Military Academy
USMC - United States Marine Corps
USMRA - United States Military Road Atlas
USN - United States Navy
USO - United Service Organizations
USS - United States Service

V
VCR - Video Cassette Recorder
VIP - Very Important Personnel
VOQ - Visiting Officers' Quarters

W
W - Water

APPENDIX B
DISCOVER AMERICA

Discover America® Tourism Offices

STATES

ALABAMA 800.ALABAMA
ALASKA 907.465.2010
ARIZONA 602.230.7733
ARKANSAS 800.NATURAL
www.ono.com/arkansas
The Natural State
Department of Parks and Tourism
One Capitol Mall
Little Rock, AR 72201
CALIFORNIA 800.TO.CALIF
COLORADO 800.COLORADO
CONNECTICUT 800.CT.BOUND
DELAWARE 800.441.8846
www.state.de.us
Do Something Different. Come to Delaware.
P.O. Box 1401
Dover, DE 19903
FLORIDA 904.487.1462
www.goflorida.com
Return to Your Senses in Florida
P.O. Box 1100
Tallahassee, FL 32302-1100
GEORGIA 800.VISIT.GA
HAWAII 800.464.2924
IDAHO 800.635.7820
ILLINOIS 800.2.CONNECT
INDIANA 800.289.6646
IOWA 800.345.IOWA
KANSAS 800.2.KANSAS Ext.131
Kansas—Simply Wonderful
700 SW Harrison, Suite 1300
Topeka, KS 66603
KENTUCKY 800.225.TRIP
LOUISIANA 800.964.7321
www.louisianatravel.com
Come As You Are. Leave Different.
P.O. Box 868
Covington, LA 70434-0868
MAINE 800.533.9595
MARYLAND 800.MD.IS.FUN
www.mdisfun.org
So Many Things to Do. So Close Together.
217 East Redwood Street
Baltimore, MD 21227
MASSACHUSETTS 800.447.MASS
MICHIGAN 800.5432.YES
MINNESOTA 800.657.3700
MISSISSIPPI 800.WARMEST
www.mississippi.org
The South's Warmest Welcome
P.O. Box 1705
Ocean Springs, MS 39566-1705
MISSOURI 800.877.1234
MONTANA 800.VISIT.MT
NEBRASKA 800.228.4307
NEVADA 800.NEVADA.8
NEW HAMPSHIRE . . . . . 800.FUN.IN.NH Ext. 159
NEW JERSEY . . . . . 800.JERSEY.7 Ext. 7963
www.state.nj.us/travel
What a Difference a State Makes
20 West State St. CN 826
Trenton, NJ 08625-0826
NEW MEXICO 800.545.2040
NEW YORK 800.CALL.NYS
NORTH CAROLINA 800.VISIT.NC
NORTH DAKOTA 800.HELLO.ND
OHIO 800.BUCKEYE
OKLAHOMA 800.652.6552
www.otrd.state.ok.us
Oklahoma Native America
Dept TN57R
P.O. Box 60789
Oklahoma City, OK 73146
OREGON 800.547.7842
PENNSYLVANIA . . . . . 800.VISIT.PA Ext. 109
www.state.pa.us
Pennsylvania Memories Last a Lifetime.
Room 456 Forum Building
Harrisburg, PA 17120
RHODE ISLAND 800.556.2484
www.visitrhodeisland.com
1 West Exchange Street
Providence, RI 02806
SOUTH CAROLINA 803.734.0122
SOUTH DAKOTA 800.SDAKOTA
www.state.sd.us
Great Faces. Great Places.
711 East Wells Avenue
Pierre, SD 57501
TENNESSEE 800.836.6200
TEXAS . . . . . 800.8888.TEX Ext. 728
www.TravelTex.com
Call for Your 288-page Texas Travel Guide.
UTAH 800.200.1160
VERMONT 800.VERMONT
VIRGINIA 800.VISIT.VA
www.virginia.org
Virginia is for Lovers.
WASHINGTON 800.544.1800
WASHINGTON, DC 202.789.7000
www.washington.org
1212 New York Avenue, NW, Suite 600
Washington, DC 20005
WEST VIRGINIA 800.225.5982
WISCONSIN 800.432.TRIP
WYOMING 800.225.5996
fax: 307.777.6904
Like No Place on Earth.
I-25 at College Drive
Cheyenne, WY 82002

U.S. TERRITORIES

AMERICAN SAMOA 684.633.1093
GUAM 800.US.3.GUAM
COMMONWEALTH OF THE NORTHERN MARIANA ISLANDS . . . www.visit-marianas.com
e-mail: mvb@saipan.com
The Rising Star of the Pacific
P.O. Box 861CK
Saipan, MP 96950
PUERTO RICO 800.223.6530
U.S. VIRGIN ISLANDS 800.372.8784

CITIES

DALLAS, TX 888.7.DALLAS
cityview.com/dallas
Dallas Has It All.
1201 Elm Street, Suite 2000
Dallas, TX 75270
HOUSTON, TX 800.4.HOUSTON
www.houston-guide.com
The Real Texas
801 Congress
Houston, TX 77002
LAS VEGAS, NV 702.892.0711
Open 24 Hours.
3150 Paradise Road
Las Vegas, NV 89109-9096
NEW ORLEANS, LA 800.672.6124
www.nawlins.com
America's European Masterpiece
1520 Sugar Bowl Drive
New Orleans, LA 70112
PIGEON FORGE, TN 800.964.8889
www.pigeon-forge.tn.us
Smokey Mountains. And More.
P.O. Box 1390
Pigeon Forge, TN 37868
PORTLAND, OR 888.606.6363
www.pova.com
26 S.W. Salmon Street
Portland, OR 97204
VALLEY FORGE, PA 888.VISIT.VF
valleyforge.org
VIRGINIA BEACH, VA 800.VA.BEACH
www.virginia-beach.va.us
2101 Parks Avenue, Suite 500
Virginia Beach, VA 23451

APPENDIX C
UNITED SERVICES ORGANIZATION DIRECTORY

CALIFORNIA

USO of Greater Los Angeles Area, Inc.
Ft. MacArthur
2400 Pacific Ave., #403
San Pedro, CA 90731
Phone: 310-514-3465
Fax: 310-514-2709

USO -LAX Gen. James H. "Jimmy" Doolittle Airport Lounge
Los Angeles Int. Airport
400 World Way, Terminal #4
Los Angeles, CA 90045
Phone: 310-642-0188
Fax: 310-642-1903

Barstow USO
220 E. Buena Vista
Barstow, CA 92311
Phone: 619-256-0102

Outreach Center
512 Barstow Rd.
Barstow, CA 92311
Phone: 619-256-1735

USO of Northern California, Inc., Admin. Offices
Naval Station
Treasure Island
San Francisco, CA 94130
Phone: 415-391-1657
Fax: 415-391-2610

San Francisco Int. Airport USO
Mezzanine, South Terminal
San Francisco, CA 94128
Phone: 415-761-4611
Fax: 415-742-6747

San Jose Int. Airport USO
Terminal "C"
1661 Airport Blvd.
San Jose, CA 95110-1285
Phone: 408-288-7603
Fax: 408-288-7621

Oakland Int. Airport USO
Mezzanine Level
1 Airport Dr., Box #20
Oakland, CA 94621
Phone: 510-562-3448

Travis AFB
AMC Passenger Terminal
P.O. Box 1663
Travis AFB, CA 94535
Phone: 707-424-3316
Fax: 707-437-9430

USO of Orange County
23421 S. Pointe Dr., Ste. #140
Laguna Hills, CA 92653
Phone: 714-581-7807
Fax: 714-588-9908

San Diego USO Family & Community Center
433 E. Harbor Dr.
San Diego, CA 92101-7825
Phone: 619-235-6503
Fax: 619-232-5520

USO Airport Center/West Terminal
3707 N. Harbor Dr., #119
San Diego, CA 92101-1040
Phone: 619-296-3192

COLORADO

USO of Pikes Peak Region
The Downtown Center
207 N. Nevada Ave.
P.O. Box 1694
Colorado Springs, CO 80901
Phone: 719-471-9790
Fax: 719-471-1723

USO Airport Information Desk
Colorado Springs Municipal Airport
5750 E. Fountain Blvd.
Colorado Springs, CO 80916
Phone: 719-574-9626

USO Outreach Center
The Meadow Park Community Center
1939 S. El Paso
Colorado Springs, CO 80906
Phone: 719-471-9790

USO Outreach Center
Deerfield Hills Community Center
4290 Deerfield Hills Rd.
Colorado Springs, CO 80916
Phone: 719-471-9790

DELAWARE

USO Delaware
500 Eagle Way, East Wing
Dover AFB, DE 19902-7507
Phone: 302-677-2491 Admin.
302-677-6905 Lounge
Fax: 302-677-2982

DISTRICT OF COLUMBIA

(Additional USO of Metropolitan Washington locations listed under Virginia and Maryland)

National Airport
Interim Terminal
Washington, DC 20001
Phone: 703-419-7705

National Airport
Main Terminal
Washington, DC 20001
Phone: 703-419-3990

FLORIDA

Dade County USO Airport Center
Miami Int. Airport
Skywalk Level, Concourse "E"
Miami, FL 33299-7266
Phone: 305-876-7585

USO of Greater Jacksonville Area, Inc.
Bldg. #1050
P.O. Box 108
NAS Jacksonville, FL 32212
Phone: 904-778-2821/ 772-3028
Fax: 904-772-5214

USO Center of Jacksonville
2560 Mayport Rd.
Atlantic Beach, FL 32233
Phone: 904-246-3481
Fax: 904-241-0463
(open Mon.-Wed. at Noon)

USO of Central Florida, Inc.
(mailing address for all USO Orlando locations)
P.O. Box 149472
Orlando, FL 32814
Phone: 407-646-4139
Fax: 407-647-2563

USO of Central Florida
Orlando USO Recruit Reception Center
Bldg. #102
Naval Training Center
Orlando, FL 32813
Phone: 407-647-2972
Fax: 407-647-2563

Brig. Emil B. Miller USO Airport Lounge
Landside "A," 3rd Level
Orlando Int. Airport
9263 Airport Blvd.
Orlando, FL 32827
Phone: 407-855-7192

Mary Boutwell USO
Bldg. #2008
Naval Training Center
Orlando, FL 32813
Phone: 407-647-0407 / 646-4377

USO of Greater Pensacola Area
Airport Lounge
Pensacola Regional Airport
Pensacola, FL 32503
Phone: 904-433-2475

USO Center
120 Entrance Rd., Unit #5
Pensacola, FL 32507
Mailing address:
P.O. Box 4321
Pensacola, FL 32507-0321
Phone: 904-455-1064

USO of St. Augustine
Lightner Bldg.
Granada St.
P.O. Box 4
St. Augustine, FL 32085
Phone: 904-778-2821
(open only on weekends)

APPENDIX C, continued

GEORGIA

USO Georgia, Inc., Admin Offices
P.O. Box 20963
Atlanta, GA 30320
Phone: 404-761-8061
Fax: 404-765-1794

USO Center Hartsfield Int. Airport
North Terminal, Int. Concourse
Atlanta, GA 30320
Phone: 404-761-8061
Fax: 404-765-1794

USO Warner Robins Outreach
Robins AFB
Smith Recreation Center
Warner Robins, GA 31099
Phone: 912-926-2105/2945

HAWAII

USO of Hawaii, Inc., Airport Center
Honolulu Int. Airport
Terminal Box #48
Honolulu, HI 96819
Phone: 808-836-3351
Fax: 808-947-2623

USO of Hawaii
P.O. Box 15788
Honolulu, HI 96830
Phone: 808-945-2024
Fax: 808-947-2623

USO Hickam AMC Center
Hickam AFB
AMC Terminal, 2nd Floor
Hickam AFB, HI 96853
Phone: 808-449-2887

USO Waikiki Family Center
Maluhia Hall
Ft. DeRussy
P.O. Box 15788
Honolulu, HI 96830
Phone: 808-945-2024

ILLINOIS

USO of Illinois, Inc., Center & Admin. Offices
Oxford House Hotel, 3rd Floor
225 N. Wabash Ave.
Chicago, IL 60601
Phone: 312-781-0730
Fax: 312-781-0740

O'Hare USO Center
O'Hare Int. Airport
P.O. Box 66434
Chicago, IL 60666
Phone: 312-686-7396

Midway USO Center
Midway Airport
5700 S. Cicero Ave.
Chicago, IL 60638
Phone: 312-582-5852

Great Lakes USO
Great Lakes Naval Training Center
Bldg. #158
P.O. Box 886935
Great Lakes, IL 60088
Phone: 708-688-5591

INDIANA

USO of Indiananapolis
1 Indiana Square, Ste. #101
Indianapolis, IN 46266
Phone: 317-241-6070

KENTUCKY

Patton USO Airport Center & Admin. Offices
13 Standiford Field
Louisville, KY 40209
Phone: 502-361-1888

MARYLAND

Indian Head Family Support Services
USO/Joint Services Support Center
Bldg. #13
Riverview Village
Naval Surface Warfare Center
Indian Head, MD 20640
Phone: 301-743-5180/5650

BWI Airport
Main Terminal
Phone: 410-859-4425

Andrews AFB
Andrews AFB, Air Terminal
Phone: 301-981-2525

MASSACHUSETTS

USO Council of New England
U.S. Coast Guard Support Center
427 Commercial St.
4th Deck, Bldg. #4
Boston, MA 02109-1027
Phone: 617-720-4949/4531
Fax: 617-720-0982

Sgt. Maj. Frederick B. Douglass USO Airport Center
Logan Int. Airport
Terminal "D"
Boston, MA 02128
Phone: 617-567-3857

USO of Pioneer Valley
Bldg. #5305
Westover Air Reserve Base
Chicopee, MA 01022-5000
Phone: 413-557-2522
Fax: 413-593-6396

MISSOURI

James S. McDonnell USO Airport Center & Admin. Offices
P.O. Box 10367
Lambert St. Louis Int. Airport
St. Louis, MO 63145-0367
Phone: 314-429-1234
Fax: 314-429-0506

NEW YORK

USO of Metropolitan New York Admin. Offices
151 West 46th St., Ste. #902
New York, NY 10036
Phone: 212-448-0455
Fax: 212-730-0870

USO Gen. Douglas MacArthur Memorial Center
151 West 46th St., 3rd Floor
New York, NY 10036
Phone: 212-719-2364

New York USO Airport Centers
Delta Flight Center
Phone: 718-656-4616
TWA, Inc.
Domestic Arrivals Area
Bldg. #58
Phone: 718-995-5539
John F. Kennedy Int. Airport
Jamaica, NY 11430

USO Ft. Hamilton Center
Bldg. #113
New York Area Command
Ft. Hamilton
Brooklyn, NY 11252
Phone: 718-630-4179

Watertown USO Center
P.O. Box 912
Watertown, NY 13601
Phone: 315-782-3082

NORTH CAROLINA

Jacksonville USO Center & Admin. Offices
9 Tallman St.
Jacksonville, NC 28540-4846
Phone: 919-455-3411/3412

OHIO

USO of Northern Ohio MEPS Center & Admin. Offices
1240 E. Ninth St., Rm. #1503-B
Cleveland, OH 44199
Phone: 216-621-4120
Fax: 216-621-4316

USO Airport Center
Cleveland Hopkins Int. Airport
Baggage Claim Level
Riverside Dr.
Brook Park, OH 44135
Phone: 216-433-7313

USO of Central Ohio Council
Port Columbus Int. Airport
4600 International Gateway
Columbus, OH 43219
Phone: 614-231-7300

MEPS USO Lounge
3333 Indianola Ave.
Columbus, OH 43214
Phone: 614-262-3044

APPENDIX C, continued

PENNSYLVANIA

USO of Philadelphia Airport Center & Admin. Offices
Philadelphia Int. Airport
Terminal "D"
Philadelphia, PA 19153
Phone: 215-365-8889
Fax: 215-365-0249

USO Navy Base Center
Bldg. #489, 2nd Deck
Naval Station
Philadelphia, PA 19112
Phone: 215-897-6910/5267
Mailing Address:
Philadelphia Int. Airport
Terminal "D"
Philadelphia, PA 19153

SOUTH CAROLINA

USO Charleston Airport Center & Admin. Offices
Charleston Int. Airport
5500 International Blvd., Ste. #120
Charleston, SC 29418-6922
Phone: 803-767-3963

TENNESSEE

USO of Metropolitan Memphis & Shelby County
7918 Church St.
P.O. Box 907
Millington, TN 38083-0907
Phone: 901-872-7722
Fax: 901-872-7330

TEXAS

Greater Houston USO, Inc.
2700 Southwest Freeway
Houston, TX 77098
Phone: 713-526-8300, x554
Fax: 713-528-2422
Mailing address:
P.O. Box 397
Houston, TX 77001-0397

Houston Airport Center
Houston Intercontinental Airport
Terminal "C"
North Concourse
Houston, TX
Phone: 713-443-2451

Houston USO Airport Center
Hobby Airport
Near Concourse "A"
Houston, TX
Phone: 713-644-1131

USO of San Antonio and Central Texas
420 E. Commerce St.
San Antonio, TX 78205
Phone: 210-227-9373
Fax: 210-227-9378

USO of South Texas, Inc.
Bldg. #3
NAS Corpus Christi, TX 78419
Phone: 512-939-2391
Autovon: 861-2391
Fax: 512-939-2391

USO of South Texas, Ingleside Center
USO Naval Station
Ingleside, TX 78362-5031
Phone: 512-776-4779/4778
Fax: 512-776-4779

VIRGINIA

USO of Metropolitan Washington
Bldg. #59, Post HQ, Rm. #B-9
Ft. Myer, VA 22211
Phone: 703-696-2628/2629
Fax: 703-696-2550

Family Programs Office
Bldg. #59, Post HQ, Rm. #B-12
Ft. Myer, VA 22211
Phone: 703-696-3279/2552

Tencza Terrace Family Support Center
Tencza Terrace, Bldg. #501
Ft. Myer, VA 22211
Phone: 703-696-3479

Woodbridge Run Family Support Services
Community Center
1400 Eisenhower Cir.
Woodbridge, VA 22191
Phone: 703-490-8880

Ft. Belvoir Family Support Services
Bldg. #200
SOSA Community Center
Ft. Belvoir, VA 22060
Phone: 703-805-2464 ITR Office 2654

USO of Hampton Roads
Coliseum Mall, Entrance "A"
1800 W. Mercury Blvd.
P.O. Box 7250
Hampton, VA 23666-0250
Phone: 804-827-1063
Fax: 804-838-9020

NAS Norfolk, AMC Terminal
Bldg. #LP-84
Norfolk, VA 23511-6691
Phone: 804-440-0939

USO Ft. Eustis
Bldg. #650
Modisett Recreation Center
Ft. Eustis, VA 23604
Phone: 804-878-2415/2407

Huntington Hall BEQ
Newport News Shipbuilding
3100 Huntington Ave.
Newport News, VA 23607
Phone: 804-928-0801

Raymond B. Bottom USO
Newport News/Williamsburg Int. Airport
Newport News, VA 23602
Phone: 804-988-0017

WASHINGTON

Admiral James S. Russell USO Center
Main Terminal, 2nd Floor
SeaTac Int. Airport
Phone: 206-433-5438

McChord USO Center
McChord AFB
Bldg. #1183
Adjacent to AMC Terminal
Phone: 206-984-2400

Admin. Offices
Main Terminal, 2nd Floor
SeaTac Int. Airport
Seattle, WA 98158
Phone: 206-246-1908

WISCONSIN

USO Milwaukee South Eastern Region, Inc.
Milwaukee County War Memorial Center
2nd Floor Lobby
750 N. Lincoln Memorial Dr.
Milwaukee, WI 53202
Phone: 414-271-3133
(closed most holidays)

U.S. VIRGIN ISLANDS

USO St. Thomas
3075 Kroprindsens Gade
Charlotte Amalie, VI 00802
Phone: 809-774-8555
Fax: 809-777-4402
Mailing Address:
Veterans Drive Station
P.O. Box 2112
Charlotte Amalie, VI 00803-2112

St. Croix USO
114 Market St.
P.O. Box 616
Frederiksted
St. Croix, VI 00841
Phone: 809-772-0523

APPENDIX D

RETIREMENT SERVICES OFFICES DIRECTORY

STATE	INSTALLATION	BRANCH	PHONE #
AL	Fort McClellan	Army	205-848-5300
AL	Fort Rucker	Army	334-255-9059
AL	Maxwell Air Force Base	Air Force	334-953-6725 or 263-1400
AL	Redstone Arsenal	Army	205-876-2022
AK	Elmendorf Air Force Base	Air Force	907-522-2337 or 5532
AK	Fort Richardson	Army	907-384-3500
AK	Fort Wainwright	Army	907-353-2102
AZ	Davis-Monthan Air Force Base	Air Force	520-228-5100
AZ	Fort Huachuca	Army	520-533-5733
AZ	Luke Air Force Base	Air Force	602-856-3923 or 6827
AZ	Phoenix	Navy	602-484-7296
AZ	Tucson	Navy	520-748-1013 or 1014
AR	Little Rock Air Force Base	Air Force	501-988-6095
CA	Beale Air Force Base	Air Force	916-634-2157
CA	China Lake Naval Air Station	Navy	619-939-0978
CA	Edwards Air Force Base	Air Force	805-277-4931
CA	Fort Irwin	Army	619-380-5603
CA	Lemoore Naval Air Station	Navy	209-998-4042
CA	Long Beach Naval Shipyard	Navy	310-547-8220
CA	Los Angeles Air Force Base	Air Force	310-363-0183
CA	March Air Reserve Base	Air Force	909-655-4077 or 4079
CA	McClellan Air Force Base	Air Force	916-643-2207 or 4309
CA	Monterey Naval Postgraduate School	Navy	408-656-3060 or 3141
CA	Onizuka Air Station	Air Force	415-603-8047
CA	Port Hueneme NCBC	Navy	805-982-1023
CA	Presidio of San Francisco	Army	415-561-3600
CA	San Diego (NAB)	Navy	619-437-2780 or 2107
CA	San Diego (NAS)	Navy	619-537-4806
CA	San Diego (NAVSTA)	Navy	619-556-7404 or 7414
CA	San Francisco	Navy	415-603-8047
CA	San Francisco (NS)	Navy	415-395-5176 or 5189
CA	Travis Air Force Base	Air Force	707-424-3904
CA	Vandenberg Air Force Base	Air Force	805-733-3430
CO	Buckley Air National Guard Base	Air Force	303-340-9160
CO	Fitzsimons U.S. Army Garrison	Army	303-361-8517
CO	Fort Carson	Army	719-526-2660
CO	Peterson Air Force Base	Air Force	719-556-7153
CT	Groton Naval Submarine Base	Navy	860-449-3284
DE	Dover Air Force Base	Air Force	302-677-4612
DC	Bolling Air Force Base	Air Force	202-767-5244
DC	Fort Myer	Army	703-696-5948
DC		Navy	202-433-6150 or 6142
FL	Eglin Air Force Base	Air Force	904-882-5916
FL	Homestead Air Reserve Base	Air Force	305-224-7580
FL	Hurlburt Field	Air Force	904-884-5443
FL	Jacksonville Naval Air Station	Navy	904-772-5783
FL	MacDill Air Force Base	Air Force	813-828-4555
FL	Mayport Naval Station	Navy	904-270-6600
FL	Orlando Naval Training Center	Navy	407-646-5288 or 4476
FL	Orlando Naval Training Center	Army	07-646-4217
FL	Patrick Air Force Base	Air Force	407-494-5463
FL	Pensacola (NAS)	Navy	904-452-5990 or 5991
FL	Tyndall Air Force Base	Air Force	904-283-2737
GA	Atlanta Naval Air Station	Navy	770-919-6735
GA	Fort Benning	Army	706-545-2715
GA	Fort Gordon	Army	706-791-2654
GA	Fort McPherson	Army	404-752-3219
GA	Fort Stewart	Army	912-767-3096
GA	Kings Bay NSB	Navy	912-673-4512
GA	Moody Air Force Base	Air Force	912-333-3209
GA	Robins Air Force Base	Air Force	912-926-2019
HI	Fort Shafter	Army	808-438-2798
HI	Hickam Air Force Base	Air Force	808-449-9896
HI	Pearl Harbor Naval Station	Navy	808-471-3345
ID	Mountain Home Air Force Base	Air Force	208-828-4878
IL	Great Lakes NTC	Navy	847-688-5434 ext. 421
IL	O'Hare International Apt/ARS	Air Force	773-825-6060
IL	Scott Air Force Base	Air Force	618-256-5092
IN	Fort Benjamin Harrison	Army	317-542-4364
IN	Grissom Air Reserve Base	Air Force	317-688-8687
KS	Fort Leavenworth	Army	913-684-2041
KS	Fort Riley	Army	913-239-3320
KS	McConnell Air Force Base	Air Force	316-652-3829
KY	Fort Campbell	Army	502-798-5280
KY	Fort Knox	Army	502-239-3320
LA	Barksdale Air Force Base	Air Force	318-456-5976
LA	Fort Polk	Army	318-531-4515
LA	New Orleans Naval Air Station	Navy	504-678-2134
ME	Brunswick Naval Air Station	Navy	207-921-2609
MD	Aberdeen Proving Ground	Army	410-278-5620
MD	Andrews Air Force Base	Air Force	301-981-2726 or 2180
MD	Annapolis Naval Station	Navy	410-293-2641
MD	Fort Meade	Army	301-677-7433
MD	Patuxent River Naval Air Station	Navy	301-342-4911
MA	Devens RFTA	Army	508-796-2285
MA	Hanscom Air Force Base	Air Force	617-377-2476
MA	Otis Air National Guard Base	Air Force	508-968-4175
MA	Westover Air Reserve Base	Air Force	413-557-3918 or 3424
MI	Detroit (Selfridge)	Navy	810-307-4317
MI	Detroit	Navy	313-824-4542
MN	Minneapolis	Navy	612-725-5737
MS	Columbus Air Force Base	Air Force	601-434-2719 or 2626
MS	Gulfport NCBC	Navy	601-871-2647
MS	Keesler Air Force Base	Air Force	601-377-3871 or 7309
MO	Fort Leonard Wood	Army	573-596-0947
MO	St. Louis	Navy	314-263-6443
MO	Whiteman Air Force Base	Air Force	816-687-6457
MT	Malmstrom Air Force Base	Air Force	406-731-3071
NE	Lincoln	Navy	402-470-2142
NE	Offutt Air Force Base	Air Force	402-294-2590 or 4566
NV	Fallon Naval Air Station	Navy	702-426-3333 or 2317
NV	Nellis Air Force Base	Air Force	702-652-8712
NJ	Earle Naval Weapons Station	Navy	908-866-2585
NJ	Fort Dix Army Garrison	Army	609-562-2666
NJ	Fort Monmouth	Army	908-532-4673
NJ	Lakehurst NAES	Navy	908-323-1224
NJ	McGuire Air Force Base	Air Force	609-724-2459
NM	Cannon Air Force Base	Air Force	505-784-2217
NM	Holloman Air Force Base	Air Force	505-475-3140
NM	Kirtland Air Force Base	Air Force	505-846-1536
NY	Amityville	Navy	516-842-6620
NY	Fort Drum	Army	315-772-6434
NY	Fort Hamilton	Army	718-630-4930
NY	Niagara Falls Air Reserve Station	Air Force	716-236-2389
NY	USMA, West Point	Army	914-938-4217
NY	Watervliet Arsenal	Army	518-266-5920
NC	Camp Lejeune MCB	Navy	910-451-5927
NC	Fort Bragg	Army	910-396-7472

APPENDIX D, *continued*

STATE	INSTALLATION	BRANCH	PHONE #
NC	Pope Air Force Base	Air Force	910-394-2174
NC	Seymour Johnson Air Force Base	Air Force	919-736-6377
ND	Grand Forks Air Force Base	Air Force	701-747-3197
ND	Minot Air Force Base	Air Force	701-723-2205
OH	Defense Supply Center	Air Force	614-692-4947
OH	Wright-Patterson Air Force Base	Air Force	937-257-3221
OK	Altus Air Force Base	Air Force	405-481-5710
OK	Fort Sill	Army	405-442-5963
OK	McAlester AA Plant	Army	918-421-7549
OK	Tinker Air Force Base	Air Force	405-739-2795
OK	Vance Air Force Base	Air Force	405-249-6330
OR	Central Point	Navy	503-772-2566
OR	Eugene	Navy	503-686-9266
OR	Kingsley Field	Air Force	503-885-6362
OR	Portland	Navy	503-285-9587 ext.548
OR	Portland International Airport	Air Force	503-335-4945
PA	Carlisle Barracks	Army	717-245-4501
PA	Charles E. Kelly Support Center	Army	412-777-1177
PA	Pittsburgh IAP/AFRS	Air Force	412-474-8559
PA	Tobyhanna Depot	Army	717-895-7019
PA	Willow Grove Naval Air Station	Navy	215-443-6038
PR	Fort Buchanan	Army	787-273-3842
PR	Roosevelt Roads Naval Station	Navy	787-865-3369 or 4566
RI	Newport NETC	Navy	401-841-4089
SC	Charleston Air Force Base	Air Force	803-566-2228
SC	Charleston NWS	Navy	803-764-7294
SC	Fort Jackson	Army	803-751-6715
SC	Shaw Air Force Base	Air Force	803-668-3036
SD	Ellsworth Air Force Base	Air Force	605-385-5050
TN	Arnold Air Force Station	Air Force	615-454-4574
TN	Millington NSA	Navy	901-873-5195
TX	Brooks Air Force Base	Air Force	210-536-2116
TX	Corpus Christi Naval Air Station	Navy	512-939-3113
TX	Dallas Naval Air Station	Navy	972-782-5442 or 5287
TX	Dyess Air Force Base	Air Force	915-672-6897 or 674-1328
TX	Fort Bliss	Army	915-568-5204
TX	Fort Hood	Army	817-287-5210
TX	Fort Sam Houston	Army	210-221-0761
TX	Goodfellow Air Force Base	Air Force	915-654-5388
TX	Houston	Navy	713-795-4109
TX	Ingleside Naval Station	Navy	512-776-4551
TX	Kelly Air Force Base	Air Force	210-925-2984 or 2976
TX	Kingsville Naval Air Station	Navy	512-595-6105
TX	Lackland Air Force Base	Air Force	210-671-2728
TX	Randolph Air Force Base	Air Force	210-652-6880
TX	San Antonio	Navy	210-225-2997
TX	Sheppard Air Force Base	Air Force	817-676-5088 or 3381
UT	Hill Air Force Base	Air Force	801-777-5735
UT	Utah Retiree Council	Army	801-584-4060
VA	Dahlgren NSWC	Navy	540-653-1839
VA	Fort Belvoir	Army	703-805-3682
VA	Fort Eustis	Army	757-878-2953
VA	Fort Lee	Army	804-734-6973
VA	Fort Monroe	Army	757-727-2093
VA	Fort Myer	Army	703-696-5948
VA	Langley Air Force Base	Air Force	757-764-7386
VA	Little Creek NAB	Navy	804-464-8101 ext 306
VA	Norfolk Naval Base	Navy	757-444-2102 or 372-5463
WA	Bangor Naval Submarine Base	Navy	360-396-4115 or 800-562-3301
WA	Bremerton (Naval Shipyard)	Navy	360-476-5113 or 800-643-4100 (WA only)
WA	Everett Naval Station	Navy	509-247-5359
WA	Fairchild Air Force Base	Air Force	509-247-5359
WA	Fort Lewis	Army	206-967-5913
WA	McChord Air Force Base	Air Force	206-984-3214
WA	Whidbey Island Naval Station	Navy	360-257-8054
WI	Fort McCoy	Army	608-388-3716
WI	Gen. Mitchell IAP/ARS	Air Force	414-482-5207 or 5208
WI	Milwaukee	Navy	414-744-9766
WI	Truax Field	Air Force	608-242-3115
WY	F. E. Warren Air Force Base	Air Force	307-775-2312

Note: Information for new United States Marine Corps (USMC) Retired Service Offices (RSO) is available at 1-800-336-4649.

★ ★ ★ ★ ★ NOTES ★ ★ ★ ★ ★

CENTRAL ORDER COUPON

P.O. Box 2347, Falls Church, VA 22042-0347, **TEL: (703) 237-0203** FAX: (703) 237-2233

Publications	ISBN	Item #	Price	QTY
R&R Space-A Report®. *The worldwide travel newsletter.* 6 issues per year. 1 yr/$15.00 - 2 yrs/$24.00 - 3 yrs/$33.00 - 5 yrs/$49.00 (Shipped by 3rd class bulk rate)				
Military Space-A Air Basic Training.	0-914862-66-9	23	$13.95	
Military Space-A Air Opportunities Air Route Map. (Folded)	0-914862-52-9	19	$13.95	
Military Space-A Air Opportunities Around the World.	0-914862-61-8	1	$18.95	
Temporary Military Lodging Around the World.	0-914862-67-7	12	$16.95	
Military RV, Camping & Rec Areas Around the World.	0-914862-65-0	24	$14.95	
U.S. Forces Travel and Transfer Guide, USA and Caribbean Areas.	0-914862-63-4	8	$14.95	
U.S Forces Travel Guide to Overseas U.S Military Installations.	0-914862-43-X	25	$17.95	
U.S. Military Museums, Historic Sites & Exhibits. (Soft Cover)	0-914862-34-0	10	$17.95	
United States Military Road Atlas.	0-914862-64-2	21	$18.95	
U.S. Military Installation Road Map. (Folded)	0-914862-62-6	14	$7.95	
COLLECTOR'S ITEM! Desert Shield Commemorative Maps. (Folded) (2 unfolded wall maps in a hard tube)	0-914862-27-8	15	$8.00 $18.00	
Assignment Washington Military Road Atlas.	0-914862-49-9	6	$10.95	
California State Military Road Map - (Folded) **Florida State Military Road Map** -(Folded) **Mid-Atlantic States Military Road Map** - (Folded) **Texas State Military Road Map** - (Folded)	0-914862-45-6 0-914862-46-4 0-914862-47-2 0-914862-48-0	22A 22B 22C 22D	$5.95 $5.95 $5.95 $5.95	
Military Living Magazine, Camaraderie Washington. *Local Area magazine.* 4 seasonal issues, $8.00/year				
Virginia Addresses add 4.5% sales tax (Books, Maps, & Atlases only)				
ALL ORDERS SHIPPED BY 1ST CLASS MAIL			**TOTAL $**	

*If you are an R&R Space-A Report® subscriber, you may deduct $1.00 per book. (No discount on the R&R Report itself or on the maps or atlas.) Mail Order Prices are for U.S. APO & FPO addresses. Please consult publisher for International Mail Price. Sorry, no billing.

We're as close as your telephone...by using our Telephone Ordering Service. We honor American Express, MasterCard, Visa, and Discover. Call us at **703-237-0203** (Voice Mail after hours) or FAX 703-237-2233 and order today! Sorry, no collect calls. Or...fill out and mail the order coupon below.

NAME:____

STREET:____

CITY/STATE/ZIP:_______________________________________

PHONE:____________________ SIGNATURE:_______________________________

RANK (or rank of sponsor):______Branch Of Service:______________________________

Active Duty:_____Retired:_____Widow/er:_____100% Disabled Veteran:_____Guard:_____Reservist:____Other:_____

Credit Card #____Card Expiration Date:_______________

Mail check/money order to Military Living Publications, P.O. Box 2347, Falls Church, VA 22042-0347
Save $$$s by purchasing any of our books, Maps, and Atlases at your military Exchange.
Prices are subject to change. Please check here if we may ship and bill the difference................................ ☐

THIS FORM MAY BE DUPLICATED